The Handbook of Asian Intelligence Cultures

SCARECROW PROFESSIONAL INTELLIGENCE EDUCATION SERIES

Series Editor: Jan Goldman

In this post–September 11, 2001, era there has been rapid growth in the number of professional intelligence training and educational programs across the United States and abroad. Colleges and universities, as well as high schools, are developing programs and courses in homeland security, intelligence analysis, and law enforcement, in support of national security.

The Scarecrow Professional Intelligence Education Series (SPIES) was first designed for individuals studying for careers in intelligence and to help improve the skills of those already in the profession; however, it was also developed to educate the public in how intelligence work is conducted and should be conducted in this important and vital profession.

1. *Communicating with Intelligence: Writing and Briefing in the Intelligence and National Security Communities*, by James S. Major. 2008.
2. *A Spy's Résumé: Confessions of a Maverick Intelligence Professional and Misadventure Capitalist*, by Marc Anthony Viola. 2008.
3. *An Introduction to Intelligence Research and Analysis*, by Jerome Clauser, revised and edited by Jan Goldman. 2008.
4. *Writing Classified and Unclassified Papers for National Security: A Scarecrow Professional Intelligence Educational Series Manual*, by James S. Major. 2009.
5. *Strategic Intelligence: A Handbook for Practitioners, Managers, and Users*, revised edition by Don McDowell. 2009.
6. *Partly Cloudy: Ethics in War, Espionage, Covert Action, and Interrogation*, by David L. Perry. 2009.
7. *Tokyo Rose / An American Patriot: A Dual Biography*, by Frederick P. Close. 2010.
8. *Ethics of Spying: A Reader for the Intelligence Professional*, edited by Jan Goldman. 2006.
9. *Ethics of Spying: A Reader for the Intelligence Professional*, Volume 2, edited by Jan Goldman. 2010.
10. *A Woman's War: The Professional and Personal Journey of the Navy's First African American Female Intelligence Officer*, by Gail Harris. 2010.
11. *Handbook of Scientific Methods of Inquiry for Intelligence Analysis*, by Hank Prunckun. 2010.
12. *Handbook of Warning Intelligence: Assessing the Threat to National Security*, by Cynthia Grabo. 2010.
13. *Keeping U.S. Intelligence Effective: The Need for a Revolution in Intelligence Affairs*, by William J. Lahneman. 2011.
14. *Words of Intelligence: An Intelligence Professional's Lexicon for Domestic and Foreign Threats*, Second Edition, by Jan Goldman. 2011.
15. *Counterintelligence Theory and Practice*, by Hank Prunckun. 2012.
16. *Handbook of Asian Intelligence Cultures*, edited by Ryan Shaffer. 2022.

The Handbook of Asian Intelligence Cultures

Edited by
Ryan Shaffer

ROWMAN & LITTLEFIELD
Lanham • Boulder • New York • London

Published by Rowman & Littlefield
An imprint of The Rowman & Littlefield Publishing Group, Inc.
4501 Forbes Boulevard, Suite 200, Lanham, Maryland 20706
www.rowman.com

86-90 Paul Street, London EC2A 4NE, United Kingdom

British Library Cataloguing in Publication Information Available

Library of Congress Cataloging-in-Publication Data

Names: Shaffer, Ryan, 1982– editor.
Title: The handbook of Asian intelligence cultures / Edited by Ryan Shaffer.
Other titles: Asian intelligence cultures
Description: Lanham : Rowman & Littlefield, [2022] | Series: Scarecrow professional
    intelligence education series | Includes index. | Summary: "The Handbook of Asian
    Intelligence Cultures explores the historical and contemporary influences that have
    shaped Asian intelligence cultures as well as the impact intelligence service have had
    on domestic and foreign affairs"—Provided by publisher.
Identifiers: LCCN 2022018312 (print) | LCCN 2022018313 (ebook) | ISBN
    9781538159996 (cloth) | ISBN 9781538197684 (paper) | ISBN 9781538160008
    (epub)
Subjects: LCSH: Intelligence service—Asia—Cross-cultural studies. | Internal security—
    Asia—Cross-cultural studies.
Classification: LCC JQ27 .H36 2022 (print) | LCC JQ27 (ebook) | DDC 327.15—dc23/
    eng/20220915
LC record available at https://lccn.loc.gov/2022018312
LC ebook record available at https://lccn.loc.gov/2022018313

Contents

Acknowledgments

Compiling a handbook is a collaborative effort that requires many different people, including authors, editors, copyeditors, and reviewers. Without them this book would not be possible. Rowman & Littlefield editors Dhara Snowden and Jan Goldman approached me about compiling a handbook and were very supportive throughout the process. Rebecca Anastasi and April Snider, also editors at Rowman & Littlefield, helped see the project to completion. The contributors provided valuable research on subjects not often written about. Kathleen Wilson and Michael Landon-Murray gave me important input. In addition, reviewers for this book gave useful feedback. Lastly, my friends and family provided support and encouragement. I am grateful for everyone's help.

Map

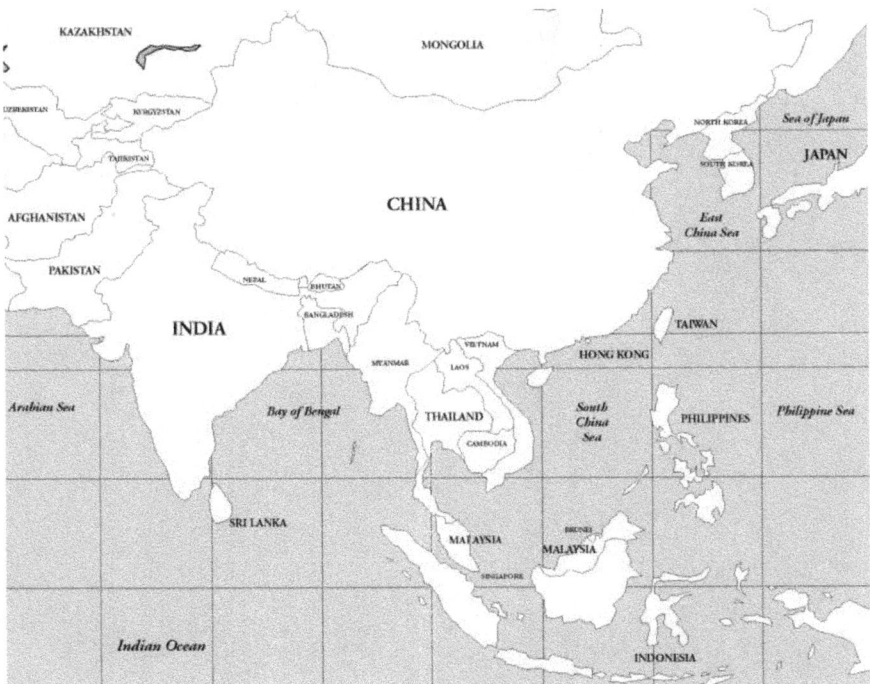

Map of Central, East, South and Southeast Asia from the Cartographic Research Laboratory at the University of Alabama.

Introduction

The Handbook of Asian Intelligence Cultures

Ryan Shaffer

Intelligence has played a significant role in Asia since at least the start of recorded history.[1] Ancient Asian texts have shaped modern statecraft, warfare, and strategy in Asia and beyond. Sun Tzu's *The Art of War* devoted a section to espionage with maxims such as "prior information enables wise rulers and worthy generals" and categorized five types of spies that an army "depends on."[2] Likewise, Kautilya's ancient treatise, the *Arthashastra*, described intelligence doctrine, providing explanations of different types of spies, methods to transmit intelligence, and counterintelligence practices. Detailing basics about the intelligence process, Kautilya explained that "intelligence gathered from roving spies shall be collected together in the establishments of spies in one place and shall be transmitted by code," including through "means of songs, speech, signs or messages in code hidden inside musical instruments or vessels."[3] Roughly 2,300 years later, the *Arthashastra* still influences South Asian intelligence today.[4] With this long history of intelligence culture and material available about Asian intelligence services, it is important to analyze and contextualize intelligence cultures in Asia for understanding the past, present, and future of Asian security.[5]

At the start of the twenty-first century, Asia emerged as a significant force in world affairs in every imaginable way. From the potential for nuclear conflict in South Asia and the Korean Peninsula to the economic power of relatively small nations like Japan and the global reach of large Chinese and Indian diasporas, Asia is at the forefront of world events. In terms of population, in 2019 the United Nations reported that Asia's population was 4.6 billion out of the world's total of 7.7 billion people.[6] Moreover, Asian countries have yet to peak in production and economic capacity, making these trends likely to continue.[7] Thus, Asian intelligence services will serve and support a range of highly impactful decision-making processes in the twenty-first century, highlighting the importance of advancing the understanding of these services.

This book is a comprehensive collection of chapters that cover intelligence services in Central, East, South, and Southeast Asia. It is meant to serve as an accessible primer on the intelligence cultures of thirty Asian nations, helping students and scholars of intelligence better understand the history, structure, and practice of each country's intelligence apparatus. Taking a broad view of intelligence as information related to government policy or security, it probes the contexts, characteristics, and customs of Asian intelligence services, demonstrating the social and political factors impacting—and impacted by—those services.

While there is a large body of literature about Asian security, policy economies, and militaries, Asia's intelligence services are not as well studied or understood.[8] Due in part to secrecy laws, undemocratic institutions, and societies weary about foreigners, there is little English-language literature on the subject compared to North America and Europe. The intelligence services throughout Asia, however, play important domestic and international security roles. This book explores Asian intelligence cultures to advance the understanding of these vital, but seemingly invisible institutions. Rather than exclusively addressing the history and practice of Asian intelligence services, it focuses on cultural aspects to highlight the norms, traditions, successes, failures, and relationships involved in intelligence.

SCHOLARSHIP

While research on Asian intelligence is growing, it is still underrepresented in the literature. India, the largest democracy in the world, with one of the oldest continually operating intelligence services, ostensibly would be the most open and permissive about studies on its intelligence community; however, a review of Indian intelligence services by subject in WorldCat, an online database of world library holdings, reveals about 250 English and non-English books, articles, videos, and other media.[9] A search for Research and Analysis Wing, India's foreign intelligence service, by subject on WorldCat reveals only forty-two results.[10] Yet, this number is misleading, as even the former Indian intelligence officers who have become authors have remained tight-lipped. One of the few books on intelligence by a former Indian intelligence leader, Vikram Sood, only mentioned India's Research and Analysis Wing "when it is relevant to the context," rather than providing a clear description or analysis of the intelligence service.[11] For comparison, a subject search for the United States' Central Intelligence Agency on WorldCat returns more than 15,300 items.[12] When one considers India is categorized as a "free" country by Freedom House, it is no surprise that there are less studies about intelligence in Asian countries ranked "not free" or "partly free."[13]

Though the literature is limited, this should not imply a complete lack of interest from scholars. Indeed, there is a body of scholarly articles in intelligence studies journals about many Asian countries as well as some excellent and groundbreaking books covering countries such as China, Indonesia, Japan, and Pakistan.[14] These books have explored intelligence operations, intergovernmental relations, and how intelligence has shaped each country's politics and history; however, there is a larger body of research addressing North American and European intelligence activity in Asia during colonialism, World War II, the Korean War, and Vietnam.[15] This is likely due to several factors, including the availability and declassification of records as well as broader interest in those wars.

In addition to articles and monographs, there are several notable anthologies. Philip H. J. Davies and Kristian C. Gustafson's anthology, *Intelligence Elsewhere: Spies and Espionage Outside the Anglosphere*, covers ancient India as well as contemporary Pakistan, Indonesia, Iran, and Japan.[16] Stephan Blancke's *East Asian Intelligence and Organised Crime* explores intelligence in the context of organized crime, examining China, Japan, Mongolia, and North Korea.[17] The most recent collection of research is Bob de Graaff's anthology, which explores select Asian countries, including the Middle East, and finds recurring themes between countries.[18] The text covers a range of countries, examining intelligence history and geopolitics in some lesser examined countries, such as Myanmar and Sri Lanka, as well as larger countries like China and India.[19] These books are significant steps in a needed direction, providing critical insights and improving our understanding of Asian intelligence services.

OBJECTIVE

This book adds to the burgeoning scholarship by exploring the mixture of history, government, institutions, and collective human behavior that inform intelligence cultures in Asia. Though national security is defined in different ways throughout Asia, the common feature is to address potential threats to the government, leadership, or territorial integrity. De Graaff's work has described some broad commonalities between Asian intelligence services in terms of function, regime support, oversight, and colonial legacy.[20] Building from those themes, the impact of globalization has also clearly affected

Asian intelligence cultures. Postcolonial intelligence structures, histories, and exchanges have been markedly shaped by modern communication, international organizations, and shared global concerns. The ability for government officials to learn from other countries, absorb international media, and respond to shared transnational concerns like terrorism have also shaped national intelligence cultures in Asia.

The primary objective of this text is to provide a comprehensive overview of the intelligence cultures in Central, East, South, and Southeast Asia. The book's purpose is not to develop a unified theory on Asian intelligence or provide comparisons between dissimilar countries. Rather, it explores intelligence cultures to understand how government, politics, culture, and societies affect intelligence institutions and, in turn, how intelligence services and communities affect government and society. In doing so, the volume draws on themes from *The Handbook of European Intelligence Cultures.*[21] The chapters examine the interactions between intelligence history and functions, on the one hand, and domestic and foreign affairs, including oversight, on the other. Thus, contributors explore successes, failures, and human rights abuses, as well as the intelligence consumer and who has oversight responsibilities for the services. Some of the cases demonstrate the link between democratic reform and intelligence oversight, but as Peter Gill and Michael Andregg have found, formal oversight "can give a false sense of security and permit continuing inefficiencies and corruption to exist for a long time."[22]

The contributors were encouraged to take approaches best suited to their expertise of a particular country and its intelligence services. As the countries range from the most populous in the world to some of the least populated, with varied approaches to governance, there is no single formula for studying their politics, cultures, and security practices. Furthermore, the book does this to avoid constructing an analytic framework that the authors would be forced into employing. This is all the more important because the book provides some of the first essays about intelligence in certain countries, such as Bhutan and Brunei. Additionally, the book seeks to broaden the readers' views about intelligence culture by drawing from British cultural studies in applying concepts from the Birmingham School of Cultural Studies that originated with Richard Hoggart.[23] It uses Stuart Hall's description that culture is "experience lived, experience interpreted, experience defined."[24] Furthermore, Hall saw cultural analysis as a way to uncover "shared ideas and forms of communication."[25] Indeed, the broader cultural turn has long been recognized for its influence in imperial studies and the new imperial history. Catherine Hall, for example, noted "cultural studies particularly has emphasized the importance of meaning to the definition of culture" with culture involving the "production and exchange of meanings."[26] This handbook looks to these concepts to probe intelligence culture as it is connected to people, experiences, and politics, as well as local and distance events.

The book covers the intelligence culture of thirty countries in Asia: Afghanistan, Bangladesh, Bhutan, Brunei, Cambodia, China, India, Indonesia, Japan, Kazakhstan, Kyrgyzstan, Laos, Malaysia, Maldives, Mongolia, Myanmar, Nepal, North Korea, Pakistan, the Philippines, Singapore, South Korea, Sri Lanka, Taiwan, Tajikistan, Thailand, Timor-Leste, Turkmenistan, Uzbekistan, and Vietnam. In terms of space, it treats all countries the same to provide each with equal coverage. Building from *The Handbook of European Intelligence Cultures* and de Graaff's anthology, this book focuses exclusively on Central, East, South, and Southeast Asia. This book does not examine North Asia (Russia) as its history and politics are more often associated with Europe. Additionally, it does not include Western Asia (South Caucasus or Middle East) as those nations' intelligence cultures should have a handbook that analyzes the region's unique cultural, historical, and linguistic connections.

SOURCES

The sources and methodologies used for the chapters vary by country and author. While some contributors are from the country they discuss in their respective chapters, this is not possible in other cases—such as North Korea—due to either internal politics that censor publications on security or a lack of access to sources. The contributors to this book were selected for their knowledge about the countries or their specific expertise on the country's intelligence. They were encouraged to take their own approaches to the subject, drawing from their research strengths and the best methodologies to utilize the sources available. This book sees the diversity of sources and approaches as a strength by demonstrating different methodologies and material that could be used to understand intelligence and security in open, closed, or "not free" societies. Indeed, most of the countries in Asia—even in the "free" ones like India—do not declassify operational intelligence records or publish official intelligence histories.

Sources are always challenging for research, but they can be especially complicated in intelligence studies. Sometimes government records are incomplete or nonexistent depending on the time period, issue, or country. In the case of studying Asian intelligence cultures, the sources available vary by country. Some of the authors for this book did draw from primary records in archives or published primary sources in foreign languages, such as memoirs of government officials or intelligence officers. Christopher R.

Moran has detailed the evolution of intelligence studies, explaining how the "first generation of serious scholarship" greatly benefited from declassified intelligence in archives during the 1980s.[27] Aside from colonial records and some postcolonial collateral intelligence-related records from other government ministries, such as in India, however, few Asian countries make archival holdings of recent intelligence documents available to the public.[28] Additionally, some authors made use of primary sources from government websites and published official records. Other authors relied on secondary works or translations, such as published scholarship, press articles, and reports from nongovernmental organizations that focus on human rights and freedom. The sources used largely depended on the country, with more closed governments that lack transparency making few or no primary sources about national security and intelligence available for analysis.

CONCLUSION

This book argues there is no single "Asian intelligence culture," but rather there are many intelligence cultures shaped by a variety of unique economic, political, geopolitical, cultural, and historical factors. The region is far too diverse in terms of populations, histories, ethnic and racial groups, and geopolitics to argue there is an archetype. To be sure, the history of colonization, decolonization, and Cold War had a significant impact in shaping Asian intelligence cultures. Yet, there is regionalism, such as in Central Asia or South Asia, where countries with shared histories and political institutions have the most similarities. The intelligence services from Bangladesh, India, and Pakistan share similarities from their British colonial roots, while Central Asia's intelligence services have commonalities from the Soviet Union's institutions.

Political structures and histories can also impact contemporary Asian countries in vastly different ways. For example, despite Bangladesh's, India's, and Pakistan's intelligence services originating in the same British India intelligence structure, domestic politics and international relations have shaped those countries' intelligence services in diverging ways, with the military playing an outsized role in Pakistani intelligence and the police shaping India's intelligence. Though there are broad similarities—in terms of politicization or corruption—between some Asian countries, they are not unique to Asia. Some countries share these commonalities with developing countries in Africa, Europe, or the Americas.

It is important to caution readers not to impose their views on foreign intelligence services' history, methods, or culture but, instead, to understand the services in their own terms. Intelligence services ostensibly serve the needs of government and society. Since governmental and societal conditions, objectives, and requirements vary, they shape intelligence cultures in different ways. This book aims not only to inform scholars and students about the intelligence cultures but also to encourage more research on Asian intelligence that advances issues surrounding the intelligence services on the world's most populous continent.

NOTES

1. Special thanks to Kathleen Wilson and Michael Landon-Murray for providing valuable comments.

2. Sun Tzu, *The Art of War*, trans. John Minford (New York: Penguin, 1992), 96, 97, 101.

3. Kautilya, *The Arthashastra*, trans. L. N. Rangarajan (Noida, India: Penguin, 1992), 471.

4. Philip H. J. Davies, "The Original Surveillance State: Kautilya's *Arthashastra* and Government by Espionage in Classical India," in *Intelligence Elsewhere: Spies and Espionage Outside the Anglosphere*, ed. Philip H. J. Davies and Kristian C. Gustafson (Washington, DC: Georgetown University Press, 2013), 50, 63.

5. One notable intelligence event that came to light was when the Indian government publicized and released transcripts of the signals intelligence from Research and Analysis Wing that confirmed Pakistan was behind the occupation of Kargil in summer 1999. See B. Raman, "Release of Kargil Tape: Masterpiece or Blunder?," Rediff, June 27, 2007, https://www.rediff.com/news/2007/jun/27raman.htm. Raman (1936–2013) was an intelligence officer in India's Research and Analysis Wing.

6. *World Population Prospects 2019*, vol. 2, *Demographic Profiles* (New York: United Nations Department of Economic and Social Affairs, 2019), 2, 62, https://population.un.org/wpp/Publications/Files/WPP2019_Volume-II-Demographic-Profiles.pdf.

7. For example, see a discussion on economic growth and military capacity in Peter E. Robertson and Adrian Sin, "Measuring Hard Power: China's Economic Growth and Military Capacity," *Defence and Peace Economics* 28, no. 1 (2017): 91–111. For a discussion on regional and growth possibilities, see Zahid Khan, Guo Changgang, and Muhammad Afzaal, "China-Pakistan Economic Corridor at the Cross-Intersection of China, Central Asia and South Asia: Opportunities for Regional Economic Growth," *Chinese Economy* 53, no. 2 (2020): 200–15. For growth and its link to energy, see Muhammad Azam, "Energy and Economic Growth in Developing Asian Economies," *Journal of the Asia Pacific Economy* 25, no. 3 (2020): 447–71.

8. For example, see Barry Eichengreen, Charles Wyplosz, and Yung Chul Park, eds., *China, Asia, and the New World Economy* (New York: Oxford University Press, 2008); Tomoo Kikuchi and Masaya Sakuragawa, *China and Japan in the Global Economy* (New York: Routledge, 2020); Dilip K. Das, *China and the Asian Economies: Interactive Dynamics, Synergy and Symbiotic Growth* (New York: Routledge,

2013); Deeparghya Mukherjee, ed., *Economic Integration in Asia: Key Prospects and Challenges with the Regional Comprehensive Economic Partnership* (New York: Routledge, 2020); Takeshi Hamashita, Mark Selden, and Linda Grove, eds., *China, East Asia and the Global Economy: Regional and Historical Perspectives* (New York: Routledge, 2008).

9. "su:Intelligence service India," WorldCat.org, 2021, https://www.worldcat .org/search?q=su%3AIntelligence+service+India.&qt=hot_subject.

10. "su:India. Cabinet Secretariat. Research and Analysis Wing," WorldCat.org, 2021, https://www.worldcat.org/search?q=su%3AIndia.+Cabinet+Secretariat.+Resea rch+and+Analysis+Wing.&qt=hot_subject.

11. Vikram Sood, *The Unending Game: A Former R&AW Chief's Insights into Espionage* (Noida: Penguin, 2018), xi.

12. "su: Central Intelligence Agency," WorldCat.org, 2021, https://www.worldcat .org/search?q=su%3A+central+intelligence+agency&qt=results_page.

13. "Countries and Territories," Freedom House, 2021, https://freedomhouse.org/ countries/freedom-world/scores.

14. For example, Richard J. Samuels, *Special Duty: A History of the Japanese Intelligence Community* (Ithaca, NY: Cornell University Press, 2019); Yatish Yadav, *RAW: A History of India's Covert Operations* (Chennai: Westland, 2020); Peter Mattis and Matthew Brazil, *Chinese Communist Espionage: An Intelligence Primer* (Annapolis, MD: Naval Institute Press, 2019); Ken Conboy, *Intel: Inside Indonesia's Intelligence Service* (Jakarta: Equinox, 2004); Owen L. Sirrs, *Pakistan's Inter-Services Intelligence Directorate: Covert Action and Internal Operations* (New York: Routledge, 2018).

15. For example, Richard J. Aldrich, *Intelligence and the War against Japan: Britain, America and the Politics of Secret Service* (New York: Cambridge University Press, 2000); C. A. Bayly, *Empire and Information: Intelligence Gathering and Social Communication in India, 1780–1870* (New York: Cambridge University Press, 2000); David M. Anderson and David Killingray, eds., *Policing and Decolonisation: Politics, Nationalism and the Police, 1917–65* (Manchester: Manchester University Press, 1992); David A. Hatch and Robert Louis Benson, *The Korean War: The SIGINT Background* (Fort Meade, MD: National Security Agency, 2000); James J. Wirtz, *The Tet Offensive: Intelligence Failure in War* (Ithaca, NY: Cornell University Press, 2013); Calder Walton, *Empire of Secrets: British Intelligence, the Cold War, and the Twilight of Empire* (New York: Overlook Press, 2013).

16. Philip H. J. Davies and Kristian C. Gustafson, eds., *Intelligence Elsewhere: Spies and Espionage Outside the Anglosphere* (Washington, DC: Georgetown University Press, 2013).

17. Stephan Blancke, ed., *East Asian Intelligence and Organised Crime* (Berlin: Verlag Dr. Köster, 2015).

18. Bob de Graaff, ed., *Intelligence Communities and Cultures in Asia and the Middle East: A Comprehensive Reference* (Boulder, CO: Lynne Rienner, 2020).

19. De Graaff, *Intelligence Communities*, 2.

20. Bob de Graaff, "Elements of an Asian Intelligence Cultures," in *Intelligence Communities and Cultures in Asia and the Middle East: A Comprehensive Reference* (Boulder, CO: Lynne Rienner, 2020).

21. Bob de Graaff and James M. Nyce, introduction to *The Handbook of European Intelligence Cultures*, ed. Bob de Graaff and James M. Nyce (Lanham, MD: Rowman & Littlefield, 2016), xxxv–xxxviii.

22. Peter Gill and Michael Andregg, "Comparing the Democratization of Intelligence," in *Democratization of Intelligence*, ed. Peter Gill and Michael Andregg (New York: Routledge, 2015), 9.

23. This was also used in Ryan Shaffer, ed., *The Handbook of African Intelligence Cultures* (Lanham, MD: Rowman & Littlefield, 2022); Richard Hoggart, *The Uses of Literacy: Changing Patterns in English Mass Culture* (Boston: Beacon, 1957).

24. Stuart Hall, *Cultural Studies 1983: A Theoretical History*, ed. Jennifer Daryl Slack and Lawrence Grossberg (Durham, NC: Duke University Press, 2016), 33.

25. Hall, *Cultural Studies 1983*, 34.

26. Catherine Hall, introduction to *Cultures of Empire, A Reader: Colonizers in Britain and the Empire in the 19th and 20th Centuries*, ed. Catherine Hall (New York: Routledge, 2001), 11. Notably, Kathleen Wilson's research explored the emergence of an extra-parliamentary political culture engaged in national issues, and the people who were tied to Britain's overseas colonies. Kathleen Wilson, *The Sense of the People: Politics, Culture and Imperialism in England, 1715–1785* (Cambridge: Cambridge University Press, 1995), 3, 26, 437.

27. Christopher R. Moran, "The Pursuit of Intelligence History: Methods, Sources, and Trajectories in the United Kingdom," *Studies in Intelligence* 55, no. 2 (2011): 40, https://www.cia.gov/static/42730af69e2fc83156316f5baeb5f268/Pursuit-of-Intel-History.pdf.

28. For example, see note on sources in Jairam Ramesh, *Intertwined Lives: P. N. Haksar and Indira Gandhi* (New Delhi: Simon & Schuster, 2018), 500.

Afghanistan: The Graveyard of Intelligence Empires

Owen Sirrs

A mountainous, landlocked state located in a vital crossroads of Asia, Afghanistan was created as a buffer between two expanding European empires at the end of the nineteenth century. Indeed, it was a byproduct of the "Great Game"—a covert power struggle between Russia and British India for mastery over Central Asia. Both powers shaped the boundaries of modern Afghanistan, while the British tried to control the country's politics with often disastrous results.[1]

Historically, Afghan governments have been fragile entities, cursed by their inability to extend state power beyond the capital, Kabul, and a few other cities. This weakness is due in large part to the notoriously difficult physical terrain, the sheer multiplicity of ethno-linguistic groups and tribes, and the tendency of Afghanistan's neighbors to meddle in its internal affairs. Afghanistan is a state in near-perpetual crisis: lacking an adequate revenue base, its governments cannot maintain the security forces necessary for internal security, let alone external defense.[2]

Given these myriad challenges it is understandable why Afghan governments rely on intelligence agencies to shield them against coups, insurgencies, and conspiracies. Inevitably, too, these governments court outside powers to fund elaborate secret police systems that frequently fail to perform as expected. At different times over the last fifty years, the Soviet Union, Iran, Pakistan, and the United States midwifed new Afghan intelligence services only to see their protégés collapse in yet another spasm of Afghanistan's chronic instability.

This chapter explores how Afghanistan's intelligence culture has been shaped by ethnic, linguistic, tribal, and religious forces since 1973. Drawing on press and published studies, it also explores how frequent regime changes impacted the evolution and effectiveness of the Afghan intelligence community. The chapter begins with an overview of Afghan intelligence history, focusing on the failures and limitations of the intelligence services as well as the role external actors played in their creation. Then it analyzes the factors shaping Afghan intelligence culture by looking at ethno-linguistic diversity, ideology, generational differences between intelligence officers, and interference by external actors. The chapter concludes by exploring how the Taliban intelligence community confronts many of the same political and cultural challenges that stymied its predecessors.

AFGHAN INTELLIGENCE HISTORY

Paradoxically, considering all that was to follow, Afghanistan was a byword for numbing stability during much of the twentieth century. King Mohammed Zahir Shah, who reigned from 1933 to 1973, kept his country out of external wars while his army and police maintained a degree of tranquility at home.[3] According to a Soviet Committee for State Security (Komitet Gosudarstvennoy Bezopasnosti, KGB) evaluation written decades later, intelligence under Zahir Shah was "extremely ineffective," lacking a central archive let alone professional training in asset recruitment and evaluation.[4] Naturally, the focus of Afghan intelligence was on internal threats to the king, such as coups and tribal rebellions; the system had scanty coverage outside of Kabul and a few other urban centers. Information sharing across the Afghan intelligence "community" was practically nonexistent.[5] Not surprisingly, in 1973, these agencies failed to detect a plot hatched by Zahir Shah's ambitious cousin, Prince Daud Khan, who sent the king into an Italian exile. This was but the first of multiple security agency failures, and the consequences for the country and its people have been devastating.

Daud's coup was facilitated by the Communist People's Democratic Party of Afghanistan (PDPA), whose operatives had entrenched themselves in the armed forces and the Interior Ministry's intelligence department. It was these moles who resisted Daud when he tried to move against the PDPA in April 1978. The result was a bloodbath and the creation of a new Communist regime in Kabul.[6] The stage was now set for the creation of a centralized and ruthless intelligence service whose number one assignment was cementing the PDPA's hold on power.

The 1978 Communist coup was an epochal event in the history of Afghanistan and its security services. The PDPA was determined to "exterminate" all vestiges of the old order by imposing land reform, nationalization, secular education, and women's rights on a rural, conservative, and largely illiterate population.[7] Lacking a mass support base, the Communists enforced their revolution with the aid of the army and a new intelligence agency known by its Pashto acronym AGSA (Afghan Interests Protection Service).

Leading AGSA was an ex–air force pilot named Asadullah Sarwari whose predilection for torture and executions quickly earned him the sobriquet "King Kong."[8] Although Sarwari was aided by veterans of Daud's counter-intelligence services, the real key to AGSA's power and reach was a KGB advisory team, which centralized all state intelligence and security functions in this agency alone. This concentration of secret police power marked a significant departure from Afghanistan's recent history.[9]

But terror begat more terror. Thousands were rounded up for interrogation in AGSA torture centers or simply "disappeared" into notorious incarceration facilities like Pul-e Charki. As for AGSA itself, its leaders preferred to personally torture prisoners rather than manage the apparatus.[10] In any case, when President Nur Mohammed Taraki was murdered in a palace coup in September 1979, Sarwari and other AGSA leaders fled into exile.

The leader of the coup, Hafizullah Amin, took a personal interest in the intelligence service. While he renamed it the Worker's Protection Service, the essential elements of the AGSA apparatus—officers, informants, interrogation centers, and archives—remained the same. Moreover, the instability infecting much of rural Afghanistan was now manifesting itself in a growing insurgency that threatened the foundations of Communist rule. Amin was losing control, and the Soviet Union decided that only an invasion by the Red Army could save the Afghan revolution.

The December 1979 Soviet invasion completed the consolidation of Afghanistan's intelligence functions in one agency called the State Information Service (Khademat-e Astakhabarat-e Dawlati, KhAD). The KGB played a dominant role in creating, funding, training, and maintaining KhAD, unwittingly setting a precedent for foreign state involvement that the Central Intelligence Agency (CIA) would follow decades later.[11] KGB officers not only staffed key KhAD directorates in Kabul but also were found in provincial secret police offices.[12] More important, the KGB finally found a man with the managerial expertise and ruthless energy to stabilize Afghan intelligence, named Mohammed Najibullah. For more than five years, Najibullah presided over this vast intelligence empire until his 1986 promotion as Afghanistan's last Communist president.

Although KhAD's core mission was safeguarding the Communist regime, it ultimately could not defeat the foreign-backed insurgency.[13] In April 1992, after years of fighting, the Communist regime collapsed when Najibullah fled to a United Nations building. His intelligence chief, Ghulam Faruq Yaqubi, a veteran secret police officer from the Daud era, was found at his desk with a bullet in his head.[14] As for the Communist-era intelligence archives, they were either destroyed or taken to the Soviet Union.[15]

But KhAD was far from dead. The rebel coalition that seized power in 1992 appointed new officials to lead the former Communist Intelligence Ministry in Kabul. Still, the secret police apparatus could not prevent the country from descending into a civil war that was fueled in part by the ambitions of Pakistan, Afghanistan's eastern neighbor.[16]

In 1995, a new force emerged on the volatile Afghan scene. Calling itself Taliban (religious students), this group benefited from considerable Pakistani and Gulf Arab largesse as it systematically overran the country. By 2001, the Taliban controlled much of Afghanistan with the aid of a Kabul-based Intelligence Ministry that included officers from the Communist-era apparatus.[17] The Taliban also relied on Pakistan's Inter-Services Intelligence (ISI) and al-Qaeda for intelligence training, and this may account for some of the group's expertise in human intelligence.[18] In any case, the Taliban's ties to al-Qaeda made it the target of American retaliation after the September 11, 2001, terrorist attacks. The history of Afghan intelligence then entered a new phase.

The CIA played a pivotal role in establishing the National Directorate of Security (NDS) as Afghanistan's "new" intelligence agency after 9/11. But, in many respects, the NDS was an outgrowth of its Communist predecessor. Like KhAD, the NDS was responsible for domestic and foreign intelligence. Furthermore, it ran powerful tribal militias against insurgents in eastern Afghanistan. Certainly, at the outset, the NDS contained a substantial cadre of former KhAD officers who had been trained by the KGB. The NDS experience paralleled that of KhAD in another area as well: it too was highly reliant on a foreign intelligence service—the CIA—for funding, training, technical equipment, and intelligence.[19]

NDS problems were evident from its inception. Its internal and external missions greatly exceeded its resources while its CIA patron sometimes withheld assistance due to corruption concerns. NDS officers came from three different traditions: the KGB-trained "elder generation," a mujaheddin cadre, and a group of younger officers trained on Western models. Synchronizing these group cultures was to be the bête noire of the NDS leadership. In addition, the NDS was chronically underfunded even as Afghan decision makers turned to it to make up for shortfalls in the Afghan National Army (ANA) and National Police (ANP).[20]

It only became clear in the last years of its existence that the NDS was still too reliant on its Western partners for funds and advice. When those partners downsized their troop contributions or pulled out of Afghanistan altogether, the Afghan security forces simply could not pick up the slack. It was a vicious circle: as the ANA and ANP security perimeter shrank, the NDS human intelligence networks disappeared. Absent adequate intelligence of the enemy, the Afghan security forces were more inclined to fall back on the cities and yield ground to the Taliban.[21]

When the government collapsed in August 2021, the NDS was bereft of effective leadership, and its remaining officers either escaped in evacuation flights or surrendered to the Taliban. In fact, when lead elements of the Taliban intelligence service captured the NDS headquarters in Kabul they found abandoned equipment, heaps of classified documents, and empty prisons in the basement. Only one senior NDS official was present to hand over the keys to what had once been a large, albeit unwieldy, intelligence apparatus.[22]

INTELLIGENCE CULTURE FACTORS

Ethno-linguistic diversity has had a major impact on Afghanistan's recent history and politics, not to mention its security services. While the Pashtuns make up a plurality of the population, their political impact is nonetheless diluted by the tribalism that invariably pits them against each other. As for the other major ethnic groups, including Tajiks, Hazaras, and Uzbeks, they too have rarely united for long to counteract preponderant Pashtun influence. The result is what some observers call *yaghestan*—a "land of the rebellious" where central governments rarely have the legitimacy or power to extend their control beyond Kabul and a few other metropolitan areas.[23]

Before its 1992 demise, the People's Democratic Party of Afghanistan (PDPA) was torn by factional discord that partially reflected the country's volatile ethnic dynamic. Whereas the Parcham ("Banner") faction represented some Pashtun, Tajik, Hazara, and Uzbek urban elites, the rival Khalq ("Masses") consisted mainly of Pashtuns from the long-ignored rural parts of Afghanistan. Much of the violence that characterized the PDPA's first months in power was based on this intra-party feud. Eventually Parcham prevailed after the 1979 Soviet invasion, and most Khalqis were purged from the secret police in the early 1980s. Yet, this did not mean that Khalq influence was eradicated: for much of the 1980s, Khalq battled Parcham in a no-holds-barred power struggle that even included using insurgent groups against each other.[24]

Ethnic politics help explain how one insurgent group led by Ahmed Shah Masood was so successful in planting informants inside the PDPA bureaucracy, the armed forces, and even KhAD itself. It turns out that Masood's best informants—the ones who warned him of upcoming offensives against his Panjsher enclave—were Tajiks like him. Moreover, as Parchamis, they rarely hesitated to expose the plans of the Khalq-dominated Interior Ministry to the Tajik resistance.[25]

Even after Communist Afghanistan succumbed to a victorious rebel coalition in April 1992, the Khalq-Parcham feud persisted. The interim Afghan government, which was dominated by Tajiks and Uzbeks (until they fell out with each other), took over a decimated secret police apparatus whose rank and file were, for the most part, Parchamis. As for ex-Khalqis, they naturally gravitated to the Pashtun-dominated insurgent groups like the Party of Islam (Hezb-e Islami), which now tried to shoot their way into power. Later, when the Pashtun-dominated Taliban took over much of Afghanistan in the 1990s, ex-Khalqis were prominent in the Taliban's security apparatus.[26]

The post-9/11 Afghan intelligence system was built around NDS. The NDS was something of a hybrid organization since its intelligence officer cadre came from three different traditions with markedly different philosophies. The first group was composed of ex-PDPA security officials who had been trained by the Soviet KGB or one of the East European satellite services. Although advanced in age by 2001–2002, this cadre not only had numbers but also possessed the requisite experience and training in intelligence operations. Not surprisingly, some of the NDS's most notorious torturers were ex-KhAD officers.[27] The second group included mujaheddin intelligence experts who learned their trade the hard way during the 1980s insurgency against the Soviets or battling the Taliban in the 1990s. A few had been trained by the United States' CIA, Britain's Secret Intelligence Service (MI6), or France's General Directorate for External Security (Direction Générale de la Sécurité Extérieure, DGSE) in the 1990s, when the West woke up to the threat posed by the Taliban's alliance with al-Qaeda. Some of these Western-trained officers formed the NDS leadership in the early 2000s.[28] The third and final group represented the post-9/11 generation of intelligence officers who were trained by Western agencies in agent tradecraft and analysis. Welding these different work cultures together proved to be an insurmountable obstacle for NDS management throughout the organization's existence.[29]

In addition to workforce cultures, ethnic politics always loomed large over the NDS. In its first decade, the NDS was perceived to be a "Tajik-dominated" organization since its first two chiefs came from that ethnic group.[30] When then president Hamid Karzai decided to clean house in 2010, he replaced the Tajik Amrullah Saleh with a Pashtun named Asadollah Khaled. Khaled's appointment and that of his Pashtun successor, Rahmatullah Nabil, were resented by non-Pashtun NDS officers who accused Karzai and his successor, Ashraf Ghani, of favoritism.[31] Still, regardless of their ethnic background, the NDS chiefs frequently chafed at the tendency of both presidents to place political and tribal favorites inside the NDS's senior ranks.[32]

When it came to the Afghan intelligence community as a whole, the CIA and its partners used the Western model as a guide, even if Western notions of separating policy from intelligence and the pursuit of "objective" analysis did not really meld well with Afghan realities. In addition to the aforementioned NDS, which was primus intra pares, there were two other major players in the nascent intelligence community: military and police intelligence. The former reported to the Defense Ministry and the Armed Forces Chief of Staff while the latter was subordinated to the Interior Ministry.[33]

None of these intelligence agencies were immune from criticism when it came to human rights. Indeed, Afghan and international human rights organizations frequently denounced the NDS and its sisters for their use of torture in interrogations, off-the-books detention practices, "disappearances" of critics, and electronic eavesdropping of Afghan citizens. Part of the problem was the relative immaturity of the Afghan justice system, which could barely handle the problems posed by illiteracy, poor infrastructure, corruption, and an active insurgency, let alone tackle human rights cases. In addition, intelligence community oversight was more of a paper exercise intended to appease Western funders than to improve the performance of the individual intelligence agencies.[34]

Poor coordination and lack of information sharing between agencies was a persistent problem that led to breakdowns like the Taliban's 2015 surprise capture of Kunduz. The other agencies resented the NDS because its officers were generally better trained and equipped than those of the defense or interior ministries. Moreover, the NDS's role in sponsoring tribal militias in eastern Afghanistan led to accusations that the intelligence service was encroaching on the ANA and ANP's turf. In this environment of mutual suspicion, it is not surprising that the NDS was reluctant to share information with its "partners" who were, in fact, rivals.[35]

Some intelligence problems were hardwired into cultural traits that were difficult to suppress. Take one crucial function of intelligence—"speaking truth to power"—as a case in point. Even in the United States, which likes to boast of the supposed "objectivity" of its intelligence process, there are numerous cases where intelligence and policy have become intermingled with dangerous consequences for both. In Afghanistan, where circumlocution is often preferred over direct, "hard facts," where saving face is inevitably a part of political (and even physical) survival, shielding objective truth from power seems patently unrealistic if not risible. When Amrullah Saleh, the CIA-trained NDS chief, conducted an in-depth analysis of the resurgent Taliban in 2006, the result was lambasted by President Karzai, who especially resented the characterization of the Taliban as an "insurgency." Curiously, the Bush administration rejected Saleh's study for the same reason.[36]

Pakistan's role in fueling the Taliban insurgency was always a contentious issue between the NDS and its political masters. Most NDS chiefs, regardless of ethnicity, were adamant that Pakistan's ISI sustained the Taliban and the Haqqani Network. This conviction ran up against the grim realities confronting each Afghan president: no long-term peace in Afghanistan was possible absent Pakistan and, sooner or later, every Afghan leader had to make the humiliating trip to Islamabad to find out what Pakistan's price for peace was. In the case of the first three NDS chiefs, Afghan-Pakistan relations featured prominently in their dismissals/resignations.[37]

The thorny Pakistan issue also bedeviled the NDS-CIA relationship. Afghan intelligence chiefs believed their American patrons were too deferential toward ISI. When the CIA tried to engineer a rapprochement between the leaders of ISI and the NDS, the result was acrimony, mud-slinging, and a sense among the Afghans that ISI was arrogant, overbearing, and patronizing. It was believed in some NDS circles that ISI pressured Karzai and Ghani into firing their "anti-Pakistan" NDS chiefs as a prerequisite for peace.[38]

NDS relations with the CIA were fraught on another level, too. In a world where trust in the intelligence "product" is imperative, the CIA questioned the objectivity of some NDS analysis. This doubt was aggravated by Langley's conviction that the Russians, Iranians, and Pakistanis had infiltrated the NDS to such an extent that any meaningful cooperation required very close counterintelligence monitoring. It is noteworthy that neither the KGB nor Soviet military intelligence placed much faith in KhAD assessments either.[39]

Another significant issue plaguing NDS-CIA ties was ranking adversaries and aligning limited resources against them. The CIA was focused heavily on al-Qaeda, and it maintained tribal militias ("counterterrorism pursuit teams" in Langley's anodyne parlance) to hunt and kill al-Qaeda operatives in eastern Afghanistan. For its part, the NDS concentrated on the Taliban and ISI.[40] As a Pakistan-backed insurgency, the Taliban unquestionably posed a more lethal threat to the Afghan government than al-Qaeda. The Taliban had not only the guns but also an organized presence in the Afghan outback, where its "shadow governments" blended a powerful mix of rough-and-ready justice with relatively low levels of corruption and a strong dose of intimidation.[41]

Taliban intelligence "departments" were found at every level of governance from the Iran- and Pakistan-based *shuras* down to the provinces and individual districts. One mission of the intelligence departments was to serve as an oversight mechanism for the shadow government. Another was to build and sustain village spy networks. It was these latter structures that constituted the heart and soul of the Taliban intelligence system. They not only enforced loyalty to the shadow government but also broadcast insurgent propaganda, uprooted government intelligence networks, executed government spies and collaborators, and monitored government and Coalition troop movements.[42] One US journalist nicely summed up the strengths of Taliban intelligence in 2001: "The Taliban is strongest where US intelligence is weakest: in the bazaars, mosques, and teahouses of Afghanistan."[43]

Some observers believed that Taliban intelligence was too decentralized to be effective at coordinating regional- and national-level intelligence operations. They also questioned the Taliban's ability to produce objective analysis, although this was a shortcoming afflicting Afghan intelligence as a whole.[44] Such criticism seems to be contradicted by the Taliban's rapid accession to power during summer 2021.

Italian researcher Antonio Giustozzi offered a more nuanced picture of Taliban intelligence that may account for some of the organization's successes on the ground. He reported that, starting in 2006, the Taliban implemented concrete measures to professionalize its intelligence cadre, including the creation of the aforementioned intelligence departments and teaching a specific course to the movement's intelligence officers. Steps were also taken to improve counterintelligence, such as an institutionalized cadre vetting process.[45]

Ultimately, the effectiveness of the government's intelligence community was checked by forces well beyond the capability of the NDS and its Western allies to master. In a society where the state is often seen as weak or irrelevant (at best) or a dangerous interloper (at worst), Afghans invariably fall back on other, horizontal hierarchies for survival. Depending on location and circumstance, those stronger claims on loyalty may be exerted by clan elders, family patriarchs, mullahs, drug lords, or charismatic militia leaders. In this environment, betraying a vague "state" or "nation" is far less important than betraying a prominent family member or community leader.[46] Thus, betrayals of the Afghan state are common since the state itself is a fungible concept and the costs of betraying it relatively insignificant.

CONCLUSION

The Taliban regime that bribed its way to power in summer 2021 will confront many of the same problems that debilitated its predecessors. If there is one thing that the last fifty years have taught us it is that coercive fear has its limits, especially in a country as complicated and difficult to govern as Afghanistan. The multiple ethnic, linguistic, and even religious cleavages will still be there, and the Pashtun-centric Taliban will be hard-pressed to accommodate them. Even the Pashtun "community," divided as it is by clan, tribe, and region, will clash with Taliban authority over how scarce state revenues are spent. As this study demonstrates, producing objective analysis, operating and maintaining technical intelligence assets, forging a common intelligence culture, and even supporting a true intelligence community will require resources and expertise that the Taliban cannot muster on its own.

The new Taliban intelligence apparatus will also struggle against multiple counterintelligence dangers. Its first order of business will be deciding what to do with the old NDS: how much of that should be incorporated into the new intelligence structure—with the attendant problems of disloyalty? How will Taliban internal security adapt to threats posed by irreconcilable NDS elements, the CIA, Russia, Iran, and India? What about Pakistan's ISI? Intelligence allies today probably will be intelligence adversaries tomorrow.

Lack of resources will be another major obstacle confronting Taliban intelligence. How will the new intelligence structure pay its officers, buy equipment, recruit informants, and fund operations? In this regard, Taliban intelligence faces the same financial problems as its NDS predecessor did, but without the deep pockets of powerful Western allies. It is doubtful that narcotics and extortion will be enough to sustain a centralized Taliban security apparatus over the long term.

A great deal will also depend on the Taliban's ability to forge an effective governance system. While Taliban "justice" supposedly worked in local areas under its control prior to 2021, it is doubtful this model can be successfully adapted to the national level. The ruling *shura* will be stressed to provide oversight of the intelligence community in the areas of corruption, extortion, and infighting. Judicial corruption and gross mismanagement badly undercut the Western-backed Afghan regime. It remains to be seen if "Taliban sharia" truly represents a viable alternative.

The Pakistan problem won't go away either. While ISI has served as the Taliban's main sponsor since the mid-1990s, its generals have grown used to playing the role of big brother. Not only can ISI arrogance grate on Taliban sensibilities, Pakistan's interests and those of the Taliban will not always coincide, especially since the latter now constitutes a government in its own right. Indeed, Taliban intelligence will probably struggle to bridge the gap between ISI demands and the natural Afghan tendency to suspect the worst of their eastern neighbor.

Finally, there will be the challenge of treason. We have already seen how this overwhelmed earlier governments, and it is safe to say it will afflict the Taliban as well. While the Taliban has always used coercion for political gain, will this be enough now that the Taliban is in power? It is reasonable to predict that under Taliban rule Afghans will be torn between different demands on their loyalty: those exerted by the Islamic Emirate versus traditionally stronger claimants at the local level. The problem of treason is, of course, closely linked to counterintelligence.

Taliban security *will* be different than that of its ousted predecessor. It will be harsher, blending intimidation, brutality, and extortion. The Taliban has long relied on an aura of fear and invincibility; however, barring positive inducements like development and education, the fear factor will eventually lose its potency. The *"yaghestan"* phenomenon—Afghanistan's historic tendency to rebellion and disorder—seems destined to return with a vengeance.

NOTES

1. On three separate occasions (1839–1842, 1878–1880, and 1919), Afghan fighters successfully resisted British India's efforts to control their country. See Peter Hopkirk, *The Great Game: The Struggle for Empire in Central Asia* (New York: Kodansha, 1992); Karl Meyer and Shareen Blair Brysac, *Tournament of Shadows: The Great Game and the Race for Empire in Central Asia* (New York: Perseus Books, 1999).

2. William Kerr Fraser-Tytler, *Afghanistan: A Study in Political Developments in Central and Southern Asia*, 3rd ed. (London: Oxford University Press, 1950).

3. Cable from Amembassy Kabul, "German Police Advisory Team: Ministry of Interior," no. 03599, May 16, 1973; Steve Coll, *Directorate S* (New York: Penguin, 2018), 124.

4. Vladimir Snegirev and Valerii Samunin, *Virus A: Kak my zaboleli Btorzheniyem v Afghanistan* (Moscow: Rossiiskaya Gazeta, 2011), translated as *The Dead End: The Road to Afghanistan*, ed. and trans. Svetlana Savranskaya and Malcolm Byrne (Washington, DC: National Security Archive, 2012), 122.

5. Gregory Feifer, *The Great Gamble* (New York: Harper, 2009), 28; Anthony Hyman, *Afghanistan under Soviet Domination, 1964–81* (New York: St. Martin's, 1982), 52–53; Harvey Smith et al., *Afghanistan: A Country Study* (Washington, DC: American University, 1973), 380; J. Bruce Amstutz, *Afghanistan: The First Five Years of Soviet Occupation* (Washington, DC: National Defense University Press, 1985), 264.

6. There were at least two PDPA moles inside Daoud's Interior Ministry: Pacha Sarbaz and Ghulam Farook Yaqubi. See Barnett Rubin, *The Fragmentation of Afghanistan* (New Haven, CT: Yale University Press, 1995), 102; Sher Zaman Taizi, *The Saur Revolution (1978–86)* (Peshawar: Frontier Post Publications, 1991), 43–44; Anthony Arnold, *Afghanistan's Two-Party Communism: Parcham and Khalq* (Stanford, CA: Stanford University, Hoover Institution Press, 1983), 59.

7. John Fullerton, *The Soviet Occupation of Afghanistan* (Hong Kong: South China Morning Post, n.d.), 33–34; Peter Tomsen, *The Wars of Afghanistan* (New York: PublicAffairs, 2011), 132–33.

8. Hyman, *Afghanistan under Soviet Domination*, 108.

9. Tomsen, *The Wars of Afghanistan*, 121; Snegirev and Samunin, *Virus A*, 127–28, 228.

10. Snegirev and Samunin, *Virus A*, 130.

11. Christopher Andrew and Vasili Mitrokhin, *The World Was Going Our Way: The KGB and the Battle for the Third World* (New York: Basic Books, 2005), 408.

12. Vadim Kirpichenko, *Razvedka: Litsa i Lichnosti* (Moscow: Mezhdunarodnie Otnosheniye, 2019), 358–59.

13. In 1986 KhAD was renamed the Ministry of State Security. Amstutz, *Afghanistan*, 266–67.

14. Feifer, *The Great Gamble*, 150; Rubin, *The Fragmentation of Afghanistan*, 154, 294.

15. Diva Patang, "Afghanistan Intelligence War," *Wild Blue Yonder*, Air University, February 17, 2020.

16. Steve Coll, *Ghost Wars* (New York: Penguin, 2004), 286–87.

17. Note from Netherlands Delegation to the Council for Information and Exchange on Asylum of the European Union, "Afghanistan—Security Services in Communist Afghanistan (1978–1992)," no. 7953/01, April 26, 2001, 30.

18. Ben Brandt, "The Taliban's Conduct of Intelligence and Counterintelligence," *CTC Sentinel* 4, no. 6 (June 2011): 20.

19. Steve Coll called the NDS a "stepchild" of the KGB: Coll, *Directorate S*, 122–23. Also see Thomas Gibbons-Neff and Julian Barnes, "To Save Peace Deal with Taliban, U.S. May Reduce C.I.A. Presence in Afghanistan," *New York Times*, April 18, 2020; and David Jolly and Mark Mazzetti, "C.I.A.-Trained Forces in Afghanistan Scrutinized after Civilian Deaths," *New York Times*, December 4, 2015.

20. Greg Miller et al., "From 'Torturer in Chief' to Life in U.S.," *Washington Post*, April 29, 2014; Matthew Rosenberg, "Afghan Spy Chief Defies Labels, Usefully," *New York Times*, January 17, 2015; Coll, *Directorate S*, 124, 192.

21. Miller et al., "From 'Torturer in Chief'"; Tamim Asey, "Intelligence Reform for Peacetime—a Call to Reform and Modernize the Afghan Intelligence Services," Atlantic Council, March 22, 2021; Jessica Donati and Margherita Stancati, "Intelligence Gap Fuels Extremist Rise in Afghanistan," *Wall Street Journal*, December 22, 2015.

22. "Videos Show Children in Airport Chaos," *New York Times*, August 21, 2021; Matthieu Aikins, "After Quick Victory, Taliban Find Governing Harder," *New York Times*, September 1, 2021.

23. Sarah Chayes, *The Punishment of Virtue* (New York: Penguin, 2006).

24. Feifer, *The Great Gamble*, 147; Amstutz, *Afghanistan*, 266, Rubin, *The Fragmentation of Afghanistan*, 151, 271; Tomsen, *The Wars of Afghanistan*, 93.

25. Andrew and Mitrokhin, *The World Was Going Our Way*, 414; Coll, *Ghost Wars*, 122, 347–48; Feifer, *The Great Gamble*, 173; Rubin, *The Fragmentation of Afghanistan*, 269; Tomsen, *The Wars of Afghanistan*, 341.

26. Coll, *Directorate S*, 124; Note from Netherlands Delegation, 30.

27. A. Rasul Amin, "The Sovietization of Afghanistan," in *Afghanistan: The Great Game Revisited*, ed. Rosanne Klass (New York: Freedom House, 1987), 323; Kirpichenko, *Razvedka*, 358–59; Andrew and Mitrokhin, *The World Was Going Our Way*, 408–9.

28. Coll, *Ghost Wars*, 123; Coll, *Directorate S*, 12–13, 19.

29. Miller et al., "From 'Torturer in Chief'"; Asey, "Intelligence Reform"; Tamim Asey, "Making Intelligence Work: A Call to Reform and Re-organize the Afghan Intelligence Community," *Small Wars Journal*, December 24, 2018; Note from Netherlands Delegation.

30. Coll, *Directorate S*, 190.

31. Coll, *Directorate S*, 118.

32. Miller et al., "From 'Torturer in Chief.'"

33. Robert Walters and Loren Traugutt, "The State of Afghanistan's Intelligence Enterprise," *Military Review*, May–June 2017, 64–71; US Department of Defense, *Enhancing Security and Stability in Afghanistan* (Washington, DC: DOD, June 2020), 51.

34. Rosenberg, "Afghan Spy Chief"; Miller et al., "From 'Torturer in Chief.'"

35. Asey, "Making Intelligence Work"; Abdul Zuhoor Qayomi, "Fall of Kunduz City: Nabil Apologizes to Nation, Tells Lawmakers Intelligence Reports Were Overlooked," *Afghanistan Times*, September 30, 2015; Bilal Sarwary, "Afghanistan's Dysfunctional Security Agencies," BBC, August 14, 2011.

36. Coll, *Directorate S*, 216–18.

37. Ernesto Londono, "Karzai Ousts Two Top Officials," *Washington Post*, June 7, 2010; Hamid Shalizi, "Afghan Spy Chief Resigns after Fallout with President," Reuters, December 10, 2015; Thomas Ruttig, "Political Cleavages over Pakistan: The NDS Chief's Farewell," Afghanistan Analysts Network, December 23, 2015.

38. Coll, *Directorate S*, 215; Londono, "Karzai Ousts Two Top Officials."

39. Coll, *Directorate S*, 122–23, 192, 215; Asey, "Intelligence Reform"; Feifer, *The Great Gamble*, 117–18.

40. Coll, *Directorate S*, 192, 215; Thomas Gibbons-Neff and Julian Barnes, "To Save Peace Deal with Taliban, U.S. May Reduce C.I.A. Presence in Afghanistan," *New York Times*, April 18, 2020; Thomas Gibbons-Neff et al., "C.I.A. to Expand Its Covert Role in Afghanistan," *New York Times*, October 23, 2017.

41. Antonio Giustozzi, *Koran, Kalashnikov, and Laptop: The Neo-Taliban Insurgency in Afghanistan* (New York: Columbia University Press, 2008), 97–139.

42. Giustozzi, *Koran, Kalashnikov, and Laptop*, 156–57; Tom Coghlan, "The Taliban in Helmand: An Oral History," in *Decoding the New Taliban: Insights from the Afghan Field*, ed. Antonio Giustozzi (New York: Columbia University Press, 2009), 142; James Astill, "Taliban Spies Keep Strong Grip on South," *Guardian*, December 10, 2003; Brandt, "The Taliban's Conduct," 19–20.

43. Tim McGirk, "Taliban Spies: In the Cross Hairs," *Time*, November 12, 2001.

44. Brandt, "The Taliban's Conduct," 20; Borzou Daragahi, "The Taliban Embraces New Intelligence Methods," *Los Angeles Times*, April 15, 2011.

45. Antonio Giustozzi, *Afghanistan: Taliban's Intelligence and the Intimidation Campaign* (Oslo: Landinfo, 2017).

46. Snegirev and Samunin, *Virus A*, 122.

2

Bangladesh: Intelligence Culture and Reform Priorities

ASM Ali Ashraf

There is phenomenal growth in the study of intelligence cultures and reforms in the post-9/11 era. Bangladesh and its South Asian neighbors are stark examples. In Bangladesh alone, more than a dozen universities now include courses on intelligence culture and history, organizational reform, and accountability issues. This was hardly seen a decade ago. Media and think tanks have also responded to growing public interest. Consequently, intelligence issues are becoming a central theme in discussions of national security rather than peripheral matters of civil-military relations.[1] Political masters have taken up the opportunity to declassify intelligence archives to glorify the independence movement. The *Secret Documents of Intelligence Branch on Father of the Nation Bangabandhu Sheikh Mujibur Rahman*, a fourteen-volume book series, is a case in point.[2] The *Secret Documents* represent the first major declassification of the intelligence archive of the Special Branch (SB) of the Bangladesh Police. They shed light on how the West Pakistani rulers tasked their Intelligence Branch to closely monitor the architect of Bangladesh's independence movement for twenty-four years (1948–1971). Serving military officials have also begun writing about intelligence in the context of United Nations (UN) peacekeeping missions.[3]

In the context of such growth in intelligence studies, two questions arise: How is the intelligence community (IC) of Bangladesh organized, and what are the salient features of intelligence culture and reform priorities in the country? Answers to these questions will address the prevailing knowledge gap on a country that has the seventh-largest population in the world, is located in the strategically important Indian Ocean Region, and now contributes the largest UN peacekeeping force.

15

The chapter begins with an overview of Bangladesh's IC with attention to specific intelligence services and their objectives. Turning to the drivers of reform, the chapter then examines key events that have shaped intelligence reform in the last several years, which mainly centers on terrorism, border, and refugee issues. Next, oversight is explored by highlighting the institutions and coordination of intelligence. Moving to international cooperation, intelligence partnerships are discussed within historical context and how geography has shaped those relations. Lastly, the chapter concludes by describing how Bangladesh's intelligence culture and reform priorities are influenced by politics.

BANGLADESH'S INTELLIGENCE COMMUNITY AND CULTURE

Bangladesh has inherited a British colonial bureaucratic system with a culture of secrecy in matters of intelligence, law enforcement, and national security. Since independence from Pakistan in 1971, successive governments have tasked the intelligence agencies to collect, analyze, and disseminate information for the purpose of both internal control and external security. Yet, concerns over regime survival, ethnic insurgency, and law and order have historically given the security and intelligence agencies an expansive mandate in internal affairs. It is only recently that the fight against terrorism, multidimensional peacekeeping and refugee influx have necessitated a growing role for external intelligence. Following several high-profile intelligence failures in the past two decades, the reform priorities have focused on capacity building, interagency coordination, and international cooperation.

The Directorate General of Forces Intelligence (DGFI), the National Security Intelligence (NSI), and the SB are the principal intelligence agencies in Bangladesh.[4] Among them the DGFI and the NSI have dual mandates of national security and internal control, whereas the SB is mandated to conduct political surveillance and manage immigration control. These three agencies rely extensively on human intelligence (HUMINT) collection efforts but differ in recruits, officer cadres, and reporting authorities.

The DGFI is a tri-service intelligence agency responsible for the assessment of secret information that concern the armed forces. It operates with nine headquarters-level bureaus and nineteen detachments throughout the country. The agency is manned by military personnel drawn from the army, navy, and air force, and permanent civilian staff. Although it was conceived of "all forces' intelligence," the functions of DGFI have evolved to include internal and external affairs, national security, counterterrorism, and counterintelligence. DGFI acquired signals intelligence (SIGINT) capabilities and maintains intelligence partnerships with a number of countries including China, India, Russia, the United Kingdom, and the United States.

As for the NSI, it collects, collates, and analyzes intelligence pertaining to internal security, domestic and international terrorism, and foreign governments. It is manned mostly by civilian officials, but the senior leadership structure comprising the director general and a few director posts are filled by serving military officials. NSI agents are stationed in all of the sixty-four administrative districts in Bangladesh and in selected foreign countries.

Turning to law enforcement and domestic issues, the SB was established during the British colonial period. It is the oldest and the largest of the three having extensive field-level collectors. It monitors the activities of opposition political parties, student movements, and trade unions due to their propensity to agitate against the incumbent government.[5] As transnational organized crime is emerging as a serious threat, SB has mounted its surveillance efforts through immigration control and open source intelligence (OSINT) to assess the complex threats of money laundering, human trafficking, and cybercrimes. It also monitors critical infrastructure and works on preventing sabotage against the government.[6]

A salient feature of the intelligence culture of Bangladesh concerns the coexistence of both political and apolitical roles of various agencies. Over the past fifty years, successive governments in Bangladesh have tasked the DGFI, NSI, and SB to monitor political dissidents for regime consolidation purposes.[7] Their roles become more pronounced ahead of the national elections. But there are other intelligence entities that maintain apolitical roles for national defense and international security. The Armed Forces Division (AFD) at the Prime Minister's Office has an Intelligence Directorate (IntD) for providing the required security and intelligence directives to the three services. It maintains liaisons with armed forces and various intelligence agencies on defense and national security. The Directorate of Military Intelligence (DMI), the Directorate of Naval Intelligence (DNI), and the Directorate of Air Intelligence (DAI) are the intelligence outfits of the army, navy, and air force, respectively. They analyze threats to sovereignty and territorial integrity originating from land, maritime, and airborne sources. The two decades of ethnic insurgency in the Chittagong Hill Tracts (CHT) of Bangladesh and Myanmar's hostile activities in the southeastern border areas are the prime concerns of DMI. The Border Security Bureau and the Coast Guard Intelligence focus on disrupting cross-border infiltration and smuggling in land and maritime areas. All of these defense and border intelligence entities operate within the country through HUMINT collectors in the field and analysts at the headquarters.[8]

Peacekeeping intelligence is a top priority for Bangladesh. The Operations and Plan Directorate (OPD) of the AFD plays a key role through its Foreign

Affairs and Protocol section to accumulate intelligence inputs for ongoing and future peace missions. The OPD assembles data from the Overseas Operations Directorate of Army HQ, Directorate of Naval Overseas Operations of Navy HQ, and the Directorate of Air Overseas Operations of Air HQ to synthesize security assessments and determine training and logistics requirements for the mission areas. The IntD at AFD is connected in the loop on an as-needed basis. In overseas missions, the Bangladeshi contingents collaborate with other troop-contributing countries and the UN HQ to make extensive use of HUMINT, TECHINT, and OSINT.[9] As the conflicts in Mali, the Democratic Republic of Congo, and the Central African Republic are becoming increasingly riskier than other missions, Bangladeshi contingents are adapting their intelligence, surveillance, and reconnaissance efforts to fulfill their mission mandates. While the AFD takes the coordinating role in peacekeeping matters, for procedural reasons, the DGFI, DMI, DNI, and DAI get connected to the intelligence process to monitor the integrity of Bangladeshi troops deployed overseas.[10]

Counterterrorism (CT) has emerged as an important area of intelligence reform.[11] The Counterterrorism and Transnational Crime (CTTC) Unit was established in 2016 as a principal CT arm of Dhaka Metropolitan Police (DMP), a model that has been replicated in other metropolitan cities. Intelligence analysts at CTTC depend on OSINT, social media monitoring, and tips from the Police HQ and its Lawful Interception Cell (LIC) for analyzing a broad spectrum of terrorist activities spanning radicalization and recruitment, funding and training, operational planning, and transnational connections.[12] The LIC operates under the Intelligence and Special Affairs (ISA) wing of Police HQ as a small SIGINT center. Additionally, the SB also provides sensitive information to CTTC for operational purposes.[13] The CTTC boosts the development of an analytical culture for Bangladeshi IC. A core team of CTTC officials are digging historical and contemporary data and archival materials, drawn from the Task Force for Interrogation (TFI) cell and various court case documents, to produce a nuanced assessment of the terrorist threat.[14]

Additionally, the government established the Anti-Terrorism Unit (ATU) in 2017 as an investigating agency and operational force. The CTTC and ATU complement each other. While the CTTC's mandate of terrorism investigation is restricted to the Dhaka Metropolitan city, the ATU has a nationwide mandate. With executive orders from the Police HQ, the CTTC can launch operations throughout Bangladesh, but its investigation remit is limited to Dhaka Metropolitan only.

The CTTC deploys its striking force, Special Action Group (SAG), to conduct its operations. Between 2016 and 2020, the SAG carried out two dozen high-risk operations targeting militants affiliated with two organizations—the Neo-Jama'atul Islam Mujahideen Bangladesh (Neo-JMB) and the Ansar al Islam (AAI). Notable among the CTTC's operations include a raid in 2016 that killed Neo-JMB leader Tamim Chowdhury, who masterminded the Holey Artisan Restaurant and Café attack in the same year that killed twenty-five people including nine Italians, seven Japanese, an American, and an Indian. In another CTTC raid in 2016, nine Neo-JMB's suicide operatives were killed in the Kalyanpur area of northern Dhaka.[15]

The Rapid Action Battalion (RAB) is another major CT entity in Bangladesh.[16] Although it was established in 2004 as a composite force of personnel drawn from civilian police and military forces, its intelligence and operational wings are dominated by military personnel attached to it. With its headquarters, battalion, and company-level intelligence collectors and analysts, RAB achieved notable successes against terrorists and organized criminals.[17] In the initial years of its founding RAB arrested top militant leaders including Mufti Abdul Hannan of Harkat ul Jihad al Islami Bangladesh (HUJI-B), Shayakh Abdur Rahman of Old-JMB, and Siddikul Islam alias Bangla Bhai of Jagrata Muslim Janata Bangladesh (JMJB).[18] The arrest of top militant leaders contributed to their judicial prosecution in several high-profile trials, such as the August 2004 attack on the Awami League rally in Dhaka that targeted then opposition leader and current prime minister Sheikh Hasina. RAB also played a key role in the arrest and prosecution of militants responsible for the August 2005 series bombings in Bangladesh, as well as the November 2005 killing of two judges in the southern Jhalakathi District.[19]

While the ATU, CTTC, and RAB are new CT actors, the "big three" agencies have also created CT units. The list includes the DGFI's Counter-Terrorism Intelligence Bureau (CTIB), the NSI's Counter Terrorism Wing (CTW), and the SB's Counter-Terrorism Section (CTS). These are in-house intelligence desks of their mother agencies created for the purpose of monitoring terrorist activities in the real and virtual worlds and for developing improved capacity to apprise the cabinet, the prime minister, and the home minister.[20]

The leadership structure of the CT agencies varies. Senior military officials from Bangladesh armed forces act as the heads of CTIB, CTW, and RAB Intelligence Wing (RIW), and as a result, interagency collaboration is very robust among them. The CTIB and CTW are headed by army brigadier-generals, while the RIW is usually directed by an army lieutenant colonel.[21] The CTTC chief is a deputy inspector general (DIG) of the police, and the ATU chief is a one-rank senior additional inspector general of Police (Addl. IGP). Intelligence sharing among the civilian police entities is very high.

Bureaucratic turf battles between the civilian and military CT units often come to the surface regarding the assessment of terrorist threats.

A new SIGINT and technical intelligence (TECHINT) agency, the National Monitoring Cell (NMC) was formed in 2008 within the DGFI. It was later expanded in 2013 as a full-fledged intelligence agency with a new name, the National Telecommunication Monitoring Center (NTMC).[22] The NTMC operates under the Ministry of Home Affairs (MOHA).[23] The founding director of NTMC is a serving brigadier in the Bangladesh army, who previously oversaw RAB's intelligence and operations. The NTMC is developing a large criminal database for interagency collaboration.

As for monitoring financial crime, the Bangladesh Financial Intelligence Unit (BFIU), the Customs Intelligence and Investigation Directorate (CIID), and the Central Intelligence Cell (CIC) have important roles.[24] Operating under the Ministry of Finance, they analyze three distinct types of threats. The BFIU monitors money laundering and terrorist financing, the CIID deals with smuggling of goods and commodities, and the CIC focuses on tax evasion by large business entities.[25] These three financial intelligence entities work closely with the Anti-Corruption Commission (ACC) and the Criminal Investigation Department (CID) of Police. Financial crimes related to money laundering are referred to the ACC, and terrorist financing are referred to the CID for further investigation and criminal prosecution.

Lastly, law enforcement intelligence involves the CID, the Detective Branch (DB), and the Police Bureau of Investigation (PBI), which are three constituent agencies of Bangladesh Police. Among these agencies, the CID is the largest and the oldest, a British legacy that it shares with the SB.[26] The PBI was established in 2012 to investigate homicides, property crimes, sexual assaults, arson, and cybercrime.[27] Although the CID, DB, and PBI are investigative agencies, their role in the investigation of organized and serious crime can contribute to national security. The Prisons Intelligence Unit (PIU) acts as a counterintelligence entity of the Prisons Department. As prison and probation services are key stakeholders in rehabilitating and reintegrating terrorists, the role of PIU can hardly be overstated.[28] The CID is headed by an Addl. IGP, whereas the DB and PBI are headed by DIGs. The PIU is overseen by a serving military official at the rank of colonel.

DRIVERS OF INTELLIGENCE REFORM

Several events in the past two decades have acted as key drivers for intelligence reform in Bangladesh. The rise of Islamist militancy has been the most significant driver. This was evident in the July 2016 Holey Artisan terrorist attack that killed innocent civilians and restaurant visitors. The victims were kept as hostages and brutally killed by five armed militants wearing Islamic State of Iraq and Syria (ISIS) garb. The twelve-hour siege at the Holey Artisan Café ended with the First Paracommando Battalion of the Bangladesh army leading a joint security forces drive that killed all of the five militants. Although ISIS claimed responsibility for the café attack, subsequent investigations and judicial trial process revealed how homegrown militants partnered with a section of the radicalized Bangladeshi diaspora to plan and execute the attack.

The café attack was the culmination of two decades of Islamist militancy in Bangladesh. During this time, four militant groups—HUJI-B, Old-JMB, AAI, and Neo-JMB—emerged as the dominant threats. Among them, the Neo-JMB claims to be a local affiliate of Iraq- and Syria-based ISIS-Central with no connections to the ISIS-Khorasan Province in Afghanistan. Intelligence analysts are puzzled by the variations in targeting strategy and attack methods of the militant groups. The HUJI-B was notorious for using grenade attacks against high-value targets. By contrast, the JMB came into the limelight in August 2005 after detonating 500 improvised explosive devices (IEDs) all over the country. The group emerged more menacing in November 2005 when one of its suicide operatives killed two judges by hurling explosives at a minivan carrying them to court. RAB succeeded in arresting most of the top HUJI-B and JMB leaders, who later received death sentences after lengthy trials. Half a decade later, the AAI emerged primarily as a social media–based platform targeting secular online activists, bloggers, and LGBT rights activists, all of whom were labeled atheists and the enemies of Islam.[29] The militant activities of the violent extremist groups reached their climax with the Neo-JMB's café attack. The group used semiautomatic rifles, suicide vests, and explosives for the café attack, but for other attacks, it deployed suicide bombers and sleeper cells armed with guns and explosives.

This rich narrative of the terrorism landscape is important to understand the emergence of an intelligence-led policing culture. Since the DGFI, NSI, and SB are purely spy agencies, and not operational forces, their intelligence outfits have rarely been public with their assessments. In contrast, the latter three operational forces—RAB, CTTC, and ATU—often hold media briefings giving details of their CT operations.

The armed rebellion at the Bangladesh Rifles (BDR) headquarters in February 2009 was another key driver for intelligence reform. A leaked probe report concluded that the NSI, DGFI, and SB lacked any collection efforts during the mutiny and before it started. Members of the Rifles Security Unit, BDR's counterintelligence entity, were also compromised as they participated in the planning of the mutiny.[30] The BDR mutiny was an embarrassment for Prime Minister Sheikh Hasina whose party came to power just a month before the mutiny in January 2009. There was no formal inter-agency coordination system at that time, which created a huge controversy over the government's crisis management strategy. The Hasina government formed the National Committee for Intelligence Coordination (NCIC) in July 2009 in response to a recommendation of the Anis Uz Zaman Committee report, part of which was leaked to the media.[31]

A third major event concerns refugee influx from Myanmar. Since August 2017, nearly 800,000 Rohingya Muslim minorities from Myanmar's Rakhine State entered Bangladesh, fleeing persecution from the Myanmar security forces. This new refugee cohort joined another batch of 300,000 Rohingya refugees who fled to Bangladesh over three decades. Apparently, the refugee influx was caused by a security drive in Rakhine state that involved destroying Rohingya houses and killing Rohingya men and women. Yet, the Myanmar government's systematic eviction remained completely unnoticed, producing no warning of an impending refugee influx in Bangladesh.

The refugee influx has demonstrated the need for integrating intelligence in foreign and security policy making. Various agencies have field-level agents in the Rohingya refugee camps to monitor the law-and-order situations. Bangladeshi agencies are aware of Indian media reports circulating news of Pakistan's Inter-Services Intelligence (ISI) Directorate attempting to recruit Rohingya refugees into terrorist groups.[32] Military intelligence agencies closely watch Myanmar's hostile and provocative activities in the border areas. On the diplomatic side, concerned area specialists at the Ministry of Foreign Affairs (MOFA) provide much of the intelligence and analysis pertaining to Bangladesh's search for repatriation as the most preferred solution to the Rohingya crisis. The NSI and DGFI also keep a close eye on the Rohingya issue by providing useful inputs to Bangladesh's attempt to internationalize the Rohingya issue.

INTELLIGENCE COORDINATION AND OVERSIGHT

There are three national-level security and intelligence coordination structures in Bangladesh. Two of them are headed by the prime minister and the third by a senior cabinet member (see figure 2.1). The principal intelligence coordination body NCIC got a legal footing through a gazette notification in March 2019.[33] While the DGFI, NSI, and SB have remained the key members of the NCIC, its membership has been extended to the Ministry of Home Affairs and the CTTC. As MOHA is the lead ministry for CT intelligence and operations, the minister and top bureaucrats of MOHA are now part of

Notes: Major counterterrorism intelligence entities are shown in bold font, among them those headed by military officials are shown in oval shape entities. In addition to the Overseas Operations Directorate (OOD) of the Army HQ, the Directorate of Naval Overseas Operations at Navy HQ, and the Directorate of Air Overseas Operations at Air HQ manage peacekeeping affairs for Bangladeshi troops. For simplicity, only OOD is shown here.

Notes on Abbreviations

Addl IGP	Additional Inspector General of Police	MOCAT	Ministry of Civil Aviation and Tourism
Addl Com	Additional Commissioner of Police	MOD	Ministry of Defense
AFD	Armed Forces Division [under Prime Minister's Office]	MOF	Ministry of Finance
ATU	Anti Terrorism Unit	DG	Director General
BFIU	Bangladesh Financial Intelligence Unit	MOHA	Ministry of Home Affairs
BGB	Border Guard Bangladesh	MOF	Ministry of Finance
BSB	Border Security Bureau	MOFA	Ministry of Foreign Affairs
CG	Coast Guard	MOI	Ministry of Information
CGI	Coast Guard Intelligence	MOInd	Ministry of Industries
CIC	Central Intelligence Cell	MOLJPA	Ministry of Law, Justice, and Parliamentary Affaires
CID	Criminal Investigation Department	MOP	Ministry of Planning
CIID	Customs Intelligence and Investigation Directorate	MOPEMR	Ministry of Power Energy and Mineral Resources
CTTC	Counter Terrorism and Transnational Crime	NCIC	National Committee for Intelligence Coordination
CTIB	Counter Terrorism Intelligence Bureau	NCSA	National Committee for Security Affairs
CTS	Counter Terrorism Section	NSI	National Security Intelligence
CTW	Counter Terrorism Wing	NTMC	National Telecommunication Monitoring Cell
DAI	Directorate of Air Intelligence	OOD	Overseas Operations Directorate
DB	Detective Branch	OPD	Operations and Plans Directorate
DG	Director General	PBI	Police Bureau of Investigation
DGFI	Directorate General of Forces Intelligence	PHQ-ISA	Police Headquarters Intelligence and Special Affairs Wing
DMI	Directorate of Military Intelligence	PSD	Public Security Division of Ministry of Home Affairs
DMP	Dhaka Metropolitan Police	PSO	Principal Staff Officer
DNI	Directorate of Naval Intelligence	RAB	Rapid Action Battalion
HQ	Headquarters	RIW	RAB Intelligence Wing
IGP	Inspector General of Police	SB	Special Branch
IntD	Intelligence Directorate	SSD	Security Services Division of Ministry of Home Affairs
MOC	Ministry of Commerce	SSF	Special Security Force

Figure 2.1. Intelligence Community of Bangladesh.
Source: Updated from ASM Ali Ashraf, "Bangladesh," in *Intelligence Communities and Cultures in Asia & the Middle East: A Comprehensive Reference*, edited by Bob de Graaff (Boulder, CO: Lynne Rienner, 2020), p. 32.

the NCIC.[34] The stature of the CTTC has been elevated with its inclusion in the NCIC.

The second coordination body, the National Committee for Security Affairs (NCSA), was revived in 2019 after it was renamed in 1992 from the National Security Council (NSC).[35] During the dictatorial regime of General H. M. Ershad (1982–1990), the NSC was dominated by the military. The current structure of NCSA establishes civilian control of the armed forces. Headed by the prime minister, it now comprises senior ministers and top bureaucrats from various ministries including MOFA and MOHA. The chiefs of staff of the army, navy and air force; the inspector general of police (IGP); and the director generals of DGFI and NSI are also members of the NCSA. The remit of the NCSA is well aligned with the *National Defense Policy* and the *Forces Goal 2030*, two strategic documents outlining Bangladesh's military modernization plans.[36] It is also charged with assessing and reviewing internal security for timely intervention.[37]

At the MOHA level, the National Committee for Militancy Resistance and Prevention (NCMRP) convenes periodic meetings of concerned ministries and intelligence agencies. Although the NCMRP does not play a role in intelligence coordination per se, intelligence officials attending the NCMRP meetings gather useful information regarding the CT role of various stakeholders. NCMRP meetings are hosted by the MOHA and chaired by a senior cabinet minister.[38]

The NCIC, NCSA, and NCMRP represent national-level, interministerial, and interagency coordination bodies in the domain of security and intelligence. Additionally, Bangladesh Police maintains a bottom-up approach to intelligence flow from the District HQ to Police HQ and SB HQ levels.[39] Given that the IGP and the SB chief are both members of the NCIC, and the IGP sits in the NCSA as well, such police-level intelligence coordination can directly inform the prime minister, who chairs both the NCIC and NCSA.

LEGISLATIVE REFORM AND PARLIAMENTARY OVERSIGHT

Unlike the United Kingdom and the United States where intelligence agencies operate on the basis of overarching written laws, Bangladesh has pursued a mixed approach of using executive orders and legislative reforms to govern the IC. For instance, the DGFI and the NSI were established in 1972 by administrative orders of the Sheikh Mujib government. Yet, no legislation has brought these two agencies under a law. The same procedure of executive order was followed in reforming the CT apparatus. Both the CTTC and

ATU were formed with executive orders of MOHA that requires the prime minister's approval rather than any parliamentary process.

Legislative reforms were initiated for other agencies. The Anti-terrorism Act 2009 was amended in 2012 to establish the legal basis for the creation of the BFIU. Prior to that the Armed Police Battalion Ordinance 1979 was amended in 2003 to establish RAB and grant it some intelligence responsibilities. The Money Laundering Prevention Act 2012 and the Digital Security Act 2018 provide various intelligence agencies with a wide-ranging power to monitor and intercept cybercrime and cyberterrorism. In contrast to these new intelligence entities, most of the intelligence and investigative agencies of Bangladesh Police operate largely under the British colonial laws such as the Police Regulations of Bengal 1943, the Penal Code of 1860, the Police Act of 1861, and the Code of Criminal Procedure of 1898. The Dhaka Metropolitan Police Ordinance 1976 and the Police Bureau of Investigations Regulations 2016 are two exceptions. They have established the DMP and the PBI, respectively.

Parliamentary oversight is an essential feature of the intelligence accountability models in the global North. Comparable accountability systems can hardly be found in the global South. It is thus no surprise that the Jatiya Sangsad (National Parliament) of Bangladesh lacks any power to oversee intelligence matters. The Parliamentary Standing Committees on Defense and Home Affairs in Bangladesh rarely discuss substantive matters having an effect on security and intelligence reform. In the absence of any parliamentary oversight, the executive branch of the government, the PMO to be more precise, has full control over the Bangladeshi IC. Although the prime minister chairs both the NCIC and the NCSA, public knowledge of how frequently these two coordination committees meet and what they discuss is almost nonexistent.

INTERNATIONAL COOPERATION

Although Bangladesh shares a border more than 4,000 kilometers (about 2,500 miles) long with India, bilateral relations between the two countries have seen ebbs and flows. In 1971 India's external intelligence agency, Research and Analysis Wing (R&AW), supported the Bangladeshi freedom fighters in their guerilla warfare against the Pakistani occupying forces. The influence of R&AW diminished after the August 1975 military coup that assassinated Sheikh Mujib and most of his family members. After Mujib's daughter Sheikh Hasina came to power in 1996, relations with India improved significantly. Hasina signed the Ganges Water Treaty with India in the same year. Next year in 1997, India supported Bangladesh in bringing the ethnic Shanti Bahini rebels back to the negotiating table that resulted in the signing of CHT Peace Accord. Bangladesh reciprocated by handing over top Indian rebel leaders affiliated with the United Liberation Front of Assam (ULFA).

Over the past decade, the need for joint investigation and capacity building have created the context for increasing CT cooperation between Bangladesh and other countries. This was evident in 2014 when an accidental explosion in West Bengal brought the Indian National Investigation Agency (NIA) closer to the Bangladeshi intelligence agencies to assess the cross-border presence of JMB militants. After the 2016 café attack, Western intelligence agencies showed an interest in the intelligence and investigative capacity building of Bangladeshi CT forces. This resulted in Bangladesh being enlisted into the US Counterterrorism Partnership Fund. Other notable attempts include US-Bangladesh security dialogue, UK-Bangladesh strategic dialogue, and Australia-Bangladesh joint counterterrorism exercises.

As a strong supporter of regional economic integration, Bangladesh has played a key role in establishing the South Asian Association for Regional Cooperation (SAARC) and the Bay of Bengal Initiative for Multi-Sectoral Technical and Economic Cooperation (BIMSTEC). The SAARC members have adopted an antiterrorism convention and formed three intelligence-sharing desks on drugs, terrorism, and cybercrime. While these desks are more than three decades old, they are yet to emerge as functional entities like the European Union's Situation Center. In a similar vein, although BIMSTEC has introduced a security dialogue forum of high-level officials, it is yet to emerge as a regional intelligence-sharing platform.

Bangladesh works closely with various multilateral institutions including the United Nations, Interpol, and the Egmont Group of financial intelligence units (FIUs). It is a founding member of the South Asian Regional Intelligence Coordination Center (SARICC), which was initiated by the UN Office on Drugs and Crime to exchange transnational crime–related intelligence. In 2013, the BFIU became a member of the Egmont Group and since then has sought to exchange financial intelligence for combating money laundering and terrorist financing. After the Bangladesh Bank lost US$101 million from its account with the Federal Reserve Bank of New York in a major cyber heist in February 2016, the BFIU worked closely with the Federal Reserve Bank and several US-based cybersecurity and law firms to recover the stolen money. So far only US$20 million was recovered from a bank in Sri Lanka, and the remaining US$81 million in a Filipino bank account has yet to be recovered.[40]

CONCLUSION

This chapter explored Bangladesh's intelligence culture and reform priorities by demonstrating how the IC comprises a wide variety of civilian- and military-controlled agencies having overlapping, and often competing, roles in maintaining public order and national security. The rise of Islamist militancy, a mutiny in the paramilitary border force, and a refugee influx from Myanmar have been the key drivers of intelligence reforms. Indeed, the growth of CT agencies, the creation of a central intelligence coordination mechanism, and the integration of intelligence in refugee policy making represent the salient features in the country's intelligence reform. Yet, Bangladesh's intelligence culture is marked by the paucity of an overarching national legislation giving legal footing to the DGFI and the NSI. Intelligence cooperation is demand driven and shaped by the political regime in power and the need for modernization and shared threat assessment.

NOTES

1. ASM Ali Ashraf, ed., *Intelligence, National Security, and Foreign Policy: A South Asian Narrative* (Dhaka: BILIA and DUIR, 2016); M. Sakhawat Hossain, "Capacity Building of Law Enforcement and Intelligence Agencies," in *Countering Terrorism in Bangladesh*, ed. Farooq Sobhan (Dhaka: UPL, 2008), 37–82; Nuruzzaman Labu, "At a Glance: Intelligence Agencies of Bangladesh," *Dhaka Tribune*, February 19, 2019.

2. Sheikh Hasina, ed., *Secret Documents of Intelligence Branch on Father of the Nation Bangabandhu Sheikh Mujibur Rahman*, vol. 10 (Dhaka: Hakkani, 2021).

3. Abu Hena Mohammad Razi Hasan, "From Taboo to Absolute Necessity—the Evolution of UN Intelligence: Experience from the UN Mission to DRC (MONUSCO)," *United Nations Peacekeepers Journal* 7, no. 7 (2021): 1–17.

4. Ministry of Defense, *Annual Report: 2014–2015 Financial Year Activities* (Dhaka: Ministry of Defense, 2015); Ministry of Home Affairs, *Shafoller Panch Bochor (January 2009–December 2013)* [Five years of success (January 2009–December 2013)] (Dhaka: MOHA, GoB, 2014); "Services and Activities," Prime Minister's Office, 2021, https://pmo.gov.bd/site/page/0c5ec6a1-cd26-49e3-8548-d84f7f2ad86b/Services-&-Activities.

5. Interview with a senior SB official, Dhaka, 2015.

6. Interview with a senior SB official, SB Headquarters, 2021.

7. Interview with a senior journalist, Dhaka, 2016.

8. Interviews with BGB and BCG officials, April 2016.

9. Interviews with former OPD officials and UN peacekeepers, September 2021.

10. Interviews with senior officials from the Bangladesh army, Bangladesh navy, and Bangladesh air force, May 2016.

11. ASM Ali Ashraf, "Bangladesh," in *Intelligence Communities & Cultures in Asia and the Middle East: A Comprehensive Reference*, ed. Bob de Graaff (Boulder, CO: Lynne Rienner, 2020), 25–50.

12. Interviews with senior CTTC officials, Dhaka, 2018, 2019, 2021.

13. Interviews with senior CTTC officials, Dhaka, 2019.

14. Over the years, the interagency TFI cell has compiled a wealth of data on faith-based extremists. Interviews with senior CTTC officials, 2019.

15. Counter-Terrorism and Transnational Crime Unit, "The Success of DMP's Counter Terrorism (CT) Unit in Anti-Militancy Operations: At a Glance," Unpublished Mimeo, Dhaka, August 2020.

16. Rapid Action Battalion, *RAB Forces Journal* (Dhaka: RAB HQ, 2014).

17. Interviews with senior officials, Legal and Media Wing, Intelligence Wing, RAB HQ, 2015, 2018.

18. Staff Correspondent, "Mufti Hannan Arrested," bdnews24.com, September 30, 2005; "Top Bangladesh Militant Arrested," BBC News, March 2, 2006; Julfikar Ali Manik and Shamim Ashraf, "Tyrant Bangla Bhai Finally Captured," *Daily Star*, March 7, 2006.

19. Interviews with ATU and CTTCU officials, 2019.

20. Interviews with DGFI and NSI officials, 2018, 2019, 2021.

21. Interviews with the former directors of CTIB and NSI director of external affairs, 2015, 2016.

22. "History," National Telecommunication Monitoring Center, 2021, https://ntmc.gov.bd/history/

23. "About Us," National Telecommunication Monitoring Center, 2021, https://ntmc.gov.bd/mission/.

24. BFIU is manned by Bangladesh Bank officials whereas CIID and CIC are manned by officials from the National Board Revenue. See "Overview of Bangladesh Financial Intelligence Unit," Bangladesh Bank, 2021, https://www.bb.org.bd/bfiu/; "Vision and Mission," Customs Intelligence and Investigation Directorate, 2021, http://www.ci.gov.bd/AboutUs.aspx.

25. Kamal Hossain, "Fighting Money Laundering and Terrorist Financing: The Role of Bangladesh Financial Intelligence Unit," in *Intelligence, National Security, and Foreign Policy: A South Asian Narrative*, ed. ASM Ali Ashraf (Dhaka: BILIA and DUIR, 2016), 95–110; Customs Intelligence and Investigation Directorate, *Goendader Chokh* [Intelligence gaze] (Dhaka: Customs Intelligence and Investigation Directorate, 2014), 15–25; Staff Correspondent, "NBR Setting Up Intelligence Cell at Income Tax Zones," *New Age*, January 4, 2017.

26. "History," Criminal Investigation Department, 2021, https://cid.gov.bd/page/history.

27. "History," Police Bureau of Investigation, 2021, http://pbi.gov.bd/pbi_history.php.

28. Council of Europe, *Guidelines for Prison and Probation Services regarding Radicalisation and Violent Extremism* (Strasbourg: Directorate General, Human Rights and Rule of Law, 2016).

29. Ryan Shaffer, "Islamist Attacks against Secular Bloggers in Bangladesh," in *Violence in South Asia: Contemporary Perspectives*, ed. Pavan Kumar Malreddy and Anindya Sekhar Purakayastha (Abingdon: Routledge, 2019), 209–23.

30. Anis Uz Zaman Khan, *Revolt at the BDR Headquarters Situated at Peelkhana: Report of the Investigative Committee Created for Investigation of the Heinous Massacre*, submitted May 21, 2009.

31. ASM Ali Ashraf, "Intelligence Reform in Bangladesh," *Daily Star*, March 27, 2014.

32. Zobaer Ahmed, "Is Pakistani Intelligence Radicalizing Rohingya Refugees?," *Deutsche Welle*, February 13, 2020.

33. Cabinet Division, Gazette Notification, No. 04.00.0000.611.06.001.19.81, dated March 27, 2019, for the creation of "National Committee for Intelligence Coordination (NCIC)."

34. Interview with a member NCIC, June 2019.

35. Mohammad Saber, "National Security of Bangladesh: Challenges and Options," *NDC Journal* 7, no. 1 (2008): 15.

36. UNB, "Cabinet Approves Draft of National Defence Policy 2018," *Dhaka Tribune*, March 19, 2018; interview with a former DGFI chief, 2021.

37. Cabinet Division, Gazette Notification, No. 04.00.0000.611.06.001.19.91, dated March 27, 2019, for the creation of "National Committee for Security Affairs (NCSA)," 2.

38. Interview with senior official, Ministry of Home Affairs, March 2020.

39. Muhammad Nurul Huda, "Capacity Building and Coordination at Field Level of the Government Agencies in Preventing Terrorism," in *Trends in Militancy in Bangladesh*, ed. Farooq Sobhan (Dhaka: UPL, 2010), 101–8.

40. Mehedi Hasan, "Bangladesh Bank: Reserve Heist Case to Be Settled in Three Years," *Dhaka Tribune*, February 3, 2019.

3

Bhutan: An Intelligence Culture amid Regional Geopolitics

Praveen Kumar

The intelligence services of Bhutan may still be in a stage where they are yet to acquire an independent status from the police and army structures and functions. The collection of data and information for the purpose of national security, of which internal security is the more significant part, is done by the security agencies themselves or organizations that exist within the larger security architecture. The available information and data in the open source sufficiently indicate that Bhutan does not have an intelligence agency with a distinct name. Intelligence, as understood in modern-day statecraft, however, does happen for Bhutan's government to make threat assessments. This is because Bhutan, like all nation-states, plans policies to meet national interests based on information that is not otherwise in the public domain. Such information is gathered by agencies especially tasked by the government to undertake such activities.

This chapter argues Bhutan's present position in regional geopolitics does not warrant an elaborate security structure, but largely shapes the country's intelligence culture. Historically, China's aggressive moves, especially since annexation of Tibet by China in 1958, remain the only external security concern for Bhutan. Other developments like the entrance of Nepali refugees or insurgency have not required creation of a vast security structure, which would require a large intelligence setup. Overall, Bhutanese intelligence must be studied by looking at the organizational setup of the Royal Bhutan Army (RBA) and Royal Bhutan Police (RBP), and in the light of the National Security Act of Bhutan of 1992 and the Royal Bhutan Police Act of 2009.

This chapter is organized into five parts. The first section examines historical intelligence requirements, demonstrating how the country's security needs evolved and why it appears not to have created a European-type intelligence service. In the second part, the chapter describes the Royal Bhutan Army's official responsibilities and size as it relates to intelligence. The third section examines law enforcement's intelligence capabilities, including the Royal Bhutan Police and the Investigation Bureau, with attention to responsibilities and security threats. In the fourth part, the intelligence culture is assessed with attention to the character and notable lack of explicit mentions about intelligence in Bhutan by the press. Lastly, the chapter concludes with final thoughts about Bhutan's intelligence requirements and those to carry out intelligence duties.

INTELLIGENCE REQUIREMENTS

Bhutan is a landlocked country with India and China as its immediate neighbors. India and Bhutan have common boundaries in the west (Sikkim), south (West Bengal and Assam), and east (Arunachal Pradesh); whereas China surrounds Bhutan on its entire northern border. A cursory glance at Bhutan's history indicates that until the 1600s, Bhutan existed as a collection of small kingdoms.[1] What actually unified Bhutan was the common reverence to Buddhism. The country was under a dual system of governance in the mid-seventeenth century, which was replaced in 1907 by the establishment of the first dynastic rule under the first king of Bhutan, Ugyen Wangchuck.[2] Bhutan, under the fourth king, Jigme Singye Wangchuck, transitioned the government into a democratic constitutional monarchy in 2008.[3]

The period preceding the establishment of the dynastic monarchy in seventeenth-century Bhutan witnessed the conflict between the rival Buddhist schools of thought, most prominently between the Ngawang Namgyal–led Drukpa School that was challenged by the ruler of Upper Tsang valley, Tsang Desi.[4] Ngawang Namgyal, who assumed the title of Zhabdrung (meaning "at whose feet one submits"), managed to consolidate his position by forming a local alliance. While some form of assessment about relative strengths and weaknesses of potential enemies or allies might have occurred at this stage while deciding on a likely course of action by the Zhabdrung, it is not clear if the beginning of intelligence services occurred at this stage.

Later developments in Bhutan's military history include conflicts with Tibet in the seventeenth century and attacks on Bhutan by combined forces of Tibetans and Mongols in 1645 and 1649.[5] By the 1620s, however, Bhutan had in place a unified system of governance combining the temporal and spiritual authority. This perhaps allowed the Zhabdrung to direct his resources to the achievement of political ends, of which unification in the western part of Bhutan by the Zhabdrung in 1649 was a notable one. By this time, it appears,

Bhutan had started paying attention to the maintenance of national security. It is believed the death of the Zhabdrung (likely in 1651) was kept secret until 1708 in the interest of national security.[6] Even at this stage, it appears unlikely that Bhutan created an organization dedicated to intelligence gathering and analysis.

Periods of instability and conflict, along with *Choesi*, the dual system of governance with separate religious and secular heads (Je Khenpo and Druk Desi, respectively), marked the historical developments of Bhutan during the period between the late seventeenth century and the early twentieth century.[7] During this period, many Druk Desis were either assassinated or deposed. This era also witnessed events like Tibetan invasion, mediation by Tibetans and the Chinese, and an alliance with Nepal. Bhutan came into contact with the British East India Company (BEIC) in 1765, which included conflicts known as the Duar War and, finally, a settlement following the treaty of Sinchula in 1865. The political instability came to an end with Ugyen Wangchuck establishing himself as the ruler of the country in 1885 after his victory in the battle of Changlimithang.[8] The recorded beginning of Bhutan's hereditary monarchy was in 1907 with *Choesi* coming to an end. It is likely that Bhutan needed some form of intelligence that European countries, for instance, might have needed. The nation-states in Europe not only had been competing with each other in the continent but also military conflicts for control over colonies, most prominently in Asia and Africa, were located geographically far away from the metropole. The colonial powers were also required to maintain an elaborate security structure to keep law and order in their respective colonies. Later developments like the two World Wars and the Cold War further intensified the culture of intelligence gathering, analysis, and operations by European countries and the United States.

In contrast, following the Treaty of Punakha in 1910, the British rendered advice pertaining to foreign affairs to the Bhutan government.[9] Bhutan also underwent a period of self-imposed isolation in the 1930s. Bhutan did not require an external intelligence service under the then existing political conditions. Although one can argue that maintenance of peace and stability would demand that the ruler should have the requisite information pertaining to matters related to governance, this most likely was accomplished by the law-and-order enforcement agencies rather than an agency modeled along the lines of France's Second Bureau (Deuxième Bureau) or the United Kingdom's Security Service (MI5).

A friendship treaty with India was negotiated by Jigme Wangchuck in 1949, wherein Bhutan agreed to conduct its external affairs in light of India's advice.[10] It is believed that an immediate cause of this agreement was the successful communist revolution in China. Modernization of police and army occurred under Jigme Dorji Wangchuck, who had succeeded to the throne in 1953.[11] China's aggressive military actions in the north, however, continued to shape Bhutan's external threat perceptions, which were only aggravated by the annexation of Tibet by China in 1958. The following year, China had seized Bhutan-administered enclaves in the vicinity of Mount Kailash and the Gartok region in western Tibet.[12] There were violations of Bhutanese territory adjacent to the southern part of the Chumbi valley by Chinese troops and Tibetan grazers. In reaction, Bhutan needed a modern, professional army to secure its international borders from external aggression.

ROYAL BHUTAN ARMY

With respect to Bhutan, it is better to identify and locate national security intelligence as an "activity" rather than "service" undertaken by dedicated agencies. It is understood that military operations are unconceivable in modern times in the absence of actionable intelligence. This applies to the Royal Bhutan Army (RBA) as well, which possibly engages in intelligence collection and analysis through the sixteen wings that are stationed in different districts of Bhutan.[13] Bhutan also negotiated mutual security arrangements with India that includes deployment of the Indian Military Training Team (IMTRAT) in Bhutan since 1961, which is an outcome of the Joint Defence Agreement with India.[14] The RBA's headquarters was established in 1963 at Draduel Makhang, which was shifted later to Lungtenphu, even though the royal militia had been in existence since the 1950s. The king of Bhutan is the supreme commander in chief of the RBA. Officially, the RBA is responsible for maintaining Bhutan's integrity and sovereignty against security threats.[15] In addition, the RBA also has independent companies, as well as companies of Special Forces and Royal Bodyguards. In total, the RBA, along with the Royal Body Guard (RBG) and the Royal Bhutan Police (RBP), were estimated to have 14,209 personnel in 2004.[16] The number of security force personnel has been reduced and currently is about 7,000 military personnel.[17] For 2021, Bhutan is ranked last out of the 140 countries considered for the annual Global Fire Power review.[18]

INTELLIGENCE-RELATED ORGANIZATIONS AND RESPONSIBILITIES

The 2009 Royal Bhutan Police (RBP) Act mentioned, perhaps for the first time, intelligence as an activity for the Investigation Bureau (IB) explicitly. The IB has been mandated to collect intelligence on all the criminal and subversive activities against the people or the king or the kingdom of Bhutan. As per the 2009 act, the IB is primarily entrusted with the task of collection of information and intelligence. As part of the RBP and under the overall charge of the police chief, the IB (and operations of any sort) would eventually be guided and controlled by the RBP (see figure 3.1). Thus, it is the RBP that should constitute the operational arm of the IB. The Royal Bhutan Police (RBP) was formed on September 1, 1965.[19] The RBP is responsible for maintaining law and order and preventing crime in Bhutan. Its independent statutory basis was initially governed by the Royal Bhutan Police Act of 1980, which was later repealed and replaced in its entirety by the Royal Bhutan Police Act of 2009.

Even in the general report for the police headquarters, the police superintendent does not send or receive intelligence reports. Clause 58, however, states that the commanding officer would maintain the village/town information register.[20] The latter possibly could become the basis of town- or village-level intelligence for the law enforcement agencies. The act further makes the provision that the RBP shall have an Investigation Bureau (IB). The IB

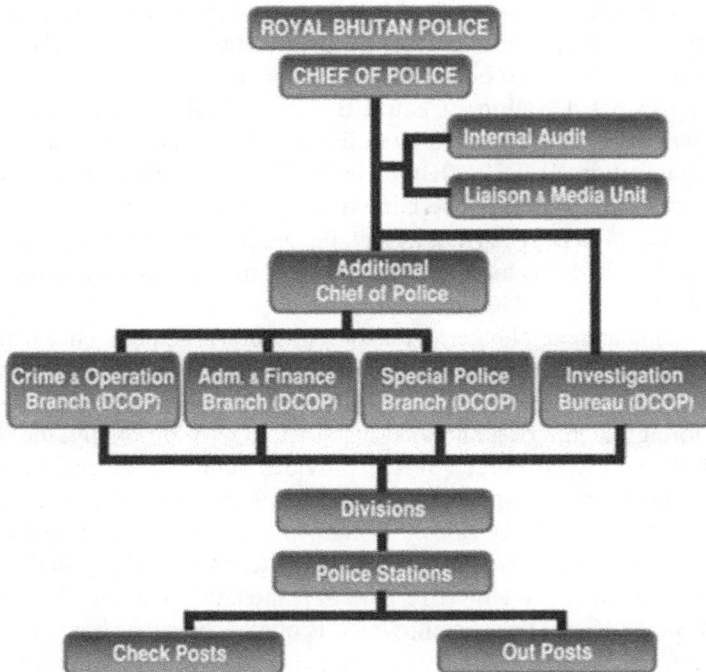

Figure 3.1. Royal Bhutan Police structure.
Source: Royal Bhutan Police, https://www.rbp.gov.bt/organo.

is directly under the chief of police and has been created "for the purpose of collecting intelligence and information relating to criminal and subversive activities against the TSA-WA-SUM (King, People and Country)."[21] According to the act, the IB shall be headed by the deputy chief.

As for the specific security issues that concern the IB, Bhutan's National Security Act (NSA) of 1992 enumerates various kinds of offenses against TSA-WA-SUM (King, People and Country) that can be considered a breach of national security and prescribes various kinds of punishments including death. The NSA of Bhutan applies on all individuals irrespective of nationality, "if the relevant offence has been committed in Bhutan or is intended to be committed in Bhutan, or is committed on an aircraft/carrier registered in Bhutan."[22] Any kind of a treasonable act (or any attempt of a treasonable act) with intent to give aid and comfort to the enemy or to harm the national interest against the TSA-WA-SUM either within or outside Bhutan is punishable with death or imprisonment for life. The act further declares that undermining or any attempt to undermine the security and sovereignty of Bhutan either through speech or in writing or by any other means whatsoever by creating or attempting to create hatred and disaffection among the people shall be punished with imprisonment up to ten years. Additionally, fomenting any hostility between the government and people of Bhutan or the government or any foreign country is also punishable under the act.[23]

Bhutan also has a National Central Bureau (NCB) located at the police headquarters. The NCB was created to liaise with the International Criminal Police Organization (INTERPOL).[24] The NCB has subregional bureaus and maintains a secure global police communication system; it also assists the RBP's Investigation Bureau (IB). In fact, the NCB-Interpol Thimphu is a part of the RBP-IB. The NCB monitors and responds to requests from subregional bureaus and the Interpol General Secretariat.

Bhutan also has several other organizations that have intelligence capabilities. Under the RBP act of 2009, the RBP has the Special Police Division (SPD) and Security Division (SD), which is responsible for providing security to VIPs, foreign dignitaries, and vital installations.[25] Additionally, the RBP's Special Police Reserve Force (SPRF) provides support services, including specialized counterterrorism response, and helps address narcotic drug trafficking and other illegal activities.[26] Bhutan also has a Financial Intelligence Department (FID), but it is in a rudimentary state.[27] Originally established as the Financial Intelligence Unit (FIU) in 2011, the latter functioned within the Financial Supervision Department, which is one of the subordinate branches of the Royal Monetary Authority of Bhutan. Later, it was upgraded to the FID under the direct supervision of the Royal Monetary Authority of Bhutan as per the Financial Service Act of July 2018.[28] The objectives of the FIU, among others, are to combat money laundering, terrorist financing, and other related crimes in line with the Financial Action Task Force (FATF) recommendations and other international standards. Intelligence management happens under the surveillance division of the FID.[29]

INTELLIGENCE CULTURE

The aforementioned agencies make up Bhutan's intelligence community. The NCB, FIU, and IB appear to have direct connections with intelligence gathering and analysis. They also have official mandates that directly reference intelligence regarding their organizational structure and objectives. In contrast, the RBA, SPD, SD, and SPRF are intelligence organizations by implication, given the nature of work that they conduct likely includes aspects of intelligence. Thus, Bhutan's intelligence culture is marked by a mixture of political or military personnel depending on their training. Their objectives are largely shaped by the regional geopolitical environment that sees India as a friend and China as a foe.

In the organizational hierarchy, the chief of the RBP reports to the minister for home and cultural affairs. The king of Bhutan, meanwhile, is the supreme commander of the RBA. The king is also the head of the state, but the executive power is vested in the cabinet headed by a prime minister; the latter is elected directly by the people through elections, which are conducted every five years under the supervision of an independent Election Commission.[30] Technically, if seen in the light of NSA of Bhutan, any action that may create "misunderstanding or hostility" in the country or any action against the king is likely punishable, but the democratic provisions do provide space for democratic deliberations since Bhutan was converted to a constitutional monarchy in 2008. Moreover, the national culture of Bhutan is purportedly directed toward what is known as Gross National Happiness (GNH). Additionally, the democratic constitution of Bhutan under Article 1 declares that "sovereign power belongs to the people of Bhutan."[31] However, the sovereignty and territorial integrity of Bhutan is inviolable. In this light, it can be argued that intelligence and analysis are requirements to ensure Bhutan's security. Being part of the larger international system, Bhutan also cannot afford to remain isolated from geopolitical happenings. Thus, intelligence analysis in some form would be inseparable from its overall security architecture.

Issues such as the presence of ethnic Nepali immigrants and Indian insurgent groups—including the erstwhile United Liberation Front of Asom (ULFA) and National Democratic Front of Bodoland (NDFB), as well as the Kamtapuri Liberation Organisation (KLO)—on Bhutan's soil require the Bhutan government to keep an eye on their activities for the country's own national security. Watching the activities of Indian insurgent groups is a particular obligation under the friendship agreement with India. It led to an armed campaign, popularly known as "Operation All Clear" in 2003 against the KLO.[32] These threats cannot be effectively managed in the absence of intelligence activities, in whatever form they may exist. There are other instances that would further corroborate the fact that even if it may not go by any specific public name, Bhutan does make use of the existing security mechanisms for intelligence gathering and analysis for the purpose of national security. Some of these events include the following:

- Doklam intrusion by China in 2017.[33]
- Twin explosions in Phuentsholing ahead of the Bhutan king's wedding in October 2011.[34]
- Bomb explosions in Thimphu and other districts prior to elections in 2008, which were claimed by the United Revolutionary Front of Bhutan (URFB).[35]
- An alleged attempt on the life of King Jigme Dorji Wangchuck in July 1965.[36]
- Assassination of Bhutan prime minister Jigme Palden Dorji in 1964, which resulted in a crisis within the government and threatened civil war in the country.[37]
- Suspected presence of a pro-China lobby in Bhutan following the closing of Bhutan's border with Tibet and imposition of a ban on trade with Tibet and China in 1959.[38]

Notably, media reports about these events did not explicitly make reference to any "intelligence" organization, with one exception. In the lone instance of the 2011 bombing, a media report made a reference to "intelligence officers" who had "reasons to believe that militant groups who are against the Bhutan monarch have planned the explosion before the king's wedding ceremony. Though intelligence officers are yet to confirm the group behind the blasts, they suspect the anti-monarchy Communist Party of Bhutan (Maoist)."[39] Such reports are rare, as demonstrated with a comparison to media reports over a similar 2008 attack described earlier. The media reported that "a spokesperson for the Royal Bhutan Police" named three militant outfits—the Bhutan Tiger Force (BTF), the Bhutan Maoist Party (BMP), and the Communist Party of Bhutan (Marxist-Leninist-Maoist) or CPB (MLM) as the suspects.[40]

CONCLUSION

Bhutan's intelligence culture must be understood as the "performance" of intelligence rather than having specific agencies responsible for intelligence to safeguard Bhutan's national security. Organizations responsible for law enforcement of military defense engage in intelligence duties, but there are other organizations that perform the task as part of the larger national security enterprise. Moreover, Bhutan's intelligence requirements are also fulfilled by security and defense agreements with India. This means there is no specific civilian intelligence service with civilian officers engaged in political intelligence collection or analysis, while a foreign country conducts vital national security missions for Bhutan. As a result, the small amount of people involved in intelligence are a mixture of law enforcement or military professionals who execute intelligence tasks based on that training.

NOTES

1. Karma Choden and Dorji Wangchuk, *Culture Smart: Bhutan* (London: Kuperard, 2018), 19.

2. C. T. Dorji, *A Political and Religious History of Bhutan, 1651–1906* (Thimphu/Delhi: Sangay Xam, in collaboration with Prominent, 1995), 33.

3. Joseph C. Mathew, "Bhutan: 'Democracy' from Above," *Economic and Political Weekly* 43, no. 19 (2008): 29–31.

4. M. S. Kohli, *Bhutan: A Kingdom in the Sky* (New Delhi: Vikas, 2004), 32.

5. Nirmala Das, *The Dragon Country: The General History of Bhutan* (New Delhi: Orient Longman, 1974), 19.

6. "Zhabdrung Ngawang Namgyal," *Chinese Buddhist Encyclopedia*, 2021, http://www.chinabuddhismencyclopedia.com/en/index.php/Shabdrung.

7. Thierry Mathou, "The Politics of Bhutan: Change in Continuity," *Journal of Bhutan Studies* 2, no. 2 (2000): 235, https://core.ac.uk/download/pdf/1323118.pdf.

8. Das, *The Dragon Country*, 38.

9. Tashi Choden and Dorji Penjore, *Economic and Political Relations between Bhutan and Neighbouring Countries* (Thimphu: Centre for Bhutan Studies, 2004), 64.

10. Dasho K. Letho and Dasho Karma, "Indo-Bhutan Relations," *Indian Journal of Asian Affairs* 7, no. 1 (1994): 53–58.

11. Kohli, *Bhutan*, 39.

12. Chen Jian, "The Tibetan Rebellion of 1959 and China's Changing Relations with India and the Soviet Union," *Journal of Cold War Studies* 8, no. 3 (Summer 2006): 54–101.

13. "Royal Bhutan Army—Order of Battle," Global Security, 2021, https://www.globalsecurity.org/military/world/bhutan/army-orbat.htm.

14. Dhurba P. Rizal, *Administrative System in Bhutan: Retrospect and Prospect* (Delhi: Adroit, 2002), 93.

15. "Army Headquarters," Royal Bhutan Army, 2021, http://www.rba.bt/ahq.php.

16. "Strengthening National Security," https:// kuenselonline.com, July 25, 2004, cited in Dorji Penjore, "Security of Bhutan: Walking between the Giants," 124, https://dorjipenjore.files.wordpress.com/2015/08/security-of-bhutan-walking-between-the-giants.pdf.

17. "2021 Bhutan Military Strength," Global Fire Power, 2021, https://www.globalfirepower.com/country-military-strength-detail.php?country_id=bhutan.

18. "2021 Bhutan Military Strength."

19. "History of Royal Bhutan Police," Royal Bhutan Police, 2013, https://web.archive.org/web/20130320165535/http://www.rbp.gov.bt/hist.php.

20. "Royal Bhutan Police Act, 2009," Government of Bhutan, 2009, 32, https://www.oag.gov.bt/language/en/resources/royal-bhutan-police-act-2009-both-dzongkha-english/.

21. "Royal Bhutan Police Act, 2009," 60.

22. "National Security Act of Bhutan, 1992," Government of Bhutan, 1992, 1–3, https://www.nab.gov.bt/assets/uploads/docs/acts/2014/National_Security_Act_1992_Eng.pdf.

23. "National Security Act of Bhutan, 1992," 1–3.

24. "Royal Bhutan Police Act, 2009," 60. Also see "Bhutan," INTERPOL, 2021, https://www.interpol.int/en/Who-we-are/Member-countries/Asia-South-Pacific/BHUTAN.

25. "Royal Bhutan Police Act, 2009," 61–62.

26. "Royal Bhutan Police Act, 2009," 63.

27. "Bhutan: Systematic Country Diagnosis," World Bank, 2021, 27, https://documents.worldbank.org/curated/en/162771580405026027/pdf/Bhutan-Systematic-Country-Diagnostic.pdf.

28. "Financial Intelligence Department," Royal Monetary Authority of Bhutan, 2021, https://www.rma.org.bt/fid/#:~:text=The%20Financial%20Intelligence%20Unit%20(FIU,of%20Financial%20Service%20Act%202011.

29. "Organizational Structure," Royal Monetary Authority of Bhutan, n.d., https://www.rma.org.bt/fid/aboutUs/org_structure.

30. "Vision and Mission," Election Commission of Bhutan, n.d., https://www.ecb.bt/vision-and-mission/.

31. "Article 1, Bhutan's Constitution of 2008," Constitute Project, 2008, https://www.constituteproject.org/constitution/Bhutan_2008.pdf?lang=en.

32. Praveen Kumar, "External Linkages and Internal Security: Assessing Bhutan's Operation All Clear," *Strategic Analysis* 28, no. 3 (2004): 390–410.

33. A. K. Bardalai, "Doklam and the Indo-China Boundary," *Journal of Defence Studies* 12, no. 1 (2018): 5–13, https://idsa.in/system/files/jds/jds-12-1-2018-doklam.pdf.

34. "Twin Blasts Rock Bhutan ahead of King's Wedding," *Times of India*, October 11, 2011, https://timesofindia.indiatimes.com/world/south-asia/twin-blasts-rock-bhutan-ahead-of-kings-wedding/articleshow/10305177.cms.

35. "Timeline," South Asia Terrorism Portal, 2008, https://www.satp.org/satpor gtp/countries/bhutan/timeline/2008.htm.

36. "Bhutan (1907–Present)," University of Central Arkansas, 2021, https://uca .edu/politicalscience/dadm-project/asiapacific-region/60-bhutan-1907-present/.

37. "Modernization under Jigme Dorji, 1952–72," in *Bhutan: A Country Study*, ed. Andrea Matles Savada (Washington, DC: GPO for the Library of Congress, 1991), http://countrystudies.us/bhutan/12.htm.

38. Rajesh Kharat, "Bhutan's Security Scenario," *Contemporary South Asia* 13, no. 2 (2004): 175.

39. "Twin Blasts Rock Bhutan ahead of King's Wedding."

40. Pramod Giri, "Serial Blasts Rock Bhutan, Woman Injured," *Hindustan Times*, January 20, 2008, https://www.hindustantimes.com/india/serial-blasts-rock-bhutan -woman-injured/story-MjG7Im0LSRYfWm9VA3AR2L.html.

4

Brunei: A Royal Intelligence Culture

Ryan Shaffer

Brunei is a small and wealthy Southeast Asian country on the South China Sea and borders Malaysia. In fact, Brunei is the smallest country by population in Asia and the second smallest—after the Maldives—by territory. With a population of less than 500,000 and ruled by a monarch, Brunei has faced extensive change in recent decades.[1] Since the country received independence from the United Kingdom in 1984, it has undergone significant economic transformation with oil and natural gas reserves accounting for a major part of the economy with citizens receiving free medical care and education. Brunei does not face any significant territorial threats from other states; rather, security concerns include threats to the monarch, terrorists, and transnational crime. Freedom House categorizes the country as "not free," concluding "Brunei is an absolute monarchy in which the sultan exercises executive power" with no elected national representatives and "significantly restricted" speech that is "monitored by authorities" online.[2] Consequently, intelligence is vital for solving crime, maintaining government security, and thwarting extremist violence.

This chapter argues that Brunei's intelligence culture is centered on supporting the monarch where security of the head of state is the main objective. It uses secondary sources, newspaper articles, and government websites to understand the country's intelligence services. The chapter is organized in three parts. The first examines the country's history with attention to security concerns. In the second part, the key security and intelligence agencies are examined. In particular, the roles, activities, and responsibilities that inform the intelligence culture are analyzed to understand broad characteristics. Lastly, oversight and foreign relations are explored with attention to military and intelligence exchanges.

Chapter 4

BACKGROUND

Brunei's official name is Negara Brunei Darussalam, which means "Nation of Brunei, Adobe of Peace."[3] The country is ruled by Sultan Hassanal Bolkiah, who became the crown prince in 1961 when he was a teenager and was crowned sultan in 1968 at age twenty-two. Since then, he has acquired significant wealth and power. According to the Brunei government, he currently serves as prime minister, minister of defense, minister of finance and economy, and minister of foreign affairs.[4] His extravagant lifestyle has been discussed by international press, such as his gold-coated Rolls-Royce and hiring Michael Jackson to perform at his fiftieth birthday, while one of his sons posts images of the family's wealth on social media.[5] A 1987 article in *People* magazine reported that Bolkiah's "gold-domed, 1,788-room palace is the largest private residence in the world," and he has "a stable of 200 polo ponies."[6]

Other key posts are occupied by the royal family with Prince Al-Muhtadee Billah serving as the senior minister in the Prime Minister's Office (PMO) since 2005.[7] Similarly, at the Ministry of Foreign Affairs the sultan's sister, Princess Hajah Masna, is the ambassador at large.[8] The monarch's personal wealth mirrors the country's status, which was ranked fourth richest in the world in terms of gross domestic product and gross national income as well as life expectancy in 2019.[9] The country has not been without controversy, however, as the Brunei Investment Agency, part of the Brunei government, owns luxury hotels throughout the world and business and celebrities have boycotted the hotels over human rights concerns.[10]

The country has a proud royal history. According to scholar Ooi Keat Gin, "The official date for conversation to Islam and the emergence of a sultanate is 1368, but Brunei as a political entity probably dates from around the tenth century."[11] Between 1888 and 1984, Brunei was a British protectorate, and its main source for exports was its oil reserves in which there was a type of "royal paternalism" wherein citizens received benefits from the state's wealth.[12] After World War II, the British gave self-government to the sultan rather than the people in 1959, which was followed by full internal sovereignty in 1971.[13] According to the sultan's official biography, he is credited with leading negotiations that led to independence from the United Kingdom in 1984 and the subsequent signing of the Treaty of Friendship and Co-operation with the United Kingdom.[14] Gin analyzed the Malay Islamic Monarchy (MIB) that was written in the country's independence proclamation, which professes Malay ethnicity (language, culture, and customs), Islam as the religion, and the sultanate as the governance.[15] MIB is "a national ideology" that is "embedded" in the citizenry "from school children to civil servants to the business community to military personnel."[16] Marie-Sybille de Vienne argues MIB "anchors the legitimacy and governance of the absolute monarchy" but is accompanied with the rule of law—civil and sharia—where the legal system is perceived as equitable and corruption is "heavily punished."[17]

Bolkiah has absolute power, with the country providing him with "supreme authority" wherein "loyalty and obedience to the Sultan" is compared to Allah for the "Muslim faithful."[18] As for the citizens, the government provides free education, free health care, subsided housing, "generous pensions" for civil servants, and no taxes;[19] however, only about 65 percent of the country's residents are citizens—mostly of Malayan descent—and the majority of the noncitizens are ethnically Chinese who did not receive citizenship when the country gained independence.[20] The key to wealth was the exportation of natural gas, starting in the 1970s from what was "the world's largest liquefied natural gas (LNG) production plant" at the time.[21] The new wealth not only rapidly transformed the infrastructure and civil servants in the country, including professionalizing personnel overseas, but also prompted corruption and the establishment of the Anti-Corruption Bureau in 1982.[22] The oil money also allowed the armed forces to be "well-equipped" with "advanced" communications systems.[23]

Despite the social welfare, Brunei's government has been harshly criticized for abuses, censorship, and arbitrary arrests. The country's Internal Security Act (ISA) lays out the security provisions of the country, allowing authorities to arrest those "acting in any manner prejudicial to the security of Brunei Darussalam or any part thereof or to the maintenance of public order."[24] The 2020 US Department of State Report on Human Rights Practices described the ISA as allowing "the government to detain suspects without trial for renewable two-year periods" in which "an independent advisory board consisting of senior security and judicial officials to review individual detentions and report to the minister of home affairs."[25] Additionally in 2019, Amnesty International condemned the country for adding provisions in the law to "allow stoning and amputation as punishments—including for children."[26] As for free expression, Amnesty International concluded: "Journalists and online activists continued to self-censor for fear of prosecution."[27] Moreover, stateless children are not afforded free education but, instead, need permission to enroll and usually have to pay.[28]

The government faces limited internal and external pressure. While serious challenges to the monarchy are not apparent due to the tight restrictions on opposition, there was an attempted coup in 1962 when the country was a protectorate.[29] The country is at low risk for transnational terrorism as there are no indigenous terror groups, but the country faces similar terrorist threats to other countries in the South China Sea.[30] Additionally, crime is limited and mostly nonviolent.[31] The penalties for breaking laws are harsh; drug trafficking, for example, is punishable by the death penalty.[32] The country depends on foreign laborers who often lack legal status in the government, and there are cases of involuntary servitude and uneven enforcement of labor laws.[33] Other issues include foreign protests to Brunei's overseas investments as the country tries to diversify its economy as well as domestic middle and educated classes seeking power and influence.[34]

INTELLIGENCE CULTURE

The sultanate depends on and makes use of intelligence to maintain power and ensure national security. The 2021 Defence White Paper—the first published in ten years—specifically highlighted the importance of intelligence as a "prerequisite" for national security.[35] Aside from law enforcement intelligence, the PMO and the Ministry of Defence have explicit intelligence components. In February 2007, the National Security Council (NSC) was established to provide advice to the prime minister and coordinate on security matters.[36] Currently, the NSC consists of an intelligence executive working committee, which is one of five committees, to inform policy.[37]

According to the International Institute for Strategic Studies, Bolkiah—who is also minister of defense—makes defense a "high priority" for the country and ensures a "well-trained and professional" military with "deterrence" efforts can protect its exclusive economic zone in the South China Sea.[38] In 2019, the defense budget was 19.7 percent, which was more than double the previous year of 9.1 percent.[39] The institute estimates the Royal Brunei Armed Forces to have 7,200 active personnel (the army has 4,900 personnel, the navy has 1,200, and the air force has 1,100) as well as a paramilitary between 400 and 500 and an army reserve of 700.[40] The Ministry of Defence also has an intelligence component and is one of the military's three directorates.[41] The current director of intelligence, Haji Mohd Muluddin bin Awang Haji Latif, has the rank of colonel; he completed officer training in New Zealand, finished undergraduate research in the United Kingdom, attended further training in Canada, and served as a defense attaché in the United States.[42] Additionally, Brunei hosts a British defense presence of 2,000 that operate training schools as well as an infantry training school from Singapore.[43] As for industry, the country lacks its own indigenous defense production and imports military equipment, but in 2010, it established a school for defense research.[44]

In addition to the military, there are several services and departments that explicitly have intelligence or national security responsibilities under the PMO. According to the office, the agencies under its authority that deal with security are the Anti-Corruption Bureau, Narcotics Control Bureau, and the Internal Security Department (ISD).[45] In 2021, the Brunei press reported that the PMO had a US$325 million budget (roughly 431.52 million in Brunei dollars), with all the aforementioned agencies, including the Brunei Research Department (BRD), under the PMO being categorized as "sensitive."[46] While other departments in the PMO list how much of the budget is allocated, the sensitive agencies do not publicly release their financial budgets.[47] Interestingly, the mission and activities of the ISD, as well as the Narcotics Control Bureau, the Anti-Corruption Bureau, and the Royal Brunei Police Force, appear on the official government web pages with one notable exception—the Brunei Research Department.[48] Indeed, while the Brunei Research Department is named in government documents, it is unclear what its responsibilities and functions are as well as where it is situated in the government hierarchy other than it is in the PMO.

The ISD has particular importance for internal intelligence. It was established on August 1, 1993, under the PMO with its headquarters at Jalan Utama Mentiri and three branches in the Tutong, Belait, and Temburong districts.[49] According to the government, the ISD's "mission is to give early warning to the government on any imminent threats to protect the country including the public and properties in Brunei. By doing so, the government would be able to take necessary precautions to avoid or reduce any harm that may be caused by such threats."[50] To do this, ISD officers "identify security threats and its sources," "collect and analyse intelligence," "carry out investigation[s] whenever necessary," and provide security plans and other "measures."[51] For internal security, it is responsible for monitoring and reporting on subversion, espionage, sabotage, and terrorism.[52] The budgets allocated for intelligence, police, and defense are not publicly available, but press reports for the 2019/2020 year state that the Ministry of Foreign Affairs had a budget of 113,041,410 Brunei dollars (about US$85 million) and 800,000,000 was allocated for development (about US$604 million).[53]

Constraints on speech and the absolute power of the sultanate explain the little information about intelligence activities and scandals; however, there are a few press reports and press releases that shed light on interagency relations and issues. First, even though it is not clear what the BRD's activities are, there is information about the leadership. As of March 2021, the head of the BRD is Haji Asmawee bin Haji Muhammad, who was previously deputy director of Brunei Research at the BRD.[54] Second, the BRD—along with

Royal Brunei Armed Forces and other Brunei departments—were involved with security exercises at the Association of Southeast Asian Nations (ASEAN) summit in Brunei during October 2013.[55] Third, the security services engage in soccer tournaments with the teams made up of the agency personnel. In 2019, the police force was the league champion defeating the ISD, while the BRD took third place out of nineteen teams.[56]

As for the future of intelligence, the 2021 Defence White Paper called for improving the collection and analysis of intelligence in the next fifteen years.[57] Specific steps include improving skills; "fusing" tactical, operational, and strategic intelligence; improving the timeliness and quality of intelligence; making "increased" use of satellite systems; and reviewing the way "intelligence is processed and disseminated" due to disinformation.[58] Lastly, the document calls for "wider networks" involving "partners, domestic and international."[59]

OVERSIGHT AND FOREIGN RELATIONS

There is no information publicly available about intelligence oversight and nonmilitary intelligence relations; however, Bolkiah's absolute power and role as sultan, prime minister, foreign minister, and defense minister gives him ultimate responsibility for oversight. Given there is no nationally elected body, any oversight duties outside of the sultan would rest with personnel he appointed and who answer to him.

In addition, there is little information about prosecution of intelligence or security officers. Though corruption in the country is low, in 2008 a BRD assistant research officer was sentenced to five months in jail after pleading guilty for "abetting" a receptionist at the Empire Hotel and Country Club who embezzled "a large amount of money."[60] It is not clear from public reports what the connection between the BRD and the hotel is, but the receptionist embezzled money and "forged five invoices from the hotel, which were addressed to the Brunei Research Department."[61] The receptionist then received "cash payments" from the BRD.

As one of the oldest kingdoms in the Malay world, Brunei developed relations with other empires for decades that were fostered through marriages, diplomacy, trade, and conquest.[62] Until the 1980s, Brunei "clung" to relations with the United Kingdom for security, but as relations loosened Brunei became a member of ASEAN; allowed Australia, Japan, South Korea, and the United States to establish diplomatic missions; and joined the United Nations and the Organization of Islamic Countries.[63]

According to Brunei's government, foreign diplomatic missions exist to "promote cooperation in political, economic, social, cultural, educational, trade and security fields."[64] As of 2021, Brunei has foreign missions in Australia, Bahrain, Belgium, Canada, China, Egypt, France, Germany, India, Indonesia, Iran, Laos, Japan, Jordan, Kuwait, Malaysia, Morocco, Myanmar, Oman, Pakistan, Philippines, Qatar, Russia, Singapore, South Korea, Switzerland, Thailand, Timor-Leste, Turkey, the United Arab Emirates, the United Kingdom, the United States, and Vietnam.[65] According to Brunei's military intelligence, it "actively" engages "in bilateral intelligence exchanges (INTELEXES) with the military intelligence agencies of friendly countries."[66] Additionally, it participates in the ASEAN Military Intelligence Informal Meeting (AMIIM), the Asia Pacific Intelligence Chiefs Conference (APICC), and the ASEAN Militaries Analysts-to-Analysts Intelligence Exchange (AMAAIE).[67]

One of the few public mentions involving intelligence meetings is a report from Brunei's Ministry of Foreign Affairs that Saudi Arabia's Prince Muqrin bin Abdulaziz, then head of Saudi intelligence, met with Brunei officials in Brunei during 2006.[68] Another publicly reported event was the Memorandum of Understanding signed between Brunei's and Bangladesh's respective Financial Intelligence Units in 2015.[69]

In 2018, the Singaporean government organized its twelfth annual conference for senior Asia-Pacific national security officers and had speakers from about a dozen countries and participants from twenty-four countries.[70] The BRD's assistant director of operations was listed on the program.[71] According to a summary of the event, Brunei's presentation on security threats stated that the country has more concerns about the Islamic State–affiliated groups in Southeast Asia rather than the Islamic State itself or al-Qaeda.[72]

CONCLUSION

The sultanate has absolute control over Brunei. Not only is Bolkiah the head of the state, but he is responsible for the country's security with the title of prime minister and minister of defense. Wealth has enabled the country to purchase foreign defense equipment, hire skilled personnel, and provide training to staff from foreign partners. These factors influence the country's intelligence culture by creating a professional class of officers who protect the monarchy above all. Though not much is directly known about the intelligence services as speech is restricted and punishment for those who break the laws are severe, it is almost certain that the head of state or close advisers make use of the intelligence services to maintain power and thwart any efforts to challenge that power.

NOTES

1. "Brunei," *World Factbook*, Central Intelligence Agency, 2021, https://www.cia.gov/the-world-factbook/countries/brunei/.

2. "Brunei," Freedom House, 2021, https://freedomhouse.org/country/brunei.

3. Ooi Keat Gin, "Monarchy in Brunei: Past, Present and Future," in *Continuity and Change in Brunei Darussalam*, ed. Victor T. King and Stephen C. Druce (New York: Routledge, 2021), 7.

4. "His Majesty Sultan Haji Hassanal Bolkiah Mu'izzaddin Waddaulah ibni Almarhum Sultan Haji Omar 'Ali Saifuddien," Prime Minister's Office, 2021, http://www.pmo.gov.bn/SitePages/minister-and-senior-officials/Prime-Minister.aspx.

5. Alan Yuhas, "The Sultan of Brunei: Opulence, Power and Hard-Line Islam," *New York Times*, April 4, 2019, https://www.nytimes.com/2019/04/04/world/asia/who-is-sultan-brunei.html.

6. Maria Wilhelm, "His $10 Million Contra-Bution Got Lost, but to the Sultan of Brunei It Was (Sigh) Only Money," *People*, June 1, 1987, https://people.com/archive/his-10-million-contra-bution-got-lost-but-to-the-sultan-of-brunei-it-was-sigh-only-money-vol-27-no-22/.

7. "His Royal Highness Prince Haji Al-Muhtadee Billah," Prime Minister's Office, 2021, http://www.pmo.gov.bn/SitePages/minister-and-senior-officials/Senior-Minister.aspx.

8. "Organisation Structure," Ministry of Foreign Affairs, 2021, http://www.mfa.gov.bn/Pages/theministry-Organisation-Structure.aspx.

9. Grant Suneson, "These Are the 25 Richest Countries in the World," *USA Today*, July 7, 2019, https://www.usatoday.com/story/money/2019/07/07/richest-countries-in-the-world/39630693/.

10. Rachel Savage, "Rising Number of Businesses Cut Ties with Brunei over Gay Sex Death Penalty," Reuters, April 5, 2019, https://www.reuters.com/article/us-brunei-lgbt-business-idUSKCN1RH1BL.

11. Gin, "Monarchy in Brunei," 8.

12. Gin, "Monarchy in Brunei," 7.

13. Gin, "Monarchy in Brunei," 9.

14. "His Majesty Sultan Haji Hassanal Bolkiah Mu'izzaddin Waddaulah ibni Almarhum Sultan Haji Omar 'Ali Saifuddien," Prime Minister's Office, 2021, http://www.pmo.gov.bn/SitePages/minister-and-senior-officials/Prime-Minister.aspx.

15. Gin, "Monarchy in Brunei," 9.

16. Gin, "Monarchy in Brunei," 13, 14.

17. Marie-Sybille de Vienne, *Brunei: From the Age of Commerce to the 21st Century* (Singapore: NUS Press, 2015), 275, 280.

18. Gin, "Monarchy in Brunei," 11, 12.

19. Gin, "Monarchy in Brunei," 13.

20. Aurel Croissant and Philip Lorenz, "Brunei Darussalam: Malay Islamic Monarchy and Rentier State," in *Comparative Politics of Southeast Asia*, ed. Aurel Croissant and Philip Lorenz (New York: Springer, 2018), 17.

21. Graham Saunders, *A History of Brunei*, 2nd ed. (New York: Routledge, 2015), 165.

22. Saunders, *A History of Brunei*, 166.

23. Saunders, *A History of Brunei*, 167.

24. "Internal Security Act," Government of Brunei, 2021, http://www.agc.gov.bn/AGC%20Images/LOB/pdf/Internal%20Security%20Act%20(chapter%20133).pdf.

25. "2020 Country Reports on Human Rights Practices: Brunei," US Department of State, March 30, 2021, https://www.state.gov/reports/2020-country-reports-on-human-rights-practices/brunei/.

26. "Brunei Darussalam: Heinous Punishments to Become Law Next Week," Amnesty International, March 27, 2019, https://www.amnesty.org/en/latest/news/2019/03/brunei-darussalam-heinous-punishments-to-become-law-next-week/.

27. "Brunei Darussalam 2017/2018," Amnesty International, 2021, https://www.amnesty.org/en/countries/asia-and-the-pacific/brunei-darussalam/report-brunei-darussalam/.

28. "Brunei Darussalam 2017/2018."

29. For more, see Harun Abdul Majid, *Rebellion in Brunei: The 1962 Revolt, Imperialism, Confrontation and Oil* (London: Tauris, 2007).

30. "Brunei 2020 Crime and Safety Report," US Department of State, March 4, 2020, https://www.osac.gov/Country/Brunei/Content/Detail/Report/368c0c1a-0a4a-4f79-805e-181e1e61beda.

31. "Brunei 2020 Crime and Safety Report."

32. "Brunei: Family Drug Ring Faces Death Penalty," *The Star*, September 27, 2020, https://www.thestar.com.my/aseanplus/aseanplus-news/2020/09/27/brunei-family-drug-ring-faces-death-penalty.

33. "2020 Country Reports on Human Rights Practices: Brunei."

34. Gin, "Monarchy in Brunei," 17; "Brunei Hotel Boycott Gathers Steam as Anti-gay Law Goes into Effect," *New York Times*, April 3, 2019, https://www.nytimes.com/2019/04/03/world/asia/brunei-hotel-boycotts.html.

35. *Defending the Nation's Sovereignty: A Secure and Resilient Future, Defence White Paper 2021*, Brunei Ministry of Defence, 2021, https://www.mindef.gov.bn/Defence%20White%20Paper/DWP%202021.pdf.

36. "Security and Enforcement," Prime Minister's Office, 2021, http://www.pmo.gov.bn/SitePages/Security%20and%20Enforcement.aspx.

37. "Security and Enforcement."

38. International Institute for Strategic Studies, "Asia," *Military Balance* 121, no. 1 (2021): 233.

39. International Institute for Strategic Studies, "Asia," 233.

40. International Institute for Strategic Studies, "Asia," 246.

41. "Directorate of Intelligence," Ministry of Defence, 2021, https://www.mindef.gov.bn/SitePages/Intelligence.aspx

42. "Directorate of Intelligence."

43. International Institute for Strategic Studies, "Asia," 247.

44. International Institute for Strategic Studies, "Asia," 246.

45. "Security and Enforcement."

46. Nabilah Haris, "PMO Gets $431 Million Budget," *The Scoop*, March 17, 2021, https://thescoop.co/2021/03/17/pmo-tables-431-million-budget/.

47. "Summary of Budget for 2019–2020," *Borneo Bulletin*, March 22, 2019, https://borneobulletin.com.bn/summary-of-budget-for-2019-2020/.

48. "Vision/Mission," Narcotics Control Bureau, 2021, http://www.narcotics.gov.bn/SitePages/Vision%20Mission.aspx; "Anti-corruption Bureau," Anti-corruption Bureau, 2021, http://www.bmr.gov.bn/Theme/Home.aspx; "Royal Brunei Police Force," Royal Brunei Police Force, 2021, http://www.police.gov.bn/Theme/Home.aspx

49. "Introduction," Internal Security Department, 2021, http://www.isd.gov.bn/SitePages/Introduction.aspx.

50. "Mission, Vision and Function," Internal Security Department, 2021, http://www.isd.gov.bn/SitePages/Mission,%20Vision%20and%20Function.aspx.

51. "Mission, Vision and Function."

52. "Roles and Responsibility," Internal Security Department, 2021, http://www.isd.gov.bn/SitePages/Roles%20and%20Responsibility.aspx.

53. "Summary of Budget for 2019–2020."

54. "New Director of Brunei Research Appointed," *Borneo Bulletin*, March 28, 2021, https://borneobulletin.com.bn/new-director-of-brunei-research-appointed/.

55. Xinhua, "Brunei's Police, Security Agencies Hold Joint Exercises for ASEAN Summit," *Global Times*, October 2, 2013, https://www.globaltimes.cn/content/815274.shtml.

56. Haniza Abdul Latif, "Royal Brunei Police Force Wins Information Department Futsal Championship," Information Department of the Prime Minister's Office, October 27, 2019, http://information.gov.bn/Lists/News/DispForm.aspx?ID=555.

57. *Defending the Nation's Sovereignty*, 80.

58. *Defending the Nation's Sovereignty*, 80, 81.

59. *Defending the Nation's Sovereignty*, 81.

60. Fadley Faisal, "Govt Servant Jailed for Abetting Embezzlement by Instigation," *Borneo Bulletin*, November 14, 2018, https://web.archive.org/web/20181121061127/https://borneobulletin.com.bn/govt-servant-jailed-for-abetting-embezzlement-by-instigation/.

61. Faisal, "Govt Servant Jailed."

62. Ampuan Haji Brahim bin Ampuan Haji Tengah, "Silsilah Raja-Raja Brunei: The Brunei Sultanate and Its Relationship with Other Countries," in *Brunei: History, Islam, Society and Contemporary Issues*, ed. Ooi Keat Gin (New York: Routledge, 2016), 48.

63. Saunders, *A History of Brunei*, 172, 179. See the original signed document at: "Association of Southeast Asian Nation (ASEAN)," Ministry of Foreign Affairs, 2021, http://www.mfa.gov.bn/Pages/association-of-southeast-asian-nation-(asean).aspx.

64. "Diplomatic Missions," Ministry of Foreign Affairs, 2021, http://www.mfa.gov.bn/Pages/Diplomatic-Mission.aspx.

65. "Missions Abroad," Ministry of Foreign Affairs, 2021, http://www.mfa.gov.bn/Pages/missions-abroad02.aspx.

66. "Directorate of Intelligence."

67. "Directorate of Intelligence."

68. "Middle East," Ministry of Foreign Affairs, 2021, http://www.mfa.gov.bn/ Shared%20Documents/politics2documents/(Final)%20Middle%20East.pdf.

69. "Bangladesh," Ministry of Foreign Affairs, 2021, http://www.mfa.gov.bn/ Pages/br_bangladesh.aspx.

70. "Event Report: Asia-Pacific Programme for Senior National Security Officers: Boundaries of National Security," Centre of Excellence for National Security, May 6–11, 2018, https://www.rsis.edu.sg/wp-content/uploads/2018/08/APPSNO-2018 -Report-3-8-18-FINAL.pdf.

71. "Event Report."

72. "Event Report."

5

Cambodia: Intelligence Mission—Regime Security

Paul Chambers

Throughout Cambodia's history, despotic regimes have almost always dominated the country. As a result, intelligence services have played more of a role of bolstering regime security rather than protecting the overall state. If anything, the development of these services evolved from being rudimentary and neocolonial to dysfunctional to divided to singularly dominated. This changing evolution owes to the fact that Cambodia experienced thirty years of civil war and constant external meddling in its internal affairs, followed by the incremental enhancement of single-party rule and eventually the personalization of authoritarian control in one person. As with Cambodia's overall security forces, the country's intelligence services have always appeared as a partisan, corporate arm of whichever political party (dominated by an authoritarian figure) has controlled the country. As of this writing, that party is the Cambodian People's Party (Kanakpak Pracheachon Kampuchea), and that figure is Prime Minister Hun Sen. While this has ensured civilian control of intelligence services as well as security forces, it is not an institutionalized form of control.

Rather, Hun Sen has succeeded in personalizing supremacy over Cambodia's politics and intelligence services by what might be termed "neo-sultanistic tendencies." Following Max Weber, Juan J. Linz defined sultanism as "personal ruler-ship . . . with loyalty to the ruler based on a mixture of fear and rewards to his collaborators. . . . The ruler exercises his power without restraint at his own discretion and above all unencumbered by rules or by any commitment to an ideology or value system."[1] Neosultanism situates such a regime behind the facade of electoral democracy, whereby "a modern-looking judiciary and legislature can be provided for."[2] Hun Sen's regime is akin to neosultanism, given his personal domination of the Cambodian polity despite what appears to be a procedural democracy. It is akin to a "hybrid" regime, which possesses the formal trappings of democracy while retaining definite authoritarian features.[3] Larry Diamond refers to this phenomenon as "electoral authoritarianism" or "pseudodemocracy."[4] Obedience by security forces to Hun Sen is based upon a managed dependence, deriving from his use of both "carrots and sticks" to keep them in line. This asymmetrical linkage, whereby a despotic leader and party serve as patron to clientelistic security forces and intelligence services, has been repeatedly reproduced in previous Cambodian regimes.

As of 2021, Cambodia possesses two intelligence services. The first is the General Directorate of Intelligence under the Ministry of National Defense.[5] The second is the Intelligence Department under the Central Security Department of the National Police General Commissioner's Office at Cambodia's Interior Ministry.

This chapter argues that the entrenched path with dependence on turbulence, foreign intervention, and autocracy—as seen in Cambodia since 1969—has produced an intelligence culture that makes it difficult to reform intelligence services so that these are under an institutionalized, elected civilian control. As a result, reforms in these services have only enhanced their repressive nature. Yet what is the history of intelligence bureaucracies in Cambodia? How has Cambodia's intelligence bureaucracy worked with other bureaucracies and other countries? What exact reforms have occurred in Cambodia's intelligence bureaucracy? This chapter addresses these questions. To do this, it is organized in four sections. The first explores the history of Cambodia and its intelligence services from French colonialism through the Khmer Rouge to the present. In the second part, it examines issues shaping Cambodia's intelligence culture, including internal and external political factors. Next, the chapter analyzes oversight, reform, and neosultanistic control by highlighting familial connections in intelligence and the increased centralization of intelligence. The chapter concludes with a summary of the findings about Cambodia's intelligence culture.

HISTORY OF CAMBODIA AND ITS INTELLIGENCE SERVICES

As with other arms of the state, Cambodia's intelligence services have always been a tool for one authoritarian regime after another. Cambodia's history of intelligence services from its 1953 independence until the 1998 election had been extremely disjointed with successive regimes establishing new intelligence agencies.

At the dawn of Cambodian independence from France in November 1953, France's Service for External Documentation and Counter-Espionage (Service de Documentation Exterieure et de Contre-Espionnage, SDECE), a carryover of the traditional French Second Bureau (Deuxième Bureau), acted as the new country's intelligence service. Norodom Sihanouk, then king of Cambodia, abdicated in 1955 to run for and become prime minister. Following the 1955 elections, he and his Popular Socialist Community (Sangkum Reastr Niyum, SRN) political party won three more elections. During this period, Sihanouk established a neosultanistic regime, becoming "dictatorial Chief of State, with his policies ratified by a rubber-stamp National Assembly" until a coup overthrew him in 1970.[6]

In 1955, Cambodia commenced its own intelligence agency, the French Second Bureau (Deuxième Bureau) of Cambodia, advised by the SDECE and the United States' Central Intelligence Agency (CIA), which was embedded within the Ministry of Interior under General Dap Chhuon. Chhoun was a mercurial political opportunist who possessed a personal militia and had gained Sihanouk's confidence. He became an immediate guarantor of regime security and intelligence gathering but was also a strident anticommunist who increasingly criticized Sihanouk's growing tilt toward neutralism. By 1956, Washington, DC, began to perceive Chhoun as a potential replacement for Sihanouk. In 1959, Chhuon became implicated in a coup attempt against Sihanouk, which was supported by Thailand and South Vietnam.[7] The "Bangkok Plot" was also tacitly supported by the United States.

In the aftermath of the failed coup, Sihanouk became ever more suspicious of his political opponents, and his regime became more authoritarian. He began to rely heavily on General Lon Nol, who in 1960 was promoted from army chief of staff to army commander. Lon Nol's military intelligence bureau succeeded in assassinating Tou Samouth, general-secretary of the Communist Party of Kampuchea (Parti Communiste du Kampuchea, CPK). Nol also served twice as prime minister while Sihanouk was head of state. Despite his overwhelming authority, Sihanouk seemed to overlook the growing array of domestic actors interested in deposing him and the intensifying unease in Washington, DC, about his persistent policy of neutralism. In 1968, the CIA agreed to endorse a coup against Sihanouk (code-named "Sunshine Park") in which "Lon Nol was to be the principal."[8] The putsch eventually occurred on March 18, 1970.

Lon Nol's usurpation of power led to the creation of the Khmer Republic, above which, like Sihanouk previously, Lon Nol exerted neosultanistic dominance. One result of the coup was that Lon Nol appointed trusted lackeys to lead governmental posts. Indeed, he elevated his own brother General Lon Non to oversee intelligence alongside General Les Kosem, as deputy chief.

The two, known for indiscriminate killings and corruption, led Lon Nol's Republican Security Battalion, Cambodia's infamous intelligence/assassination unit.[9] Meanwhile, Cambodia increasingly receded into a destructive civil war, but it could not prevent the 1975 Khmer Rouge revolution.

Once in power, the Khmer Rouge began a reign of terror that turned into a genocide. It reorganized state intelligence directly under the new Revolutionary Army of Kampuchea (RAK), closely connected to the National United Front of Kampuchea (Front Uni National Khmer, FUNK). The totalitarian regime's secret police was called Santebal ("keeper of peace"). It was responsible for internal security as well as running torture camps such as S-21 (Tuol Sleng) in Phnom Penh where thousands of Cambodians were tortured and murdered.[10] Though Santebal's initial commander was Son Sen, it was tightly dominated by Khmer Rouge leader Pol Pot.[11] Indeed, intelligence collection was of principal importance to the extremely paranoid 1975–1979 Khmer Rouge government.

In 1979, Vietnam intervened in Cambodia, occupying the country until 1989. Vietnam installed the puppet People's Republic of Kampuchea (PRK) regime, led by the Kampuchean People's Revolutionary Party (KPRP). During this period, Hanoi entrenched its own intelligence services in Cambodia while reconstructing Cambodia's bureaucratic institutions in Vietnam's own image. The Vietnamese Ministry of Defense's Tổng Cục 2 (General Department 2), which answers to the Communist Party of Vietnam and Vietnam's president, became heavily involved in building the new General Directorate of Intelligence of the Kampuchean People's Revolutionary Armed Forces. In 1983, the military intelligence unit of Vietnam's Front 479 imprisoned thousands of Cambodians thought to be hostile to Vietnamese government.[12] In 1985, Vietnam endorsed Hun Sen to become prime minister of its puppet PRK Cambodian government. At that point, Hun Sen was not yet dominant over Cambodian politics but shared power with other post-1979 figures— such as Interior Minister Chea Sim—under Vietnam's tutelage.

Insurgent organizations fighting this government coalesced under the Coalition Government of Democratic Kampuchea (Roathaphibal Chamroh Kampuchea Pracheathipatai, CGDK), comprising Sihanouk's FUNCINPEC party, the Khmer Rouge, and anticommunist Son Sann's Khmer People's National Liberation Front (KPNLF). The KPNLF was to propagandize the local population and gather intelligence through its Khmer Information and Security Agency, which was reorganized in 1987 as the Bureau of Intelligence, Research and Documentation.[13]

In 1991, the year of the Paris Peace Accords, General Pol Saroeun, loyalist to Hun Sen and chief of the Supreme Command's General Staff, became the de jure commander over all of Cambodia's armed forces. Saroeun controlled the "Research Commissariat" or military intelligence branch (code-named Q101) of the State of Cambodia (as the Vietnam-supported regime had been called since 1989). General Mol Roeup was appointed commander of military intelligence in 1992. That same year, the Ministry of Interior's Defense of Political Security Directorate 1 (unit S21) and Defense of Political Security Directorate 2 (unit S22) were renamed the Anti-Terrorism Directorate and the Intelligence Directorate, respectively.[14] Other covert groups under the Interior Ministry included units A-91 and A-92, which "could kill, arrest secretly, and kidnap [and were] also expected to generate revenue."[15] A Hun Sen partisan Sok Phal directly headed up S22 as well as units A-91 and A-92.

During 1992–1993, Cambodia was administered by the United Nations Transitional Authority in Cambodia (UNTAC), with the military restructured as the Royal Cambodian Armed Forces (RCAF). During this time, Sok Phal informally continued on as chief of intelligence at the Ministry of Interior;[16] however, a 1993 sub-decree restructured the Ministry of Interior, creating a Supreme Directorate of National Police, under which was the General Information Unit, itself under the Security Central Directorate. This Information Unit oversaw intelligence and its name rapidly reverted to Intelligence Directorate under Sok Phal's command.[17]

The UNTAC-administered 1993 elections resulted in Sihanouk's son Norodom Ranariddh of FUNCINPEC becoming "first" prime minister while Hun Sen (Cambodian People's Party, CPP) became "second" prime minister. From 1993 until 1997, the FUNCINPEC and CPP shared control over the government and security services. Though Cambodia's five military regions were formally under the Supreme Command, each possessed its own military intelligence battalion and answered to Pol Saroeun. The most abusive was Q101 subunit S91 of Military Region 5, which became infamous for abductions, kidnaps-for-ransom, torture, and extra-judicial executions. S-91's then-commander Yon Youm was investigated by UNTAC for multiple human rights abuses but given his political connections, was never prosecuted. In 1993, the name of S-91 was changed to B-2.[18] It remained dominated by the CPP, but formally under the Ministry of National Defense. In 1996, Cambodian military intelligence developed two branches formally under the Supreme General Staff: Cambodia's Intelligence Second Bureau and the separate Intelligence Research Group (Q101) that was famous for mass arrests and torture.

In July 1997, "second" prime minister Hun Sen carried out a bloody coup against "first" prime minister Norodom Ranariddh. Assuming office as prime minister following a chaotic, unbalanced 1998 election, Sen thereupon centralized the Supreme Command's (and his own) control over all security units, including the Research and Intelligence Directorate.[19] Hun

Sen's entrenchment in power has continued through 2021. His authoritarian domination has ensured the embedding of a partisan, repressive intelligence apparatus that ably serves his regime.

ISSUES SHAPING CAMBODIA'S INTELLIGENCE CULTURE

Cambodia's intelligence culture is shaped by a plethora of issues. These include relations with international actors, general security issues, governmental structure, and interagency coordination with other governmental branches.

As the smallest country in mainland Southeast Asia, Cambodia is hemmed in by Thailand and Vietnam, which have much larger militaries. At the same time, great powers such as the United States, China, and Russia have taken an interest in Cambodia. All of these countries have, at one time, meddled in Cambodia's internal affairs, through invasion, bombing, or propping up proxy insurgent forces. From 2008 until 2014, Cambodia and Thailand came close to war over a disputed ancient border temple called Preah Vihear (Khao Phra Vihaan) temple.[20] Cambodia and Laos experienced tense border disputes in 2019. From its 1979–1989 occupation of Cambodia until today, Vietnam has been heavily influential in Cambodia's politics, military and economy. Vietnam and Cambodia engage in yearly armed forces exercises, among other areas of military cooperation.[21] Vietnam's military intelligence apparatus (Tổng Cục 2) has also continued to work closely with that of Hun Sen.

Yet, it is China that currently is Cambodia's leading investor as well as trade and military partner. China has also become Cambodia's leading supplier of military hardware and associate in military trainings (though these were suspended in 2021).[22] Moreover, Chinese and Cambodian intelligence have closely colluded together, an association that helped lead to Cambodia's 2009 extradition of twenty Uighur activists from Phnom Penh back to Beijing.[23] Meanwhile, Cambodia used to conduct annual military exercises with the United States until 2017.[24] For purposes of oversight, Cambodia's intelligence agencies have collected intelligence about the movements of foreign troops near Cambodia's borders as well as external interests within Cambodia.

Along with other Cambodian security actors, the country's intelligence services are tasked with guaranteeing "peace, stability, security, sovereignty, territorial integrity and the nation's development."[25] In terms of building up nontraditional security, Cambodia's intelligence agencies formally support Cambodia's security sector in terms of confronting such issues as counterterrorism, maritime security, border frictions/instability, anti-narcotics trafficking, land disputes, response to national health emergencies (such as the COVID-19 pandemic), union/unemployment issues, and environmental difficulties and ethnic problems.[26] As for counterterrorism, intelligence services have been a major part of efforts against al-Qaeda and Jemaah Islamiyah.[27] Regarding minorities, intelligence agencies have continuously monitored the Vietnamese diaspora within Cambodia while Muslim Cham people have often suffered eviction from their homes.[28] Intelligence agencies have monitored protests by political parties and nongovernmental organizations (NGOs) critical of the CPP, often working to identify the demonstrators for later arrest.

The same agencies have been used to gather intelligence about labor union leaders, striking workers, and other civil society leaders. Security forces have sometimes imprisoned or even killed such workers.[29] Almost assuredly, intelligence officials were involved in the 2004 assassination of Cambodian labor leader Chea Vichea. During protests marking the second anniversary of his death, military police intelligence officials mingled in the crowd.[30] Overall, intelligence and other state agencies have tended to follow Hun Sen's preferences on security issues, however partisan or repressive they may be. Intelligence agents have assisted in other targeted assassinations. Most likely they were involved in the murders of environmentalist Chut Wutty (2012) and journalist Kem Ley (2016), both of whom had been critical of Hun Sen's government.

Cambodia's governmental structure is such that intelligence agencies' activities are not transparent or accountable to courts, the legislature, or other parts of the executive branch. Indeed, there has never been any public scrutiny of intelligence activities because the country has always either been under autocracy or in the midst of civil war. Though both the Intelligence Department under the Ministry of Interior as well as the Defense Ministry's Intelligence Department formally report to ministry heads Sar Kheng and Ban Teah, respectively, they must also directly answer to Prime Minister Hun Sen, who has appointed perceived loyalists to lead each ministry's intelligence units. By personally dominating intelligence agencies, Hun Sen can "monitor potential opposition" and "spy on" Cambodia's Interior and Defense personnel.[31]

Cambodia's two intelligence services coordinate and work with other government branches when they are commanded by Hun Sen or his representatives in the military and police, which have also worked to further the interests of the CPP. Such cooperation oscillates around the prime minister, being highly hierarchical and personal and representing the neosultanistic leadership style characteristic of all post-1953 rulers. Cambodian intelligence

agencies have cooperated with other state agencies in several areas. These
have included counterterror operations; monitoring Thai and Vietnamese
troop movements along the borders; assisting in repressing demonstrations;
and guaranteeing security for the prime minister and his family.[32]

Yet another area of intelligence service activity has involved assisting
Cambodia's neighbors in attacking, "disappearing" or deporting dissidents
from those countries residing in Cambodia, in return for such services
from its neighbors. Since 2014, Cambodia, Thailand, Vietnam, Laos, and
Malaysia all seem to have avidly assisted each other in these matters. For
example, in 2017 four Vietnamese dissidents suffered an acid attack in Cambodia, purportedly ordered by Vietnamese authorities.[33] In 2018, "Thailand
detained and rendered two Cambodian exiles . . . at the apparent request of
the Cambodian government."[34] In 2020, Thai dissident Wanchalearm Sat-
saksit disappeared in broad daylight in Phnom Penh. Reports suggest that
Cambodian intelligence collaborated with Thai authorities in "disappearing"
Wanchalearm.[35]

Ultimately, while Cambodia's intelligence community formally prioritizes
challenges to state and societal security, the country's heavily politicized
intelligence culture has pressured intelligence officials to place regime security over all other national interests. As a result, intelligence officers have
become mere clients to the personalistic, neopatrimonial rule of Hun Sen.

OVERSIGHT, REFORM, AND NEOSULTANISTIC CONTROL

Hun Sen has increasingly maintained oversight and personalized domination
over Cambodia's intelligence services since his 1997 coup. He has appointed
reliable sycophants to lead intelligence agencies from the 1990s until the
present.

In the Ministry of Interior, General Sok Phal led the Intelligence Directorate from 1992 until 2003, becoming the director of the Central Security
Directorate in 2003, which also oversees Intelligence.[36] A new Intelligence
Department opened in 2007 under the Central Security Department of the
National Police General Commissioner's Office. It was formally tasked with
collecting foreign intelligence for national security; placing officials in Cambodian embassies abroad for intelligence operations; recommending security
proposals to the Ministry of Interior; working with foreign intelligence
services; and combating terrorism.[37] The department's director was General
Khem Sambo.[38] Though Sambo is a loyalist of Hun Sen, he was also close to
his patron and boss, powerful police chief General Hok Lundy. Lundy was
killed in a mysterious helicopter crash in 2008. In 2010, Lundy's son Dy

Vichea (also an executive of Sokha Helicopters) married Hun Sen's daughter Hun Mana, and in 2014, the prime minister appointed Vichea to become director of the Interior Ministry's Central Security Directorate, succeeding Sok Phal. The post ensured Vichea was "in charge of the National Police, internal intelligence and the police's bodyguard unit."[39] It also helped Hun Sen monitor potential opposition within the Ministry of Interior.[40] In 2017, Vichea became a general and was appointed as deputy director of the police. Though Sambo remains head of the Interior Ministry's Intelligence Department, Vichea oversees Sambo.

Turning to the Royal Cambodian Armed Forces' (RCAF) Intelligence Department, General Mol Roeup was its director from 1992 until 2012. A Hun Sen crony, he was described as "the architect of 'dirty tricks' campaigns against the prime minister's political opponents," and his military intelligence agency profited from illegal logging.[41] Upon Roeup's 2012 death, he was succeeded by General Chea Dara, another Hun Sen loyalist. That same year, the prime minister's son, General Hun Manith, was appointed deputy director of the Intelligence Department.[42] Interestingly, just as General Dy Vichea is married to Hun Sen's daughter, Hun Manith is married to Dy Vichea's sister Hok Chendavy. In 2015, Manith became the department's director.[43] In this capacity, he oversaw the spy agency's growth in human resources and "broad jurisdiction over national security affairs."[44] Manith has been rumored to have generated the "evidence" of a plot by the Cambodian National Rescue Party (the country's pre-2017 chief opposition party), which led to the legal dissolution of the party by Cambodia's judiciary in 2017. Evidence in 2017 also linked Manith to discussions on financing for the *Khmer Times* newspaper.[45] Manith's control over military intelligence has enabled Hun Sen to maintain close surveillance of potential adversaries, external and internal, while permitting "him to monitor his top generals' activities."[46] In August 2017, the prime minister appointed his son to become general director of a new General Directorate of Intelligence, which reports directly to Hun Sen and has five departments. It collects internal and external intelligence to build military strategy, strengthen cooperation with foreign intelligence and other units, and engage in counterterrorism. It also trains Cambodians to be spies for combat purposes against foreign and domestic foes while inculcating soldiers and police officers in intelligence-gathering techniques.[47] Interestingly, one role of the directorate is in Cambodia's elections. Former RCAF Supreme Commander General Pol Saroeun explained the 2018 election is "an absolute priority, so the intelligence director will have an important role to play."[48] See table 5.1 for a summary of the evolution of Cambodia's Intelligence Services.

Table 5.1.   The Disjointed Evolution of Cambodia's Intelligence Services

Regime	Agency/Agencies	Chief/Chiefs	Years
King Norodom Sihanouk	SDECE	French officials	1953–1955
Prince Norodom Sihanouk	Deuxième Bureau of Cambodia	Dap Chhuon, Lon Nol	1955–1970
Lon Nol	Republican Security Battalion	Lon Non, Les Kosem	1970–1975
Khmer Rouge	Santebal	Son Sen; Nuon Chea	1975–1979
PRK/SOC	Intelligence Directorate	Vietnamese domination	1979–1992
UNTAC	Information Department	Interior: Sok Phal	1992–1993
	Research Commissariat	RCAF: Mol Roeup	
Norodom Ranariddh / Hun Sen	Intelligence Directorate	Interior: Sok Phal	1993–1997
	Intelligence Second Bureau; Intelligence Research Group	RCAF: Mol Roeup	
Hun Sen regime	Intelligence Department	Interior: Sok Phal, Khem Sambo, Dy Vichea	1997–Present
	Intelligence Department/ Directorate	RCAF: Mol Roeup Hun Manith	

CONCLUSION

This chapter has argued that the entrenched path with dependence on turbulence, foreign intervention, and hybrid regime autocracy has dramatically impinged upon the history of Cambodia. These factors have ensured the perseverance of personalized control over intelligence services by an autocratic leader rather than institutionalized civilian control, which has dramatically shaped the intelligence culture to be loyal to an individual and his loyalists rather than the state.

At the beginning of the chapter, three questions were asked. First, what is the history of intelligence bureaucracies in Cambodia? Second, how has Cambodia's intelligence bureaucracy worked with other bureaucracies and other countries? Third, what exact reforms have occurred in Cambodia's intelligence bureaucracy? The evolution of Cambodian intelligence agencies has been piecemeal, chaotically disjointed, externally influenced, controlled by partisan interests, and invariably used for regime rather than national security. As for inter- and intra-agency collaboration, given that Cambodia is a relatively small country relative to its neighbors and vulnerable to great powers, intelligence services in France, the United States, Vietnam, and China (in that historical order) have worked closely with and provided training for Cambodian intelligence agencies. While Cambodian intelligence has monitored borders for dangers from its neighbors, it has also worked with other countries in counterterrorism and other issues. To appease outside powers, it has specifically helped monitor, attack, "disappear," or rendition those countries' dissidents when they reside in Cambodia. As for reform, given that Cambodia's regime authority over intelligence services has always been personalized by different rulers, the reforms implemented by Hun Sen since 1997 have only evolved from placing regime stalwarts in control of intelligence to positioning his family in charge of them. The latter can be seen in his appointment of his son Hun Manith as chief of the RCAF intelligence directorate and his appointment of his son-in-law Dy Vichea to establish indirect control over the Ministry of Interior's Department of Intelligence. These reforms show that Hun Sen is seeking to establish tightfisted authority over Cambodian intelligence.

Ultimately, through the years, there have been three principal factors that have shaped and continue to influence the intelligence culture in Cambodia. These have included external pressures from outside powers; transnational challenges (such as terrorism and, most recently, monitoring Cambodians who might be susceptible to the COVID-19 pandemic); and the fears of ruling elites, who have politicized intelligence to bolster their hold on power.[49] Having led or co-led Cambodia since 1985 (longer than any previous Cambodian leader), Hun Sen has incrementally reformed intelligence to make it his personalized tool assisting his survival in power. Since the charade 2018 election, after which Hun Sen's post-2018 electoral authoritarianism devolved into simple dictatorship, he will have to rely increasingly upon intelligence to monitor members of his own government and civil society to sustain power. Intelligence services in Cambodia thus matter more than ever: Hun Sen's neosultanistic fiefdom depends upon their capabilities.

NOTES

1. Juan J. Linz, "Totalitarian and Authoritarian Regimes," in *Handbook of Political Science*, vol. 3, *Macropolitical Theory*, ed. Nelson Polsby and Fred Greenstein (Reading, MA: Addison-Wesley, 1975), 259.

2. Paul Zagorski, *Comparative Politics: Continuity and Breakdown in the Contemporary World* (London: Routledge, 2009), 469.

3. See Kheang Un, "Patronage Politics and Hybrid Democracy: Political Change in Cambodia, 1993–2003," *Asian Perspective* 29, no. 2 (2005): 203–5.

4. Larry Diamond, "Thinking about Hybrid Regimes," *Journal of Democracy* 13, no. 2 (April 2002): 24.

5. Until 2017 it was called the Cambodian Intelligence and Research Department; in 2009 it had a budget of US$10,756,644.16. See Christian Hippner, "A Study into the Size of the World's Intelligence Industry" (MA thesis, Mercyhurst College, October 2009), 87.

6. Michael Vickery, "Kambodscha," in *Südost Asien Handbuch*, ed. Bernhard Dahm and Roderich Ptak (München: Verlag C. H. Beck, 1999), 252.

7. "Prince Sihanouk and the New Order in Southeast Asia," US Central Intelligence Agency, Office Service No. 20, April 1, 1962, 47–50, https://www.global security.org/military/library/report/other/esau-25.pdf.

8. Matthew Jagel, "Son Ngoc Thanh, the United States, and the Transformation of Cambodia" (PhD diss., Northern Illinois University, 2015), 190, https://commons.lib.niu.edu/bitstream/handle/10843/18583/Jagel_niu_0162D_12197 .pdf?sequence=1&isAllowed=y.

9. Kenton Clymer, *The United States and Cambodia, 1969–2000: A Troubled Relationship* (London: Routledge, 2004), 69.

10. Ben Kiernan, *The Pol Pot Regime: Race, Power and Genocide in Cambodia under the Khmer Rouge, 1975–1979* (New Haven, CT: Yale University Press, 2008), 315.

11. Luke Hunt, "Khmer Rouge: A Family Affair," *The Diplomat*, May 8, 2012, https://thediplomat.com/2012/05/khmer-rouge-a-family-affair/.

12. Kosal Path, "Lustration," in *Memory of Nations—Democratic Transitions Guide: The Cambodian Experience* (Washington, DC: National Endowment for Democracy and CEVRO, 2018), 13, https://www.researchgate.net/publication/ 329504662.

13. Timothy Carney, "Kampuchea in 1982: Political and Military Escalation," *Asian Survey* 23, no. 1 (January 1983): 76, https://online.ucpress.edu/ as/article-abstract/23/1/73/21912/Kampuchea-in-1982-Political-and-Military ?redirectedFrom=fulltext; Kenneth Conboy, *The Cambodian Wars: Clashing Armies and CIA Covert Operations* (Lawrence: University Press of Kansas, 2013), 233–35.

14. "Cambodia's Dirty Dozen: A Long History of Rights Abuses by Hun Sen's Generals," Human Rights Watch, June 2018, 48–49, https://www.hrw.org/ report/ 2018/06/27/cambodias-dirty-dozen/long-history-rights-abuses-hun-sens-generals.

15. "'Tell Them That I Want to Kill Them': Two Decades of Impunity in Hun Sen's Cambodia," Human Rights Watch, November 13, 2012, https://www .hrw.org/report/2012/11/13/tell-them-i-want-kill-them/two-decades-impunity-hun -sens-cambodia.

16. "Cambodia's Dirty Dozen," 18–19.

17. "Cambodia's Dirty Dozen," 169.

18. "'Tell Them That I Want to Kill Them.'"

19. "'Tell Them That I Want to Kill Them,'" 26.

20. See Charnvit Kasetsiri, Pou Sothirak, and Pavin Chachavalpongpun, *Preah Vihear: A Guide to the Thai-Cambodian Conflict and Its Solutions* (Bangkok: White Lotus, 2013).

21. Mech Dara, "Cambodia-VN Disaster Rescue Drills Come to End," *Phnom Penh Post*, December 19, 2019, https://www.phnompenhpost.com/national/cambodia-vn-disaster-rescue-drills-come-end.

22. Umair Jamal, "Cambodia Signals Foreign Policy Shift by Halting Military Drills with China," *ASEAN Today*, March 10, 2021, https://www.aseantoday.com/2021/03/cambodia-signals-foreign-policy-shift-by-halting-military-drills-with-china/.

23. "Chinese Agencies Rule Roost in Phnom Penh," Intelligence Online, December 24, 2009, https://www.intelligenceonline.com/grey-areas/2009/12/24/chinese-agencies-rule-roost-in-phnom-penh,76855433-art.

24. Reuters Staff, "Cambodia Suspends Annual Military Drill with United States," Reuters, January 16, 2017, https://www.reuters.com/article/us-cambodia-usa-idUSKBN1501YK.

25. "Defending the Kingdom of Cambodia" (White Paper), Kingdom of Cambodia, 2006, https://www.files.ethz.ch/isn/156829/Cambodia-2006.pdf.

26. "Defending the Kingdom of Cambodia," 15–52.

27. "Cambodian Linked to Jemaah Islamiyah Terrorist Group," Voice of America, October 28, 2009, https://www.voanews.com/a/a-13-a-2003-06-12-1-cambodian-66854872/375960.html.

28. Leonie Kijewski, "Beautifying Phnom Penh: Muslim Cham Face Eviction in Cambodia," *Aljazeera*, December 13, 2019, https://www.aljazeera.com/news/2019/12/13/beautifying-phnom-penh-muslim-cham-face-eviction-in-cambodia.

29. David Hutt, "How Cambodia Killed Its Unions," *Asia Times*, May 2, 2018, https://asiatimes.com/2018/05/how-cambodia-killed-its-unions/.

30. Kuch Naren and Lee Berthiaume, "Over 100 March in Memory of Chea Vichea," *Cambodian Daily*, January 23, 2006, https://english.cambodiadaily.com/news/over-100-march-in-memory-of-chea-vichea-memory-52045/.

31. Jonathan Sutton, "Hun Sen's Consolidation of Personal Rule and the Closure of Political Space in Cambodia," *Contemporary Southeast Asia* 40, no. 2 (August 2018): 186.

32. "Defending the Kingdom of Cambodia," 46; "Updated: Still Missing," Political Prisoners in Thailand, October 5, 2020, https://thaipoliticalprisoners.wordpress.com/2020/10/05/still-missing/.

33. "Enforced Disappearance and Regime Lies," Political Prisoners in Thailand, February 8, 2021, https://thaipoliticalprisoners.wordpress.com/tag/cambodia/.

34. "Enforced Disappearance and Regime Lies."

35 "Updated: Still Missing," Political Prisoners in Thailand, October 5, 2020, https://thaipoliticalprisoners.wordpress.com/2020/10/05/still-missing/.

36. "Cambodia's Dirty Dozen," 164–79.

37. "Intelligence Department Established," *Phnom Penh Post*, November 1, 2007, https://www.phnompenhpost.com/national/intelligence-department-established.

38. Douglas Gillison and Yun Samean, "Gov't Names Head of New Intelligence Service," *Cambodian Daily*, November 7, 2007, https://english.cambodiadaily.com/news/govt-names-head-of-new-intelligence-service-56096/.

39. May Titthara, "Key Post to PM's Son-in-Law," *Phnom Penh Post*, August 11, 2014, https://www.phnompenhpost.com/national/key-post-pm%E2%80%99s-son-law.

40. Titthara, "Key Post to PM's Son-in-Law."

41. Global Witness, "Cambodia's Family Trees: Illegal Logging and the Stripping of Public Assets by Cambodia's Elite," Cambodia.org, June 2007, 64, http://www.cambodia.org/downloads/pdf/cambodias_family_trees_med.pdf.

42. Saing Soenthrith, "Hun Sen's Second Son in Meteoric Rise through RCAF Ranks," *Cambodia Daily,* January 30, 2012, https://english.cambodiadaily.com/news/hun-sens-second-son-in-meteoric-rise-through-rcaf-ranks-1560/.

43. "Cambodia's Hun Sen Names Son Head of Military's Intelligence Department," Radio Free Asia, October 22, 2015, https://www.rfa.org/english/news/cambodia/appointment-10222015170944.html.

44. Kosal Path, "Consolidating the State Apparatus," in *Memory of Nations— Democratic Transitions Guide: The Cambodian Experience* (Washington, DC: National Endowment for Democracy and CEVRO, 2018), 8.

45. Ben Paviour, "Leaks Link Hun Manith, NagaCorp CEO to *Khmer Times*," *Cambodia Daily*, March 2, 2017, https://english.cambodiadaily.com/news/link-alleged-between-newspaper-hun-manith-nagacorp-ceo-126010/.

46. Path, "Consolidating the State Apparatus," 8.

47. May Titthara, "Prime Minister Sets Up Spy Training School," *Khmer Times*, December 13, 2017, https://www.khmertimeskh.com/95669/prime-minister-sets-spy-training-school/.

48. Khy Sovuthy, "Hun Sen's Son Gets Intelligence Chief Job," *Khmer Times*, August 24, 2017, https://www.khmertimeskh.com/79682/hun-sens-son-gets-intelligence-chief-job/.

49. Sorpong Peou, "Hun Sen's Power Paradox," *East Asia Forum*, November 7, 2018, https://www.eastasiaforum.org/2018/11/07/hun-sens-power-paradox/.

6

China: The Fearful Intelligence Culture

Matthew Brazil

The Chinese Communist Party (CCP) has placed priority on its intelligence and security operations for almost a century. This core business of the party significantly contributed to the CCP's 1949 victory and to the maintenance of the party's current power. Most recently, the internet and artificial intelligence (AI) have enabled previously unimaginable foreign espionage successes. Yet there are cracks in the facade: unending existential fear about enemies within; fear of being caught between CCP general secretary Xi Jinping's never-ending anticorruption drive and a culture that still fosters graft, as well as fear of being insufficiently loyal to Xi's "thought" and to his status as the CCP "core." These factors may stifle intelligence analysis.

Drawing from Chinese-language publications and interviews with former Western security officials who had regular contacts with their Chinese counterparts, this chapter argues that these are old problems but, under Xi, have become more pronounced in recent decades. It shows how China's espionage organs will likely continue to achieve successes in cyberespionage, agent recruitment, and technology theft, but dispassionate intelligence analysis may be hindered by pressure to conform to the party line. Thus, Chinese intelligence culture in the 2020s may sometimes make it difficult for Beijing's senior leaders to see the forest through the trees.

This chapter is organized in six sections. The first examines the roots of Communist China's intelligence and security with attention to early support and operations. Next, it explores more recent cases of corruption and power struggles. The third section analyzes the intelligence culture's state-centric approach in contrast to the United States' national security focus. Then it turns to the lasting influence of two key leaders, which stresses the importance of loyalty within the intelligence culture. Shifting to a few key cases, the fifth section provides an overview of competence versus ideology in Chinese intelligence services. Lastly, the chapter concludes by highlighting the evolution of Chinese intelligence and how the culture of fear will likely persist.

THE SHELL-SHOCKED ROOTS OF CHINESE COMMUNIST INTELLIGENCE AND SECURITY

The drone of escalating fear in the CCP's intelligence and security organs—and in the party more generally—has its roots almost 100 years ago in the early years of the Chinese Revolution. The fear of enemies within, the campaigns to dig them out, and the genuine threat of enemy espionage prompted the CCP Central Committee to directly control intelligence and security from its first decade. Although the CCP "did not know how to organize intelligence" before 1927, according to early Chinese intelligence officer Chen Yun, it quickly adapted by placing intelligence and security at the head table.[1]

Chen was referring to the first six years of the CCP after its 1921 founding, leading up to the day everything changed. On April 12, 1927, the CCP was betrayed by its erstwhile "united front" allies, the Chinese Nationalist Party (国民党, Kuomintang, aka the KMT/GMD) led by Chiang Kai-shek (蒋介石, Jiang Jieshi). In his "party cleansing" (清党, *qingdang*) operation that month, Chiang's forces rounded up and executed a significant percentage of the CCP's urban cadre.[2] It was arguably the CCP's first major intelligence failure and came close to destroying the party's leadership.

Late that summer, after the bloodletting had eased and secret meetings resumed, the CCP Central Committee directed Zhou Enlai to reorganize its departments to meet the challenge of operating as an urban "underground" while maintaining a military effort in the countryside. Party leaders considered it vital that they remain in the cities, close to China's tiny proletariat. Marxist doctrine maintained that organizing workers was the key to advancing revolution, and for practical reasons, an urban underground was key to receiving funds from Moscow. In November, Zhou established the Central Special Services Section (SSS), which he gradually built over the next twenty-four months to include logistical, administrative, intelligence, and special operations branches.[3] The SSS reported directly to the CCP leadership, a promotion from being subordinate to the Military Department. But as an independent section (科, *ke*), SSS was not yet an equal to the higher-ranking departments (部, *bu*) at the Central Committee conference table.

The decade that followed underlined the necessity to build a more thorough knowledge of the party's enemies. SSS officers were assigned a variety of dangerous and daring tasks, principally to penetrate the Chinese Nationalist Party and central government organizations and military commands, assassinate traitors, and harass and kill particularly effective police and other security officials in Shanghai and other cities—including Hong Kong.[4] As the weaker contestant in the struggle for national power, it needed high-quality information about enemy capabilities and intent.

Selected operations from these early days are lauded today as examples of clever and courageous action—important to modern intelligence culture because espionage after the 1949 Communist victory is almost never publicly discussed. Model operations include the "Three Heroes of the Dragon's Lair" (龙潭三杰, *Longtan sanjie*), a Communist spy ring that kept the CCP underground headquarters in Shanghai one step ahead of the Nationalist police for two short years. It was also known as the Li Kenong Small Group (李克农小组, Li Kenong xiaozu), after its head.[5] Other celebrated operations include the Mo Xiong (莫雄) network inside the Nationalist Army that enabled the Red Army under Mao Zedong (毛泽东) and Zhu De (朱德) to break out of Chiang Kai-shek's "Fifth Encirclement" in 1934.[6] Additional operations in Shanghai, Hong Kong, and Macau involved Dr. Ke Lin (柯林), who maintained the natural cover of a physician for decades beginning in 1928.[7] There were also assassinations against traitors such as Bai Xin (百鑫).[8]

The Three Heroes ring performed a last vital act as they were exposed in April 1931. The event carries great cultural significance even today because it was the second time in four years that an intelligence failure almost destroyed the party. That month the head of operations for the SSS, Gu Shunzhang (顾顺章), accompanied a Red Army leader, Zhang Guotao (张国焘), from Shanghai to the Eyuwan Soviet, 500 miles to the west. Once Gu delivered Zhang, he went to Wuhan for a rendezvous but was captured by Nationalist intelligence.

Gu quickly defected to avoid torture, raising an important question for the CCP's leaders that may still resonate today. That is, if the intelligence chief immediately defects to the enemy upon capture, what hope is there of resistance by the rank and file? Gu began naming names of underground Communist leaders and their hiding places while begging the Nationalists to protect his family in Shanghai. A member of the Three Heroes Ring, Qian Zhuangfei (钱壮飞), spotted the first reporting telegrams at Nationalist intelligence headquarters. He alerted his network, saving some party members who were underground. Zhou Enlai, today considered the father of CCP intelligence, organized and carried out the revenge execution of Gu's entire family, sparing only an infant.[9]

Those events happened before modern communication capabilities. While some Communists could be quickly contacted in time to flee for their lives, the Nationalist central government soon captured and killed thousands of Communists in Shanghai and other cities. Their investigations may also have led to the arrest on June 1 of "the Noulens Couple," a husband-wife team of Soviet agents who controlled distribution of funds from Moscow to Communist groups throughout East Asia.[10]

By 1934, Nationalist raids against Communist cells in Shanghai and other cities were like a relentless mudslide that subsumed everything Red in its path. Meanwhile, in faraway Jiangxi Province, the Red Army was surrounded and forced to embark on the Long March, its calamitous escape to China's northwest in which the forces of Mao and Zhu De sustained losses of nearly 90 percent over thirteen months. In November 1935, upon arrival at the CCP's new headquarters of Bao'an, the Central Committee decided to scrap the SSS because few assets remained in China's cities.[11] The surviving agents and officers were transferred to the Red Army's State Political Protection Bureau (PPB, 国家政治保卫局, *Guojia zhengzhi baowei ju*, 1931–1939), known more for massive purges of enemies within than for producing intelligence.[12]

A balance of sorts was in motion. During the Long March, Li Kenong, the former head of the Three Heroes ring, ran the production of signals intelligence (SIGINT) and analysis that kept the Red Army intact as the Nationalist army subjected it to constant attack. Li may have thus outperformed his boss in the PPB, Deng Fa, because after arrival in Bao'an, the Central Committee decided to promote Li and transfer his boss, Deng, to the Grains Bureau. Deng was suddenly yesterday's man. A dyad was in the making: quality military and political intelligence on the enemy versus digging out (铲除, *chanchu*) internal enemies. Yet, even with Li in charge and enemy intelligence a priority, the purges continued.[13]

Back in Shanghai, one hard-core remnant held out: the "dog beating squad" (打狗队, *dagou dui*) assassination ring in Shanghai of Gong Changrong (龚昌荣), known as "general two-gun" (双枪将, *Shuang qiang jiang*) because of his ability to simultaneously handle two pistols. Gong had a distinguished record of kills in Hong Kong, Guangzhou, and Shanghai from 1927 until his capture in November 1934. He and his team were hanged the following April after being continuously tortured. In today's propaganda it is said that he and his comrades did not talk. A cultural symbol, indeed, he has been lionized in print and a five-minute dramatized video posted on Baidu.[14] Meanwhile, Zhang Meixiang (张美香), Gong's spouse, had acted as the group's armorer, maintaining weapons and ammunition in their residence while raising two small children. Party propaganda claims that she and the children escaped to Hong Kong, where Zhang with the family ran a secret radio station for the CCP.[15]

Whether strictly true or exaggerated, the story of Gong, his group, and his family is one of many that hint at the high level of commitment and discipline expected of officers, and probably also of families, in *approved* CCP intelligence culture. As former Central Intelligence Agency (CIA) director Leon Panetta expressed in an interview, while the CIA's culture stresses nonpartisan public service, CCP intelligence culture stresses discipline, particularly in China's premier civilian foreign intelligence and counterespionage agency, the Ministry of State Security (MSS).[16] Others with experience in China, including the author, have observed that MSS officers are more careful in their comments, especially at social functions, than are Public Security officials or military intelligence officers of the Chinese People's Liberation Army (PLA).[17] Such discipline is displayed today by the apparently tight-lipped Xu Yanjun (徐燕军), an MSS officer from the Jiangsu State Security Bureau. Xu was arrested in Belgium and extradited to the United States in October 2018, where he was charged with trade secret theft under the US Economic Espionage Act and convicted in November 2021.[18]

CORRUPTION, ANTICORRUPTION, AND POWER STRUGGLES

A counterpoint to discipline is corruption, sown far and wide in the 1980s and 1990s as Chinese responded to Deng Xiaoping's idea, expressed in 1985, that the CCP should "let some people become rich first" (让一部分人先富起来, *rang yi bufen ren xian fu qilai*).[19] His utterance soon became known everywhere in China and told the population that the party would not oppose economic activity that heretofore had been previously condemned as capitalist.

Yet, there were downsides. First, the bulk of the population remained poor, and years later the CCP was still struggling to fit the idea of capitalist activity into a socialist model.[20] Second, corruption blossomed into a threat against the CCP's legitimacy. While the number of poor in China declined, demands for graft increasingly affected daily life for ordinary people. Growing corruption infected the security services and the military, with some units in the PLA and MSS fostering side businesses that enriched senior officers. Bribes were routinely demanded for promotions and assignments. The problem continued under Xi Jinping, particularly in support units, according to PLA expert Dennis Blasko, and in PLA military intelligence itself, according to the Australian China analyst Alex Joske.[21]

Xi was intent on solving China's corruption crisis, at least among those opposed to him, when he ascended to national leadership in 2012. A spy scandal earlier that year involving MSS vice minister Lu Zhongwei (陆忠伟) and his confidential assistant Li Hui (李辉) must have drawn Xi's attention. Li was discovered to be an agent of the US Central Intelligence Agency—apparently responsible for the compromise of an uncertain, but perhaps substantial, number of Chinese secret agents in the United States. Li's boss, MSS vice minister Lu, was apparently not charged, but he was ousted.[22]

Li's fate is not certain, but he likely was executed, one of perhaps twenty CIA agents discovered by Chinese authorities between 2010 and 2012 (possibly viewed as corrupt activity because of the payments they likely received). A Chinese mainland source commented that it was a rare instance of two nations simultaneously destroying each other's clandestine networks in their own countries.[23]

Further investigations followed, leading to the arrest of MSS vice minister Ma Jian (马健) in January 2015. Ma had ties to the Chinese billionaire Guo Wengui (郭文贵), exiled in the United States and a target of the MSS for repatriation and trial on corruption charges of uncertain veracity. On top of that, Ma was said to have engaged in wiretapping Xi at the behest of Zhou Yongkang (not related to Zhou Enlai), then the CCP's overseer of security affairs.[24] The apparent ally of Ma and Zhou was Bo Xilai, a rival of Xi Jinping for the CCP leadership. The trio received long prison sentences.

These events highlighted the risk that China's security services, in the wrong hands, could be used against the party's leadership in a power struggle. Xi subsequently brought in the highly skilled Chen Wenqing (陈文清) to lead MSS. Though he had no background in foreign intelligence, Chen did serve substantial time in Public Security bureaus in his home province of Sichuan. He also had a tour of duty in State Security as a senior official in the Chengdu State Security Bureau: a vital post, managing counterespionage work in a city with numerous foreign consulates that is also a center for defense production. Chen's subsequent duties in the CCP Discipline Inspection Commission, attacking party corruption, allowed him to get to know X's associates. When Xi needed a "broom" to clean up the MSS, Chen's experience in police, counterespionage, and anticorruption work made him a timely choice. Chen appears to be an important, and powerful, Xi loyalist, who has promoted a culture in the MSS of discipline and loyalty to today's great leader.[25]

STATE SECURITY, NOT NATIONAL SECURITY

Chen Wenqing's elevation to head of the MSS, with no foreign intelligence experience, underlines the fact that the primary mission of the MSS, "state security" (国家安全, *guojia anquan*), is different than the United States' concept of "national security." For Washington, DC, national security is about preventing hostile foreign acts against the United States and its citizens and organizations abroad. For Beijing, state security means preserving the CCP's leading position in Chinese society, mostly against enemies within. It means suppression of even the most minor threats against the Party State before they metastasize into existential problems.[26]

This causes Beijing's agencies to use their substantial resources, with hundreds of thousands, if not more, direct employees and numerous additional contractors, to attack issues that are generally ignored by nonauthoritarian states. The MSS prioritizes seemingly minor matters such as Chinese overseas who criticize Beijing, be they from the Han majority or the Tibetan and Uyghur diasporas. For certain, the MSS pursues foreign intelligence and advanced technology, as is often reported. Meanwhile, many of their officers abroad spend substantial time seeking to divide, depoliticize, and eventually demobilize anticommunist activists, often by placing pressure on their families in China to cease criticizing the regime.[27]

This is not to say that the MSS devotes fewer resources to foreign political and military intelligence compared to other major powers. But their operations do not always appear professional or organized. Nigel Inkster, the former head of operations and intelligence for the British Secret Intelligence Service (MI6) explained:

> We don't see a predictable MO [modus operandi]. The Russians, for example, would always carefully kit out the agents that they ran, but the Chinese don't do that, they're more hit and miss. That seems to include training of their own officers. The lack of standards and lack of care seems, at least in part, to indicate a disrespect for the U.S.[28]

Inkster cited as an example of "hit and miss" the case of Kevin Mallory, a former CIA officer turned Chinese spy. The MSS equipped him with a mobile phone that was supposed to erase the secret messages between Mallory and his handler—but it failed to do so, providing the Federal Bureau of Investigation with crucial evidence leading to Mallory's conviction.[29]

THE LASTING LEFTIST INFLUENCE OF MAO ZEDONG AND KANG SHENG

The roots of today's CCP intelligence culture of total loyalty to Xi, and the use of the intelligence and security infrastructure to promote that loyalty in society at large, extend back to Mao Zedong. Though Zhou Enlai is considered to be the father of CCP intelligence, Mao minimized Zhou's control of that work as much as possible from 1935 to 1945 and during the Cultural Revolution beginning in 1966. Mao, his preferred intelligence chief, Kang Sheng, and their acolytes emphasized digging out enemies within the party and wider society as much as obtaining quality intelligence, aspiring to the "both red and expert" (又红又专, *you hong you zhuan*) policy formula—that is, being competent both at Communist ideology and professional matters with an emphasis on complete loyalty to the leader.

Kang Sheng hewed to Mao's inclinations at all times, pursuing a broad attack on perceived enemies—including Zhou Enlai himself in 1943 during the brief but raucous "Salvation" campaign (抢救运动, *Qiangjiu yundong*). Kang claimed that he could personally sniff out spies without recourse to actual evidence, more a terror technique than a claim to supernatural abilities. Modern CCP propaganda blames Kang for initiating the practice of "forcing a confession and believing it" (逼供信, *bigong xin*).[30]

Though Mao sidelined Kang Sheng in 1946 due to pressure from Moscow and the fact that his erstwhile security chief was widely hated in the party, Kang did not permanently lose favor.[31] Kang began his comeback to national-level politics in 1962, when he denounced Xi Zhongxun, the father of China's current leader, in an invented political controversy. Mao responded by denying office to the elder Xi for sixteen years, and soon Kang allied himself with Mao's spouse, Jiang Qing, in her drive to attain leadership of the party's extreme Left.[32] When the Cultural Revolution began in 1966, Kang took over political oversight of intelligence and security. He was ailing by 1972 and died a year later—but not before engineering the rise of Luo Qingchang (罗青长), a figure important even today in CCP intelligence culture.[33]

Luo was the only top officer of the Central Committee Investigation Department (CC/ID) who was not purged and struggled against at the beginning of the Cultural Revolution in 1966.[34] He became its leader after a brief period of military control and stayed in the top position until 1983, three years after the rise of Deng Xiaoping as China's paramount leader. Luo's resilience in office and his ability to resist Deng's reforms were remarkable in itself. Even though Luo developed a deserved reputation during the Cultural Revolution for betraying his mentors and colleagues, he remains an officially respected figure today.[35] This indicates that the red and expert model, if not radical leftism itself, may retain a place in the culture of Beijing's spy apparatus and in the CCP at large.[36]

COMPETENT SPY VERSUS REAR AREA IDEOLOGUE

During the Anti-Japanese War (1937–1945), the cultural dyad in CCP intelligence that began in 1927 matured. On the one hand, there were politically correct, redder than red ideologues pursuing counterespionage work (i.e., catching spies) in the rear areas. On the other hand, there were pragmatic intelligence officers operating undercover behind enemy lines in the dangerous, gray world of espionage.

In some systems and intelligence cultures, such a dyad might produce coequal groups. In Communist China's intelligence culture, however, counterespionage officers in the safety of the rear areas were strongly advantaged. Competent spies, rubbing shoulders with noncommunist access agents and others in enemy areas, were vulnerable to even the wildest allegation because the demands of clandestine work and CCP intelligence methods prohibited record keeping that might provide contrary evidence.[37]

That imbalance was Mao's responsibility. As the late CCP historian Gao Hua described:

> The basic reasons for the vicious circle leading to brutal campaigns against counterrevolutionaries were:
> 1) Mao's exaggerated estimation of the enemy situation within the Party, which rendered the ultra-Leftist mentality against counterrevolutionaries a permanent mindset; and
> 2) Mao's misrepresentations regarding elimination of counterrevolutionaries due to his personal motivations. . . . Even the founder of the CCP's intelligence and anti-counterrevolutionary apparatus, Zhou Enlai, did not hold Mao's extreme appraisal of the "enemy situation."[38]

This aspect of CCP intelligence culture was promoted by Mao solely to benefit his personal power. As a result, CCP intelligence officers and agents sent undercover into enemy areas during the 1930s and 1940s were vulnerable to being victimized by accusations of treason for simply doing their jobs—in particular during extreme Left movements in 1943, in 1955, and in 1966 onward with the Cultural Revolution. Whether that is also true today is a question for future research.

Three prominent cases illustrate the dyad. Liu Shaoqi, who worked many years in enemy areas, and Pan Hannian, a senior intelligence officer who spent most of his career in occupied cities, suffered terribly during the Cultural Revolution.[39] By contrast, Deng Xiaoping was relatively immune from charges of being a hidden traitor because he had seldom worked in enemy areas.[40] Lastly, Larry Wu-tai Chin (金无怠, Jin Wudai), one of the most damaging Chinese spies ever to penetrate the United States government, was an exception. He apparently endured no hostile examination by Beijing during his long career as an agent inside the US government (1947–1983), perhaps for the simple reason that he was not able to travel to China during periods when extreme campaigns against counterrevolutionaries were in progress. Additionally, the information he provided was exceptionally valuable.[41]

CONCLUSION

In the early years of the People's Republic of China, the Investigation Department, which began its existence working on both foreign intelligence and domestic security, had a hard time maintaining consistent reporting. Good policy-related intelligence collection only began to develop in the 1980s, with the founding of the MSS and the increased activity of PLA intelligence. The rise of Chinese cyber operations beginning in 2005 had a great impact. After a number of impressive results in capturing huge amounts of data in the United States and elsewhere, Beijing's agencies may be developing a superior understanding of big data compared to Western countries.[42]

Given China's rise and its more aggressive foreign policy, there is likely an increased demand for quality intelligence on the United States and on China's neighbors and trading partners. While suppressing dissent and running agent operations will remain important—and indeed seem to be on the rise outside of China—cyber operations may garner an ever-greater share of resources in the future.

In the next decade, the ranks of MSS and the PLA Intelligence Bureau will gradually fill up with recruits born during and after the 1990s, raised in an era of heightened nationalism and suspicion of foreigners. If the legacy of fear in CCP intelligence culture persists, combined with more and more big data, raw intelligence could become overwhelming while the ability declines to make sense of it and clarify the truth through unrestricted internal discussion. Such shortcomings in intelligence analysis could leave Beijing's decision makers less able to make sense of the outside world, not to mention crucial and controversial domestic developments, in the 2020s and 2030s.

NOTES

1. Chen was one of the early CCP's senior intelligence officers. He is better known as China's leading socialist economist during the first five decades of the People's Republic. Jin Chongji, *Chen Yun Zhuan* [Biography of Chen Yun] (Beijing: Zhongyang Wenxian Chubanshe, 2005), 105; Hao Zaijin, *Zhongguo Mimi Zhan* [China's secret war] (Beijing: Zuojia Chubanshe, 2005), 2–3.

2. "1927 nian Jiang Jieshi we he turan dui Gongchandang dakai shajie" [Why did Chiang Kai-shek suddenly begin murdering communists in 1927?], *Sina Jinlang Junbao*, November 5, 2015, http://mil.news.sina.com.cn/2015-11-05/1447843115.html.

3. SSS: 中央特别任务科, Zhongyang tebie renwu ke, often abbreviated as 特科 (*te ke*). Hao, *Zhongguo Mimi Zhan*, 5. *Zhou Enlai Nianpu, 1898–1949* [The annals of Zhou Enlai, 1898–1949] (Beijing: Zhongguo Wenxian Chubanshe, 2007), 128. Xue, "Guanyu Zhonggong Zhongyang Teke Ruogan Wenti de tantao" [An investigation

into certain issues regarding the CCP Central Special Services Section], *Zhonggong Dangshi Yanjiu* [Investigations in Chinese Communist history], no. 3 (1999), https://xuewen.cnki.net/CJFD-ZGDS199903012.html.

4. Zhang Yiyu, ed., *Shanghai Yinglie Zhuan Qi Zhuan* [Biographies of Shanghai's brave martyrs] (Shanghai: Zhongguo Shanghai Shiwei Dangshi Yanjiushi, 1991), 7:149–50. "Provisional List: Hong Kong Police Deaths in the Course of Duty, 1841–1941," Police.Gov.HK, 2021, https://www.police.gov.hk/offbeat/788/eng/n10.htm.

5. Kai Cheng, *Li Kenong* [Biography of Li Kenong] (Beijing: Zhongguo Youyi Chubanshe, 1995), 2, 8–10, 15, 34–40; Hao, *Zhongguo Mimi Zhan*, 9.

6. Wang Zuohua, "Yifen juemi qingbao cushi hongjun tiaoshang changzheng lu" [The piece of top secret information that prompted the Red Army to embark on the Long March], *Shijie Junbao*, September 22, 2009, http://xibaipo.com/news2007/News/shmw/2009/22/09221635764G566DEEK8594HC086B.html.

7. "Legend of an Era: Dr. Ke Lin," YouTube, uploaded by China Documentary, September 2021, https://www.youtube.com/watch?v=gYJx1HBQRbY; "Hongse yisheng Ke Lin de dixia dang rensheng" [The party underground life of the Red doctor Ke Lin], Phoenix Television, October 7, 2009, http://phtv.ifeng.com/program/nyjs/200910/1007_5364_1378071_2.shtml.

8. Mu Xin, *Yinbi Zhanxian Tongshuai Zhou Enlai* [Commander in chief of the secret battlefront, Zhou Enlai] (Beijing: Zhongguo Qingnian Chubanshe, 2002), 156–61, 170–78; *Zhou Enlai Nianpu, 1898–1949*, 166–67; Warren Kuo, *Analytical History of the Chinese Communist Party* (Taipei: Institute of International Relations, 1969), 2:293–94.

9. Liu Wusheng, *Zhou Enlai Da Cidian* [The big dictionary of Zhou Enlai] (Nanchang: Jiangxi Renmin Chubanshe, 1997), 31–32; *Zhou Enlai Nianpu, 1898–1949*, 166–167 and 210–211.

10. Frederick S. Litten, "The Noulens Affair," *China Quarterly* 138 (June 1994): 492–512, https://www.cambridge.org/core/journals/china-quarterly/article/abs/noulens-affair/4535CF06E82F2D3FED24C36414F050CC.

11. Frederick Wakeman, *Spymaster: Dai Li and the Chinese Secret Service* (Berkeley: University of California Press, 2003), 42–45, 128; Liu, *Zhou Enlai Da Cidian*, 31–32; Hao, *Zhongguo Mimi Zhan*, 8–10; Jin, *Chen Yun Zhuan*, 104.

12. Xu Zehao, *Wang Jiaxiang Nianpu* [The annals of Wang Jiaxiang] (Beijing: Zhongyang Wenxian Chubanshe, 2001), 56–57; Zhao Shaojing, "Suqu 'Guojia Zhengzhi Baowei Ju' yu sufan kuodahua wenti banzheng" [The Soviet Area State Political Protection Bureau and the question of enlarging the purge of counterrevolutionaries], CNKI, accessed May 16, 2020, https://www.cnki.com.cn/Article/CJFDTOTAL-BFFX200804011.htm; Hao, *Zhongguo Mimi Zhan*, 10.

13. Hao, *Zhongguo Mimi Zhan*, 10, 13–15, 20; He Jinzhou and Li Huimin, *Deng Fa Zhuan* [The Biography of Deng Fa] (Beijing: Zhonggong Dangshi Chubanshe, 2008), 70–71; Kai, *Li Kenong*, 74–80; Wang Fang, *Wang Fang Huiyi Lu* [The memoirs of Wang Fang] (Hangzhou: Zhejiang Renmin Chubanshe, 2006), 14.

14. Zhang, ed., Shanghai Yinglie Zhuan, 7:179. See the video at https://baike.baidu.com/item/龚昌荣/15900704.

15. "Zhōngyāng tè kē 'shuāng qiāng jiāng' gōngchāngróng" [Gong Changrong, "Double Gun General" of Central Teke], 163.com, February 11, 2021, https://www.163.com/dy/article/G2J9T5VT05129QAF.html; *"Gōngchāngróng: Yǐnbì zhànxiàn jiéchū de qiáo xiāng yǐngxióng"* [Gong Changrong: Outstanding overseas Chinese hero on the hidden front], Jiangmen Municipal People's Government, April 13, 2020, http://www.jiangmen.gov.cn/home/zwyw/content/post_2028949.html.

16. Author interview with Leon Panetta, former US defense secretary and CIA director, August 30, 2021.

17. Author confidential interviews, 2021.

18. "Jury Convicts Chinese Intelligence Officer of Espionage Crimes, Attempting to Steal Trade Secrets," US Department of Justice, November 5, 2021, https://www.justice.gov/opa/pr/jury-convicts-chinese-intelligence-officer-espionage-crimes-attempting-steal-trade-secrets.

19. "Deng Xiaoping: rang yi bufen ren xian fuqilai" [Deng Xiaoping: Let some people become rich first], *News of the Communist Party of China*, n.d., http://cpc.people.com.cn/gb/34136/2569304.html.

20. Wu Jun Huang Shiqing, "Deng Xiaoping lilun: Zui ke baogui de caifu" [Deng Xiaoping theory: A most valuable asset], *People's Daily*, July 26, 2013, http://theory.people.com.cn/n/2013/0726/c367101-22340560.html.

21. Miles M. Evers, "The Greatest Threat to China's Military Might," *National Interest*, July 16, 2014, https://nationalinterest.org/blog/the-buzz/the-biggest-threat-chinas-growing-military-might-10891; Dennis Blasko, "Corruption in China's Military: One of Many Problems," *War on the Rocks*, February 16, 2015, https://warontherocks.com/2015/02/corruption-in-chinas-military-one-of-many-problems/; Minnie Chan, "China's Military Needs Checks on Power to Stamp Out Corruption, Top Military Advisor Says," *South China Morning Post*, February 22, 2019, https://www.scmp.com/news/china/military/article/2187366/chinas-military-needs-checks-power-stamp-out-corruption-top; Jichang Lulu, "The PLA and CCP Influence Abroad: Business, Intelligence, Crime and Interference Enmeshed," *Sinopsis*, December 6, 2019, https://sinopsis.cz/en/joske-pla/.

22. "Jin Wudai shi zisha de ma? Ci shi qian chu Zhongguo Guo'an Bu jiandie Li Hui de xiachang" [Did Jin WuDai commit suicide? The incident led to the fate of Li Hui, a spy of the Ministry of State Security of China], GreatChinese.com, December 16, 2016, http://www.greatchinese.com.cn/law/shehuixinwen/20161216/17431.html.

23. Liang Haoming [梁浩明], "Zhongguo cuihui Meiguo Zhongyang Qingbao Ju jiandie huodong neimu" [The inside story of China's destruction of the CIA's activities], *The Kunlun*, June 7, 2017, http://www.kunlunce.com/myfk/fl1111/2017-06-07/116546.html.

24. David Ignatius, "China's Intelligence Shakeup Mirrors Its Political Tumult," *Real Clear Politics*, April 1, 2016, https://www.realclearpolitics.com/articles/2016/04/01/chinas_intelligence_shakeup_mirrors_its_political_tumult_130158.html#!.

25. Matthew Brazil, "China's Top Spy Is a Working-Class Hero," *SpyTalk*, January 4, 2021, https://www.spytalk.co/p/chinas-top-spy-is-a-working-class.

26. Peter Mattis and Samantha Hoffman, "Managing the Power Within: China's State Security Commission," *War on the Rocks*, July 28, 2016, https://warontherocks .com/2016/07/managing-the-power-within-chinas-state-security-commission/.

27. Tenzin Dorjee, "Divide, Depoliticize, and Demobilize: China's Strategies for Controlling the Tibetan Diaspora," *China Brief* 21, no. 18 (September 2021), https:// jamestown.org/program/divide-depoliticize-and-demobilize-chinas-strategies-for-co ntrolling-the-tibetan-diaspora/.

28. Author interview with Nigel Inkster, London, July 2021.

29. Adam Goldman, "Ex-CIA Officer Is Convicted of Spying for China," *New York Times*, June 8, 2018, https://www.nytimes.com/2018/06/08/us/politics/cia -officer-kevin-mallory-convicted-spying.html.

30. Gao Hua, *Hong Taiyang Zenyang Shengqi de* [How the Red sun rose over Yanan] (Hong Kong: Chinese University of Hong Kong Press, 2008), 509; "Zhong-yang guanyu shencha ganbu de jueding" [Central Committee decision concerning cadre examination], August 15, 1943, in *Zhonggong Zhongyang Wenjian Xuanji* [Selected documents of the Chinese Communist Central Committee] (Beijing: Renmin Chubanshe, 2013), 14:89–96; "Jing diaocha ta mingling ben shi yilu bu kaizhan Qiangjiu yundong" [After investigation he ordered his division not to carry out the Salvation movement], Sohu.com, March 2019, https://www.sohu.com/a/ 300948725_120015077.

31. Gao, *Hong Taiyang Zenyang Shengqi de*, 465; Roger Faligot, *Les services secrets chinois de Mao aux Jo* [The Chinese secret services of Mao and Zhou] (Paris: Nouveau Monde, 2008), 81–82. Faligot, *Chinese Spies* (London: Hurst, 2015), 47.

32. "Xi Zhongxun yi: Kang Sheng yige tiaozi rang wo shiliu nian meiyou gong-zuo" [Xi Zhongxun remembers: A note from Kang Sheng (to Mao) kept me unem-ployed for 16 years], *Shijiazhuang Ribao*, May 23, 2012, http://news.sohu.com/ 20120523/n343923544.shtml.

33. Peter Mattis and Matthew Brazil, *Chinese Communist Espionage: An Intel-ligence Primer* (Annapolis, MD: Naval Institute Press, 2019), 92–95.

34. 调查部, *Diaochabu*, then China's civilian foreign intelligence agency.

35. Shen Xueming and Zheng Jianying, eds., *Zhonggong Diyi Jie zhi Di Shiwu Jie Zhongyang Weiyuan* [Central Committee Members from the First to the Fifteenth Chinese Communist Central Committees] (Beijing: Zhongyang Wenxian Chubanshe, 2001), 513; Michael Dutton, *Policing Chinese Politics: A History* (Durham, NC: Duke University Press, 2005), 218–21, 227–30; Roderick MacFarquhar and Michael Schoenhals, *Mao's Last Revolution* (Cambridge, MA: Belknap Press, 2006), 98, 415; "Luo Qingchang: Cengren Zhongyang Diaocha Bu buzhang, Zhou Zongli linzhong qian zhaojian" [Luo Qingchang, former director of the investigation department whom Premier Zhou summoned before his death], *Renmin Wang*, April 21, 2014, http://dangshi.people.com.cn/n/2014/0421/c85037-24920819.html.

36. See Mattis and Brazil, *Chinese Communist Espionage*, 92–95.

37. David Chambers, "Edging in from the Cold: The Past and Present State of Chi-nese Intelligence Historiography," *Studies in Intelligence* 56, no. 3 (September 2012): 41, https://www.cia.gov/resources/csi/studies-in-intelligence/volume-56-no-3/edging -in-from-the-cold-the-past-and-present-state-of-chinese-intelligence-historiography/.

38. Gao Hua, *How the Red Sun Rose: The Origins and Development of the Yan'an Rectification Movement, 1930–1945*, trans. Stacy Mosher and Guo Jian (Hong Kong: Chinese University Press, 2018), 504.

39. Chambers, "Edging in from the Cold," 39–41; Mattis and Brazil, *Chinese Communist Espionage*, 129–34.

40. Author interview with CCP historian, 2016; author interview with David Chambers, 2018.

41. Mattis and Brazil, *Chinese Communist Espionage*, 203–4.

42. Inkster interview.

7

India: Managing Challenges in an Evolving Security Environment

Sameer Patil and Arun Vishwanathan

Like most constitutional democracies, India has a vast intelligence apparatus. The country inherited parts of it along with the security establishment from the British colonial rule. Yet, India has had a rich history of espionage, as evident from the works of Kautilya, the key political adviser to the Mauryan Empire (ca. 323–185 BCE), who emphasized the role of intelligence in statecraft.[1]

This chapter takes a broad overview of India's intelligence establishment. It argues that India's intelligence community is expansive and well established, with its structure and capabilities shaped by the unique demands put forth by India's "quasi-federal" polity and the multiple security challenges the country faces. India's agencies face several challenges but have managed to largely fulfill India's security needs. The chapter begins by providing an overview of key intelligence services and the structure of India's intelligence community. After discussing the principal elements of this establishment, it highlights some of the important historical developments that shaped this apparatus. It then discusses unique factors that influence India's intelligence culture. Finally, it reviews the operational challenges faced by the intelligence agencies and how they have been addressed.

KEY INTELLIGENCE SERVICES AND STRUCTURE

At present, two agencies dominate India's intelligence structure in matters of resources, influence in decision-making, and personnel strength—Intelligence Bureau (IB), the domestic intelligence agency, and Research and Analysis Wing (R&AW), the external intelligence agency (see figure 7.1). IB was created in 1887, on the recommendation of Lord Dufferin, then British viceroy of India.[2] Apart from domestic intelligence, it is responsible for internal security, counterintelligence, and counterterrorism. R&AW was created out of IB, decades later, on September 21, 1968.[3] Besides foreign intelligence gathering, it is also responsible for counterterrorism and counterproliferation and operational missions abroad focusing on India's neighbors.

The National Technical Research Organisation (NTRO) is another agency that has acquired prominence in recent years. Established in 2004, it is India's technical intelligence agency and reports to the National Security Advisor (NSA).[4] The functioning of these three intelligence agencies is governed by the Intelligence Organisations (Restrictions of Rights) Act of 1985.[5] A former senior IB official, Maloy Krishna Dhar (1937–2012), noted that the Indian government took the step of amending Article 33 of the constitution to place the intelligence agencies like IB, R&AW, Director General of Security in R&AW, and NTRO at par with the military in terms of constitutional rights and organized trade activities.[6] The legislation bars staff of these agencies from forming any unions or associations, restricts their freedom of speech, prohibits any communication with media, and prevents publication of a book or other document without the approval of the head of the agency.[7]

Additionally, there are multiple specialized intelligence agencies or, in some cases, units/divisions. The three wings of the Indian military have their respective intelligence agencies—Directorate of Military Intelligence (Indian army), Directorate of Air Intelligence (Indian air force), and Directorate of Naval Intelligence (Indian navy). Besides these, the Defence Intelligence Agency (DIA) is responsible for providing and coordinating intelligence for the military.[8] Another inter-services agency is the Joint Cipher Bureau, which is responsible for crypt-analysis and encryption.[9]

Each of India's paramilitary forces under the Ministry of Home Affairs (MHA), like the Central Reserve Paramilitary Force and Border Security Force, has its dedicated intelligence units. In the civilian domain, there is the Department of Revenue Intelligence (DRI) under the Ministry of Finance, which is described as the "apex anti-smuggling agency" tasked with preventing the trafficking of contraband including drugs and checking evasion of customs duty.[10] There is also the Financial Intelligence Unit-India, which tracks suspicious financial transactions, including instances of money laundering and terrorist financing.[11]

The newest addition to this structure is the Multi-Agency Centre (MAC), which was strengthened after the 2008 Mumbai attacks for counterterrorism-related information sharing among the security agencies. It is located within the IB and has auxiliary units in all state capitals.[12] This information sharing was enabled to a great extent by establishing the National Intelligence Grid,

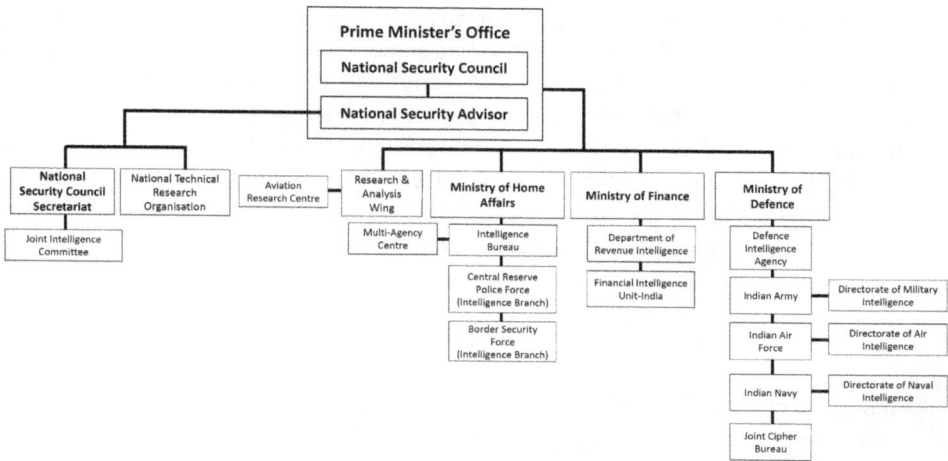

Figure 7.1. India's Intelligence Apparatus
Source: Compiled by the authors.

known better by its acronym NATGRID, which consolidates databases of all intelligence agencies.[13]

At the top of this structure sits the Joint Intelligence Committee (JIC), which has gone through ups and downs during its existence. Currently, it is part of the National Security Council Secretariat (NSCS), which was set up in April 1999 as part of the revived National Security Council (NSC) system headed by the NSA. The JIC analyzes intelligence inputs received from IB, R&AW, NTRO, and other intelligence agencies. In 2018, it was subsumed within the newly created Internal Security division of the NSCS. A deputy NSA–level officer reports to the NSA who heads it.

Together these agencies tackle India's multiple security challenges, many of which can be attributed to a troubled neighborhood. Externally, border disputes and activities of Pakistan-based anti-India terrorist groups dominate India's security concerns, while internally, New Delhi tackles terrorism in Jammu and Kashmir, insurgency in the northeast, and left-wing extremists in the hinterlands. Punjab, too, has remained a focus with the activities of the *Khalistani* terrorist groups, which demand a separate homeland for the Sikhs. An ever-persistent threat is domestic or homegrown terrorism, manifested through the extended networks of Pakistan-based terrorist groups and the Islamic State's efforts to radicalize Indian youth. Linked with these threats are smuggling syndicates and organized criminal gangs that have taken advantage of India's porous borders. An emerging concern on this threat landscape is cybersecurity.

India's intelligence structure is extensive and wields enormous influence and power in the Indian system. It also had some notable successes, as will be discussed later in the chapter. Yet, like many large bureaucracies elsewhere, this apparatus is afflicted by poor coordination, interagency turf battles, ad hoc and reactive decision-making, and interference from the political executive. Moreover, despite repeated shocks of intelligence failures, India's intelligence establishment has resisted foundational reforms, owing to its clout in the bureaucracy and direct access to the apex political establishment.

HISTORY

George Santayana is credited with an oft-repeated adage: "Those who cannot remember the past are condemned to repeat it."[14] A historical overview of India's intelligence establishment proves this. Many of the committees and commissions set up by the government to investigate the intelligence failures were more often than not narrowly focused on identifying the causes or drawing lessons from the intelligence failure or a particular crisis. Yet they failed to pay sufficient attention to the larger macro, structural issues, which possibly resulted in the failure or crisis in the first place. This was evident right from the Henderson Brooks–Bhagat Report on the 1962 India-China war.[15]

After facing a humiliating defeat in the war, the government set up the committee comprising Lieutenant General T. B. Henderson Brooks and Brigadier Premindra Singh Bhagat, then commandant of the Indian Military Academy. The committee's report, popularly known as the "Henderson Brooks Report," has not been publicly released by successive Indian governments.[16] The committee, tasked with looking at the operational aspects of the 1962 war, essentially blamed the military leadership and intelligence apparatus for the debacle. It noted that there was enough evidence pointing to China's road-building activities along the entire Himalayan frontier, especially in the Aksai Chin area, and that the government was aware of it.[17] Yet, the political leadership and military and intelligence establishment did not consider it and failed to recognize China's aggressive intentions and continued their focus on Pakistan instead of China, which proved to be a costly mistake.[18]

Despite the experience of the 1962 war, it appeared that India's intelligence establishment learned little as intelligence sharing remained mired in interagency turf battles. In the aftermath of the war with Pakistan in 1965, the government set up a committee to look at the reasons for the intelligence lapse under B. S. Raghavan, a senior MHA official. The Indian army had blamed IB for not having provided advance intelligence about Pakistan's plans to open the Ichogil canal to flood tankable approaches.[19] IB, however, countered the allegations. Former R&AW director (but then serving in IB) K. Sankaran Nair noted in his memoirs that he went before the committee with "some fifty reports sent over the year, about the Ichogil canal including Pakistan's plans about its utilization in war."[20] After deliberations, the committee concluded that Army Intelligence had not adequately disseminated these reports and the information therein to the field units. The deliberations of the committee and the Henderson Brooks Report contributed to the eventual creation of the R&AW.[21]

While intelligence agencies, including IB, were primarily focused on tackling India's security challenges during the initial decades, a worrying trend that acquired salience during the tenure of Prime Minister Indira Gandhi in the late 1960s and early 1970s was the use of IB for political purposes. This trend peaked when Gandhi imposed the state of emergency in June 1975 that lasted until March 1977.[22] Post-emergency, when Gandhi lost the Lok Sabha elections, her successor, Morarji Desai, constituted a committee to investigate the allegations of widespread misuse of intelligence agencies by Gandhi and her son, Sanjay Gandhi. The committee, under the chairmanship of former home secretary L. P. Singh, especially looked at the role of IB and the Central Bureau of Investigation (CBI), the principal federal investigative agency. The committee looked into the ethical and legal aspects of the work done by the IB and the CBI but left out R&AW from its scrutiny.[23]

The L. P. Singh committee in its report recommended that IB and CBI adopt institutional charters.[24] But it was never acted upon, and after Gandhi's return to power in 1979, the report was buried and never made public. While the R&AW had been left out of the ambit of the L. P. Singh committee, Prime Minister Morarji Desai was very suspicious of the organization and "considered it to be Mrs. Gandhi's Gestapo."[25] Desai harbored a staunchly hostile attitude toward intelligence agencies in general.[26] He, therefore, sought to cut the organization and rolled back its extensive human intelligence network and foreign operations, including in Pakistan. Desai's repeated expressions of lack of trust in R&AW chief R. N. Kao led the latter to decide to retire prematurely.[27]

The next milestone in India's security and intelligence establishment came more than two decades later when Prime Minister Atal Behari Vajpayee set up the K. C. Pant Task Force in 1998. The task force's recommendations resulted in the constitution of the NSC chaired by the prime minister.[28] It also created the post of NSA, a single point source of advice for national security–related issues to the prime minister.[29]

Yet the problem of information sharing and intelligence analysis persisted, as was seen months after the NSC's establishment when the Pakistan army regulars and militants supported by the army occupied the heights in the Kargil and Drass sectors of the Line of Control virtually undetected. These developments surrounding the Kargil conflict of 1999 brought another intelligence failure and prompted the government to establish the Kargil Review Committee (KRC) under the chairmanship of strategic expert K. Subramanian to examine issues of national security and intelligence reforms. A high-level Group of Ministers (GoM) examined the committee's recommendations under the chairmanship of then deputy prime minister L. K. Advani.[30] Unlike previous review committees, this committee's report was a landmark because it was tabled in Parliament and a redacted version published as a book.[31]

One of the taskforces that the GoM established dealt with intelligence issues. The GoM's recommendations yielded some crucial changes in the Indian intelligence setup.[32] These included the following:

- Institution of a formal charter outlining the responsibilities and role of the IB and the R&AW;
- Restructuring of R&AW by moving the Seema Suraksha Bal (a border security agency deployed along Nepal and Bhutan borders) to the MHA and ensuring greater involvement of the military in the Aviation Research Centre (ARC), R&AW's imaging intelligence wing;
- Establishment of the NTRO, on the lines of the US National Security Agency as the technical intelligence collection agency;
- Establishment of the DIA as the military intelligence agency under the Integrated Defence Staff, Ministry of Defence. In addition, the DIA was also put in charge of the Defence Image Processing and Analysis Centre (which handled India's satellite image acquisition capability) and the Signals Intelligence Directorate (which handled interception and decryption of enemy communications).

FACTORS SHAPING INDIAN INTELLIGENCE PERFORMANCE

In political science terms, India is categorized as a "quasi-federal" polity where the powers of the states (the constituent units) are not symmetric with the union (the whole).[33] As per the provision of the Indian constitution, "public order" and "police" are in the "State List," which illustrates the list of items states can legislate.[34] This does not ensure a complete say for the states in managing security issues, however, because another related matter, "Defence of India," is in the "Union List," which gives powers to the union government and Indian Parliament to legislate on specific issues, even by overriding states' objections. This asymmetric federalism impedes efficient intelligence management as states are wary of powerful central intelligence agencies.

Symbolic of the state's wariness was how the National Counter Terrorism Centre (NCTC) issue played out in 2012. The 2008 Mumbai attacks revealed a key lacuna in interagency information sharing on counterterrorism issues.[35] To remedy this, the Indian government revived the MAC on December 31, 2008, within the MHA to collate and disseminate counterterrorism-related information.[36] As the next step, the government rolled out the NCTC, which would have acted as a unified center for information sharing, intelligence analysis, and joint operational planning.[37] It was vested with operational powers so far given only to the state police and central investigation agencies. Fearful of NCTC's powers encroaching upon their police force, several states, including Gujarat, West Bengal, Odisha, Tamil Nadu, Madhya Pradesh, and Bihar, strongly opposed the NCTC. In the face of strong opposition from states, the government put the NCTC proposal on hold, and it has not been revived so far. According to the former chairman of the JIC, S. D. Pradhan, copying the American NCTC model would not work for India as the organization would not have powers to arrest, and without the cooperation of the states and presence of district-level collation centers, the NCTC would largely be ineffective.[38]

An additional issue that has shaped India's intelligence culture is the fiercely secretive attitude of the Indian government toward intelligence agencies to maintain the confidentiality of their work. India's intelligence apparatus is strictly under the control of the executive with no parliamentary oversight.[39] Both the premier agencies, IB and R&AW, do not have statutory recognition.[40]

Another unique aspect of the intelligence culture is the dominance of personalities in national security decision-making. The example of R. N. Kao's influence during Prime Minister Indira Gandhi's tenure and his role in shaping the initial progress of R&AW demonstrates the key role of an individual decision maker.[41] This aspect has been reinforced with the creation of the NSA's post in 1999. Being one of the close aides of the prime minister and a senior IPS or Indian Foreign Service (IFS) officer, the NSA wields unprecedented influence over all intelligence agencies and within the security establishment. This is particularly the case with the IPS appointees and former IB heads—M. K. Narayanan (2005–2010) and Ajit Doval (2014–present)—who have been appropriately described as "security czars."[42] This dominance of individual actors has also resulted in less emphasis on processes.

OPERATIONAL ISSUES

There are five key issues surrounding Indian intelligence operational issues. The first is the absence of statutory recognition and legislative oversight, which has impeded democratic transparency and government accountability. The second is the inadequate staff and recruitment challenges that have resulted in the usage of temporary staff to address shortfalls. The third is interagency turf battles and absence of coordination that leads problems in intelligence sharing. The fourth is inadequate intelligence collection and analysis capability that harms the quality of output provided to the government leadership. Lastly, there is deficient intelligence analysis training.

India is possibly the only democracy of its size and importance where the intelligence agencies continue to function without statutory recognition and parliamentary (legislative) oversight. According to former senior R&AW official B. Raman (1936–2013), despite support from the intelligence agencies and senior security officials, not much headway has been made on this front.[43] This is possibly due to the lack of will on the part of the political executive that desires to keep the intelligence agencies under its control and to continue using them for gathering political intelligence.

As noted earlier, the L. P. Singh Committee (1977–1979) had also recommended that IB and CBI adopt institutional charters, which was never implemented. Former intelligence officer V. K. Singh noted that the only possible attempt to put in place legislative oversight of intelligence agencies took place during Prime Minister V. P. Singh's short tenure in 1989. It was also during this period when R&AW had asked the government to approve basic tasks for the agency.[44] These initiatives could not get much traction, however, possibly due to the short tenure of the government. The legal vacuum that the IB and R&AW was functioning in was noted by the KRC in 1999, which recommended a specific and formal charter of duties for both agencies.[45] This reform, however, still left unattended the matter of parliamentary oversight.

Speaking in 2010 at the R&AW headquarters, then Vice President Hamid Ansari raised the need for oversight of intelligence agencies.[46] This was followed by the tabling of a private member bill called the Intelligence Services (Powers and Regulation) Bill in 2011 by Manish Tewari, a Lok Sabha member of the then ruling Indian National Congress party.[47] The proposed bill had sought to create a legal basis for three intelligence agencies: the IB, the R&AW, and the NTRO. In addition, it had envisaged a legislative and regulatory framework for these three agencies and the creation of two bodies to monitor their functioning: the National Intelligence Tribunal and the National Intelligence and Security Oversight Committee.[48] The bill, however, did not make it through Parliament and lapsed in October 2012. Tewari reintroduced it in 2020, but it was not taken up for discussion.[49]

While there are differences about the extent of legislative oversight—whether to limit it to policy issues or cover financial, operational matters—there is a broad agreement in the agencies over the need for such a mechanism under the Indian Parliament. The political executive, however, does not seem to be making efforts at pursuing this.[50]

Another issue faced by Indian intelligence agencies is the endemic shortage of staff. In 2013, then minister of state for home, R. P. N. Singh, had told Parliament that the IB had a shortfall of close to 8,000 staff at various levels: the agency having 18,795 personnel on its rolls, against a sanctioned strength of 26,867.[51] Likewise, the R&AW is short by about 5,000 personnel and finds itself in a similar situation, especially in the middle run of its leadership and technology domains.[52]

With no dedicated central cadre, civilian intelligence agencies like IB, R&AW, and NTRO have resorted to irregular recruitment of employees, including taking officers, particularly from the IPS, on deputation/secondment from various other services. As a result, the IPS officers rule the roost at the middle to higher levels in these agencies.[53] The IPS officers—who are essentially federal police officers—are generally deputed from their state/province cadre to the central intelligence agencies for short periods, ranging up to a couple of years. The dominance of the IPS officers at the top echelons is compounded by the lack of a central or organization-specific cadre of intelligence officers, which is one of the most serious challenges for the intelligence agencies. As is the practice, many of the IPS officers join the central intelligence agencies on deputation to "cool off" while searching for better opportunities or because of differences with the political leadership at the states/provincial level.[54]

The practice of deputation of IPS officers first began in the IB during the 1970s when Indira Gandhi was in office. Before that, officers were "earmarked" for working in the IB at the time of their initial training.[55] Such officers continued to work in the IB throughout their careers and even rose to head the organization. According to Dhar, the discontinuance of this practice of "earmarking," coupled with reliance on officers on short-term deputations, caused "maximum damage to the organization and transformed it to a mundane and controlled central police organization or any other uniformed force under the control of the Ministry of Home Affairs."[56]

This assessment is echoed by the Task Force on Intelligence Reforms set up by the Ministry of Defence–funded think tank, the Institute for Defence Studies and Analyses, which lamented that the dominance of the IPS officers blurred the lines between field policing and intelligence gathering, and stymied areas where specialized skill sets were required like language specialists and science and technology specialists. A senior R&AW official, V. Balachandran, put it succinctly when he said: "You can't run your space programme, or Army, with people on deputation. You can't run your intelligence services that way, either."[57]

Recruitment challenges are particularly acute for R&AW. The agency had relied on the IPS and its newly created Research and Analysis Service (RAS, created in 1971) along with some lateral recruitment.[58] Yet the IPS maintained its dominance and cornered most of the apex postings within the organizations and abroad, creating considerable resentment among the non-IPS officers of the R&AW.

To alleviate this factionalism, Prime Minister Rajiv Gandhi appointed a committee under former R&AW chief, K. Sankaran Nair, in the 1980s. The committee focused not just on R&AW but also on other intelligence services.[59] It not only tried to alleviate factionalism between IPS and non-IPS officers within the organization but also attempted to find ways to tide over the resentment over lack of opportunities to get promoted, more so among the non-IPS officers and Class Two (the lower level) personnel within the R&AW and also the IB.[60] The IPS lobby frustrated these reform efforts, however.

R&AW engaged in direct recruitment into the RAS echelons between 1971 and 1977 and later in the mid-1980s to 1992.[61] Yet, this recruitment was frozen between 2004 and 2010 with continued debates about how the personnel should be recruited, whether through centralized all-India examinations or direct campus recruitment.[62]

Some R&AW officers like former chief Vikram Sood have argued that the civil services that provide for India's bureaucracy are unlikely to provide the best intelligence officers given the need for multiple skill sets, including foreign language skills, weapons handling knowledge, interrogation skills, and intelligence tradecraft. He therefore suggests the need to hire domain specialists from different areas like economics, political science, journalism, and sciences to be recruited into intelligence agencies via the lateral, direct-entry route.[63]

Similar to any other country that has a vast security establishment, India too faces the challenge of interagency turf battles and bureaucratic politics.[64] This has had its impact on interagency coordination and information sharing. The fight between the R&AW and NTRO over aerial intelligence and satellite imagery is symbolic of this turf battle. Since the creation of NTRO in 2002, R&AW has actively guarded the ARC and its aerial assets, fearing that those might be taken over by the NTRO. In 2015, NSA Doval made a decision to shut down the ARC and divide its aerial assets between NTRO and the IAF.[65] Given the recent reports of the use of ARC ariel reconnaissance assets as late as in 2020, it seems the R&AW has managed to hold on to its assets.[66]

Turf battles have also been seen between the IB and R&AW. These are partly a function of the lack of coordination and overlapping roles of the organizations. The IB, which is the nodal agency for domestic counterintelligence, is often in the crosshairs of other agencies and their personnel. Issues like cross-border terrorism, arms smuggling, *hawala* transactions, and cross-border terror funding come under the domain of both IB and R&AW, leading to continued efforts by the agencies to secure their spheres of interest. The Ministry of External Affairs (MEA) and the R&AW too have had their share of differences over timely sharing of political intelligence collected by its officers while being posted in the Indian diplomatic missions abroad. V. K. Singh has noted that previously an arrangement was followed whereby an IFS officer was appointed as foreign service adviser in the R&AW. The aim was to "act as a link between the MEA and R&AW and assist in the implementation of political intelligence tasks assigned to the latter, as well as evaluation of its output."[67] This arrangement helped bring much-needed coordination between the MEA and the R&AW, but it fell into disuse over a period of time.

Saikat Datta has pointed out that modern intelligence processes are based on the twin pillars of intelligence collection and a robust analytical capability, both of which remain challenges for Indian intelligence agencies.[68] While India has raised an extensive structure, intelligence agencies, barring IB, R&AW, and MI, have been found deficient on the intelligence collection front. This is particularly so with paramilitaries such as the BSF. Technical intelligence collection capabilities have vastly improved.[69] But the agencies' human intelligence network remains dismal, with few human assets to monitor subversive, anti-India activities.[70] Top officials have repeatedly raised questions on the quality of intelligence received, in particular the human intelligence.[71]

This is combined with the lack of dedicated intelligence analysis capability. Consequently, substandard and uncorroborated intelligence inputs often make their way through the system to the apex decision makers. This inability to separate "the signal from the noise" has resulted in the agencies missing vital clues in many cases.[72] The 2008 Mumbai attacks highlighted this. Despite having multiple pieces of information pointing to the possibility of such an attack, agencies did not detect the threat and prevent the attacks. Former NSA Shivshankar Menon remarked that, when it came to the Mumbai attacks, "no one put together the whole picture."[73]

The JIC, which was supposed to perform the job of intelligence collation and analysis at the apex level, has also often found it difficult to get intelligence agencies, particularly IB and R&AW, to reveal the quality of their sources. As strategic expert K. S. Subramanian wrote, assigning labels such as "secret" or "top secret" also helps agencies avoid questions about their sources.[74]

In many cases, these agencies themselves perform the task of producing intelligence assessments, violating the basic principle that the collecting agency should not assess its own inputs.[75] This absence of intelligence analysis capability has also contributed to strategic thinking, where the focus is mainly on daily operational-tactical intelligence.[76]

Training of fresh inductees and regular updating of tradecraft, technical skills, or on-the-job training for junior and middle-rung staff is a crucial aspect that has been often overlooked in the Indian intelligence apparatus. As per one study, the IB training facilities can process only about 600–700 staff every year, which is woefully short to meet its workforce requirements.[77] Adequate training of recruits and on-the-job training of existing staff becomes notably critical due to the growing complexity of threats faced by India.[78] This is especially true for cyberspace, where IB and R&AW have actively tracked espionage campaigns, but their efforts to counter the same have fallen short due to lack of training and capacity.[79] Consequently, India lags far behind in projecting power in cyberspace. According to the Belfer National Cyber Power Index, among the thirty countries measured for cyber power, including offensive cyber operations, India stood at twenty-seven.[80]

The challenges in imparting training are multifold, ranging from archaic and police-centric curriculum to outdated equipment, to lack of well-trained instructors in adequate numbers at the intelligence training centers.[81] Another challenge has been the shortage of instruction in foreign languages like Arabic, Chinese, Pashto, and Dari, where well-trained and proficient instructors are few.[82] There have been suggestions to hire external experts wherever necessary for imparting training, especially in specialized areas, and to establish common training facilities for all intelligence agencies. Implementing these suggestions, however, will require a push from the apex political and national security leadership.

NOTABLE SUCCESSES

Notwithstanding these challenges, Indian agencies have had some notable successes that have strengthened India's national interest and foreign policy objectives. Among the major success stories is the R&AW's covert operations in 1971 in what was then Eastern Pakistan, which eventually led to the division of Pakistan and the creation of Bangladesh.[83] Similarly, in 1986, an operation by IB weakened a northeastern insurgent group, the Mizo National Front, forcing it to sign a peace accord with the government of India.[84] In another success for the IB, the agency ran an "aggressive" counterintelligence campaign in the run-up to the 1998 nuclear tests.[85] The campaign successfully prevented the detection of India's test preparations by the US intelligence community.[86] In recent years, India's growing global engagement has yielded valuable foreign intelligence collaborations for India from countries such as the United States, the United Kingdom, Israel, the United Arab Emirates, and Saudi Arabia. These have brought major success for India on the counterterrorism front. In the face of the 2008 Mumbai attacks, IB and R&AW have successfully apprehended several anti-India terrorist masterminds and operatives from the Persian Gulf, Nepal, and Bangladesh.[87] Successful intelligence partnerships in the region with Bangladeshi and Nepalese agencies have also contributed to this. This counterterrorism success has caused a major decline in terrorist incidents in India's hinterland.

CONCLUSION

As this chapter described, India has an expansive and well-developed intelligence setup. These are a function of the multiple security challenges faced by the country from its neighborhood, unresolved boundary disputes, cross-border terrorism, and involvement of external powers in internal security challenges faced by India. The chapter highlighted the successes of the agencies in light of very real challenges that they face—ranging from poor coordination, lack of statutory recognition, challenges with recruitment, and training of staff—as they work toward furthering Indian national interests and protecting the country from various security threats.

It is disappointing, however, that the public only knows and discusses their failures and not their successes. In August 2008 during an interview, former NSA M. K. Narayanan had mentioned that Indian intelligence agencies had "uncovered at least 800 terrorist cells in the country operating with 'external support' . . . and had disrupted several modules."[88] These successes, however, were quickly forgotten following the November 2008 terror attacks by the Lashkar-e-Taiba terrorists in Mumbai. That is the nature of the world that intelligence agencies work in the world over, and their counterparts in India are no different.

NOTES

1. Kaushik Roy, *Hinduism and the Ethics of Warfare in South Asia: From Antiquity to the Present* (Cambridge: Cambridge University Press, 2012).
2. "23rd December 1887: The Journey Begins," *Indian Police Journal* 59, no. 4 (December 2012): v.

3. V. K. Singh, *India's External Intelligence: Secrets of Research and Analysis Wing RAW* (New Delhi: Manas Publications, 2007), 30; Jairam Ramesh, *Intertwined Lives: P.N. Haksar and Indira Gandhi* (New Delhi: Simon & Schuster India, 2018), 376–77.

4. R. S. Bedi, "NTRO: India's Technical Intelligence Agency," *Indian Defence Review*, March 2008, http://www.indiandefencereview.com/spotlights/ntro-indias-technical-intelligence-agency/.

5. "The Intelligence Organisations (Restriction of Rights) Act, 1985," Pub. L. No. 58 of 1985 (1985), https://legislative.gov.in/actsofparliamentfromtheyear/intelligence-organisations-restriction-rights-act-1985. According to Maloy Krishna Dhar, this legislation was necessitated by unrest in both the premier intelligence agencies over pending personnel and administrative grievances. See Maloy Krishna Dhar, *Open Secrets: India's Intelligence Unveiled* (New Delhi: Manas, 2018), 16.

6. Dhar, *Open Secrets*, 16.

7. Vijaita Singh, "NTRO Now under Intelligence Act," *The Hindu*, May 18, 2017, https://www.thehindu.com/news/national/ntro-now-under-intelligence-act/article18475771.ece.

8. Tribune News Service, "Lt Gen KJS Dhillon Is DG of Defence Intelligence Agency," *The Tribune*, March 10, 2020, https://www.tribuneindia.com/news/j-k/lt-gen-kjs-dhillon-is-dg-of-defence-intelligence-agency-53560.

9. Chris Ogden, *Indian National Security*, Oxford India Short Introductions (New Delhi: Oxford University Press, 2017), 47.

10. "About Us, Directorate of Revenue Intelligence," Directorate of Revenue Intelligence, April 12, 2018, http://dri.nic.in/main/aboutus.

11. "Functions of FIU-India," Financial Intelligence Unit—India, 2019, https://fiuindia.gov.in/files/About_FIU-IND/About_FIUIND.html.

12. Writing in the special issue of the *Indian Police Journal* in November 2018, Home Minister Rajnath Singh stated that the MAC is "electronically connected between the National Capital, 25 Central Member Agencies and all the State Capitals. In the State Capitals this network links the Subsidiary Multi Agency Centre (SMACs), State Police Special Branches and offices of all the Central and other Counter Terror Agencies. The network is also being extended to District Police Headquarters wherever found feasible. At present, total of 429 SMAC nodes and 251 District Police Offices are connected to the MAC/SMAC Network." Rajnath Singh, "Towards a More Secure Nation," in "Special Issue on Police Martyrdom," special issue, *Indian Police Journal* (November–December 2018): 9; Government of India, Ministry of Home Affairs, "Loksabha: Unstarred Question No. 643" (Lok Sabha: Parliament of India, December 19, 2017), http://164.100.24.220/loksabhaquestions/annex/13/AU643.pdf; Singh, "Towards a More Secure Nation," 7.

13. Ryan Shaffer, "Centralizing India's Intelligence: The National Intelligence Grid's Purpose, Status, and Problems," *International Journal of Intelligence and CounterIntelligence* 31, no. 1 (2018): 160.

14. George Santayana, *The Life of Reason: Reason in Common Sense* (New York: Scribner, 1905), 1:284, https://www.gutenberg.org/files/15000/15000-h/15000-h.htm#vol1CHAPTER_XII_FLUX_AND_CONSTANCY_IN_HUMAN_NATURE.

15. Sameer Suryakant Patil, "India's China Policy in the 1950s: Threat Perceptions and Balances," *South Asian Survey* 14, no. 2 (December 2007): 283–301.

16. Copies of the report are believed to be in the safe custody of the Indian defense secretary; however, in February 2014, Australian academic and journalist Neville Maxwell released sections of the report on an Indian website. See IDR News Network, "The Henderson-Brooks Report Is Out by Neville Maxwell," *Indian Defence Review*, July 11, 2014, http://www.indiandefencereview.com/news/the-henderson -brooks-report-is-out-by-neville-maxwell/.

17. Sameer Patil, "Lessons from the Henderson Brooks Report," Gateway House, March 26, 2014, https://www.gatewayhouse.in/lessons-from-the-henderson -brooks-report/.

18. Patil, "India's China Policy in the 1950s," 293–94.

19. B. Raman, "Why India Should Declassify Historical Documents," *Rediff*, May 10, 2010, http://news.rediff.com/column/2010/may/10/why-india-should-declassify -historical-documents.htm.

20. K. Sankaran Nair, *Inside IB and RAW: The Rolling Stone That Gathered Moss*, 2nd ed. (New Delhi: Manas Publications, 2016), 153.

21. Ryan Shaffer, "Unraveling India's Foreign Intelligence: The Origins and Evolution of the Research and Analysis Wing," *International Journal of Intelligence and CounterIntelligence* 28, no. 2 (2015): 258–60.

22. Ryan Shaffer, "Significant Distrust and Drastic Cuts: The Indian Government's Uneasy Relationship with Intelligence," *International Journal of Intelligence and CounterIntelligence* 30, no. 3 (2017): 525–26.

23. B. Raman, "Making Intelligence Agencies Accountable," *Outlook*, January 20, 2010, http://www.outlookindia.com/website/story/making-intelligence-agencies -accountable/263866; B. Raman, *Intelligence: Past, Present & Future* (New Delhi: Lancer, 2002), 62, 79.

24. Manoj Shrivastava, *Re-energising Indian Intelligence* (New Delhi: Vij Books, 2013), 14; Raman, *Intelligence*, 79–80.

25. "Torture by Indira's Gestapo," *Marxist Review* 10, no. 10–11 (May 1977): 329–35.

26. Ryan Shaffer, "Indian Spies inside Pakistan: South Asian Human Intelligence across Borders," *Intelligence and National Security* 34, no. 5 (2019): 727–42.

27. Vappala Balachandran, *National Security and Intelligence Management: A New Paradigm* (Mumbai, India: Indus Source Books, 2014), 170.

28. Cabinet Secretariat, "Cabinet Secretariat Resolution No. 281/29/6/98/TS," *Gazette of India*, April 16, 1999, 4–7, https://ia600601.us.archive.org/13/items/in.gaz ette.e.1999.383/E_94_2013_050.pdf.

29. S. D. Pradhan, "National Security System—Evolution," in *India's National Security Annual Review 2010* (New Delhi: Routledge, 2011), 444; IDSA Task Force, "A Case for Intelligence Reforms in India: IDSA Task Force Report," in *Task Force Report* (New Delhi: Institute for Defence Studies and Analyses, 2012), 89–90, http:// www.idsa.in/book/ACaseforIntelligenceReformsinIndia. The NSA is a crucial link between the intelligence agencies and the prime minister. He wears several hats in addition to the essential role of being the security adviser to the prime minister. The

NSA chairs the National Intelligence Board, created in 2002 to monitor civilian and military intelligence agencies' functioning. In addition, he heads the Technical Coordination Group and the Intelligence Coordination Group. The NSA is also the Special Representative on Border Talks with China, chairman of the Executive Council of the Nuclear Command Authority, and the link between the Executive and the Political Council (IDSA Task Force, "A Case for Intelligence Reforms in India," 89–90).

30. L. K. Advani et al., *Report of the Group of Ministers on National Security* (New Delhi: Government of India, February 19, 2001), 137.

31. Kargil Review Committee, *From Surprise to Reckoning: The Kargil Review Committee Report* (New Delhi: Sage, 2000).

32. Singh, *India's External Intelligence*, 35–36.

33. K. Venkataramanan, "Explained: India's Asymmetric Federalism," *The Hindu*, August 11, 2019, https://www.thehindu.com/news/national/the-forms-of-federalism-in-india/article28977671.ece.

34. Ministry of Law and Justice Government of India, "The Constitution of India," Article 246 § Seventh Schedule (1977), sec. Seventh Schedule, https://legislative.gov.in/sites/default/files/COI.pdf.

35. Sameer Patil, "Counter-Terrorism and Federalism," Gateway House, August 14, 2014, http://www.gatewayhouse.in/counter-terrorism-and-federalism/.

36. Singh, "Towards a More Secure Nation," 7.

37. "National Counter Terrorism Centre (Organisation, Functions, Powers and Duties) Order," Government of India, March 1, 2012, https://www.satp.org/satporgtp/countries/india/document/papers/2012/NCTC_2012.pdf.

38. Brijesh Pandey, "Too Many Spooks Spoil the Case," *Tehelka*, March 28, 2013, http://old.tehelka.com/too-many-spooks-spoil-the-case/.

39. Srinath Raghavan, "After 50 Years of RAW, There Are Still No Declassified Documents or an Official History," *ThePrint*, September 18, 2019, https://theprint.in/opinion/why-was-raw-formed-and-what-has-india-learnt-after-50-years-of-its-existence/119811/.

40. In practical terms, this attitude has manifested in the government's reluctance to make public reports of multiple investigative commissions such as the Henderson Brooks Report or the Raghavan committee report. The only exception to the rule is the KRC report, which was tabled in the Parliament, and the redacted version of the report was published in the form of a book. See Raman, "Making Intelligence Agencies Accountable"; Kargil Review Committee, *From Surprise to Reckoning*.

41. Shaffer, "Significant Distrust and Drastic Cuts," 523–24.

42. Siddharth Varadarajan, "More Effective Externally Than Internally," *The Hindu*, January 20, 2010, https://www.thehindu.com/opinion/columns/siddharth-varadarajan/More-effective-externally-than-internally/article16838476.ece; Shekhar Gupta, "The New Doval Durbar Reduces India's Layered Security System to a Top-Down Caliphate," *ThePrint*, October 13, 2018, https://theprint.in/national-interest/india-gets-a-national-security-adviczar-it-is-ajit-doval/133795/.

43. Raman, "Making Intelligence Agencies Accountable"; IDSA Task Force, "A Case for Intelligence Reforms in India," 34.

44. Raman, *Intelligence*, 11–12; Singh, *India's External Intelligence*, 37.

45. Singh, *India's External Intelligence*, 36–37.

46. Avtar Singh Bhasin, ed., *India's Foreign Relations 2010 Documents* (New Delhi: Public Diplomacy Division, Ministry of External Affairs; Geetika, 2010), 3–12.

47. Manish Tewari, "The Intelligence Services (Powers and Regulations) Bill, 2011: Bill No. 23 of 2011," accessed May 17, 2022, http://164.100.24.219/billstexts/lsbilltexts/AsIntroduced/7185LS.pdf.

48. Manish Tewari, "State of the Union: Time for Intelligence Reforms?," *Deccan Chronicle*, March 19, 2016, https://www.deccanchronicle.com/opinion/op-ed/190316/state-of-the-union-time-for-intelligence-reforms.html; "Bill on Intelligence Agencies Reforms," *Event Report* (New Delhi: Observer Research Foundation, March 29, 2011), https://www.orfonline.org/research/bill-on-intelligence-agencies-reforms/.

49. Manish Tewari, "Parliament Oversight Key for Reforms in Intelligence Agencies," *Deccan Chronicle*, July 20, 2020, https://www.deccanchronicle.com/opinion/columnists/200720/manish-tewari-parliament-oversight-key-for-reforms-in-intelligence-a.html.

50. IDSA Task Force, "A Case for Intelligence Reforms in India," 109–10.

51. Praveen Swami, "Five Years after 26/11, Intelligence Services Still Crippled by Staff Shortage," *The Hindu*, November 26, 2013, https://www.thehindu.com/news/national/five-years-after-2611-intelligence-services-still-crippled-by-staff-shortage/article5391698.ece.

52. Swami, "Five Years after 26/11."

53. IDSA Task Force, "A Case for Intelligence Reforms in India," 45.

54. Dhar, *Open Secrets*, 16.

55. IDSA Task Force, "A Case for Intelligence Reforms in India," 44–45; Dhar, *Open Secrets*, 12.

56. Dhar, *Open Secrets*, 12–13.

57. Swami, "Five Years after 26/11."

58. Rana Banerji, "Bharath Asked: How about a Website for RAW and Can We Recruit More People from Outside UPSC Route? We Got to Change | Manohar Parrikar Institute for Defence Studies and Analyses," Manohar Parrikar Institute for Defence Studies and Analyses, accessed May 17, 2022, https://www.idsa.in/askanexpert/HowaboutawebsiteforRAWandcanwerecruitmorepeoplefromoutsideUPSCroute.

59. Nair, *Inside IB and RAW*, 201; Raman, "Why India Should Declassify Historical Documents."

60. A. S. Dulat and Aditya Sinha, *Kashmir: The Vajpayee Years* (Noida: HarperCollins, 2015), 133; Prem Mahadevan, *The Politics of Counterterrorism in India: Strategic Intelligence and National Security in South Asia*, South Asian ed. (London: Tauris, 2012), 243.

61. IDSA Task Force, "A Case for Intelligence Reforms in India," 43; Banerji, "Bharath Asked."

62. Swami, "Five Years after 26/11."

63. Vikram Sood, *The Unending Game: A Former R&AW Chief's Insights into Espionage* (New Delhi: Penguin Viking, 2018), 250–51.

64. Ramesh, *Intertwined Lives*, 122.

65. Praveen Swami, "RAW to Shut down Its Covert Air Wing, Assets Will Go to NTRO and IAF," *Indian Express*, September 18, 2015, https://indianexpress.com/article/india/india-others/raw-to-fold-its-covert-air-wing/.

66. Snehesh Alex Philip, "India's Oldest Flying Aircraft in Spotlight after Radar Website Shows It Going to Pakistan," *ThePrint*, May 14, 2020, https://theprint.in/defence/indias-oldest-flying-aircraft-in-spotlight-after-radar-website-shows-it-going-to-pakistan/421757/.

67. Singh, *India's External Intelligence*, 163–64.

68. Saikat Datta, "India's Intel Agencies Make No Use of Big Data Analytics," *Deccan Chronicle*, June 26, 2020, https://www.deccanchronicle.com/opinion/columnists/260620/saikat-datta-indias-intel-agencies-make-no-use-of-big-data-analytic.html.

69. Neeraj Chauhan, "India's Agencies Increasingly Depend on Tech Intel," *Hindustan Times*, January 9, 2021, https://www.hindustantimes.com/india-news/indias-agencies-increasingly-depend-on-tech-intel-101610160966455.html.

70. Patil, "Counter-Terrorism and Federalism"; Chauhan, "India's Agencies Increasingly Depend on Tech Intel"; Kamal Davar, "Re-energising Indian Intelligence: A National Imperative," *Journal of the United Service Institution of India* 148, no. 613 (September 2018), https://usiofindia.org/publication/usi-journal/re-energising-indian-intelligence-a-national-imperative/.

71. The Kargil Review Committee comments on the lack of good HUMINT, which affected the intelligence agencies' capabilities to detect the Pakistan army's plans to intrude in the Kargil and Drass sector and occupy the heights during the winter. See Kargil Review Committee, *From Surprise to Reckoning*, 26; N. K. Bhatia, "Human Intelligence (HUMINT) as a Driver for Intelligence Operations," Issue Brief (New Delhi: Centre for Land Warfare Studies, June 2016), https://www.claws.in/static/IB79_Human-Intelligence-HUMINT-as-a-Driver-for-Intelligence-Operations.pdf.

72. Saikat Datta, "Intelligence, Strategic Assessment, and Decision Process Deficits," in *Investigating Crises: South Asia's Lessons, Evolving Dynamics, and Trajectories*, ed. Sameer Lalwani and Hannah Haegeland (Washington, DC: Stimson Center, 2018), 99.

73. James Glanz, Sebastian Rotella, and David E. Sanger, "In 2008 Mumbai Attacks, Piles of Spy Data, but an Uncompleted Puzzle," *New York Times*, December 21, 2014, https://www.nytimes.com/2014/12/22/world/asia/in-2008-mumbai-attacks-piles-of-spy-data-but-an-uncompleted-puzzle.html.

74. K. S. Subramanian, "Intelligence Bureau, Home Ministry and Indian Politics," *Economic and Political Weekly* 40, no. 21 (May 21, 2005): 2147–50.

75. Raghavan, "After 50 Years of RAW."

76. Vinayak Dalmiya, Vindra Kapoor, and Saikat Datta, "India's Enduring Challenge of Intelligence Reforms," ORF Issue Brief (New Delhi: Observer Research Foundation, December 2020), https://www.orfonline.org/research/indias-enduring-challenge-of-intelligence-reforms/.

77. Swami, "Five Years after 26/11."

78. Dhar, *Open Secrets*, 49.

79. Sameer Patil, interview with Indian Police Service officers in Mumbai and Delhi (English), June 2017.

80. Julia Voo et al., "National Cyber Power Index 2020: Methodology and Analytical Considerations," China Cyber Policy Initiative, Harvard Kennedy School, Belfer Center for Science and International Affairs, September 2000, https://www .belfercenter.org/sites/default/files/2020-09/NCPI_2020.pdf.

81. IDSA Task Force, "A Case for Intelligence Reforms in India," 49–50.

82. Shibani Mehta, "RAW Thinks Espionage Can Be Taught in 6-Month Crash Course—It Clearly Needs Training Reforms," *ThePrint*, April 24, 2019, https://the print.in/opinion/raw-thinks-espionage-can-be-taught-in-6-month-crash-course-it-clea rly-needs-training-reforms/225576/.

83. B. Raman, *The Kaoboys of R&AW: Down Memory Lane* (New Delhi: Lancer, 2013), 19–24.

84. Yatish Yadav, "Return of the Superspy," *New Indian Express*, June 8, 2014, https://www.newindianexpress.com/magazine/2014/jun/08/Return-of-the-Superspy -622565.html.

85. Jeffrey T. Richelson, *Spying on the Bomb: American Nuclear Intelligence from Nazi Germany to Iran and North Korea* (New York: Norton, 2006), 444–45.

86. A few years earlier in December 1995, similar plans by India to carry out a test was derailed after the US intelligence community had gotten a whiff about it. See PTI, "Pokhran: US Detected Indian Nuclear Test Buildup at Pokhran in 1995," *Economic Times*, February 23, 2013, https://economictimes.indiatimes.com/news/ politics-and-nation/us-detected-indian-nuclear-test-buildup-at-pokhran-in-1995/ articleshow/18636491.cms.

87. PTI, "Suspect in Akshardham Attack Held," *India Today*, July 19, 2009, https://www.indiatoday.in/latest-headlines/story/suspect-in-akshardham-attack- held-52390-2009-07-19; Sandeep Joshi, "Arrest of IM Operatives a Rare Success for Indian Intelligence Agencies," *The Hindu*, August 31, 2013, https://www.thehindu .com/news/national/other-states/arrest-of-im-operatives-a-rare-success-for-indian -intelligence-agencies/article5080013.ece.

88. PTI, "800 Terror Cells Unearthed in India: NSA," *Outlook India*, August 12, 2008, https://www.outlookindia.com/newswire/story/800-terror-cells-unearthed-in -india-nsa/598398.

8

Indonesia: Intelligence Culture in Turbulent Times

Mark Briskey

On December 27, 1949, Indonesia gained its independence, which was four years after the Second World War's end and a war for independence first against the British and then the Dutch, who had returned to seize back their colonial possessions. After significant pressure especially from the United States, the Dutch relinquished all control of their former Dutch East Indies Empire except West Papua. Yet this was not the end of the new country's challenges as a never-ending litany of rebellions, separatist movements, conspiracies by various political actors, and internecine military problems emerged. Fears of a Balkanization of the disparate ethnicities and regions within the archipelago were and continue to be an enduring concern for the Indonesian state.[1] Links between the military as well as other security services along with regional violence were staples of Indonesian security issues from the early 1950s.[2] The evolution of Indonesia's national security and intelligence services continued apace during these turbulent times.

Any writing on Indonesia's intelligence services makes for compelling reading and involves detailed studies; notable is Ken Conboy's book, *INTEL: Inside Indonesia's Intelligence Service*, which traverses the history of these services and their work in addressing a myriad of state security challenges. His work provides descriptive examples of specific cases involving espionage or terrorism including Iranian, Vietnamese, North Korean, and Russian covert recruitment operations, terrorist entities, and figures, such as Riduan Isamuddin (aka Hambali).[3] Conboy's research provides a focused examination about the significant intelligence matters and the services themselves including the State Intelligence Agency (Badan Intelijen Negara, BIN).

Building from that earlier research, this chapter examines Indonesia's intelligence culture by exploring the BIN's background, role, and functions. In particular, it argues that, even though BIN is not the most powerful state actor involved in security, throughout its various iterations BIN has been focused on the internal security of the Indonesian state and ensured that the unity of the multiethnic and culturally religious diverse states was guarded from a host of threats. In this process, BIN and its partners engaged in egregious human rights abuses and crimes, which demonstrates aspects of its intelligence culture. This chapter connects BIN and its predecessor agencies, the Indonesian National Military (Tentara Nasional Indonesia, TNI) and the National Police of the Republic of Indonesia (Kepolisian Negara Republik Indonesia, Polri).

The chapter begins by analyzing BIN's legislated objectives and mission. Next, it provides a brief history of Indonesia's national security challenges and BIN's evolution as well as some discussion of the structure, personnel, and institutional culture of Indonesian security agencies. Subsequently, it explores BIN's role in addressing crime, espionage, and counterterrorism, as well as internal operations, such as the contentious role in West Papua and departmental malfeasance. Lastly, the chapter concludes by explaining how Indonesian state intelligence has been continuously evolving and responding to national security priorities from its inception and that BIN's challenges remain in addressing current security issues, such as issues in West Papua and the return of foreign fighters. Moreover, it also highlights how BIN continues to negotiate its place in the security hierarchy of Indonesia with other powerful actors, such as TNI and Polri, subject to the sometimes arbitrary and competing budgetary restraints in a new democracy.

BACKGROUND AND BIN'S EMERGENCE

The earliest intelligence capabilities of Indonesian state intelligence owe much to the Japanese occupation of the Dutch East Indies during World War II. The Dutch East Indies became Indonesia through their training of a local auxiliary force known by its acronym PETA (Pembela Tanah Air) as well as from other sources including stranded German submariners.[4] Between 1953 and 1958, the United States was an early mentor for Indonesia's new intelligence service and provided training to Sulawesi- and Sumatran-based rebels and opponents of the state when the United States became worried by the leadership of Indonesian president Sukarno.[5]

Early Indonesian intelligence services undertook foreign operations against the Dutch in Papua until 1962 when it was absorbed into the Indonesian state. Likewise during *Konfrontasi* (a conflict over Indonesia's opposition to Malaysia's establishment from 1963 to 1966), Indonesian forces undertook insurgency and intelligence operations against British and Commonwealth forces defending the new Federation of Malaya. Indonesia's efforts were successfully disrupted by Commonwealth intelligence efforts primarily through a flow of "real time" signals intelligence (SIGINT) from Jakarta to Commonwealth intelligence agencies, such as Government Communications Headquarters (GCHQ), forewarning them of Indonesian plans.[6]

The anticommunist purges that occurred between 1965 and 1966 caused an estimated loss of 500,000 lives and many more detentions and torture conducted by the military, militia allies, and others. Indeed, these are characteristics that defined Indonesia's response to the Cold War.[7] In fact, the systematic nature of the killings during this period led by military and police units included execution quotas.[8] These issues were tied to a militarized effort aimed at the unity of the new republic in its early years and more recent national security concerns in the form of autonomy movements in West Papua and recent returning Islamic State fighters.[9] A significant actor in ensuring the continuity of post-independence unity up to the current time were the intelligence agencies of the new state. These included the following:

1. Indonesian State Secret Agency (Badan Rahasia Negara Indonesia, BRANI)
2. Intelligence Coordinating Agency (Badan Koordinasi Intelijen, BKI)
3. Central Intelligence Agency (Badan Pusat Intelijen, BPI)
4. State Intelligence Command (Komando Inteligen Negara, KIN)
5. State Intelligence Coordinating Board (Badan Koordinasi Intelijen Negara, BAKIN)
6. State Intelligence Agency (Badan Intelijen Negara, BIN)

The BIN, which superseded BAKIN in 2001, is the focus of this chapter due to its size and importance, but other state security services are also examined here.[10] In the 2011 Law on State Intelligence, the act noted the aims of state intelligence were to protect every Indonesian citizen, advance general prosperity of the country, contribute to enlightening the life of the nation, and help "maintain a global order based on independence, lasting peace and social justice as mandated in the Preamble to the 1945 Constitution of the Republic of Indonesia."[11] In this regard, the preamble to the law noted, "it is essential to have early detection and warning capable of supporting efforts to ward off any form of threats that may endanger the existence and integrity of the Unitary State of the Republic of Indonesia." Additionally, part 2 of Article 5 of the 2011 draft noted:

The objective of the State Intelligence [is] to detect, identify, assess, analyse, interpret, and present Intelligence in order to provide early warning for anticipating various forms and characteristics of potential and real threats against the safety and existence of the nation as well as the existing opportunities for national interests and security.[12]

This demonstrates the BIN's objectives are not dissimilar to other national intelligence services whether they be democratic or undemocratic states with different ethical guidelines to "deliberately equip themselves with specialist agencies to access and analyze information that can help them make better decisions."[13] Most recently, BIN's medical intelligence department has also become involved in assisting the Indonesian COVID-19 rapid response task force by undertaking analysis and estimates of COVID-19 infection rates in Indonesia.[14]

In Indonesia, Intelligence Law No. 17/2011 provides the Indonesian parliament with authority and powers to oversee BIN. At the time of the law's enactment, it was noted that an intelligence subcommittee had yet to be formed. Consequently, BIN's accountability was not subject to effective scrutiny despite the oversight role of Commission 1 of the National Parliament.[15]

INDONESIAN NATIONAL SECURITY AND THE BIN'S EVOLUTION

Indonesian president Sukarno, from 1945 to 1967, was responsible for the number of intelligence services. These services were dominated by the military, including most significantly the Strategic Intelligence Agency (Badan Intelijen Strategis, BAIS) responsible for military and BAKIN for foreign intelligence. After the fall of the Suharto regime, BAKIN became BIN.[16] TNI additionally has an intelligence function through its Armed Forces Military (Komando Daerah Militer, KODAM) system that reports to the armed forces commander. TNI maintained an internal security and intelligence role in the post-Suharto period via Law No. 34/2004, which stipulates that TNI can undertake a military operation in the support of other government agencies in combating terrorism, separatist movements, and rebellion. This law allowed TNI to be the primary agency in combating the Free Papua Movement (Organisasi Papua Merdeka, OPM), a separatist movement, and its armed wing in West Papua.[17] During the Suharto period, BAIS and BAKIN also provided personnel for the Coordination of Support for National Stability (Bakorstanas), which was subsequently dissolved after the fall of Suharto. Bakorstanas was led by the armed forces commander, who monitored the existence of any political threats against the regime.[18]

Turning to BIN's size and structure, a source involved in the 2016 parliamentary budget discussions noted that the agency had 3,000 agents within twenty different organizational departments.[19] Indonesian House of Representatives member Tubagus Hasanuddin described the number as insufficient following hearings with the BIN chair.[20] The chair argued that the agency was under pressure to address a diverse range of security issues across the archipelago, making staffing levels manifestly insufficient.

The minimum requirement to be recruited into BIN is for the candidate to hold an undergraduate degree. The BIN's primary source for personnel is its intelligence college, State Intelligence Institute (STIN), which provides a four-year undergraduate degree in intelligence. STIN is reportedly progressive and produces high-quality graduates for BIN. It also is similar to other state intelligence agencies that develop skills commensurate with existing and developing hybrid threats.[21]

BIN's website provides details on its structure, history, and some of its public-facing work.[22] The chair of BIN is supported by a number of deputies, and BIN's structure incorporates a primary coordinating secretariat that supports administrative and functional units. BIN's administrative and operational units worked to develop policy and implement foreign and domestic intelligence activities as well as addressing technology development, cyber intelligence and communications, and analytic and governance security functions to maintain governance integrity.

BIN also maintains members with expertise in several key areas including politics and ideology, defense, society and culture (especially important in an ethnically and socioculturally diverse state as Indonesia), law, human rights, environment, and natural resources. BIN is also supported by specific centers, such as the Intelligence Professional Development Center, the Research and Development Center, Education and Training Center, Medical Intelligence Center (being drawn upon in BIN's public outfacing role for the COVID-19 pandemic), and the Psychology Center.[23]

It is important to note that Indonesia, like many other countries, has a number of intelligence agencies in the military and civilian spheres that overlap and interconnect. Every *Angkatan* (force) in TNI possesses its own intelligence service, and then these separate services also have multiple intelligence units frequently siloing their information. They are also involved in internal rivalries with other intelligence units as well as intelligence units within government ministries. Though BIN is a civilian intelligence service, it has predominantly been led and staffed by TNI officers. This has significant impact on Indonesia's intelligence culture. In particular, the connection to TNI by those commanding BIN is important due to allegations of TNI's human rights abuses, violence, and murder. This factor is important in understanding what

Geoffrey B. Robinson describes as the "institutional culture" of the Indonesian military and security services, police and cognate agencies. He explains:

> [T]heir internal norms and patterns of behavior, which depending on their historical experience and training, may be more or less violent. An important dimension of an institutions culture is its "repertoire of violence" . . . the routines of violence learned and employed by all of those associated with the institution.[24]

These allegations, such as that involving the murder of human rights activist Munir Said Thalib, have focused on the BIN's propensity to flout laws and human rights norms in what it perceives as the real and paramount national security interests of the state.

In an environment in which TNI still dominates the national security infrastructure and even Polri are becoming ever more influential, BIN must compete for state resources against other agencies that generate their own income through legal and sometimes illegal ventures. In 2015, Sutiyoso, then the chief of BIN, announced the ambitious plan to recruit an additional 1,000 officers and supporting staff would be postponed due to the government's budget proposal that drastically cut BIN's budget from Rupiah 2.6 trillion (subject to fluctuations, about US$184 million) to less than Rupiah 1.6 trillion for 2016. In lamenting this decision, Sutiyoso stated: "We are at the forefront of the nation's security. But we have so little in terms of a budget and now it's up for another cut."[25] In 2016, BIN had hoped to spend up to Rupiah 700 billion (subject to fluctuations, about US$49.5 million) on new personnel for more effective training and qualifications, which would then be deployed to regional (Binda) intelligence bureaus proportionate to the population and geographic size of the region as well as threat levels.[26]

Though the Indonesian National Policing Agency has primary responsibility for crime, there is cooperation with BIN on transnational crimes, especially where matters involving terrorism, international collusion, corruption, and the criminal financing of terrorist entities overlap. This cooperation can also involve foreign police and intelligence services posted to Jakarta and who are frequently involved in multilateral joint agency investigations and intelligence sharing. Indonesia is host to a number of international ventures that enhance international operational and training cooperation. These include the Jakarta Centre for Law Enforcement Cooperation (JCLEC) in Semarang as well as historic initiatives, such as the Transnational Crime Coordination Centre (TNCCC) at Mabes Polri Headquarters in Jakarta to address transnational crime and terrorism. Apart from BIN's primary source of agents being STIN, there are also a number of other intelligence schools that exist, including Polri's School of Criminal Intelligence, which was located in Bandung.

Like all state intelligence services, BIN must attempt to counter foreign agencies' efforts at conducting intelligence collection against key Indonesian political, military, and economic targets. Reports of industrial espionage being conducted on Indonesian Defence Industries, such as P. T. Pindad, were raised as a security issue in 2012 by then BIN chair Lieutenant General Marciano Norman.[27] The bilateral relationship between Indonesia and Australia suffered in the wake of the Edward Snowden revelations that Australian intelligence agencies had been spying on the cell phones of President Susilo Bambang Yudhoyono, his wife Ani, and a number of his close confidants in 2009.[28] The revelations added to previous discomforts for BIN when, during a 2007 visit to Australia, the future chief of BIN, retired lieutenant-general Sutiyoso, was upset when approached without notice by an Australian police officer and court official asking him to testify at an inquiry into the deaths of five Australian journalists killed during the Indonesian invasion of Timor-Leste in 1965.[29]

Regarding the Australian spying revelations, Marciano Norman, the chief of BIN at the time, directly engaged the Australian agencies and sought assurances that it would not happen again.[30] The matter had serious repercussions for Australia as Indonesia scaled down bilateral cooperation. Since the 2002 Bali bombings, Australian and Indonesian counterterrorism cooperation between Polri and the Australian Federal Police (AFP) was significant. The AFP maintain their largest overseas presence in Indonesia, as well as cooperation between BIN and the Australian Secret Intelligence Service (ASIS) and military cooperation.

A joint intelligence agreement signed in 2014 clarified and reset the bilateral arrangements upon intelligence sharing between the two states. Apart from a statement of principles and regular intelligence agency meetings, the document established two commitments; first, that Australia and Indonesia "will not use any of their intelligence, including surveillance capacities, or other resources, in ways that would harm the interests of the parties" and, second, that "the parties will promote intelligence cooperation between the relevant institutions and agencies in accordance with their respective national laws and regulations."[31]

Conversely, Indonesians tried to get intelligence from Australia. Hendro Priyono, a former BIN chief, described the targeting of Australian military, diplomatic, and civilian targets particularly at the time of the separation of Timor-Leste in 1999. Priyono claimed he had never managed to recruit Australians to betray their country. This contention, however, was rebutted by Warren Reed, a former member of the Australian Secret Intelligence Service

(ASIS), who claimed the Indonesians had a long history of successful infiltration into Australian intelligence agencies.[32]

Indonesia is the world's most populous Muslim nation. With a population of nearly 274 million, Indonesia is socioculturally and ethnically diverse; 87 percent are Sunni Muslim, and the next largest confessional group is Protestant Christian, followed by smaller populations of Hindus and Buddhists.[33] In addition to internal matters concerning internal separatist movements, Indonesia intelligence focused heavily on terrorism after the 2002 Bali bombings, the J. W. Marriott hotel bombing, and a number of other acts throughout the archipelago. More recently, BIN has been addressing terrorism involving returned Islamic State fighters as well as combatting pro–Islamic State ideologues such as Aman Abdurrahman and publications in Bahasa Indonesian such as *Dabiq*, *Rumiyah*, and *An-Naba* that have inspired both coordinated and lone wolf attacks in Indonesia.[34] The threats in the second decade of the new millennium were in some ways similar to earlier threats that emerged when Indonesians returned from Afghanistan after fighting as mujahideen. Some of these returned fighters, also referred to as the "Afghan Alumni," took part in the violent Christian–Muslim religious conflicts in Ambon, Maluku, and Poso Central Sulawesi between 1998 and 2001.[35]

Terrorism from returning Islamic State fighters has created some unanticipated scenarios for BIN and other agencies involved in detection and interdiction. Those sympathetic to the Islamic State have conducted lone wolf attacks involving family units and children. Other problems have involved ensuring that Indonesian legislation has kept pace with the developing threats responded to by BIN and other agencies. Earlier in the century, Indonesian law suffered from gaps in its ability to interdict and prosecute terrorists. A lack of general laws prohibiting conspiracies to commit criminal acts in Indonesia meant that the terrorist entity had to commit a criminal act, such as a bombing, before being found guilty.[36]

BIN works collaboratively with a host of international intelligence, security, and policing agencies in developing intelligence on both domestic and foreign terrorist entities of interest. The 2011 arrest of Umar Pakek—who had fought with the Moro Islamic Liberation Front (MILF) in the Philippines in 1995 and was wanted for his alleged involvement in the Bali bombing of 2002—is one public example of collaboration among BIN, the Pakistan's Inter-Services Intelligence, and the United States' Central Intelligence Agency.[37] Indonesian intelligence has a long history of working with and undertaking training activities with foreign partners. Indonesian agencies involved in counterterrorism duties experienced an exponential growth in their relationship, for example, with Australian agencies in the wake of the 2002 Bali bombings. Indonesian agency personnel have visited Australia and other states on extended joint-operational visits, in such locations as the International Law Enforcement Academy (ILEA) in Thailand.

Violent religious radicalism remains a priority national security issue with BIN. In 2018, Budi Gunawan, the head of BIN, noted the infiltration of Indonesian universities by radical Islamists, claiming that up to 39 percent of undergraduates have been indoctrinated and up to 25 percent were supportive of establishing an Islamic state.[38] The 2019 arrests of ISIS terrorist members of Jama'ah Anshorut Daulah, an Indonesian ISIS affiliate in Jayapura West Papua, found with laptops, explosives, and other weapons, is an example of the ongoing threat.[39]

As for internal operations and malfeasance, in 2008 Muchdi Purwopranjono, the deputy head of BIN and a former Kopassus (Indonesian Special Forces officer), was charged with the premeditated murder of Munir Said Thalib, who was arguably Indonesia's best-known human rights and anticorruption activist.[40] He died of arsenic poisoning during a flight to Amsterdam in 2004. Former Garuda pilot Polycarpus Priyanto was jailed for twenty years for administering the poison with Polri, alleging that it was Muchdi who had coordinated the assassination. The implication of Muchdi's involvement in the killing was connected to previous allegations of his involvement in the abduction of democracy activists. Muchdi was acquitted at trial among allegations of the judiciary being intimidated. Calls for reinvestigating Munir's assassination have been made by human rights activists in Indonesia as well as foreign figures such as John Kerry, then US secretary of state, on the tenth anniversary of Munir's death in 2014.[41]

More broadly, the United States' 2020 human rights report notes that Indonesia continues engaging in human rights violations, including unlawful or arbitrary killings, arbitrary arrest or detention, and detention of political prisoners.[42] The report does not specifically mention BIN but noted torture by the police and the state. The police and TNI were especially criticized for deployments in Papua, which continues to be the focus of the Indonesian security services. Given the early history of separatists across the archipelago and those seeking to carve out autonomous states, BIN's role continues its predecessors' objectives, looking at effective methods of addressing national security threats.

In early 2013, TNI bought US$6.7 million worth of surveillance equipment from British firm Gamma TSE. Indonesia's military stated the equipment would be used for "strategic" intelligence gathering. Human Rights Watch (HRW), however, claimed the equipment would be used "against Indonesian citizens, dissidents, human rights defenders and West Papuans" by Indonesian security agencies.[43] HRW stated that a tranche of leaked documents had made clear that Indonesia's security services were heavily involved in monitoring the activities of West Papuan activists. HRW claimed the triangulation equipment allowed the security services to identify the owners of mobile phones.

HRW was correct in that Indonesian agencies do use triangulation and other high-technology electronic surveillance equipment, which was extremely effective in multinational police and intelligence operations that captured many of the Jemaah Islamiyah terrorists wanted for the Bali 2002 bombing, as well as subsequent terrorist acts and conspiracies in Indonesia including the Australian embassy bombing in 2004 and the J. W. Marriott bombing.[44] Newer portable technology provided by allies, including advanced technology from companies such as Rohde & Schwarz and the technical and physical services of companies such as the Gamma Group, offer effective national security technical options for BIN.[45] BIN and other Indonesian agencies received a great deal of technical support after the Bali bombings of 2002 from Australian, British, American, and other agencies to assist in operations against Jemaah Islamiyah and other terrorist entities in Indonesia.[46] The Gamma Group supplied high-technology intelligence-gathering equipment to Indonesian services. A newsletter released by the Gamma Group, based in Britain and Germany with offices in Singapore, advertise their equipment and services as

> providing advanced technical surveillance monitoring solutions and advanced government training as well as international consultancy to National and State Intelligence Departments and Law Enforcement Agencies.[47]

The Gamma Group specializes in a range of physical and surveillance technologies equipment and courses including magnetic lock–picking equipment, IT information, warfare and exploitation solutions, equipment to test for food poisoning, and a range of courses such as concealment and surveillance.[48] These would all be useful to BIN.

Indonesian services, such as TNI, Polri, or BIN, also rely on human intelligence (HUMINT) and engage in methods that would seem both unconventional as well as possibly illegal for other states' national security and/or policing agencies. In the wake of the Bali bombings, for example, Indonesia utilized the services of captured terrorists to exploit intelligence leads and on occasion to deploy them with personnel in a surveillance capacity to identify persons of interest.

Indonesia continues to suffer archipelago-wide instances of regional instability such as what occurred in Poso since the independence of Timor-Leste in 1999 and the signing of the Helsinki Peace Accord regarding Aceh and the Free Aceh Movement (Gerakan Aceh Merdeka, GAM) in 2005. Currently though the region referred to outside of Indonesia as West Papua and within Indonesia as Papua and Papua Barat provinces remains a focus for Indonesian security services including BIN. While there has been no definitive study, some reports allege that more than 100,000 Papuans have been killed since May 1963.[49] Each of the BIN headquarters in the two provinces is held by a brigadier general–level equivalent officer known as a Kabinda (Kepala BIN Daerah), head of regional BIN.[50] Violent incidents and human rights infringements involving the security forces and separatists occur frequently with deaths on both sides. The alleged April 2021 beating to death of three Papuan brothers by the army for trying to steal weapons from soldiers is illustrative of the situation the Indonesian government is trying to manage.[51]

CONCLUSION

This chapter reviewed the Indonesian intelligence culture and the intelligence services tasked with protecting national security. While BIN was the focus of this chapter, it was also noted that TNI continues to be the dominant national security actor in Indonesia. The provenance of BIN is found in those first nascent security agencies established initially by the Japanese before independence and then more fully developed after independence with the assistance in particular from the United States. While the United States provided early assistance, it also contributed to fomenting revolt during the 1950s when concerned with Sukarno's leadership. Indonesian services were involved in external activities against the Dutch until 1962 in Papua as well as against the British Commonwealth during *Konfrontasi*, also in the early 1960s.

The Indonesian Communist Party's destruction and the deaths of more than 500,000 Indonesians by Indonesian security forces and their proxies established the Cold War credentials of the Indonesian security services and demonstrate the early violent intelligence culture. The post-Suharto period and the new millennium saw the establishment of BIN and new challenges— including Islamist terror; espionage by states including Australia, Russia, and North Korea among others; insurgencies; and the problems of new democratic institutions—brought to the security sector.[52] BIN arguably continues to evolve and respond to these challenges, though it has been revealed to have committed egregious human rights violations and has been suspected of other malfeasance. With some exceptions, BIN has successfully contributed to maintaining the unity and sovereignty of the Indonesian state.

NOTES

1. Michelle Ann Miller, "Self-Governance as a Framework for Conflict Resolution in Aceh," in *Autonomy and Armed Separatism in South and Southeast Asia*, ed. Michelle Ann Miller (Singapore: Institute of Southeast Asian Studies, 2012), 40.

2. Arianto Sangaji, "The Security Forces and Regional Violence in Poso," in *Renegotiating Boundaries: Local Politics in Post-Suharto Indonesia*, ed. Henk Schulte Nordholt and Gerry Van Klinken (Leiden: Brill, 2007).

3. Ken Conboy, *INTEL: Inside Indonesia's Intelligence Service* (Jakarta: Equinox, 2004).

4. Conboy, *INTEL*, 15–18.

5. Conboy, *INTEL*, 26–28.

6. Richard J. Aldrich, *GCHQ, the Uncensored Story of Britain's Most Secret Intelligence Agency* (London: HarperPress, 2011), 168.

7. Geoffrey B. Robinson, *The Killing Season: A History of the Indonesian Massacres, 1965–1966* (Princeton, NJ: Princeton University Press, 2018), 118.

8. Robinson, *The Killing Season*, 127.

9. Sidney Jones, "Yudhoyono's Legacy on Internal Security: Achievements and Missed Opportunities," in *The Yudhoyono Presidency: Indonesia's Decade of Stability and Stagnation*, ed. Edward Aspinall, Marcus Mietzner, and Dirk Tomsa (Singapore: Institute of Southeast Asian Studies, 2015).

10. "History," Badan Inteligen Negara, 2020, https://www.bin.go.id/en/Profile/Tentang_Kami; "Organizational Structure," Badan Inteligen Negara, 2020, https://www.bin.go.id/Profile/Struktur_Organisasi.

11. "The Republic of Indonesia Draft Law Number 17, Year 2011 on State Intelligence," CYRILLA, 2011, https://cyrilla.org/en/document/iu66vgcpll?page=1.

12. "The Republic of Indonesia Draft Law Number 17."

13. David Omand, *How Spies Think: Ten Lessons in Intelligence* (London: Viking, 2020), 3.

14. "Spy Agency: Indonesia's COVID-19 Cases May Surpass 106,000 by July," *The Star*, April 4, 2020, https://www.thestar.com.my/news/regional/2020/04/04/spy-agency-indonesia039s-covid-19-cases-may-surpass-106000-by-july.

15. Beni Sukadis, "Indonesia State Intelligence Agency Reform and Its Challenges," Centre for Security Governance (CSG), September 16, 2014, https://secgovcentre.org/2014/09/indonesias-state-intelligence-agency-reform-and-its-challenges/.

16. Angel Rabasa and John Haseman, *The Military and Democracy in Indonesia: Challenges, Politics and Power* (Santa Monica, CA: RAND, 2002), 31.

17. Tentara Pembebasan Nasional (TPN; National Liberation Army). Despite being poorly armed, the TPN has conducted low-level insurgency attacks against Indonesian security personnel and government targets.

18. Rabasa and Haseman, *The Military and Democracy in Indonesia*, 31.

19. APR Editor, "Wanted: 2000 More Spies in Indonesia, Says BIN Chief," *Asia Pacific Report*, March 4, 2016, https://asiapacificreport.nz/2016/03/04/wanted-2000-more-spies-in-indonesia-says-bin-chief/.

20. APR Editor, "Wanted."

21. Sukadis, "Indonesia State Intelligence Agency Reform and Its Challenges."

22. "Organizational Structure."

23. Peraturan Badan Intellijen Negara (BIN), Organisasi Dan Tata Kerja Badan Intelijen Negara, Republik Indonesia, 2020 (BIN Organisation 2020).

24. Robinson, *The Killing Season*, 16.

25. "BIN Budget Cuts to Jeopardize Regional Election Security, Says Spy Chief," *Jakarta Globe*, September 10, 2015, https://jakartaglobe.id/context/bin-budget-cuts -jeopardize-regional-election-security-says-spy-chief/.

26. APR Editor, "Wanted."

27. Hasyim Widhiarto, "Indonesia a Growing Target for Economic Espionage," *Jakarta Post*, April 16, 2012.

28. Kimberley Ramplin, "Should We Be Outraged That Australia Spied on Indonesia? No," *The Guardian*, November 19, 2013, https://www.theguardian.com/ commentisfree/2013/nov/19/should-we-be-outraged-that-australia-spied-on -indonesia-no.

29. Catriona Croft-Cusworth, "This Week in Jakarta: Chief Concerns," *The Interpreter*, July 10, 2015, https://www.lowyinstitute.org/the-interpreter/week-jakarta -chief-concerns.

30. "Indonesia Told Phone Taps Won't Happen Again," Special Broadcasting Service (SBS) Australia, November 20, 2013, https://www.sbs.com.au/news/indonesia -told-phone-taps-won-t-happen-again.

31. "Australia and Indonesia Sign Spying Code of Conduct," *Guardian Australia*, August 28, 2014, https://www.theguardian.com/world/2014/aug/28/australia-and -indonesia-sign-spying-code-of-conduct.

32. "New Rules in the Great Game," *Australian Defence Magazine*, January 10, 2008, https://www.australiandefence.com.au/D2A14720-F806-11DD-8DFE 0050568C22C9.

33. "Pew-Templeton Global Religious Futures Project," Pew Research Center, 2021, http://www.globalreligiousfutures.org/countries/indonesia#/?affiliations _religion_id=0&affiliations_year=2020&region_name=All%20Countries&restrictions_year=2016.

34. Julia Ebner, *Going Dark: The Secret Social Lives of Extremists* (London: Bloomsbury, 2020), 79.

35. Kirsten E. Schulze, "From Ambon to Poso: Comparative and Evolutionary Aspects of Local Jihad in Indonesia," *Contemporary Southeast Asia* 41, no. 1 (April 2019): 35–62.

36. Kent Roach, "The Case for Defining Terrorism with Restraint and without Reference to Political or Religious Motive," in *Law and Liberty in the War on Terror*, ed. Andrew Lynch, Edwina MacDonald, and George Williams (Sydney, Australia: Federation Press, 2007), 40.

37. Kathy Gannon and Kimberly Dozier, "Official: CIA Tipoff Led to Pakistan Arrest," Associated Press, March 30, 2011, http://archive.boston.com/news/world/ asia/articles/2011/03/30/officials_praise_arrest_of_bali_terror_suspect/; Aubrey Belford, "Indonesia Headed to Pakistan to Identify Possible Bali Bombing Suspect," *New York Times*, March 30, 2011, https://www.nytimes.com/2011/03/31/world/ asia/31indonesia.html.

38. Francis Chan, "Radical Groups Targeting Campus Environment to Mobilise New Terrorist Candidates: Indonesia's Spy Chief," *Straits Times* (Singapore), April 30, 2018, https://www.straitstimes.com/asia/se-asia/radical-groups-targeting-campus -environment-to-mobilise-new-terrorist-candidates.

39. "Indonesian Police Arrest 7 Suspected Militants in Papua," *Straits Times*, December 14, 2019, https://www.straitstimes.com/asia/se-asia/indonesian-police -arrest-7-suspected-militants-in-papua.

40. Geoff Thompson, "Former Indonesian Military Chief Charged with Murder," Australian Broadcasting Corporation (ABC), Sydney, Australia, June 20, 2008.

41. Margareth S. Aritonang and Bagus BT Saragih, "Kerry Calls for Justice for Munir," *Jakarta Post*, September 8, 2014, https://www.thejakartapost.com/news/ 2014/09/08/kerry-calls-justice-munir.html.

42. Bureau of Democracy, Human Rights and Labor, "2020 Country Reports on Human Rights Practices: Indonesia," US Department of State, 2020, https://www .state.gov/reports/2020-country-reports-on-human-rights-practices/indonesia/.

43. Cameron Stewart, "Jakarta Boosts Spying Powers despite Natalegawa's Claims, Former Intelligence Chief Admits Spying on Neighbours," *The Australian*, November 22, 2013.

44. "The Right to Privacy in the Indonesia Stakeholder Report Universal Periodic Review 27th Session," Institute for Policy Research and Advocacy (ELSAM) and Privacy International, September 2016, https://uprdoc.ohchr.org/uprweb/download-file.aspx?filename=3914&file=EnglishTranslation; Gamma Group, *Gamma Group Newsletter*, January 2011.

45. "The Right to Privacy in the Indonesia Stakeholder Report."

46. William M. Wise, *Indonesia's War on Terror* (Washington, DC: United States– Indonesia Society, 2005), https://jko.jten.mil/courses/atl1/courseFiles/resources/Anti terrorism_Electronic_Library/Indonesia's_War_on_Terror.pdf.

47. Gamma Group, *Gamma Group Newsletter*, January 2011.

48. "Products & Services," Gamma Group, 2021, https://www.gammagroup.com/ ProductsServices.aspx?m=p.

49. Bilveer Singh, "Autonomy and Armed Separatism in Papua: Why the Cendra-wasih Continues to Fear the Garuda," in *Autonomy and Armed Separatism in South and Southeast Asia*, ed. Michelle Ann Miller (Singapore: Institute of Southeast Asian Studies, 2012), 63.

50. Antonius Made Tony Supriatma, "TNI/Polri in West Papua: How Security Sector Reforms Work in the Conflict Region," *Indonesia* (Southeast Asia Program Publications, Cornell University), no. 95 (April 2013).

51. "3 Brothers Killed by Indonesian Soldiers at Papuan Health Clinic," *Business Standard*, April 12, 2021, https://www.tbsnews.net/world/3-brothers-killed -indonesian-soldiers-papuan-health-clinic-227398?amp.

52. Sheena Chestnut Greitens, "North Korea's Activities in Southeast Asia and the Implications for the Region," Brookings, November 29, 2017, https://www.brookings .edu/articles/north-koreas-activities-in-southeast-asia-and-the-implications-for-the-region/; "Police to Investigate North Korean Restaurant on Spy Activity," *Jakarta Post*, February 20, 2017, https://www.thejakartapost.com/news/2017/02/20/police-to -investigate-north-korean-restaurant-on-spy-activity.html; "US Accuses Three North Koreans of Conspiring to Steal More Than $1.3 Billion in Cash and Cryptocur-rency," *Washington Post*, February 17, 2021, https://www.washingtonpost.com/ national-security/north-korea-hackers-banks-theft/2021/02/17/3dccf0dc-7129-11eb -93be-c10813e358a2_story.html.

9

Japan: The Rise, Fall, and Reinvention of the Intelligence Community

Richard J. Samuels

The beginning of modern Japanese intelligence gathering is often attributed to the spies dispatched by the Tokugawa Shogunate (1603–1868) to report on corruption and sedition in the provinces.[1] Although this was a time of enforced isolation from the rest of the world, the government gathered intelligence on foreign developments through reports from the Dutch at Dejima, its only official window on the outside world. It also monitored developments through visiting Korean embassies. Its cadre of elite undercover agents were the "ninjas" who have been celebrated in endless period dramas in theaters, on television, and in the movies—in Japan and worldwide.[2]

The now fetishized throwing stars (*shuriken*) and swords (*katana*) of Japan's "samurai culture" began receding into pop culture soon after Japan began to establish a professional intelligence bureaucracy in the late nineteenth century. Japan's modern intelligence community began taking shape in much the same way that other Japanese institutions did—leaders of the new government identified the need for timely and accurate information about foreign adversaries, closely studied foreign practices and technologies, and selectively applied what they believed would best serve the national interest. In 1869, the young Meiji government dispatched its first students—including Yamagata Aritomo, who would become Japan's most influential grand strategist—to study Germany's military. This visit convinced Yamagata that Japanese security required a powerful state at home protected by a powerful and well-informed military abroad. He soon became war minister and, wasting little time, sent Japan's first military attachés and diplomats to practice tradecraft in China in 1875 and set up a "system of espionage in North China."[3]

Yamagata, however, neglected to establish a professional track for career intelligence officials, and at least until the 1930s, Japanese intelligence relied as much on expatriate freelancers as on military intelligence officers. Danny Orbach aptly refers to the network of (often criminal, sometimes pan-Asianist and nationalist) freelance spies and their secret government and business sponsors as a "military-adventurous complex [in] a multi-layered system of deniability."[4] These now storied "continental adventurers" (*tairiku rōnin*) enjoyed extraterritorial privileges and consular protection in China—a textbook breeding ground for moral hazard. In the early twentieth century, Japan's intelligence resources were devoted to covert action as much as to intelligence analysis and collection.

The expansion of the Japanese intelligence community at the turn of the last century and for the next several decades was overdetermined. It was, after all, a time of empire and technological revolution. Japan was an early adopter of technology-intensive signals intelligence (SIGINT) and had early success using it in the first Sino–Japanese War in 1895, and Japan's first military intelligence successes were technological triumphs in its victory over tsarist Russia a decade later. After Russian cruisers sank several Japanese troop transports in successive raids in the Sea of Japan in early 1904, the Imperial Navy broke Russian codes and set up its first SIGINT unit, using wireless intercepts to monitor the Russian transmissions and cut off successive raids throughout the war.[5] Japan's senior diplomats and general officers pioneered "area studies" in the service of intelligence collection and analysis, nurturing careers of deeply knowledgeable area specialists who developed impressive open source intelligence capabilities.

Yet at just the moment when European states were beginning to professionalize their intelligence services, Japan began to consign its analytical intelligence officers to a backbench, depending instead on the operations of innumerable "special duty units" in the Imperial Japanese military. In the run-up to the Asia-Pacific War, and throughout the fighting, they supported coups d'état in Korea, assassinated warlords in China, and nurtured nationalist resistance movements in colonial South and Southeast Asia.

Civilian-military intelligence cooperation was famously limited. Having grown concerned about the size and relative influence of military intelligence, the Foreign Ministry moved to create its own intelligence unit in 1931. But the costliest of all stovepipes were fed by competition within the Imperial Japanese military itself. The bill for the inability of the Imperial Army and Imperial Navy to coordinate intelligence collection and analysis came due after Midway in June 1942 and during the Battle of Leyte Gulf in October 1944, when each actively sabotaged—or at a minimum ignored—the other's intelligence.

There were a great many other failures, most notably in counterintelligence, as in the case of Richard Sorge, who operated under the impeccable cover of the German embassy in Tokyo during World War II. Working with well-placed and idealistic Japanese colleagues, Sorge passed on Japan's Manchurian order of battle to Moscow and provided advance warning of both Japan's 1937 invasion of China and Germany's 1941 invasion of the Soviet Union.

In an oft-repeated Japanese joke, during the Cold War Japan had no Central Intelligence Agency (CIA), but it did have a "KGB": Keisatsu (National Police Agency), Gaimushō (Foreign Ministry), and Bōeichō (Defense Agency). These separate government agencies—like those in intelligence communities abroad—seem to have been engaged in intense and sometimes petty jurisdictional competition, captive in silos inhibiting central coordination. After the Asia-Pacific War, the Japanese intelligence community, like the US and British ones, took a sharp bureaucratic turn—perhaps even earlier and more sharply than in Washington or London. Many intelligence professionals had been cashiered soldiers from the former Imperial Japanese military rehired by the US military occupation that shared their anti-Soviet views. They were joined later by diplomats in the Ministry of Foreign Affairs (MOFA), crime fighters in the National Police Agency (NPA), economists in the Ministry of International Trade and Industry (MITI) and the Ministry of Finance (MOF), and lawyers in the Justice Ministry's Public Security Intelligence Agency (PSIA). Even when seconded to an underpowered Cabinet Intelligence Research Office (CIRO), they belonged as much to their home units as to the central Japanese state. Japan's intelligence units operated in an environment of mutual distrust with limited central authority and even more limited public support. Ken Kotani, a leading historian of Japanese intelligence, tells us that the government "never succeeded in managing the central intelligence system effectively," and even today many observers simply throw up their hands and declare "Japan has no intelligence community."[6]

Not all the problems encountered (or created) by the postwar Japanese intelligence bureaucracies should be connected to the domestic structure of strategic policy making. Subordination to Washington also muted interest in developing Japan's postwar intelligence. During the Occupation (1945–1952)—and even well after Japan regained sovereignty—its intelligence function was aimed narrowly at domestic enemies and foreign firms. The larger strategic horizon was monitored by its ally, the United States. Resentment of Japan's subservience to its US partner—what one intelligence journalist has called a persistent "master-servant relationship"—never independently forced the shape and pace of Japanese intelligence reform, but it did become a more persistent problem than normally is acknowledged.[7] Most Cold War Japanese intelligence and security professionals accepted that they had little choice but to accommodate US power.

While this was a defining feature of the first decades after the war, the Japanese intelligence community—like the military overall—was also stifled by clear and insistent public opposition to any practice redolent of wartime governance. Above all, this meant that engaging in or even debating the merits of intelligence—especially counterintelligence—was problematic. Every plan and each discussion of the topic raised hackles among those who feared (not without cause) that Japan could slide down a slippery slope back to unrestrained practices like domestic surveillance and foreign aggression that destroyed millions of lives and their nation.

TAKING INTELLIGENCE SERIOUSLY AGAIN

After the Cold War, thoughtful Japanese national security strategists—both bureaucrats and politicians—took up intelligence reform with new energy. They began to tinker, reconceive, and, finally, to restructure Japan's national security apparatus—and with it, Japan's intelligence community.

Three factors propelled reform of the Japanese intelligence community after the Cold War. The first—and most persistent—were shifts in the regional strategic balance. The most conspicuous was the stunning rise of China and, perforce, the relative decline of the United States. Many Japanese strategists are quite naturally concerned that continued dependence for security and intelligence on a United States in relative decline renders Japan vulnerable in new ways. As we shall see, this was evident to many well before Donald Trump's campaign and 2016 election accelerated these concerns. Nearly a decade earlier—even before China's military threat became palpable and North Korea's acquisition of nuclear weapons openly challenged the US position—a former chief of MOFA's Intelligence and Analysis Bureau argued that Japan could not effectively reform its intelligence community until it realized that Washington, DC, would not necessarily provide for Japan's security.[8] Just as Prime Minister Shinzō Abe was preparing to reengineer Japan's foreign policy and intelligence system in 2013 by creating a National Security Council (NSC) and National Security Secretariat (NSS), three Diet representatives from different parties—one of whom would become Abe's foreign minister in 2017 and defense minister in 2019—issued a vigorous call for an independent Japanese intelligence service, justifying it with the following assessment, rhetorical question, and prescription:

> Japan's diplomacy and national security have never been in such a tight fix. America's relative power is declining and China's military rise, as well as its expanding claims in the ocean, are striking. . . . Is Japan responding effectively

to the historic shift in world order? . . . Even if an NSC is established, there is still a missing piece—a foreign intelligence [unit].[9]

The second driver of intelligence reform was technological change. The most prominent intelligence-related technologies have been related to the way intelligence is collected: human intelligence (HUMINT), radio and other SIGINT, and image intelligence (IMINT) are the most widely known and are all widely practiced. Cyber-based intelligence harvesting is just the latest tool to which Japanese intelligence officials have had to adjust.

Even if Japan's counterintelligence capabilities sometimes trailed its collection technologies, Tokyo was never too slow off the technological mark. Despite self-imposed constraints on the military use of space, Japan deployed transponders on the satellites of civilian agencies to transmit images for the use of military intelligence starting at least as far back as the 1980s. Today, Japanese analysts use many of the most advanced image-processing technologies—in one instance reportedly being able to differentiate between five pilots and a lone protocol officer standing in line on the deck of China's aircraft carrier.[10]

Failure was the third, and most proximate, driver of intelligence reform. Failure drives intelligence reform everywhere, but nowhere has it been more plentiful or storied than in Japan. The nineteenth-century shogunate was shaken to its knees once the capabilities of Commodore Perry's "black ships" became known; imperial militarists and pan-Asianists were unprepared for US resolve in the Asia-Pacific War; and the most famous tactical intelligence failure of that conflict occurred after a US signals unit located Admiral Yamamoto Isoroku near the Solomon Islands in April 1943, allowing Admiral Nimitz's pilots to ambush his plane. In the early 1970s, President Richard Nixon pulled the rug out from under Japan not once, but *twice* in "shocks" that upended the global financial community and that brought China in from the cold. Subsequent unannounced and unanticipated visits by a Soviet MIG-25 in 1976 and by a North Korean missile in 1998 justified immediate changes in the way Japan practiced intelligence. More recent failures, as in the Algerian hostage crisis in 2013, made intelligence reform more urgent.

It is tempting to assume that the sudden end of the Cold War left the underdeveloped Japanese intelligence community and Japan's political class clueless about what was in store. That was not the case, however. Without waiting for external provocation, senior Japanese bureaucrats and politicians had already begun thinking about how to enhance Japan's intelligence collection. Their first target was military intelligence; they had already begun making plans to tinker with it before the Soviet Union collapsed.

With the support of Prime Minister Hashimoto Ryūtarō and other Liberal Democratic Party (LDP) heavyweights—as well as with allies embedded in senior bureaucratic posts—intelligence reformers like Gotōda Masaharu hitched plans for military intelligence reform to the popular effort to achieve more comprehensive and popular administrative reform. They were betting that the Japanese public became almost as disenchanted with the policy dominance of bureaucrats as they were with the militarists who by then had receded further in their rear-view mirrors. They read the mood clearly—there was support for budgeting to be more transparent and for the administrative state to be more streamlined. Moving intelligence reform forward in tandem with—and under the cover of—major administrative reform, Gotōda and Nishihiro Seiji (Japan's most senior defense bureaucrat) engineered consolidation of military intelligence—specifically signals and imaging—by shepherding the January 1997 formation of their long-sought Defense Intelligence Headquarters (DIH) that consolidated most military image and signals intelligence for the first time.

This new early warning unit failed its first major test. One of the justifications for its creation had been the Japanese Defense Agency's inability in May 1993 to anticipate and warn Japan of the first test by North Korea of an indigenous ballistic missile, the Nodong-1, which landed short of, but uncomfortably near, the Noto peninsula that juts into the Sea of Japan from central Japan. The Japanese public took notice but did not rise in indignation to demand better tools, much less a military response. In September 1998, the DIH, however, failed to detect preparations for the launch of a longer-range North Korean Taepodong-1 that flew through Japanese airspace. This time, echoing the way Washington set up NASA in July 1958 after the Soviets put Sputnik into orbit, Tokyo's politicians took the bit between their teeth. Within months, the government retreated (informally for the time being) from its decades-long policy banning the military use of space and initiated an indigenous spy satellite program. In an awkward arrangement entirely consistent with Japan's history of fractured intelligence, however, the program was placed under the nominal control of the National Police Agency. This was just more evidence that during this first post–Cold War decade Japan would content itself with tinkering with its underpowered and dependent intelligence community. Comprehensive intelligence reform would have to wait until greater threats manifested themselves and until new leaders emerged who were willing to expend the political capital necessary for comprehensive reform.

As in the past, there were also famous counterintelligence failures, as when politicians stood aside as bureaucratic obstacles blocked the Public Security Intelligence Agency, Japan's major counterintelligence organization, from disabling the murderous Aum Shinrikyō cult before it snuffed out thirteen lives on a Tokyo subway in March 1995.

Taking stock of the state of the intelligence community in 2008, one influential analyst judged that considerably more work needed to be done "to conquer" three critical, persistent "bottlenecks"—each conforming to elements explored in this study. Kaneko Masafumi called for improvement in the circulation and sharing, presentation, and the end to leaks—*mawatte, agate*, and *morenai* in Japanese.[11] Indeed, a small industry emerged dedicated to intelligence reform and strengthening.[12] These and multiple other exhortations from media, think tanks, and scholars undergirded a cascade of government reports and recommendations from the political class that began to argue seriously, substantively, and compellingly for comprehensive intelligence reform. For its part, moreover, public opinion seemed to be becoming more accustomed to—and accepting of—formal discussion of the threat.

As Japan slowly became engaged in operations abroad, collection, analysis, and communication functions were each enhanced—but not with much fanfare. The Ground Self-Defense Force's experience in Iraq after 2003 stimulated calls to enhance the ground forces' tactical intelligence capabilities, and contracts were let for significant new ISR capabilities, including large numbers of a new indigenous maritime patrol aircraft. And the long-standing fiction regarding the nonmilitary use of space was formally abolished. A new generation of political leaders, impatient with the slow pace of their pragmatic predecessors, emerged to advocate Japan's becoming a "normal nation" and displayed an open and unselfconscious eagerness to enhance Japanese defense capabilities and the intelligence community that would support them.

Although Japan's intelligence community was actively reimagined during this period, there was still no consensus on the best way forward in part because this eagerly pro-reform generation of leaders had yet to fully consolidate power. Indeed, Japan's political leadership remained quite unsteady. In just the first six years after the retirement of Prime Minister Koizumi Junichirō in 2006, Japan had seven prime ministers, eleven foreign ministers, and sixteen defense ministers from two different major parties. Not surprisingly, then, intelligence reform initiatives undertaken by some were undone by others, as when Prime Minister Abe's 2006 effort to overhaul Japan's foreign policy decision-making apparatus was blocked the following year by Fukuda Yasuo, his immediate successor.

Several non-LDP governments favored intelligence reform, but their efforts were blocked by the LDP, which was eager to regain power. Until Abe returned to power in early 2013, the endemic failures of intelligence units to communicate with one another and the intelligence community as a whole to communicate with the political class continued to define Japanese intelligence and undermine national policy.

ACHIEVING NORMALCY

By the second decade of this century, however, a new world order—one characterized by the diffusion of global power—came into sharper focus for Japanese strategists. Post–Cold War threats, at first limited to nonstate actors and to terrorism, gave way to an even more consequential shift in the strategic environment—the rise and expansion of China, the nuclearization of North Korea, and the concomitant relative decline of the United States. Japanese strategists have had to consider what one scholar has aptly called the "strategic insolvency" of the United States—the possibility that Washington would lose its capacity to effectively manage the gap between its strategic commitments and its national objectives.[13]

Even if they could not openly declare it, Japanese strategic planners, led by Prime Minister Abe and his closest allies in the LDP and the foreign ministry, seemed finally to appreciate that America's unipolar moment was receding. Without an obvious alternative to the alliance with Washington, they worked diligently to shore it up without boxing themselves in. Judging a security hedge to be the most prudent course in the face of declining US capabilities relative to China, they eagerly accepted US exhortations to improve their military and their intelligence systems. Washington was pushing on an open door.[14]

The Japanese government moved in several directions simultaneously to expand its own intelligence capabilities. The boldest move was the simultaneous creation in 2013 of the "twin pillars" of intelligence reform—the Designated State Secrets Law and the NSC. The former created postwar Japan's first official document classification system, something long sought by Washington. The latter was an even more sweeping reform of foreign policy decision-making—including the NSS to streamline communication across intelligence units and between the intelligence community and the policy community. This was a direct frontal assault on long-standing, widely recognized impediments to effective intelligence in a system in which there was diminished, but still lingering, resistance to national security issues within the general public. The political costs were contained, however, and these institutional reforms were accepted by the public without damaging the Abe administration.

So, too, were other, less controversial initiatives. Determined to extend defense to outer space and bring indigenously developed and domestically produced space-based intelligence resources in line with Japan's new security infrastructure, the Abe government rewrote its predecessor's Basic Space Plan in late 2013 even before the ink had dried. It followed a year later with a Cybersecurity Basic Law that created a Cybersecurity Headquarters to engage formally with the brave new, dangerous, world of cyber threats. The

Abe administration proceeded thereupon to establish a new Counterterrorism Unit ahead of the 2016 G-7 Summit in Ise Shima and the planned 2020 Tokyo Olympics. Then, in late 2017—a year in which cyberattacks had increased by 20 percent—the MOD announced plans to create a joint cyber and space command under the direct control of the minister on the same reporting level as the Ground, Air, and Fleet Commands. It also announced an increase in the number of military attachés deployed to Southeast Asia to cooperate with the Philippines, Vietnam, and Malaysia to coordinate intelligence operations regarding China. In December 2017, the government announced plans for research on space-based quantum cryptography communications. Suddenly intelligence reform and enhancement had a new spring in their steps.[15] The SDF revealed in April 2018 that it would deploy a new long-range radar system in the Ogasawara island chain 1,000 kilometers south of Tokyo to monitor the South China Sea, and for its part, the Japan Coast Guard (JCG) announced it would install radar sites on twenty-three remote southwestern islands explicitly to monitor Chinese and North Korean maritime activity. The JCG's 2018 budget also included new patrol aircraft and a significant increase in its personnel—including sixty new pilots, radar technicians, and mechanics to enhance aerial surveillance near the disputed Senkaku Islands in the East China Sea.[16] Clearly, these initiatives were driven by newly ener- gized political leaders and accepted by a newly amenable public concerned about shifts in the strategic environment and technology.

This forward motion notwithstanding, the ambitions of Japan's intelligence reformers still were not fulfilled, making it difficult to be overly optimistic about the prospects for enhanced coordination within the Japanese intelli- gence community. Even after periods of intense reimagination and substan- tive reengineering, the Japanese intelligence community remained riven by familiar, long-standing jurisdictional competition. Importantly, this condition was owed not only to the nature of bureaucratic politics in general or to secrecy in the specific case of intelligence everywhere. Rather, the problem has a Japanese character to it—the well-documented Japanese predilection for stove-piping in every bureaucratic endeavor, what the Japanese refer to as "the evils of bureaucratic sectionalism." In the intelligence domain, there was no law requiring cooperation across constituent units until 2013, and LDP plans in 2015 to resurrect a serious HUMINT capacity and centralize intelli- gence by launching a "Japanese-style CIA" were rejected by the Abe govern- ment as moving too far and too fast.[17] Even after intelligence cooperation was identified as crucial to national policy, the law creating the National Security Council only required intelligence units to submit their data and analyses to the NSS. NSS officials could provide feedback but could not share it across the intelligence community or generate their own analyses.

Meanwhile, CIRO continued to enjoy direct access to the prime minister in parallel to the NSS. CIRO officials—all from the Police Agency—sit atop most of the recently established intelligence units—even those in the military. Indeed, not only did silos persist after the National Security Secretariat was established in 2013, but military intelligence reverted to its stove-piped norm in 2018 when the MOD stepped back from its 2007 commitment to joint intelligence by transferring supervision of its Military Intelligence Command from the civilians in the ministry to the officers in the Ground Self-Defense Force's Ground Component Command. Consequently, despite the recognition of the problem, the demands of many, and the expectations of some, stovepipes never went away and a robust HUMINT capability has yet to be consolidated.

CONCLUSION

This chapter focused on the standard elements of intelligence in Japan—its organization and mission, its successes and failures, and its relations with the political class. One element remains—oversight. Formal intelligence oversight never existed in authoritarian Japan, of course. It emerged slowly as a norm in the postwar system and was not established legally for decades. Several efforts to surveille Japanese citizens—both on the left and the right—and successive efforts to protect state secrets mobilized the public and led to court challenges that resulted in legal changes that limited state power. Intelligence oversight is not as robust in Japan as in some other industrial democracies, which also, it must be noted, came to it rather late. But due to an engaged public, neither has it been moribund.

NOTES

1. This chapter is derived from Richard J. Samuels, *Special Duty: A History of the Japanese Intelligence Community* (Ithaca, NY: Cornell University Press, 2019). A portion was published as "La communauté de renseignement japonaise," in *Le renseignement: Approches, acteurs et enjeux* [Intelligence: Approaches, actors and issues], ed. Jean-Baptiste Jeangène Vilmer, Jean-Vincent Holeindre, and Paul Chareon (Paris: Institut de Recherche Stratégique de l'École Militaire, 2020). It is republished here with permission of the publisher.

2. See John Whitney Hall, *The Cambridge History of Japan*, vol. 4 (Cambridge: Cambridge University Press, 1988).

3. Ken Kotani, *Japanese Intelligence in World War II* (Oxford: Osprey, 2009), 6; Kiyoichi Tachikawa, "Japan's Pre-war Military Attaché System," *NIDS Journal of*

Defense and Security 16 (December 2015): 147–85; Louis Allen, "Japanese Intelligence Systems," *Journal of Contemporary History* 22, no. 4 (October 1987):547–62.

4. Danny Orbach, "The Military-Adventurous Complex: Officers, Adventurers and Japanese Expansion in East Asia, 1884–1937," *Modern Asian Studies* 53, no. 2 (2018): 10. These business ties included sponsorship of many of Japan's most ambitious *zaibatsu* leaders, such as Iwasaki Hisaya of Mitsubishi and Baron Ōkura Kihachirō of the Ōkura Group.

5. Edward J. Drea, "Missing Intentions: Japanese Intelligence and the Soviet Invasion of Manchuria, 1945," *Military Affairs* 48 (April 1984): 186; Nakamuda Kenichi, *Jōhō Shikan no Kaisō* 情報士官の回想 [Reminiscences of an intelligence officer] (Tokyo: Asahi Sonorama, 1985), 25–47, 82.

6. Ken Kotani, "A Reconstruction of Japanese Intelligence: Issues and Prospects," in *Intelligence Elsewhere: Spies and Espionage Outside the Anglosphere*, ed. Philip J. Davies and Kristian C. Gustafson (Washington, DC: Georgetown University Press, 2013), 189.

7. Kuroi Buntarō 黒井文太郎, "Wārudowaido Interijensu" ワールドワイドインテリジェンス [Worldwide intelligence], *Gunji Kenkyū*, September 2005, 236.

8. See interview with Magosaki Ukeru 孫崎享 in Kuroi Buntarō 黒井文太郎, *Interijensu no Gokui* インテリジェンスの極意 [The mysteries of intelligence] (Tokyo: Takarajimasha, 2008), 261.

9. Kōno Tarō 河野太郎, Mabuchi Sumio 馬淵澄夫, and Yamauchi Kōichi 山内 康一, "Nihongata 'Supai Soshiki' no Tsukurikata" 日本型スパイ組織の作り方 [How to build a Japanese-style spy organization] *Chūō Kōron*, May 2013, 94–101.

10. Author interview with a former MOD official, November 29, 2017, Tokyo.

11. Kaneko Masafumi 金子史将, "Kantei no Interijensu Kinō wa Kyōka Sareru Ka" 官邸のインテリジェンス機能は強化されるか [Will the cabinet's intelligence function be strengthened?], *PHP Policy Review* 2, no. 62008 (February 29, 2008): 4.

12. Shigeta Hiroshi 茂田宏, "Nihon no Jōhō Kinō ni kansuru Genjō to Kadai" 日本の情報機能に関する現状と課題 [The present circumstances and problems with Japan's intelligence functions], *Seiron*, May 2006, 296.

13. Michael J. Mazarr, "The Risks of Ignoring Strategic Insolvency," *Washington Quarterly* 35, no. 8 (2012): 7–22. See also Richard J. Samuels and Corey Wallace, "Introduction: "Japan's Pivot in Asia," *International Affairs* 94, no. 4 (July 2018): 703–10.

14. The first public US exhortation is credited to Joseph S. Nye and Richard L. Armitage, *The U.S.-Japan Alliance: Anchoring Stability in Asia* (Washington, DC: Center for Strategic and International Studies, August 2012).

15. For more on the proliferation of these offices, see Richard J. Samuels, *Special Duty: A History of the Japanese Intelligence Community* (Ithaca, NY: Cornell University Press, 2019), chap. 6. The increase in attacks was reported in *Nihon Keizai Shimbun*, February 28, 2018, and the increase in attachés is from *Taiwan Times*, March 7, 2018. Also, note that there was less bounce in that step when the government's 2018 cybersecurity budget allocated less than $700 million for cybersecurity to support just 150 staff. See *Yomiuri Shimbun*, December 27, 2017, for the new unit

and the quantum cryptography initiative, and February 2, 2018, for JCG's radar plans. The 2018 budget is here: https://www.misc.go.jp/active/kihon/pdf/yosan2018.pdf. For the cabinet announcement of the new strategies document, see *Mainichi Shimbun*, January 18, 2018.

16. *Mainichi Shimbun*, April 13, 2018.

17. *Sankei Shimbun*, December 28, 2015; author interview with LDP Diet representative Iwaya Takeshi, November 10, 2017, Tokyo.

10

Kazakhstan: A Circular Revolution in Intelligence Culture

Elizabeth Van Wie Davis

The Republic of Kazakhstan's intelligence services have been forming and reforming since independence and appear to have returned to their original model of the Soviet Union's Committee for State Security (Komitet Gosudarstvennoy Bezopasnosti, KGB). Under the Soviet Union, Kazakhstan operated the Kazakh KGB. Shortly after independence, Kazakhstan formed the first independent Kazakh foreign intelligence service, Barlau, in 1992 to replace the Kazakh KGB. The National Security Committee (NSC) was also founded in 1992. Under perceptions that Barlau was too weak, it was replaced with another foreign intelligence agency, Syrbar, in 2009, which was modernized and expanded. The Republic of Kazakhstan put Syrbar directly under the NSC with a June 17, 2019, decree by the new president, Kassym-Zhomart Tokayev, shortly after taking office. The NSC is now a supra intelligence agency, like the earlier Soviet KGB. Consequently, the intelligence services have come full circle.

The NSC is under the jurisdictional authority of the Office of the President and headed by the powerful former president Nursultan Nazarbayev. Originally focused on domestic issues of human and society security, the constitutional system, state sovereignty, territorial integrity, and economic, scientific-technical, and defense potential of the country, it expanded to include military counterintelligence and counterterrorism including the border service and the Lions (*Arystan*) commando unit.[1] The 2019 intelligence consolidation—where the foreign intelligence agency now also reports to the all-encompassing NSC—increases the focus on Kazakhstan's relationships with the great powers of China, Russia, and the United States. Additionally, the NSC focuses on domestic issues, including the strengths and weaknesses of shifting government and intelligence online, potential movements capable of destabilization, and market reforms that concentrate wealth in the hands of the elite. This resource-rich country imposes few restrictions or nonexecutive oversight of its intelligence.

The intelligence services of the Republic of Kazakhstan are meant to serve the head of the government specifically and, through the leadership, serve the state. Like other political systems throughout the world, including most post-Soviet states, Kazakhstan retains authoritarian origins. The main element of the authoritarian system in Kazakhstan is the combination of limiting political input to those supporting the government and of economic reforms that are not fully distributed through the population.[2] It has also meant that domestic and foreign intelligence returned as a tightly controlled arm of the executive branch as the authoritarian origins reemerged.

This chapter explores the intelligence culture in the Republic of Kazakhstan by providing an analysis of its history, including the recent consolidation that put these services directly under the control of Nazarbayev, tightened recruitment into the Kazakh intelligence services, and its concerns with presidential succession and government stability. The chapter also reviews the Kazakh intelligence culture's recent domestic developments and global and regional neighborhood. Finally, the chapter discusses the impact of Kazakhstan's imposition of few restrictions and little oversight of its intelligence services that directly report to the president. Overall, the Kazakh intelligence agencies have been strengthening, mirroring an earlier model and culture in response to this environment.

HISTORY OF KAZAKH INTELLIGENCE

The history of intelligence services in the Republic of Kazakhstan centers on several impactful moments. The first, and perhaps most important, is the multistep consolidation of the intelligence services over the past three decades. Additionally, the recruitment into Kazakh intelligence has modified. Finally, the presidential succession is a vital concern for the intelligence services as it has consequential implications for domestic stability.

The most impactful moment in the recent history of Kazakh intelligence is the final consolidation of its intelligence services. The NSC, the main intelligence agency in Kazakhstan, accepted the ultimate consolidation into its understructure of the foreign intelligence service, the most secretive of the intelligence services. Based on the Soviet KGB, there persists within the NSC a culture of corruption and privilege that leaves enormous potential for abuse of power and unjust use of the intelligence services.

The NSC directly reports to the president of Kazakhstan.[3] Kazakhstan and its post-Soviet neighbors largely inherited the idea of a presidential advisory body on foreign policy and national security from Russia.[4] The consolidation specifically establishes the NSC as the executive branch body responsible for foreign policy and national security matters, reinforcing and restructuring Kazakhstan's intelligence services' approach into a structure comparable to the earlier Kazakh KGB.[5]

Consolidated and renamed as the Foreign Intelligence Service of the National Security Committee, this intelligence agency has an expansive portfolio.[6] It oversees obtaining information and providing intelligence and analytical assessments of the political, financial, economic, military, political, scientific, technical, humanitarian, and environmental fields. It also has the objectives of promoting economic development and scientific and technological progress of the country and the military, participation in the development and creation of conditions conducive to national security, and of preventing damage to the national interests and security from foreign states, individuals, terrorists, and extremist organizations abroad. Moreover, it secures Kazakh diplomatic missions, coordinates with other countries' foreign intelligence agencies, and performs other tasks determined by the laws and acts of the Kazakh president. Finally, the Foreign Intelligence Service includes operational, training, analytical, and technical units; scientific research institutions; and legal departments.[7]

The 2019 consolidation and strengthening of the NSC, days after the election of President Tokayev, is one of several actions taken in these early days; others include two decrees on the creation of new ministries and several trips to Central Asian organizations.[8] Such activity suggests that the new president simply signed the documents worked out during the Nazarbayev administration. Former president Nazarbayev is unlikely to allow his successor to immediately operate in sensitive areas like the state apparatus and the manpower deployment inside it with such autonomy.[9]

Recruitment into the Kazakh intelligence services was strengthened in 2016. Specifically, the change included tightening the procedure for admission to the Academy of the National Security Committee of the Republic of Kazakhstan. The academy of the NSC is a special, multidisciplinary educational institution in the field of training, retraining, and advanced training of operational, technical, and managerial staff of national security bodies. Selection and admission to the academy is regulated by Article 10 of the Law of the Republic of Kazakhstan titled "On Special State Bodies," and the order of the chairman of the National Security Committee no. 2 of January 13, 2016.[10] This gives the NSC one more order of magnitude to control all aspects of the intelligence services and intelligence culture.

Finally, the three decades of Kazakhstan intelligence services history centers on presidential succession and government stability. Nursultan Nazarbayev retains sweeping powers as head of the NSC and leader of the ruling Radiant Fatherland (Nur Otan) party. Nazarbayev's right to head the NSC for life went through several steps for constitutional approval in summer 2018, the year before he resigned as president of Kazakhstan.[11] Nazarbayev's lifelong right to head the NSC follows the constitutional reform of 2017 and argues that this role will strengthen Kazakhstan's stability. The law also expands the NSC's role as a constitutional body responsible for a unified state policy both domestically and internationally. The decisions of the NSC and its chairman are mandatory and subject to strict execution by the government.[12] So there has been a presidential succession, but the first president maintains considerable power, including controlling the intelligence services.

The Nur Otan party continues its decades-long domination of Kazakhstan and is also headed by Nazarbayev—who had been the Kazakh prime minister under the Soviet Union in 1984 and became the first president of Kazakhstan in 1990. He will provide President Tokayev with guidance on both domestic and foreign affairs.[13] The Nur Otan party "won a landslide victory" in the 2019 election; observers from the Organization for Security and Co-operation in Europe (OSCE) asserted that the vote was uncompetitive since no opposition groups ran in the vote.[14]

The second presidential succession is widely assumed to be from President Tokayev to Nazarbayev's eldest daughter. Nonetheless, Dariga Nazarbayeva left her position as speaker of the Senate, which led some observers to note that Tokayev held this same position before he ascended to the presidency. President Tokayev is the one who nominated Ms. Nazarbayeva to the role of speaker. Under the Kazakh constitution, the speaker of the Senate is first in line to take over the presidency in the case of the sitting president's resignation or death. In fact, Tokayev was speaker of the Senate when then president Nazarbayev resigned. It is less clear whether former president Nazarbayev will use his role as the head of the NSC and the Nur Otan party to quietly assist his daughter in the presidential succession before his death.[15] The intelligence services may well argue that Nazarbayev's daughter would continue national stability as the third president.

INTELLIGENCE CULTURE DOMESTICALLY AND INTERNATIONALLY

The Kazakh intelligence culture reflects both its global and regional neighborhood and recent domestic developments. Domestic issues have pushed

Kazakh intelligence culture to focus on, first, e-government and cybersecurity; second, domestic economic inequality; and, third, dissidents and radicalization and illegal drugs. Internationally, Kazakhstan's intelligence services navigate its position as the biggest country in Central Asia, as well as its great power neighbors, China and Russia, and considerable American investments. Domestically, Kazakhstan reveals its authoritarian past, and internationally, Kazakhstan reflects the fate of a middle-sized power with borders with great powers.

First, one of Kazakhstan's central domestic issues is its decision to move toward an e-government structure in 2006 and to implement Digital Kazakhstan in 2017 (and the inherent vulnerability to cyberattacks).[16] The NSC continues to amass power needed to protect e-government, manage information and communications technology infrastructure, and surveil online content. A secretive cybersecurity body named the National Coordination Center for Information Security, under the NSC, was known to exist as of 2018.[17] In addition to the NSC leadership, there are at least two other ministries—the Ministry of Digital Development, Innovation, and Aerospace Industry and the Ministry of Information and Social Development—that have direct presidential responsibilities of cybersecurity.[18] With so much government and governmental services online, a country becomes susceptible, like Estonia, to cyberattacks that can shut down government and close down cyberespionage that is more important than ever to the intelligence services.[19]

The online move has internal and external ramifications. Kazakhstan is ranked twenty-ninth in the United Nations' global ranking according to the level of development of e-government.[20] Yet, the population still has limited access to broadband or the digital economy, and issues of internet freedom persist.[21] President Tokayev halted the rollout of its national security certificate, enabling it to monitor citizens' online activities, after a few weeks of public objection in 2019.[22] Its basis in legislation remained so that it can be reintroduced at any time, however.[23]

The government also has started implementing advanced video surveillance technologies, even as multiple high-profile data breaches raise concerns over the security of citizens' personal data. Additionally, online content continues to be censored.[24] Externally, Kazakhstan is vulnerable to cyberattack. For instance, a report at the end of 2019 revealed an extensive cyberattack campaign hit a wide range of targets including government agencies and military personnel.[25] The cyber attacker is linked to Russia and similarly attacked Kazakhstan in 2018 but used a different malware strain.[26]

The intelligence services' second domestic concern is the failure of the successful market reforms to be spread among the population. The 2020–2022 fiscal plan focuses on modernizing the economy and reducing its oil production concentration on economic development.[27] Although 2020 economic reforms involved both weaker export demand due to the COVID-19 pandemic and the crash in oil prices, the government is determined to continue supporting infrastructure building, the development of special economic zones, and the agro-industrial complex.[28] In March 2020, the government unveiled a US$10 billion anti-crisis program, which is partially meant to mitigate economically motivated antigovernment protests. Kazakh socioeconomic disparities are creating conditions for occasional outbreaks of communal violence, including the anti-Dungan riots in the impoverished Zhambyl region in February 2020.[29] Moreover, anticorruption measures are unlikely to mitigate high-level bribery, which is widespread across state institutions.[30] Ultimately, governmental use of authoritarian force to suppress dissents can trigger violent repercussions as the national poverty rate rose to 12–14 percent in 2020.[31]

Third, dissidents, radicalization, and illegal drugs are important domestic concerns for the NSC and most clearly reveals its authoritarian past. The NSC practices fighting dissidents, including outside their borders.[32] Dissidents include exiles, political opposition, journalists, academics, civil society activists, former regime insiders, and alleged religious extremists.[33] Dissidents are subjected not only to physical attacks and online surveillance and harassment but also to extradition attempts, INTERPOL Red Notices, kidnapping and other forms of illegal rendition, and even assassination.[34] Other concerns are youth turning to radical Islam, despite increased de-radicalization initiatives and criminalization of participation in radical organizations. Radical Islam is more widespread in the impoverished southern regions of Kazakhstan.[35]

The illegal trade and transit in narcotics to Russia and Europe for growing unlawful shipments of Afghan opiates can help finance dissidents and radical adherents. Counternarcotic measures have produced limited results as main trafficking operations evade detection due to corruption in law enforcement and customs.[36] Shortly after the collapse of the Soviet Union, the United Nations Office on Drugs and Crime set up offices in Central Asia in 1994 followed by the Central Asia Regional Information and Coordination Centre inauguration in Almaty, Kazakhstan, in 2010.[37] According to estimates from the United Nations Office on Drugs and Crime, fifty-nine kilograms of heroin and morphine, trafficked from Afghanistan through Kazakhstan en route to Russia, was seized in 2018.[38] Moreover, there are always domestic drug use problems that arise in transit states.[39] Drug flow is increasingly posing a threat to the stability and security of the Central Asian states, affecting their relations with the great powers of Russia, China, and the United States.[40]

Of central importance to almost every intelligence service's culture is its position in foreign relations. Former president Nazarbayev's policy of amity with all the great powers, a position President Tokayev is continuing, seems sensible, especially toward Russia. While Kazakh intelligence services have significant cultural overlap with Russia and the former Soviet Union, the Kazakh government has kept a close eye on Russia's aggressions with Georgia and Ukraine.[41] Intelligence cooperation between Russian and Central Asian intelligence services were formalized in April 1992 with an agreement not to spy on each other. The relationship put Russia in a superior position, and the Central Asia countries each had different responses to this dominance.

Kazakhstan, long suspicious of ethnic Russians who had migrated during Soviet times, signaled their independence by purging Russians from the ranks of their intelligence services. The Federal Security Service (Federal'naya sluzhba bezopasnosti Rossiyskoy Federatsii, FSB) became the dominant intelligence player in Central Asia and the most powerful Russian intelligence service. Although the Russian foreign intelligence service had promised not to spy on the former Soviets, the FSB had never signed any such agreement and felt free of any obligation.[42] As a result, in late 1999, the FSB was granted permission to establish a new directorate—the Directorate of Operative Information (UKOI) inside the Department of Analysis, Forecasting, and Strategic Planning—to focus on Central Asia.[43] Furthermore, Kazakhstan is not above using FSB intelligence in aiding its own intelligence gathering.[44]

Kazakhstan's intelligence services balance a national desire for Chinese investment with popular fears of encroachment by their giant eastern neighbor.[45] China is an important consumer of Kazakhstan's oil and gas industries, and there is concern over Chinese expansion. A wave of anti-China protests in Kazakhstan in 2019 focused on increasing debt to China, the growing presence of Chinese enterprises and goods, the inevitable scheme of trading oil for technology, and the persecution of Muslims in neighboring Xinjiang.[46] China now runs fifty-five projects worth US$27.6 billion, half in oil and natural gas.[47] The sophisticated transport lines being built from China into Kazakhstan is another indicator of China's influence, even though there is local resistance to it.[48]

There appears to be little cooperation between China and Kazakhstan's intelligence services. Kazakh counterintelligence officers detained a senior Kazakh government adviser (who was also a former intelligence officer) on charges of passing classified documents to China in 2019.[49] The fact that the Kazakh government allowed the case to leak to the local media is interpreted as a rare public pushback against China's growing influence in Kazakhstan.[50] On the one hand, China clearly uses its intelligence services to gather information on Kazakhstan, and it is reasonable to assume that Kazakhstan does the same. On the other hand, there is cooperation between Kazakhstan and

China through the Shanghai Cooperation Organization, which also includes Russia and other Central Asian states. Kazakhstan's government is shrewd in its diplomatic activities and excels in establishing good relations with the great powers.[51]

As the United States was the first country to recognize Kazakhstan's independence, positive relations with the United States are important to balance China and Russia. From the US perspective, a cornerstone of the cooperation is security and nuclear nonproliferation, as evidenced by Kazakhstan renouncing its nuclear weapons in 1993, participating in the Nuclear Security Summits from 2010 to 2016, participating in US-funded military exercises, and removing nuclear warheads, weapons-grade materials, and supporting infrastructure.[52] From the Kazakh perspective, there is residual resentment over Russia conducting nuclear tests in Kazakhstan and fears of Chinese expansion, so the more distant United States can create a balance. While it is highly likely that there were interactions between the Kazakh and American intelligence services during the US war in Afghanistan, there is no open-source evidence to confirm this. Notably, American troops left Afghanistan, and US military and intelligence services are discussing where to reposition forces, possibly to Kazakhstan.[53] A better approach for the United States may be increasing economic engagement with Kazakhstan to give it room to flex between the great powers, a marquee goal of the United States Strategy for Central Asia 2019–2025.[54]

Regionally, Kazakhstan enjoys amicable relations with its Central Asian neighbors over security, borders, and intelligence cooperation.[55] There are a series of bilateral security agreements among the former Soviet republics such as the strategic partnership agreement with Uzbekistan in 2013. Borders have been enhanced by the Convention on the Legal Status of the Caspian Sea in 2018 with Azerbaijan, Iran, Russia, and Turkmenistan as a positive step in the oil-rich region. Kazakhstan also has maritime border agreements with Azerbaijan, Russia, and Turkmenistan.[56] Intelligence cooperation between Kazakhstan and Kyrgyzstan includes exchanges of military intelligence and specialist assessments on vital topics, as well as information about terrorist and other organizations. The cooperation agreement also covers joint activities to counter further challenges and threats.[57]

Thus, the Kazakh intelligence services have a culture of authoritarianism at home and amiable relations abroad. This does not mean that domestic authoritarian crackdowns do not risk domestic unrest or that positive relations with great powers precludes fears of cyberattacks or need for careful balancing among the United States, Russia, and China. With a consolidated intelligence service that serves the executive, the next issue is oversight and reform.

OVERSIGHT OF THE INTELLIGENCE SERVICES

Kazakhstan imposes few restrictions on or oversight of its intelligence, which undoubtedly shapes the intelligence culture. Not only do the intelligence services directly report to the president, but also the ministries charged with supplemental oversight are appointed by the president. The result is that the intelligence services are not transparent or subject to independent oversight outside of the Office of the President.[58]

There are other elements limiting oversight of the intelligence services as well. The first is the lack of vibrant political diversity. For instance, the political opposition parties to the ruling Nur Otan party, including the banned Democratic Choice of Kazakhstan (DVK) party, have little voice. For instance, the DVK was reduced to calling for demonstrations in urban centers across Kazakhstan in May 2021. The DVK also denounce the arrests of political activists ahead of those rallies.[59] The lack of true political opposition eliminates pressure on the ruling party to provide intelligence service oversight.

Second, the power of the intelligence services themselves also limit citizens' ability to promote oversight. For instance, facial recognition, biometric identification, artificial intelligence, and video surveillance technologies have been rapidly emerging domestically to keep close watch on the citizenry. It is the intelligence services that are providing oversight of the Kazakh citizens with hundreds of thousands of cameras installed by 2022, a nationwide fingerprint collection, and a biometric identification system in 2021.[60]

Third, the concept of independent oversight of the intelligence services has been extended to include the role played by civil society.[61] Despite this, the intelligence community is generally viewed as within the exclusive domain of the executive. Where civil society plays a role in overseeing the intelligence sector, it generally does so through traditional means of public oversight. Under certain conditions, the interests of intelligence services and civil society may coincide, but in general the roles of civil society and intelligence services are separated to ensure the independence of the intelligence services.[62]

Finally, while in some countries the judicial branch provides some oversight of the intelligence services, Kazakh law does not provide for an independent judiciary.[63] The country's judiciary remains heavily dependent upon the executive branch, according to the NGO Freedom House's Nations in Transit 2020 report.[64] Judges are subject to political influence, and corruption is a problem throughout the judicial system. [65] Additionally, prosecutors have the authority to suspend court decisions.[66] It seems highly unlikely that the judiciary will either play a role in oversight of the intelligence services themselves or provide an avenue for other organizations' attempts to provide oversight.

In short, the intelligence services remain under the direct service of the Office of the President and the direct control of the powerful former president Nursultan Nazarbayev as chairman for life of the NSC. Whatever oversight of the intelligence agencies that exists is run by Nazarbayev. Given the consolidated power and existing corruption, it is reasonable to assume that oversight of the Kazakh intelligence services is minimal.

CONCLUSION

The Republic of Kazakhstan's intelligence culture has evolved over its three-decade history from a fairly weak intelligence service as a reaction against the Soviet KGB into a strong intelligence service under absolute control of the president and the chair of the NSC, an agency that has become remarkably similar to the KGB. Kazakhstan attempts to project an image of increased democratization and openness with the 2021 election's three slogans—transition, competition, and pluralism—in a "post-Nazarbayev" era.[67] Yet, these slogans do not appear to reflect the actual direction of either the Kazakh government or the intelligence culture.[68]

While the Kazakhstan intelligence agencies have formed and re-formed over the past three decades, they appear to reemerge in a model not inconsistent with the Kazakh KGB. Most telling is former president Nazarbayev's decision to consolidate all intelligence services under the NSC, have his chairmanship of the NSC confirmed for his lifetime, and only then step down from the presidency in favor of his chosen successor. This reflects neither transition, competition, nor pluralism.

The history of intelligence use in Kazakhstan, including the recent consolidation putting these services directly under Nazarbayev's control, tightened recruitment into the Kazakh intelligence services, and its concerns with presidential succession and government stability will likely continue into the foreseeable future. Intelligence culture is shaped by Kazakhstan's global and regional neighborhood and domestic developments. Domestically, the intelligence services are reflecting their authoritarian roots with intensified surveillance of their citizenry and suppression of opposition political parties and domestic uprisings. Internationally, Kazakhstan gets along well with its Central Asian neighbors as the largest and most successful state in the region. It also has amicable relations with its great power neighbors of Russia and China, although fears and suspicions remain. The relationship with the United States is one of balancing those great power neighbors.

The domestic and international demands on the Kazakhstan intelligence services occurs in an environment where there are few restrictions and little oversight of its intelligence. Not only are the intelligence services directly controlled by the powerful former leader and directly report to his chosen presidential successor, but also the ministries in charge of aspects of intelligence are neither transparent nor subject to their own independent oversight. As the Kazakh intelligence agencies have formed and re-formed over the past three decades, they appear to have returned to their original model and culture of the KGB, where all intelligences services are in tight control of the leadership.

NOTES

1. Anna Gussarova, "Kazakhstan Moves to Expand, Strengthen National Security Council," *Jamestown Foundation Eurasia Daily Monitor* 15, no. 22 (February 13, 2018), https://jamestown.org/program/kazakhstan-moves-expand-strengthen-national-security-council/.

2. Dosym Satpaev, "An Analysis of the Internal Structure of Kazakhstan's Political Elite and an Assessment of Political Risk Levels," in *Empire, Islam, and Politics in Central Asia*, ed. Tomohiko Uyama (Sapporo, Japan: Hokkaido University, Slavic Research Centre, 2007), 283–300.

3. Gussarova, "Kazakhstan Moves to Expand, Strengthen National Security Council."

4. Gussarova, "Kazakhstan Moves to Expand, Strengthen National Security Council."

5. Gussarova, "Kazakhstan Moves to Expand, Strengthen National Security Council."

6. "On Approval of the Regulation on State Security Service of the Republic of Kazakhstan—Decree of the President of the Republic of Kazakhstan Dated May 4, 2014 No. 814, and updated June 13, 2019," Ministry of Justice of the Republic of Kazakhstan, 2019, https://adilet.zan.kz/eng/docs/U1400000814.

7. "On Approval of the Regulation on State Security Service of the Republic of Kazakhstan."

8. "Kazakhstan Country Report," Crisis 24, 2021, https://crisis24.garda.com/insights-intelligence/intelligence/country-reports/kazakhstan.

9. "Why They Assigned Syrbar to the NSC," KazakhSTAN 2.0, June 21, 2019, https://kz.expert/en/news/analitika/1514_why_they_assigned_syrbar_to_the_nsc_.

10. "How to Enter the Academy of the National Security Committee of the Republic of Kazakhstan and the Academy of the Border Guard Service of the National Security Committee of the Republic of Kazakhstan," e.gov, April 14, 2021, https://egov.kz/cms/en/articles/wkola_fknb.

11. Aigerim Seisembayeva, "Kazakh President Given Right to Head National Security Council for Life," *Astana Times*, July 13, 2018, https://astanatimes.com/2018/07/kazakh-president-given-right-to-head-national-security-council-for-life/.

12. Seisembayeva, "Kazakh President Given Right to Head National Security Council for Life."

13. "Kazakhstan Country Report."

14. Reuters Staff, "Kazakh Ruling Party Sweeps Vote Criticized as Uncompetitive," Reuters, January 10, 2021, https://www.reuters.com/article/us-kazakhstan-election-result/kazakh-ruling-party-sweeps-vote-criticised-as-uncompetitive-idUSKBN29F0K5.

15. Reuters Staff, "Daughter of Former Kazakh Leader Leaves Key Senate Post," Reuters, May 2, 2020, https://www.reuters.com/article/us-kazakhstan-nazarbayeva/daughter-of-former-kazakh-leader-leaves-senate-speaker-post-idUSKBN22E080.

16. E. S. Petrenko and A. L. Shevyakova, "Features and Perspectives of Digitization in Kazakhstan," in *Ubiquitous Computing and the Internet of Things: Prerequisites for the Development of ICT*, ed. E. Popkova, Studies in Computational Intelligence 826 (Cham: Springer, 2019), https://doi.org/10.1007/978-3-030-13397-9_91.

17. "Freedom on the Net 2020—Kazakhstan," Freedom House, 2021, https://freedomhouse.org/country/kazakhstan/freedom-net/2020.

18. "Freedom on the Net 2020—Kazakhstan."

19. "Estonia Hit by 'Moscow Cyber War,'" BBC News, May 17, 2007, http://news.bbc.co.uk/go/pr/fr/-/2/hi/europe/6665145.stm.

20. United Nations, "E-Government Survey 2020," United Nations Publications, 2020, https://publicadministration.un.org/egovkb/Portals/egovkb/Documents/un/2020-Survey/2020%20UN%20E-Government%20Survey%20(Full%20Report).pdf.

21. Petrenko and Shevyakova, "Features and Perspectives of Digitization in Kazakhstan."

22. "Freedom on the Net 2020—Kazakhstan."

23. "Freedom on the Net 2020—Kazakhstan."

24. "Freedom on the Net 2020—Kazakhstan."

25. Catalin Cimpanu, "Extensive Hacking Operation Discovered in Kazakhstan," *ZDNet*, November 23, 2019, https://www.zdnet.com/article/extensive-hacking-operation-discovered-in-kazakhstan/.

26. Pierluigi Paganini, "Russia-Linked APT Group DustSquad Targets Diplomatic Entities in Central Asia," Security Affairs, October 16, 2018, https://securityaffairs.co/wordpress/77165/apt/russia-linked-apt-dustsquad.html; Catalin Cimpanu, "Extensive Hacking Operation Discovered in Kazakhstan," supra.

27. "Kazakhstan Country Report."

28. "Kazakhstan Country Report."

29. "Kazakhstan Country Report."

30. "Kazakhstan Country Report."

31. "Kazakhstan's Economy to Recover Modestly in 2021, but COVID-19-Induced Poverty on the Rise, Says World Bank," World Bank, January 29, 2021, https://www.worldbank.org/en/news/press-release/2021/01/29/kazakhstan-economic-update-december-2020.

32. "Why They Assigned Syrbar to the NSC."

33. Adam Hug, ed., "No Shelter: The Harassment of Activists Abroad by Intelligence Services from the Former Soviet Union," Foreign Policy Centre, November 2016, https://fpc.org.uk/publications/noshelter/.

34. Hug, "No Shelter."

35. "Kazakhstan Country Report."

36. "Kazakhstan Country Report."

37. UN Office on Drugs and Crime, "Central Asia Intelligence-Sharing Centre Inaugurated in Kazakhstan," *UNODC Milestones Newsletter*, January 2010, https://www.unodc.org/documents/centralasia/Newsletter13_eng.pdf.

38. "World Drug Report 2021," UN Office on Drugs and Crime, 2021, https://www.unodc.org/unodc/en/data-and-analysis/wdr2021.html.

39. "UNODC Presents the Concept of the Survey of Kazakhstan's High-Risk Drug Use," UN Office on Drugs and Crime, March 4, 2021, https://www.unodc.org/centralasia/en/news/unodc-presents-the-concept-of-survey-of-kazakhstans-high-risk-drug-use.html.

40. "Central Asia Intelligence-Sharing Centre Inaugurated in Kazakhstan."

41. James Pach, "Interview: Victor Robert Lee," *The Diplomat*, November 6, 2015, https://thediplomat.com/2015/11/interview-victor-robert-lee/.

42. Andrei Soldatov and Irina Borogan, "Russia's Very Secret Services—Analysis," Institute of World Politics, May 2019, https://www.iwp.edu/wp-content/uploads/2019/05/20131119_SoldatovBoroganRussiasVerySecretServicesAnalysis.pdf.

43. Soldatov and Borogan, "Russia's Very Secret Services."

44. Hug, "No Shelter."

45. Thomas Grove, "A Spy Case Exposes China's Power Play in Central Asia," *Wall Street Journal*, July 10, 2019, https://www.wsj.com/articles/a-spy-case-exposes-chinas-power-play-in-central-asia-11562756782.

46. Temur Umarov, "What's behind Protests against China in Kazakhstan?," Carnegie Moscow Center, October 30, 2019, https://carnegie.ru/commentary/80229.

47. James Durso, "U.S. Bases in Central Asia: Where Will They Go?," Defense. Info, May 5, 2021, https://defense.info/re-shaping-defense-security/2021/05/u-s-bases-in-central-asia-where-will-they-go/.

48. Pach, "Interview: Victor Robert Lee."

49. Grove, "A Spy Case Exposes China's Power Play in Central Asia."

50. Grove, "A Spy Case Exposes China's Power Play in Central Asia."

51. OSC Analysis, "Kazakhstan—Opening Up for Nuclear Collaboration," Open Source Center via FAS.org, October 6, 2009, https://fas.org/nuke/guide/kazakhstan/osc100609.pdf

52. Bureau of South and Central Asian Affairs, "U.S. Relations with Kazakhstan: Bilateral Relations Fact Sheet," US Department of State, January 20, 2021, https://www.state.gov/u-s-relations-with-kazakhstan/; Jonathan S. Landay, "US and Kazakhstan Complete Secret Transfer of Soviet Nuclear Materials," *Christian Science Monitor*, November 17, 2010, https://www.csmonitor.com/World/Asia-South-Central/2010/1117/US-and-Kazakhstan-complete-secret-transfer-of-Soviet-nuclear-materials.

53. Eric Schmitt and Helene Cooper, "How the U.S. Plans to Fight from Afar after Troops Exit Afghanistan," *New York Times*, April 15, 2021, https://www.nytimes.com/2021/04/15/us/politics/united-states-al-qaeda-afghanistan.html.

54. Durso, "U.S. Bases in Central Asia."

55. Kanat Altynbayev, "Kazakhstan Approves Military Intelligence Deal with Kyrgyzstan in Sign of Closer Regional Ties," Central Asia News, May 28, 2019, https://central.asia-news.com/en_GB/articles/cnmi_ca/features/2019/05/28/feature-01.

56. "Kazakhstan Country Report."

57. Altynbayev, "Kazakhstan Approves Military Intelligence Deal with Kyrgyzstan."

58. "Freedom on the Net 2020—Kazakhstan."

59. "Kazakhstan: Banned Opposition Group Calls for Protests in Multiple Cities May 7–9," Crisis 24, May 6, 2021, https://www.garda.com/crisis24/news-alerts/475536/kazakhstan-banned-opposition-group-calls-for-protests-in-multiple-cities-may-7-9.

60. Anna Gussarova, "Kazakhstan Experiments with Surveillance Technology to Battle Coronavirus Pandemic," *Jamestown Foundation Eurasia Daily Monitor* 17, no. 47 (April 8, 2020), https://jamestown.org/program/kazakhstan-experiments-with-surveillance-technology-to-battle-coronavirus-pandemic/.

61. "Rethinking Engagement between Intelligence Services and Civil Society," DCAF Thematic Brief, Geneva Centre for Security Sector Governance, March 17, 2021, https://www.dcaf.ch/rethinking-engagement-between-intelligence-services-and-civil-society.

62. "Rethinking Engagement between Intelligence Services and Civil Society."

63. "2020 Country Reports on Human Rights Practices: Kazakhstan," US Embassy in Kazakhstan, January 2021, https://kz.usembassy.gov/2020-country-reports-on-human-rights-practices-kazakhstan/

64. "2020 Country Reports on Human Rights Practices."

65. "2020 Country Reports on Human Rights Practices."

66. "2020 Country Reports on Human Rights Practices."

67. Paolo Sorbello, "The Illusions of Post-Nazarbayev Kazakhstan," *The Diplomat*, February 1, 2021, https://thediplomat.com/2021/01/the-illusions-of-post-nazarbayev-kazakhstan/.

68. Sorbello, "The Illusions of Post-Nazarbayev Kazakhstan."

11

Kyrgyzstan: Seeking Stability in a Complex Region

Réjeanne Lacroix

Kyrgyzstan is a unitary parliamentary republic centrally located on the Eurasian steppes. The rise and fall of regional empires, local tribal interactions, and later experiences with imperialism have all played notable roles in the history and development of what has come to be known as the modern conception of the Kyrgyz Republic. This chapter explores the development of Kyrgyz intelligence culture from its republican origins to ongoing challenges in its post-Soviet existence. A reliance on Russian intelligence services for development and guidance on operational intelligence as a distinctive factor; however, domestic crises within the Central Asian republic have subsequently compelled Kyrgyz practitioners to look inward and focus on domestic political security. At the same time, the strategic location—between regional powers China and Russia—has compelled foreign actors, as well as regional intergovernmental security organizations, to seek a foothold in the Kyrgyz security sector.

This chapter is organized in four sections that highlight how Kyrgyzstan's intelligence culture is demonstrative of a state that prioritizes stability because it has withstood a turbulent postindependence experience. The first part provides a background on Kyrgyzstan's past being intertwined with Russian and Soviet history. The second section provides a historical overview of intelligence with special attention to the Soviet Union's role. Then the chapter examines country-specific issues, as well as key events, including a series of political upheavals. Lastly, it explores oversight, the limits of reform, and international intelligence relations.

BACKGROUND

In October 1864, the Treaty of Tarbagatai (or Chuguchak) established Central Asian boundaries that favored the Russian Empire, thus causing the Qing Dynasty to lose a significant part of Kyrgyz territory and constituent population.[1] Kirghizia became a subordinate subject of the Russian Empire formally in 1876 and liable to follow Russian decrees. Decades later, during the tumultuous period of the Russian Revolution (1917–1923), Kyrgyzstan had its most notable interactions with a secret police agency—the Extraordinary Commission to Combat Counter-Revolution or the Cheka.

Central Asian borders shifted during the early decades of Soviet development. To emphasize this point, the dissolution of the Turkestan Autonomous Soviet Socialist Republic (April 30, 1918–October 27, 1924) resulted in the foundation of the diverse Central Asian Soviet Socialist republics and autonomous oblasts, including the Kara-Kyrgyz Autonomous Oblast (now Kyrgyzstan and a section of Uzbekistan), the Tajik Autonomous Soviet Socialist Republic (ASSR—replaced by the Tajik Soviet Socialist Republic in 1929), Uzbek SSR, and the Turkmen SSR. Shortly after, the territory was renamed the Kirghiz Autonomous Oblast, and it was successively updated to the position of an Autonomous Socialist Soviet Republic in 1926.

Soviet intelligence and secret police services similarly transformed during this time as well. From the early 1920s to the early 1950s, intelligence services were dismantled and reconfigured numerous times, with such organizations as the Joint State Political Directorate (OGPU) (1923–1934) and later the notorious People's Commissariat for Internal Affairs (NKVD) (1934–1946) affecting Kyrgyzstan. Additional intelligence services followed, but it was only until the creation of the Committee for State Security (KGB) in 1954 that the Soviet Union found a lasting intelligence service. Membership in the Union of Soviet Socialist Republics (USSR) resulted in the creation of regional KGB offices, which meant the individual Central Asian republics gained preliminary proficiencies in the creation and management of intelligence operations. Modern visions of the future Central Asian republic continued to mature as its final configuration as the Kirghiz Soviet Socialist Republic emerged in 1936 and lasted until the disbandment of the USSR in its entirety in 1991.

The Soviet experience expedited the modernization of Kirghizia, not only regarding infrastructure but also in organizational structures related to bureaucracy and intelligence. Still, since independence, Kyrgyzstan has struggled with domestic political insecurity, the threat of Islamist terrorism, and uneasy internal relations with minority ethnic groups. Each of these issues have shaken recent Kyrgyz history and therefore highlight the role of intelligence in its journey as a sovereign state. The State Committee for National Security (UKMK) is the top intelligence agency that manages security threats related to terrorism, deals with transnational organized crime, and conducts counterterrorism operations.[2] This unique set of challenges coupled with its status as a post-Soviet state have contributed to the conception of a novel Kyrgyz intelligence culture and its subsequent maturation.

HISTORY OF INTELLIGENCE

The early twentieth century witnessed Kyrgyzstan emerge as a subordinate territory under early Soviet leadership. As a result of the challenges in establishing administrative divisions, perpetual crises and rebellions stemming from frustration in the predominant agrarian class, deportations, and organized resistance against Soviet policies followed. Intelligence was a vital aspect for these events to keep leadership informed and counter threats to security.

The roots of Kyrgyz intelligence extend to the establishment of a local presence of early Soviet secret police and intelligence affiliates. Agencies such as the Cheka were tasked to defend the Bolshevik revolution thus resulting in broad responsibilities as well as absolute authority over civil and military society.[3] It was their duty to root out any subversion in Red Army ranks as well as any anti-Soviet sentiment espoused by former tsarist officials, the clergy, the aristocracy, or any organized groups.[4] Membership in the secret police ballooned by the tens of thousands over the course of the Russian civil war as officers were present at the national, provincial, city, or town level, therefore allowing it to reach the farthest flung regions of the empire, including Kyrgyzstan.[5] In the same vein, the OGPU facilitated the deportations of respected Kyrgyz tribal elders.[6] This was done so that entrenched tribal hierarchies that were considered an impediment to further Sovietization were removed. It may be daunting to imagine the breadth of surveillance and infiltration needed to reach the fringes of the Central Asian constituent territories, but these early encounters paved the way for modern intelligence practices to take root in regions lacking administrative frameworks.

A lack of qualified ethnic Kyrgyz authorities meant that the secret police relied on Russian leadership and cadres to facilitate intelligence operations. This factor combined with the Stalinist-era push for centralization meant that the promise of Kyrgyz republican autonomy acquired in 1936 was largely meaningless.[7] The USSR, however, continued to develop its organs across its empire within its diverse republics, including its intelligence and security services.

The establishment of the KGB in 1954 meant that the creation of a republican office of the Committee for State Security of the Kyrgyz Soviet Socialist Republic immediately followed. At the republican level, the Kyrgyz KGB was tasked with the suppression of any internal dissent by way of information collection against those engaged in opposition movements and counterintelligence activities. Nearly seventy years of Soviet engagement in Kyrgyzstan mostly resolved the issue of a lack of trained intelligence and security officials in the Central Asian republic. This left an apparatus for the establishment of new agencies once the USSR collapsed. At the same time, the intelligence apparatus that was developed during the Soviet period has resulted in KGB-trained intelligence officers who remain active in former republics like Kyrgyzstan.[8]

Askar Akayev became the first president of the independent Kyrgyz Republic in 1991 and moved swiftly to establish intelligence functions in the country. On November 20, 1991, he signed a presidential decree that dismantled the regional KGB office and established the State Committee for National Security. Duties centered on specific issues relevant to Kyrgyz national security interests such as the collection of intelligence to counter terrorism, subversion by disenchanted groups, and organized crime. It cooperates with the Ministry of the Interior to ensure national security. Changes in structure and integrated agencies have occurred since its foundation, and these moves have typically aligned with regime changes as well as the need to centralize objectives.

Kyrgyzstan has experienced severe instances of political insecurity that have resulted in leaders being toppled from power. Askar Akayev—who faced serious allegations of corruption, authoritarianism, and a fraudulent parliamentary election—was overthrown during the Tulip Revolution that lasted between March 22 and April 11, 2005. Soon after, Kurmanbek Bakiyev was elected with an overwhelming majority in the July 2005 elections, obtaining a mandate that prompted changes in all areas of governance, including the military and security sector. The objective of presidential protection led to the creation of a special division of the security services known as Arstan in 2009. Under the direction of Bakiyev, Arstan was tasked with the protection of the president and his closest associates while also being engaged in operations to neutralize any threat of the military or security services opposing him.[9]

Bakiyev centralized power around the presidency and filled key positions with loyalists.[10] For instance, he named his brother, Zhanysh Bakiyev, as head of the state security service—a role he would resign from in 2006 upon his implication in a scheme where heroin was planted in the luggage of an opposition leader.[11] Zhanysh Bakiyev later sought protection in Belarus;

however, additional scandals plagued the family (including the former president's son Maksim). His conviction in absentia for murder, graft, and corruption by Kyrgyz authorities also followed his time in the highest-ranking Kyrgyz intelligence position.[12]

The year 2010 was another explosive political one for Kyrgyzstan, and the intelligence community experienced modifications as well. First, in the early days of April, a series of violent protests and counteractions by security forces began in the capital of Bishkek, only to reach other regions of the country, particularly Issyk-Kul, Naryn, and Tokmok. On April 15, Bakiyev—under fire for allegations of authoritarianism, economic mismanagement, and a hike in energy rates unsustainable for the majority of the impoverished country—resigned from the presidency and sought exile, first in Kazakhstan and later in Belarus. This series of events came to be known as the People's April Revolution. Tensions continued, and on June 9, violence reached the southern Kyrgyz districts of Osh and Jalal-Abad, which consequently resulted in ethnic clashes between Kyrgyz citizens and the Uzbek minority. Interim president Roza Otunbayeva advised the security forces to use deadly force to neutralize the riots.[13] It was telling that Artsan was unable to protect Bakiyev and the security forces struggled to contain the riots.

Intelligence and security services were undoubtedly affected during this tumultuous period. The interim government of Otunbayeva dismantled the state security service due to its compromised history and previous complaints of nefarious behavior, such as widespread corruption.[14] This political crisis was shortly followed by a national constitutional referendum in June 2010 in which Kyrgyz citizens decided the path forward rested in a parliamentary system.

A peaceful transition of power from the Otunbayeva administration to the elected Almazbek Atambayev administration occurred in December 2011, and Atambayev's leadership endured until November 2017. During this period, there was generally good political security, but matters of terrorism and the role of Kyrgyz foreign fighters affiliated with the Islamic State (IS) dominated Central Asian discourse. It was also a time in which Kyrgyz intelligence was focused on countering the threat of terrorism and the government stoked fears of IS infiltration to counter political oppression.[15]

Political crisis returned to Kyrgyzstan in 2020. On October 6, violent protests swept Bishkek over the results of the parliamentary elections held two days prior. Protesters contended that then prime minister Sooronbay Jeenbekov bought votes and felt that the numbers did not reflect the support for the Mekenchil (Patriotic) opposition party.[16] Voters were drawn to the nationalist party as their platform touched on their frustrations rooted in perpetual economic stagnation that had been escalated in light of the COVID-19 pandemic and the inability of the government to manage the crisis. During the skirmishes, Jeenbekov ordered the security forces not to use lethal force, which differed from previous political responses to unrest.[17] Jeenbekov eventually resigned on October 15, and Sadyr Japarov—a former member of Parliament and Kyrgyz nationalist who had been released from serving a prison sentence when protesters captured a government building—was eventually elected to the highest office in Kyrgyzstan on January 10, 2021.[18]

This brief overview of contemporary Kyrgyz history demonstrates that its intelligence and security services have been called to act in periods of political destabilization and when threats of terrorism emerged. At the same time, personal pursuits for power have influenced the responsibilities and abilities of the intelligence services. Kyrgyz political culture is centered on personal connections and interest, which likely is also true of the mentality in the national intelligence culture. Even still, the intelligence services remain aware of regional developments as state instability can easily be exploited by those with disreputable agendas.

COUNTRY-SPECIFIC ISSUES

Kyrgyzstan is unique in a Central Asian context as it has struggled with seamless transitions of power in comparison to its neighbors. This is primarily because the country instituted constitutional reforms and engages in regular elections, unlike regional leaders who retain power for lengthy periods. As a result, academic literature and journalistic discussions refer to Kirghizia as an "island of democracy" in Central Asia.[19] Roles of the intelligence and security services have been amended during specific presidential periods to suit the needs of the relevant leader or state objectives. Indeed, the security services have come under scrutiny for their links to corruption and their inability to defend the state internally during political convulsions. The lack of political security, a reliance on outside help—primarily Russian—as well as the threats stemming from Islamist terrorism and transnational crime are the main country-specific issues.

The stability of the seventy-year Soviet period provided Kyrgyzstan with the means to develop a modern intelligence apparatus that has undoubtedly left an influence on how information gathering and operations are conducted. Unexpected revolutions and a political system based on personal connections, however, disrupted any continuity that facilitated unified state security objectives. Thus, Kyrgyz intelligence culture continues to be in its developmental stages as it has not been provided with enough consistency to become truly nationally entrenched.

National character of any state activities requires time to manifest and become intrinsic to the understanding of how a state organizes itself internally and how it interacts externally. As demonstrated with the political eruptions in Kyrgyzstan, the intelligence culture has not been provided with the adequate means to take root because it has remained basically in flux since independence. While the Soviet system left foundations and an ethos on how intelligence services were to conduct themselves, the services transitioned to being either a political tool for personal politicking by particular presidents and their inner circle or attempting to manage oppositional forces that perpetually threatened the unity of the state. Disruption has become such a hallmark of the Kyrgyz situation that Russian president Vladimir V. Putin noted, "Every time they have an election, they practically have a coup . . . this is not funny" when remarking about the COVID-19-related protests and election of Japarov.[20]

Since Kyrgyzstan lacked the internal footing to establish intelligence services immediately after its independence, it sought guidance from known efficient state practitioners. The new Kyrgyz republic intelligence services found themselves in a conundrum as departing KGB officers who once staffed their local republican branch removed classified operational files, which left an informational void. Additionally, intelligence officers stationed in the region worked not only in Kyrgyzstan but also in neighboring countries. This created a situation in which knowledge of state matters could be easily compromised.[21] The National Security Service faced informational isolation because it did not possess the staff nor established streams of incoming information to continue the gathering of relevant intelligence.[22] It is a significant challenge to inaugurate a new agency without the guidance of an established and extremely knowledgeable partner.

The Russian Federation, through its leadership of the Commonwealth of Independent States (CIS), provided an avenue for the authorities in Bishkek to receive intelligence assistance and cooperate with regional partners. Member states entered into cooperative intelligence agreements—as well as the Collective Security Treaty of the CIS that led to the creation of the intergovernmental military alliance of the Collective Security Treaty Organization (CSTO) in 2002—that permitted states to engage regionally but maintain their sovereignty. For Kyrgyzstan, engagement with the CIS offered the ability to engage regionally at the same level as its neighbors, the means to skirt away from contradictions over security matters, and maintain enough distance to protect its independence.[23] At the same time, Russian leadership meant that its intelligence agencies were prioritized. Moscow had the ability to connect not only with Bishkek through regional security channels but also bilaterally with the Federal Security Service (FSB) and the Foreign

Intelligence Service (SVR), acknowledged as regional leaders that could provide expertise. Indeed, Russian and Kyrgyz intelligence ties are strong particularly for this reason.

The risk of terrorism and the broad reach of transnational organized crime have been noteworthy security threats to Kyrgyzstan, and its intelligence services view them as timely country-specific issues. Bishkek emerged as a willing participant in the early days of the global war on terror. Soon after its commencement, Kyrgyzstan declared international terrorism and religious extremism as primary threats against national, regional, and international security.[24] This has been a contentious issue as scholars argue over the validity of these claims in regard to Central Asia. Recent developments, such as the infiltration of IS, its franchising of once localized extremist groups, and the issue of foreign fighters from Central Asian republics denote that security risks are perceptible. Nonetheless, some academics contend that the Kyrgyz authorities began viewing all sociopolitical activities related to Islam as fundamentalist activity preluding conflict.[25] This led to the view that the risk has been inflated not only by governments but also by Islamist extremists themselves as a means to appear more powerful.[26]

The Islamic Movement of Uzbekistan (IMU) was the most prominent violent nonstate actor in southern Kyrgyzstan. The IMU were internationally notorious for their deadly attacks across Central Asia as part of their overall objective to destabilize governments, overthrow leadership, and establish an Islamic state in the Ferghana Valley—a parcel of land spanning territory included in Kyrgyzstan, Tajikistan, and Uzbekistan. During the 2001 US intervention in Afghanistan, the IMU suffered severe losses of foot soldiers, which began a slow disintegration and abandonment of its state-building objectives. At first, Kyrgyz authorities acknowledged the threat from the IMU drastically declined, but later, the intelligence services highlighted the risks of regional Islamist terrorism and intensified their counterterrorism operations.[27]

While the original IMU may have been defeated, its remnants continue engaging in violent extremism. In 2016, a new faction emerged that used the IS name but remained independent from the organization overall. It stated that it remained loyal to the Taliban, al-Qaeda, and other traditional Islamist extremist groups active in Pakistan, Afghanistan, and Central Asia.[28] Other groups, such as Hezb-ut-Tahrir and the East Turkestan Liberation Organization (ETLO), have also been designated as terrorist organizations in Kyrgyzstan.

Transnational organized crime continues plaguing Kyrgyzstan and demands the attention of the security services. Narcotics trafficking remains the main criminal threat, and Kyrgyzstan's central location—as well as its remote and porous borders—allows for the uncomplicated transit of illicit goods. In a typical scenario, narcotics begin their journey in Afghanistan, transit through Kyrgyz territory, thus making their way to Russian and European black markets.[29] Membership in the CSTO has subsequently resulted in Kyrgyz involvement in long-term endeavors that focus on the trafficking of narcotics and other illicit goods, such as Operational Kanal (Channel). In 2018, Kanal was undoubtedly deemed a success with the United Nations Office on Drugs and Crime (UNDOC) commenting it "made significant inroads into blocking illegal drug smuggling from Afghanistan to Europe."[30] Nonetheless, organized crime and black market activities remain active threats that must be proactively contended by the collection of relevant information by Kyrgyz law enforcement, intelligence agencies, and security services.

OVERSIGHT, REFORM, AND INTERNATIONAL CONNECTIONS

Intelligence oversight and reform are more nuanced in Kyrgyzstan than in other Central Asian countries. More often than not, calls for enhanced supervision and changes to the security services are linked to the attitudes about holding onto power. In the Kyrgyz context, those who promote good governance and democratization prioritize holding intelligence agencies to account for their actions while those who prefer personalized politics that typically broaden the scope of the services' apparatuses to provide political security.

In the traditional sense, the UKMK is a member of the Security Council of Kyrgyzstan. The Security Council is a constitutional body with advisory duties that is part of the presidential office tasked with providing timely counsel to leadership on intelligence, military, and law enforcement matters. Its meetings have even been broadcast live on Kyrgyz national television.[31] One can easily deduce that since the UKMK is a member of the Security Council (which in turn is a branch of the Office of the President), then the Kyrgyz president is the true overseer of Kyrgyz intelligence.

In the period following the People's April Revolution in 2010, political momentum focused on the creation of good governance, transparency, and liberalization meant that the actions of the security services were scrutinized. In March 2011, under the guidance of Otunbayeva, a series of volunteer-led Public Advisory Councils (PACs) were created. These councils have the ability to monitor executive branch activities, including the Ministry of Internal Affairs, and have access to relevant government records.[32] Indeed, this was an initiative to ensure citizen participation in the supervisory process of particular government bodies that directly influenced civilian lives.[33] The PACs creation was undoubtedly a laudable effort to ensure a semblance of transparency, but it has been a difficult endeavor to remain relevant in subsequent changes of presidential authority. Advisory councils remain active in Kyrgyz political affairs despite these obstacles.

There has been little perceptible intelligence reform in Kyrgyzstan, but there have been attempts to remedy intelligence community problems. One can easily reflect upon Akayev's establishment of the first intelligence service in the early days of Kyrgyz independence as well as the 2010 constitutional amendments where the security services were dismantled and subsequently recreated as a similar government organ that it replaced. For the most part, intentions to reform the security services have been policy objectives without any sort of political will or initiative to compel changes to come to fruition. There are two reasons for this stalemate. First, it is difficult to pursue such a thorough endeavor when state and political security is threatened on a routine basis due to factors related to sociopolitical deficiencies. Second, the UKMK is entangled in the Kyrgyz political culture based on personalities and their political power. Additionally, the continued threat and mind-set espoused by the global war on terror compels authorities in Central Asia to strengthen the abilities of their intelligence services, rather than audit their performance and take up significant changes. Dismissal of staff, including those in high-ranking positions, has been the typical remedy for accusations of corruption in the security services.

The Kyrgyz intelligence and security services demonstrate their international connections through active engagements in regional partnerships and bilateral dialogue. Moscow remains the undisputed closest partner of Bishkek in all matters related to military, security, and intelligence. At the same time, the UKMK has dealt with Turkey, the United States, and Uzbekistan, albeit with varying degrees of closeness.[34] Intelligence sharing and objectives to streamline interagency cooperation with Tajikistan have happened as well.[35] It is easily deduced that these relationships are rooted in the need to collaborate against the cross-border national security threats of ethnic extremism, terrorism, and organized crime. For instance, it has been noted that though Bishkek has an occasionally rocky relationship with Tashkent, they have engaged bilaterally as an act of mutual convenience to counter terrorist organizations, such as the IMU.[36]

The United States keeps a keen eye on Kyrgyzstan as it offers a strategic location for its regional military objectives. Shortly after the terrorist attacks of September 11, 2001, and the United States' intervention in Afghanistan, Bishkek—with the agreement of Moscow—permitted the US military to use the airfield at Manas as a logistics and refueling center. This arrangement lasted until June 2014. The United States consequently believed that opportunities for deeper engagement would result from the tilt toward greater democratization during the 2010 political upheavals and constitutional changes; however, that was not the case. Kyrgyzstan continues relying on Russia, and its security sector will continue to work closely with them.

Membership in regional organizations, primarily the CSTO and the Shanghai Cooperation Organisation (SCO), are perhaps the strongest avenues for Kyrgyzstan to concurrently engage with regional powers and neighbors regarding intelligence sharing. Security threats stemming from transnational organized crime and terrorism have been prioritized in both organizations. In the late 1990s, the Shanghai Five framework of the SCO was established to include major powers China and Russia along with the Central Asian republics of Kazakhstan, Kyrgyzstan, and Tajikistan in a collaboration mechanism to share intelligence and cooperate on regional security matters. Additionally, Kyrgyz involvement in the SCO—and closer relations with Beijing—expanded to inclusion in the Regional Anti-terrorism Structure, with the main objectives to counter extremism and armed groups, as well as manage a database of known terrorist organizations.

Involvement with the CIS and the CSTO remains the touchstone of regional intelligence cooperation in the Kyrgyz context. Early in its origins, all member states of the CIS agreed to share intelligence and collaborate on security matters. This move consequently led to the creation of the CIS Council of Directors of Security Agencies and Special Services that regularly meets under the chairmanship of the Russian FSB.[37] Further regional connections centered on Russian leadership began to take shape as well. For instance, the Anti-Terrorism Center (ATC) in Moscow was established in June 2000 as a hub for all member states to coordinate activities and engage in intelligence exchanges.[38] Bishkek received even greater attention with the establishment of an ATC branch in 2002. Its director is a Russian colonel, and besides Kyrgyz authorities, it shares the space with representatives from Kazakhstan and Tajikistan.[39] In conclusion, it is evident that through involvement with intergovernmental organizations and bilateral relations, Kyrgyz authorities are well tuned to engage with partners that hold similar intelligence and security objectives, both domestically and regionally.

CONCLUSION

Kyrgyz intelligence culture is difficult to pinpoint as a stand-alone phenomenon. It remains tied to Soviet foundations and a challenging political environment since independence. While the post-Soviet state has a functional intelligence apparatus, a lack of political security due to eruptions of popular discontent resulted in a situation where important government bodies have not had time to mature or develop a uniquely Kyrgyz ethos. Key intelligence services remain influenced by personal politicking characteristic of Kyrgyz power dynamics and a reliance on external mentorship remains the norm for the foreseeable future.

This arrangement may be the best solution for Kyrgyzstan for the time being as stable governance seems elusive due to concerns over government inefficacies and a myriad of socioeconomic problems. The identifiable security threats of extremism, terrorism, and transnational crime require the attention of the intelligence services and security forces on an immediate and ongoing basis. Cooperation with regional security alliances that foster intelligence sharing and strong bilateral relationships—primarily with Russia—strengthen the abilities of the Kyrgyz intelligence services so that they are indeed the guarantors of republic security.

Though Kyrgyzstan has struggled to foment a distinguishable intelligence culture since its independence, an intrinsic Kyrgyz philosophy will emerge as the state continues its development as a sovereign entity, realizes a political routine, and achieves a foothold in the Central Asian neighborhood.

NOTES

1. Chia Ning, "Kyrgyz," in *Encyclopedia of Chinese History*, ed. Michael Dillon (New York: Routledge, 2017), 360.

2. "Antïterror" [Anti-terror], Gosudarstvennyy Komitet Natsional'noy Bezopasnosti Kyrgyzskoy Respubliki [State Committee for National Security of the Kyrgyz Republic], 2021, https://gknb.gov.kg/antiterror.

3. Tim Wilson, "Cheka (Chrezvychaynaya komissiya)," in *Russian Revolution of 1917: The Essential Reference Guide*, ed. Sean N. Kalic and Gates M. Brown (Santa Barbara, CA: ABC-CLIO, 2017), 32.

4. Wilson, "Cheka (Chrezvychaynaya komissiya)," 32.

5. Wilson, "Cheka (Chrezvychaynaya komissiya)," 32.

6. Benjamin H. Loring, "Rural Dynamics and Peasant Resistance in Southern Kyrgyzstan, 1929–1930," *Cahiers du Monde Russe* 49, no. 1 (2008): 200.

7. John Anderson, *Kyrgyzstan: Central Asia's Island of Democracy?* (New York: Routledge, 1999), 9.

8. Stéphane Lefebvre and Roger N. McDermott, "Russia and the Intelligence Services of Central Asia," *International Journal of Intelligence and CounterIntelligence* 21, no. 2 (2008): 254.

9. Erica Marat, *Security Sector Reform in Central Asia* (Geneva: Geneva Centre for Democratic Control of Armed Forces, 2012), 26, https://issat.dcaf.ch/download/15983/187285/RPS_13_SSR_Central_Asia.pdf.

10. Marat, *Security Sector Reform in Central Asia*, 21.

11. C. J. Chivers, "Kyrgyzstan: President's Brother Ousted," *New York Times*, September 13, 2006, https://www.nytimes.com/2006/09/13/world/asia/13briefs-002 .html.

12. "Former Kyrgyz Leader's Son Sentenced in Absentia for Graft," Reuters, March 27, 2013, https://www.reuters.com/article/us-kyrgyzstan-sentence-idUSBRE 92Q0UF20130327.

13. Fred Weir, "Kyrgyzstan Authorizes Deadly Force on Wave of Riots, Looting," *Christian Science Monitor*, April 21, 2010, https://www.csmonitor.com/World/ Asia-South-Central/2010/0421/Kyrgyzstan-authorizes-deadly-force-on-wave-of-riots -looting.

14. Marat, *Security Sector Reform in Central Asia*, 26.

15. Thomas F. Lynch III, Michael Bouffard, Kelsey King, and Graham Vickowski, *The Return of Foreign Fighters to Central Asia: Implications for U.S. Counterterrorism Policy* (Washington, DC: Institute for National Strategic Studies, 2016), 13, https://inss.ndu.edu/Portals/68/Documents/stratperspective/inss/Strategic -Perspectives-21.pdf.

16. Olga Dzyubenko and Olzhas Auyezov, "Coronavirus Lit Fuse in Kyrgyzstan, Spreading Unrest in Putin's Backyard," Reuters, October 8, 2020, https://www .reuters.com/article/us-kyrgyzstan-protests-pandemic-analysis-idUSKBN26T2ML.

17. Oleg Burunov, "All You Need to Know about Protests in Kyrgyzstan," *Sputnik*, October 6, 2020, https://sputniknews.com/asia/202010061080680389 -all-you-need-to-know-about-protests-in-kyrgyzstan/.

18. "Ex-MP Sadyr Japarov Freed from Prison, Arrives at Ala-Too Square," *AKI Press*, October 6, 2020, https://akipress.com/news:649116:Ex-MP_Sadyr_Japarov _freed_from_prison,_arrives_at_Ala-Too_square/.

19. Anderson, *Kyrgyzstan*, 23.

20. Mariya Gordeyeva and Andrew Osborn, "Pandemic Protests Test Putin's Influence in Ex-Soviet Space," Reuters, November 2, 2020, https://www.reuters.com/ article/us-health-coronavirus-russia-kyrgyzstan-idUSKBN27I0F5.

21. Lefebvre and McDermott, "Russia and the Intelligence Services of Central Asia," 270.

22. Lefebvre and McDermott, "Russia and the Intelligence Services of Central Asia," 270.

23. Lefebvre and McDermott, "Russia and the Intelligence Services of Central Asia," 271.

24. Mariya Y. Omelicheva, *Counterterrorism Policies in Central Asia* (New York: Routledge, 2014), 69.

25. Omelicheva, *Counterterrorism Policies in Central Asia*, 27–28.

26. Omelicheva, *Counterterrorism Policies in Central Asia*, 69.

27. Omelicheva, *Counterterrorism Policies in Central Asia*, 69.

28. Bill Roggio and Caleb Weiss, "Islamic Movement of Uzbekistan Faction Emerges after Group's Collapse," *Long War Journal*, June 14, 2016, https:// www.longwarjournal.org/archives/2016/06/islamic-movement-of-uzbekistan-faction -emerges-after-groups-collapse.php.

29. Overseas Security Advisory Council, "Kyrgyzstan 2019 Crime and Safety Report," US Department of State, June 27, 2019, https://www.osac.gov/Country/Kyrgyzstan/Content/Detail/Report/ac8fa4f9-e878-4c0c-b059-161f682cc4e1.

30. "UNODC Participates as an Observer in the Regional Anti-narcotic Operations Channel," United Nations Office on Drugs and Crime, June 1, 2018, https://www.unodc.org/rpanc/en/Sub-programme-1/unodc-participates-as-an-observer-in-the-regional-anti-narcotic-operation-channel.html.

31. Anastasia Mokrenko, "Meeting of Security Council of Kyrgyzstan to Take Place Today," *24.kg*, December 24, 2020, https://24.kg/english/177806__Meeting_of_Security_Council_of_Kyrgyzstan_to_take_place_today/.

32. Marat, *Security Sector Reform in Central Asia*, 21.

33. Marat, *Security Sector Reform in Central Asia*, 21.

34. Lefebvre and McDermott, "Russia and the Intelligence Services of Central Asia," 277.

35. "Working Meeting of Reps of Intelligence Agencies and Border Guards of Kyrgyzstan, Tajikistan," *Kabar*, November 4, 2019, http://en.kabar.kg/news/working-meeting-of-reps-of-intelligence-agencies-and-border-guards-of-kyrgyzstan-tajikistan/.

36. Lefebvre and McDermott, "Russia and the Intelligence Services of Central Asia," 278.

37. Lefebvre and McDermott, "Russia and the Intelligence Services of Central Asia," 258.

38. Lefebvre and McDermott, "Russia and the Intelligence Services of Central Asia," 258.

39. Lefebvre and McDermott, "Russia and the Intelligence Services of Central Asia," 259.

12

Laos: Intelligence Culture with Internal Threats and External Actors

Hans Lipp

It is challenging to write about Lao intelligence because the services' structure is hidden under the visible structure of the internal security apparatus of the Lao People's Revolutionary Party (Phak Pasaxon Pativat, LPRP). The party is a small and self-contained community with its own rules, which is mirrored in the intelligence and security services. While the country's population is small, the Laotian informant and informer network for the intelligence and security services is nearly unlimited in size. Every person is a potential small cog in the state's machinery, and most people do not know their respective roles because they were never asked for their participation. Laos is an autocratic state, comparable to North Korea in terms of systemic structures in Asia, which may come as a surprise to those traveling through the seemingly easy-going country.[1]

This chapter explores Laos's intelligence and security culture by tracing its history and draws from secondary sources, including academic studies and media outlets. Organized in seven sections, it argues that Laos's intelligence culture throughout history has been marked by internal security concerns but involves outside actors for training, information, and operations. The first section provides a brief background, providing an overview about the country and population. In the second section, the chapter explores the intersection between French colonialism and security. The third section examines security and intelligence shortly after Laos's independence with attention to security challenges and internal stability. In the fourth section, the Lao monarchy and its security is analyzed with attention to the United States' influence and its limitations in security. The fifth section explores the establishment of the Communist Lao People's Democratic Republic government with attention to coercion and its efforts in dismantling the royalist structures. The sixth section reviews Communist countries' relationships with Laos and influence in the security sector. In the seventh section, the chapter examines the main ministries involved in security and intelligence with attention to their leadership and the role ethnicity plays. The conclusion describes the intelligence culture by highlighting the permissive environment where state actors behave with impunity and foreign actors have an important role in security.

BACKGROUND

The origins of Laos's intelligence and security culture begin with the country's history as a largely empty territory without major population centers but having scattered and small communities in a rugged landscape. The people tried to protect themselves against enemies from outside the local community. The need for knowledge about the potential dangers led to the creation of information networks so the villagers could protect themselves. From this, an all-and-everything culture of surveillance and intelligence emerged in the local community that did not end with the relative security during the colonial period.

During the first half of the nineteenth century, the population was less than 150,000 men, women, elders, and children, as well as fewer "men of military age" in a territory more than two and a half times the size of present-day Austria. Indeed, large parts of Southeast Asia appeared to European travelers as "space without people."[2] Scholar Volker Grabowsky argues that the rulers of that time were less concerned with the control of the country than with the people living in the country.[3] The regional rulers regarded the indigenous, local population as a resource of immense importance for their military and economy. Thus, every member of the local communities was significant for the rulers' ambitions.

Taking into account the relationship among the country's size, topographical structure, dense forestation, and thin population density, the theory of "tribal security" can be applied to Laos's intelligence culture to understand the performance of intelligence, security-related tasks. Tribal security can only be performed by people who were local residents from birth.[4] In fact, there was a special designation for the administration of the royal, aristocratic security structures within the *phrai* or *lek* (quasi serfs of the king or local rulers). These were the *lek dan* (border leks), who were designated to patrol the vaguely defined borders (mandala states) of the kingdom and between the *muang* (administrative units, principalities).[5]

COLONIAL DREAMS AND REALITY

External security was the main focus in signing treaties that shaped the Laotian principalities into a French protectorate. For the French, the security of Vietnam depended on denying rebels the use of sanctuaries. Colonel Tournier, the first resident-general of Laos, argued that taking possession of Laos was a political necessity for the security of Vietnam and Cambodia.[6] The internal security and relationship with the indigenous population remained essentially a matter for the local rulers. In fact, the relationship between the local population and the colonial power was established by the Indigenous Guard (Garde Indigène); the few French in the country depended on themselves for security, and the military had only a limited role with Indigenous Guard officers and partly with the Security (Sûreté) officers.

The country became structured in two parts: a northern part (with its capital Luang Prabang) and a southern part (its capital is today a rather unimportant town, Khong at Khone Island). Both were headed by a *commandant supérieur* who answered to the *gouverneur general* of Indochina, who resided in Hanoi. The north was structured into six commissariats, and the south had seven with administrators responsible for security in their areas.[7] An October 20, 1911, decree for the Indochinese Union provided administrative and financial autonomy. This decision had far-reaching consequences in terms of personnel and material for Laos's internal security.

After January 1, 1914, military detachments for Laos, Yunnan, and Quang-Tcheou-wan were connected to the detachment in Annam Tonkin. The Annam Tonkin Division, under a captain and headquartered in Hanoi, had a strength of 140 soldiers. Although personnel adjustments were made over the following years, the ratio of personnel to the region's size reveals much about the limited presence of the police force.[8]

The establishment of a civilian police force was largely an illusion during Laos's colonial era. It failed because no civilian administration gained a foothold in large parts of the country. Policing for internal security remained the Garde Indigène's task until February 27, 1909, when the gendarmerie arrived in Laos, first in Luang-Prabang. More posts were established later but were constrained by budget cuts.[9] Executive power in colonial Laos remained militarized despite some agents of the National Security (Sûreté Nationale) and the Garde Indigène's power. They were commanded by French officers who were subordinate to the governor-general in Hanoi, who delegated authority to the *résident supérieur* (minister) in Vientiane that consisted of two-thirds to three-quarters of "civilized" Vietnamese. The Guard—though poorly trained, armed, and paid—was the first modern police force in Laos.[10] The colonial period consisted of a succession of rebellions and uprisings by mostly ethnic groups. These were usually triggered by various types of tax demands (often paid with *corvée*—forced labor) to finance the establishment of the colony and thus also the security apparatus.

World War II led to the 1941 establishment of the Laotian Hunter Battle (Batallion de Chasseurs Laotiens, BCL), which was equally an army and general security force.[11] Indeed, the Franco-Thai War and World War II brought about the militarization and civilian regression of state structures, which were only weakly developed on Laotian territory. Intelligence structures had always been mostly militarized and remained so under the Vichy and Japanese occupation regimes.

While the occupations initially brought little change, it led to the dismantling of French administrative and security structures. This was triggered by the liberation of metropolitan France in Europe and the short-lived takeover by Japanese troops that lasted only five months. The reconstruction of French administration proved nearly impossible after the war and ultimately led to decolonization. Thus, the colonial security apparatus was not invincible but showed the population that it was based on their cooperation. Following World War II and the first Indochina War until Laos's 1953 independence, the country proved to be extremely unstable and offered "some room for adventurous and even criminal procedures and structures, especially in the secret and security service sector."[12]

FROM EARLY INDEPENDENCE

By 1947, the first Lao police service named the Indochinese Police and Immigration Service (Service de la Police et de l'Immigration Indochinoise) under the command of Pheng Souvannavong was established in the Lao Ministry of Interior under French control. It never exceeded thirty personnel, and its main objective was to "control aliens and maintaining law and order."[13] In December 1949, it was absorbed by the newly founded Lao National Police. That same year a rural police force called Laotian Gendarmerie Forces (Forces de Gendarmerie Laotiennes) was created under the Ministry of Defense; however, it never reached more than half of its authorized personnel strength and suffered from the poor education and training of its members (about 20 percent were illiterate). In 1950, it was dissolved with members partly integrated into the newly established Gendarmerie Royal during February 1951.

Attempts at modernizing the police force proved challenging due to the ethnic-rooted police forces in Xieng Khouang. In particular, "Lao ethnic policemen performed their police duties starting in 1949" when France offered autonomy leading to independence, making police separate from the military.[14] After 1950, training was given to police officers throughout the Laos kingdom, and Hmong police training started in 1955. Additionally, independent urban police forces founded in the few bigger cities and the Federal Security (Sûreté Federale) were probably part of the administrative coordination for internal security in the final period of French colonialism.[15]

On November 9, 1948, the Lao National Police's new French administrator, Jean Deuve, who organized the police force, was appointed and served until he was replaced by Lao officials in late 1952. Meanwhile, the United States began supporting French security efforts until the 1960 Kong Le coup. Deuve, an officer with the External Documentation and Counter-Espionage Service (Service de Documentation Extérieure et de Contre-Espionnage, SDECE) created the Intelligence Service of Laos in 1945 and was its director until 1948. He also led the Psychological Warfare Service of the Royal Government of Laos and then served as political adviser to the president of the Council of Ministers of the Royal Government of Laos until 1964.[16]

In 1953, a large air base was established near Savannakhet, in southern Laos at Seno, by military and policy makers who realized that the French Empire in Indochina was ending. After 1954, the air base served as a training center for the newly formed Laotian army but was also a surveillance center for Communist forces' communication lines in China. This role remained under French army control until the 1960 Kong Le coup, which marked a steady reduction of French personnel until the complete occupation by Laotian socialist forces at the end of June 1963.[17] The August 10, 1960, attempted coup was led by Kong Le, a young paratrooper captain who belonged to the neutralist faction in Laos. Possibly with implicit support from the French still in the country, his ire was directed against rampant corruption in the government and US influence. Kong Le was defeated, but nonetheless his attempted coup ushered in the end of French influence over the military and security services in Laos.

The coup did not achieve its objectives but marked a turning point as the country entered a phase of lawlessness and loss of French influence. This notably included the expulsion of French units from their last significant Lao base. The police forces were removed from control of the Ministry of Interior and placed under the Ministry of Defense. In reality, the paramilitary groups of the Directorate of National Coordination commanded by Colonel Siho were criminal gangs operating outside existing laws. Subsequently, an exodus of personnel left a gutted, dysfunctional police force.

In September 1962, a high-profile public security official reported that there was inadequate leadership, poor management and training, improper communications, lack of resources, "poor rapport with the population," and negative consequences of military control after January 1961.[18] Thus, during the Second Indochina War, there was no centrally controlled, functioning police and security structure in Laos. The inability to monitor remote settlements and border areas created room for China and Vietnam to take over areas near the border and extend influence into Laotian territory. It also enabled actors to engage in a wide range of illegal activities, such as drug production and smuggling.

FROM UNITED STATES INFLUENCE TO LAOTIAN MONARCHY

The United States took over French positions and believed that the internal security problem in Laos could be solved with substantial financial support. This was a serious misunderstanding of the country's security situation in the 1960s. The 1965 Walton Report demonstrated how US donors saw security issues from a perspective and ignored basic facts about the country's structural-, educational-, and population-related reality. Most specialists, technicians, and qualified theorists were sent to Laos for just a few months and had limited contact with local officials, which impeded their ability to learn about the actual security environment. Moreover, there was only a small number of foreign citizens living throughout the country.[19]

The Walton Report laid out a new structure for a Lao national police force but did not describe how to implement the plan.[20] Frank Walton, a high-ranking officer working for the US State Department, also ignored to a large extent the Laotian reality. This is why the United States sought to use methods, organization, and technology that were incompatible with Laotian conditions. As the specialists and consultants changed with regularity, the United States became frustrated with the lack of success. Between the United States' official withdrawal in October 1973 and the final Communist takeover on December 2, 1975, the national police rapidly disintegrated.

The problems were not so much the personnel and hierarchical structures of the police force implemented by foreign influence but, rather, the curricula at the police academy that was grossly out of step with the reality of the country.[21] Indeed, the security structures installed by the United States and the royal Laos government provided clear evidence of the lack of sustainability. The paramilitary forces set up by General Siho Lanphouthacoul as the Directorate of National Coordination (Directorate National de Coordination, DNC) and the Hmong army maintained by the Central Intelligence Agency and General Vang Pao in mountainous northeastern Laos were the only quasifunctioning elements of a security apparatus. Both forces were financed and operated outside the existing legal framework. Although they were focused on military operations, they also took on police tasks and were financed in significant parts by illegal activities such as drug trafficking and extortion, among other things.[22]

THE COMMUNIST TAKEOVER

Following a civil war, the Communist forces overthrew King Savang Vat-thana, and Kaysone Phomvihane emerged as the country's leader in December 1975. With the successive, mostly non-sudden displacement of pro-royal forces, the security apparatus was increasingly indoctrinated even before the final seizure of power through infiltration, gradual undermining of existing structures, or by simply taking willing existing employees and adapting them to the new emerging system. Indeed, senior members of the former royal Lao government apparatus who resisted "reeducation" in camps, called *semana*, often faced execution.

Before the Communist forces of the Lao People's Liberation Army (Pathet Lao) completely took over the government, members of the royal police forces and representatives of the royal Laotian administration had the choice of retreating to government-controlled territory or actively integrating into the Pathet Lao forces due to the lack of support from the official government during the 1960s.

The Communist influence started during the first Indochina war with the Soviet Union's support, and from the mid-1950s East Germany's state security provided development aid.[23] The destruction of the weakly developed structures of the royal Laotian government was gradual over the decades. It was a "step-by-step" takeover of the remaining legal framework until it transformed into the socialist Sino-Vietnamese administrative apparatus.

SOCIALIST LINKS FOR SECURITY

The new security structure involved appointing personnel to command a military region. China and Vietnam reacted to these practically lawless areas near their borders with efforts to control them by sending in its own military and security forces as well as administrative units. Border provinces, such as Phongsali, Udomxai, and Luang Namtha, came under Chinese influence, while Hua Phan, Xieng Khouang, and large areas of southeastern Laos fell under Vietnamese control. This was accompanied by the development of relatively open transportation, communications, and security structures.

Vietnam extended its communication networks far across the border. It is also likely extended the use of methods and technologies of internal as well as external reconnaissance received from East Germany.[24] To avoid the appearance of colonization, development tasks, including security, were led by smaller satellites of the Soviet Union. Yet as far as the role of development aid, East Germany was dominant in Vietnam and Laos. Additionally, China increased involvement in the northern part of Laos by building camps that had been transformed into settlements and later even cities as well as large-scale military and social infrastructure.[25] Since German-Laotian contacts were on a personal basis due to the lack of conventional administrative structures, however, they acquired an extraordinary quality and proved enduring.[26] Until the Soviet Union's and Communist Europe's collapse, the Lao People's Democratic Republic was closely connected to Communist Europe. In fact, news reports in the late 1980s discussed Viktor M. Chebrikov, head of the Soviet Committee for State Security (Komitet Gosudarstvennoy Bezopasnosti, KGB), visiting Vietnam and Laos in coordinating socialist intelligence services.[27]

The conflict between Vietnam as a regional power and China's strategy began with the second Indochina war. After the 1975 Communist takeover of Laos, the new government borrowed heavily from Vietnamese military, security, and intelligence structures. In fact, Vietnam was seen as the big brother of Laos until the collapse of the socialist bloc. Vietnam's strategy in Laos could be seen as a slow "reintegration" of land into its national territory as it developed the Laotian administration to Vietnamese standards. The Soviet Union's collapse created space for China taking over the leadership of Laotian structures in Laos and territory.

The Laotian security apparatus structure is mostly speculation because its internal structures are at best laid down in nonpublic party documents. Since Vietnam has been the dominant force in administrative development in Laos, Laos's security structure could be described based on Vietnamese structures by taking Laotian conditions into account (see figure 12.1).

The Vietnamese influence is currently weakening because parts of Laos's administration have been under Chinese influence, and Chinese-dominated areas of Laotian territory gain aid from China under highly politicized auspices.[28] China, as many observers noted with the Belt and Road Initiative, follows a stricter colonial pattern for control than France ever could. The Chinese influence sometimes goes directly and deeply into government structures.

In 2021, there was a notable indication of Chinese influence. The Lao People's Revolutionary Party (Phak Pasaxon Pativat, LPRP) bureau issued a directive on February 15, 2021, for dissolving the Ministry of Science and Technology, and its different departments were integrated into five different other ministries such as the Post, Telecom and Communications; Ministry

Lao Security Intelligence & Complex (Speculative Theory)

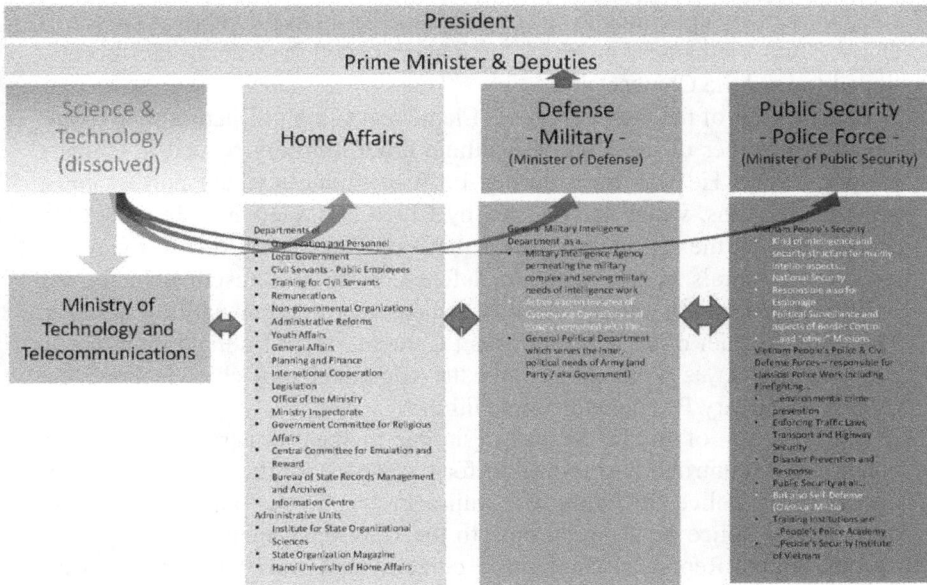

President

Prime Minister & Deputies

Science & Technology (dissolved)	Home Affairs	Defense - Military - (Minister of Defense)	Public Security - Police Force - (Minister of Public Security)

Ministry of Technology and Telecommunications

Departments of
- Organization and Personnel
- Local Government
- Civil Servants - Public Employees
- Training for Civil Servants
- Remuneration
- Non-governmental Organizations
- Administrative Reforms
- Youth Affairs
- General Affairs
- Planning and Finance
- International Cooperation
- Legislation
- Office of the Ministry
- Ministry Inspectorate
- Government Committee for Religious Affairs
- Central Committee for Emulation and Reward
- Bureau of State Records Management and Archives
- Information Centre

Administrative Units
- Institute for State Organizational Sciences
- State Organization Magazine
- Hanoi University of Home Affairs

General Military Intelligence Department as a:
- Military Intelligence Agency permeating the military complex and serving military needs of intelligence work
- Action system involved in Covert area Operations and assets connected with the
- General Political Department which serves the inner, political needs of Army (and Party / aka Government)

Vietnam People's Security
- Kind of intelligence and security structure for mainly interior aspects...
- National Security
- Reconnaissance also for Espionage
- Political Surveillance and aspects of Border Control ...and "other" Missions

Vietnam People's Police & Civil Defense Forces – responsible for classical Police Work including Firefighting
- ...environmental crime prevention
- Enforcing Traffic Laws, Transport and Highway Security
- Disaster Prevention and Response
- Public Security at air...
- Riot and Self-Defense (Combat Militia)
- Training Institutions are: People's Police Academy, People's Security Institute of Vietnam

Figure 12.1. Speculative model of the Laotian security and intelligence complex.
Source: Phaybounе Thanabouasy, 'Government of Laos Dissolves Ministry of Science and Technology," *The Laotian Times*, March 1, 2021, https://laotiantimes.com/2021/03/01/government-of-laos-dissolves-ministry-of-science-and-technology; Yasmina Yap, "Who is Who in the Laotian Government," *The Laotian Times*, May 6, 2018, https://laotiantimes.com/2018/05/06/whos-who-in-the-lao-government.

of Industry and Commerce; Ministry of Agriculture and Forestry; and the Ministry of Energy and Mines.[29] This appeared to move closer to China's administrative structures. Though China has consistently had influence in northern Laos, China has been extending its regional dominance southward by building strategic infrastructure, roads, bridges, and airfields. Indeed, there appears to be an ongoing displacement of traditional Vietnamese–Lao ties. Chinese interest groups in Laos have been preparing to replace more Vietnamese-oriented political leaders, especially those in the strategically important executive sector, with those more beholden and socialized to the Chinese world.

SECURITY AND INTELLIGENCE MINISTRIES

There are three ministries directly involved in intelligence. These are the ministries of public security, defense, and interior with personnel reflecting ethnic-political fault lines. For the past several years, there have been attempts to balance ethnic composition. There are indications of efforts within the Laotian security apparatus to strike a balance between the representatives of Chinese and Vietnamese interests, but it appears that the balance has recently tipped toward the Chinese side.

The minister of national defense is Lieutenant General Chansamone Chanyalath, a member of the Kim Mun ethnic group (closely related to China's Hmong-Mien). He was born during 1949 in Phongsaly, the northernmost province of Laos, which is enclosed by China and Vietnam. He joined the "revolution" at the age of fourteen in 1963. Besides being one of the country's few generals and minister of defense, he is also responsible for the militias used for both internal security and partially external national defense. The military chief of staff is Lieutenant General Suvon Luongbunmi, whose adoptive mother is Vietnamese, and the commander in chief is President General Secretary Bounnhang Vorachith.

The Ministry of Public Security (similar to the Ministry of Interior in many other countries) is responsible for the police forces, traffic, immigration, security police (including riot, railroad, and border police), as well as other armed police units. According to the US Department of State's 2020 Human Rights Report, it "monitored citizens' activities through a surveillance network that included secret police," and "laws allow the government to monitor individuals' movements and private communications, including via mobile telephones and email without a warrant."[30] The relatively unknown Vilay Ladkhamfong holds the position of minister and has been additionally appointed deputy prime minister.[31] He was born and raised in the Chinese-founded and heavily Chinese-dominated Muang Xai, the capital city of the northern Laos province of Oudomxai.

The Ministry of Interior (similar to the Ministry of Home Affairs in many other countries) has a complicated portfolio because it was previously two ministries in the seventh government. The tasks of the interior and secret services are directly under the Office of the Prime Minister. From April 2015 until October 2020, the minister of interior has been Khammanh Sounvileuth; born on April 12, 1952, in Khoua District of Phongsaly Province, he belongs to the Lao Theung ethnic group. Sounvileuth previously served as governor of Bokeo and Phongsaly provinces and vice president of the Control Council of the Party Central Committee. Another notable former minister of interior who served until 2002 was Asang Laoly. Born on February 2, 1941, in Phongsaly Province, Laoly has been the deputy prime minister since 2002. His previous positions include minister of interior and deputy minister of interior with responsibilities consistently being intelligence.

CONCLUSION

Laos's pervasive security complex is apparent throughout its history, and the power of the military is present in all spheres of daily life. More recently, there has been a marked change toward a more "civilian" orientation within the culture. In 2000, SIPRI's published financial allocations of Laos's defense sector showed decreasing budgets until 2013 (which was the last year figures were published).[32] Since then, there has been a shift from the military budget to militias, which are controlled by the military but are not in the military budget. Financial aspects, however, are more a matter of detail in Laos as the power of the security apparatus can best be seen with the numerous dissidents who have disappeared at home and abroad.

Sombath Somphone is an internationally known land rights activist, agricultural scientist, and development worker. Following his December 2002 arrest, kidnapping, and eventual disappearance without a trace from a busy street in the middle of Vientiane at an alleged police check, Sombath has become a symbol of the unpredictability of Laos's police and security services.[33] Sombath remains missing, which is reflective of a deeper trend. Thai dissidents are not only disappearing in Laos, but also Laos is a place where people disappear and sometimes their bodies are later found on the banks of the Mekong. The number of dissidents of both nationalities who have "disappeared" and are "disappearing" is growing.[34]

Meanwhile, a 2020 ceremony in Vientiane with Minister of Public Security Lakhamfong and the Chinese ambassador was marked by a symbolic gift that demonstrates joint Lao–Chinese security concerns. The ambassador gave a gift of emergency vehicles to the Laos police for fighting civil unrest and suppressing demonstrations.[35] The ceremony was held at a time of growing unrest in the Laotian population at the increasing Chinese dominance in the country. This event demonstrates two broader issues in Laotian intelligence culture: first, the intelligence and security services' orientation toward the "internal enemy" and, second, that such activities have been carried out or aided by external actors. Indeed, it appears Laos has returned to the times of Colonel Siho, the era of Vietnamese emperors, when foreign exchanges of intelligence training, information, agents, and wanted individuals was not unusual.

NOTES

1. Ralph Jennings, "See Who's Asia's No. 2 Police State after North Korea, and It's Not China," *Forbes*, December 27, 2016, https://www.forbes.com/sites/ralph jennings/2016/12/27/behind-the-smiles-laos-is-known-as-asias-no-2-police-state/?sh =2f7cf1295eda.

2. Volker Grabowsky, *Bevoelkerung und Staat in Lan Na* [Population and state in Lan Na: A contribution to population history] (Wiesbaden, Germany: Harrassowitz Verlag, 2004), xvii.

3. Grabowsky, *Bevoelkerung und Staat in Lan Na*.

4. Ted Shackley and Richard A. Finney, *Spymaster: My Life in the CIA* (Dulles, VA: Potomac Books, 2006), 142, 143.

5. Puangthong R. Pawakapan, "Warfare and Depopulation of the Trans-Mekong Basin," in *Warring Societies of Pre-colonial Southeast Asia: Local Cultures of Conflict within a Regional Context*, ed. Michael W. Charney and Kathryn Wellen (Copenhagen, Denmark: NIAS Press, 2017), 25.

6. Martin Stuart-Fox, "The French in Laos, 1887–1945," *Modern Asian Studies* 29, no. 1 (1995): 116.

7. Geoffrey C. Gunn, *Rebellion in Laos* (Bangkok, Thailand: White Lotus, 2005), 20–22.

8. Georges Lelu (via Le Cahier Toulousain), *La gendarmerie colonial: Grand livre d'or historique de la Gendarmerie Nationale* [The colonial "gendarmerie": The golden book of the National Police] (Toulouse, France: Le Cahier Toulousain; Tenue Bleu-Gendarme, Online Summary, 2018), http://tenuebleugendarme.free.fr/departe mentale/colonies_20s.html.

9. Lelu, *La gendarmerie colonial*.

10. Paul Chambers and Hans Lipp, "Earning Their Keep: The Political Economy of the Military in Laos," in *Khaki Capital: The Political Economy of the Military in Southeast Asia*, ed. Paul Chambers and Napisa Waitoolkiat (Copenhagen, Denmark: NIAS Press, 2017), 220.

11. Chambers and Hans Lipp, "Earning Their Keep," 220.

12. Alfred W. McCoy, *Politics of Heroin: CIA Complicity in the Global Drug Trade* (New York: Harper Colophone Books, 1991), 48, 131–46; Alfred W. McCoy, Catleen B. Read, and Leonard P. Adams II, *Politics of Heroin in Southeast Asia* (New York: Harper Colophone Books, 1973), 90–126.

13. Jean Deuve, *Histoire de la Police Nationale du Laos* [History of the Laos National Police] (Paris, France: L'Harmattan, 1998), 8.

14. Vang Geu, *Unforgettable Laos* (Mount Gilead, NC: n.p., 2011), https://www.unforgettable-laos.com/governing-system-in-m-rii/the-lao-hmong/.

15. Jean Marc Le Page, "Le renseignement politique en Indochine à l'épreuve de la vietnamisation de la Sûreté (1949–1955)" [Political intelligence in Indochina Put to the Test of the Vietnamization of the Sûreté (1949–1955)], *Guerres Mondiales et Conflits Contemporains* (September 2018): 1; Frank E. Walton, Paul H. Skuse, and Wendell Motter, *A Survey of the Lao National Police* (Washington, DC: Office of Public Safety, May 15, 1965), 31, 32.

16. Pierre Le Roux, "Avant-propos: Un homme tranquille" [Foreword: A quiet man], foreword to "La remontée du Mékong de Vientiane à Luang Prabang en 1947" (by Jean Deuve), *Moussons* 2 (2000), https://journals.openedition.org/moussons/4791?lang=en.

17. Le Page, "Le renseignement politique en Indochine," 16.

18. Walton et al., *A Survey of the Lao National Police*, 37.

19. Walton et al., *A Survey of the Lao National Police*, 99. The report discusses roughly sixty Westerners officially registered in Laos. Yet this is not accurate as US staff based in Laos exceeded the confirmed number by twenty-six. Additionally, French citizens apparently were not counted separately. Thus, official statistics are unreliable (Walton et al., *A Survey of the Lao National Police*, 99). The French population in 1907 reached 189 people. Other sources state around 350 French citizens on Lao territory at the peak in the 1930s. Grant Evans, *A Short History of Laos: The Land in Between* (New South Wales, Australia: Crows Nest, 2002), 59.

20. Walton et al., *A Survey of the Lao National Police*, 37–62. The report has seventeen charts and tables explaining the state of the country's national police at the time the report was written.

21. Walton et al., *A Survey of the Lao National Police*, 67–96.

22. Kenneth Conboy and James Morrison describe these forces as "the most competent military unit outside the CIA's Hmong guerilla program." Kenneth Conboy and James Morrison, *Shadow War: The CIA's Secret War in Laos* (Boulder, CO: Paladin, 1995), 105.

23. Martin Grossheim, "The East German 'Stasi' and Vietnam: A Contribution to an Entangled History of the Cold War," *International History Review* 42, no. 1 (2021): 136–52.

24. Grossheim, "The East German 'Stasi' and Vietnam."

25. Udom Xai was previously just a loose collection of villages that merged into a city under the influence of military road and supply base construction.

26. In December 2019, I had a conversation with a medical doctor (presumably almost seventy years old) at Wat Phousy in Luang Prabang. He spoke in good German about his positive experiences regarding the education in Halle an der Saale during the last years of the civil war—before 1975. He even rudimentarily performed German songs.

27. For example, "KGB Chief Off to Vietnam," *Los Angeles Times*, December 21, 1987, https://www.latimes.com/archives/la-xpm-1987-12-21-mn-20267-story.html.

28. Phayboune Thanabouasy, "Phongsaly Province Provides Assistance to Vietnam to Fight COVID-19," *Laotian Times*, June 2, 2021.

29. Phayboune Thanabouasy, "Government of Laos Dissolves Ministry of Science and Technology," *Laotian Times*, March 1, 2021.

30. Bureau of Democracy, Human Rights, and Labor, "2020 Country Reports on Human Rights Practices: Laos," US Department of State, March 30, 2021, https://www.state.gov/reports/2020-country-reports-on-human-rights-practices/laos/.

31. Ministry of Public Security, Government of Laos, 2021, http://www.laosecurity.gov.la/. Manyphone Vongphachanh, "Laos National Assembly Approves Cabinet Reshuffle and New Appointments," *Laotian Times*, June 20, 2022.

32. Data for Laos are available from 2000 to 2013 in "SIPRI Military Expenditure by Country as Percentage of Government Spending, 1988–2019," SIPRI, 2020, https://www.sipri.org/sites/default/files/SIPRI-Milex-data-1949-2019.xlsx.

33. Simon Creek, "Distressing Developments in Laos," *New Mandala* (Canberra, Australia), December 23, 2012, https://www.newmandala.org/distressing-developments-in-laos/; Richard Finney and Max Avary, "Lao Democracy Activist

Still Missing after a Year, as Thai Police Investigation 'Stalls,'" Radio Free Asia's Lao Service, August 25, 2020, https://www.rfa.org/english/news/laos/missing-08252020101554.html; James Giggacher, "What Happened to Sombath Somphone?," *New Mandala* (Canberra, Australia), March 27, 2014, https://www.newmandala.org/what-happened-to-sombath-somphone/.

34. Hanna Beech, "Thai Dissidents Are Disappearing, and Families Are Fighting for Getting Answers," *New York Times*, June 26, 2020. https://www.nytimes.com/2020/06/26/world/asia/thailand-dissidents-disappeared-military.html; Michael Sullivan, "Thai Dissidents Disappear or Turn Up Dead, Even after Escaping Nation," NPR, May 27, 2019, https://www.npr.org/2019/05/27/727358670/thai-dissidents-disappear-or-turn-up-dead-even-after-escaping-nation; "Thailand: Lao Refugee Feared 'Disappeared,'" Human Rights Watch, September 7, 2019, https://www.hrw.org/news/2019/09/07/thailand-lao-refugee-feared-disappeared; Eugene Wong and Sidney Khotpanya, "Few Answers on Missing Lao Citizens as World Marks Enforced Disappearance Victims," Radio Free Asia's Lao Service, August 28, 2020, https://www.rfa.org/english/news/laos/dissappeared-08282020173331.html.

35. "China Hands over Law Enforcement Vehicles in Assistance to Laos," Xinhua, October 25, 2020, http://www.xinhuanet.com/english/2020-10/25/c_139464967.htm.

13

Malaysia: Between Untenable Intelligence Tradition and Unrealized Reform

Scott Edwards

Malaysia's intelligence culture has been strongly defined by its historical development. Inheriting structures of colonial control and facing significant domestic turmoil in its formative years, the country's intelligence community is now centralized, secretive, and largely focused on internal political "threats."[1] The consolidation of rule by the leading National Front (Barisan Nasional, BN) coalition, until its first election loss in 2018, saw the development of a "partified" community that operates with general impunity under the control of the executive.[2] Despite successes in tackling perceived legitimate threats, it has largely served the political purposes of Malaysia's former ruling party with little democratic oversight. The distinction between regime protection and national security became increasingly blurred throughout its development. As a result, while intelligence officials are well trained and well organized—and possess strong expertise—the norms of the community have been problematic and its accountability to Malaysian society questionable.

Such practices, however, are increasingly being challenged. Malaysia's intelligence community has found itself the target of significant criticisms following the unprecedented defeat of the National Front regime. While Malaysia's politics remain turbulent—with the breakdown of the 2018 democratically elected coalition due to political infighting and maneuvering—appetite for reform and accountability seemingly continues to exist. This places the intelligence community at a difficult crossroads between increasingly untenable traditions of partified regime protection and unrealized reforms centered on de-politicizing the intelligence community.

This chapter primarily focuses on organizational and systemic variables—specifically history and traditions, organizational demographics, security issues, and external influences.[3] First, it maps Malaysia's intelligence agencies and their strong centralization under the executive. Second, it centers on the historical foundations of the community in line with the recognition that a community's early years are extremely important to its contemporary culture. In particular, it demonstrates why the intelligence culture is defined by secrecy and its inwardly political orientations.[4] Third, it highlights how these have become entrenched under the National Front's control as the community has responded to various significant events in Malaysia. Finally, the chapter focuses on reform attempts following the 2018 election. It demonstrates that, while there has been some movement toward reform and accountability, this has largely stalled, and the traditional norms underpinning the culture remain dominant.

MALAYSIA'S INTELLIGENCE COMMUNITY

Malaysia's intelligence community is constituted by three primary agencies: the Special Branch (Cawangan Khas, SB), the Defense Intelligence Staff Division (Bahagian Staf Perisikan Pertahanan, BSPP), and the Research Division of the Prime Minister's Department (Bahagian Penyelidikan Jabatan Perdana Menteri), also known as the Malaysian External Intelligence Organization (MEIO). There are other agencies with intelligence functions, though they tend to be more limited in scope or do not exclusively focus on intelligence. The Senoi Praaq (War People), for example, operates under the police and has a mandate for intelligence gathering among Malaysia's indigenous peoples (Orang Asli).[5] Many agencies also have their own intelligence units. Examples include the Malaysia Maritime Enforcement Agency, who has a surveillance unit and processes its own intelligence, and Malaysia's national bank's (Bank Negara) Financial Intelligence Unit.

The Special Branch is responsible for developing intelligence on a broad array of internal and external threats "to maintain law and public order."[6] As a part of the Royal Malaysian Police (Polis Di Raja Malaysia), it retains policing powers, such as authority to arrest, and has its own detention centers. The SB has reported either to the minister of home affairs or to the prime minister, directly through the Special Branch's director or the inspector general of the police.[7] It has roughly 8,000 personnel.[8] The BSPP is the military agency under Malaysia's Royal Intelligence Corps (Kor Risik Diraja) in Malaysia's armed forces. It provides intelligence to support defense functions, while also focusing on cyber threats, Malaysia's border regions, and surveillance.[9] The director reports to the minister of defense directly or through the chief of the armed forces.[10] Finally, the MEIO is focused in theory on external intelligence, though there are some overlaps and domestic focus due to the current emphasis on combatting terrorism. It has around 1,000 personnel.[11] As part of the Prime Minister's Department, the director general of the Research Division reports directly to the prime minister. The Special Branch remains the primary intelligence agency.

While some question the utility of referring to multiple agencies as a community due to the potential fragmented nature, Malaysia's intelligence community is highly coherent due to the centralized institutional structures that direct it. Intelligence in Malaysia is coordinated by a National Intelligence Council (Jawatankuasa Perisikan Negara).[12] This is chaired by the prime minister and supported by the National Intelligence Division.[13] The National Intelligence Council itself is a subdivision of the broader National Security Council (Majlis Keselematan Negara), supported by a staff in the National Security Division (Bahagian Keselematan Malaysia).[14] Through these bodies, which are also constituted by ministers of defense, foreign affairs, and communication and media, alongside the chief of defense forces and inspector general of the police, the prime minister ultimately wields executive control over intelligence. The National Security Council is effectively shielded from oversight due to a 2015 law that allows it to operate in absolute secrecy and blocks actions from being taken against it.[15]

COLONIAL FOUNDATIONS

The core cultural aspects of the community—its inward focus, prioritization of political affairs, secrecy, and relative impunity—all stem from its formative colonial years. The intelligence community, particularly the SB, emerged in response to the Malayan Communist Emergency that ran from 1948 to 1960. Countering this largely domestic pro-independence movement, the SB was established and staffed primarily by the British. When it replaced the Malayan Security Services, it began understaffed and under-resourced, with no independence from the Criminal Investigation Department (CID).[16] It emerged as an organization that significantly assisted the efforts against the Malayan Communist Party's guerrilla war: helping the military search for jungle camps and ambush enemy forces, guard settlements, and "turn" Communists to successfully map Communist forces.[17]

This had several implications. The SB was, first and foremost, a colonial entity that focused on colonial control to ensure a stable decolonization process. It secretly targeted sections of the Malayan population. While communism was its primary remit, it also focused Malay nationalism, the surveillance of public organizations and political leaders, and different ethnic "political matters."[18] This "intelligence trauma" had a lasting impression, driving the intelligence community to be inwardly focused and primarily concerned with political policing long after the fall of communism.[19] Practices that were used in the Emergency have continued in the postcolonial state, including the ability to detain without trial and "strong-arm" interrogation practices.[20] These were facilitated by the controversial Internal Security Act (ISA) that allowed for two-year detention that could be reviewed at the discretion of the home minister absent any input from the judiciary. While this was repealed in 2012, many of the practices are allowed for in the replacement Security Offences (Special Measures) Act (SOSMA) of 2012 with only minor judicial adjustments to the detention process.[21] Thus, the norm of impunity to act as required was facilitated by legal protections established during the Emergency.

INTERNAL CRISES

Malaya gained independence in 1957, but there was little in the way of significant changes for its intelligence community. The SB largely avoided the immediate "Malayanization" of the bureaucracy due to a lack of qualified personnel.[22] Many British officers carried on their duties, and it was only in 1960 that the SB gained its first Malay head.[23] As Ong Weichong argues, Malay elites chose to adopt virtually identical procedures and institutions.[24] While the next security threat was external in nature—armed confrontation (*konfrontasi*) with Indonesia—it was quickly resolved, and much of the intelligence focus was on the borders.[25] Instead, domestic crises once again raised to the fore. With the ruling "Alliance" coalition losing much of its support in the 1969 elections to what were perceived to be Chinese-dominated parties, sectarian violence broke out in Kuala Lumpur. This led to an emergency proclamation, which was only revoked in 2011, and concerns that Malay dominance of Malaysia was collapsing.

The riots have had several impacts on the intelligence community's culture. First, the riots, as well as the Second Communist Emergency running between 1968 and 1989, reinforced that Malaysia's primary "threats" and orientation were internal in nature.[26] It was not just the SB mobilized domestically but also the BSPP—with notable successes during the Second Emergency.[27] Second, these threats were seen along communal lines, and Malaysia's multiethnicity was presented as a significant security challenge.[28] The concept of Malay supremacy (*Ketuanan Melayu*) emerged as a result, which prioritized the Malay control of Malaysia. It aimed to legitimize the United Malay National Organization's (UMNO) rule by presenting itself as the only viable protector of Malay rights with the wider National Front coalition as the only viable means for ongoing stability.[29] Beyond influencing the community's threat perception, this also impacted on the organizational structure of the intelligence services. Like many of Malaysia's uniformed services they remain dominated by Malay personnel, and promotion prospects are poor for Chinese personnel—limiting non-Malay leadership.[30] At times, this lack of officers from other backgrounds has limited the effectiveness of the community.[31] Third, the riots led to the institutionalization of many ongoing structural features of the intelligence community, including the formation of the National Security Council (then called the National Operation Council).

PARTIFICATION

These dynamics have allowed for the partification of the intelligence services to emerge, which has resulted in the entrenchment of impunity and secrecy at the core of the community's culture. Timothy Edmunds refers to partification as the "rapaciously partisan co-option of security sector actors to a particular political party or personality."[32] As such, it goes beyond politicization, especially in terms of the severity of its excesses when working with a particular party. Following the 1969 riots, the Malaysian intelligence community was structured in a way that made it particularly vulnerable to co-option along these partisan lines. On a practical level, UMNO had held power since independence and centralized state apparatus under its control. This resulted in a regime referred to as hybrid or competitive authoritarian, where elections are held but the playing field is structured unequally to ensure the dominance of one party.[33] Intelligence was one of these apparatuses contributing to its maintenance of power.

Such centralization was difficult to criticize. The specter of 1969 has not been fully exorcised, and concerns of communal conflict are strategically manipulated to retain the veneer of legitimacy.[34] The National Front presented itself as the most viable means for ongoing stability, and Malaysia's national security was increasingly strategically intertwined with the need to protect the regime. With the legislature having no role in the formulation of defense policy—there is no parliamentary defense committee despite calls from opposition political parties—there have been few obstacles to this conflation.[35] Furthermore, even the opposition has generally accepted this justification of requiring order in the multicommunal society.[36] The broad acceptance of the need for order has resulted in a willing and mutually supportive relationship between Malaysia's primary political party and the intelligence community.

During the National Front's rule, multiple laws and instruments furthered the powers of the intelligence community due to challenges to its rule.[37] The

ISA and SOSMA were not the only controversial instruments that allowed the intelligence agencies to be used against Malaysian society. The Official Secrets Act of 1972, for example, has been heavily criticized for the breadth of documents that can be classified as secret. With primarily executive control and without any form of substantial legislative oversight, including of their budgets,[38] the agencies have been empowered to act without significant accountability.[39] Indeed, a 2005 Royal Commission into Police Reform noted that there were significant allegations that SB officers ill-treated ISA detainees and recommended that to make the SB more accountable its responsibilities needed to be clearly defined in law.[40]

As a result of this, the political functions of the intelligence agencies developed during the emergencies, and crises were well suited and well placed to be wielded against legitimate political opposition. This political function can be observed in numerous repressive actions. In 1988, for example, Operation Lalang saw the SB execute a major crackdown on more than 100 people including nongovernmental organization (NGO) activists and opposition politicians. While the justification was to prevent ethnic conflict, the targets were primarily those critical of then prime minister Mahathir Mohamad, and there is a general acceptance it was for political purposes.[41] It is not just those in the opposition that have allegedly been targeted. There are allegations that former home minister Ghazali Shafie utilized the SB to try and discredit Mahathir during UMNO's 1978 party elections, demonstrating the alleged willingness to employ state intelligence functions for political purposes.[42] In 1998, the SB gained significant attention when senior officers testified about their role in deputy prime minister Anwar Ibrahim's arrest for sodomy—a charge pursued due to the breakdown of his and Mahathir's relationship.[43] These are not merely isolated or historical cases. While many authoritarian actions aimed toward regime protection have been executed by the SB, such as surveillance of politicians and attending public gatherings, concerns have been raised by opposition politicians that the BSPP also has an increasingly political and domestic role.[44] The most controversial case in recent years saw a leaked letter demonstrating that the MEIO had requested support from the United States Central Intelligence Agency to buttress the ruling government in the 2018 election.[45]

This is not to say the intelligence community is absolutely and solely political. The Malaysian intelligence community has seen strong areas of success in more legitimate realms, especially terrorism and organized crime. Terrorism is a significant sector for the intelligence community with Malaysia taking seriously its perceived identity as a moderate Muslim country. In the years after 9/11, Malaysia arrested more than 100 suspects, including individuals connected to Jemaah Islamiyah, al-Qaeda, and the Islamic State.[46]

Malaysia has endured only a few attacks since 9/11, and the BSPP's focus on the borders and SB's intelligence-led activities have been significant in the effort to disrupt the use of Malaysia as a transit route.[47] They have also had strong success in tackling organized crime with a particular focus on human trafficking. Intelligence-led arrests have been made and corruption at Malaysia's borders was uncovered by the SB.[48] These successes have largely depended on the same tools and practices that enable the more controversial aspects of its culture, which demonstrates the difficulties of any potential transformations in the future. The repealing of ISA, for example, led to arguments that the SB was unable to do its job against organized crime.[49] It seems, furthermore, that co-option has played a role in limiting the legitimate activities of the intelligence community and that its successes are despite it, rather than because of it. There have been accusations from a retired general, for example, that the BSPP failed to detect militant movements because it was wrongly focused on internal political operations.[50] When investigating corruption in the 1Malaysia Development Berhad (1MDB) fund, which eventually implicated former prime minister Najib Razak, the deputy of the SB was dismissed, which halted the investigations.[51]

TOWARD REFORM?

Following the downfall of the National Front and the election of the opposition Alliance of Hope coalition (Pakatan Harapan), there were strong expectations that the culture of Malaysia's intelligence community would change. The shock of the MEIO letter permeated Malaysian society, and many of the now-ruling coalition leadership were those who had been targeted in the past. Significant reform—or a "de-partification"—faces continuing challenges, and it is unclear whether the culture of secrecy, impunity, and political involvement will be able to meaningfully change. So far only tentative steps have been taken.

Timothy Edmunds argues there are three levels required to attain a degree of Intelligence Security Sector Reform—political, organizational, and international—of which this chapter focuses on the political and organizational levels.[52] Broadly, the political level consists of the establishment and consolidation of civilian and democratic rule through independent legislative, judicial, or public oversight of its propriety or budget.[53] This is central to de-partification, as well as wider democratizing processes, because agency capabilities give them a powerful role in domestic politics, so some degree of accountability is required.[54] While Thomas Bruneau, Kenneth Dombroski, and Fred Schreier demonstrate that overseeing intelligence under the executive can work in some contexts, it is problematic in a context where executive control has led to partification.[55] In such circumstances, a well-equipped parliamentary oversight body for the budget and propriety provides separation of powers, but it is challenging to establish.[56] Norms of secrecy that define the intelligence community are in tension with norms of transparency that define democracy, and it requires parliamentary expertise that is difficult to develop.[57] Civil society can also provide a degree of oversight if there is a degree of dialogue and transparency established.[58] The organizational level is focused on internal reforms that shift these agencies from their authoritarian-era roles.[59]

So far, Malaysia has only met the bare minimum in terms of reform. The primary objective has been to remove the most politicized and compromised personnel and focus on the organizational level. The former head of the MEIO was dismissed from government service almost immediately after the election and was later arrested for corruption—as have some BSPP staff.[60] The director general of the BSPP, Lieutenant General Abdul Hadi Bin Haji Hussin, was removed shortly after. There was even discussion of shutting down the MEIO due to its overt political role.[61] The intelligence agencies also seem to have reorientated for their new roles.[62] They demonstrate greater degrees of responsibility by emphasizing, on the surface at least, the contribution they make to more legitimate threats such as terrorism and organized crime.[63] The SB, in particular, gives relatively regular media updates on its counterterrorism efforts and announced that it had successfully stopped assassination attempts against members of the new government.[64]

There has been no institutionalization of independent legislative oversight, including of intelligence budgets or propriety. As a result, impunity and secrecy remain central to the intelligence culture and continues to diminish its legitimacy. This makes it difficult to assess internal control, and an absence of transparency has prevented media and NGOs from providing analysis of the agencies' activities. As an example, SUHAKAM, Malaysia's Human Rights Commission, has accused the SB of being behind the enforced disappearance of multiple individuals.[65] Mahathir announced his intention to investigate once the inspector general of police (who was SB director at the time) retired. There has been no such investigation. The SB said it will not declare itself when monitoring political events such as news conferences, even if state ministers object.[66] Democratic principles do not seem to have yet permeated Malaysia's intelligence community, and it is therefore difficult to assess whether any sort of organizational changes have occurred more broadly or the extent to which they have instead created a blockage to reform. There has been the suggestion that some state institutions have been frustrating the reform process more broadly, especially as many police and military personnel are UMNO supporters or have enjoyed the benefits of corruption under UMNO's patronage. The SB, however, has apparently had the lowest corruption rates of all police branches.[67]

The limitations of reform may result from it being too soon. Oversight needs expertise to be effective, and this has not had the opportunity to develop in the Malaysian context.[68] Malaysia's turbulent political context, however, suggests that the continuity of the intelligence community's culture results just as much from the contemporary political dynamics it finds itself in—especially as there are significant constraints to transformation. For one, the Alliance of Hope prime minister in 2018 was Mahathir. He was accused of utilizing the intelligence apparatus for his own political means when he was prime minister for the former National Front coalition. The transformation from a state that had been ruled by one coalition had more continuity than other states may experience. Furthermore, the Alliance of Hope's rule was extremely short, and the coalition is no longer in power. While UMNO is not formally part of the new coalition, Perikatan Nasional, it depends on UMNO's support. Such political instability has the potential to stall willingness not just from politicians but also from the intelligence community. It further demonstrates why there have been significant limitations despite hopes for reform. How far the agencies are ready to embark on a genuine process of organizational reform remains unclear. The Malaysian intelligence community instead finds itself in a problematic crossroads. The agencies lack the initiative and desire to reform from within, and politicians seem reluctant to tackle reform head-on, whether due to their own complicity or general divisions.

CONCLUSION

Malaysia's intelligence community, constituted by three primary agencies, is heavily influenced by its history. Founded in a time of "intelligence trauma," practices enacted during the Communist Emergency were sustained well into the postcolonial state's development. With the former trauma of the 1969 riots, and continuing specter of communal conflict influencing national security perceptions, the intelligence agencies were directed internally as one of the tools to maintain domestic stability. They were also empowered to play this domestic role. With this role and the centralization of command under the executive, as well as a lack of democratic oversight, it made the intelligence community vulnerable to co-option by the dominant UMNO party. Its usage for regime maintenance and political control means that for much of its history it labored within a partified culture.

While the intelligence community is well trained, well resourced, and cohesive—which has contributed to some significant successes in the realms of counterterrorism and organized crime—there remain problematic norms of secrecy, impunity, and a political focus. Despite the fall of UMNO in 2018, the privileges and prerogatives that resulted from the community's historical development have not been significantly transformed. This puts the culture of the intelligence community in tension with increasing democratic norms. While there are some promising signs that the intelligence community could meet a more responsible role in a time of greater democratic governance, these have been limited. Instead, an entrenchment of the dominant norms is only weakly challenged due to the ongoing political maneuvering in Malaysia, which limits the political willingness and capacity to establish or consolidate democratic oversight and accountability. With democratic backsliding a real risk, demonstrated during suspicions concerning the motivations behind Malaysia's declared state of emergency in response to COVID-19, it is unlikely that these norms will be further challenged. Instead, the intelligence community will be defined by them for at least the short to medium term in the future.

NOTES

1. I would like to thank Timothy Edmunds (University of Bristol) and Albrecht Schnabel (DCAF) for their inputs to this chapter. Any mistakes remain my own.
2. Timothy Edmunds, *Security Sector Reform in Transforming Societies* (Manchester: Manchester University Press, 2007); Timothy Edmunds, "Intelligence Agencies and Democratisation: Continuity and Change in Serbia after Milosevic," *Europe-Asia Studies* 60, no. 1 (2008): 25–48.
3. Rob Johnston, "Developing a Taxonomy of Intelligence Analysis Variables," *Studies in Intelligence* 47, no. 3 (2003): 1–19.
4. Bob de Graaff and James Nyce, eds., *Handbook of European Intelligence Cultures* (Lanham, MD: Rowman & Littlefield, 2016).
5. Roy Jumper, "Malaysia's Senoi Praaq Special Forces," *International Journal of Intelligence and Counterintelligence* 13, no. 1 (2000): 63–93.
6. "Cawangan Khas," PDRM, 2021, https://www.rmp.gov.my/infor-korporate/jabatan---jabatan/cawangan-khas.
7. Mark Beeson and Alex Bellamy, *Securing Southeast Asia: The Politics of Security Sector Reform* (Oxon: Routledge, 2008).
8. Liew Chin Tong, "Did the Special Branch Spy or Not?," *Free Malaysia Today*, May 13, 2016, https://www.freemalaysiatoday.com/category/opinion/2016/05/13/did-the-special-branch-spy-or-not/.
9. Phillip Davies, "All in Good Faith? Proximity, Politicization, and Malaysia's External Intelligence Organization," *International Journal of Intelligence and*

CounterIntelligence 32, no. 4 (2019): 691–716; "Fungsi," *Tentera Darat Malaysia*, 2021, https://army.mod.gov.my/index.php/ms/about-us/profile/fungsi.

10. Dzirhan Mahadzir, "Securing Southeast Asia: The Politics of Security Sector Reform (review)," *Contemporary Southeast Asia* 30, no. 2 (2008): 338–39.

11. "Secretive Agency Has over 1000 Personnel Worldwide," *The Star*, August 1, 2018.

12. Bob de Graaff, *Intelligence Communities and Cultures in Asia and the Middle East* (Boulder, CO: Lynne Rienner, 2020).

13. Davies, "All in Good Faith?"

14. "Sejarah," MKN, 2021, https://www.mkn.gov.my/web/ms/sejarah-mkn/.

15. "The National Security Council Bill 2015 Is a Lurch towards an Authoritarian Government," *Malaysian Bar*, December 3, 2015, https://www.malaysianbar.org.my/article/news/press-statements/press-statements/press-release-the-national-security-council-bill-2015-is-a-lurch-towards-an-authoritarian-government.

16. Roger Arditti and Philip Davies, "Rethinking the Rise and Fall of the Malayan Security Service, 1946–48," *Journal of Imperial and Commonwealth History* 43, no. 2 (2015): 292–316.

17. Roger Arditti, *Counterinsurgency Intelligence and the Emergency in Malaya* (London: Palgrave Macmillan, 2019); Leon Comber, *Malaya's Secret Police: The Role of the Special Branch in the Malayan Emergency* (Victoria: Monash University Press, 2008); Georgina Sinclair, "'The Sharp End of the Intelligence Machine': The Rise of the Malayan Police Special Branch 1948–1955," *Intelligence and National Security* 26, no. 4 (2011): 460–77.

18. Arditti, *Counterinsurgency Intelligence*; Comber, *Malaya's Secret Police*.

19. De Graaff, *Intelligence Communities*; Sinclair, "'The Sharp End of the Intelligence Machine.'"

20. Comber, *Malaya's Secret Police*; "Malaysia: Amnesty International Submission to the UN Periodic Review," Amnesty International, February 2009, https://www.amnesty.org/en/documents/asa28/003/2008/en/.

21. "Malaysia: Repeal Abusive Security Law: SOSMA Denies Right to Fair Trial," Human Rights Watch, October 31, 2019, https://www.hrw.org/news/2019/10/31/malaysia-repeal-abusive-security-law.

22. Comber, *Malaya's Secret Police*.

23. Comber, *Malaya's Secret Police*.

24. Ong Weichong, *Malaysia's Defeat of Armed Communism: The Second Emergency, 1968–1989* (Oxton: Routledge, 2014).

25. Davies, "All in Good Faith?"

26. Kamarulnizam Bin Abdullah, "Emerging Threats to Malaysia's National Security," *Journal of Policing, Intelligence and Counter Terrorism* 5, no. 2 (2011): 55–70.

27. Ong, *Malaysia's Defeat of Armed Communism*.

28. Alan Collins, "The Ethnic Security Dilemma: Evidence from Malaysia," *Contemporary Southeast Asia* 20, no. 3 (1998): 261–78.

29. Collins, "The Ethnic Security Dilemma"; John Funston, "UMNO—from Hidup Melayu to Ketuanan Melayu," in *The End of UMNO*, ed. Bridget Welsh (Kuala Lumpur: SIRD, 2016).

30. Ong, *Malaysia's Defeat of Armed Communism*; Scott Edwards, "Government and Defence Anti-corruption Index—Malaysia," Transparency International, 2015, http://government.defenceindex.org/countries/malaysia/.

31. Comber, *Malaya's Secret Police*; Ong, *Malaysia's Defeat of Armed Communism*.

32. Edmunds, *Security Sector Reform*, 30–31.

33. Dan Slater, *Ordering Power* (Cambridge: Cambridge University Press, 2010); Lucian Way and Steven Levitsky, *Competitive Authoritarianism* (Cambridge: Cambridge University Press, 2010).

34. John Funston, "Change and Elections: 1969 and 2013 Similarities," in *Regime Resilience in Malaysia and Singapore*, ed. Greg Lopez and Bridget Welsh (Kuala Lumpur: SIRD, 2018); Amanda Whiting, "Rebooting the Emergency: Najib's Law 'Reform' and the Normalisation of Crisis," in *Illusions of Democracy*, ed. Sophie Lemiere (Kuala Lumpur: SIRD, 2017).

35. Edwards, "Government and Defence Anti-corruption Index—Malaysia."

36. Slater, *Ordering Power*.

37. Whiting, "Rebooting the Emergency."

38. The defense budget is aggregated with no released breakdown to parliament.

39. Edwards, "Government and Defence Anti-corruption Index—Malaysia."

40. "Malaysia: Amnesty International Submission to the UN Periodic Review."

41. Whiting, "Rebooting the Emergency"; "Malaysia: Stop Torture and Ill Treatment in the 'War on Terror,'" Amnesty International, March 1, 2006, https://www.amnesty.org/en/documents/ASA28/003/2006/en/.

42. Graham Brown, *Balancing the Risks of Corrective Surgery: The Political Economy of Horizontal Inequalities and the End of the New Economic Policy in Malaysia* (London: Centre for Research on Inequality, Human Security, and Ethnicity, 2005).

43. Thomas Fuller, "Anwar's Trial Brings Tactics of Malaysia's 'Special' Police to Light," *International Herald Tribune*, November 13, 1998, https://www.nytimes.com/1998/11/13/news/anwars-trial-brings-tactics-of-malaysias-special-police-to-light.html; Slater, *Ordering Power*.

44. Amnesty International 2009; "Malaysia's Special Branch and the Deep State," *Asia Sentinel*, July 11, 2019, https://www.asiasentinel.com/p/malaysia-special-branch-deep-state.

45. Davies, "All in Good Faith?"

46. "No Confirmed Link between Malaysia Terror Suspects and Christmas Attack," Voice of America, January 27, 2010, https://www.voanews.com/east-asia/no-confirmed-link-between-malaysia-terror-suspects-and-christmas-attack; Leslie Lopez, "Police Arrest 14 Suspects Linked to Banned Group," *Wall Street Journal*, April 19, 2002. https://www.wsj.com/articles/SB1019120256745777040.

47. Bureau of Counterterrorism, "Malaysia: Country Reports on Terrorism 2018," US Department of State, 2018, https://www.state.gov/reports/country-reports-on-terrorism-2018/#Malaysia; "Malaysia Cuts Off Transit Route for Militants to Join ISIS in Syria," *Strait Times*, January 13, 2015, https://www.straitstimes.com/asia/se-asia/malaysia-cuts-off-transit-route-for-militants-to-join-isis-in-syria.

48. Farrah Naz Karim, "Exclusive: 80pc of Enforcers Manning Borders on the Take," *New Straits Times*, June 3, 2015, https://www.nst.com.my/news/2015/09/exclusive-80pc-enforcers-manning-borders-take.

49. Karim, "Exclusive: 80pc of Enforcers Manning Borders on the Take."

50. Hazlan Zakaria, "Complete Intelligence Failure in Lahad Datu," *MalaysiaKini*, March 13, 2013, https://www.malaysiakini.com/news/223718.

51. Nadirah Rodzi, "Malaysia's Police Chief Claims Corruption within Senior Ranks of Force," *Straits Times*, March 24, 2021, https://www.straitstimes.com/asia/se-asia/malaysias-police-chief-claims-corruption-within-senior-ranks-of-force.

52. Edmunds, *Security Sector Reform in Transforming Societies*; Edmunds, "Intelligence Agencies and Democratisation."

53. Ibid. Thomas Bruneau and Kenneth Dombroski, "Reforming Intelligence: The Challenge of Control in New Democracies," in *Who Guards the Guardians and How*, ed. Thomas Bruneau and Scott Tollefson (Austin: University of Texas Press, 2006); DCAF, *Intelligence Services: Roles and Responsibilities in Good Security Sector Governance* (Geneva: DCAF, 2017); DCAF, *Intelligence Oversight—SSR Background Series* (Geneva, DCAF, 2017); Hans Born, "Parliamentary and External Oversight of Intelligence Services," in *Democratic Control of Intelligence Services*, ed. Hans Born and Marina Caparini (Hampshire: Ashgate, 2007).

54. Edmunds, "Intelligence Agencies and Democratisation."

55. Bruneau and Dombroski, "Reforming Intelligence"; Fred Schreier, "The Need for Efficient and Legitimate Intelligence," in *Democratic Control of Intelligence Services*, eds. Hans Born and Marina Caparini (Hampshire: Ashgate, 2007).

56. Born, "Parliamentary and External Oversight of Intelligence Services"; Marina Caparini, "Controlling and Overseeing Intelligence Services in Democratic States," in *Democratic Control of Intelligence Services*, ed. Hans Born and Marina Caparini (Hampshire: Ashgate, 2007).

57. Ibid. DCAF, *Intelligence Services: Roles and Responsibilities in Good Security Sector Governance*; Hans Born and Fairlie Jensen, "Intelligence Services: Strengthening Democratic Accountability," in *Democratic Control of Intelligence Services*, ed. Hans Born and Marina Caparini (Hampshire: Ashgate, 2007); Grazvydas Jasutis, Teodora Fuior, and Mindia Vashakmadze, *Parliamentary Oversight of Military Intelligence* (Geneva: DCAF, 2021).

58. DCAF, *Rethinking Engagement between Intelligence Services and Civil Society* (Geneva: DCAF, 2021).

59. Edmunds, "Intelligence Agencies and Democratisation."

60. Davies, "All in Good Faith?"; "Ex-military Intel Chief, 2 Senior Army Officers Charged with Corruption," *Free Malaysia Today*, October 27, 2020, https://www.freemalaysiatoday.com/category/nation/2020/10/27/ex-military-intel-chief-2-senior-army-officers-charged-with-corruption/.

61. Hazlin Hassan, "New Malaysian Cabinet to Slash Costs," *Straits Times*, May 24, 2018, https://www.straitstimes.com/asia/se-asia/new-malaysian-cabinet-to-slash-costs.

62. Bruneau and Dombroski, "Reforming Intelligence"; Edmunds, "Intelligence Agencies and Democratisation."

63. Mohd Azam Shah Yaacob, "Police Cripple Human Trafficking Syndicate Masterminded by M'sian Man," *New Straits Times*, September 26, 2019, https://www.nst.com.my/news/nation/2019/09/524762/police-cripple-human-trafficking-syndicate-masterminded-msian-man; R. Loheswar, "Special Branch Reveals Assassination Attempts against Dr Mahathir, Guan Eng, Mujahid Rawa, Tommy Thomas," *Malay Mail*, March 25, 2021, https://www.malaymail.com/news/malaysia/2021/03/25/special-branch-reveals-assassination-attempts-against-dr-m-guan-eng-mujahid/1960942; "IGP: Elements of Corruption in Malaysia's Borders, Integrity Dept to Conduct Probe," *Malay Mail*, December 10, 2020, https://www.malaymail.com/news/malaysia/2020/12/10/igp-elements-of-corruption-in-malaysias-borders-integrity-dept-to-conduct-p/1930850.

64. Loheswar, "Special Branch Reveals Assassination Attempts."

65. "Public Inquiry into the Disappearance of Pastor Raymond Koh," SUHAKAM, 2019, https://suhakam.org.my/publications/national-public-inquiry-reports/.

66. Thasha Jayamanogaran, "Special Branch Won't Entertain Request for Its Men to Identify Selves at Political Events," *Malay Mail*, May 15, 2019, https://www.malaymail.com/news/malaysia/2019/05/15/igp-special-branch-wont-entertain-request-for-its-men-to-identify-selves-at/1753076.

67. Rodzi, "Malaysia's Police Chief Claims Corruption"; "Corruption Highest in Criminal Investigation Dept, Says Malaysian Police Chief," *Today Online*, August 14, 2018, https://www.todayonline.com/world/corruption-highest-criminal-investigation-dept-says-malaysian-police-chief; Ida Nadhirah Ibrahim, "Deep State Impedes Pakatan Institutional, Political Reforms for New Malaysia, Says Kit Siang," *Malay Mail*, July 30, 2019, https://www.malaymail.com/news/malaysia/2019/07/30/deep-state-impedes-pakatan-institutional-political-reforms-for-new-malaysia/1776104; Auriel Croissant and Philip Lorenz, *Comparative Politics of Southeast Asia: An Introduction to Governments and Political Regimes* (London: Springer, 2018).

68. Edmunds, "Intelligence Agencies and Democratisation"; Caparini, "Controlling and Overseeing Intelligence Services in Democratic States."

14

Maldives: Connections between Intelligence Culture and Oversight

Abdulla Phairoosch

On October 25, 2015, Maldivian president Abdulla Yameen delivered a public statement that he had not received intelligence from the police since July, but "the Vice President has been collecting police intelligence, officially and privately."[1] He made the remarks following the arrest of his deputy on the previous day. Other than asserting impropriety and transfer of senior police officers, no new measures were taken by his administration to strengthen the intelligence culture with enhanced oversight. Four years later, intelligence misuse came to light again in the island state, following the release of a draft report of the Presidential Commission on Disappearances and Death in September 2019.[2] In both instances, the allegation was the exploitation of intelligence for political purposes. Despite these revelations, a formal process was never created to hold the intelligence regime accountable, minimize intelligence abuse, and understand capacity gaps.[3] These events indicate the existing oversight system either lacks capacity or has a narrow understanding of accountability.

This chapter examines the oversight gap. The chapter argues that an absence of a professionally rooted intelligence culture in the Maldives has hindered not only the development but also oversight of the intelligence profession. Another factor that contributes to the poor intelligence oversight is the unfamiliarity of the policy makers with the fundamentals of intelligence. This chapter draws from Hans Born and Ian Leigh's three-layered framework of intelligence oversight, comprising executive oversight, parliamentary oversight, and nonpolitical oversight.[4] The chapter focuses only on the judiciary in their framework because inspectorates have such a limited role in the Maldives. Before discussing the oversight in these three aspects, the chapter provides an overview of the intelligence culture, which is followed by a section on the intelligence community. After discussing the oversight elements, the last section concludes the chapter with the findings.

INTELLIGENCE ROOTS

Irrespective of the governance system in the Maldives, use of covert agents to collect information about political opponents remained a dominant activity in the political realm. Yet it was only in 1999 after an increased demand for the right to dissent that dedicated officers were used to collect information for the first time in the Maldives. Four junior military officers were enlisted to collect information about political opposition and dissent. They were assigned to the investigation division of Police Headquarters under the guise of "administrative officers." The four officers frequented places where the public gathered, such as teashops and parks, and reported what they saw or heard in those places to the in-charge of the division.[5]

During this time, all security and policing duties were performed by the National Security Service (NSS), renamed the Maldives National Defence Force (MNDF) on April 21, 2006, under the Ministry of Defence and National Security.[6] The Police Headquarters was the NSS unit responsible for the policing function. The number of "administrative officers" performing intelligence work in the investigation division grew in 2001 following increased political activism, particularly after the submission of a petition to form political parties.[7] To analyze the political landscape and assess the support for the president, before the 2003 presidential election, a project code-named Omega was launched in the Police Headquarters. Shortly after, Omega was made responsible for monitoring dissidents and transcribing key conversations. During this time, religious extremists were attempting to exploit the space created by dissidents to promote their extremist ideology. To curb religious extremism, monitoring such subjects was added to the mandate of the fledgling intelligence setup. In 2003, Omega was renamed the Police Intelligence Division, and office space and resources were allocated along with funds for intelligence operations for the first time. Even after this change, Omega was retained as the name of Police Intelligence Division, and use of the term *intelligence* in official communications was prohibited. Consequently, other officers were unaware of the existence of an intelligence division in their agency, which deprived detectives of the ability to contact the intelligence function for support.[8]

For the first time in the history of the Maldives, a debate on intelligence took place during the high-level discussions in 2004 about separating the policing function (Police Headquarters) from the NSS to create a civil police agency. Both the police and military leadership wanted the intelligence division. To convince the political and military leadership about the importance of having an intelligence setup in the police, the police change-managers linked intelligence with modern policing through the philosophy of intelligence-led policing, although they lacked an understanding of the fundamental elements of intelligence and the philosophy. The outcome was the clearance to keep the intelligence division in the police after separation from the military. Upon creation of the Maldives Police Service (MPS) on September 1, 2004, the Police Intelligence Division was renamed the Internal Intelligence Department. According to the architects of the change, the term *internal* was added to the name of the department to delineate its role (to internal security) and gain approval of the military leaders and policy makers.[9] Following the agreement on the allotment of the intelligence function to the police, an intelligence division was created in the military (NSS). Though the exact date of the military's intelligence department creation cannot be stated with certainty, it is presumed to be in March 2004.[10]

The Sultan Park bombing in 2007 that injured twelve foreign tourists became the catalyst for modernizing intelligence craft in the Maldives. Since then, all security policies maintain a focus on Islamic extremism and terrorism. The bombing enabled cooperation with Western intelligence and security agencies for the first time. Additionally, they provided training opportunities. Intelligence desks designated for various categories of crimes in the Internal Intelligence Department were elevated to units. In 2012, the intelligence department was moved to a command entity, and in 2013 it was renamed the Directorate of Intelligence.[11] The directorate was responsible for preventing crime; identifying offenders involved in organized crime and recidivism; providing intelligence support to other policing functions; collecting national security intelligence and determining the countermeasures for preventing or reducing threats; advising the commissioner, government, and MPS Executive Board; and developing the intelligence function of the MPS.[12] The directorate functions as the state's intelligence arm but is not officially designated.[13]

Despite those opportunities and close collaboration with Western intelligence agencies, the analytic profession still appears primitive. This is due to the emphasis on collection and obliviousness to the application of intelligence in policy making. Most of the short trainings offered by friendly countries addressed tradecraft (surveillance and monitoring), but instruction on analysis is a rarity.[14] The first structured intelligence course, called Intelligence Foundation Course, was conducted on May 3, 2012, by the MPS training wing. It lasted three weeks, and fifteen participants from various agencies attended.[15] Around the same time, the MNDF commenced its eleven-week-long Military Intelligence Basic Course.[16] In July 2019, the MPS started a twelve-month Diploma in Intelligence Management course that addressed intelligence management, analysis, and application.[17] No other intelligence service conducts nationally recognized intelligence trainings.

INTELLIGENCE COMMUNITY

The military (MNDF) and police (MPS) are the only security services recognized in the constitution of the Maldives. The security services are in charge of the following constitutional responsibilities: protecting the national sovereignty, maintaining territorial integrity, defending the constitution and democratic institutions, upholding law and order, and rendering assistance during emergencies. The constitution requires the two forces be organized as two separate agencies functioning independently from each another, operating on the basis of accountability, subjected to the authority of the People's Majlis (the unicameral parliament) through a committee of the People's Majlis (hereafter referred to as 241 Committee as it was created under section 241 of the constitution), which has representation from all the different political parties within the People's Majlis.[18] Prior to the ratification of the constitution in 2008, the legislative branch had no direct mandate over national security policies and services.

The Armed Force Act, ratified in 2008, defines the responsibilities, powers, and general principles of the military. Other than protecting the sovereignty, national interest, and the government, the force is also mandated to lead in disasters and crises, provide firefighting services, carry out search and rescue of individuals stranded at sea, protect ports, and collect and analyze information pertaining to national security.[19] To perform these different roles, the military serves as a combined force of combat divisions, Coast Guard, and Fire and Rescue Service.[20]

The Armed Force Act added a new element to the security regime, the National Security Council (NSC). The NSC's primary responsibility is to advise the president on matters related to national security. The NSC is composed of the commander in chief (president), vice president, defense minister, foreign minister, home affairs minister, atolls minister (the ministry is now abolished), attorney general, and chief of MNDF.[21] The law offers the commander in chief the discretion to add temporary NSC members. Utilizing this discretion, the president has included the commissioner of police in the NSC. Owing to this limitation and creating a "holistic interagency approach towards defense, national security and public safety," the government pledged to enact a national security law by 2020.[22] This was delayed, likely due to more immediate concerns caused by COVID-19.

The MPS attained legal status in 2008 with the enactment of the Police Act. In 2012, the Police Service Bill was submitted before the People's Majlis to grant operational autonomy to the police leadership and limit political interference in operational policing.[23] Ratified on December 27, 2020, the bill is scheduled to be in effect after three months. Once the Police Service Act comes into force, the Police Act will become invalid.[24] Also in 2012, the Maldives published its first National Security Policy (NSP), which identified threats faced by the country, emphasized the need to increase coordination and communication among national security agencies, highlighted the need for demarcation of MPS and MNDF's mandates (as their legal responsibilities overlap), and identified intelligence as one of the six national apparatuses for protecting and advancing national interests.[25]

Despite the operational focus since 2007 on religious extremism, threats have multiplied. Numerous policies and laws were adopted to give teeth to enforcement, including a special law to prevent terrorism financing in 2014 and a new antiterrorism law in 2015. Under the terrorism financing law, the Financial Intelligence Unit (FIU) was created under Maldives Monetary Authority (MMA). The FIU is the national center for collection, analysis, and dissemination of information concerning money laundering, terrorism financing, and proceeds of crime. It receives transaction reports from various financial/banking institutions and disseminates suspicious transaction reports to law enforcement agencies.[26] Like the FIU, the National Counter Terrorism Centre (NCTC) was created in 2016, under the Ministry of Defence, to coordinate the national counterterrorism effort. The NCTC is responsible for advising the government, president, and NSC on matters related to terrorism based upon its analysis of the information received from other agencies.[27] Other than these intelligence services, intelligence departments exist in the Maldives Customs Service and Maldives Immigration.

Thus, these six intelligence departments form the Maldives intelligence community, although the Second Amendment to Terrorism Act (ratified on 10 October 2019) does not recognize NCTC as an element of the Maldives intelligence community. Strategic attention given to the intelligence departments in Immigration and Customs is far less due to their narrow role in the Maldives' national security.

EXECUTIVE OVERSIGHT

The executive branch has an operational and political responsibility over the intelligence services. The operational responsibility is to create essential policies, define priorities, provide guidance, allocate budgets (and special funds), equip the intelligence services to the extent they can contribute to the requirements of national interest and policy, authorize sensitive operations, and initiate inquiries in cases of impropriety. The political responsibility is to the parliament and public to ensure the intelligence agencies operate within the legal boundaries and are effective.[28] Despite the NSC and NSP, a coherent intelligence culture remains largely unrealized owing to overlap of responsibilities between the police and military, competition for authority and resources among the security services and NCTC, the NSC's limited role, and the NSP's lack of guidance.

The executive providing guidance is the most important aspect for effective oversight and accountability.[29] Guidance—the starting point of the intelligence cycle—defines the objectives for collection (i.e., second phase of the intelligence cycle) within a public policy framework and supports the allocation of resources based on threat assessments. In the Maldives, guidance can be provided by chiefs of the agencies, responsible cabinet ministers, and the NSC. My own experience is that the NSC (and its subcommittee) hears strategic and operational intelligence produced by police intelligence (Directorate of Intelligence) and military intelligence, which are mostly about terrorism, and offers operational guidance. The guidance was usually limited to sanctioning tactical response or collecting additional information on the specific threat under discussion. The NSC, therefore, appreciates the intelligence put before it but refrains from getting directly involved in the ways intelligence capabilities are used.

The police and military ordinances offer legal authority to the responsible minister to exercise powers available to any superior officer at any time and command any individual officer or group of officers. Further, the minister is also accountable for ensuring the forces are compliant to the provisions of their respective laws. The Customs Law vests with the minister the power to articulate policies and make regulations for ensuring accountability,[30] while the Immigration Act assigns that authority to the in-charge of the overseeing institution.[31] Despite these provisions, the extent that ministers direct the intelligence process is unclear. Even in cases of intelligence abuse, the ministers were never formally questioned. The FIU is the only intelligence service not under a minister. Its parent body is the MMA, which is governed by the Authority's Board of Directors. As with all other state institutions, the MMA must submit its annual report before the president.[32]

In the foreword to the *Capstone Doctrine 2020*, the Maldives' overarching military doctrine, the defense minister emphasized the administration's commitment to provide strategic advice and guidance to the military, including defining national interests. The minister also identified a key effort undertaken in ensuring a civilian control over the military, which involved the publication of military policies, procedures, and processes.[33] Nevertheless, the seventeen regulations required to be drafted under the Armed Force Act have not been published.

The absence of these regulations means it is unclear whether the defense minister has any role in authorizing intelligence collection, but it is explicit that the military employs clandestine tactics for collection. In contrast, published police regulations and policies establish that the commissioner of police must approve clandestine communication interceptions and intrusive surveillance. The ordinances also illustrate a responsibility on the police intelligence chief and commissioner of police for the use of special funds. The *Policy on Spending for Intelligence Collection* describes the process of auditing special funds allocated for clandestine work. The new Police Service Act requires the officers to obtain a court warrant before employing intrusive surveillance tactics. To review the legality of the tactic, the new law creates a three-member committee, composed of the attorney general, prosecutor general, and commissioner of police. Any violations observed by this committee must be stopped and reported to the 241 Committee and minister.[34] Other special laws on crime also authorize officers to intercept communications based on a court warrant. A court's refusal to issue a warrant can be appealed in a higher court; however, the laws do not require the enforcement agencies to submit details of those applications rejected by the courts before a third agency for scrutiny.

PARLIAMENTARY OVERSIGHT

The People's Majlis can call cabinet ministers to account for the actions of the agencies they oversee.[35] In theory, this process should provide a reliable oversight process as the ministers are vested with adequate powers in the laws. Furthermore, the ministers can make the agencies accountable to any extent through the regulations they are authorized to make under the laws. Yet, for the People's Majlis, holding the ministers of security services accountable has been challenging. The commissioner of police and chief of defense force declined to attend before the 241 Committee thrice in 2010, which prompted the committee to summon them on August 26, 2010. They refused again and informed that the respective minister must be the person responding to queries of the People's Majlis.[36] The issue was submitted before the Supreme Court on December 2, 2010, under a motion assented by the Majlis. The pronouncement (advice) of the apex court was in favor of the People's Majlis.[37]

The actions of the People's Majlis often have been motivated by political interests rather than the best interests of the people. Politically aligned groups "exploit the complexities of politics to disguise the action they take on behalf of the party agendas."[38] The People's Majlis and the executive had always remained on a collision course when the ruling party fails to get a majority of seats in the People's Majlis. The aforementioned confrontation occurred after the arrest of two senior opposition lawmakers at a time the opposition had the Majlis majority.[39] In 2013, when the opposition could not call security services' officers before the 241 Committee because they lacked the majority of the seats in the committee, the opposition attempted to use the Government Oversight Committee of the Majlis to call them. Based on the legal advice of the attorney general, officers abstained from attending the hearing.

The People's Majlis raises concerns about intelligence abuses but has not led any genuine effort in holding the intelligence services accountable except for political interest. For instance, in the debate of the Telecommunications Bill on August 13, 2014, the issue of unlawful phone tapping by security services was raised.[40] The same issue was briefly touched on again by the speaker on December 6, 2020.[41] On November 23, 2020, the speaker informed the People's Majlis that the Directorate of Intelligence attempted to install listening devices in his chamber, the deputy speaker's chamber, and another chamber. The matter was forwarded to the 241 Committee for investigation.[42] All facts surrounding this remain unknown, and the home minister was not called to the Majlis or 241 Committee regarding this matter.

The People's Majlis approves the government budget, and any supplementary budgets, and may approve or amend the budget submitted in its discretion as it deems fit.[43] The People's Majlis can ensure special funds are used properly and in the most cost-efficient manner. In none of the budget finalization sessions has there been a focus or discussion on special funds. The independent institutions (such as the Auditor General's Office and National Integrity Commission) must table their annual reports and any special reports before the People's Majlis. The laws do not require redaction of operationally sensitive information in the reports submitted to the legislator and executive.

The auditor general is responsible for auditing all state enterprises, ministries, and institutions, including the security services. This duty appears to be duly performed, and as required under the constitution, reports are submitted to the president and the People's Majlis. On behalf of the People's Majlis, the Public Accounts Committee is responsible for reviewing the audit reports. On September 5, 2019, the speaker admitted more than 608 audit reports were pending before the Public Accounts Committee, and the review of the audit report of state-owned enterprise Maldives Marketing and Public Relations Company (MMPRC) was completed on the previous day.[44] Upon review of the MMPRC audit report, the committee realized that money was laundered by involving the central bank (MMA) and national bank.[45] Nevertheless, in 2017, the Anti-Corruption Commission compiled a detailed report on the grand corruption through the MMPRC. The report established abuse of authority in a number of government agencies, including the FIU, and that money was laundered.[46]

Irregularities of around US$6 million in MMPRC was initially reported in 2014 by the auditor general, and the findings were shared with the executive and legislator.[47] Following the report, the auditor general was removed from office through an amendment introduced to the Audit Law by the ruling party-controlled People's Majlis.[48] This blocked further inquiry into the corruption. In 2016, a banking official from the national bank disclosed further details related to the corruption. He was arrested and charged for unauthorized disclosure of information.[49] The MMPRC scandal turned out to be the largest of its kind in the history of the Maldives, hitting US$220 million.[50] After an explosion on the president's speedboat *Finifenma* in 2015, an alleged attempt on President Yameen's life, on October 27, 2015 the president ordered a fresh audit into MMPRC. The new audit uncovered embezzlement, fraud, forgery, and failure of oversight bodies (including the FIU), confirming that it was planned by officials in all arms of the state.[51]

JUDICIAL OVERSIGHT

The judiciary plays a limited role in establishing accountability over the Maldives' intelligence community. The courts adjudicate constitutional, administrative, and criminal claims pertaining to intelligence. The courts authorize the use of special investigative techniques but have never reviewed the legality of an intelligence operation. This could be due to the absence of specially designated courts to hear surveillance applications and freedom of information cases with national security aspects. It is publicly unknown whether military intelligence has ever submitted an application before a court seeking authorization.

On two occasions, in 2015 and 2016, the Employment Tribunal decided that it was unlawful to dismiss government employees from office based on intelligence reports. When the decisions were appealed in the courts, the rulings provided different conclusions. In the 2016 case, the High Court ruled that an intelligence product alone is not sufficient to establish an offense.[52] The appeal was mainly based on the tribunal's repudiation of a police intelligence report by not offering adequate weight to the document, although the report falls within the limits of documentary evidence under the Evidence Act. The verdict identified the need to corroborate the "facts" in intelligence reports. In the 2015 case of the dismissal of an employee of Aviation Security Command based on a security assessment of military intelligence on grounds of national security, the High Court also accepted that the dismissal by the Civil Service Commission amounted to procedural unfairness. The appellant court merely required the state to compensate the defendant's financial loss and accepted his dismissal as reasonable on grounds of losing trust between the employer and employee. In 2018, the defendant appealed the High Court's decision at the apex court. At the Supreme Court hearing, the Civil Service Commission's argument was that the commission cannot challenge or question an intelligence assessment of intelligence services. The commission also held the belief that it must take action upon receipt of intelligence assessments. In the judgment, upholding the decision of the tribunal, the Supreme Court noted that the intelligence assessment failed to identify the act committed or will be committed by the defendant that could be considered as breach of laws, regulations, and procedure that the employee was obliged to uphold.[53]

In 2019, the Criminal Court refused to issue a search warrant based only on an intelligence report. When the state appealed, the High Court overruled the lower court's decision on March 14, 2019, recognizing that the intelligence report established a probable cause for issuing a search warrant.[54] Nevertheless, the Criminal Court had been issuing warrants based on intelligence reports. The search warrant issued on January 18, 2015, for Enif building is notable in this regard because it was the then defense minister's residence. Police raided the minister's apartment around 03:30 hours, recovering a pistol and three bullets. He challenged the legality of the search warrant at the appeal court. The High Court concluded the case without providing a remedy on the grounds that the defendant can raise that issue in the ongoing trial in the Criminal Court.[55] On March 26, 2015, he was sentenced to eleven years in prison without an assessment of the grounds for generating the intelligence report.[56] He appealed his sentence, claiming that the lower court rejected a review of the search warrant's basis flouting the appeal court's previous decision. Nevertheless, the High Court upheld the lower court's decision without looking into that plea.[57] Three lawmakers submitted a motion before the 241 Committee on January 18, 2015, regarding the search. Without reviewing, the committee closed the case on June 18, 2019.[58] On January 30, 2015, the commissioner of police provided insights about the search operation at a press conference. He said that the MPS had received "intelligence" about the presence of weapons and explosives in a house, and that the MPS was unaware of whose residence it was before the raid. Replying to a reporter's question, he further stated that police do "not have to find whose dwelling it was, before conducting a search," which removed the processing phase of the intelligence cycle.[59]

CONCLUSION

This chapter examined the Maldives' intelligence culture by exploring its intelligence oversight and processes. Reviewing the oversight mechanism reveals massive gaps that detrimentally affect the public and governance. These gaps are due to a lack of understanding of intelligence in all arms of the state (executive, legislative, and judiciary) and nonpolitical bodies because of the relatively new establishment of intelligence in the country. Another factor that contributes to a weak intelligence machinery in terms of oversight and production is the absence of a rooted intelligence culture. Intelligence craft is relatively new in the Maldives with the steppingstones laid in 1999 as a political tool to monitor and control dissidence. Later, it was also used against religious extremists. Efforts taken to professionalize the processes have proven unsatisfactory as intelligence analysis took a backseat in the developmental process.

Furthermore, the actors in the oversight machinery do not fully understand their roles. The executive, despite enjoying enormous legal powers, fails to fully comprehend the importance, meaning, and craft of intelligence oversight. Guidance is essential for the security and intelligence services to use resources and financial planning efficiently and ethically. Clearly identified national intelligence priorities and guidance are essential. Unfortunately, the NSP and NSC do not offer these. The judiciary and other state institutions (such as the Civil Service Commission) remain unfamiliar with intelligence work, consequent to which they offer evidentiary weight to intelligence assessments.

The legislature lacks the will and capacity to hold the intelligence services accountable, which is necessary for a democracy. The lawmakers oftentimes subordinate the democratic order to party interests, which erode public confidence not only in the security sector but also in good governance. The People's Majlis should step up its performance in reviewing the annual budget and audit reports, especially those of the intelligence services. It should also enact a law for the NSC's effective and efficient administration as envisaged in the national development plan 2019–2023. Abuse will take place if the agencies are allowed to operate without scrutiny. The longer the agencies can evade oversight and operate without scrutiny, the greater the abuse is going to be.

NOTES

1. Abdulla Yameen, *Address of President Abdulla Yameen on the Prevailing Situation in the Country on 25 October 2015* (Malé: President's Office, 2015), para 19.

2. *Summary of the Enforced Disappearance of Ahmed Rilwan Abdulla* (Malé: People's Majlis, 2019), https://majlis.gov.mv/storage/action_files/341/2Na4UKzzRE llDCVfGHBRFrlq7z7fsxfFC0lDHixC.pdf.

3. In mid-2020, however, after the submission of the draft report to the People's Majlis, an intelligence professional from the United Kingdom was added to the Presidential Commission on Disappearances and Death so as to discern covert operations and intelligence practices followed in the Maldives Police Service, implying that the members of the commission lacked that mastery. The People's Majlis also voted on September 5, 2019, to set up a special task force in the Majlis, with representation of all relevant state bodies, to review the issues identified in the commission's report. Such a task force has not been formed yet. See *Report of the Proceedings of the People's Majlis on 5 September 2019* (Malé: People's Majlis, 2019), 136–37.

4. Hans Born and Ian Leigh, *Democratic Accountability of Intelligence Services* (Geneva: Geneva Centre for the Democratic Control of Armed Forces, 2007).

5. Abdulla Phairoosch, "Intelligence-Led Policing: Interpretation, Implementation and Impact" (PhD diss., Macquarie University, Sydney, Australia, 2019).

6. *Presidential Directive 2006/28* (Malé: President's Office, 2006).

7. Forming political parties and engaging in political activities was legalized on June 2, 2005.

8. Phairoosch, "Intelligence-Led Policing," 109–10.

9. Phairoosch, "Intelligence-Led Policing," 110–14.

10. This estimation is based on a draft organigram of the military (Office of the Chief of the Staff) found with the documents that were produced for the high-level discussions on sharing and allotting NSS resources to the new police agency to be created on September 1, 2004.

11. Phairoosch, "Intelligence-Led Policing," 110.

12. *Annual Report 2013* (Malé: Maldives Police Service, 2014), 1149–50.

13. The MNDF *Capstone Doctrine* fails to identify military intelligence as a core function of the military despite recognizing information as one of the elements of national power in safeguarding the country's national interest.

14. Phairoosch, "Intelligence-Led Policing," 136–37.

15. *Annual Report 2012* (Malé: Maldives Police Service, 2013), 32.

16. College of Defence and Security Studies, *Military Intelligence Basic Course* (Malé: Maldives Qualification Authority, 2021), http://www.mqa.gov.mv/ institutes/16/courses/424.

17. ISLES, "Diploma in Intelligence Management," Institute for Security and Law Enforcement Studies, 2019, http://www.isles.edu.mv/page/fsot/1640.

18. Maldives Constitution, chapter 9.

19. Armed Force Act (Law 1/2008) § 7.

20. Integrated Headquarters, *Capstone Doctrine* (Malé: Maldives National Defence Force, 2020).

21. Armed Force Act § 13(b).

22. *Strategic Action Plan 2019–2023* (Malé: President's Office, 2020), 389.

23. National Security Services Committee, *Report Number 6-R/2012/SG—Assessment Report of the First Amendment Bill of Law 5/2008* (Malé: People's Majlis, 2012).

24. Police Service Act (Law 34/2020) §135.

25. *National Security Policy* (Malé: President's Office, 2012), 40.

26. FIU, *Annual Report 2019* (Malé: Maldives Monetary Authority, 2020).

27. *Presidential Directive 2016/3* (Malé: President's Office, 2016).

28. DCAF, *Intelligence Oversight: Ensuring Accountable Intelligence within a Framework of Democratic Governance* (Geneva: Geneva Centre for the Democratic Control of Armed Forces, 2017).

29. Jack Davis, "A Policymaker's Perspective on Intelligence Analysis," *Studies in Intelligence* 38, no. 5 (1995): 7–15.

30. Customs Act (Law 8/2011) §110(a).

31. Immigration Act (Law 1/2007) § 35.

32. Maldives Monetary Act (Law 1/1981) §35(b); Official Proceedings Act (Law 2/68) §14.

33. Integrated Headquarters, *Capstone Doctrine*, iii.

34. Police Service Act (Law 34/2020), chapter 18.

35. Maldives Constitution § 98(a).

36. *Report of the Security Services Committee of the People's Majlis on Their Refusal to Attend before the Committee* (Malé: People's Majlis, August 26, 2010).

37. *Advice to the People's Majlis under Article 95 of the Constitution* (Malé: Supreme Court, 2011).

38. Kathleen Bawn, Martin Cohen, David Karol, Seth Masket, Hans Noel, and John Zaller, "A Theory of Political Parties: Groups, Policy Demands and Nominations in American Politics," *Perspectives on Politics* 10, no. 3 (September 2012): 571.

39. Abdulla Yameen vs State (2010), Case 2010/SC-A/20, Maldives Supreme Court; Qasim Ibrahim vs State (2010), Case 2010/SC-A/19, Maldives Supreme Court.

40. *Report of the Proceedings of the People's Majlis on 13 August 2014* (Malé: People's Majlis, 2014), 20.

41. *Report of the Proceedings of the People's Majlis on 6 December 2020* (Malé: People's Majlis, 2020), 30–31.

42. *Report of the Proceedings of the People's Majlis on 23 November 2020* (Malé: People's Majlis, 2020), 2.

43. Maldives Constitution § 96.

44. *Minutes of the 40th Meeting of the Public Accounts Committee* (Malé: People's Majlis, 2019), 3.

45. *Minutes of the 40th Meeting of the Public Accounts Committee*, 5.

46. *Investigation Report Number TR-2017/275* (Malé: Anti-corruption Commission, 2017).

47. *Special Audit of the Transactions Pertaining to MVR 77.1 Million of Maldives Post Limited and USD 1 Million of Maldives Tourism Development Corporation through MMPRC* (Malé: Auditor General's Office, 2014).

48. First Amendment to Audit Act (Law 30/2014) § 2(e).

49. "Gasim Abdul Kareem: The Hand That Rocked the Boat," Transparency Maldives, September 22, 2016, https://transparency.mv/2016/09/gasim-abdul-kareem-the-hand-that-rocked-the-boat/.

50. *Investigation Report Number TR-2017/275.*

51. *Report of the Special Audit of MMPRC* (Malé: Auditor General's Office, 2016).

52. Aminath Areej Hussain vs. Prosecutor General's Office (2018), Case 2016/HC-A/376, Maldives High Court.

53. Hussain Nazeef vs Civil Service Commission (2019), Case 2019/SC-A/22, Maldives Supreme Court.

54. Judgment for Case Number 2019/HC-A/186, Maldives High Court, April 18, 2019.

55. Mohamed Nazim vs State (2015), Case 2015/HC-A/72, Maldives High Court.

56. Mohamed Nazim vs State (2015), Case 137/Cr-C/2015, Maldives Criminal Court.

57. Mohamed Nazim vs State (2016), Case 2015/HC-A/172, Maldives High Court.

58. 241 Committee, *Report Number M19/SKH/2019/01* (Malé: People's Majlis, 2019).

59. Hussain Waheed, "Press Briefing by the Commissioner of Police on Three Cases Being Investigated by the Police on 30 January 2015," video recording (Malé: Maldives Police Service, 2015).

15

Mongolia: Democratization and Intelligence

Jargalsaikhan Mendee, Adiya Tuvshintugs, and Julian Dierkes

In comparison to any political aspects of modern nation-states in Asia, Mongolia stands out for the institutionalization of democracy for more than twenty years.[1] It is, in fact, the only democratic country in post-state socialist Asia on a continent that includes the most populous democracy in India but, beyond that, offers few examples of recent democratization processes. Mongolia stands in stark contrast to various Southeast Asian countries broadly aligned with China, or the Central Asian countries that emerged out of the former Soviet Republics. It is this democratization that has shaped the role of Mongolia's intelligence services over the past twenty years.

The role of intelligence services in democratization processes has been addressed to some extent in academic discussions.[2] Yet, this has not become a focus of investigations for scholars and does not receive much public attention unless it is associated with violence. This chapter explores the interplay between the intelligence services in Mongolia and the consolidation of democracy. Since 1990, electoral democracy has become the "only game in town," a vibrant civil society exists, and the security services have remained aloof from political contestation.[3] The passage of a law on conflicts of interest and a broader judicial reform agenda, revisions of election laws, and apparently free and fair elections are signs of a healthy democracy.[4] That is not to say that there is no room for improvement in democratic institutions and citizens' participation, but particularly when viewed from a comparative perspective, Mongolian democracy seems firmly entrenched. In particular, Mongolia has been categorized as "free" by the Freedom in the World report and moved into the highest category for "political rights."[5]

Unique in the region, Mongolia's security apparatus, including the military, intelligence agencies, paramilitary forces (such as border troops and internal troops), and police have mostly remained outside of the analysis of this political transformation. Some scholars tend to ignore the role of these security institutions for democratization because of misperception about their roles and centrality, as well as the Soviet military presence in the Cold War.[6]

During the Cold War, the huge presence of the Soviet military was explicitly directed against a Chinese military threat; it had little impact on and involvement in Mongolian domestic politics. In fact, the hosting of the Soviet military served as leverage to elicit material support from the Soviet Union in an exchange of economic aid for the burden of hosting a military presence. At the same time, the Mongolian government maintained its own military and intelligence institutions to enhance its defense capabilities and to control society. Accordingly, an important question is why this security apparatus did not become involved in state matters during the democratization process, as they did in so many other new democracies. Why, for example, did Mongolian intelligence agencies not follow the Russian path of siding with political and economic interest groups and undermining democracy? What prevented the emergence of security-sponsored economic interests to become a significant actor in privatization and political decision-making?

This chapter provides three interrelated answers. First, political elites reached a historic consensus not to politicize the security institutions from the beginning of the democratic transition in 1990. Second, the intelligence professionals, like other security institutions, preferred to remain politically neutral and began their own self-structuring to survive in a democratic, free market society. Third, at the time that democratization and privatization were pursued simultaneously, there were few economically attractive pieces of the former state-run sector to inspire the greed of state cadres and to turn such pieces into the economic bases of a linking among resources, the security apparatus, and organized crime.

MONGOLIAN INTELLIGENCE SERVICES DURING THE STATE-SOCIALIST PERIOD

Mongolia gained its independence from Chinese colonial rule in 1911 under the Bogd Khaan theocracy. A national intelligence service was formed within the Internal Ministry and the Military Ministry. Although the Bogd Khanate only lasted a short period of time before the turmoil that ultimately led to the people's revolution of 1921, Mongolia attempted to develop its own intelligence capabilities from scratch without any foreign influence.

During the state-socialist period (1921–1989), the development of the security apparatus was marked by its parallels with the intelligence services of the Soviet model. After 1921, Mongolia adopted Soviet political, economic, and cultural institutions, and this mimicry extended to the intelligence services as well. Intelligence cadres were educated in the Soviet Union or in Soviet-style training programs in Ulaanbaatar. Under the direct guidance from the Soviet Union through its resident advisers, Mongolian intelligence also committed atrocities against its population and in particular against Buddhist clerics in the 1930s.[7]

Following the end of World War II, the Ministry of Internal Affairs and the Military Ministry were amalgamated under the Ministry of Military and Public Security in 1955, and both ministries encountered massive personnel and resource reductions in the 1950s. But four years later, the Ministry of Public Security was separated from the military. The Ministry of Public Security oversaw the intelligence, police, border troops, firefighters, and penitentiary facilities. Intelligence and other security services were built up again from 1960 as Mongolia sided with the Soviet Union in the Sino-Soviet split and thus became a frontier state. During this Sino-Soviet confrontation, the main focus of the Mongolian intelligence services was China, which had been seen as a historic external threat for Mongolian sovereignty.

While the *cheka* image became widespread in Soviet and Mongolian literature, movies, and media, this image was linked to the heroism of Mongolian intelligence against Japanese and Chinese aggressions.[8] With this depiction, the Mongolian intelligence was able to recruit the best and brightest and to project an image as the protectors of independence. Given the tight state control and repression in all walks of life, organized crime was not a threat to the Mongolian state during the state-socialist period.

MONGOLIAN INTELLIGENCE SERVICES IN 1990

The end of the Soviet Union and state socialism in Mongolia is the most recent distinct period in the development of the intelligence services in Mongolia. This period began in 1989 when the Soviet Union lost its interests and influence over Communist bloc states. The democratization process in Mongolia was closely linked with the "third wave" of democracy movements in Central and Eastern Europe and "perestroika" in the Soviet Union via its political and intellectual links.[9] The most historic moment of the Mongolian democratic revolution occurred in March 1990 when the Politburo of the Mongolian People's Revolutionary Party (MPRP, known as the Mongolian People's Party since 2011) agreed to resign collectively, to conduct multiparty elections, and to remove party organs from the security organization.

The intelligence services played several key roles during this period. For one, intelligence officers were providing updates and analysis of democratic revolutions in state-socialist states, including the Soviet Union and China, to party officials. Second, the minister of public security, A. Jamsranjav, proposed not to use the force against demonstrators for political and economic liberalization.[10] This stance was also favored by the secretary-general of the Central Committee of the MPRP, J. Batmunkh, even though some members of the party leadership were proposing to suppress the demonstrators. Third, military units of the Ministry of Internal Security as well as some army units were on high alert during the democratic revolution. Finally, like other security organizations, the intelligence leaders remained neutral in the ongoing political turmoil and restricted its personnel's participation in demonstrations and political events.

Since the rest of this chapter analyzes the democratization of governance of the intelligence services in detail, a few important features of this period need to be highlighted. First, the core of the Ministry of Public Security was the Committee for State Security, which was the most sophisticated, networked security institution in Mongolia. According to interviews with former ministers, the intelligence services were the only reliable source for the party officials on both domestic and external matters by the late 1980s. Second, the Soviet-style process of intelligence institution building had been completed within two decades (1960–1980), and the Mongolian intelligence services were fully interoperable with its Soviet allies. Like many other Mongolian ministries (except the Ministry of Foreign Affairs), the Soviet advisory group at the Ministry of Public Security served as a conduit in this alliance.

Third, the level of public awareness and understanding about intelligence was low and misleading. The disclosure of archival materials documenting political purges in the 1930s, 1950s, and 1980s in response to public pressure discredited the intelligence organizations. Additionally, there were fears about the intelligence services' potential involvement in repression of the democratization movement. Past Soviet repressions in Eastern Europe, the purges executed by the Mongolian intelligence agencies during the state-socialist period, as well as the Tiananmen incident and the events of the 1989–1990 winter in Romania surely contributed to public unease. Finally, this period provided opportunities for the Mongolian new political leaders to reform the intelligence institutions.

DEMOCRATIC REFORM OF THE MONGOLIAN INTELLIGENCE SERVICES

The democratic reform of Mongolian intelligence organizations started in April 1990. Following the agreement between the MPRP and democratic leaders, the Ministry of Public Security (including the Committee for State Security, police, border and internal troops, and marshal services) was dismantled. The police and the Committee for State Security became separate government agencies.[11] In addition to this sudden, unplanned structural change, the intelligence activities required a new legal framework.

Several new acts concerning roles and missions of the intelligence services were approved by parliament to reorient intelligence operations in the newly emerging democratic society and free market economy. All government institutions were restructured under the 1992 constitution. The mission of security organizations was defined in the *1994 National Security Concept*, a fundamental statement of national security policy.

The General Intelligence Agency (GIA) was established in 1994 and its jurisdiction over other security organizations such as the Border Troops and Internal Troops was transferred to the Ministry of Justice and Internal Affairs. As with many other government ministries and agencies, intelligence professionals provided a lot of input in formulating and defining the new legal basis for the intelligence organizations. In other words, because parliament was overwhelmed with the immense and urgent demand for new legislation, to justify and coordinate the existence of any government institutions, most government ministries and agencies drafted the laws pertaining to their organization based on their expertise and lobbied for these drafts in parliament. It is unlikely that parliament members and their staff had either enough expertise or interest in intelligence matters at that time. No foreign experts offered advice on restructuring Mongolia's intelligence services.

Within this new structure, today there are three intelligence agencies. The GIA is the overarching agency for intelligence and counterintelligence while the Military Intelligence Agency and Border Intelligence Service are tasked with specific mandates for military and border intelligence, respectively. The GIA is tasked to conduct intelligence and counterintelligence operations, to protect state secrecy and communication, to provide security of state dignitaries, and to provide professional advice to political leaders and other intelligence services (military and border).

LEGISLATION GOVERNING INTELLIGENCE OPERATIONS

By 1999, activities of these intelligence services came to be governed by a specific set of legislation. The Law on Intelligence Operations (1997) set the legal limits and mechanisms to control covert intelligence operations. The law also framed the parameters and procedures for the Marshal Service, the police, and the Anti-Corruption Agency to conduct covert operations in addition to the three intelligence services. Moreover, the law prohibits high-ranking public servants from engaging in covert intelligence operations and provides rights to the president, parliament, and the prime minister to implement civilian control over the intelligence operations.

There were several laws governing intelligence operations. The Law on Intelligence (1999) is the overarching legislation for all three intelligence agencies that defines organizational structures, rights and responsibilities of intelligence professionals, and ways of overseeing the intelligence activities. In 1995, the parliament passed two other important laws: the Law on State Secrecy and the Law on State Protection designating the GIA the principal agency to protect state secrecy, state officials, and facilities. The GIA also is the lead agency to implement the Law on Terrorism, which was approved in 2004 in response to the United Nations (UN) Security Council resolution 1373. Under this law, the GIA chief chairs the National Council for Coordinating Antiterrorist Action. Legislation continues to be reviewed and revised by the parliament and its relevant committees. For example, the 1999 Law on Intelligence has undergone substantial reviews in 2001 and 2011.[12]

Although the legal framework has been well institutionalized, L. Batdolgor makes several important observations. First, there has not been any substantial judicial analysis of the legal environment for the intelligence activities. Second, no work has been done to educate public servants and the public to increase awareness of their legal rights and responsibilities vis-à-vis laws governing the intelligence services. Finally, intelligence professionals themselves still lack legal skills to use these laws.[13] However, the new institutional setting demonstrates Mongolia's departure from its Soviet and state-socialist origins as well as a striking contrast with intelligence reform in Russia and many former Soviet republics.

INTELLIGENCE OPERATIONS AND THE DEMOCRATIC STATE

Mongolia was not a Soviet republic and maintained its independent statehood during the Soviet period. Even after the collapse of the Soviet Union, Mongolia did not seek intelligence ties with the European Union or the United

States—ties that played an important role in reforming the intelligence services of postcommunist states in Central and Eastern Europe. Instead, Mongolian institutional reforms of the intelligence services were homegrown. While reformers looked around the world for models and examples, they were based on endogenous dynamics. The new structures of civilian oversight of the intelligence services exemplify this point.

Prior to 1990, the intelligence services were one of the most important instruments for party leaders to control society and to marginalize dissent. Under the 1992 constitution, Mongolia had chosen a semi-parliamentary system of government with substantial checks and balances between branches of the government. The winning party in parliamentary elections runs the executive office while the popularly elected president enjoys some leverage over the prime minister. The seventy-six-member, unicameral legislative body, the State Great Khural (*Улсын Их Хурал*), approves laws and budgets concerning intelligence, oversees the intelligence services through the Special Inspection Sub-Committee, requests intelligence and information, and audits the intelligence budget through the National Audit Office.

The president and prime minister, who leads the cabinet, have a shared responsibility over the GIA's chief. The prime minister appoints the chief in consultation with the president; in turn, the chief serves as a member of the cabinet under the prime minister. The president, on the other hand, has authority to seek intelligence and information from the chief of the GIA because he is the commander in chief of the Armed Forces and chair of the National Security Council. The National Security Council is the highest decision-making forum for the president, prime minister, and chairman of parliament; however, decisions are based on a consensus among these three members.[14] The chief of the GIA reports to the National Security Council.

The judiciary has extensive independent control over intelligence activities. Under the Law on Intelligence Activities, all types of surveillance activities require permission from the special prosecutor of the General Prosecutor's Office. The Investigative Service of the General Prosecutor's Office investigates crimes committed by the intelligence organizations. The Military Intelligence Agency and Border Troops Intelligence Service are also subject to civilian control of legislative, executive, and judiciary branches in addition to professional directives from the GIA. For instance, the prime minister can make organizational changes in the Military Intelligence Agency only in consultation with the president as commander in chief of the Armed Forces. The standard operating procedures and regulations for the Military Intelligence Agency need joint approval from the chief of the General Staff and chief of the GIA. Thus, Mongolia has institutionalized its intelligence services in line with the democratization process.

CHALLENGES

The reformed governance structure of the intelligences services has faced challenges for more than twenty years. First, the most acute challenge in a democracy is how much power and authority democratically elected officials have over the intelligence services versus officials' temptation to use intelligence for political and personal gains. Since 1997, the chief of the GIA has been a civilian public servant. But this opened opportunities for the winning political parties, for example, to assert their influence over the GIA by appointing their own members to senior intelligence posts. For instance, in 1996, the Democratic Party appointed Major General Jaalkhuugiin Baatar chief of the GIA.

A second challenge is the education and training of intelligence personnel.[15] In the early 1990s, the intelligence services lost many professionals as a result of the drawdown policy as well as economic hardship. At the same time, Russia was no longer offering educational and training assistance to Mongolia.[16] Although the Academy of the Ministry of Public Security was the main educational and training institution for intelligence professionals at the national level during the state-socialist period, its resources were split between new institutions like the Border Troops Academy and particularly the Police Academy in the early 1990s.[17]

The National Intelligence Academy was established in 1997 to improve professional development.[18] The academy offers a four-year bachelor's degree as well as master's degree program. From 1997 to 2011, 164 students received bachelor's degrees (and 52 of those students earned master's degrees) in security and legal affairs. These programs are approved by the Ministry of Education and Science. As stated in an interview with the chief of the GIA, about 70 percent of the intelligence personnel now have less than ten years of experience—the training and education needs are still important for the Mongolian intelligence community.[19] The number of foreign-educated intelligence professionals is still low, while the percentage of graduates from domestic programs is on the rise.[20] In contrast, the Military Intelligence Agency was able to train a few officers through the US International Military Education and Training (IMET) program, as the demand for interoperable military intelligence officers for Mongolian peacekeeping contingents increased. Because the military lacks regional (country-specific) and counterterrorism experts for the increasing number of deployments to UN and coalition missions, the GIA had to dispatch its personnel as embeds to peacekeeping contingents in Iraq, Afghanistan, Kosovo, and UN missions in Africa.

A third challenge is the enormous tasks that require close collaboration among civilian and military organizations with limited resources. During the Cold War, Mongolia enjoyed "protection" under the Soviet security and intelligence umbrella. Today, in addition to traditional tasks in the country, Mongolian intelligence agencies need to think about safety and security of its diplomatic missions, peacekeeping contingents, and citizens (more than 200,000 Mongolians live abroad); organized and transnational crimes; cyber threats; and economic and environmental crimes. One of the major differences of the Mongolian intelligence services from other intelligence services is the focus on provision of intelligence to decision makers rather than law enforcement; intelligence services are tasked to deal with twenty-one types of crimes.[21] Because of its increasing globalization, Mongolia is fighting against transnational crimes and economic crimes (smuggling precious minerals, endangered species, and explosives).[22]

Turning to Mongolia's neighbors, foreign countries pose a fourth challenge. Notably, the 2008–2009 Intelligence Report highlighted a noticeable increase in activities of foreign intelligence service in Mongolia to gain intelligence on domestic politics, foreign and defense policies, and high-ranking officials.[23] Moreover, two cases of treason have gained substantial attention in Mongolia. The first case related to a Mongolian diplomat who had passed secret foreign policy documents to Russia. A Mongolian diplomat received a prison term in 2011 while, according to the GIA official, Russia withdrew a diplomat as the investigation started.[24] The latter ongoing case involves a former counterintelligence officer who allegedly sold geological data to Chinese mining companies and businesses linked with the Chinese security services.[25]

Organized crime is another challenge. While drug busts are reported in the Mongolian media on occasion, there is not much evidence of cross-border flows through Mongolia. The somewhat antagonistic attitude of Mongolia's neighbors means that while the border is very long and not heavily guarded, cross-border flows of goods and people are monitored on all borders. Mongolia is regularly accused of being used in human trafficking, but the country is regarded as a source country of victims rather than as a destination for criminal activities, rendering this a concern primarily for the protection of Mongolian nationals against efforts to abduct them rather than a confrontation with organized crime.

Lastly, transparency is the fifth challenge as parliamentarians, their staffs, state auditors, and lawyers acquire more interest and expertise in intelligence and security matters. The Mongolian intelligence services seem to be aware of these challenges. The GIA has responded by reaching out to the public. The intelligence chiefs and experts have made themselves available for media interviews.[26] The GIA's press office was established in 2001, and later in 2008, it expanded their Public Relations Service, which responds to public inquiries, publicizes activities, and provides official explanations. The Public Relations Service organizes several open days per year to allow the public to visit the agency and to meet its senior intelligence leadership. Additionally, the National Intelligence Academy has evolved into a venue to engage civilian universities and think tanks and to conduct public opinion polls about public perceptions of intelligence activities and national security matters on an annual basis. The Research Center of the academy now serves as a key research hub on intelligence and security matters. Researchers and faculty members of the academy conduct projects to develop strategic and policy documents, organize academic conferences, and supervise graduate research. Notably, the National Intelligence Academy began publishing a peer-reviewed academic quarterly journal, *Independence*, in 2006.

CONCLUSION

Democratization and reforms of state-orchestrated intelligence operations have been mutually supportive in the case of Mongolia. Although the Mongolian intelligence services had an umbilical relation with Russia over seven decades, they did not follow the Russian example after the Soviet Union's collapse in using the intelligence services for political power and economic wealth. Nor were Mongolian reforms sponsored or designed by new allies or foreign advice. Instead, the Mongolian intelligence services have become more and more apolitical instruments in line with the desire of politicians and intelligence professionals. Importantly, the intelligence services did not play a hindering or violent role during the democratic revolutions and have not sided with politicians and business interest groups as in many former Soviet republics. The brief attempts of the politicization of the intelligence in the mid-1990s led politicians and intelligence professionals to depoliticize the service and to limit the involvement of the intelligence services in domestic matters despite contrary desires expressed by some political leaders. The clear test was the July 1, 2008, riots when the intelligence services remained neutral and did not take sides.

The endogenous reforms and democratization of the intelligence services was possible in the geopolitical context in which Mongolia found itself in the early 1990s. No immediate territorial disputes or threats, as well as a lack of attention paid to Mongolia by Russia, China, and other nations, allowed for a gradual reform process that paralleled the institutionalization of democratic institutions in other areas of Mongolian society. Macroeconomic destitution at the moment of democratization meant that democratic institutions were established before economic interests crystallized around mineral resources or other assets controlled by the state. This sequencing also played an important role in preventing the emergence of organized crime.

There are immense tasks waiting for the Mongolian intelligence services as Mongolia begins to attract economic and political interests of its neighbors and others. According to the action plans of each government since 2000, the emphasis appears to be on education and training of intelligence professionals and enhancement of the intelligence capacities to deal with new threats. Mongolians are in charge and responsible for the design, effectiveness, and efficiency of intelligence activities. Even if it is hard to measure the effectiveness of any intelligence activity unless there is a failure, the Mongolian case could serve as a useful example of building democracy-friendly, noncorrupt institutions.

NOTES

1. This chapter was reprinted with permission. It is a condensed version of "Intelligence Services in Democratic Mongolia," in *East Asian Intelligence and Organised Crime*, ed. Stephan Blancke (Berlin: Verlag Dr. Köster, 2015). Sections were previously published in Jargalsaikhan Mendee and Adiya Tuvshintugs, "Consolidating Democracy: The Reform of Mongolian Intelligence," *International Journal of Intelligence and CounterIntelligence* 26, no. 2 (2013): 241–59. The authors thank doctors Ravdan Bold, Thomas Bruneau, and L. Batdolgor for their extremely helpful and constructive comments on the draft and D. Narantsetseg and B. Enkhtuya for research assistance.

2. Gregory F. Treverton and Wilhelm Agrell, *National Intelligence Systems: Current Research and Prospects* (New York: Cambridge University Press, 2009); Florina Cristiana Matei and Thomas C. Bruneau, "Policymakers and Intelligence Reform in the New Democracies," *International Journal of Intelligence and CounterIntelligence* 24, no. 4 (2011): 656–91; Larry L. Watts, "Intelligence Reform in Europe's Emerging Democracies," *Studies in Intelligence* 48, no. 1 (2004): 11–25; Thomas C. Bruneau and Florina Cristiana Matei, "Intelligence in the Developing Democracies: The Quest for Transparency and Effectiveness," in *The Oxford Handbook of National Security Intelligence*, ed. Loch K. Johnson (Oxford: Oxford University Press, 2010); Thomas Bruneau and Kenneth Dombroski, "Reforming Intelligence: The Challenge of Control in New Democracies," in *Who Guards the Guardians and How: Democratic Civil-Military Relations*, ed. Thomas Bruneau and Scott Tollefson (Austin: University of Texas Press, 2006); Florina Cristiana Matei, "The Legal Framework for Intelligence in Post-communist Romania," *International Journal of Intelligence and CounterIntelligence* 22, no. 4 (2009): 667–98; Thomas C. Bruneau, "Controlling Intelligence in New Democracies," *International Journal of Intelligence and CounterIntelligence* 14, no. 3 (2001): 323–41.

3. Since the 1990 transition to democracy, Mongolia has been rated as "free" by the Freedom House, available at www.freedomhouse.org. Samuel P. Huntington, *The Third Wave: Democratization in the Late Twentieth Century* (Norman: University of Oklahoma Press, 1991), 24, 178–80; Verena Fritz, "Mongolia: The Rise and Travails of a Deviant Democracy," *Democratization* 15, no. 4 (2008): 766–88; Steven M. Fish, "Inner Asian Anomaly: Mongolia's Democratization in Comparative Perspective," *Communist and Post-communist Studies* 34, no. 3 (September 2001): 323–38.

4. Parliament passed the Law on Conflict of Interest on March 9, 2012, along with a series of legislation concerning the reform of the national judicial system. The parliament revised the election law and made a number of modifications in the current electoral system to increase accountability, to promote gender equality, and to limit populist politics.

5. "Freedom in the World 2013—Mongolia," Freedom House, March 16, 2013, http://www.freedomhouse.org/report/freedom-world/2013/mongolia-0.

6. Resnke Doorenspleet and Cas Mudde, "Upping the Odds: Deviant Democracies and Theories of Democratization," *Democratization* 15, no. 4 (2008): 817. For instance, Doorenspleet and Mudde argue that Mongolia had a weak military and Soviets were protecting Mongolian borders.

7. The totalitarian regimes in Moscow and Ulaanbaatar systematically massacred 30,000 people and kept the society under total fear until 1952. Out of 30,000 people who were executed in the 1930s, 17,000 were monks; in addition, 20,000–25,000 monks were persecuted in the 1920s. Most intellectuals, many of them graduates of Soviet schools, were persecuted during this time. See Bat-Erdene Batbayar, *Twentieth Century Mongolia* (Cambridge: Cambridge University Press, 1999), 309, 315–17; 361–65; Shagdariin Sandag and Harry Kendall, *Poisoned Arrows: The Stalin-Choibalsan Mongolian Massacres, 1921–1941* (Boulder, CO: Westview, 2000), 63; Chris Kaplonski, "Resorting to Violence: Technologies of Exception, Contingent States and the Repression of Buddhist Lamas in 1930s Mongolia," *Ethnos* 77 (2012): 72–92.

8. *Cheka* was an abbreviation of the Soviet State Security organization, Extraordinary Commission (*ЧК - чрезвычайная комиссия*), which was established immediately after the October revolution in 1917. Members of the commission were called *chekisty*. Here again, Mongolia closely paralleled the Soviet Union, and admission to this service was the most competitive among youths.

9. Fritz, "Mongolia."

10. Even in the late 1980s, intelligence officials were concerned about potential usage of the intelligence for personal interests of the party leaders. The public security minister, Agvaanjantsagiin Jamsranjav, raised this issue in his article "Reform— Goals of the State Security Organization," in the central party newspaper, *Unen*, no. 276, 1988.

11. Adiyagiin Altankhuyag and Yadamsurengiin Batsuuri, *Ayulgui Baidliin Manaand—80 jil* [Guarding the security—80 years] (Ulaanbaatar: Government Press, 2002).

12. "Revision of the Law on Intelligence," *State Bulletin*, no. 26 (2011).

13. Lanjiin Batdolgor, *Legal and Ethical Aspects of Intelligence Operations* (Ulaanbaatar: Intelligence Academy Press, 2012).

14. Thomas C. Bruneau, Florina Cristiana (Chris) Matei, and Sak Sakoda, "National Security Councils: Their Potential Functions in Democratic Civil-Military Relations," *Defense & Security Analysis* 25, no. 3 (September 2009).

15. Lanjiin Batdolgor, "Selection and Training of the Intelligence and Counterintelligence Professionals" [in Mongolian], *Bulletin Journal*, no. 1 (1995).

16. Between 1951 and 1990, the majority of Mongolia's key intelligence professionals were educated and trained in the Soviet Union. Most Soviet intelligence schools and short specialized courses were open to Mongolian intelligence professionals. But from 1934 onward, the Ministry of Internal Security had its own intelligence training and educational programs. These programs were modeled after the Soviet style (authors' interview on June 26, 2012).

17. Most intelligence professionals were educated at the Academy of the Ministry of Public Security in the years 1956–1994.

18. *Report of the National Intelligence Academy* (Ulaanbaatar, 2011).

19. Ravdan Bold, *Implementation of Law on Intelligence and Reforming Work Methods* (Ulaanbaatar: General Intelligence Agency Press, 2009); Ravdan Bold, *Improvement of Intelligence Analysis* (Ulaanbaatar: General Intelligence Agency Press, 2011).

20. Vaanchigiin Chuluunbat, "About Requirements for Intelligence Professionals" [in Mongolian], *Independence Journal*, no. 3 (2010): 12–18.

21. Under the Criminal Code of Mongolia, the intelligence services are tasked with conducting criminal investigations regarding treason, espionage, assassination of state and public dignitaries, conspiracy for the unlawful takeover of the state power, armed violence, sabotage, attempts against national unity, disclosure and loss of state secrecy, illegal border crossings, contraband, terrorism, armed conflicts, weapons of mass destruction, genocide, and mercenaries.

22. "Annual Country Report," in *The Minerals Yearbook*, vol. 3, *Area Reports: International* (Reston, VA: US Geological Survey, 2012), http://minerals.usgs.gov/minerals/pubs/country/asia.html#mg.

23. *Statement and Report 2008–2009* (Ulaanbaatar: General Intelligence Agency of Mongolia, 2010).

24. *Udriin Sanin* [Mongolian Daily Newspaper] 11 (3713), January 13, 2011.

25. "The Case Related to B. Nyamkhand Will Be Transferred to the Prosecutor," *NewsMN*, [Mongolian Online Newspaper], February 22, 2011, http://www.news.mn/content/55234.shtml.

26. The chief of the General Intelligence Agency gave interviews to the *Uptown Journal* and *Daily Newspaper* in 2010, *De facto* TV series and *Daily Post* newspaper in 2011, and *Eagle* TV series and *Public Official's Hour* of National TV in 2012, and he provided detailed responses to questions and explained about the changing roles of the intelligence services.

Myanmar: Security through Surveillance

Prem Mahadevan

Intelligence in Myanmar has three objectives: to preserve regime stability against dissidence, maintain political unity against ethno-nationalism, and uphold national sovereignty against external powers. Underlying these objectives is fear of foreign subversion and dominance, which in turn is driven by three factors. First, Myanmar is a developing country with a diverse and disunited population (eight major ethnic groups, 135 subgroups, and at least seventeen armed rebel organizations). More than seven decades after independence, the country is still developing a shared national identity. Second, memories of colonial rule and the accompanying drain of natural resources have fostered abundant caution in dealing with foreigners. In addition to the exploitation of forest and mineral resources, the ethnically divisive practices of government administrators remain a historical grievance inherited from colonialism. Third, Myanmar has three demographically larger neighbors (China, India, and Thailand) that have imperial histories and/or self-perceptions of civilizational greatness. The cumulative risk of cultural assimilation or economic expansionism posed by them is real, but it can also be exaggerated for political ends.

Since 1962 the Myanmar military, known as the Tatmadaw, has followed a state-consolidation model that emphasizes strategic neutrality under military-led governance. This model has survived regime changes in 1988, 2011, and 2016, albeit with modifications. It is likely to survive the 2021 coup as well. Military-led governance is preserved by a surveillance machinery that has both partisan and utilitarian purposes. Although associated with stratocratic authoritarianism, it may also prevent domestic ruptures. Such reasoning is unpopular among those who romanticize the pro-democracy movement led by Aung San Suu Kyi, daughter of the modern Myanmar state's founder,

Aung San. After Suu Kyi took over as state councillor in 2016, many of her admirers were disappointed by her unwillingness to condemn systemic violence against the Rohingya minority. Suu Kyi herself defended the state machinery, which she led over the next five years. With the February 2021 coup, political power has once again been overtly concentrated under the military leadership. Yet this time there has been less international idolization of Suu Kyi herself, perhaps because her foreign supporters are wary of championing her too strongly at the expense of wider principles.

Why, despite the transition to civilian rule, has political and intelligence change in Myanmar proved less dramatic than expected? This chapter examines how Myanmar's intelligence community has evolved and what its intelligence cultural characteristics are. To set the strategic context, it opens with an introduction to the country's tumultuous history, describing a covert operation whose two main results were a militaristic personality cult centered on Aung San as well as the genesis of the surveillance state.[1] Next, the chapter outlines the intelligence architecture and explains how there has been more continuity than change despite political transitions. Finally, it closes with an assessment of Myanmar's strategic position within the China-India rivalry in Asia. The chapter argues that political surveillance not only serves the Tatmadaw's interests but also keeps Myanmar unified in a context where military balances favor other states and historical tensions between various ethnic groups are yet to be fully addressed.

ASIA'S LAWRENCE OF ARABIA

In May 1940, a middle-aged man arrived in Yangon. His identification papers described him as Minami Masuyo, a correspondent for the Japanese newspaper *Yomiuri Shimbun*.[2] His real name was Suzuki Keiji, and he was an intelligence officer in the Japanese army, with the rank of colonel. Previously based in Bangkok, he had spent much of the 1930s cultivating long-distance contacts with the Thakin group, a gathering of ethnic Bamar nationalists seeking to end British colonial rule in Myanmar.

Under the British, the Bamar majority had been inflicted with one humiliation after another. First, the colonizers had seized Yangon and the coastal region in two wars between 1824 and 1852. In a third and final clash, they had marched to the seat of the Bamar monarchy in Mandalay in 1885 and deposed the king. The capital was shifted to Yangon to facilitate the extraction of natural resources by sea, a move that undermined the already fragile cohesion of the Bamar-led state. Ethnic minorities who had previously been repressed were prioritized for job recruitment in the new colonial administration. As a final insult, Indians were encouraged to emigrate to Myanmar, taking away jobs that Bamars thought were rightfully theirs. The 1930s had seen a backlash, in the form of attacks by Bamar nationalists on Indian workers, a trend that worsened as the aftershocks of the Great Depression began to create widespread agrarian unrest. Myanmar was ripe for revolt, and Colonel Suzuki, who enthusiastically espoused the Japanese slogan "Asia for Asians," was keen to lead one.

Officially, Suzuki's mission was to block off the Burma Road, through which the British were sending military aid from India to General Chiang Kai-shek's Kuomintang resistance fighters in Japanese-occupied China.[3] The Japanese spymaster learned of a Thakin leader called Aung San, who was seeking help from Mao Zedong's Chinese communists to fight the British. Suzuki discovered that Aung San was in China and dispatched agents to meet the Bamar leader and arrange for him to visit Tokyo. There, Aung San was cultivated by Suzuki and agreed to cooperate in fighting the British.

In February 1941, a resistance organization called Minami Kikan was established under Japanese tutelage. That same summer, a group of Thakin activists, later remembered as the "Thirty Comrades," assembled for paramilitary training on Japanese-occupied Hainan Island. They constituted the core of the future Burma Independence Army (BIA), which was formed in December 1941, three weeks after the Japanese attack at Pearl Harbor. The BIA was led by Suzuki, who adopted the pseudonym Bo Mogyo ("Thunderbolt") to exploit a popular legend in Myanmar that one day a thunderbolt would burst from the sky and strike down an "umbrella," a coded reference to British colonialism. The Japanese officer additionally styled himself as a descendant of the deposed Bamar monarchy to give respectability to his position as BIA leader. The myth was reinforced by his chief of staff, Aung San.

Together with the Japanese Fifteenth Army, the BIA invaded Myanmar with 2,300 men in early 1942. Within weeks, they had taken Yangon as a panicky colonial administration evacuated Europeans to India. But independence proved elusive. The Japanese high command was in no hurry to grant self-determination to the Bamar people. Over the next three years, Aung San bided his time, avoiding an open clash with his patrons. The BIA during this time served as a collaborationist force, pursuing ethnic minorities who had benefited from British rule and who were perceived as conniving for an eventual return of the colonial power. In a series of massacres, BIA troops razed 400 villages populated by the Karen minority in the Irrawaddy Delta, killing at least 1,800 people. Other attacks took place across the country.[4]

After retreating from Myanmar, the British had played their favorite tactic—divide and conquer—by relying remotely on the country's minorities to tie down the Japanese occupation. Meanwhile, British commanders prepared to launch a counteroffensive from India. Besides the Karens, Kachin tribesmen in the north and Rohingyas in the west were used to harass Japanese troop movements. The long-term impact of these operations would poison ethnic relations between the Bamar and various ethnic groups for decades to come.

As the tide of war turned against Japan, Aung San made his move in 1945. Keiji had long since been posted out of the country, and thus the interpersonal ties that had previously stayed Aung San's hand were no longer relevant. He revolted against the occupation force and soon emerged as the preeminent military figure in the country. As Myanmar transitioned toward independence, he took over the reins of government, only to be assassinated less than a year later along with six cabinet colleagues. This event killed not just the prospective leadership of the soon-to-be-sovereign state but also political initiatives aimed at containing ethnic tensions. Forty-one years after his death, Aung San's daughter emerged as a pivotal figure in the country's politics. In the interim, the reins of power moved into the hands of another member of the Thirty Comrades: General Ne Win, who set the state machinery on its present course.

RISE OF THE SURVEILLANCE STATE

Following independence, Ne Win became commander in chief of the Tatmadaw, the successor organization to the Burma Independence Army. For the first decade of Myanmar's existence, he served under a civilian prime minister. Having been trained by the Japanese *Kempeitai* (military police) as an intelligence and subversion specialist, he was mindful of the contribution that counterintelligence could offer regime security. In 1958, he forced the civilian government to hand over power to the Tatmadaw, pending new elections. Under a military-run caretaker government, Ne Win established the Military Intelligence Service (MIS) as a powerful branch within the armed forces.

Ne Win ultimately seized power in a coup in March 1962. The MIS became his favored instrument for quelling political dissent. In the early 1950s, the civilian regime had created a Bureau of Special Investigations to pursue corruption suspects, but in 1964 Ne Win subordinated that agency, as well as the police Special Branch and the Criminal Investigation Department, to military control by creating a National Intelligence Bureau (NIB).[5] The NIB was dominated by MIS officers, although the three other agencies were represented. In 1974, as the Tatmadaw handed power to the nominally "civilian" Burma Socialist Programme Party (also led by Ne Win), the NIB was granted formal status under law.

Under Ne Win, the Myanmar state retreated into itself. There were plenty of challenges left over from independence, most notably pacification of the hill tribes in remote border regions. This task gained urgency because during the 1950s Kuomintang remnants had moved into the Wa Hills following Communist victory in the Chinese civil war. Expelling them from Myanmar was a challenge, not least because they enjoyed covert support from the United States' Central Intelligence Agency (CIA). One of Southeast Asia's most notorious drug traffickers today, a man called Wei Hsueh-kang, first gained prominence through covert operations with the Kuomintang. A 2011 Thai commentary states:

> The CIA catalyzed the explosion of opium in the Golden Triangle (a 950,000 square kilometre mountainous region spread over parts of Burma, Thailand, Laos and Vietnam) in the 1950s where it backed first the Kuomintang (KMT)—remnants of General Chiang Kai-shek's Chinese nationalist forces—and then a host of other militias as part of the US' "anti-communist" covert wars in Indochina. US support for the KMT's drug-funded fifth army ignited a race to control this expansive trade, with Burma, Thailand and later Laos competing for a share of the burgeoning business.[6]

Wei Hsueh-kang went on to become chief financier of the United Wa State Army (UWSA), the largest ethnic rebel organization in Myanmar, with a militia of 30,000 fighters.[7] The UWSA has a self-administered zone in northern Shan state, along the border with China's Yunnan province. The area under their control is described as "roughly the size of Belgium."[8]

The connection among the KMT, the Wa, and Myanmar's domestic security is crucial because KMT bases on Myanmar territory triggered a Chinese proxy invasion in January 1968. Using the Communist Party of Burma (CPB) as a cover, Beijing sent in so-called "volunteers" to fight the KMT.[9] The invading forces consisted of Chinese nationals and carried Chinese weapons and rations but were front-ended by Myanmar Communist leaders.[10] This made them appear to be an "indigenous" entity, rather than a manifestation of cross-border aggression. Between 1968 and 1972, the CPB conquered the Wa Hills and dislodged the KMT. The Tatmadaw, meanwhile, clashed with the invaders and later with locally recruited guerrillas who were supported by China. Such engagements bred suspicion about Beijing among young army officers, which might explain why Myanmar sought to reduce its economic dependence on China during the 2010s, as many of these officers rose to the top of the army leadership.[11]

Aware that his military capability was no match for China and with the memory of colonialism still fresh, Ne Win pursued a policy of strict neutrality and isolationism during the Cold War. He expelled most of the Indian minority and, in the 1970s, intensified surveillance of university campuses. Teachers at higher education institutions were obliged to report suspicious student activity. Among students in the Yangon region, one in every four was thought to be a government informer. The level of paranoia may not have been unjustified, as plots against the military dictator, originating within the military, were uncovered during this period.

The Military Intelligence Service was rechristened the Directorate of Defence Services Intelligence (DDSI) in 1969, only to be renamed the Office of the Chief of Military Intelligence in 2001 and renamed yet again as the Office of the Chief of Military Security Affairs in 2004, a name it still holds today. When it was known as the DDSI, the service underwent a radical overhaul in 1983–1984, after a terrorist bombing in Yangon by North Korean operatives killed twenty-one people. The bomb had been intended to assassinate the visiting South Korean president but detonated early.[12] Ne Win treated the embarrassing security lapse as an opportunity to get rid of the head of military intelligence, who was seen as too ambitious, replacing him with an upcoming protégé called Khin Nyunt. For the next twenty years, the latter would be the intelligence czar of Myanmar, overseeing some of the harshest repression against the pro-democracy movement that emerged in 1988.

The so-called "Four Eights Uprising" of 1988 caught the regime by surprise. Although the MIS/DDSI had been considered "one of Asia's most efficient secret police forces," Andrew Selth, a leading expert on Myanmar's intelligence apparatus, later pointed out that the service's coverage has tended to be "wider than it is deep."[13] This seems a fair assessment. In the late 1980s, there was a broader trend of competent intelligence agencies failing to warn policy makers about the risk of public unrest, such as the Stasi in East Germany and the Israeli Shin Bet in the Occupied Territories. While protest movements elsewhere were either partially or wholly successful in prompting political change, in Myanmar the result was far less dramatic. Although Ne Win stepped down and handed power back to the Tatmadaw leadership, he continued to be influential behind the scenes.

A twenty-three-year period of direct military rule ensued with the government, led by the senior-most general of the Tatmadaw and eighteen colleagues, ruling as a council. The "junta" arrangement lasted until 2011, when a quasi-civilian government under a retired general took power. The next four years (2011–2015) were spent rebuilding Myanmar's ties with the international community, which led to an easing of sanctions that had been imposed by Western countries after 1988. Aung San Suu Kyi, who had emerged as leader of the pro-democracy movement, was released from house arrest in 2010. Her party, the National League for Democracy (NLD), was allowed to contest the 2015 election and won it by a landslide. The following year, Suu

Kyi took office as "state councillor," a position that granted her governing powers. She was ineligible to be president because members of her immediate family were foreign nationals.

Perceptions of Myanmar's intelligence apparatus have been heavily informed by accounts of ruthless suppression of pro-democracy activists during the period of 1988 to 2011. In part, this view was colored by close ties that developed between the Tatmadaw junta and the Chinese Communist Party. Both were willing to crush popular protests by force, going against the dominant tide of regime change that was sweeping across Eastern Europe at around the same time. In need of an international patron, the Tatmadaw set aside its suspicions of Beijing and opened Myanmar to Chinese investors, forging business ties based on crony capitalism.

The perception of a brutal garrison state was also partly real. The military intelligence machinery, operating both independently and through the police Special Branch, is alleged to have interrogated up to 10,000 dissidents using methods amounting to torture. After 1988, the number of MIS/DDSI detachments across the country went up from twelve to thirty. Five were based in Yangon, where they reported on specific targets (for example, detachment MI-6 reported on underground groups, while MI-7 reported on student activism).[14] Arrests of civilian politicians were common. To show solidarity, international advocacy groups based in Thailand began running couriers to opposition figures. Called "pigeons," these couriers were Western citizens (whose passports afforded them at least some protection from summary execution or harsh physical treatment). They would obtain a visitor visa for Myanmar, surreptitiously contact opposition activists as instructed, and deliver supplies or funds. Some, like future CIA officer Amaryllis Fox, smuggled out multimedia that was broadcast to the outside world.[15]

MORE CONTINUITY THAN CHANGE

Supporters of Suu Kyi would argue that her ability to govern after becoming state councillor was circumscribed by Myanmar's constitution, and there was some merit to this argument. Under the present constitution introduced in 2008, three ministries—defense, home affairs, and border affairs—remained under direct military control. Their heads reported to the Tatmadaw commander in chief, not to Suu Kyi. She had no control over the Office of the Chief of Military Security Affairs (as military intelligence is called now), nor over the Bureau of Special Investigation, the police Special Branch, or any other intelligence units. She only controlled the Ministry of Foreign Affairs because she held this portfolio personally.

Furthermore, 25 percent of seats in parliament were reserved for serving Tatmadaw officers under the 2008 constitution. Since constitutional amendments could only be introduced by a 75 percent majority vote, this meant that the military had (and still has) veto power over the legislative process at any time. Thus, the political transition from military to civilian rule in 2011–2016 was incremental and, as was demonstrated by the February 2021 coup, easily reversible. In part, this has been because of the institutional stability of the post-1988 military-led junta system as a collective dictatorship rather than a regime built on a personality cult. The latter was the fatal weakness of Ne Win's government, and it has also been a factor that limited Suu Kyi's own credibility among sections of the Myanmar population during her 2016–2021 stint as state councillor.

But for being Aung San's daughter, Suu Kyi herself would likely not have been the people's choice to lead the country. Andrew Selth has observed that Suu Kyi's long period of house arrest left her incommunicado and allowed legions of far-removed supporters to casually project their own values and beliefs onto her. Selth noted that Suu Kyi herself tried to temper expectations and may have been genuinely uncomfortable with the burden that was being imposed on her to enact sweeping changes. She also played a double-game during her years in the political wilderness, leveraging the benefits of an influential fan-following in the West. Influential voices in the United Kingdom romanticized her since she was educated in England and married to an Englishman.[16] Her subsequent unwillingness to publicly condemn violence against the Rohingya minority caught admirers by surprise, even though it was consistent with the "real" Suu Kyi.

An academic article from 2013 commented that Suu Kyi's approach to ethnic tensions has always been to gloss over real grievances that minorities had—and subordinate these to her larger objective of coming to power at the helm of a Bamar-dominated government.[17] An Indian journalist opined in 2018, once international criticism of "the Lady" had mounted, that as Suu Kyi's father had also been the founder of the Tatmadaw, she may have reflexively held the military as an institution in high regard.[18] In any case, expectations that she would usher in a liberal transformation of Myanmar politics have proven to be seriously misplaced, even before the 2021 coup demonstrated how circumscribed her power was.

Regardless of whether or not elections are held, the historical legacy and political architecture of Myanmar ensures that it remains a garrison state with a sharp division of labor between civilians and soldiers. At the best of times, civilians can only hope to handle international perception management and nonsensitive issues of governance. Soldiers would meanwhile deal with domestic security, which is going to remain a concern so long as ethnic rebel groups located near the China border refuse to enter into a cease-fire agreement with the government (rebels elsewhere in Myanmar have accepted the cease-fire).[19] Even prior to the 2021 coup, members of Suu Kyi's own party, the National League for Democracy, were being monitored by the police Special Branch, which came under the Home Affairs Ministry and therefore under Tatmadaw control.[20] The main difference between the 1988–2011 and 2016–2021 periods was that, while surveillance intensified, especially through technical collection, physical intimidation became less common.[21] Even so, foreign journalists reported reluctance on the part of interviewees to speak openly, due to worries about official harassment. Visiting delegations from international agencies alleged that their freedom to travel within the country was curtailed (a charge refuted in suitably vague terms by the NLD).[22]

The technological upgrade of surveillance methods began in the early 2010s as Myanmar opened up to foreign businesses. An Israeli security company supplied mobile "phone-hacking systems" to the police. Malware developed by a German company was found in mobile devices within the country. The same company had previously sold malware to Arab governments to hack journalists and dissidents.[23] Owing to Myanmar's extraordinarily high growth rate of internet access, electronic tracking proved to be more comprehensive than surveillance based on human informers. At the start of the decade, even as political transition was yet to begin, the government had stipulated that internet cafés provide records on user activity, banned transferring information from or onto storage devices, such as USB, and barred Voice over Internet Protocol (VoIP).[24]

While the NLD administration lasted, the civilian-staffed but military-controlled police were the main tools for exercising mass political control. Previously military intelligence personnel had directly handled this task, a situation that has possibly repeated itself in 2021. The shift from military to civilian spying in the domestic sphere was not a nod to institutional changes. It represented a preexisting tendency by the Tatmadaw to occasionally restrict the power of the military intelligence establishment. In 1983–1984, the then DDSI was overhauled under a new chief, Khin Nyunt. Over the next two decades, this man eventually rose to become the prime minister of Myanmar and the third most powerful figure in the junta, after the Tatmadaw commander in chief and his deputy. He allegedly collected compromising material on rival generals. Then in 2004, Khin Nyunt was abruptly arrested and sentenced to forty-four years' imprisonment (he was granted house arrest and pardoned within eight years).[25] The trigger for his fall, according to some speculation, was he grew too powerful (the same perception had brought down his predecessor). Most of his appointees in the military intelligence community were imprisoned, and 1,500 personnel were forced into retirement while another 2,500 were transferred back to line infantry units. The purge greatly weakened the service's collection capability.

Khin Nyunt's successor had no experience in intelligence work. Beginning from 2005, the service was unable to prevent a series of bombings in the country.[26] The National Intelligence Bureau was abolished, and for the first time in four decades, there was no overall leader of the intelligence apparatus. Power among spies was decentralized; this suited the Tatmadaw leadership, who are wary and resentful of the relatively urbane and slick operators of the intelligence community and seem to relish in periodically reminding them of their place.

THE ROLE OF EXTERNAL FACTORS

Andrew Selth has pointed out that intelligence in Myanmar is overwhelmingly a domestic-oriented affair. The country is not known to have a dedicated foreign intelligence service.[27] On the one hand, this feeds into the popular image of a state ruled by a corrupt junta that is more concerned with the perpetuation of its elite privileges than about public welfare. But there is also another factor at play: the sense of vulnerability that comes from having porous borders with militarily more powerful neighbors. To the west, India has long been tarnished not just in Myanmar but also elsewhere in Asia, as having previously "collaborated" with colonialism by providing the mercenary manpower base that enabled British conquests. To the west, China is also viewed with suspicion because awareness of eighteenth-century invasions by the Qing dynasty lingers within the Myanmar historical consciousness. The invasions were militarily unsuccessful, which added a heroic spark in the minds of later Myanmar generations.

Together with Beijing's support for the CPB from the 1960s to the late 1980s, and its ongoing involvement with ethnic rebel groups (some of which splintered from the CPB), it is unsurprising that an undercurrent of multi-directional xenophobia runs in Bamar politics. The pro-democracy movement, which has been supported by the West (and to a lesser extent, India), is viewed as a destabilizing agent. Concern over destabilization is anyway what pushed the Tatmadaw closer to Beijing after 1988. In return for diplomatic and economic support, China gained preferential access to mineral and forest resources. Rebel organizations along the Yunnan border cut deals with Chinese authorities, allowing thousands of low-skilled Chinese workers to cross the border without visas and harvest timber to feed China's construction industry. Their activities were illegal according to Myanmar law, but the

Tatmadaw lacked the ability to enforce border control. Instead, it relied on ill-funded militias to do the same. These militias, in turn, have been implicated in the drug trade and likely serve as cutouts for local Tatmadaw officials to receive kickbacks from illicit cross-border flows.

In all this, there remains the Sino-Indian geopolitical rivalry. Myanmar lies at the fringes of both countries' civilizational spheres, and its position is vaguely analogous to that of Switzerland in the Franco-German rivalry prior to 1945. Since Myanmar is caught between two mutually opposed neighboring powers, its most sensible policy is one of neutrality. Yet, the weak state capacity of the central government means that it cannot prevent Myanmar territory from being used as a battleground for covert operations.

During the 1960s, China supported separatist rebels in India's northeast region by providing their leadership with paramilitary training. The rebels would travel in batches through Myanmar to Yunnan. Their travel was facilitated by Kachin guerrillas. The latter had initially hoped for support from India in their own struggle against the Tatmadaw, but when their overtures were rebuffed by New Delhi, they turned to Beijing. In return for Chinese assistance, they agreed to allow anti-Indian guerrillas to travel through their strongholds to reach China. Stung by this turn of events, India henceforth was careful to track Chinese contacts with ethnic rebel groups inside Myanmar, which necessitated expanding intelligence coverage of that country but also fed the Tatmadaw's concerns about foreign intrigues.[28]

During the 2010s, India was a quiet beneficiary of rapprochement between the Tatmadaw and the NLD. The previous tension between extending moral support to a democratic movement in a neighboring country and simultaneously staying on good terms with that country's politically active security establishment momentarily disappeared. New Delhi was hoping to compete with China for economic access to Myanmar. That competition continues and is playing out in the covert realm to some degree: media commentary suggests that the Arakan Army, a rebel organization in western Myanmar, is sabotaging Indian infrastructure projects at the insistence of Beijing. The Chinese state-owned company Norinco has been alleged to supply weapons to rebel organizations in both Myanmar and India.[29] Thus, eighty years on, the game played by Colonel Suzuki Keiji is being resurrected: Myanmar remains crucial to strategists outside its borders because of its pivotal location and abundant resources. As a link between the landlocked southern Chinese hinterland and the openness of the Indian Ocean, it is too important for Beijing to lose. As the only land bridge between South Asia and the "tiger economies" of Southeast Asia, it is too important for New Delhi to ignore. With its vast timber reserves (the country accounts for half of the world's natural teak), it offers tremendous scope to drive development and poverty alleviation in

Asia. In this context, it is unsurprising that the Tatmadaw finds it necessary to remain vigilant against domestic developments that threaten its own entrenched power base, which it considers inseparable from the economic and security interests of Myanmar as a whole.

CONCLUSION

Surveillance will remain the primary instrument for preserving the domestic status quo in what might become a crucial battleground in any larger Sino-American contest for dominance over Asia. Unlike Switzerland, which by the late nineteenth century was both rich enough and institutionally strong enough to resist external interference in its affairs, Myanmar is far from being a fully sovereign nation. Like Switzerland lying on a vital north-south and east-west trade axis across Europe, Myanmar lies on trade routes that are vital to both Chinese and Indian geoeconomic aspirations. Without having the military might and international goodwill to defend its unity and stability against foreign-controlled actors, the country will have little choice but to use its intelligence apparatus for political policing.

NOTES

1. Timothy McLaughlin, "Mythmaking in the New Myanmar," *Foreign Policy*, November 6, 2015, https://foreignpolicy.com/2015/11/06/mythmaking-in-the-new -myanmar-aung-san-suu-kyi-elections-burma-movie/.

2. Andrew Thomson, "Keiji Suzuki: The Japanese Lawrence of Arabia Who Helped End British Rule in Myanmar," *Tea Circle Oxford*, July 26, 2018, https:// teacircleoxford.com/2018/07/26/keiji-suzuki-the-japanese-laurence-of-arabia-who -helped-end-british-rule-in-myanmar/.

3. Wei Yan Aung, "The Day Myanmar Said Farewell to Japan's Maverick Wartime Spy," *The Irrawaddy*, July 12, 2020, https://www.irrawaddy.com/specials/on -this-day/day-myanmar-said-farewell-japans-maverick-wartime-spy.html.

4. Aung Zaw, "The Man behind the Burma Independence Army," *The Irrawaddy*, August 25, 2017, https://www.irrawaddy.com/opinion/commentary/man-behind -burma-independence-army.html.

5. Andrew Selth, "Myanmar's Intelligence State," *Australian Outlook* (Australian Institute of International Affairs), September 20, 2018, https://www.international affairs.org.au/australianoutlook/myanmars-intelligence-state/.

6. "The DEA Hunt for Wei Hsueh-kang?," *Chiang Rai Times*, June 15, 2011, https:// www.chiangraitimes.com/thailand-national-news/the-dea-hunt-for-wei-hsueh-kang/.

7. Aung Zaw, "Shadowy Drug Lord Wei Hsueh-kang's Influence Still Felt in Myanmar's Wa Region and Beyond," *The Irrawaddy*, March 9, 2020, https://www

.irrawaddy.com/opinion/commentary/shadowy-drug-lord-wei-hsueh-kangs-influence
-still-felt-myanmars-wa-region-beyond.html.

8. Dominique Dillabough-Lefebvre, "The Wa Art of Not Being Governed," *The Diplomat*, May 28, 2019, https://thediplomat.com/2019/05/the-wa-art-of-not-being
-governed/.

9. Bertil Lintner, "The United Wa State Army and Burma's Peace Process," *Peaceworks*, no. 147 (April 2019): 6, https://www.usip.org/sites/default/files/2019
-07/pw_147-the_united_wa_state_army_and_burmas_peace_process.pdf.

10. Sithu Aung Myint, "The UWSA: 30 Years of Going Its Own Way," *Frontier Myanmar*, March 10, 2019, https://www.frontiermyanmar.net/en/the-uwsa-30-years
-of-going-its-own-way/.

11. Aung Zaw, "Myanmar's Generals Make a Show of Displeasure at China's Arming of Rebels," *The Irrawaddy*, November 26, 2019, https://www.irrawaddy
.com/opinion/commentary/myanmars-generals-make-show-displeasure-chinas
-arming-rebels.html.

12. Andrew Selth, "Burma's Intelligence Apparatus," *Intelligence and National Security* 13, no. 4 (1998): 45, 60–63.

13. Selth, "Burma's Intelligence Apparatus," 142.

14. Kyaw Zwa Moe, "Bye Bye, Big Brother," *The Irrawaddy*, October 20, 2020, https://www.irrawaddy.com/from-the-archive/bye-bye-big-brother.html.

15. In her autobiography, Fox may have used artistic licence to considerably exaggerate her derring-do while couriering for the Myanmar democracy movement. See David Scott Mathieson, "One Flew over the Pigeon's Nest," *The Irrawaddy*, May 11, 2020, https://www.irrawaddy.com/culture/books/one-flew-pigeons-nest.html; Allie Jaynes, "Former CIA Agent Talks Smuggling Video Out of Myanmar and Working Undercover in New Memoir," CBC Radio, November 5, 2019, https://www.cbc
.ca/radio/thecurrent/the-current-for-nov-5-2019-1.5348042/former-cia-agent-talks
-smuggling-video-out-of-myanmar-and-working-undercover-in-new-memoir-1.534
8242.

16. Andrew Selth, "The Fallen Idol: Aung San Suu Kyi and the Politics of Personality," ABC (Australia), September 12, 2017, https://www.abc.net.au/religion/the
-fallen-idol-aung-san-suu-kyi-and-the-politics-of-personality/10095394.

17. Matthew J. Walton, "The 'Wages of Burman-ness': Ethnicity and Burman Privilege in Contemporary Myanmar," *Journal of Contemporary Asia* 43, no. 1 (2013): 16.

18. Abhijit Dutta, "Why We Misread Suu Kyi and Her Refusal to Demonise the Burmese Army," *Economic Times* (India), November 25, 2018, https://economic
times.indiatimes.com/news/international/world-news/why-we-misread-suu-kyi-and
-her-refusal-to-demonise-the-burmese-army/articleshow/66786330.cms?from=mdr.

19. "China's Role in Myanmar's Internal Conflicts," US Institute of Peace, September 14, 2018, 22, https://www.usip.org/publications/2018/09/chinas-role
-myanmars-internal-conflicts.

20. Zaw Zaw Htwe, "In Myanmar, Even a Chief Minister Is Prone to Military-Controlled Intelligence," *The Irrawaddy*, July 21, 2020, https://www.irrawaddy.com/

news/burma/myanmar-even-chief-minister-prone-military-controlled-intelligence
.html.

21. Karin Dean, "Myanmar: Surveillance and the Turn from Authoritarianism?,"
Surveillance & Society 15, nos. 3/4 (2017): 500.

22. Simon Lewis, "U.N. Envoy Complains of State Surveillance, Access Restrictions in Myanmar," Reuters, July 21, 2017, https://www.reuters.com/article/us
-myanmar-un-idUSKBN1A61ZR.

23. "German Spyware Tools Being Used in Myanmar," *Mizzima*, July 11,
2019, http://mizzima.com/article/german-spyware-tools-being-used-myanmar; Patrick Howell O'Neill, "The Spyware Used by Arab Dictators Has Now Shown up in
Myanmar," *MIT Technology Review*, July 10, 2019, https://www.technologyreview
.com/2019/07/10/65585/spyware-dealers-spotted-in-myanmar/.

24. "Surveillance of Media and Internet Stepped up under New Civilian
President," *Reporters without Borders*, May 17, 2011, https://rsf.org/en/news/
surveillance-media-and-internet-stepped-under-new-civilian-president.

25. Wei Yan Aung, "The Day Myanmar's Military Intelligence Chief Was
Sacked," *The Irrawaddy*, October 19, 2020, https://www.irrawaddy.com/specials/
on-this-day/day-myanmars-military-intelligence-chief-sacked.html.

26. Aung Zaw, "A Burmese Spy Comes in from the Cold," *The Irrawaddy*, June
2006, https://www2.irrawaddy.com/article.php?art_id=5828&page=1.

27. Andrew Selth, "Myanmar," in *Intelligence Communities and Cultures in Asia
and the Middle East: A Comprehensive Reference*, ed. Bob de Graaff (London: Lynne
Rienner, 2020), 200–203.

28. Avinash Paliwal, "India's Kachin Connection in Myanmar," *Raisina Debates*,
October 7, 2020, https://www.orfonline.org/expert-speak/indias-kachin-connection
-in-myanmar/.

29. "The Easy Flow of Illicit Chinese Weapons into Myanmar Poses Threats to
Regional Security and Stability," *EFSAS Commentary*, July 24, 2017, https://www
.efsas.org/commentaries/the-easy-flow-of-illicit-chinese-weapons-into-myanmar/.

Nepal: A Developing Intelligence Culture

Bishnu Raj Upreti

Nepal is a landlocked country in South Asia. According to the preliminary results of the 2021 national census, it has a population of roughly 29 million people and a total area of about 147,516 square kilometers.[1] Known as the country of Mount Everest and birthplace of Buddha, it is situated between two powerful neighbors, China and India. Being the nexus of these two major powers, this key geopolitical location makes intelligence important for the Nepali government. In this sense, intelligence is broadly interpreted as a process and outcome as well as an essential tool for public order and national security. The security issues that make intelligence vital in Nepal range from radicalization to geopolitical issues to terrorism to organized crime.

This chapter approaches intelligence in a broad context beyond dealing with public order and covering intelligence activities of nonstate actors like insurgent groups. It argues that Nepal's intelligence culture has been shaped by a variety of characteristics, including the country's unique geostrategic location, and the culture is in flux. In particular, intelligence challenges and ineffectiveness as well as a change in politics have made the intelligence culture fluid. To understand this, the chapter proceeds with three sections. The first examines the history of intelligence in Nepal with the emergence of informal and then formal structures. Next, the chapter explores the factors that shape Nepali intelligence and then analyzes oversight and Nepal's collaboration with foreign countries. Lastly, it provides a conclusion that describes the features that influence Nepal's intelligence culture and demonstrates that the culture is in transition.

The chapter takes a wide-ranging approach to understanding intelligence because Nepal has several intelligence services with a variety of responsibilities. The National Intelligence Department (NID) is the dedicated and specialized state institution for intelligence collection. Other services that directly and/or indirectly engaged in intelligence-related activities are the following: the Department of Military Intelligence (DMI) of the Nepali Army (NA), Crime Investigation Department (CID), Anti-Terrorism Cell and Special Taskforce of the Nepal Police (NP), the Armed Police Force (APF), and the National Vigilance Centre (mainly responsible to check corruption, irregularity, and inefficiency in government offices). Topically, the state's intelligence services are focused on national security, terrorism, narcotics and drug trafficking, economic embezzlement, human trafficking, money laundering, cross-border crime, cybercrime, and organized crime.

The private sector in Nepal also has an intelligence role. Private security companies (PSC) are growing in Nepal. The PSCs are operating under the conceptual framework of new public management wherein private security companies handle security demands of public and private companies, which necessitate collecting information related to their work. Banks, multinational companies, and telecommunication agencies also invest in collecting and analyzing intelligence for their internal purposes. Additionally, political parties gather information for internal and external party purposes. Likewise, other private agencies also collect relevant information related to their activities to perform threat and risk assessments.

Non-statutory forces (NSF) who took the law into their own hands and organized intelligence services for their activities were frequently observed during the time of the insurgency. Some of the violent NSF observed during the time of the armed conflict from 1996 to 2006 that needed intelligence included Limbuwan Krantikari Sangathan, Limbuwan Rajya Parishad, Limbuwan Jana Parishad, Limbuwan Swayamsevak Sangh, Madhes Rastra Janatantrik Party (Krantikari), Janatantric Tarai Mukti Morcha (Pratik), Akhil Tarai Mukti Morcha (Goit), Janatantric Tarai Mukti Morcha (Prithvi group), Tarai Army, Madhesi Mukti Tigers, Tarai Tigers, Janatantric Tarai Mukti Morcha (Jwala Singh group), Janatantric Tarai Mukti Morcha (Rajan), Janatantric Madhesh Mukti Tigers, Samyukta Tharuhat Sangharsa Samiti, Samyukta Madhesi Morcha, Tharuhat Swayatta Rajya Parishad, Tharu Kalyankari Sabha, and Madhesi Virus Killers.[2] Most of these groups no longer exist, however, as they handed over their arms and integrated into mainstream politics, while only a few exist in name without any activity.

BRIEF HISTORY OF INTELLIGENCE

The reign of King Prithvi Narayan Shah the Great (1769–1775) was considered the beginning of modern Nepal, and intelligence was strategically used in this era for state affairs and national unification. He initiated a unification campaign after 1743 and continued this effort until his death in 1775. During his rule, he strategically and tactically used intelligence to capture different fiefdoms and principalities to establish the modern state. Subsequently, intelligence continued to be utilized in Nepal but was mostly informal. His successors used intelligence in expanding the territory and later in internal power struggles.

There was a powerful intelligence-gathering mechanism named the Royal Intelligence Bureau (RIB) during the Panchayat era (1960–1990), serving as a counterintelligence service to verify the secret information coming from other state intelligence services.[3] Later, the Palace created the Panchayat Policy and Research Centre under the leadership of the crown prince to gather information about pro-Panchayat and anti-Panchayat political groupings. Leo Rose highlighted Nepal's strategy for survival indicating the strategy of the then king of Nepal to balance the two big neighbors, China and India.[4] These institutions, however, gradually became ineffective and dissolved with the partyless Panchayat political system and restoration of democracy in Nepal in 1990.

The establishment and institutionalization of contemporary intelligence services are relatively new in Nepal because they were started only after the end of the Rana Oligarchy in 1950. The Central Intelligence Bureau (CIB) was established in 1951 and the Nepal Police (NP) was established in 1952, but CIB was not integrated into the police service. In 1956, the government established the Intelligence Department. In 1992, the Central Investigation Department (CID) of Nepal Police was established, and the CIB's functions were integrated into the CID. The CIB's responsibilities include conducting effective investigations into complex and serious criminal offenses, contributing to compliance, and protection and promotion of Nepal's laws and acts.[5] Thus, the CIB's public objective is providing security through effective criminal prevention and investigation. Additionally, the Anti-terrorism Cell in the Nepal Police focuses on monitoring terrorist activities beyond the security and criminal offenses. Furthermore, the Special Taskforce of NP often operates covertly to collect information on professional criminal activities, such as cybercrime and other new forms of crimes.[6]

Though the *jasusi karya* (intelligence) was prevalent since the creation of the Nepal Army, the Department of Military Intelligence (DMI) was created in 1952 under the Chief of General Staff to strengthen its own specialized intelligence collection about security threats.[7] Indeed, the CIB and the DMI of Nepal Army were established around the same time. This occurred immediately after the Rana Regime's end in 1951, and Nepal's contemporary intelligence collection system was started and gradually advanced in capabilities.[8]

Though different state intelligence services and mechanisms were active for long periods, the intelligence capabilities were criticized for their poor performance, especially during the time of the insurrection (1996–2006) waged by the then Communist Party of Nepal-Maoist (CPNM). This criticism was mainly due to the state's inability to get information about possible attacks by the CPNM and lacking counterintelligence capacities to nullify any CPNM attacks against the NP, NA, and other state institutions.[9] Security lapses and excesses were the result of poor security sector reform.[10] The CPNM insurgency was marked by frequent and large-scale attacks on the barracks of security forces and vital infrastructures, including telecommunications, bridges, and roads. The state's intelligence services failed to adequately assess the CPNM's strategies and operational plans, which resulted in the state security forces facing difficulties in countering the insurgency.

There has been regular criticism about the NID's functions. In this context, Kiran Nepal explained, "The department has now depressingly turned into a 'recruitment center' by various coalition governments formed after the parliamentary elections held in 1994."[11] The glaring intelligence failures during the armed conflict include the CPNM attacks in Dang, Gaam, Mangalsen, and Sandhikharka that proved to be a severe setback for Nepal's security forces.

There were public concerns about the effectiveness of Nepal's intelligence services during the armed conflict due to the lack of intelligence coordination among the NA, APF, and NP. Specifically, there was concern they were not properly coordinating, which was compounded by problems of having different chains of command. The Nepal Police was supplying intelligence it collected to the home minister / prime minister, but the NA's intelligence was directly passed to the Palace.[12] Another reason for the ineffectiveness was the disruption of the established communication networks and politicization of intelligence agencies. In reality, the NID was used by home ministers as a recruitment center for their own workers rather than recruiting professionals and the best people in the country. Thus, a growing debate for security sector reform emerged, including the need for intelligence reorganization.[13]

Similar to insurgent groups in other countries, the CPNM made special efforts to strengthen its intelligence capability by establishing a Central Intelligence Bureau (CIB) to collect information for the senior most political and army leadership.[14] In particular, the CPNM adapted the Peruvian insurgency strategy.[15] Even though it is difficult to find any written procedures about the CPNM's intelligence, one strength observed during the armed conflict was its intelligence.[16] Often the CPNM's CIB collected raw information from the local CPNM commanders, processed the information, and then passed it to the higher command for action.[17] CPNM had an approach that maximized the utilization of communication, which was also used by Hezbollah as an important tool.[18] The CPNM expanded and advanced its insurgency, unlike the Provisional Irish Republican Army that was defeated by the effective use of intelligence.[19]

As Paul Jackson described, the CPNM's CIB developed a semiprofessional intelligence cadre by training its intelligence personnel (covering such areas as strategic intelligence, tactical military targeting, field operations, and liaison) and then posted them in strategic areas.[20] This allowed them to collect information and effectively respond to the state's counterinsurgency plans. Jackson explained, "Decisions in general within the Maoists were highly centralized and doctrine was extremely important in guiding discipline of the movement."[21] Consequently, the organization was similar to a cell structure used by other insurgent movements and "based on Mao's 'Organization of a Guerrilla Company' in his Appendix to 'On Guerrilla War.'"[22] In particular, this was centered on "an intelligence officer" who is "one of the five executive members supporting the Company Commander, the Executive Officer and the Political Officer."[23]

The intelligence cadres trained and assigned for operations formed "an inner circle" who were "hardcore" and from the "first revolutionary cell," and "all six battalion commanders of the Maoist Army were drawn from this group, along with several Politburo members with special status, including Prachanda, Battarai, Ananta, Pasang, Prabhakar and Baldev amongst others, and they all had intelligence responsibilities at [a] strategic level."[24]

The main reasons for the CPNM's effective intelligence were a combination of a separate, centralized intelligence operations involving senior leaders in intelligence collection and tactfully utilizing networks of local sympathizers. In rural remote areas, they used the intelligence collected by local supporters and utilized professional intelligence in urban areas, towns, and cities. Similar to the Revolutionary Armed Forces of Colombia (FARC) in Colombia, the CPNM recruited militants mostly from rural areas and marginalized communities, which helped them expand their influence in rural areas.

Jackson explained, "Operational environment faced by the Maoists was largely positive since the Government intelligence system was effectively falling apart."[25] He described how Nepal's main intelligence agencies—DMI, SB, and NID—rarely "talked to each other" and had "little accountability."[26] As a result, this proved counterproductive, and the services "may even have provided information to the Maoists as part of this rivalry."[27] Though this seems extreme, there is little doubt the state's intelligence services were largely ineffective during this period. The role of intelligence determining a victory in armed conflicts varies on the context and time period.[28] Yet, the importance of intelligence in conflict and civil war is evident in Nepal's decade-long armed insurrection.[29]

FACTORS SHAPING INTELLIGENCE CULTURE

The major factors shaping intelligence culture in Nepal are the government's priorities, national laws and legal frameworks, intelligence stakeholders, political parties, different ethnic groups, and civil society groups. The most prominent example was during the armed insurrection when the government's highest priority was to contain and therefore collect information about the activities of the CPNM.[30] Additionally, high-level international visits by foreign heads of state are important events shaping the need for security-related intelligence.[31] The national laws and legal frameworks, such as the Anti-Terrorist Ordinance imposed by the government in 2001 against the CPNM, shaped intelligence priorities against the CPNM.[32] Indeed, intelligence effectiveness was influenced by frequent attacks from radical groups.[33] As for legal mandate, the Nepal Special Service Act, 2042 (1985), for example, provides the NID with broad powers to act in protecting the country's national security.[34] The activities of international nongovernmental organizations (NGOs) have prompted government reviews of internal activity that necessitate intelligence.[35] Political parties have politicized intelligence through the recruitment of party cadres and supporters in intelligence.[36] Additionally, there are different caste and ethnic groups—Nepal has about 125 ethnicities—with different interests, expectations, and frustrations that the government must track.[37] Lastly, the linguistic plurality (there are about 127 languages spoken in the country) is notable because only eight or nine major languages are influential. Communication in other local languages is limited to the individual community. Thus, language has led to difficulties in collecting intelligence, and the domination of certain languages in intelligence culture is connected to barriers of certain linguistic groups.[38]

The armed conflict was also influential in shaping intelligence. Ethnic and geographical radicalization, forceful extraction, human rights violations (kidnapping, torture, and murder), capturing of public and private properties, large-scale attacks, and counterattacks were influential in shaping intelligence culture.[39] The activities of ethnic leaders and radical groups in particular geographical regions threatened the social fabric and challenged national unity through the insurgents' use of violence and external assistance.[40] Once the CPNM publicly declared a specific ethnic identity in November 2001, including Tamunwan, Limbuwan, Khambuwan, Tamangsaling, and Tharuhat, the ethnic radicalization process became rapid and posed several threats, such as local ethnic conflict, disruption of social harmony, and escalated intercommunal mistrust. The CPNM used its intelligence in achieving these goals. As a result, the state's intelligence activities were focused on minimizing or controlling ethnic radicalization and extremism, which changed after the promulgation of Nepal's constitution in 2015.

The frequent political changes in Nepal during the last three decades also had a direct impact in the intelligence community. Once the partyless Pan-chayat political system changed and the country moved to a constitutional monarchy in 1990, the formal intelligence reporting system for all intel-ligence services was altered, and they reported to the Office of the Prime Minister. The influence of the Palace in the intelligence remained, howev-er.[41] Moreover, once Nepal became a constitutional monarchy, politicization of the National Intelligence Department and government polices under the Home Ministry led to the deterioration of the quality of intelligence gathering of these agencies.[42]

Once the CPNM started an insurgency in 1996 and its influence expanded, the intelligence landscape changed, and the Royal Nepal Army took on a coordination role.[43] In particular, intelligence collected from different agen-cies was synthesized, and appropriate strategies developed under the Royal Nepal Army with integrated security mechanism.

After signing the Comprehensive Peace Agreement on November 21, 2006, Nepal's intelligence services were seriously affected due to a disrup-tion of intelligence collection and dissemination. The intelligence services were working in an atmosphere of confusion and chaos when the agreement led to the prime minister becoming the most powerful leader. Unsettled issues with the rebel leaders remained even after the peace agreement because their actions were largely similar to the insurgency era. Moreover, there was widespread suspicion about the intelligence services because of their role when the king ruled directly. In fact, the king took over the government on February 1, 2005, based on information from the intelligence services, which assessed that the political parties were corrupt and unpatriotic, working for vested anti-national interests. In response to the king's actions, an alliance between the main political parties with the radical CPNM emerged. In the process, Nepal's intelligence services were weakened and demoralized, and their activities were limited for years after the peace agreement. Once the first meeting of the Constituent Assembly on May 2, 2008, formally ended 240 years of the monarchy, the new intelligence structure and process under the presidential federal republic system became clear. Yet the degree and inten-sity of politicization in the police and CID increased, while only the army was unaffected by politicization.

The effectiveness of the intelligence services, especially the work of CID and police, are also affected when the home minister changes. If a new gov-ernment in Nepal is a coalition of different parties, this has a different impact then if it is a majority government. In the case of a majority government, a party usually has a ruling mandate and results in a more direct line of intelligence requirements and reporting. The king was no longer above the constitution after 1990 but had a major impact on intelligence, and this continued to a lesser degree when he was the constitutional monarch until his total power was removed in 2006. As for the end of the monarchy in May 2008, the impact on intelligence was negligible because all power of the king was transferred to the prime minister, and he lacked any political power from November 2006 to May 2008 while the prime minister became the head of state. Thus after 240 years, the monarchy's end had no actual effect on the intelligence culture. In contrast, a more observable change was the demonstrably improved intelligence effectiveness when the new majority (nearly two-thirds) government formed on February 15, 2018. The prime minister moved the CID from the Ministry of Home Affairs to the Office of the Prime Minister and Council of Ministers, which improved intelligence coordination and effectiveness under the head of government.

Intelligence challenges remain due to the overlap of several agencies. The government agencies that engage in intelligence activities are the NID, DMI, Crime Investigation Department, Anti-Terrorism Cell and Special Taskforce of the Nepal Police, intelligence unit of the Armed Police Force, and National Vigilance Centre operating in the field of intelligence. Overlap has impeded the coordination of activities and, in a few instances, caused lapses. Coordination among the intelligence agencies has a mixed record. In the early stage of the insurgency, coordination was relatively weak but strengthened as the conflict continued. Regarding the coordination with external intelligence agencies, Nepal's intelligence agencies are coordinating on an ad hoc basis. For example, in 2020, coordination and collaboration have been observed between the Indian border security forces and Nepal's security services to address crime on the Nepal-India borders.[44] The security agencies in both countries work in border areas and periodically meet to tackle cross-border crime and address security information requirements.[45]

Nepal's intelligence is also shaped by activities of other actors. For example, the Indian blockade of 2015 immediately after the earthquake constrained the bilateral relationship, which also limited security relations.[46] Nepal's finite resources for competent personnel and financial and legal frameworks in a small, landlocked, and developing country are also influential factors in the intelligence community. Further, Nepal's intelligence culture has also been shaped by the interpersonal characters of key stakeholders, such as their intelligence experiences, their ideological orientation, their connection to and networks with power, and their personal goals (e.g., accumulating wealth or prestige for their families and relatives).

OVERSIGHT AND FOREIGN RELATIONS

Nepal's intelligence culture is informed by a combination of multiple factors involving constitutional and regulatory oversight provisions and foreign relations. There are three key government bodies that provide oversight or review intelligence or intelligence-related activity. There is only minor intelligence relations with foreign governments, but competing global powers undoubtedly play a role in shaping Nepal's intelligence priorities.

The three key bodies are Nepal's parliament, the Office of the Prime Minister, and the Commission for the Investigation of Abuse of Authority (CIAA) to address corruption and abuse. First, the parliament's role (both National Assembly and House of Representatives) is that of an influential oversight agency in shaping operation of intelligence because of the assertive and proactive role of the committee members. The six different committees of the National Assembly and the eleven committees of the House of Representatives perform oversight actions. In particular, the committees debate and discuss national security issues related to intelligence activities, invite the intelligence officials and security officials to the committee to answer public concerns and questions related to intelligence and/or security, scrutinize annual reports, and instruct government to take specific actions. Regarding security and oversight, the State Affairs and Good Governance Committee and Public Account Committee of the House of Representatives are particularly important regulatory bodies.

Second, the Office of the Prime Minister and Council of Ministers (OPMCM) is another influential agency shaping intelligence culture in Nepal, especially after the National Intelligence Department was moved from the Ministry of Home Affairs to the OPMCM. The Ministry of Home Affairs also has a role in shaping intelligence related to government structures under the Nepal Police and Armed Police Force.

Third, the CIAA is an apex constitutional body to combat corruption. It is another important oversight agency because it allows citizens to file complaints and acts as an investigative and prosecutorial agency.[47]

Intelligence relations are not an important feature for Nepal's intelligence community. Except during the armed conflict from February 1996 to November 2006, no significant international partners have been observed shaping intelligence culture by providing foreign assistance in Nepali infrastructure or capability development. Yet the direct or indirect influence from foreign diplomatic missions cannot be ignored because Nepal's geostrategic location attracts powerful countries and their intelligence agencies.

At present, growing geostrategic interests in Nepal are observed with the competing interests between China and the United States in the form of the

Indo-Pacific Strategy (IPS) and Belt and Road Initiative (BRI). For instance, the United States' Millennium Challenge Cooperation support of UD$500 million in Nepal is not only contested but also interpreted by some groups as strategic foreign intervention; it passed in parliament during 2022.[48] Other groups in Nepal perceive the BRI to be dangerous for the country, citing Sri Lanka and arguing the BRI support to Nepal could lead to a debt trap. Thus, the functioning of intelligence in small countries surrounded by powerful neighbors, like India and China, is not only complex but also affected by different external and internal actors' interests and opportunities.

CONCLUSION

There are a wide variety of factors that shape Nepal's intelligence culture. From its informal origins to the more recent Maoist insurgency, Nepal's intelligence culture has developed unique characteristics under dramatic political and social changes. Indeed, Nepal's intelligence culture from senior leadership to the rank and file is shaped by the country's historical legacies, domestic power dynamics, ethnic and linguistic groups, and system of government. Additionally, Nepal's geostrategic position situated between India and China informs the intelligence culture by shaping skeptical attitudes toward foreigners. The interests of bilateral and multilateral partners, international activity of NGOs, the residual effects of the decade-long armed conflict, the relatively weak national intelligence service, and the state-building process demonstrate Nepal's intelligence culture has continually been in flux.

NOTES

1. "Preliminary Report of National Population Census 2021," National Planning Commission, Central Bureau of Statistics, Government of Nepal, January 27, 2022, http://censusnepal.cbs.gov.np/Home/Details?tpid=1&dcid=0f011f13-7ef6-42dd-9f03-c7d309d4fca3; Bhuwan Sharma and Basanta Khadka, "Nepal's New Map Covers an Area of 147,516 sq km, 10,000 Copies Being Printed," My Republica, May 21, 2020, https://myrepublica.nagariknetwork.com/news/nepal-s-new-map-covers-an-area-of-147-516-sq-km-10-000-copies-being-printed/. I would like to express my sincere thanks to Dr. Yamuna Gahle and General Himalaya Thapa (retired) for their help during the preparation of this chapter. I also appreciate the hard work of Dr. Ryan Shaffer in editing my chapter and the support of Mr. Ayush Upreti (Marist College) and Ms. Asmita Upreti (Kathmandu) while preparing this work.

2. Ajaya Bhadra Khanal, "Non-statutory Forces," in *Nepal Security Sector: An Almanac*, ed. Bishnu Sapkota (Geneva: Geneva Centre for the Democratic Control of Armed Forces, 2009), 209–23.

3. Kiran Nepal, "The National Intelligence Department," in *Nepal Security Sector: An Almanac*, ed. Bishnu Sapkota (Geneva: Geneva Centre for the Democratic Control of Armed Forces, 2009), 191–207.

4. Leo E. Rose, *Nepal: Strategy for Survival* (Berkeley: University of California Press, 1971).

5. "Central Investigation Bureau (CIB) Overview / Background," Central Investigation Bureau, 2021, https://cib.nepalpolice.gov.np/index.php/about-us/introduction?id=892.

6. Nepal, "The National Intelligence Department."

7. General Himalaya Thapa, interview with the author, February 27, 2021.

8. Bishnu Raj Upreti, *Nepal: The Role of the Military in Politics, 1990–2020* (Oxford: Oxford Research Encyclopedias, Politics, 2021), 1–25.

9. Nepal, "The National Intelligence Department."

10. Safal Ghimire, "Making Security Sector Reform Organic: Infrastructures for Peace as an Entry Point?," *Peacebuilding* 4, no. 3 (2016): 262–81; Safal Ghimire, "Reforming Security Sector Governance in Nepal: Achievements and Arrears," *Third World Quarterly* 38, no. 6 (2017): 1415–36.

11. Nepal, "The National Intelligence Department," 193.

12. Upreti, *Nepal: The Role of the Military in Politics, 1990–2020*.

13. Rajan Bhattarai and Rosy Cave, eds., *Changing Security Dynamics in Nepal* (Kathmandu: Nepal Institute for Policy Studies, 2009); Rajan Bhattarai and Geja Sharma Wagle, eds., *Emerging Security Challenges of Nepal* (Kathmandu: Nepal Institute for Policy Studies, 2010); Bishnu Raj Upreti and Peter Vanhautte, "Security Sector Reform in Nepal: Challenges and Opportunities," in *Security Sector Reform in Challenging Environments*, ed. Hans Born and Albrecht Schnabel (Münster: LIT, 2009), 165–87.

14. J. Bowyer Bell, "The Armed Struggle and Underground Intelligence: An Overview," *Studies in Conflict and Terrorism* 17, no. 2 (1994): 115–50; John A. Gentry and David E. Spencer, "Colombia's FARC: A Portrait of Insurgent Intelligence," *Intelligence and National Security* 25, no. 4 (2010): 453–78; Gaetano Joe Ilardi, "Al Qaeda's Operational Intelligence—a Key Prerequisite to Action," *Studies in Conflict and Terrorism* 31, no. 12 (2008): 1072–1102; Gaetano Joe Ilardi, "Irish Republican Army Counterintelligence," *International Journal of Intelligence and CounterIntelligence* 23, no. 1 (2009): 1–26; Gaetano Joe Ilardi, "Al Qaeda's Counterintelligence Doctrine: The Pursuit of Operational Certainty and Control," *International Journal of Intelligence and CounterIntelligence* 22, no. 2 (2009): 246–74; Lincoln B. Krause, "Insurgent Intelligence: The Guerrilla Grapevine," *International Journal of Intelligence and CounterIntelligence* 9, no. 3 (1996): 291–311; Paul Jackson, "Intelligence in a Modern Insurgency: The Case of the Maoist Insurgency in Nepal," *Intelligence and National Security* 34, no. 7 (2019): 999–1013.

15. R. Andrew Nickson, "Democratization and the Growth of Communism in Nepal: A Peruvian Scenario in the Making?," *Journal of Commonwealth & Comparative Politics* 30, no. 3 (1992): 358–86.

16. Bishnu Raj Upreti, "External Links of the Maoist Insurgency in Nepal," in *Terrorism: Patterns of Internationalization*, ed. Jaideep Saikia and Ekaterina Stepanova

(New Delhi: Sage, 2009), 93–117; Bishnu Raj Upreti, "Restructuring Nepal Army: Conflict Transformation Perspective," *Nepal Journal of Contemporary Studies* 7, no. 1 (2007): 69–94; Bishnu Raj Upreti, *Armed Conflict and Peace Process in Nepal: The Maoist Insurgency, Past Negotiation and Opportunities for Conflict Transformation* (New Delhi: Adroit, 2006).

17. Jackson, "Intelligence in a Modern Insurgency."

18. Carl Anthony Wege, "Hezbollah's Communication System: A Most Important Weapon," *International Journal of Intelligence and CounterIntelligence* 27, no. 2 (2014): 240–52.

19. William Matchett, *Secret Victory: The Intelligence War That Beat the IRA* (London: Matchett, 2016).

20. Jackson, "Intelligence in a Modern Insurgency."

21. Jackson, "Intelligence in a Modern Insurgency," 1003–4.

22. Jackson, "Intelligence in a Modern Insurgency," 1003–4.

23. Jackson, "Intelligence in a Modern Insurgency," 1003–4.

24. Jackson, "Intelligence in a Modern Insurgency," 1004.

25. Jackson, "Intelligence in a Modern Insurgency," 1004.

26. Jackson, "Intelligence in a Modern Insurgency," 1004.

27. Jackson, "Intelligence in a Modern Insurgency," 1004.

28. John A. Gentry, "Intelligence in War: How Important Is It? How Do We Know?," *Intelligence and National Security* 34, no. 6 (2019): 833–50.

29. Upreti, *Armed Conflict and Peace Process in Nepal*; Upreti, "Restructuring Nepal Army;" Bishnu Raj Upreti and R. K. Nepali, eds., *Nepal at Barrel of Gun: Proliferation of Small Arms and Light Weapons and Their Impacts* (Kathmandu: South Asia Small Arms Network–Nepal, 2006).

30. See Upreti and Nepali, *Nepal at Barrel of Gun*; Dil Bikram Subbha, "Government's Strategy against the Maoist Insurgency in Nepal (MA thesis, US Army Command and General Staff College, Fort Leavenworth, KS, 2010).

31. Shuvam Dhungana, "Security is Tightened as Xi Jinping Arrives Today," *Kathmandu Post*, October 11, 2019, https://kathmandupost.com/national/2019/10/11/with-xi-jinping-arriving-kathmandu-beefs-up-security.

32. See Deeptima Shukla, "Insurgency in Nepal and Role of State," *Indian Journal of Political Science* 64, no. 1/2 (2003): 61–78, http://www.jstor.org/stable/41855770.

33. For example, see Shuvam Dhungana, "Police's Intelligence Continues to Fail Them as Chand Party Claims Explosion," *Kathmandu Post*, January 17, 2020, https://kathmandupost.com/national-security/2020/01/17/police-s-intelligence-continues-to-fail-them-as-chand-party-claims-explosion.

34. See "Nepal Special Service Act, 2042," Law Commission, August 28, 1985, http://www.lawcommission.gov.np/en/wp-content/uploads/2018/10/nepal-special-service-act-2042-1985.pdf.

35. "INGOs Campaigning Christianity," *People's Review*, April 20, 2019, https://www.peoplesreview.com.np/2019/04/20/ingos-campaigning-christianity/.

36. Dinesh Bhattarai, "Intelligence and Nepal's Foreign Policy," *MyRepublica*, February 13, 2020. https://myrepublica.nagariknetwork.com/news/intelligence-and-nepal-s-foreign-policy/. Kiran Nepal wrote, "[T]he then Home Minister Khum

Bahadur Khadka was at the forefront in misusing the intelligence gathering service after 1995" (Khanal, "Non-statutory Forces," 196).

37. See Bishnu Raj Upreti, "Nationalism and Militarization in Nepal: Reactive Response or Long-Term Phenomenon?," *Asian Journal of Peacebuilding* 2, no. 2 (2014): 217–39.

38. Ram Ashish Giri, "The Politics of 'Unplanning' of Languages in Nepal," *Journal of NELTA* 14, no. 1–2 (December 2009): 32–44, https://www.nepjol.info/index .php/NELTA/article/view/3089.

39. Jackson, "Intelligence in a Modern Insurgency"; Upreti, "External Links of the Maoist Insurgency in Nepal."

40. Upreti, "External Links of the Maoist Insurgency in Nepal."

41. See Nepal, "The National Intelligence Department."

42. Nepal, "The National Intelligence Department."

43. See Jackson, "Intelligence in a Modern Insurgency."

44. Manoj Paudel, "Nepal and India Begin Joint Security Patrol along Border in Kapilvastu," *Kathmandu Post*, September 21, 2020. https://kathmandupost.com/ province-no-5/2020/09/21/nepal-and-india-begin-joint-security-patrol-along-border -in-kapilvastu.

45. "Security Agencies of Nepal and India Agree to Work Jointly to Control Criminal Activities," Himalayan News Service, August 21, 2018, https://thehima- layantimes.com/nepal/security-agencies-of-nepal-and-india-agree-to-work-jointly-to -control-criminal-activities.

46. "Nepal Blockade: Six Ways It Affects the Country," British Broadcasting Corporation, December 12, 2015, https://www.bbc.com/news/world-asia-35041366.

47. "About CIAA," Commission for the Investigation of Abuse of Authority, 2021, http://www.ciaa.gov.np/page/7.

48. "MCC Statement on Nepal Compact Ratification," Millennium Challenge Corporation, March 1, 2022, https://www.mcc.gov/news-and-events/release/stmt- 030122-nepal-compact-ratification.

18

North Korea: An Agile and Adaptable National Intelligence System

Joseph Fitsanakis

Contemporary scholarship on the Democratic People's Republic of Korea (DPRK), commonly known as North Korea, is an exercise in contesting dominant narratives of the country as obdurate and reclusive. A study of the DPRK's intelligence services, in particular, demonstrates a reality that is different from the stereotype of the North Korean state as an outmoded international pariah.[1] Indeed, the North Korean intelligence system has a long and well-chronicled history of recognizing, and quickly responding to, international challenges. It has done so historically with a degree of astuteness that many Western intelligence services would envy. North Korea's intelligence responses to internal pressures have largely mirrored the North Korean governing elite's brutal efforts to subjugate the country's population and neutralize the regime's domestic enemies. Responses to outside pressures reflect Pyongyang's delicate maneuvering as a reluctant, yet shrewd, participant in the international system of nations.[2]

Within these conditions, the North Korean intelligence system has learned to survive by rapidly adapting to challenges stemming from its relations with policy makers and decision makers. Most of these challenges have stemmed from internal power struggles among governing elites, which at times favored and at times disadvantaged the national intelligence system. Despite its key position within the state apparatus and its centrality in ensuring the very survivability of the state, the North Korean intelligence system cannot be seen as an autonomous praetorian guard. On the contrary, its operational subordination to the country's political leadership has been undeviating. Additionally, it has always been subjected to a stringent mechanism of political oversight, which has arguably remained the most enduring factor throughout the many stages of its development.

This chapter is organized in four thematic parts. The first section examines the historical evolution of the North Korean intelligence apparatus, paying attention to its origins in the anti-Japanese struggle, the civil war, and North Korea's postwar reconstruction. The second part explores the current structure of North Korean intelligence and provides an outline of the different intelligence agencies and their missions as well as their respective areas of responsibility. The third section analyzes North Korea's highly peculiar intelligence culture, which features strong elements of interagency infighting, intra-agency antagonism, and informal power clusters that report to individual government officials. The final part examines the current operational scope of the intelligence services with emphasis on internal and external intelligence activities.

HISTORICAL EVOLUTION

Western accounts of the evolution of the North Korean intelligence establishment tend to show partiality toward external factors—namely, those associated with the DPRK's role in the Cold War. In reality, the development of North Korean intelligence is the history of enduring power struggles between rival factions in the uppermost echelons of the country's governing apparatus. It was indeed as a direct response to infighting within the Workers' Party of Korea (WPK)—the DPRK's foremost political institution—that the country's intelligence system emerged in 1946. That year marked the establishment of the Bureau of Protection and Security, which was quickly renamed Bureau of Internal Affairs (BIA). Control over the BIA was nominally exercised by an oversight committee of the WPK; however, actual power within the BIA was contained within a single unit, known as the Political Security Department (PSD). The PSD was directly accountable to North Korea's founder and premier, Kim Il-sung, who used the PSD to neutralize—often physically—rival factions within the WPK, notably the pro-Chinese Yan'an faction, and even rivals within his own pro-Soviet Kapsan faction.[3] In 1951, once his rivals in the WPK were seemingly eliminated (they briefly reemerged in the 1960s), Kim transformed the PSD into the new Ministry of Public Security (MPS). Most intelligence observers of North Korea trace the origins of the country's modern-day secret police to the emergence of the MPS.[4]

The secret police system set up by Kim in the early 1950s proved instrumental in implementing extensive purges of alleged "counterrevolutionaries." These started in 1953. Among the hundreds of thousands who were tried, blacklisted, executed, or sent to labor camps were at least half of all WPK card-carrying members.[5] In the second half of the 1960s, the MPS became the central coordinating body of a new round of nationwide purges. This resulted in the unprecedented institutional growth of the MPS: by the end of the decade, its employee ranks had expanded to nearly 200,000.[6] The experience of consecutive purges was also instrumental in expanding and reinforcing the MPS's networks of informants. These were intricate in both composition and structure and were handled by equally elaborate configurations of MPS case officers who were stationed in field offices throughout the country. It can be reasonably estimated that, at the height of its power, the MPS maintained informant networks amounting to at least 100,000 and possibly as many as 500,000. The high-end estimate would place the MPS's informant network at about 100,000 more than the estimated number of North Korean informants during the start of the Korean War in 1950.[7]

While recognizing the predominance of domestic factors in shaping the institutional character of North Korean intelligence, the influence of external factors must also be acknowledged. By the mid-1950s, having emerged from a succession of brutal wars, the siege mentality of the North Korean leadership brought Pyongyang closer to the Union of Soviet Socialist Republics (USSR). At that time, North Korean intelligence and security institutions were largely staffed by thousands of ethnic Koreans from the USSR, most of whom spoke fluent Russian and had been trained by Soviet intelligence officers.[8] Among these bilingual apparatchiks was Kim Il-sung himself, who had been trained in intelligence as an officer of the Soviet Red Army's Eighty-Eighth Special Brigade, a reconnaissance unit that specialized in intelligence collection behind enemy lines.[9] Yet by no means can this be described as "Sovietization." Scarred by the experience of the Korean War, in which the Soviet Union refused to intervene militarily, North Korea's leaders deeply mistrusted Moscow.[10] They shielded the country's armed forces from Soviet influence, which meant that the DPRK's military intelligence components— arguably the country's most powerful—developed largely outside of Soviet domination. Pyongyang was somewhat more trusting of the Chinese leadership, which, unlike the Soviet Union, had deployed its People's Volunteer Army in support of North Korean forces during the Korean War.[11] But even in that case, the DPRK regime went out of its way to avoid an overly close association with the Communist Party of China. Broadly speaking, at no point after 1953 did North Korea's intelligence leadership view China and the Soviet Union as trusted allies.[12]

CURRENT INSTITUTIONAL STRUCTURE

The North Korean intelligence establishment is structured along internal and external operational missions. Its internal components focus largely on counterintelligence with a concentration on defensive and offensive operations. Following a number of high-profile defections in the 2010s, vetting North Korea's diplomatic corps has taken center stage among internal intelligence operations. Another aspect of internal intelligence work centers on domestic security and counterterrorism. It is concerned largely with the organization and maintenance of civil defense structures and with the protection of North Korea's crucial infrastructure from attacks and sabotage. The physical protection of North Korea's senior leadership is also part of the domestic security and counterterrorism mission.[13] The intelligence community's external components provide informational support to the country's decision makers, both regionally and at the national level. The collection, analysis, and dissemination systems of the intelligence services largely resemble those of other countries with comparable intelligence apparatuses. Additionally, the type of information collected by North Korea's external intelligence services mirrors the political, military, economic, and technical themes that one sees in other nations.[14]

The supreme leader of North Korea is nominally at the helm of all institutions that perform intelligence oversight functions. These are the Cabinet, the Central Committee of the WPK, and the National Defense Commission. The Cabinet—North Korea's highest executive organ—has administrative jurisdiction over the MPS, whose operations are internal in nature. They include, aside from basic counterintelligence and counter-sabotage functions, law enforcement and the management of the country's prison system.[15] Alongside regular policing functions, the MPS has historically performed elementary political-policing functions. It is therefore responsible for a sizeable network of informants throughout the country.[16] In recent decades, however, the MPS has been rivaled—and in many ways superseded—by the Ministry of State Security (MSS). Founded in 1973 by the then supreme leader, Kim Il-sung, the MSS today administers North Korea's labyrinthine network of political prisons, including labor camps. Aside from running its own networks of informants, the MSS exercises extensive undercover functions aimed at combatting smuggling networks. These smuggling networks are known to facilitate mass defections of North Korean citizens to South Korea and to China, which the regime sees as damaging to its reputation and security.[17] In recent years, the MSS has also concentrated on the Cheollima Civil Defense, which is also known as Free Joseon. Following its emergence in 2017, this group has operated semi-openly as North Korea's first known active resistance movement since the 1960s. In February 2019, the group claimed responsibility for a violent raid on North Korea's embassy in Madrid.[18]

The Central Committee of the WPK administers the Secretariat in Charge of South Korean Affairs, whose United Front Department (UFD) operates as a public-relations bureau for communicating with pro-Pyongyang communities of North Koreans abroad. Among those is the strongly pro-DPRK General Association of Korean Residents in Japan—also known as Chongryon. Members of Chongryon, who are Japanese citizens, have at times come under scrutiny by South Korean, Japanese, and Western intelligence services as possible non-official-cover (NOC) intelligence officers of North Korea.[19] Additionally, along with the Liaison Department of the Secretariat in Charge of South Korean Affairs, the UFD is the primary coordinating body of the Korean Friendship Association (KFA). Headquartered in Spain and with chapters in more than thirty nations, the KFA brings together networks of foreign nationals who are supportive of the North Korean regime. These support networks operate in countries such as Brazil, Canada, Germany, Mexico, Turkey, and the United Kingdom. South Korean and Western intelligence agencies tend to view the KFA as the outreach component to a broader intelligence effort, which aims to spot and recruit potential assets for North Korean intelligence.[20]

Notably, KFA president Alejandro Cao de Benós, a Spanish citizen, was arrested by Spanish police in 2016 on gun-trafficking charges. In 2020, Cao de Benós was featured in the documentary *The Mole: Undercover in North Korea*, in which he is allegedly seen mediating between North Korean diplomats and an investigative reporter posing as a KFA supporter and potential foreign investor in North Korea. The film features surreptitiously filmed footage of a meeting between the undercover reporter and North Korean diplomats stationed in Uganda. During the meeting, the North Korean diplomats are seen proposing a plan to purchase an island in Lake Victoria to build a luxury hotel that would function as a cover for an underground factory that would manufacture illicit narcotics and weapons.[21] In 2018, another KFA member, Benoît Quennedey, a French civil servant who served as president of the French branch of the KFA, was arrested by the French General Directorate for Internal Security on suspicion of spying for North Korea.[22]

Until 2009, the Secretariat in Charge of South Korean Affairs maintained a little-known human intelligence (HUMINT) and covert-action training center, known as the Operations Department.[23] In 2009, this secretive outfit was amalgamated into the Reconnaissance General Bureau (RGB), which today operates under the command of the DPRK's armed forces, the Korean People's Army. The armed forces are controlled by the National Defense Commission, which by default is the overseeing body of the RGB.[24] The RGB is North Korea's foremost military intelligence agency and is broadly comparable to the Main Directorate of the General Staff of the Russian Armed Forces (previously known as GRU), or the United States' Defense Intelligence Agency (DIA). Unlike the GRU or DIA, however, the RGB is primarily driven by special operations and today commands most of the DPRK's Special Operations Force of more than 100,000 soldiers.[25] This makes the RGB a cross between the United States' Central Intelligence Agency and the Joint Special Operations Command, but incomparably larger in size, and with special operations as the more dominant element in that partnership.

INTELLIGENCE CULTURE

The North Korean intelligence establishment forms a central pillar of what can be described as a security state. As is commonly the case with security states, it features domestic surveillance, largely formalistic mechanisms of social control, and a relatively centralized command structure. This ultimately emanates from the uppermost echelons of what is essentially a monarchical-style dynasty. Yet the North Korean intelligence services are vast in size and labyrinthine in complexity. It follows that the command of the state's intelligence apparatus is, by necessity, nowhere close to absolute. Rather, it is dispersed between a host of WPK committees, the National Defense Commission, and the Cabinet. Undoubtedly, such institutions often "act as rubber stamps in sanctioning what the Great Leader declares to be good for Korea."[26] At the same time, the day-to-day running of the country's intelligence establishment is far more diffused and decentralized than what outside observers generally assume. Notably, there is ample evidence of bitter interagency turf wars, intra-agency discord, and "duplication of effort[s] and a waste of precious resources, with operations frequently displaying overlapping and sometimes conflicting areas of responsibilities."[27]

Arguably the most prominent features of this intra-agency discord are the individual lines of command that often exist within North Korean intelligence agencies. These are agency units that are controlled by, and report directly to, individual government officials. This largely informal structure has historically enabled specific members of the DPRK's political leadership to maintain personalized clusters of power that coexist within the state's official intelligence apparatus. There are ample examples of such units being accountable to different government apparatchiks and spying against each other, or even against rival cliques in non-intelligence state agencies. During particularly contentious times, such rivalries have resulted in purges of entire wings of state agencies, especially the case in times of transition in the country's top leadership.[28] For instance, during the first months of Kim Jong-un's reign, it was reported that only about half of the country's senior leadership was spared by sweeping purges, which were implemented by Kim's inner circle of advisers. These are believed to have resulted in at least sixty executions of high-profile officials—among them General Hyon Yong-chol, head of the Korean Armed Forces.[29] During such times of uncertainty, intra-agency rivalries intensify, as physical survival becomes the primary concern of senior intelligence officials. As scholars have observed, the existence of these informal centers of administrative power promotes a culture of antagonism and institutional fragmentation within North Korean intelligence institutions. What is more, this parallel superstructure has become ingrained in the system. Today it is at the root of a fundamentally corrupt institutional culture that prioritizes the pursuit of personal career ambitions and narrow bureaucratic privileges over broader national security goals.[30]

The siege mentality of the North Korean leadership has shaped the country's political culture as well as its intelligence culture. Throughout their existence, the DPRK's intelligence institutions have operated under "a garrison state worldview of imminent threat."[31] A major byproduct of this worldview has been the theory of *juche*. Translated loosely as "self-reliance," the term is often described as embodying the ideological foundations of North Korea's quasi-socialist state doctrine.[32] It was initially articulated in late 1955 by Kim Il-sung in response to the realization that the DPRK could not trust even its closest ideological allies. It favors the development of a state-run national economy that does not respond to the pressures of the international economic system. This goes hand in hand with the development of an idiosyncratic political ethos that is built around isolationist perceptions of North Korean national identity. Lastly, *juche* advocates for the development of sovereign national defense and intelligence systems.[33] In the following years, in what can be described as a landslide change in North Korea's strategy, the country severely curtailed contacts with the Communist bloc and started systematically reaching out to members of the Non-Aligned Movement.[34]

This dramatic shift in North Korea's international strategy became a principal influence on the nation's external intelligence posture. Its impact can be seen today, as agencies like the RGB base most of their operations in the developing world—notably in Africa and Latin America, as well as in some parts of Asia. Indeed, the RGB's intelligence activities occur almost entirely in the developing world where the DPRK built substantial diplomatic and economic relationships during the Cold War. Additionally, the shortage of foreign hard currency, which resulted from the loss of foreign patronage, prompted North Korean spy agencies to abandon large-scale intelligence operations in favor of small-scale special activities, adapted from Chinese and Vietnamese models.[35] The *juche* doctrine is also at the heart of the DPRK's elaborate covert-operations doctrine, which was developed in the 1960s and 1970s. This doctrine is responsible for the long list of infiltrations of South Korean territory over a thirty-year period, a host of brazen kidnappings and assassinations abroad, and the development of a wide array of intelligence collection methodologies that include the 1968 capture of the US naval intelligence vessel USS *Pueblo*.

OPERATIONAL SCOPE

The nationalistic rhetoric of the North Korean government consistently portrays foreign actors—notably Japan and the United States—as the greatest nemeses to the survival of the DPRK. In reality, the foremost threat to the regime consists of the very population it claims to represent. In fact, mistrusting the general population is the single most unifying element of the state apparatus. It permeates its culture and has historically allowed it to overcome its endemic sectarianism. The near-universal mistrust of the population also shapes the operational priorities of the DPRK's intelligence community, prompting it to dedicate immense resources to domestic intelligence collection. Indeed, the intelligence community's emphasis on domestic surveillance is a defining parameter of its operational scope and today constitutes its most intensive activity.[36] Its principal aim is to force the general population to comply with North Korean state doctrines, thus ensuring near-absolute obedience on a mass scale. When dissidents are detected, this mechanism gives way to a rigorous system of political policing, consisting of political instructors, interrogators, and *gulag* administrators. This system rests on extensive networks of informants, who serve on the front lines of this elaborate system of social control.

Informants are far more important to the system than outside observers generally assume, given that the telecommunications penetration in North Korea remains low. This means that most communication happens in face-to-face settings. It follows that the state's signals-intelligence apparatus is ineffective in monitoring political exchanges between citizens. For this reason, domestic intelligence agencies that have strong HUMINT components are prioritized when it comes to the allocation of state funds. Statements by North Korean defectors regularly confirm this. One example is Kang Myong-do, son-in-law of North Korea's late prime minister, Kang Song-san, who in 1994 became "the most damaging defector ever to escape from North Korea."[37] In 2015, Kang stated: "North Korea considers spies as very important." The defector, who worked in an intelligence capacity for the UFD, added that loyal HUMINT operatives "are treated on the same level as generals, their education is to a similar high level."[38] The prominence of HUMINT in North Korea's social control landscape has prompted intelligence agencies to utilize this method of intelligence collection as a means of augmenting their budget, resources, and status within the state apparatus.

On the external front, the operational scope of North Korean intelligence agencies has been severely hampered in recent years by the weak state of the country's economy and its dwindling diplomatic presence abroad. The latter poses major logistical problems for North Korea's intelligence operations planners, given that much HUMINT intelligence activity is based out of diplomatic representations. To counteract this logistical hurdle, the RGB has increasingly utilized NOC actors, mostly in Asia, with mixed success. A notorious example of such activity was the February 2017 assassination of Kim Jong-nam, half brother of DPRK supreme leader Kim Jong-un, in Kuala Lumpur. The operation relied on a network of North Korean NOCs, who recruited foreign assets for the assassination.[39] Many of these NOCs have been known to make use of third-country passports, notably Austrian, Brazilian, Japanese, Thai, and South Korean, to travel unabated.[40] These efforts are assisted by an international network of front companies, which allows the North Korean regime to evade international sanctions against it and to coordinate the activities of hundreds of NOC operatives.[41] In March 2021, a Singapore-based NOC officer of the RGB, identified as Mun Chol-myong, who was detained by Malaysian authorities, was extradited to the United States on charges of laundering money for North Korea.[42] To protest Mun's extradition, the North Korean government shut down its embassy in Kuala Lumpur.

Alongside the use of NOCs, North Korea continues to utilize its diplomatic network for intelligence purposes. This was made clear in 2018, when German authorities uncovered an extensive operation to procure dual-use technologies, which was based out of North Korea's embassy in Berlin.[43] In 2020, Czech intelligence foiled a secret plan by North Korea to smuggle weapons parts and surveillance drones from the Czech Republic via Africa, leading to the expulsion of a North Korean diplomat from the country.[44] A few years earlier, Ukrainian authorities had barred all North Korean citizens from entering the country after they caught three North Korean diplomats surreptitiously photographing classified documents relating to weapons systems.[45]

The newest element in the North Korean intelligence establishment's external activities centers on efforts to ameliorate its dire financial situation by securing foreign currency. In previous years, such activities involved the production and smuggling of illicit narcotics, counterfeit currency, and precious stones, using the DPRK's diplomatic facilities as transit and distribution centers.[46] Most of these activities were facilitated by the WPK Central Committee Bureau 39.[47] In recent years, however, the regime has dedicated much effort to cyberespionage and cybercrime operations targeting international banking institutions. In 2017, a senior US National Security Agency official appeared to confirm reports that North Korea was behind an attempt to steal nearly $1 billion from the Bangladesh Bank—Bangladesh's state-owned central bank—using the SWIFT network.[48] Observers said at the time that the attempted heist showed that North Korea's cyber capabilities were among the most advanced in the world.[49] In the following year, a report by leading cybersecurity firm FireEye warned that previously little-known North Korean cyberespionage groups had widened their sophistication and scope and were now threatening targets worldwide. One such group, dubbed "Lazarus" by cybersecurity researchers, was believed to have been behind the infamous Sony Pictures attacks in 2014, as well as the worldwide wave or ransomware attacks known as "WannaCry" in 2017. FireEye warned that a subelement within Lazarus, known as "APT37," was systematically targeting human rights groups and North Korean defectors living in South Korea. Other targets of the group consisted of aerospace companies, financial institutions, and telecommunications service providers on at least three continents.[50] In 2020, Lazarus was almost certainly behind a sophisticated "spear-phishing" campaign against at least eleven officials of national delegations belonging to the United Nations (UN) Security Council. It appears that the hackers selected specific UN staff members for penetration and approached them online using fake identities.[51]

CONCLUSION

To a large extent, the North Korean regime owes its survival to its expansive, well-funded, and sophisticated national intelligence system. Today, more than three decades after the fall of the Berlin Wall, the intelligence apparatus of the DPRK continues to display institutional agility, by quickly and effectively responding to both internal and external pressures. Having been trained under the *juche* system, North Korean intelligence administrators have learned to prioritize operations that require minimal resources but have high-impact results—such as the 2014 Sony Pictures attacks or the 2017 assassination of Kim Jong-nam. Domestically as well as externally, North Korean intelligence has historically relied on extensive networks of HUMINT operatives, who are well trained and have advanced operational skills. Yet the system has been willing to incorporate new, technologically advanced methods of intelligence collection, as can be seen from the development of its cyber arsenal in recent years.

The survival of the ruling dynasty remains the central priority of the North Korean intelligence system. It pursues this goal with notable intensity through the utilization of a highly efficient and carefully calibrated domestic security apparatus. At the same time, the system has learned to maneuver on the often-perilous shifting sands of the North Korean government bureaucracy and respond to the needs of the ruling elite with a mixture of subservience and autonomy. This has ensured its continued survival within the state apparatus, which remains largely unchallenged to this day. No matter what is in store for the North Korean regime in the coming years, it is highly probable that its intelligence system will continue to demonstrate adaptability and responsiveness and will therefore survive without existential threats to its integrity.

NOTES

1. In-kang Wha, "The Media-Government Relations: Comparative Analysis of the United States, South Korea and North Korea's Media Coverage of Foreign Policy" (PhD diss., Rutgers University, 2007), 243.

2. Daniel Wertz, J. J. Oh, and In-sung Kim, *DPRK Diplomatic Relations*, Documentation Project Issue Brief (Washington, DC: National Committee on North Korea, 2014), 1.

3. Jae-cheon Lim, *Kim Jong-il's Leadership of North Korea* (London: Routledge, 2008), 447.

4. Andrei Lankov, *From Stalin to Kim Il Sung: The Formation of North Korea, 1945–1960* (New Brunswick, NJ: Rutgers University Press, 2002), 134.

5. Robert A. Scalapino and Chong-sik Lee, *Communism in Korea* (Berkeley: University of California Press, 1972), 833–34.

6. Kenneth E. Gause, *Coercion, Control, Surveillance and Punishment: An Examination of the North Korean Police State* (Washington, DC: Committee for Human Rights in North Korea, 2012), 110.

7. Gause, *Coercion, Control, Surveillance and Punishment*, 91.

8. James M. Minnich, *The North Korean People's Army: Origins and Current Tactics* (Annapolis, MD: Naval Institute Press, 2005), 24.

9. Jasper Becker, *Rogue Regime: Kim Jong Il and the Looming Threat of North Korea* (New York: Oxford University Press, 2005), 205.

10. Gwang-oon Kim, "The Making of the Juche State in Postcolonial North Korea," in *Origins of North Korea's Juche: Colonialism, War and Development*, ed. Jae-jung Suh (Lanham, MD: Lexington Books, 2013), 68.

11. Charles K. Armstrong, *The North Korean Revolution, 1945–1950* (Ithaca, NY: Cornell University Press, 2003), 245.

12. Office of the Secretary of Defense, *Military and Security Developments Involving the Democratic People's Republic of Korea* (Washington, DC: US Department of Defense, 2013), 4.

13. Joseph G. Bermudez, "SIGINT, EW, and EIW in the Korean People's Army: An Overview of Development and Organization," in *Bytes and Bullets in Korea: Information Technology, Revolution and National Security on the Korean Peninsula*, ed. Alexander Y. Mansourov (Honolulu: Asia-Pacific Center for Security Studies, 2005), 236.

14. Office of the Secretary of Defense, *Military and Security Developments*, 13.

15. Bermudez, "SIGINT, EW, and EIW," 274.

16. Daniel Schwekendiek, *A Socioeconomic History of North Korea* (Jefferson, NC: McFarland, 2011), 87.

17. Dong-gu Suh, *North Korean Intelligence and Security Apparatus to Protect the Kim Jonh-un Regime* (Seoul: Korea Institute for National Unification, February 16, 2015), 13.

18. Joseph Fitsanakis, "Analysis: Who Was behind the Raid on the North Korean Embassy in Madrid?," IntelNews, March 18, 2019, https://intelnews.org/2019/03/18/01-2514.

19. Joseph Fitsanakis, "S. Korea Police Says Professor Was Secret Handler of N. Korea Spies," IntelNews, February 3, 2016, https://intelnews.org/2016/02/03/01-1854; Joseph Fitsanakis, "North Koreans Are Studying Nuclear Physics in Japan, Say Human Rights Activists," IntelNews, December 23, 2016, https://intelnews.org/2016/12/23/01-2030.

20. Suh, *North Korean Intelligence*, 2.

21. Paul Adams, "Documentary Claims to Expose North Korea Trying to Dodge Sanctions," BBC, October 11, 2020, https://www.bbc.com/news/world-asia-54464581.

22. Joseph Fitsanakis, "French Senior Civil Servant Arrested on Suspicion of Spying for North Korea," IntelNews, November 27, 2018, https://intelnews.org/2018/11/27/01-2444.

23. Bermudez, "SIGINT, EW, and EIW," 267.

24. Joseph Fitsanakis, "N. Korean Dictator Had Army Chief Publicly Executed, Say Intel Sources," IntelNews, May 13, 2015, https://intelnews.org/2015/05/13/01-1694.

25. Joseph G. Bermudez, *A New Emphasis on Operations against South Korea?* (Baltimore, MD: U.S.-Korea Institute, Johns Hopkins University, 2010), 4.

26. Edward A. Olsen, *Korea: The Divided Nation* (Westport, CT: Praeger, 2005), 117.

27. Joseph G. Bermudez, *Shield of the Great Leader: The Armed Forces of North Korea* (St. Leonards, NSW: Allen & Unwin, 2001), 177.

28. Sung-chull Kim, *North Korea under Kim Jong Il: From Consolidation to Systemic Dissonance* (New York: State University of New York Press, 2006), 103.

29. Simon Mundy, "Kim Jong UN Purge Suggests Struggle for Loyalty in North Korea," *Financial Times*, May 14, 2015, https://www.ft.com/content/690d17d6-fa15-11e4-b432-00144feab7de.

30. Kong-dan Oh and Ralph C. Hassig, *North Korea through the Looking Glass* (Washington, DC: Brookings, 2000), 114.

31. Office of the Secretary of Defense, *Military and Security Developments*, 4.

32. Kim, *North Korea under Kim Jong Il*, 8.

33. Gause, *Coercion, Control, Surveillance and Punishment*, 98.

34. Olsen, *Korea: The Divided Nation*, 123.

35. Taik-young Hamm, *Arming the Two Koreas: State, Capital and Military Power* (London: Routledge, 1999), 71–79; Oh and Hassig, *North Korea through the Looking Glass*, 108.

36. Oh and Hassig, *North Korea through the Looking Glass*, 114.

37. James Sterngold, "Defector Says North Korea Has 5 A-Bombs and May Make More," *New York Times*, July 28, 1994, https://www.nytimes.com/1994/07/28/world/defector-says-north-korea-has-5-a-bombs-and-may-make-more.html.

38. Paula Hancocks, "Former North Korea Operative Reveals Secret Spy Tactics," CNN, May 22, 2015, https://www.cnn.com/2015/05/21/asia/north-korea-spies/index.html.

39. Joseph Sipalan, "Four North Korean Suspects Fled Malaysia after Airport Murder: Police," Reuters, February 19, 2017, https://www.reuters.com/article/us-northkorea-malaysia-kim-police-idUSKBN15Y068.

40. Guy Faulconbridge, "Exclusive: North Korean Leaders Used Brazilian Passports to Apply for Western Visas—Sources," Reuters, February 27, 2018, https://www.reuters.com/article/us-northkorea-kim-passports-exclusive/exclusive-north-korean-leaders-used-brazilian-passports-to-apply-for-western-visas-sources-idUSKCN1GB2AY.

41. Scott Snyder, "How North Korea Evades UN Sanctions through International 'Front' Companies," *Forbes*, March 3, 2017, https://www.forbes.com/sites/scottasnyder/2017/03/03/how-north-korea-evades-un-sanctions-through-international-front-companies/.

42. Michael Balsamo, "North Korean Man Extradited to US in Sanctions Case," ABC News, March 21, 2021, https://abcnews.go.com/Politics/wireStory/north-korean-man-extradited-us-sanctions-case-76590063.

43. Ian Allen, "North Korea Used Berlin Embassy to Acquire Nuclear Tech, Says German Spy Chief," IntelNews, February 5, 2018, https://intelnews.org/2018/02/05/01-2263.

44. Joseph Fitsanakis, "Czech Intelligence Foiled North Korean Plan to Smuggle Arms through Africa," IntelNews, January 31, 2020, https://intelnews.org/2020/01/31/01-2715.

45. Joseph Fitsanakis, "Ukraine Releases Rare Footage Showing Arrests of North Korean Nuclear Spies," IntelNews, August 28, 2017, https://intelnews.org/2017/08/28/01-2164.

46. David L. Asher, "The North Korean Criminal State, Its Ties to Organized Crime, and the Possibility of WMD Proliferation" (lecture, Nautilus Institute for Security and Sustainability, Berkeley, CA, November 15, 2005).

47. David Rose, "North Korea's Dollar Store," *Vanity Fair*, August 5, 2009, https://www.vanityfair.com/style/2009/09/office-39-200909.

48. Ben Buchanan, *The Hacker and the State: Cyber Attacks and the New Normal of Geopolitics* (Cambridge, MA: Harvard University Press, 2020), 272–75.

49. Elias Groll, "Bank Thefts Show North Korea's Hacking Prowess," Yahoo! News, May 27, 2016, https://www.yahoo.com/news/bank-thefts-show-north-korea-211412162.html.

50. Joseph Fitsanakis, "Previously Obscure North Korean Hacker Group Is Now Stronger Than Ever, Say Experts," IntelNews, February 21, 2018, www.intelnews.org/2018/02/21/01-2274.

51. Kaori Yoshida, "North Korea Spied on 11 Security Council Officials Using Gmail," *Nikkei Asia*, April 5, 2020, www.asia.nikkei.com/Spotlight/N-Korea-at-crossroads/North-Korea-spied-on-11-Security-Council-officials-using-Gmail.

Pakistan: The Multidimensional Culture of the Inter-Services Intelligence

Nasir Mehmood

Inter-Services Intelligence (ISI), also known as the "Agency," is Pakistan's principal external intelligence collection organization with the mandate and capacity to operate across the width and breadth of the country. Throughout the course of more than seventy years, it grew from a modest beginning to a point in the twenty-first century where it has become a modern and internationally recognized versatile intelligence service. ISI is fundamentally concerned with national security rather than law and order issues.[1] It has demonstrated its capacity by strengthening Pakistan's defense against India, containing communism during the Cold War, and fighting the global War on Terror.[2]

The Agency possesses a unique status and culture in Pakistan, which this chapter argues is multidimensional owing to its composition, mission, and history. In particular, ISI provides and coordinates strategic intelligence with the armed forces of Pakistan and other state bodies. By virtue of this, it has an intimate relationship with all the military services chiefs. Concurrently, ISI seeks its mandate and higher policy directions from the Chief Executive (prime minister / president) of Pakistan. In line with this, the Agency outlines the policy options and their consequences to the political leadership, which contributes to the policy execution by generating favorable conditions. As for oversight, both political and military leadership inevitably engage and evaluate the Agency's delivery in their own right.

The Agency's unique status is mirrored in its organizational makeup. It has a relatively small staff recruited directly from society through an elaborate selection process and some specialized training for the envisaged task of each individual and team. Selected deputations from military and civil bureaucracy make it versatile with rich experience and expertise. With better integration than other aspects of the government, the Agency channels power from all-state machinery to improve its delivery and has a cohesive culture.

Owing to its external connections, integration with state machinery and society, quick access of the Chief Executive, and better human, technological, and financial resources, the Agency views itself as the front line and last line of the country's defense. Despite notable exception, there is little scholarly literature on ISI even though it regularly plays a vital role in Pakistan's national security. Within the available literature, there are confusions and contradictions about the Agency. To help address these issues, this chapter analyzes available sources, including interviews with former intelligence, military, and political heads. Additionally, it makes use of secondary sources, including relevant books, journal articles, and press commentaries.

This chapter explores Pakistan's intelligence culture by largely focusing on ISI. It begins by tracing the Agency's origins. Next, it outlines ISI's basic organizational structure. Then the chapter discusses the other major national intelligence agencies and illuminates their interaction with ISI. It then concludes by discussing the intelligence culture broadly and ISI specifically as well as highlights new challenges in the emerging security landscape.

ISI ORIGINS

As a secular Muslim-majority state, Pakistan was born to conflict, intimidation, and existential threats. Pakistan and India simultaneously succeeded the British Raj in the subcontinent in August 1947. India's leadership did not embrace the idea of partition enthusiastically despite consenting to it. Instead, India saw partition as an injury to its soul.[3] India created a whole range of security issues for Pakistan during and after partition. For example, it harmed Pakistan by undermining the division of key assets, annexation of princely states, boundary awards, water resources, and mass migration.[4] The hasty, unprofessional, and tainted partition aggravated the underlying animosity instead of mitigating it.[5] The British government analyzed Pakistan-India security relations in the following words:

> Even if present bitterness between India and Pakistan lessens somewhat, it can hardly be doubted that for some years to come, at all events, it will be the policy of the Indian government (or most of its members), whether by obstruction or core positive methods, to make it as difficult as possible for Pakistan to exist as a separate Dominion, in the hope that it will collapse within a measurable period.[6]

Similarly, the neighboring Kingdom of Afghanistan was the only country that opposed Pakistan's admission to the United Nations. It laid irredentist claims over a large swath of Pakistani territory and sponsored armed secessionist movements across the border. Pakistan's threat perception was compounded with the formidable threat of communism from northwestern and northeastern borders. With relatively powerful and aggressive India on its eastern borders, Pakistan inherited a vulnerable northwestern frontier with Afghanistan. Thus, Pakistan was established under the shadows of three large states: India, China, and the Soviet Union. Meanwhile, Pakistan lacked a functioning civil administration, armed forces, intelligence community, and well-defined borders.

Under those regional and extra-regional geostrategic circumstances, the Pakistan government needed a dedicated external intelligence collection agency. By summer 1948, India was launching military operations in the Indian-held Jammu and Kashmir. To have accurate and actionable intelligence, the Pakistan government asked the then secretary of the Joint Services Commanders Committee, Major General Bill Cawthorne, the most experienced intelligence officer in the British Commonwealth, and Lieutenant Colonel Shahid Hamid, a graduate of Sandhurst and head of the Pakistan National Guards, to raise an intelligence organization. They drew up a "Directorate of Forces Intelligence, forerunner of the Inter-Services Intelligence Directorate" (ISID) from scratch in the latter half of 1948.[7] The Directorate was housed in Karachi and staffed by both military and civilian personnel. Along with this, a few suitable positions were also created for women. Broadly, the Agency selected its staff from the three services of the Pakistan armed forces, the former Indian Intelligence Bureau, and civil society. Cawthorne sought institutionalized help and support from the British Secret Intelligence (MI6) for training and equipment purposes. In the following years, it had also received substantial support from the US Central Intelligence Agency (CIA).[8]

During its early years, the Agency was essentially a small organization with the mandate of tracking external threats. One of the early successes was the timely detection of the mobilization of an Indian offensive during the 1950 and 1951 military crises.[9]

BASIC ORGANIZATIONAL STRUCTURE

Intelligence is a hidden dimension of policy and strategy. It has a diversified and profound impact on military power, strategic decisions, and relations between states.[10] In its simplest terms, intelligence is foreknowledge about the surrounding world and involves what Sun Tzu called "divine manipulation of the threads."[11] Intelligence agencies serve strategy and policy in a manner that other government organizations cannot. Conventionally, they remain tight-lipped about their composition, as organizational hierarchies and structures provide clues about their function and agenda. ISI invariably maintains ambiguity about its organizational layout. No two opinions and information about its layout are similar, which reflects that ISI frequently modifies its flexible organization and changing methodologies.

The ISI Directorate presumably consists of several divisions and departments. A serving three-star general, usually from the army, heads as Director General ISI. He is assisted by several two-star generals from the three armed services, with the majority from the army. They are called directors general who head different divisions and departments, and each division/department has many subsections with exclusive and focused responsibilities.[12]

All Directorates General divisions handle different subject areas. The Directorate General Personnel looks after administrative, financial, recruitment, training, promotions, postings, transportation, and miscellaneous works. The Directorate General Analysis observes and evaluates important events and aspects of the realm of regional and international politics. It constantly coordinates with the foreign and defense ministries. The Directorate General Counter Intelligence thwarts foreign spying. It is responsible for the surveillance of unwanted or doubtful individuals from a counterintelligence perspective and regularly updates political leadership on significant developments.[13]

One of the Directorates General is entrusted with observing important developments and trends in governance, economy, and religion at the national level. It has tentacles across all provinces, including the Capital Territory of Pakistan. The Directorate General Counter Terrorism, established in the wake of the 9/11 terrorist attacks, exclusively concerns terrorism and counterterrorism operations. The Directorate General Media deals with print and electronic media that are involved in shaping societal perception on key policy issues. Lastly, the Directorate General Technical provides technical assistance to intelligence operations and is responsible for the secure normal, secret, and emergency communication requirements of political and military leadership. It also protects important buildings against listening devices.[14]

The structure and responsibilities demonstrate the Agency's multidimensional culture with its ability to operate against different threats and technologies for several decades. With limited resources, it seeks high gains from these adaptive workflows. Furthermore, the organization has a centralized and decentralized execution. The Director General ISI maintains central command over the organization, but the different divisions operate independently and orthogonally from each other. The personnel comprise a mix of armed forces, core intelligence officers, and some retired personnel on a contractual basis. With a largely military ethos and staff with seemingly frequent reorganization, the culture is also marked by discipline to the military. The actual size and composition of the directorate's staff in unknown. According to some estimates, it has more than 10,000 staff members. The Agency's main headquarters is situated in Islamabad with operational offices across the width and breadth of the country.[15]

COLLABORATING WITH OTHER INTELLIGENCE ORGANIZATIONS

There are more than a dozen intelligence organizations in Pakistan. Apart from ISI, the most notable are the Intelligence Bureau (IB), Air Intelligence (AI), Naval Intelligence (NI), and Military Intelligence (MI). They operate in different domains and with different mandates. Together they forge a substantive part of the national intelligence. Various new structures to aid security have reportedly been developed following the December 2014 Army Public School Peshawar attack and subsequent National Action Plan (NAP) drafted to counter terrorism in the country.

Intelligence Bureau (IB) Directorate

Intelligence Bureau Directorate, commonly known as the Intelligence Bureau (IB), is the oldest and preeminent civilian intelligence agency of Pakistan. IB is a lineal descendant of the Raj ancestral intelligence setup of the same name. At the time of independence, IB was entrusted with a massive agenda of foreign, strategic, and domestic intelligence. The IB's responsibility has been reduced to Pakistan's internal security as other intelligence agencies have emerged. The directorate exclusively works under the Chief Executive (prime minister / president) of Pakistan. It is headed by the highest-ranked civil servant, especially from the Police Services of Pakistan (PSP), who is addressed as the Director General Intelligence Bureau (DGIB). Occasionally, senior military officers have also held the position of DGIB.[16]

The Director General Intelligence Bureau (DGIB) is assisted by several joint director generals (JDGs). These JDGs head different wings/sections at headquarters. These wings include external, internal, counterintelligence, security, counterterrorism, and administration. IB underwent major expansion following the September 11, 2001, attacks in the United States and received substantial technical and training assistance. With better technology and training, IB has effectively administrated countless intelligence-based operations against nonstate actors across the country.[17]

Fundamentally, the IB updates the Chief Executive Office about currents of society and state institutions. It monitors political, religious, governance, financial, and law and order issues. Arguably, the IB has the most effective human intelligence (HUMINT) network and reaches the lowest level of state institutions and society. Besides, it runs counterintelligence operations to protect the state from hostile foreign agents.[18] The IB headquarters, located at Pakistan Secretariat, Islamabad, comprises four provincial headquarters and two regional headquarters in Gilgit Baltistan and Azad Jammu and Kashmir. The IB Directorate inducts officers and staff on a permanent as well as on a deputation basis.

Air Intelligence (AI) Directorate

Air Intelligence Directorate, commonly known as Air Intelligence (AI), is the intelligence arm of the Pakistan Air Force (PAF). AI was established along with the PAF's inception and housed in the Air Headquarters (AHQ), Islamabad. With the operationalization of nuclear deterrence and expansion of air bases, the Air Intelligence Directorate was upgraded and refurbished during the 1990s. It is currently led by a serving two-star officer (air vice marshal), who is designated as the Director General Air Intelligence (DGAI). The director general simultaneously performs three functions. He acts as the principal staff officer to the chief of Air Staff, commander of air intelligence operations, and administrative head of Air Intelligence School. He is assisted by two deputy directors general (DDGs), who usually are one-star officers (air commodore); they are focused on external intelligence and counter/internal intelligence.[19]

The office of Deputy Director General External performs different tasks during peace and war. During peacetime, it provides intelligence about air force development, deployment, and employment plans on the eastern border. Apart from the eastern border, it keeps an eye on the western borders with Afghanistan and Iran. During crisis or war, it furnishes information about the enemy's order of air battle to the Pakistan Air Force. In addition, it runs reconnaissance for potential targets, as air operational strategy is primarily concerned with the selection of targets. Simultaneously, it discerns morale and vital social issues bothering the enemy troops.[20] The office of Deputy Director General Internal is tasked with counterespionage, counterterrorism, and security matters. With the help of exclusive and highly trained teams, it concurrently runs all three operations in each air base, including adjacent areas. Its activities and scope during the War on Terror have increased, as air force assets became the priority of hostile nonstate actors.

Naval Intelligence (NI) Directorate

Naval Intelligence Directorate, commonly known as Naval Intelligence (NI), is the intelligence branch of the Pakistan Navy. It is headquartered in the Naval Headquarters (NHQ), Islamabad. It came into being along with the establishment of the Pakistan Navy. Like AI, it was headed by a one-star officer (commodore) but is now led by a serving two-star officer (rear admiral), who is appointed as Director General Naval Intelligence (DGNI) and is a principal staff officer to the Chief of Naval Staff (CNS). The Naval Intelligence Directorate inducts human resources from other branches of the Pakistan Navy, including submarines, surface, aviation, and special services group.[21] NI has gone through a major overhaul in the wake of the global War on Terror and the nuclearization of the Pakistan Navy.

Director General Naval Intelligence (DGNI) is assisted by a Deputy Director General Naval Intelligence (DDGNI). He administers several directorates, including operations, counterintelligence, security, and analysis. The Directorate Operations concentrates on the adversary's armed forces' naval component and monitors its force development and procurement plans. It keeps an eye on the disposition of the opposing naval forces. During crisis or war, it provides real-time information about the position/location of the critical naval war fighting machinery of the enemy, including other hostile naval forces in the Arabian Sea, Persian Gulf, Bay of Bengal, and the Indian Ocean widely. Along with this, it offers intelligence about an adversary's naval order of battle to the Pakistan Navy and observes the morale of the enemy troops.[22]

The Directorate Counterintelligence directs a whole range of counterespionage operations, including counterterrorism within and in the vicinity of naval installations across the country. The Directorate of Analysis is the NI's think tank. It closely follows salient developments and ideas across the realms of naval doctrine, naval strategy, naval governance, and politics widely.[23]

Military Intelligence (MI) Directorate

Military Intelligence (MI) Directorate, commonly known as Military Intelligence (MI), is the main intelligence service of the Pakistan Army. It was established soon after the inception of the Pakistan Army. The MI Directorate is located at the General Headquarter (GHQ), Rawalpindi. Like the AI and the NI, the Military Intelligence was headed by a serving one-star officer (brigadier general) for a long time; however, it underwent major refurbishment and expansion following the 1979 Soviet invasion of Afghanistan, domestic political upheaval, the nuclearization of the strategic forces, and the global War on Terror. It is led by a serving two-star officer (major general).

He is called Director General Military Intelligence (DGMI). He simultaneously performs three functions as the general staff officer to the Chief of Army Staff, commander of military intelligence operations, and administrative head of the School of Military Intelligence. He reports to the Army Chief. Military Intelligence exclusively enlists highly qualified and trained staff from the Corps of Military Intelligence (CMI).[24]

Director General Military Intelligence (DGMI) is supported by several deputy director generals (DDGs). They supervise the following directorates: Operations, Counterintelligence, Security, Technical, Counterterrorism, and Coordination. The Operations Directorate observes force development, deployment, and employment plans and activities of the hostile arming. It also monitors Pakistan's operational borders with India, Afghanistan, and Iran. During crisis or war, its intelligence operations track the mobilization and maneuvering of the critical warfighting machinery of the adversary. MI determines form and composition of the hostile formations directed toward the Pakistani borders.[25] It even reports tactical encounters within the battle space. Lastly, MI updates the morale and harmony of enemy troops.

The Counter-Intelligence Directorate primarily runs activities on Pakistan's soil. It counters threats from acquiring information about capabilities, operational preparedness, deployment, and war plans of the Pakistan Army. It also works to mitigate subversive activities of the enemy. Similarly, the Counter-Terrorism Directorate runs intelligence-based operations against hostile nonstate actors. Both the Security and Counter-Terrorism directorates have their own respective setup and teams across the width and breadth of the country. The Technical Directorate provides all kinds of technical assistance to all intelligence operations. The Coordination Directorate handles all the administrative, financial, and logistic requirements of Military Intelligence.[26]

Regarding the exchanges between and among the IB, AI, NI, MI, and ISI, they routinely interact at the tactical, operational, and headquarters levels to synergize their intelligence operations and efforts. These interactions are both formal and informal, and they have an impact on the overall national intelligence culture. Conventionally, the DGs of these organizations decide what is shared and approve intelligence sharing only on a needed basis. At times, the Chief Executive and the Services Chiefs' offices may also act as a communication bridge between and among these intelligence organizations. These interactions were streamlined and intensified in the wake of the global War on Terror. During times of war, these organizations may even shorten the bureaucratic procedures to expedite intelligence cooperation. Recently, the government of Pakistan has formed the National Intelligence Coordination Committee to integrate collective intelligence sharing and synchronize response.[27]

CONCLUSION

These intelligence services, along with ISI, constitute a significant part of the Pakistani intelligence community. Overall, Pakistan's national intelligence culture is a set of paradoxes. First, there is an element of exclusiveness as well as inclusiveness. On the one hand, these organizations tend to act as a single community and attempt to pursue integrated intelligence policy lines. On the other hand, these organizations prioritize their independent mandate and indulge themselves in the sense of healthy competition. Second, the intelligence community simultaneously reflects a culture of sharing and keeping intelligence. They essentially rely on subjectivity—such as an immediate or institutional perception of the need—for intelligence sharing. Third, all these intelligence services have military color. Therefore, their working environment and ethics are strongly reflective of military organizations. Fourth, there is an element of overlapping in the domain of other intelligence agencies to augment each other's responsibility.

For ISI specifically, it is the country's continuously surviving prime external intelligence collection organization. Due to its mission, history, geopolitical context, and politics, ISI has a multidimensional intelligence culture. In particular, the Agency works in multiple domains with fixed resources and optimal gains, which reflects an adaptive-workflow model. Although it intimately serves all the Services Chiefs, ISI seeks its mandate and policy directions from the Chief Executive of Pakistan. Both political and military leadership assign tasks to the Agency and evaluate its delivery in their own right. Furthermore, it has integrated with the armed services, civil bureaucracy, and civil society, bolstering the Agency's delivery.

The Agency improved its ability to work with other national intelligence agencies following the 9/11 attacks. ISI has enabled Pakistan's defense against adversaries, including terrorism, which continues to pose a serious threat to the country. In comparison to agent-based intelligence, ISI needs to further develop to tackle the security challenges. In the same vein, national cohesion, food security, climate change, energy security, cybersecurity, partnership with the private sector, and interaction with the public require priority in the Agency's agenda.

In particular, ISI has been subject to enormous challenges after the withdrawal of US and Western forces from Afghanistan as well as India's presence in Afghanistan. Indeed, the types of threats and challenges are expanding and getting complicated in the domestic, regional, and global milieu. To meet these affecting challenges, the Agency's culture needs to adapt along three lines, which Robert John Sawers, as the new chief, has messaged to the Secret

Intelligence Service (MI6) in 2009. These can be described in three themes: reputation, alignment, and delivery.[28]

In continuation of a good record, the Agency's culture also needs to catch up with the impending technological revolution. To do this, the Agency requires an innovative and imaginative intelligence doctrine. The analytical effort is crucial—from the collection of raw intelligence to processing to final intelligence and application. The analytical tools help collectors, processors, and policy makers determine reliability, meaning, and intelligence content.[29] Building on this, there is a need to increase the interest and skills of the policy makers and military strategists to properly interpret and comprehend the intelligence. Indeed, there must be consideration to think beyond immediate and short-term needs.

NOTES

1. Zulfiqar Khan (former senior analyst at ISI HQ), in discussion with the author, February 2, 2021.

2. Raza Muhammad (former major general and senior official at ISI HQ), in discussion with the author, March 9, 2021.

3. Jawaharlal Nehru, "Our Foreign Policy," speech at Indian Council of World Affairs, New Delhi, March 22, 1949, reproduced in *Nehru: The First Sixty Years,* ed. Jawaharlal Nehru and Dorothy Norman (London: Bodley Head, 1965), 465.

4. Papers of Field Marshal Sir Claude Auchinleck, University of Manchester Library, GB 133 AUC/1262.

5. Stanley Wolpert, *India and Pakistan: Continued Conflict or Cooperation?* (Berkeley: University of California Press, 2010), 7–9.

6. Analysis from British Government on Likely Future Relations India and Pakistan, October 20, 1947; National Archives, UK, DO 121/69.

7. Syed Ali Hamid, "The Early Years of the ISI," *Friday Times*, May 7, 2021.

8. Owen L. Sirrs, "The Perlis of Multinational Intelligence Coalition: Britain, America and the Origins of Pakistan's ISI," *Intelligence and National Security* 33, no. 1 (2018): 40–43.

9. Iqbal Akhund, *Trial & Error: The Advent and Eclipse of Benazir Bhutto* (Oxford: Oxford University Press, 2000), 136–37.

10. Geoffrey Sloan (director, Ways of Warfare Centre, University of Reading, UK), e-discussion with the author, December 3, 2020.

11. Sun Tzu, *The Art of War*, trans. Lionel Giles (Leicester: Allandale, 2000), 60.

12. Hein G. Kiessling, *Faith, Unity, Discipline: The Inter-Services-Intelligence (ISI) of Pakistan* (Noida: HarperCollins, 2016), 168–70.

13. Syed A. I. Trimazi, *Profiles of Intelligence* (Lahore: Intikhab-e-Jadeed Press, 1995), 7.

14. Kiessling, *Faith, Unity, Discipline*, 172.

15. Anonymous (former official at ISI HQ), in discussion with the author, April 5, 2021.

16. P. C. Joshi, *Main Intelligence Outfits of Pakistan* (New Delhi: Anmol, 2008), 15–17.

17. Anonymous (former senior official at IB HQ), in discussion with the author, June 12, 2021.

18. Anonymous, June 12, 2021.

19. Anonymous (former senior Pakistan Air Force officer), in discussion with the author, March 15, 2021.

20. Anonymous, March 15, 2021.

21. Anonymous (former Pakistan Naval Intelligence officer), in discussion with the author, February 17, 2021.

22. Anonymous, February 17, 2021.

23. Anonymous, February 17, 2021.

24. Anonymous (former Pakistan Military Intelligence officer), in discussion with the author, March 18, 2021.

25. Anonymous (former Pakistan Military Intelligence officer), in discussion with the author, March 25, 2021.

26. Anonymous, March 25, 2021.

27. Baqir Sajjad Syed, "Prime Minister Okays Creation of Liaison Body for Spy Agencies," *Dawn*, November 24, 2020.

28. War Studies, King's College London, "Conversations with Strategy: Former MI6 Chief, John Sawers on Intelligence and Diplomacy," YouTube, March 25, 2021, https://www.youtube.com/watch?v=2MANsEfe5uw&t=1348s.

29. Philip H. J. Davies and Kristian Gustafson, "Intelligence and Military Doctrine: Paradox or Oxymoron?" *Defence Studies* 19, no. 1 (2019): 26–27.

The Philippines: Knowing, Hurting, and Intelligence Culture

Amador IV Peleo

Any description of an intelligence culture is also an assessment of how surveillance and covert operations are valued in a particular culture of governance. The claim that intelligence services are not unlike other line agencies that contribute useful information to the government is commonly encountered in introductions to histories of security communities.[1] Indeed, it is possible to argue that the intelligence services are not the only government agencies that have "secrets and mysteries" options when conducting their operations. More important, the recurrent use of covert action to evade official oversight mechanisms, including counterintelligence capabilities, indicate that the intelligence community is inherently politicized or at least retains the ability to exercise political influence if intelligence officers decide.[2] This chapter on the Philippines' intelligence community is an account of the origins and direction of this politicization. The prevailing view is that the professional integrity of the intelligence services risks damage by politicization.[3] Yet in the Philippines at least, this politicization norm is consistent with the broader political culture in which the instruments of governance can be subverted to satisfy the narrow interests of government officials and other members of a "political elite."

FROM COLONY TO COUNTRY

The intersection of the security sector with governance issues has been an enduring feature of politics in the Philippines since its colonial period in the sixteenth century. Security forces are still used to suppress political subversives and armed secessionist movements that have been active since the late 1960s and were directly involved in the removal of two incumbent presidents in 1986 and 2001.[4] The main intelligence organizations that are currently operating were formed under highly politicized circumstances. The Intelligence Service of the Armed Forces of the Philippines (ISAFP) as well as the Criminal Investigation and Detection Group (CIDG) and Intelligence Group (IG) under the Philippine National Police (PNP) trace their origins to the Information Section of the Philippine Constabulary (PC) that was formed on August 8, 1901.[5] The PC was not technically a military organization as it was commanded by the civilian United States authorities of the Philippine Commission.[6] But, the Filipino troops of the PC proved so effective in the paramilitary role of exterminating Filipino nationalist rebels that, by 1904, the number of US Army personnel deployed in the Philippines was reduced to less than a fourth of the number deployed in 1901.[7]

The National Bureau of Investigation (NBI) has its origins in the Division of Investigation (DI) under the Department of Justice (DOJ) of the Philippine Commonwealth formed on November 13, 1936.[8] Although it gained control of the PC and its intelligence capabilities through the National Defense Act of 1935,[9] the Commonwealth government still chose to form the DI as an analogue of the New York Police Department (NYPD) and the Federal Bureau of Investigation (FBI) to be deployed for police work in Manila, the national capital.[10] In 1949, the National Intelligence Coordinating Agency (NICA) was formed, according to Philippine president Elpidio Quirino, "to provide for a central agency to coordinate the intelligence gathering activities of the various branches and instrumentalities of the government."[11] The appropriateness of this timing can be attributed to the conclusion of two bilateral security treaties between the US and Philippine governments in 1947, and to a subsequent assessment by the US State Department in 1948 that identified the Philippines as a key recipient of military aid for anticommunist operations.[12] Several hundred Communist Huk cadres, who fought the Japanese during World War II, continued their subversion and appeared to threaten the reestablishment of a pro-American and capitalist-driven Philippine government.

During the Cold War, the Criminal Investigation Service (CIS), the precursor of the CIDG and IG, was reorganized in 1953 to operate a crime laboratory[13] in support of the Philippine Army (PA), which, with US direction, had been changed from an external defense force to a counterinsurgency force in 1950.[14] The body that advises the president on matters of national security, currently the National Security Council (NSC), uses the intelligence that is ideally provided or vetted by the NICA[15] and has also been reconfigured by almost every president since the creation of the original Council of National Defense on December 21, 1935.[16] General Douglas MacArthur, a US citizen, was appointed as military adviser of the Philippine government by president

Manuel Quezon on December 16, 1935, prior to the creation of the Council of National Defense, and since then every security advisory council has been convened through executive orders to allow for the modification of the council as the president has seen fit.[17]

The current politicization of the intelligence services can be seen from an operational perspective. Depoliticizing entails the improvement of the functional and organizational characteristics of these agencies, ideally to prevent security operatives from exploiting their government posts for personal enrichment. This was the perspective from which the Security Sector Reform (SSR) goal in the 2011–2016 National Security Policy was identified. Specifically, professionalism in the security sector reflects the professionalization of all other government agencies to which it is linked.[18] The operationalization of this in the intelligence services was to have been an improvement of guidance and support capabilities mainly for combat operations against Communist and Islamist subversives[19] and for coordination with US military forces.[20] The improvement of support for "anti-illegal drug and anti-criminality campaigns" was added to the 2018 Armed Forces of the Philippines' (AFP) Development Support and Security Plan.[21]

Underpinning this professionalization campaign was a renewed concern for "transparency and accountability," as the entire security sector had been attempting to expunge its reputation for corruption and brutality that persisted from the 1965–1986 Marcos presidency.[22] The Philippine constitution adopted in 1987 listed oversight mechanisms that cover all government operations, including those of the security sector. The most prominent are the Civil Service Commission, Commission on Audit, Office of the Ombudsman, and the National Police Commission (NAPOLCOM).[23] These mechanisms, however, appear to operate with a "plain oversight" approach—that is, wrongdoing is investigated only after complaints are officially reported, typically by concerned citizens, rather than prevented through the inputs of officials and internal specialists who monitor operations in real time.[24] Institutional oversight specifically for the intelligence services appears to have been initially limited to the Senate Oversight Committee on Intelligence and Confidential Funds, Programs and Activities that was first convened in 1997.[25] Several bills have since been filed in the Senate that proposed the formation of a Joint Congressional Intelligence Committee (JCIC) composed of delegates from the Senate and the House of Representatives.[26] To date, this committee does not appear to be operational, causing oversight responsibilities to remain mainly with agencies to which the intelligence units are immediately attached; these are the AFP for the ISAFP, the PNP for the CIDG and IG, the DOJ for the NBI, and the Executive Committee of the NSC for the NICA.

THE CORRUPTION OF INTELLIGENCE

The politicization of the Philippine intelligence services can also be assessed from a structural perspective. *Policing America's Empire* (2009) by Alfred McCoy is the definitive account about how eleven decades of "sliding political boundaries between police and army, crime and war"[27] created the Philippine "mafia state"[28] system. Also instructive is *Philippine Politics and Society in the Twentieth Century* (2000) by Eva-Lotta Hedman and John Sidel. Systems of governance operate not so much as the means through which social services are delivered but, rather, as extensions of the operations through which political elites—ostensibly, "gangster-politicians" and business oligarchs—accumulate, legitimize, and advertise their wealth and prestige.[29] More incisive is the argument of Nathan Quimpo that governance in the Philippines has been devolving from the parochial "patron-clientelism" in the early twentieth century to an aggressive "predatory regime" in the early twenty-first. Political elites have become more cynical and opportunistic; they are thereby more willing to defraud the state of its resources and to resort to coercion, violence, and other covert "dirty tricks."[30] From this perspective, the issue is no longer about whether the information and covert services provided by the intelligence community are accurate, concise, timely, and fair—that is, as politics free as possible. Rather, the issue is about whether the resources available to the intelligence services match the interests that the incumbent political elites intend to be satisfied.

In this intelligence culture, the primary objects of investigation are instances of organizational deviance, which, in this case, refer to failure to achieve organizational goals or abide by administrative procedures set by the government.[31] Commonly termed in the Philippines as "corruption," this behavior is generally accepted as "victimless crimes," the harm of which is identified not with the accrual of unfair advantage but with the subterfuge through which advantage is gained.[32] The intelligence services being utilized as internal police could, in principle, deter racketeering in government; however, the intelligence operatives' involvement in corruption scandals likely indicates the persistence of the belief that patronage from the political elite guarantees against discovery, investigation, and prosecution.

On February 17, 2020, a Senate investigation with the PNP and NBI into the involvement of Philippine Offshore Gaming Operators (POGOs) with sex trafficking and prostitution uncovered a scheme through which millions of Chinese nationals entering the Philippines, including POGO workers, were each extorted 10,000 pesos (about US$208) by Bureau of Immigration (BI) officials to waive their vetting at the Ninoy Aquino International Airport (NAIA).[33] The BI, like the NBI, is under the jurisdiction of the

DOJ. Although five BI officials were "immediately relieved from their posts due to command responsibility,"[34] the Office of the President neither acknowledged a need for an immediate investigation[35] nor suspended BI commissioner Jaime Morente, a political ally of President Rodrigo Duterte and former police chief of Duterte's hometown, Davao City.[36] On March 3, 2020, testimony from BI officer Allison Chiong, a witness at the Senate inquiry into the scandal, identified former DOJ secretary Vitaliano Aguirre II as the "protector" of the racket.[37] Aguirre is a "brother" of Duterte in the Lex Talionis fraternity based at the San Beda College of Law and the Ateneo de Davao College of Law, and other "brothers" of the fraternity were involved in a multimillion-peso bribery scandal at the BI in 2016, when Aguirre was the incumbent DOJ secretary and commanded the BI.[38] Aguirre also appointed Marc Red Mariñas, who was identified by Morente as a key person in the scheme,[39] to the Ports Operation Division (POD) of the BI in 2016 and, later, to its Board of Commissioners in 2018.[40] Yet neither Aguirre, Mariñas, nor Morente were included in a list, issued by the NBI on September 2, 2020, of twenty individuals to be prosecuted for involvement in the scam.[41]

At a sting operation conducted by the NBI on September 21, 2020, NBI Legal Assistance Section chief lawyer Joshua Paul Capiral and his brother, BI Medical Section officer Christopher John Capiral, were arrested after they received marked money from BI officer Jeffrey Dale Ignacio, another witness of the Senate hearing. The money, worth 200,000 pesos (about US$4,156), was presumed by the brothers as payment for their help to reduce or remove the culpability of the individuals included in the list issued by the NBI on September 2.[42] The investigation also appears to have indicated the interference of Joshua Paul Capiral in other cases of the NBI, particularly those involving drug trafficking.[43]

A consequence of this culture is that intelligence operatives are reduced to being instruments and casualties when the Philippine government "denounces itself for breaking its own laws."[44] On June 29, 2020, nine members of the PNP who were manning a checkpoint in Jolo, Sulu, gunned down four Philippine Army (PA) intelligence operatives. These operatives were coordinating with a PA combat unit to capture two suspected suicide bombers and a bomb maker with links to the Abu Sayyaf terrorist group.[45] A subsequent investigation by the NBI refuted the claim made by the policemen that an exchange of gunfire between the two groups occurred at the checkpoint; it also revealed that the policemen planted evidence to give the appearance that PA soldiers intended to shoot first.[46] At a Senate hearing on the incident held on August 19, 2020, one of the policemen involved, Staff Sergeant Iskandar Susulan, testified that the soldiers were attacked as they were believed to be involved with the Abu Sayyaf or drug traffickers,[47] and evidence was presented that linked one of the casualties, Corporal Adbal Asula, to a drug syndicate.[48] At a hearing on August 24, 2020, however, AFP Western Mindanao Command chief Major General Corleto Vinluan Jr. testified that the Jolo police believed the intelligence operatives suspected, and could have exposed, some of the policemen as being related to, and thereby somehow protecting, the terrorists under investigation.[49] Furthermore on November 21, 2020, Lieutenant Colonel Walter Annayo, the chief of police in Jolo during the incident, was shot dead by an unidentified gunman in Maguindanao, where he was reassigned after the relief of his command.[50] The killing of Annayo has yet to be linked to the killings in Jolo. What is certain is that local politicians in Sulu have been linked to drug smuggling, corruption, and support for the Abu Sayyaf,[51] and that President Rodrigo Duterte personally endorses a "shoot to kill" approach to dealing with drug criminals[52] and terrorists.[53]

CONCLUSION

The Philippine intelligence community is vulnerable to corruption, infighting, and co-option by political elites. Indeed, its politicization more closely resembles the differential association processes similar to those by which criminal gangs are created.[54] More significantly, this politicization likely diminishes the ability of the intelligence services to identify and assess security threats that are not immediately linked to local political interests. The Philippine security sector would not have discovered the "Bojinka plot" to assassinate Pope John Paul II and bomb eleven airliners had not Police Officer Aida Farsical, on January 6, 1995, decided to personally look into a smoke alarm report in a Manila apartment apparently caused by "just some Pakistanis playing with fireworks." This resulted in the arrest of a Pakistan passport-bearing Kuwaiti, Abdul Hakim Ali Hashim Murad, who was later subjected to a "tactical interrogation"—a euphemism for torture—after having first attempted to bribe and mislead Farsical and other PNP officers.[55] He eventually confessed his involvement not only with the Bojinka plot but also with the bombing of the Cebu-Tokyo Philippine Airlines flight 434 on December 11, 1994.[56]

In another case, the AFP was first alerted to the presence of Chinese structures at the Mischief Reef in the South China Sea area claimed by the Philippines only by Filipino fishermen, who gave their eyewitness accounts in February 1995.[57] The expectation that Filipino fishermen, who are among the most impoverished in Philippine society, are to provide intelligence seems to be recurrent in Philippine security circles.[58] This can be inferred from the details of the militarized confrontation between the Philippine Navy (PN) ship BRP *Gregorio del Pilar* and eight unarmed Chinese fishing vessels in the Scarborough Shoal on April 10, 2012,[59] and from the proposed "fishermen militia" involving fishermen volunteers who already augment PN forces in the South China Sea.[60]

Lastly, the Battle of Marawi—involving Philippine security forces against Islamist terrorists from May 23 to October 23, 2017, and considered the longest case of urban warfare in modern Philippine history,[61]—has been acknowledged by President Duterte as a failure of intelligence.[62] This failure is due, in part, to a failed analysis of the influence held by the Maute family of Lanao del Sur, which organized and partly sponsored the Islamist militants involved in the conflict.[63] As these three cases demonstrate, for the Philippine intelligence community to become more adept at preventing threats, a complete reimagining of the intelligence culture may be required.

NOTES

1. Thomas Fingar, *Reducing Uncertainty: Intelligence Analysis and National Security* (Stanford, CA: Stanford University Press, 2011), 37–38; Loch K. Johnson, "National Security Intelligence," in *The Oxford Handbook of National Security Intelligence*, ed. Loch K. Johnson (New York: Oxford University Press, 2010), 5–6; J. Ransom Clark, *Intelligence and National Security: A Reference Handbook* (Westport, CT: Praeger Security International, 2007), 1.

2. Peter Gill, "Theories of Intelligence," in *The Oxford Handbook of National Security Intelligence*, ed. Loch K. Johnson (New York: Oxford University Press, 2010), 51–52.

3. Fingar, *Reducing Uncertainty*, 44–45.

4. Jennifer Santiago Oreta, "Dreaming of a Modern Defense Force," in *Security Sector Reform: Modern Defense Force, Philippines*, ed. Jennifer Santiago Oreta et al. (Quezon City: Ateneo de Manila University Press, 2014), 3–5.

5. "CIDG History," Criminal Investigation and Detection Group, August 29, 2018, https://www.cidg.pnp.gov.ph/index.php/about-us/cidg-evolution-from-cis-to-cidg.

6. William K. Emerson, *Encyclopedia of United States Army Insignia and Uniforms* (Norman: University of Oklahoma Press, 1996), 295.

7. Vic Hurley, *Jungle Patrol: The Story of the Philippine Constabulary, 1901–1936* (Salem, OR: Cerberus Books, 2011), 63–64.

8. Commonwealth Act 181, Corpus Juris, November 18, 2020, https://thecorpusjuris.com/legislative/commonwealth-acts/ca-no-181.php.

9. Commonwealth Act No. 1, *Official Gazette of the Republic of the Philippines*, November 18, 2020, https://www.officialgazette.gov.ph/1935/12/21/commonwealth-act-no-1/.

10. "Overview," National Bureau of Investigation, November 18, 2020, https://web.archive.org/web/20180902015743/http://nbi.gov.ph/transparency-seal/overview/.

11. Executive Order No. 235, s. 1949, *Official Gazette of the Republic of the Philippines*, November 18, 2020, https://www.officialgazette.gov.ph/1949/07/10/executive-order-no-235-s-1949/.

12. Alfred W. McCoy, *Policing America's Empire: The United States, the Philippines, and the Rise of the Surveillance State* (Madison: University of Wisconsin Press, 2009), 375–76.

13. "CIDG History," Criminal Investigation and Detection Group, August 29, 2018, https://www.cidg.pnp.gov.ph/index.php/about-us/cidg-evolution-from-cis-to-cidg.

14. William C. Moore, "The Hukbalahap Insurgency, 1948–1954," Defense Technical Information Center, March 1, 1971, 38–42, https://apps.dtic.mil/sti/citations/AD0773529.

15. Administrative Order No. 68, s. 2003, *Official Gazette of the Republic of the Philippines*, November 19, 2020, https://www.officialgazette.gov.ph/2003/04/08/administrative-order-no-68-s-2003/.

16. Commonwealth Act No. 1, *Official Gazette of the Republic of the Philippines*, November 18, 2020, https://www.officialgazette.gov.ph/1935/12/21/commonwealth-act-no-1/.

17. Executive Order No. 3, s. 1935, *Official Gazette of the Republic of the Philippines*, November 19, 2020, https://www.officialgazette.gov.ph/1935/11/16/executive-order-no-3-s-1935/

18. *2011–2016 National Security Policy: Securing the Gains of Democracy*, National Security Council, November 19, 2020, 10, https://www.nsc.gov.ph/attachmentsarticle/NSP/NSP-2011-2016.pdf, 10.

19. "Bayanihan: Internal Peace and Security Plan," Armed Forces of the Philippines, 2010, 10, 15, 24, 32, https://www.army.mil.ph/home/images/bayanihan.pdf.

20. "Philippine Defense Transformation," Department of Defense, Republic of the Philippines, July 23, 2012, 11, 15–16, 20, https://www.dnd.gov.ph/pdf/PDT%20White%20Paper_Final_23Jul12.pdf.

21. "AFP Development Support and Security Plan 'Kapayapaan' 2017–2022," MR Online, September 2018, , 38, 43, https://mronline.org/wp-content/uploads/2018/09/AFP-Development-Support-and-Security-Plan-Kapayapaan-2017-2022.pdf.

22. Rodel A. Cruz, "Security Sector Reform: Way Forward for Democracy and Development," in *National Security Review* (Quezon City: National Defense College of the Philippines, 2013), 113–14.

23. Noel Del Prado, "Mapping Out the Legal Terrain of the Philippine Security Sector," in *Security Sector Reform: Modern Defense Force, Philippines*, ed. Jennifer Santiago Oreta et al. (Quezon City: Ateneo de Manila University Press, 2014), 29–36.

24. Francis Domingo, "Philippine Intelligence Community: A Case for Transparency," in *Security Sector Reform: Modern Defense Force, Philippines*, ed. Jennifer Santiago Oreta et al. (Quezon City: Ateneo de Manila University Press, 2014), 84–85.

25. Resolution No. 36, Senate of the Philippines, February 10, 2020, 1, http://legacy.senate.gov.ph/18th_congress/resolutions/resno36.pdf.

26. Senate Bill No. 765, Senate of the Philippines, July 7, 2010, 3, http://legacy.senate.gov.ph/lisdata/81246596!.pdf; Senate Bill No. 1384, Senate of the Philippines, March 13, 2017, 4, http://legacy.senate.gov.ph/lisdata/2558822071!.pdf;

Senate Bill No. 377, Senate of the Philippines, July 11, 2019, 5, http://legacy.senate .gov.ph/lisdata/3066927523!.pdf.

27. Paul Kramer, "Review: Alfred McCoy, *Policing America's Empire*," *American Historical Review*, October 2011, 1089, https://www.academia.edu/27342794/ Review_Alfred_McCoy_Policing_Americas_Empire.

28. Patricio Abinales, "Book Review: Alfred W. McCoy, *Policing America's Empire*," *Critical Asian Studies* 44, no. 2 (2012): 339, https://doi.org/10.1080/14672 715.2012.644895.

29. Eva-Lotta E. Hedman and John T. Sidel, *Philippine Politics and Society in the Twentieth Century: Colonial Legacies, Post-colonial Trajectories* (London; New York: Routledge, 2000), 28–29, 80–83, 89.

30. Nathan Gilbert Quimpo, "The Philippines: Predatory Regime, Growing Authoritarian Features," *Pacific Review* 2, no. 3 (2009): 347–48.

31. Penny Green and Tony Ward, *State Crime: Governments, Violence and Corruption* (London; Sterling: Pluto, 2004), 5–6.

32. Graham Brooks, *Criminology of Corruption: Theoretical Approaches* (Wolverhampton: Palgrave Macmillan, 2016), 32–33.

33. Michelle Abad, "'Magkano at hanggang kanino?' Hontiveros Reveals Bribery in Entry of POGO Workers," *Rappler*, February 17, 2020, https://www.rappler.com/ nation/hontiveros-reveals-bribery-entry-pogo-workers.

34. Cathrine Gonzales, "5 Immigration Officers Sacked over 'Pastillas' Bribery Scheme for Pogo Workers," Inquirer.net, February 18, 2020, https://newsinfo.inquirer .net/1230159/5-immigration-officers-relieved-from-posts-due-to-pastillas-scheme.

35. Krissy Aguilar, "Palace to Probe 'Pastillas' Scheme in Airport Only if Complaints Are Filed," Inquirer.net, February 18, 2020, https://newsinfo.inquirer .net/1230320/palace-to-investigate-pastillas-scheme-but-complaints-should-be-filed.

36. Krissy Aguilar, "Duterte Pal Morente Not off the Hook on 'Pastillas' Scheme, Says Palace," Inquirer.net, February 21, 2020, https://newsinfo.inquirer.net/1231721/ fwd-palace-morente-not-safe-from-being-fired-by-duterte.

37. Leila B. Salaverria, "Ex-Justice Secretary Linked to Immigration Racket," Inquirer.net, March 3, 2020, https://newsinfo.inquirer.net/1236005/ ex-justice-secretary-linked-to-immigration-racket.

38. Ina Reformina, "Two Duterte Frat Brods Figure in Corruption Scandal," ABS-CBN News, December 13, 2016. https://news.abs-cbn.com/focus/12/13/16/ two-duterte-frat-brods-figure-in-corruption-scandal.

39. Michelle Abad, "'Pastillas' Scheme Top Gun Appointed by Former Justice Secretary Aguirre—Morente," *Rappler*, February 20, 2020, https://www.rappler.com/ nation/pastillas-scheme-top-gun-appointed-by-former-doj-secretary-aguirre.

40. Ferdinand Patino, "Bureau of Immigration Names New Deputy Commissioner," Philippine News Agency, Republic of the Philippines, May 2, 2018, https:// www.pna.gov.ph/articles/1033891.

41. Jodee A. Agoncillo, "NBI Presses Raps vs 20 Tagged in 'Pastillas' Scam," Inquirer.net, September 3, 2020, https://newsinfo.inquirer.net/1330521/nbi-presses -raps-vs-20-tagged-in-pastillas-scam.

42. Benjamin Pulta, "NBI Lawyer, Brother in BI Face Extortion, Graft Raps," Philippine News Agency, Republic of the Philippines, September 23, 2020, https://www.pna.gov.ph/articles/1116337.

43. Kristine Joy Patag, "Raps Filed vs NBI Exec, Brother over Alleged Extortion in 'Pastillas' Scheme Probe," Philstar Global, September 23, 2020, https://www.phil star.com/headlines/2020/09/23/2044549/raps-filed-vs-nbi-exec-brother-over-alleged -extortion-pastillas-scheme-probe; "Duterte Orders Drug-Accused Mayor to Surrender within 24 Hours," ABS-CBN News, August 1, 2016, https://news.abs-cbn.com/ news/08/01/16/duterte-orders-drug-accused-mayor-to-surrender-within-24-hours; "Leyte Mayor Rolando Espinosa Killed in 'Firefight' inside Jail," Inquirer.net, November 5, 2016, https://newsinfo.inquirer.net/841271/rolando-espinosa-killed-in-jail.

44. Green and Ward, *State Crime*, 1.

45. Jeannette I. Andrade, "Army Loses Track of 2 Jolo Bombers after Agents' Slay," Inquirer.net, July 2, 2020, https://newsinfo.inquirer.net/1300483/army-loses -track-of-2-jolo-bombers-after-agents-slay; Jeannette I. Andrade and Julie S. Alipala, "Another Army Team Misses Abu Targets after Agents' Killing," Inquirer.net, July 3, 2020, https://newsinfo.inquirer.net/1301095/another-army-team-misses-abu-targets -after-agents-killing.

46. Kristine Joy Patag and Marianne Enriquez, "NBI Files Murder, Planting of Evidence Raps vs Jolo Cops over Killing of Soldiers," Philstar Global, July 21, 2020, https://www.philstar.com/headlines/2020/07/21/2029609/nbi-files-murder-planting -evidence-raps-vs-jolo-cops-over-killing-soldiers.

47. Rambo Talabong, "Jolo Cop Shot Army Intelligence Officer Thinking He Was 'Abu Sayyaf, Drug Lord,'" *Rappler*, August 19, 2020, https://www.rappler.com/ nation/cop-jolo-killed-army-intelligence-officer-thinking-abu-sayyaf-drug-lord.

48. Christia Marie Ramos, "'Matrix' Links to Drug Syndicate One of 4 Army Men Killed in Sulu—Police," Inquirer.net, August 19, 2020, https://newsinfo.inquirer .net/1324440/matrix-links-one-of-the-4-army-men-killed-in-sulu-shooting-to-drug -syndicate-police-claims.

49. Christia Marie Ramos, "Sulu Cops Connected with Suicide Bombers? Military Official Cites Possible Motive on Jolo Shooting," Inquirer.net, August 24, 2020, https://newsinfo.inquirer.net/1326222/sulu-cops-connected-with-suicide-bombers-mi litary-official-cites-possible-motive-on-jolo-shooting.

50. Consuelo Marquez, "Ex-Jolo Police Chief Annayo Shot Dead in Maguindanao," Inquirer.net, November 21, 2020, https://newsinfo.inquirer.net/1363364/ ex-jolo-police-chief-annayo-shot-dead-in-maguindanao.

51. Carolyn O. Arguillas, "Sulu Mayor in Duterte's 'Validated' List Passed Away in 2014," Mindanews, August 8, 2016, https://www.mindanews.com/top -stories/2016/08/sulu-mayor-in-dutertes-validated-list-passed-away-in-2014/; Jamela Alindogan, "Inside Abu Sayyaf: Blood, Drugs and Conspiracies," Al Jazeera, July 24, 2016, https://www.aljazeera.com/news/2016/7/24/inside-abu-sayyaf-blood -drugs-and-conspiracies; Linda Robinson, Patrick B. Johnston, and Gillian S. Oak, *US Special Operations Forces in the Philippines, 2001–2004* (Santa Monica, CA: RAND, 2016), 66–67.

52. "More Than 7,000 Killed in the Philippines in Six Months, as President Encourages Murder," Amnesty International UK, May 18, 2020, https://www.amnesty.org.uk/philippines-president-duterte-war-on-drugs-thousands-killed.

53. Nick Aspinwall, "After Signing Anti-terrorism Law, Duterte Names His Targets," *Foreign Policy*, July 10, 2020, https://foreignpolicy.com/2020/07/10/philippines-law-terrorism-duterte/.

54. Brooks, *Criminology of Corruption*, 68–75; George B. Vold, Thomas J. Bernard, and Jeffrey B. Snipes, *Theoretical Criminology*, 4th ed. (New York: Oxford University Press, 1998), 183–87.

55. Matthew Brzezinski, "Bust and Boom," *Washington Post*, December 30, 2001, https://www.washingtonpost.com/archive/lifestyle/magazine/2001/12/30/bust-and-boom/1109903e-3762-4b78-90a6-d191efd39920/.

56. John Hatzadony, "Oplan Bojinka Revisited: The Plot and Its Legacy," *Aviation Security International*, October 16, 2019, https://www.asi-mag.com/oplan-bojinka-revisited-the-plot-and-its-legacy/.

57. Michael Studeman, "Calculating China's Advances in the South China Sea Identifying the Triggers of 'Expansionism,'" *Naval War College Review* 51, no. 2 (Spring 1998), https://www.globalsecurity.org/military/library/report/1998/art5-sp8.htm.

58. Lisa Grace Bersales, "Farmers, Fishermen and Children Consistently Posted the Highest Poverty Incidence among Basic Sectors—PSA," Philippine Statistics Authority, 2020, https://psa.gov.ph/content/farmers-fishermen-and-children-consistently-posted-highest-poverty-incidence-among-basic.

59. "Philippines Asserts Sovereignty over Panatag (Scarborough) Shoal," *Official Gazette of the Republic of the Philippines*, April 11, 2012, https://www.officialgazette.gov.ph/2012/04/11/philippines-asserts-sovereignty-over-panatag-scarborough-shoal/.

60. Raissa Robles, "'We Are Not at War with China': Philippines' Fishermen Militia Plan Put on Pause," *South China Morning Post*, November 4, 2020, https://www.scmp.com/week-asia/politics/article/3108475/we-are-not-war-china-philippines-fishermen-militia-plan-put.

61. Agence France-Presse, "Marawi: City Destroyed in Philippines' Longest Urban War," Inquirer.net, October 19, 2017, https://newsinfo.inquirer.net/939202/marawi-war-maute-terrorism-duterte-isnilon-hapilon-is-islamic-state.

62. Trisha Macas, "Duterte Admits Failure of Intelligence in Marawi City," *GMA News Online*, July 24, 2017, https://www.gmanetwork.com/news/news/nation/619295/duterte-admits-failure-of-intelligence-in-marawi-city/story/.

63. Rommel C. Banlaoi, "The Maute Group and Rise of Family Terrorism," *Rappler*, June 15, 2017, https://www.rappler.com/voices/thought-leaders/maute-group-rise-family-terrorism.

21

Singapore: Developing Intelligence Power from Third World to First

Alexander Nicholas Shaw

Singapore in the twenty-first century is affluent, modern, and global.[1] Since its emergence as an independent state in 1965, the island city has, to borrow Lee Kuan Yew's metaphor, jumped from "third world" to "first world" status.[2] As an increasingly global power, Singapore is reliant for national security upon a powerful intelligence apparatus capable of projecting influence through sharing communication intelligence with the Western powers, providing strategic confidence in conducting relations with troublesome neighbors, or safeguarding Singapore from terrorism.

As an island of around 280 square miles with a growing population of more than 5.6 million, Singapore is a densely populated city-state. In 1947, census results showed that 78 percent of Singapore's population was ethnically Chinese, followed by 12 percent Malay and 7 percent Indian.[3] More than seventy years later, although Singapore's population has grown sixfold, the ethnic balance remains deliberately constant.[4] British colonial officials used ethnic categories as a way of understanding their subject population through ideas about race and loyalty. This form of colonial knowledge was inherently linked with intelligence analysis, and modern Singapore has inherited this obsession with maintaining consistent ethnic proportions.[5]

The nature of Singapore as a paternalist democracy has brought significant benefits. Consistency in government has facilitated huge economic growth through state intervention and long-term planning, remarkably low levels of crime and corruption, and a stable approach to national security. Conversely, paternalist politics justify the employment of a semi-authoritarian model of policing and justice where free speech is not absolute and security suspects can be detained without trial. These contradictions do not cause civil disruption because of an implicit social contract by which the Singapore government provides prosperity and safety in return for political acquiescence. Based on the assumption that Singapore faces consistent military, economic, or terrorist threats, the social contract justifies compulsory national service, systemic state intervention in the economy, and the development of a system of intelligence, surveillance, and preventative detention. The intelligence services benefit from this contact as it legitimizes their powers while they also support its perpetuation by defining national security threats and decisively responding to them, fulfilling the government's bargain to protect its citizenry while eliminating political challenges to the government.

This chapter proposes the existence of a uniquely Singaporean intelligence culture, with the social contract at its center, that has retained continuity between the colonial state of the 1950s and the paternalist democracy of the People's Action Party (PAP), which has governed Singapore continuously since the first self-governing elections in 1959. It begins by introducing the context of Singapore and its principal intelligence services before evaluating the features of the colonial intelligence culture in the 1950s. Subsequently, the chapter explores developments since Singapore achieved independence and how this intelligence culture has enabled Singapore to respond to jihadist terrorism.

The Internal Security Department (ISD) and the Security and Intelligence Division (SID) are Singapore's principal intelligence services. The ISD is responsible for security intelligence, counterterrorism, and counterespionage while the SID covers external and strategic intelligence. These agencies both evolved from the British colonial Special Branch and inherited an intelligence culture sustained through the influence of British and Australian advisers in the early years of independence. Singapore continues to have close defense relations with these countries as well as Western intelligence services, such as the Five Eyes partners.[6]

Both the ISD and SID were formally inaugurated on February 17, 1966. The ISD was initially subordinate to the Ministry of the Interior and Defense until that ministry was split in 1970 and the ISD became part of the Ministry of Home Affairs. As a security intelligence agency, the ISD has much in common with the United Kingdom's Security Service (MI5), although it is distinguished by the application of the Internal Security Act. While the British norm is to separate intelligence gathering from policing or enforcement, the ISD has the power to detain suspects independently from the Singapore police. This Singaporean model of security intelligence reflects the colonial origins of the ISD in its predecessor, the police Special Branch.

As Singapore's external intelligence service, the activities of the SID rarely enter public discourse. Reporting to the Ministry of Defense, its activities include providing strategic intelligence to the Singapore Armed Forces, collecting information relating to external threats, and liaising with foreign intelligence services. According to former SID director Eddie Teo, "we don't like to use the word 'spy' . . . we don't do the sort of things that some people think intelligence services do—go round assassinating people, covert action and black ops."[7] Teo's dismissal of covert action reflects the SID's preference to be seen as a research-focused, professional, and highly specialized aspect of the defense services. Speaking to a *Straits Times* journalist, another former SID officer described its activities as falling into three categories: collection of intelligence (human and technical), analysis and evaluation of intelligence, and secret diplomacy. The latter included the SID's involvement in training noncommunist Cambodian resistance forces and supplying them with weapons to oppose the Vietnamese invasion of Cambodia in 1979.[8] While these operations were precisely the sort of covert action that Eddie Teo denied, such practices demonstrate that Singapore has used its intelligence services to build clandestine alliances with ideologically aligned neighbors and to project power on the quiet. This is unsurprising given that Britain's intelligence services used Singapore as a base to conduct exactly this type of covert diplomacy during the 1940s and 1950s.[9]

COLONIAL LEGACIES

The Malayan Emergency commenced in June 1948, beginning a period of counterinsurgency in Malaya and counter-subversion in Singapore as British security forces sought to outwit the Communist Party of Malaya (CPM). British policy makers blamed the Malayan Security Service, which had operated in both colonies since 1946, for the perceived intelligence failure to predict the CPM uprising and replaced it with Special Branches in Malaya and Singapore.[10] The Singapore Special Branch developed a colonial intelligence culture during its confrontation with the CPM, which was defined by three inheritances that continue to define modern Singapore: police activity as intelligence activity; gathering intelligence for enforcement purposes; and colonial paternalism.

Unlike the short-lived Malayan Security Service, the Special Branch was an integral part of the Singapore police. This reprised a model of security intelligence first introduced to Singapore in 1918 to combat Indian revolutionary nationalism. Consequently, more quotidian police activity, antismuggling and antinarcotics operations contributed to the intelligence cycle. During the first six months from June 1948, only two-thirds of emergency detentions resulted from active Special Branch cases. The others resulted from other police operations where suspects were found to have ties to the

Communist Party.[11] In December 1950, Special Branch detained the complete Singapore Town Committee (the controlling organization of the CPM) following informant tip-offs and alert surveillance by the ordinary police. Previously Special Branch had enjoyed high-level agent penetration of the CPM, but after December 1950, the Communists became more security conscious and moved to a decentralized hierarchy, which left Special Branch on the backfoot.[12] In November 1952, the next major intelligence breakthrough originated when a random police stop-and-search of bus passengers found a nervous Chinese man carrying incriminating documents that identified the location of CPM safehouses.[13] Locating security intelligence within the police therefore expanded the flow of intelligence and scope of information-gathering methods.

Conversely, just as police operations were channeled into intelligence, Special Branch also provided intelligence to guide operations in enforcing law and order. This gave its intelligence culture a more operational edge than that of the discredited Malayan Security Service. In the mid-1950s, Special Branch activities against the CPM's united front culminated on the night of October 26–27, 1956, when Special Branch officers led simultaneous police raids upon several addresses linked to the Middle Road group of unions. This was a coalition led by the Singapore Factory and Shop Workers Union whose secretary, Lim Chin Siong, was implicated as a CPM agent.[14] Blurring the lines between intelligence collection and the enforcement of public order was advantageous in speeding up intelligence dissemination, but it also embroiled Special Branch in political disputes. In April 1948, the colonial government arrested members of the Communist-controlled Singapore Federation of Trade Unions. This was before the declaration of Emergency in June 1948, and public opinion was unlikely to accept these strict measures without justification, so the Singapore governor authorized the release of intelligence that proved the unions had acted illegally.[15] Similarly, during the period of self-government from 1959 to 1963, Prime Minister Lee Kuan Yew used Special Branch intelligence to justify political decisions. In a series of radio talks in 1961, Lee disclosed intelligence that demonstrated that Lim Chin Siong (released from detention in 1959 and the leader of the opposition party Barisan Sosialis) had been a Communist subversive in the 1950s. Lee's use of intelligence in the public sphere garnered popular support for the contentious policy of merging with Malaysia.[16] Because Singapore's intelligence culture is built upon blurred lines between intelligence input and government or police action, national security intelligence can easily be politicized in this manner.

This politicization of intelligence alludes to the existence of Special Branch within an environment of colonial paternalism in which there was no easy distinction between the national security of Singapore and the regime security of the colonial state. The CPM was both a national security challenge, engaging in a violent terrorist campaign during the year 1950, and a political challenge to British supremacy. Consequently, Special Branch was bequeathed extensive surveillance powers, including posting detectives within the Singapore Post Office to intercept suspect mail and tapping telephones belonging to nationalist political parties.[17] The Emergency Regulations also allowed the police to hold Communist suspects indefinitely in detention centers such as that on the former disease quarantine center on St. John's Island, at first with no oversight beyond the Governor's Office.[18] In 1960, similar colonial regulations in Malaya were updated through the Internal Security Act, a critical piece of legislation that was applied to Singapore in 1963 and remains in operation into the twenty-first century. The Internal Security Act enables Singapore's ISD, no longer part of the police but closely cooperating with them under the Ministry of Home Affairs, to carry out preventative detention of suspects for two years without judicial oversight. Singapore's first prime minister, Lee Kuan Yew, cited these detention powers as the critical factor in explaining Singapore and Malaysia's victory over Communist terrorism (a security problem that persisted into the 1970s through occasional bombings by CPM affiliates in Singapore). Lee said: "Could we have defeated them if we had allowed them habeas corpus and abjured the powers of detention without trial? I doubt it. Nobody dared speak out against them, let alone in open court."[19] In this regard, colonial legacies continue to shape Singapore's contemporary intelligence culture and the relationship between national security intelligence and the enforcement of law and order.

ADAPTING TO INDEPENDENCE

Singapore became a fully independent republic on August 9, 1965, and gained the opportunity to rethink its intelligence organization. Despite significant structural changes, however, Singapore's intelligence culture remained largely constant. Securitization, or the process of framing national security threats, is almost always an elite-driven process. In Singapore, this is especially marked because the boundaries between regime security and national security are somewhat indistinct. Like the colonial state, the PAP has successfully securitized political opponents as subversive threats to national security and ensured its continued dominance. In turn, the lack of a credible opposition enables the intelligence agenda to develop without concern for transparency.[20] This was particularly notable during the period of transition between self-government in 1959 and merger with Malaysia in 1963. As a precondition to merger, the Malayan Tunku wanted Lee Kuan Yew to arrest members of the leftist opposition party Barisan Sosialis. Both Malaysia and Singapore framed Operation Coldstore in security terms, suggesting that Barisan, led by released detainee Lim Chin Siong, was a subversive Communist organization. British observers disagreed, suspecting that the Malaysian and Singaporean governments were exaggerating security fears for political benefit. Somewhat reluctantly, Britain acquiesced to a program of mass detentions after Special Branch produced evidence that Lim Chin Siong had met with A. M. Azahari, the leader of the December 1962 anti-Malaysian insurgency in Brunei.[21]

After achieving independence, the Ministry of the Interior and Defense was founded in November 1965, and three months later the ISD and SID were formally inaugurated under its auspices. The combined nature of this ministry emphasized how the PAP government saw an inherent link between internal and external security. This was unsurprising given the context of the Indonesian confrontation from 1963 to 1966, where an external conflict mainly fought in Borneo led to terrorist attacks in Singapore. By 1970, the combined ministry was split into the Ministry of Defense and the Ministry of Home Affairs. The former took responsibility for external intelligence through the SID, and the latter assumed control of security intelligence through the ISD. This split reflected an increased confidence that internal security threats could be handled without military intervention.[22]

Demonstrating continuity with the colonial past, the ISD continues to exercise considerable surveillance powers in the digital age. Court warrants are not required to tap telephones, intercept data, or access CCTV feeds, and the Computer Misuse and Cybersecurity Act allows the government to compel cyber organizations to conduct preemptive surveillance: a digital counterpart to the preemptive detention powers established in the 1950s and retained by the ISD. Journalists have also alleged that the ISD can track individuals using car toll units (a ubiquitous gizmo that Singaporeans keep on their dashboard and that automatically applies tolls).[23] The lack of public debate over such powers reflects the importance of Singapore's social contract to its paternalist intelligence culture.

The broader defense agenda that frames Singapore's intelligence culture has undergone significant development since 1965. At the time of independence, Singapore's leaders were acutely aware of their own vulnerability as a small city-state in a region beset by international conflicts and Communist insurgencies. Committed to defense expansion and modernization, the Singapore Armed Forces engaged Israeli and Australian advisers to help construct an external intelligence apparatus with human, signals, and communication intelligence potential. Israel may seem an unusual mentor given the lack of religious, cultural, or historic ties but had appropriate synergy as a small state surrounded by hostile neighbors. This advice was particularly important because strategic and foreign intelligence were comparatively new to Singapore, having been previously handled by the United Kingdom's Secret Intelligence Service (MI6) and GCHQ before independence.[24]

Pessimistic about the plausibility of holding Singapore against invasion, the Singapore Armed Forces of the 1980s adopted a "poisoned shrimp" doctrine of deterring aggression by making Singapore strong enough to inflict serious damage on an attacker before its inevitable defeat. From the 1990s, however, the Ministry of Defense became confident in its ability to win a future war swiftly and decisively. In the 2000s, the government committed to a 6 percent GDP ceiling on defense spending: three times the GDP target agreed on by the North Atlantic Treaty Organization (NATO) member-states in Europe and North America. This expenditure ensured that the Singapore Armed Forces were equipped with the most modern and sophisticated weapons systems. While Singapore lacks the population size or geographic depth to win a war by traditional military superiority, technology has provided the solution. Singapore has the financial resources to simply out-spend and out-tech its rivals.[25]

Geography remains a vital cornerstone of Singapore's defense policy and strategic intelligence agenda, particularly with regard to Singapore's status as an island and major trading port. During the 1950s, Singapore and Djakarta exchanged intelligence relating to counter-piracy—the key maritime security issue of the day and an economic as well as security threat—despite rising political tensions between Britain and Indonesia. In the twenty-first century, Singapore's investment in sophisticated defense hardware guarantees maritime security. The Republic of Singapore Air Force first acquired Grumman Hawkeye airborne early warning aircraft in the 1980s and subsequently upgraded to the Gulfstream 550. These air assets provide Singapore with an electronic intelligence (ELINT) and signals intelligence (SIGINT) capability that are ideally suited for maritime surveillance.[26]

Across the sea, Singapore's geographical security is framed by its complex relations with its Islamic neighbors. Since expulsion and independence in 1965, relations with Malaysia have been governed by economic interdependence, political tension, and disputes over Singaporean access to Malaysian fresh water. Across the Malacca Strait, Indonesia represents a similar dichotomy of challenge and opportunity. During the 1960s, Indonesia's policy of confrontation represented a nadir in relations typified by state-sponsored terrorism against Singapore. Unsurprisingly Indonesia is often depicted as a geostrategic and ideological threat, yet Singapore relies upon Indonesian migrant workers for low-paid jobs. Being encircled by neighbors that represent both threat and opportunity has impacted Singapore's intelligence culture by emphasizing the importance of strategic intelligence to national security. An SID officer explained that "we are surrounded by countries and people not of the same mind as ourselves. But we have the maturity to realize that we are all different countries, with different interests, and we don't have to be disagreeable about it. There is a great need to understand and interpret them in a [methodical] way."[27] Beyond threat posturing and rhetoric, on a practical basis Singapore engages in bilateral security cooperation with Malaysia and Indonesia on several levels. As well as joint military exercises, cooperation is most durable in maritime surveillance through the Eyes in the Sky program to protect the Melaka Straits and joint Singaporean-Malaysian surveillance of the South China Sea.[28] The transition from rivalry to cooperation with Malaysia and Indonesia has been accelerated by the emergency of transnational terrorism as Singapore's principal security concern. The cross-border and sub-state threat of Islamic jihadism has forced Singapore and its neighbors to engage in more substantive intelligence sharing against a common enemy.

SINGAPORE'S WAR ON TERROR

Terrorism has constituted a recurrent security threat to Singapore since the year 1950, when the CPM allied with criminal secret societies to perpetrate assassination and arson. The MacDonald House bombing in 1965 constituted Indonesian state-sponsored terrorism, and in 1974, left-wing terrorists affiliated with the Japanese Red Army and the Popular Front for the Liberation of Palestine attacked an oil refinery and escaped by hijacking the ferry boat *Laju*. This incident was resolved when SID director S. R. Nathan led a team who offered themselves as exchanges for the *Laju* hostages and negotiated with the terrorists. Although this incident was resolved through conciliation, when a team of Pakistani leftist terrorists hijacked a Singapore Airlines flight in 1991, special forces stormed the aircraft and killed all the hijackers. In responding to isolated terrorist incidents before 2001, Singapore's mode of response was situationally specific rather than conforming to an overarching doctrine.

In contrast, jihadist terrorism represents a more insidious challenge to Singapore's national security and intercommunal relations and, therefore, requires a more systematic response. From the early 1990s, the terrorist landscape was dominated by al-Qaeda and its Southeast Asian affiliate Jemaah Islamiyah (JI). In late 2001, the ISD and SID began disrupting a JI plot that would likely have brought 9/11-levels of carnage to Singapore. A JI group led by condominium manager Ibrahim Maidin and Indonesian-born bus mechanic Mas Selamat Kastari planned simultaneous attacks in Singapore using truck bombs against Western embassies and other targets including Mass Rapid Transit metro stations and naval bases.[29] In December 2001 and January 2002, the ISD used the Internal Security Act to detain suspected JI members and succeeded in neutralizing al-Qaeda's operational capacity in Singapore before the attacks could be launched.[30]

After 2013, the direct threat from JI was eclipsed by the ideological challenge of the Islamic State (IS) that seized power in parts of Iraq and Syria. This represented a substantially different jihadist challenge, shifting the focus away from international terrorists infiltrating Singapore and toward Singaporean Muslims becoming radicalized, traveling to the Levant, and returning with terrorist ideas. Singapore's reliance on foreign workers for manual labor, many of whom come from Islamic nations like Indonesia or Bangladesh, compounded security fears regarding the influence of IS-inspired ideology on migrant workers as well as Singapore's Muslim residents.[31] The new jihadism of IS thereby constituted a dual threat of transnational and homegrown terrorism. With regard to the former, in August 2016, an IS-inspired Indonesian terrorist cell was arrested before they could execute a plot to fire a rocket at Singapore's iconic Marina Bay Sands hotel and casino from Batam Island around eighteen miles away.[32]

Intelligence is central to Singapore's response to jihadism at the national and international levels. Nationally, the ISD gathers intelligence about terrorist organizations and enforces counterterrorism by applying the Internal Security Act to detain terrorists. This is a clear indication that the colonial intelligence culture founded on the principles of intelligence for enforcement and strict preventative security measures has adapted to the contemporary world. In another example of successfully adapting colonial intelligence practices, the government formed the Religious Rehabilitation Group, a volunteer organization of Muslim clerics and scholars, to engage the detained JI members. During the Malayan Emergency, the British implemented a highly successful campaign of reeducation, using psychological intelligence methods to persuade detained insurgents to repudiate communism and embrace democracy. Acting on almost identical principles, the Religious Rehabilitation Group has enabled some detainees to be progressively released on restriction orders.[33]

Meanwhile, reflecting the importance of intelligence and security to Singapore's social contract, the government has embarked on a broader societal response to Islamic extremism. This social resilience is a significant aspect of Singapore's counterterrorism strategy, exhibited through the development of Inter-racial and Religious Confidence Circles, again reviving a colonial policy first promulgated by the British Commissioner General Malcolm

MacDonald. Educating the public about the terrorist threat and counteracting extremist ideology is equally important. In 2009, the Singapore Armed Forces took part in Exercise Northstar VII, a major counterterrorism exercise designed to grab public attention and restore faith in the social contract following the embarrassing escape of Mas Selamat.[34]

Internationally, Singapore's intelligence services have embarked upon revitalized regional partnerships, benefiting from a legacy of colonial and postcolonial intelligence liaison about communist terrorism in Southeast Asia. In May 2002, the Association of South East Asian Nations (ASEAN) agreed to a Singaporean proposal for each member to appoint a special antiterrorist team to act as a contact point in security liaison. Nevertheless, multilateral intelligence cooperation has failed to gather as much traction as bilateral liaison with Malaysia, Indonesia, Thailand, and the Philippines. Bilateral intelligence sharing was instrumental in the arrest of Mas Selamat Kastari, one of the Singapore JI leaders. Mas Selamat fled shortly before he could be detained in 2001 but was arrested in Indonesia and extradited to Singapore in 2006. To the public embarrassment of the Singapore government, Mas Selamat escaped from the ISD detention center on Whitley Road in February 2008. In May 2009, acting on intelligence supplied by Singapore, the Malaysian Special Branch rearrested Mas Selamat in Johore and handed him back to Singapore for detention under the Internal Security Act.[35]

Singapore's engagement with an increasingly globalized intelligence order extends beyond counter-terrorism issues.[36] As a self-defined "first world" nation, Singapore pursues cooperation with the Five Eyes alliance. SingTel is a significant corporate intelligence asset for the Singaporean government, owning equity in several other Asian mobile networks, and it also took over the Australian network Optus in 2001 which included the satellite carrying Australian military communications. The fact that Australia allowed this takeover is likely indicative of the close communications intelligence partnership which has persisted since the colonial period and through the Australian Defense Signals Directorate (DSD) helping the SID develop its independent signals intelligence capacity in the 1960s and 1970s.

CONCLUSION

Intelligence, particularly security intelligence, was of vital importance in Singapore's transition to independence. The British-controlled Special Branch of the 1950s reassured decolonizing decision makers that Lee Kuan Yew was a trustworthy anticommunist successor. While rallying nationalist support against the colonial regime, Lee nevertheless cooperated with Special Branch by passing on information relating to the CPM as it attempted to court an alliance with the PAP in 1955.[37] As Singapore prepared for merger with Malaysia in 1963, Special Branch again played a decisive role by carrying out the arrest program agreed by Lee Kuan Yew and Tunku Abdul Rahman.

With intelligence having played a significant role in the emergence of independent Singapore, it is perhaps unsurprising that Singapore's intelligence culture continues to be intertwined with the social contract that shapes political society. This contract is a Hobbesian pact with the Leviathan whereby citizens surrender their right to defend themselves to the state, which provides security in return for acquiescence. The ISD wields powers to enforce law and order, which distinguishes it from other security intelligence services like the United Kingdom's MI5, while the SID has been implicated in significant communications intelligence tapping. The lack of dissent surrounding these issues testifies to an intelligence culture that is both a beneficiary of the social contract and, as Singapore's most important means of countering jihadist terrorism, constitutes one of the main pillars supporting it.

The Singaporean social contract has evolved from the legacies of the colonial state: an inherently paternalistic entity with a blurry distinction between national security and regime security. The key features of the Special Branch system developed during the 1950s, such as the conflation of intelligence gathering and security enforcement, have persisted through legislation and inherited organizational practices. In responding to the threats of JI and IS-inspired terrorism in the twenty-first century, Singapore's intelligence culture has replicated effective practices introduced by the British to combat communism in the 1950s. This continuity is symptomatic of Singapore's pragmatic approach to its colonial past and the enduring intelligence relationship between Singapore and the Western powers. Consequently, Singapore's intelligence community has successfully capitalized on their sound colonial inheritance, geostrategic position, and the PAP's stable political vision to become a "first world" intelligence power with regional and global influence.

NOTES

1. I would like to thank Scott Ramsay for his assistance in editing this chapter.
2. Lee Kuan Yew, *From Third World to First* (Singapore: Times Editions, 2000).
3. Minute by E. C. S. Adkins, June 11, 1947, FCO 141/14359, The National Archives, (TNA), Kew, United Kingdom.
4. National Population and Talent Division, *Population in Brief 2020* (Singapore: Government of Singapore, 2020), 20.

5. Alexander Nicholas Shaw, "The British Intelligence Community in Singapore, 1946–1959: Local Security, Regional Coordination and the Cold War in the Far East" (PhD diss., University of Leeds, 2019), 10.

6. James S. Cox, *Canada and the Five Eyes Intelligence Community* (Calgary: Canadian Defence & Foreign Affairs Institute and Canadian International Council, 2012). http://citeseerx.ist.psu.edu/viewdoc/download?doi=10.1.1.357.5576&rep=rep1&type=pdf; Christian Leuprecht and Hayley McNorton, *Intelligence as Democratic Statecraft: Accountability and Governance of Civil-Intelligence Relations Across the Five Eyes Security Community* (Oxford: Oxford University Press, 2021), 21; Richard J. Aldrich, *GCHQ: The Uncensored Story of Britain's Most Secret Intelligence Agency* (London: Harper Press, 2010), 96, 166, 167.

7. Sumiko Tan, "Eddie Teo, a Very Civil Servant," *Straits Times Online*, November 19, 2017, https://www.straitstimes.com/singapore/lunch-with-sumiko-eddie-teo-a-very-civil-servant.

8. Yap Chuin Wei, "Examining the World's Second Oldest Profession," *Straits Times*, May 19, 2001, 14.

9. Alexander Nicholas Shaw, "Propaganda Intelligence and Covert Action: The Regional Information Office and British Intelligence in South-East Asia, 1949–1961," *Journal of Intelligence History* 19, no. 1 (2020): 51–76.

10. Roger Arditti and Philip H. J. Davies, "Rethinking the Rise and Fall of the Malayan Security Service, 1946–48," *Journal of Imperial and Commonwealth History* 43, no. 2 (2015): 93–94.

11. Singapore Intelligence Liaison Committee report, December 20, 1948, FCO 141/15667, TNA.

12. Special Branch memorandum, December 22, 1952, CO 1022/250, TNA.

13. Special Branch weekly summary, November 15, 1952, FCO 141/15659, TNA.

14. Letter from Alan Blades to William Goode, October 31, 1956, FCO 141/14773, TNA.

15. DSO Malaya and Singapore report for April 1948, FCO 141/15439, TNA.

16. Lee Kuan Yew, *The Battle for Merger*, 2nd ed. (Singapore: Straits Times Press, 2014), 90–101.

17. Interview with Richard Corridon, oral history 000044, National Archives of Singapore, Singapore.

18. David Bonner, *Executive Measures, Terrorism and National Security: Have the Rules of the Game Changed?* (Aldershot: Ashgate, 2007), 142.

19. Lee, *From Third World to First*, 134–35.

20. Norman Vasu and Bernard Loo, "National Security and Singapore: An Assessment," in *Perspectives on the Security of Singapore*, ed. Barry Desker and Ang Cheng Guan (Singapore: World Scientific, 2016), 28.

21. Matthew Jones, "Creating Malaysia: Singapore Security, the Borneo Territories, and the Contours of British Policy, 1961–63," *Journal of Imperial and Commonwealth History* 28, no. 2 (2000): 100.

22. Carlyle A. Thayer, "Security Relations," in *Across the Causeway: A Multidimensional Study of Malaysia-Singapore Relations*, ed. Takashi Shiraishi (Singapore: ISEAS, 2009), 169.

23. "Is Singapore Western Intelligence's 6th Eye?"

24. Kwa Chong Guan, "The Challenge of Strategic Intelligence for the Singapore Armed Forces," in *Perspectives on the Security of Singapore*, ed. Barry Desker and Ang Cheng Guan (Singapore: World Scientific, 2016), 87–88.

25. N. Ganesan, "Regional Security: The Singapore Perspective," in *Across the Causeway: A Multi-dimensional Study of Malaysia-Singapore Relations*, ed. Takashi Shiraishi (Singapore: ISEAS, 2009), 176–78.

26. "Is Singapore Western Intelligence's 6th Eye?"

27. Wei, "Examining the World's Second Oldest Profession," 14.

28. Bilveer Singh, "Singapore's Security in the Context of Singapore-Malaysia-Indonesia Relations," in *Perspectives on the Security of Singapore*, ed. Barry Desker and Ang Cheng Guan (Singapore: World Scientific, 2016), 121–34.

29. Andrew Tan, "Terrorism in Singapore: Threat and Implications," *Contemporary Security Policy* 23, no. 3 (2002): 1.

30. Rohan Gunaratna, "The Changing Terrorist Threat Landscape in Singapore," in *Perspectives on the Security of Singapore*, ed. Barry Desker and Ang Cheng Guan (Singapore: World Scientific, 2016), 233–34.

31. Kumar Ramakrishna, "The Threat of Terrorism and Extremism: A Matter of 'When' and Not 'If,'" *Southeast Asian Affairs* (2017): 336–37.

32. Bilveer Singh, "Why Singapore Is a Terrorist Target," *The Diplomat*, June 28, 2017, https://thediplomat.com/2017/06/why-singapore-is-a-terrorist-target/.

33. Gavin Chu Hearn Yuit, "Singapore's Approach to Counterterrorism," *Counter Terrorist Centre Sentinel* 2, no. 12 (2009): 23.

34. Yuit, "Singapore's Approach to Counterterrorism," 23.

35. Gunaratna, "The Changing Terrorist Threat Landscape," 236.

36. Austin Gee and Robert G. Patman, "Small State or Minor Power?: New Zealand's Five Eyes Membership, Intelligence Reforms, and Wellington's response to China's growing Pacific role," *Intelligence and National Security* 36, no. 1 (2021): 36.

37. Corey Pfluke, "A History of the Five Eyes Alliance: Possibility for Reform and Additions," *Comparative Strategy* 38, no. 4 (2019): 302–315.

38. Becky Gaylord, "In Optus Deal, Australians Ponder How to Trust Singapore," *New York Times*, August 13, 2001.

39. Desmond Ball, *Signals Intelligence in the Post–Cold War Era: Developments in the Asia-Pacific Region* (Singapore: Institute of Southeast Asian Studies, 1993), 58.

40. "People's Action Party," in supplement to *Singapore Police Intelligence Journal*, April 1955, FCO 141/15951, TNA.

22

South Korea: The Outsize Influence of the National Intelligence Service

Charlie Lizza

The Republic of Korea (ROK or South Korea) refers to itself as a "shrimp amongst whales" due to its position among regional powerhouses, including China, and threats from the Democratic People's Republic of Korea (DPRK or North Korea).[1] Despite its small size, South Korea occupies a crucial geographic position and relies heavily on its national intelligence apparatus to ensure its security. South Korean intelligence was originally influenced by the United States (US) military, taking on a counterintelligence and internal security mission in addition to a foreign intelligence role.[2] This legacy persists today. The major players are the National Intelligence Service (NIS) and military intelligence, which is composed of the Korea Defense Intelligence Agency (KDIA) and the Defense Security Command (DSC). This chapter largely focuses on the NIS. The service has a broad mandate, responsible for foreign and domestic collection and analysis and criminal investigations. Further, NIS has clear superiority in the intelligence establishment with limited oversight, classified budgets, and influence over others' budgets.[3] This outsized impact is problematic, however. Since its inception, NIS has been embroiled in controversy, including a campaign against a 2012 presidential election candidate and a 2017 bribery scandal.[4] In 2020, South Korea announced plans for changes at NIS. These included a new name, the External Intelligence and Security Service (EISS), and a reduction in authorities to remove its internal security missions and allow for enhanced government oversight.[5] While a good first step, this chapter argues that more must be done to improve the quality of South Korea's intelligence culture, including increasing oversight of the NIS, enhancing the stature of the other intelligence agencies, and improving information sharing between the agencies.

The chapter begins with a brief overview of the NIS and Korean military intelligence and exploration of South Korean intelligence history. In particular, it highlights three key events: the initial creation of intelligence agencies with the help of the United States in 1945, the establishment of the Korean Central Intelligence Agency (KCIA) in 1961, and the more recent issues that have plagued the NIS. It then describes issues facing the South Korean intelligence apparatus with attention to scandals stemming from the NIS's dominant position within the country's intelligence structure. Finally, it examines how South Korean intelligence integrates with the international community within the region and without, as well as proposed reform measures.

SOUTH KOREAN INTELLIGENCE COMMUNITY

North Korea has been South Korea's primary threat since 1945, and current fears include intelligence operations, kidnappings, and various military aggravations.[6] Consequently, the mission for South Korean intelligence includes monitoring North Korean activities and providing indications and warning of potential dangers. To do so, there are three main agencies within South Korea's intelligence community. The NIS operates at the national level, while the DSC and KDIA focus on military intelligence. Further, there are at least four entities that perform intelligence activities but are not considered official, including the Security Bureau of the National Police Agency.[7] This section explores the three primary agencies, of which the NIS is the most important.

The two military organizations are KDIA and DSC. The KDIA's responsibilities are to "integrate and manage defense intelligence policies and planning" for military intelligence, including activities at all parts of the intelligence cycle. Subordinate to the Ministry of National Defense and the Joint Chiefs of Staff, it consists of three other entities: the National Geospatial-Intelligence Agency; 777 Command, responsible for signals collection (SIGINT); and the Defense Intelligence Command, which collects human intelligence (HUMINT) as well as MASINT and SIGINT. It also has a large military attaché component, which facilitates exchanges with foreign governments.[8] To illustrate the control the NIS has over the intelligence community, while the KDIA director manages the agency's budget, the NIS reportedly can exercise control over KDIA funding.[9] Further, while NIS staff have access to the military intelligence apparatus, it is not reciprocal.[10]

The DSC is also subordinate to the Ministry of National Defense, but the KDIA manages DSC's intelligence actions. These activities include "supporting military security, military counterintelligence, intelligence collection on military units and military affairs, and investigation on specific crimes."[11] In 2018, however, disclosures of political meddling and illegitimate surveillance led President Moon Jae-in to dismantle the DSC, replace it with the Defense Security Support Command, and enforce oversight.[12] The new agency kept a similar mission, but with greater prohibitions on domestic and political interference.[13]

Critics allege that Korean military intelligence broadly suffers from groupthink in that great deference is shown to the opinions and conclusions of senior analysts. In the same vein, career progression often depends on personal connections rather than objective performance.[14] Military intelligence has been known to leak classified information, an issue seen throughout South Korea's intelligence community. In 2020, following the killing of a South Korean government employee by North Korea, the military disclosed sensitive SIGINT to lawmakers and other officials. They, in turn, revealed that information to the public, which possibly compromised future intelligence efforts.[15] Military intelligence is also subject to personnel problems. In September 2020, two officers were charged with raping a North Korean defector.[16]

The NIS Act describes the NIS's responsibilities, charging it with "handl[ing] the duties pertaining to information, protection of public peace and criminal investigation related to national security." To do so, it is empowered "to collect, produce, and distribute foreign intelligence and domestic security intelligence."[17] This broad remit combines intelligence and investigatory authorities; includes leadership of certain investigations, such as insurrection and rebellion; internal oversight, like investigations into staff misconduct; and "the planning and coordination of intelligence and public security services."[18] Little is publicly known regarding the NIS structure, which is classified; however, it is likely divided into three sections: external intelligence activities, primarily focused on North Korea; domestic activities focusing on anticommunism, counterintelligence, counterterrorism, and crime; and technical intelligence, including SIGINT.[19]

South Korea's intelligence track record is mixed. In the Cold War period, collaboration with Western powers and a well-developed HUMINT network allowed notable successes, including the revelation that North Korea conducted public executions.[20] However, its failures are also well documented. Among other things, it failed to warn of the Northern invasion in summer 1950 and did not learn that Kim Jong Il had died in winter 2011.[21] While its foreign capabilities are lacking, its domestic surveillance capacities, honed in on authoritarian regimes since the 1960s, are well established. These powers, and the abuses and scandals that have stemmed from them, are discussed in further detail later in the chapter.

MILITARY INTELLIGENCE PRE-1961

Formalized intelligence practices originated in 1946, under the US Army Military Government that occupied South Korea following the Second World War's end via the US Counter Intelligence Corps.[22] After a presidential government was established in 1948, the Army Headquarters Intelligence Bureau (AHIB)—the only intelligence service at the time—was responsible for counterintelligence, military intelligence, and special operations.[23] Due to the heavy influence of the US military, South Korean intelligence in the early years was predominantly concerned with military issues.[24] When the Korean War began in 1950, the AHIB split in two: counterintelligence (CIC) and Headquarters of Intelligence Detachment.[25] Myriad touchpoints between US and Korean intelligence existed throughout the war, including collection and guerilla operations in the north. South Koreans also provided significant translation assistance to SIGINT collection.[26] Throughout the decade, however, the CIC performed a regime security role in addition to its military security and counterintelligence mission, including removing political opposition to President Rhee Syngman.[27] This legacy of intelligence involvement in domestic politics and internal security have persisted throughout South Korea's intelligence history.

HISTORY OF THE KCIA AND ANSP, 1961–1999

In May 1961, members of the military, led by Major General Park Chung-hee, assumed control of the country via a coup d'état and established the KCIA in June.[28] Created to monitor and preserve internal security, the KCIA's mandate was "to prevent the aggression of the communists and to eliminate the obstacles of the tasks of the revolution."[29] Given expansive powers, including the ability "to receive support from all state instructions when necessary," it was further insulated due to a lack of oversight. The KCIA director was empowered to ignore oversight requests, and its "budget, facilities, and organizational structure were state secrets."[30] It quickly became the most powerful intelligence agency in South Korea and carried out abuses against regime opponents, including torturing students and democracy advocates, kidnapping opposition figures from Japan and Germany, and interfering in elections.[31]

In October 1979, in the midst of political unrest, KCIA director Kim Chae-gyu assassinated President Park. The DSC, led by Major General Chun Doo-hwan, then assumed control of the KCIA.[32] During this period, the KCIA's remit expanded to include domestic criminal investigations, becoming "the dominant domestic intelligence service."[33] Pressure from democracy advocates and whistleblowers, however, led to its rebranding as the Agency for National Security Planning (ANSP) in December 1980 under the ANSP Act.[34] The ANSP was placed under the DSC and stripped of its abilities to supervise fellow intelligence agencies but retained its planning and coordination functions.[35] This reduced stature lasted for four years, until it regained its leadership position and began to reinsert itself in state affairs, "unlawfully meddling in domestic politics, abusing its authority, and violating human rights."[36]

In 1994, the first nonmilitary government since 1961 revived and bolstered the ANSP Act to curtail the agency's ability to interfere with domestic politics. These reforms included a mandate to maintain political neutrality, removing ANSP's ability to coordinate state policies, and the creation of an Intelligence Oversight Committee.[37] These reforms were ineffective, however. In 1997, a former ANSP director was convicted for conducting a disinformation campaign against an opposition party candidate.[38] The opposition won the election anyway and enacted reforms in 1999. These changes included cutbacks in the office monitoring national affairs, removing the agency's ability to investigate opposition politicians, and renaming it the NIS.[39]

THE NIS (1999–PRESENT)

Like all previous attempts at reform, these efforts were short-lived, and the NIS has been involved in scandals since its inception. In 2012, NIS staffers were indicted on charges of wrongdoing related to a campaign against Moon Jae-in, an opposition candidate, to guarantee that conservative Park Geun-hye would win that year's presidential election. The NIS was implicated in at least three specific instances of misconduct. First, following a leak of a portion of a classified transcript that reflected negatively on Moon, the NIS director released the full document, which was widely considered to be done to support President Park.[40] Second, the NIS posted more than a million online messages either championing President Park or disparaging Moon throughout the presidential campaign, a violation of the NIS Act.[41] It was later revealed that a former director, Won Sei-hoon, directed a campaign that involved more than thirty teams of NIS personnel as well as civilians. He was convicted of violating both the NIS Act and the Public Official Election Act.[42] Sei-hoon was also convicted of bribery and corruption related to personal dealings.[43]

Problems were not limited to election interference, either. In 2013, the NIS arrested a suspected North Korean spy, Yu Woo-seong; however, the suspect was acquitted both due to lack of evidence and untrustworthy testimony by the key witness—his sister, who accused the NIS of abuse while she was imprisoned during the investigation.[44] The NIS appealed, citing new documentation of Yu's travel to China as evidence that he was indeed a spy. The Chinese embassy quickly confirmed that the documents were forgeries, leading Yu to accuse the NIS of framing him.[45] A subsequent investigation led to the indictment of three associated with the NIS and the resignation of a deputy chief.[46] Yu, however, was stripped of South Korean citizenship, and the prosecutors who brought the case against him escaped with minimal administrative sanctions.[47]

The final scandal was bribery. In 2016, President Park was removed from the presidency and sentenced to twenty-four years in prison following accusations of corruption and abuse of power.[48] In 2017, three ex-directors were accused of paying 4 billion won (about US$3.5 million) of NIS funds to Park and her associates. Later investigations would reveal that Park and her aides collected nearly 30 billion won (US$26.4 million) from the NIS for personal spending and illicit political actions. The directors took the money from NIS's special activities fund, which is suspected to hold 500 billion won (US$440 million) annually, and, like the rest of NIS's budget, is not subject to oversight or audit. All three former directors involved received prison terms, and President Park was sentenced to an additional eight years in jail.[49]

In response to this scandal, President Moon—elected following President Park's impeachment in 2017—announced another set of reforms. In 2020, the NIS was renamed the External Intelligence and Security Service (EISS), and its authorities were significantly reduced, including removing its domestic investigatory powers, which were given to South Korea's police agency.[50] As past precedent has demonstrated, however, such a change might not be enough to solve Korea's intelligence ills. For example, the administration did not repeal the National Security Law, a 1948 emergency anticommunism act that outlaws antigovernment activities, which critics allege the NIS has used to justify previous misuse of authorities.[51] Additionally, while the reforms do remove the agency's investigatory authorities, they remain in place until 2024. EISS also retains its domestic intelligence and counterintelligence responsibilities, so the possibility for illicit domestic surveillance remains.[52] Thus, it is likely that the underlying problems remain. Further, prior iterations of the NIS were able to reclaim lost authorities, as the ANSP did in 1984. It is possible the EISS will do the same.

The NIS and its predecessor organizations have continually interfered in domestic affairs, including election and political meddling, illegal surveillance, and human rights abuses. This stems from its original conception as an instrument of regime security rather than a bulwark against external threats. Since the 1980s, various governments have tried to limit the intelligence community's ability to interfere in domestic politics, but reforms have seen limited success. In part, this is due to its broad mandate and powers: "the NIS has strong authority equivalent to the combined functions of the US CIA, FBI, and NSA."[53]

The usefulness and pitfalls of these powers can be illustrated by the NIS's counterintelligence functions. The agency has always possessed "the authority to investigate crimes or criminal activities related to national security and the subversion of the South Korean government."[54] The South Korean constitution further provides that "the freedoms and rights of citizens may be restricted by law only when necessary for national security, the maintenance of law and order or for public welfare."[55] This provision, in conjunction with the Criminal Law and National Security Act, allows NIS and its predecessors (as well as other intelligence agencies) to conduct investigations.[56] Placing both intelligence and investigatory powers within a single agency can limit stovepiping, or poor communication between agencies with different responsibilities. These powers have been put to good use several times throughout South Korea's history, enabling the NIS to uncover plots against the state and allowing for the arrest and prosecution of North Korean agents and their associates.[57]

On the other hand, these expansive powers, the intelligence community's broad latitude to define those activities it considers threats, and lack of civilian oversight have led to abuse. These violations include continual instances of "political intimidation, arbitrary arrests, preventive detention, and brutal treatment of prisoners," as well as unlawful surveillance of citizens and politicians.[58] These violations are enabled by the lack of civilian government oversight of South Korea's intelligence community generally and the NIS specifically. Appointed by and reporting to the president, the NIS director is not subject to approval by the National Assembly and does not have an obligation to testify before it.[59] Further, NIS budgets are classified. The only approval and oversight authority is the president.[60] This close relationship between the South Korean president and the NIS is no accident. Indeed, the loyal aides are often named NIS directors.[61]

COLLABORATION WITH THE INTERNATIONAL COMMUNITY

Given the country's strategically important position, the international community is heavily invested in South Korea's intelligence efforts. Korea and the United States have a long-standing intelligence relationship going back to the US Army Military Government in 1945, which was reinforced by a collective self-defense pact following the Korean War. The Korean military intelligence apparatus was originally created out of US military units, and their expertise and the KCIA was also bolstered with advice from the US Central Intelligence Agency.[62] As of 2021, US Forces Korea (USFK) comprises 28,500 personnel at an average cost of US$3.35 billion per year.[63] South Korea's military intelligence operates closely with USFK's intelligence components through a joint intelligence command center.[64] South Korea, further, is host to significant SIGINT assets, which are primarily owned by the United States.[65]

USFK supports both the United Nations Command (UNC), which is the UN's multinational military contingent in South Korea, and the Combined Forces Command (CFC).[66] During peacetime, USFK, UNC, and South Korean forces operate as separate commands. In war, they combine under CFC with the USFK commander in charge.[67] While discussions regarding transferring Operational Control Authority to South Korea have taken place over the years, the USFK commander remains in charge of the CFC. The parties have agreed on conditions for the transfer, including improving South Korea's missile defense capabilities, but time is required for the improvements to manifest.[68]

For non-US-specific cooperation, South Korea has identified international collaboration as a way to enhance security.[69] It is party to intelligence-sharing agreements with the United States and Japan to enhance cooperation on the DPRK military and nuclear matters as well as agreements with Australia, India, Indonesia, the Philippines, and Vietnam.[70] For example, the South Korea–Australia alliance has roots in the Korean War. The two have combined military exercises and training, and Australia provides intelligence support.[71]

Japan, however, is South Korea's most important and vexing partner. The two have a long, complex history—Japan ruled Korea as a colony between 1910 and 1945 and used Koreans as conscript labor and sex slaves. This legacy has not been overcome, despite Japanese arguments that a 1965 agreement to restore diplomacy and a US$800 million payment for reparations has rectified the past.[72] In 2014 and 2016, South Korea entered into intelligence-sharing agreements with Japan, the latter of which was called the General Security of Military Information Agreement (GSOMIA). South Korea threatened to pull out of GSOMIA in 2019 after a tit for tat with Japan involving a court case for uncompensated colonial laborers and several rounds of trade sanctions.[73] After criticism from both the United States and Japan, South Korea remained in the arrangement, but the rift demonstrates the ease with which regional security agreements can be eroded. This places South Korea at risk of isolation from its partners.[74] More broadly, South Korea's intelligence failures—from lack of adequate warning, to leaking sensitive information, and to domestic interference—undercut the trust of its partners and weaken its ability to collaborate effectively with the international community. Reform is required not only to rebuild trust in the intelligence agencies but also to shore up international support and assistance for a key regional ally.

CONCLUSION

It is clear South Korea's intelligence community is in need of reform. Indeed, prior efforts have failed to overcome the institutional prerogatives and cultures as well as legacies of internal meddling and human rights violations. Reform is not incumbent on the intelligence community alone. The institutional legacies and powers of the NIS and other agencies are augmented by South Korea's political dynamic: liberals want change, but conservatives believe that significant authority reduction would inhibit performance and limit national security efforts. As of April 2020, the Democratic Party holds a legislative supermajority as well as the presidency, giving hope of reform for some.[75]

Any reform attempt would need to be substantially broader than the typical remedies of name changes and authorities reduction and would need to account for removing responsibilities from one agency by bolstering them in another. Scholars have put forth many theories as to the issues facing South Korea's intelligence community and the steps required to fix them. For example, critics allege the NIS is prone to "abuse of power due to the concentration of power without adequate monitoring and control" with the recommendation to break the NIS into smaller agencies by role.[76] This sentiment is present in other scholarship, along with reducing the domestic role of the NIS and establishing oversight mechanisms, including allowing the legislature to confirm directors and more transparency on budgetary matters.[77]

This chapter echoes those sentiments to improve the intelligence culture. Greater legislative and civilian oversight will provide much-needed transparency and break the close and oft-abused link between the presidency and the NIS. A permanent stripping of NIS authorities for domestic investigations and in the political arena will bolster the first recommendation by preventing interference in the oversight process. These responsibilities can then be vested in either new or existing agencies. It appears South Korea has decided upon the latter, as investigations are now assigned to the police service.[78] To ensure this change endures, the government needs to invest in the police's counterintelligence investigatory capacities and establish formal mechanisms between the police and the intelligence community to limit gaps in information sharing and assuage concerns of capability loss from transferring authorities between agencies. Leveraging the NIS's existing authorities to oversee intelligence classification, and sharing by shifting the agency from a frontline investigator to a background enabler, may help the NIS retain its historical leadership role but distance it from the conditions that led to abuses. Other efforts should include repealing and replacing the National Security Law, which has provided avenues for abuse of power.[79] While anticommunism authorities are crucial, these must be balanced with appropriate oversight. This should come in the form of legal burden-of-proof requirements to be established in front of courts before proceeding with investigations.

As the chapter has demonstrated, South Korea's intelligence culture has a long history of intelligence abuses, followed by promises of reform, before the cycle repeats. Thus, more fundamental changes are needed, as is a sincere commitment to follow through on the reforms. Time will tell if these efforts are sufficient, but South Korea likely will need to implement more sweeping reforms to ensure sustained improvements to its intelligence community and move past its abusive legacies.

NOTES

1. David Shim, "A Shrimp amongst Whales? Assessing South Korea's Regional-Power Status," GIGA Working Paper 107, German Institute for Global and Area Studies, August 2009, www.jstor.org/stable/resrep07655; Woong Chun, "National Intelligence," in *Routledge Handbook of Korean Politics and Public Administration*, ed. Chung-in Moon and M. Jae Moon (Abington: Routledge, 2020), 193.

2. Chun, "National Intelligence," 193–94.

3. "Risks of Intelligence Pathologies in South Korea," Asia Report 259, International Crisis Group, August 5, 2014, https://www.files.ethz.ch/isn/182589/259-risks-of-intelligence-pathologies-in-south-korea.pdf.

4. Chun, "National Intelligence."

5. Yosuke Onchi, "South Korea Revamps Notorious Spy Agency for Reconciliation," *Nikkei Asia*, August 12, 2020, https://asia.nikkei.com/Politics/South-Korea-revamps-notorious-spy-agency-for-reconciliation.

6. Chun, "National Intelligence," 200.

7. Chun, "National Intelligence," 196.

8. Chun, "National Intelligence," 197–98; Dolf-Alexander Neuhaus, "South Korea," in *Intelligence Communities and Cultures in Asia and the Middle East: A Comprehensive Reference*, ed. Bob de Graaff (Boulder, CO: Lynne Rienner, 2020), 318–20.

9. "Risks of Intelligence Pathologies in South Korea," 13.

10. "Risks of Intelligence Pathologies in South Korea," 13.

11. Chun, "National Intelligence," 198.

12. Chun, "National Intelligence," 198; Kyu-Seok Shim, "Military Unit Reborn with More Oversight," *Korea JoongAng Daily*, August 14, 2018, https://koreajoon-gangdaily.joins.com/2018/08/14/politics/Military-unit-reborn-with-more-oversight/3051899.html; "S. Korea Launches Team to Create New Military Intelligence Unit," *Xinhua News*, August 6, 2018. http://www.xinhuanet.com/english/2018-08/06/c_137371184.htm.

13. "Our History," Defense Security Support Command, 2021, https://www.dssc.mil.kr/dsscen/329/subview.do.

14. "Risks of Intelligence Pathologies in South Korea," 13–14.

15. Jung Da-min, "Concerns Grow over Leaking of Military Intelligence," *Korea Times*, October 12, 2020, https://www.koreatimes.co.kr/www/nation/2021/02/205_297345.html.

16. Reuters, "South Korea Charges Intelligence Officers with Raping North Korean Woman," U.S. News, September 1, 2020, https://www.usnews.com/news/world/articles/2020-09-01/south-korea-charges-intelligence-officers-with-raping-north-korean-defector.

17. "Risks of Intelligence Pathologies in South Korea," 9–12; National Intelligence Service Act, Law Viewer, accessed May 5, 2021, 197, https://elaw.klri.re.kr/eng_mobile/viewer.do?hseq=33396&type=part&key=4; Chun, "National Intelligence."

18. Chun, "National Intelligence," 197.

19. Chun, "National Intelligence," 196–97; "Risks of Intelligence Pathologies in South Korea," 11.

20. Chun, "National Intelligence," 200.

21. Chun, "National Intelligence," 200; "Risks of Intelligence Pathologies in South Korea," 1.

22. Paul Chamberlin, "Korea 2010: The Challenges of the New Millennium," *CSIS Press* (Washington, DC: CSIS), 37; "Division of Korea," *Encyclopedia Britannica*, 2021, https://www.britannica.com/place/Korea/Division-of-Korea; Hyesoo Seo, "Intelligence Politicization in the Republic of Korea: Implications for Reform," *International Journal of Intelligence and CounterIntelligence* 31, no. 3 (2018): 453.

23. Chun, "National Intelligence," 193–94; Seo, "Intelligence Politicization in the Republic of Korea," 453.

24. "Risks of Intelligence Pathologies in South Korea," 6.

25. Seo, "Intelligence Politicization in the Republic of Korea," 453.

26. "Risks of Intelligence Pathologies in South Korea," 6–7.

27. Seo, "Intelligence Politicization in the Republic of Korea," 453.

28. Chun, "National Intelligence," 193–94.

29. Chun, "National Intelligence," 194.

30. They remain so today. "Risks of Intelligence Pathologies in South Korea," 8; Chun, "National Intelligence," 194; Igor Set al Oleynik, ed., *Korea South: Intelligence & Security Activities and Operations Handbook* (Washington, DC: International Business Publications, 2010), 69.

31. Nam Eun-joo, "Former KCIA 'Room of Death' at Namsam Opens to Public," *Hankyoreh*, August 17, 2017, http://english.hani.co.kr/arti/english_edition/e_national/807239.html; Donald P. Gregg, "Korea's Rough Road to Democracy," *Asian Studies* 19, no. 1 (2014), https://www.asianstudies.org/publications/eaa/archives/koreas-rough-road-to-democracy/; Richard Halloran, "Korea Intelligence: Eyes Seem Everywhere," *New York Times*, October 28, 1979, https://www.nytimes.com/1979/10/28/archives/korea-intelligence-eyes-seem-everywhere-one-of-only-two-power.html.

32. Chun, "National Intelligence," 194.

33. Chun, "National Intelligence," 194; Oleynik, *Korea South*, 90.

34. Chun, "National Intelligence," 194.

35. Chun, "National Intelligence," 194; Oleynik, *Korea South*, 83.

36. Chun, "National Intelligence," 195.

37. Chun, "National Intelligence," 195.

38. Chun, "National Intelligence," 195.

39. Chun, "National Intelligence," 195.

40. "Risks of Intelligence Pathologies in South Korea," 16–23.

41. "Risks of Intelligence Pathologies in South Korea," 16–23; Kim Rahn,"NIS Accused of Anti-Moon Campaign," *Korea Times*, December 12, 2012, http://www.koreatimes.co.kr/www/news/nation/2012/12/116_126786.html; National Intelligence Service Act.

42. Seo, "Intelligence Politicization in the Republic of Korea," 460; Jesse Chase-Lubitz, "South Korean Spy Agency Admits to Meddling in 2012 Election," *Foreign Policy*, August 4, 2017, https://foreignpolicy.com/2017/08/04/south-korean-spy-agency-admits-to-meddling-in-2012-election/.

43. "Risks of Intelligence Pathologies in South Korea," 16–23.

44. "Sister of Alleged N. Korean Spy Says She Was Illegally Detained," *The Hankyoreh*, April 30, 2013, http://english.hani.co.kr/arti/english_edition/e_national/585202.html; Yoonjung Seo and Chico Harlan, "Prominent North Korean Defector Acquitted of Espionage by South Korean Court," *Washington Post*, August 22, 2013, https://www.washingtonpost.com/world/prominent-n-korean-defector-acquitted-of-espionage-by-s-korean-court/2013/08/22/642b3712-0b19-11e3-89fe-ab b4a5067014_story.html.

45. "Did Prosecutors Use Photoshop to Make Spying Charges Stick?," *The Hankyoreh*, December 7, 2013, http://english.hani.co.kr/arti/english_edition/e_north korea/614393.html; "Chinese Government Says Korean Officials Forged Immigration Documents," *The Hankyoreh*, February 15, 2014, http://english.hani.co.kr/arti/english_edition/e_national/624285.html; "N. Korean Refugee Accused of Spying Brings Charges against Investigators," *The Hankyoreh*, January 8, 2014, http://english.hani.co.kr/arti/english_edition/e_northkorea/618883.html.

46. "South Korea Spy Agency 'Overhaul' amid Forgery Row," BBC News, April 15, 2014, https://www.bbc.com/news/world-asia-27030769.

47. Steven Borowiec, "The Spy Who Wasn't a Spy: A Tale of Two Koreas," *Los Angeles Times*, May 17, 2016, https://www.latimes.com/world/asia/la-fg-south -korea-spy-20160517-snap-story.html; "Two Years Later, the NIS's Fabricated Spy Case and Two Upended Lives," *The Hankyoreh*, March 19, 2016, http://english.hani .co.kr/arti/english_edition/e_national/735810.html.

48. "South Korea President Park Geun-hye Ousted by Court," BBC News, March 10, 2017, https://www.bbc.com/news/world-asia-39202936; Park Si-soo, "Ex-President Park Sentenced to 24 Years in Prison," *Korea Times*, April 6, 2018, http:// www.koreatimes.co.kr/www/nation/2018/04/251_246856.html.

49. "Two South Korean Ex-spy Chiefs Arrested over Corruption," *Straits Times*, November 17, 2017, https://www.straitstimes.com/asia/east-asia/two-south-korean -ex-spy-chiefs-arrested-over-corruption; Jo He-rim, "Two Ex-NIS Chiefs Arrested in Bribery Scandal," *Korea Herald*, November 17, 2017, http://www.koreaherald .com/view.php?ud=20171117000598; Haejin Choi, "South Korean Court Sentences President Park to Another Eight Years in Jail," Reuters, July 20, 2018, https:// www.reuters.com/article/us-southkorea-politics-park/south-korean-court-sentences -president-park-to-another-eight-years-in-jail-idUSKBN1KA0HC.

50. Won-Gi Jung, "South Korea's Intelligence Agency Loses Power to Investigate North Korea Ties," NK News, December 14, 2020, https://www.nknews.org/2020/12/ south-koreas-intelligence-agency-loses-power-to-investigate-north-korea-ties/; Onchi, "South Korea Revamps Notorious Spy Agency for Reconciliation."

51. National Security Act, Korea Legislation Research Institute, Korea Law Translation Center, 2021, https://elaw.klri.re.kr/eng_service/lawView .do?hseq=26692&lang=ENG; "South Korea: Revise Intelligence Act Amendments," Human Rights Watch, December 22, 2020, https://www.hrw.org/news/2020/12/22/ south-korea-revise-intelligence-act-amendments#.

52. "South Korea: Revise Intelligence Act Amendments."

53. Chun, "National Intelligence," 201.

54. Chun, "National Intelligence," 202; "Risks of Intelligence Pathologies in South Korea," 16.

55. See Article 37, Section 2 of "Constitution of the Republic of Korea," Republic of Korea, July 12, 1948, https://www.refworld.org/docid/3ae6b4dd14.html.

56. National Security Act; Criminal Act, Korea Legislation Research Institute, Korea Law Translation Center, 2021, https://elaw.klri.re.kr/eng_service/lawView .do?hseq=28627&lang=ENG.

57. Chun, "National Intelligence," 202.

58. Chun, "National Intelligence," 202.

59. "Risks of Intelligence Pathologies in South Korea," 9.

60. National Intelligence Service Act.

61. Chun, "National Intelligence," 201.

62. Chun, "National Intelligence," 193–94; Seo, "Intelligence Politicization in the Republic of Korea," 453; Neuhaus, "South Korea," 321.

63. Hyonhee Shin and Joyce Lee, "Factbox: U.S. and South Korea's Security Arrangement, Cost of Troops," Reuters, March 7, 2021, https://www.reuters.com/article/us-southkorea-usa-alliance/factbox-u-s-and-south-koreas-security-arrangement-cost-of-troops-idUSKBN2AZ0S0; "Burden Sharing: Benefits and Costs Associated with the U.S. Military Presence in Japan and South Korea," US Government Accountability Office, GAO-21-270, March 17, 2021, https://www.gao.gov/products/gao-21-270.

64. "ACOFS J2, FKJ2," United States Forces Korea, 2021, https://www.usfk.mil/Organization/ACofSJ2,FKJ2.aspx.

65. Desmond Ball, "Signals Intelligence (SIGINT) in South Korea," Canberra Papers on Strategy and Defence 110 (Canberra: Strategic and Defence Studies Centre, Research School of Asian Studies, Australian National University, 2015), http://sdsc.bellschool.anu.edu.au/sites/default/files/publications/attachments/2016-03/110_signals_intelligence_%28sigint%29_in_south_Korea_Desmond_Ball_P100.pdf.

66. "Risks of Intelligence Pathologies in South Korea," 3; "History of the Korean War," United Nations Command, 2021, https://www.unc.mil/History/1950-1953-Korean-War-Active-Conflict/.

67. "Risks of Intelligence Pathologies in South Korea," 3–4.

68. Jina Kim, "Military Considerations for OPCON Transfer on the Korean Peninsula," Council on Foreign Relations, March 20, 2020, https://www.cfr.org/blog/military-considerations-opcon-transfer-korean-peninsula.

69. "2016 Defense White Paper," Ministry of Defense of the Republic of Korea, 2016, 11, https://www.mnd.go.kr/user/mndEN/upload/pblictn/PBLICTNEBOOK_201705180357180050.pdf; Scott W. Harold et al., *The Thickening Web of Asian Security Cooperation* (Santa Monica, CA: RAND, 2019), 71–72, https://www.rand.org/content/dam/rand/pubs/research_reports/RR3100/RR3125/RAND_RR3125.pdf.

70. "Signing of Trilateral Information Sharing Arrangement Concerning the Nuclear and Missile Threats Posed by North Korea," Department of Defense, December 28, 2014, https://www.defense.gov/Newsroom/Releases/Release/Article/605331/signing-of-trilateral-information-sharing-arrangement-concerning-the-nuclear-an/; "South Korea, Japan Extend Military Intelligence Pact," *Nikkei Asia*, August 26, 2017, https://asia.nikkei.com/Politics/South-Korea-Japan-extend-military-intelligence-pact2.

71. Harold et al., *The Thickening Web of Asian Security Cooperation*, 91–94.

72. "South Korea and Japan's Feud Explained," BBC News, December 2, 2019, https://www.bbc.com/news/world-asia-49330531.

73. Andrew Yeo, "South Korea Pulled out of a Military Intelligence Sharing Agreement with Japan: That's a Big Deal," *Washington Post*, August 27, 2019, https://www.washingtonpost.com/politics/2019/08/27/south-korea-pulled-out-military-intel-sharing-agreement-with-japan-thats-big-deal/; "South Korea, Japan Extend Military Intelligence Pact."

74. Kim Tong-Hyung, "South Korea Keeps Its Military Intelligence Pact with Japan—for Now," *The Diplomat*, November 23, 2019, https://thediplomat.com/2019/11/south-korea-will-keeps-its-military-intelligence-pact-with-japan-for-now/.

75. "South Korea's Governing Party Wins Election by a Landslide," Al Jazeera, April 16, 2020, https://www.aljazeera.com/news/2020/4/16/south-koreas-governing -party-wins-election-by-a-landslide.

76. Chun, "National Intelligence," 205.

77. Terence Roehrig, "South Korea, Foreign Aid, and UN Peacekeeping: Contributing to International Peace and Security as a Middle Power," *Korea Observer* 44, no. 4 (2013); Seo, "Intelligence Politicization in the Republic of Korea," 466.

78. Onchi, "South Korea Revamps Notorious Spy Agency for Reconciliation."

79. National Security Act; "South Korea: Revise Intelligence Act Amendments."

23

Sri Lanka: The Evolution of an Offensive Intelligence Culture

Rohan Gunaratna and Bodhana Perera

Sri Lankan intelligence served the nation during the direst and hardest times. The nation stood above its regional counterparts. The nation's history demonstrates the greatness of Sri Lankans in battle and strategy with the inability of colonial empires to martially conquer the island nation. Sinhalese people were known for their deep spirituality and intellect in the past. These traits produced high levels of loyalty toward their nation, race, and rulers. The cultural bond created togetherness, which raised the need for defense and strategy. In the effort of developing strategy, the necessity of knowing the threat created the need for intelligence. The origins of intelligence can be traced back to defensive strategy, which bears the roots of Sri Lankan intelligence.

Culture plays a significant role in shaping intelligence services. Laura Chappelli has explained that "strategic culture can be defined as a set of beliefs, attitudes and norms towards the use of military force" influenced by historical encounters.[1] Additionally, Kerry Longhurst has described how strategic culture "is persistent over time, tending to outlast the era of its original inception, although it is not a permanent or static feature. It is shaped and influenced by formative periods and can alter, either fundamentally or piecemeal, at critical junctures in that collective's experiences."[2] Therefore, cultural beliefs, values, and attitudes collectively influence the decision-making process of the national security apparatus in the course of safeguarding the nation-state. Indeed, the strategic culture determines the "strategic posture" of the country, inducing a "defensive" or "offensive" approach in the national security framework. Policy decisions are articulated through strategic intelligence, which is produced from a rigorous process of intelligence collection. Therefore, the intelligence mechanism of a country is influenced by the strategic culture, and its functionality will be based on the strategic posture that the country upholds through a national security agenda.

This chapter analyzes the strategic culture of intelligence in Sri Lanka and its interconnectivity to the theory of social contract, which illuminates the necessity of intelligence in ensuring security to the citizens by the ruler/ government. The study makes use of government policy documents, secondary literature, and press. The chapter is organized into seven parts, providing a concise briefing of Sri Lanka's strategic and intelligence cultures. The first section describes the background of Sri Lankan intelligence. The second section provides broad discussion about the ancient era and the relevance of social contract to intelligence. The third section examines the precolonial era, and the fourth reviews the colonial era with attention to the importance of intelligence. Turning to the post-colonial era, the fifth section explores key moments in terms of successes and failures in Sri Lanka's history. The sixth section analyzes contemporary intelligence with more recent transformations. The seventh section explores power and geopolitics with attention to the impact of politics and regional powers on intelligence. Finally, the chapter concludes with an analysis about the vital role Sri Lanka's intelligence services have played in ensuring national security.

BACKGROUND

Sri Lankan intelligence dates back before the Common Era with the academic literature presenting factual evidence based on archeological findings and inscriptions. According to ancient records predating modern intelligence culture, Sri Lanka was ahead of many Western intelligence models. During the ancient period, Sri Lanka was governed by monarchs, which was the same ruling system for many South Asian countries. The monarch possessed absolute power to govern, and he/she was responsible in securing the nation alongside its people and cultures. The responsibility has been cited by many historians, including Senarath Paranawithana (1896–1972) and C. W. Nicholas (1898–1961), encompassing the sociocultural perception of authority being responsible for the governed. This is reflected in the theory of social contract put forth by Thomas Hobbes (1588–1679). The Lankan populace gave up their rights and freedoms to the ruler in the belief they were being protected by the monarch, which they have reciprocated in favor of the populace by providing security.[3]

This can be understood as a mutual transfer of power and natural rights by the citizens to the ruler for protection from enemies. The academic literature recognizes that contemporary intelligence provides knowledge of foreseeable events so policy makers can adapt strategy to ensure the rights and securities of the population and, thereby, strengthen the relationship between the ruler and the citizens. Hobbes, however, wrote that "if other men will not lay down their right as well as he, then there is no reason for anyone to divest himself from his: for that were to expose himself to prey, which no man is bound to, rather than dispose himself to peace."[4] The Hobbesian theory posits the necessity to act against the divestment of one's rights and theoretically enabling the people to act in the preservation of self-interest.

PRECOLONIAL INTELLIGENCE IN SRI LANKA

The arrival of Prince Vijeya (543–505 BCE) and the subsequent conquest of Tambapanni (precolonial Ceylon) marks an important strategic juncture of Sri Lankan intelligence history. According to popular belief, Vijeya's conquest is the first recorded espionage and intelligence collection event in recorded Sri Lankan history. Prince Vijeya utilized "Kuveni," a Yakkha princess to acquire strategic intelligence before conquering Lanka at the time. The conquest, however, raises the question about the existence of an advanced intelligence culture before their arrival in Tambapanni. Historian Wilhelm Geiger wrote that Yakkha inhabitants launched a defensive against Vijeya's conquest, which made use of early human intelligence (HUMINT) in Sri Lanka before recorded history.[5]

Geiger's history also cites other uses of intelligence in the transitions of many kingdoms, most notably in the account of King Dutugemunu (161–137 BCE). He outwitted King Ellalan (235–161 BCE) and his armies, capturing and unifying the three kingdoms of Ceylon, using arguably the most noted strategies of the Anuradhapura period. Geiger and Senarat Paranawithana analyzed accounts that involved intelligence strategies under the rule of King Dutugemunu during the conquest to recapture Anuradhapura at the legendary battle in Vijithapura.

Scholar Bandu Edussuriya explained "from spies and agents who got back from Rajarata he knew that Ellalan's towns were well fortified," which allowed Dutugemunu's strategic intelligence network to stretch deep within enemy territory.[6] Yet because Dutugemunu's spies were caught at Anuradhapura, it demonstrates the scope of intelligence and counterintelligence. Indeed, the nature of intelligence at the time had been strictly strategic and less informative but, nonetheless, had an aggressive role in operations. Building from Edussuriya's work, Paranawithana and Geiger also noted the use of intelligence deception and deployment of forces based on intelligence. Thus, the battle is a notable example of strategy shaped by the intelligence networks and how intelligence was also offensively used in ancient Sri Lanka.

EVOLUTION DURING THE COLONIAL PERIOD

Sri Lanka's intelligence culture was also informed at the critical juncture of modern colonialism. Portuguese colonizers in 1505 introduced a foreign element to the monarchial power struggle, making intelligence strategically defensive rather than being offensive. The Portuguese had a religious culture and used religion as a mechanism to expand power. This strategy can be seen as the initial development of communal intelligence networks in Sri Lanka, creating a community-based intelligence culture in the capital of Colombo.[7] The Portuguese were ousted from the island by the Dutch, followed by the assistance of King Wimaladharmasuriya I (1592–1640) in 1640. An important initiative taken by the Dutch was establishing law enforcement that used intelligence, which created the concept of policing in colonial Ceylon. The first records of policing in Ceylon indicate the involvement of Dutch army officers on horses.[8]

The British, who later succeeded the Dutch, were the most impactful in institutionalizing the police and decisively constitutionalized intelligence in Sri Lanka through the police force. By introducing an ordinance for the police force, the British government created the legal capacity for intelligence in 1864 with the police ordinance Act 16 of 1964. Inculcated by the British ideology of intelligence, the police force further developed the existing model of formal intelligence in colonial Ceylon. The police "Special Unit" was a successful byproduct of this endeavor. It was the first national intelligence agency under the Western model in colonial Ceylon.

The Special Unit of police served its purpose through the period between 1870 and 1948 as a clandestine intelligence operations cell. As an organization that needed improvement, the intelligence community heavily relied on a defensive intelligence strategy. This period is arguably the first significant development phase of intelligence in Ceylon as the British had a keen interest in training police officers with intelligence techniques and made use of their own intelligence bodies. Being trained by British intelligence officers periodically, intelligence efforts were fully revamped and restructured. The creation of the Criminal Investigation Division (CID) under the Special Unit in 1870 was a notable advancement in law enforcement and intelligence. The British successfully shaped defense culture of Ceylon, which also informed the intelligence culture to become aggressive and proactive in operations.

POSTCOLONIAL INFLUENCE ON INTELLIGENCE

After independence from the British in 1948, a Sri Lankan government came to power under British crown rule with defensive intelligence culture.

Intelligence was stable and robust with the influence of the British, and the country had solid national security. The period between 1948 and 1960 is considered a calmer period for Sri Lanka due to its relative political stability and economic perseverance despite the Cold War between the United States and the Soviet Union. Soon after independence, the Special Unit deviated from its original focus and was being utilized for political espionage on the ruling party's opposition.

The era between 1950 and 1960 was famous for the use of telephone wire-taps for political espionage due to the Cold War. Concerned by the emergence of political opposition, the Special Unit's politicization was due to political insecurities and breaches in national security. It encountered a major intelligence failure with the unsuccessful 1962 coup d'état that was revealed by an insider of the coup. The scenario repeated itself with the 1971 People's Liberation Front (Janatha Vimukthi Peramuna, JVP) insurrection, which proved that the Special Unit and the Criminal Investigation Department (CID) were unable to prevent major threats to internal security. As a result, this led to the transformation of the Police Special Branch (PSB).

During the latter part of the 1960s, the PSB became a pivotal advance in intelligence. Its creation marked the first dedicated intelligence agency in Sri Lanka. The body consisted of police officers who were trained specially under intelligence and counterintelligence. Senior deputy inspector General Cyril Herath, the founding director of the Special Branch, was a notable visionary in this domain.[9] Under his guidance, the Special Branch was trained under British and Israeli veterans and experts. These efforts proved successful when PSB crushed the armed insurrection in 1971.

The 1971 JVP Communist insurgency was a watershed moment for national intelligence. The insurgency spontaneously targeted strategic military outposts nationwide, and the PSB apprehended several insurgent leaders by extracting intelligence from detained prisoners. Upon their interrogation, PSB managed to capture the leaders, and this curbed the insurrection movement within three months. This was singlehandedly the PSB's biggest achievement; however, it sent the nation into a military and intelligence conundrum, which took more than fifty days to recover. The failure to stop the JVP before the attacks was blamed on PSB. In particular, the PSB's inability in recognizing the threat even though the JVP's bomb factory had a number of accidental explosions was not investigated by the PSB. In response, the intelligence officers deployed different strategies to counteract the increasing number of threats against the nation, which led to a change in intelligence structure.

The insurrection flared a long-awaited wake-up call for intelligence. The government took steps rapidly to develop internal capacity with assets and operatives. The 1971 insurrection is the pivotal event in the shift of intelligence strategy toward defending national interests. As a result, the Intelligence Services Division (ISD) was established between 1973 to 1975 to inculcate a better intelligence service in Sri Lanka.[10] A separate body from the PSB, ISD was formed to address lacunas of the PSB by coordinating the wider involvement between intelligence experts outside the police force. The intelligence agency focused on "developing threats" and Tamil extremism that was growing nationwide at the time. Following the increased threats, the government equipped the ISD with operational capabilities.

To improve these capabilities during the Cold War, collaborative exercises were conducted with the United Kingdom's Security Service (MI5) and the United States' Central Intelligence Agency (CIA).[11] Developing intelligence and strategic communications alongside tactical capabilities were aided by the Israeli internal intelligence agency, Shin Bet. Thus, the training program included foreign instruction and exchange programs with MI5 and CIA as well as affiliated agencies from the Asian region and Europe. The period between 1972 and 1983 is considered the expansion period of modern intelligence structures, indicating a clear shift of paradigms in the Sri Lankan strategic culture and movement toward proactive engagement of intelligence and national security.

The intelligence cultures in South Asia evolved around the influence of regional and extra-regional powers during the Cold War. Diplomatic arms of capitalist and socialist global powers aimed to influence South Asian nations by developing strategic relationships. The South Asian intelligence dynamic was adopted by three major intelligence models: the Russian, American, and British. India and Pakistan became followers of the CIA model presented by the United States, while Sri Lanka, Malaysia, and Indonesia were influenced by the British MI5 and Secret Intelligence Service (MI6). In contrast, the Soviet Union was not directly a contender as an intelligence model but still introduced a pragmatic footprint in every sovereign nation. These influences escalated into an interregion intelligence race to develop intelligence bodies within South Asian nations, indicating rapid growth in the realm of South Asian intelligence between 1950 until the end of the Cold War. Thus, Sri Lanka was at a crossroads between the existing superpowers and their littoral cousins, India and Pakistan, after independence. Sri Lankan intelligence was a result of sandwiched national interests between influential regional politics and global power politics from 1948 to the end of Cold War.

CONTEMPORARY INTELLIGENCE DEVELOPMENT

The emergence of terrorism in Sri Lanka can be understood in two widely disparate perspectives. Most academic research claims that the anti-Tamil riots of 1983 caused a jacquerie of radical Tamil youth. A minority opinion sees the involvement of Indian intelligence in Sri Lanka causing instability in the north by developing terror cells under India's foreign intelligence service, Research and Analysis Wing (R&AW).[12] The People's Liberation Organization of Tamil Eelam (PLOTE) and Eelam Revolutionary Organization of Students (EROS) were two of the groups who armed themselves for conflict against the central Sri Lankan government. Velupillai Prabhakaran broke off from the PLOTE, forming the Liberation Tigers of Tamil Eelam (LTTE), which launched a three-decade-long armed conflict against the government. Between 1975 and 1983, Tamil extremists conducted several assassinations in the north, including politicians and police officers in which the most prominent was the murder of the mayor of Jaffna, Alfred Duraippah. At the time, such assassinations were closely followed by the ISD, but it was unable to apprehend or track down those responsible in multiple occasions.

In 1983, the Police Special Task Force (STF) was created due to the requirements of the elite Counter Revolutionary Warfare (CRW) unit that functioned as guards for very important persons (VIPs). The unit was trained under supervision of former British Special Air Service veterans and international private military contractors during 1984. The STF was developed with the strict purpose of being a counterinsurgency unit and was trained as a strategic deployment unit for tactical intelligence operations.[13] The STF played a major role in the north and east during the heightened war period between 1983 and 1987 and aided the offensives to recapture Elephant Pass and Mannar.

The tenure of President J. R. Jayewardene (1906–1996) was pivotal in professionalizing intelligence in Sri Lanka. President Jayewardene issued directives to reevaluate intelligence mechanisms. The process identified certain areas requiring development, which resulted in the formation of the National Intelligence Bureau (NIB) in 1984 to involve the military into a domain predominantly governed by the police.[14] The military dimension provided the much-needed operational edge to the NIB. While creating the position of DGIS (Director General Intelligence and Security), President Jayewardene centralized the intelligence community under the wing of a DGIS. The position was later changed to the head of national intelligence, which was above all the directorates of national and military intelligence.

Centralizing intelligence morphed the organization into an active body. Empowered by the highest authority, the NIB became able to turn national defensive strategies aggressively active. The military elements created a robust intelligence agency, prompting a transformation in the intelligence dynamics of Sri Lanka. The NIB was a key element in securing national interests from 1983 until 2005. The agency established footholds in regional and extra-regional arenas during the period of heightened conflict. Additionally, the NIB's capabilities were further improved during the period of 1984 to 1990 with British MI6 and SAS as well as Israeli Special Forces and Soviet Union Committee for State Security (KGB) consultants. This era also saw the close coordination of both internal and external intelligence. The JVP insurrection in 1987 and anti-LTTE offensives with the STF are key achievements in NIB history.[15] NIB developed capabilities in targeting LTTE leaders outside of the country. In fact, the bombing of LTTE's political adviser in India during 1985 demonstrated the strength of the NIB in nonterritorial arenas. Furthermore, NIB's inception juncture marked the transformation period of an actively defensive strategic culture in Sri Lanka.

The Directorate of Internal Intelligence (DII) and the Directorate of Foreign Intelligence (DFI) were created within the NIB between 1985 and 1987. Operations focused on internal and external affairs and counterintelligence as the organizations delivered comprehensive intelligence in their respective domains. The DFI had specially extended support from the CIA and Mossad in earlier development stages. The DII functioned with the purpose of securing Sri Lanka from foreign threats inside the country. Both bodies successfully managed to uncover the local LTTE links to an international terrorist network in multiple instances.[16] A major achievement of the DFI was breaking the LTTE's finance chain. This led to the apprehension of Nagendram Seevaratnam, head of finance for the LTTE in the United Kingdom.[17] Much remains unknown, however, as the majority of DII and DFI operations were labeled classified and were overseen by the head of national intelligence.

The genesis of combat intelligence marks an important development in Sri Lanka's intelligence culture. Military Intelligence (MI) was established formally around the early 1980s when the war was at the preliminary stage. MI was structured through existing informal army networks of intelligence. Following its formalization, the level of intelligence became timelier and more accurate than what was received by the NIB. MI's capability was further extended extensively by communal intelligence in their operational areas. This factor was developed by the NIB as a ground resource in the conflict areas. The ability to gather intelligence behind enemy lines was considered an asset by the NIB to develop foresight into enemy movement.

MI developed the special operational capabilities through Deep Penetration Units (DPUs) during the latter 1980s. The DPUs became self-sustaining intelligence units, which developed the capability to deliver precision attacks on crucial enemy targets. The DPU named "LRRP" (Long Range Reconnaissance Patrol) is widely known by its nom de guerre "Mahasohon Brigade." The LRRP units operating behind enemy lines had visibility on LTTE movement in the territory controlled by the enemy. By identifying LTTE convoys with LTTE leaders and important functionaries, the LRRP strategically placed claymore mines and ambushed vital LTTE assets, which included Shanmuganathan Ravishankar (better known as "Charles"), the head of LTTE's military intelligence. Charles was responsible for most of the major attacks in Colombo, both as the head of national intelligence under Shanmugalingam Sivashankar (known as Pottu Amman) and the subsequent head of LTTE military intelligence. The LRRP's tenacity in intelligence and tactical operations became a prominent factor leading the LTTE to the peace process in 2002.[18] LTTE demands to abolish the LRRP during initial peace negotiation bears evidence to the efficiency of MI and DPUs in low-intensity aggressive operations. Operations Vadamarachchi, Riviresa, and Balavegaya are just a few of MI's significant victories. MI currently functions at the capacity of eight military corps, under fully fledged operational centers within military establishments throughout the country.[19]

As for Naval Intelligence (NI), it is under the command of the Sri Lanka Navy and is believed to be established in parallel to MI. NI was responsible for securing the seas of Sri Lanka during the period of war and ensuring safety of Sri Lanka's maritime borders. Through the NI, the navy played a crucial role in preventing arms procurement of the LTTE through maritime channels during the war. This effort was furthered later by an operation backed by the State Intelligence Service and MI to destroy four floating armories of the LTTE. NI was also responsible for suppressing LTTE's sea tiger fleet while safeguarding the coast of Sri Lanka from LTTE infiltrations. Additionally, Sri Lanka Air Force Intelligence (AI) played a similar role to NI. The AI command provided aerial support with LTTE target coordinates. Sri Lankan Air Force and Ground operations command benefited fully from AI. They developed aerial surveillance, real-time target tracking, and payload delivery systems during the war. AI also developed surveillance capabilities, which aided the government to outmaneuver terrorists. Their capabilities were later demonstrated in the assassination of LTTE's head of politics, Suppayya Paramu Thamilselvan, with a precision payload delivery.

Intelligence standards were improved due to the war with the LTTE. In 2006, the NIB was rechristened the State Intelligence Service (SIS) in 2006.[20] NIB strategy to countermand the strategic capabilities of the Tamil Tigers were developed by the SIS. The fourth phase of war against the LTTE was instrumental to national intelligence. The defensive strategic culture observed previously had proved ineffective, and orders were issued for an offensive against the LTTE. This marks the most important juncture of Sri Lankan intelligence culture throughout modern history. The SIS played a crucial role in the offensive and in the rescue of civilians who were held hostage by the LTTE. National intelligence was directly responsible for the rescue and evacuation of more than 100,000 innocent civilians through strategic operations conducted by the Sri Lankan armed forces. Intelligence was a vital battle asset as there was at least a single intelligence officer in the battle room of every major war offensive.[21] Moreover, the intelligence services remained active after the LTTE's defeat during the rehabilitation and reconciliation period after the war. The SIS was responsible for tracking and integrating ex-cadres and LTTE sympathizers during the rehabilitation process. The SIS's capacity was demonstrated by successfully tracing and tracking ex-combatants and LTTE-related personnel as well as war-affected families and individuals. Indeed, SIS and MI were crucial elements behind curtailing terrorism from the end of war in 2009 until the present day.

NEGLECT OF INTELLIGENCE AND EASTER SUNDAY

From 2015 to 2019, intelligence was disregarded and the services were undermined by the government. As a result, the Islamic State was able to carry out a series of attacks during Easter Sunday in 2019. The magnitude of the attack highlighted clear lacunas between intelligence and national security. Sri Lanka's intelligence abilities were questioned by global and local communities alike. Investigations into the attacks revealed that the government obtained intelligence identified and reported the threats prior to the incident.[22] SIS traced the networks but was blamed for not preventing the attack by failing to take independent actions. After 2020, intelligence was yet again brought to the attention of the National Security Council (NSC), which needed authority to independently function. As a result, the National Intelligence Act (NIA) was promoted by the NSC to provide the necessary backing to restore intelligence capability. A noteworthy shift of paradigms in the intelligence culture can be expected with intelligence by 2030 at the current pace if the changes continue at the current rate.

INTELLIGENCE, POWER, AND GEOPOLITICS

Regional powers have always exerted extensive pressure on Sri Lanka in strategic and diplomatic fronts. This was evident with the prolonged Eelam war and the involvement of India. The Indian government was accused of training and arming the LTTE, which Sri Lankan intelligence verified by sending operatives to India. The NIB gathered evidence of Indian intelligence interventions during the Indian Peace Keeping Force (IPKF) mission in Sri Lanka.[23] In the effort to eliminate LTTE leaders sheltered by R&AW, operatives were sent to India by the NIB between 1983 and 1985. The evidence gathered by the NIB enabled Sri Lanka to force the Indian government to stop aiding the LTTE. The Indian government in 1990 withdrew the IPKF. Although the force was considered withdrawn, Indian influence on Sri Lanka continued on the sidelines, especially during the final phase of the war. Thereby R&AW's presence played a major factor in transforming Sri Lanka's intelligence culture from 1975 to the present. Yet this did not undermine other regional and extra-regional powers, including Pakistan, the United States, Russia, and China. Those countries and the presence of their intelligence networks in Sri Lanka pose a threat to the nation's security and intelligence solidarity.

Politicization also had a detrimental role in the development of intelligence. The political bureaucracy in the country during early post-independence employed intelligence as a mechanism to control political and ideological opposition. This tradition was first observed during the period of the late 1950s with telephone tapping. Suppression of political rivals became the main deterrents that drove the quality of intelligence further below standards. This was mostly seen during the period between 1956 and 2005 in which political interference was part of the national security framework. Intelligence was made vulnerable by these decisions, opening avenues for foreign and rival networks to exploit the gaps. Incidents similar to the 1971 and 1987 insurgencies and the assassinations of Terrance Perera, director of the NIB, were the result of constant political meddling in intelligence.[24] Subsequent politically appointed officers led to further dilution in the quality of national intelligence, with the transfer of experienced intelligence officers to desk appointments.[25] Politicization was also responsible for the discouragement of officers' involvement in intelligence, creating uncertainty about career progression. Therefore, intelligence capability was limited due to political influence and framework alterations by shifting political governments to suit their political conveniences. As a result, this took a negative toll, which resulted in the deaths of thousands of innocent civilians, including the third president of Sri Lanka, Ranasinghe Premadasa.

CONCLUSION

Intelligence culture in Sri Lankan history can be characterized as highly dynamic and politically driven, which ensured national security. The

framework for intelligence was designed to self-sustain and function autono-
mously. The vision was created by the colonial British government to ensure
a high caliber breed of intelligence officers. Equipped with a wealth of
knowledge, expertise, and experience, Sri Lanka is currently in the process
of bringing expertise together under a future strategic plan for Sri Lankan
intelligence. Indeed, the nation understood the value of intelligence in the
light of past incidents. Governments are compelled by the people to provide
security, and intelligence empowers this duty. The reciprocal effects of the
social contract were observed in Sri Lanka. The intelligence culture in Sri
Lanka has been an offensive actor to threats despite intelligence failures.
Standards were challenged during the postcolonial and modern eras by internal and external actors. With significant junctures in its history, the citizens
of the country have urged the rulers to become aggressive in intelligence to
promote an active culture. Therefore, Sri Lankan strategic and intelligence
cultures can be seen as reactive during the precolonial period and proactive
during the postcolonial periods.

NOTES

1. Laura Chappelli, "Differing Member State Approaches to the Development of
the EU Battlegroup Concept: Implications for CSDP," *European Security* 18, no. 4
(2009): 417–39.
2. Kerry Longhurst, "The Concept of Strategic Culture," in *Military Sociology*,
ed. Gerhard Kummel and Andreas D. Prufert (Baden-Baden: Nomos Verlagsgesell-
schaft, 2000), 301–10.
3. Interview with S. Jayarathne on the historical narrative of Sri Lankan strategic
culture, Institute of National Security Studies, 2021.
4. Thomas Hobbes, *Leviathan, or The Matter, Forme and Power of a Commonwealth Ecclesiastical and Civil* (Baltimore, MD: Penguin, 1980), 126–27.
5. C. W. Nicholas and Senarath Paranavitana, *A Concise History of Ceylon*
(Colombo: Colombo University Press, 1961), 30–31.
6. Bandu Edussuriya, "Sabotage," Dailynews.lk, August 28, 2006, http://archives
.dailynews.lk/2006/08/28/fea07.asp.
7. Interview with D. Corea on the historical evolution of intelligence in the colonial era, Sri Jayawardenapura, 2021.
8. Sri Lanka Police, "Police History," Police.lk, 2021, https://www.police.lk/
index.php/police-history?tmpl=component&print=1&page=.
9. Interview with M. Gunarathne on the history of police intelligence, Colombo,
2021.
10. Interview with M. Gunarathne on the history of intelligence.
11. Interview with R. Latiff on the influence of Western intelligence to the NIB,
Mount Lavinia, 2021.

12. Interview with anonymous, 2021.

13. Interview with R. Latiff on the inception of the Police Special Task Force.

14. Interview with M. Gunarathne on the history of the National Intelligence Bureau.

15. Walter Jayawardhana, "Elite Commando Forces of the Police Over Runs [*sic*] a Large Tamil Tiger Base in the Eastern Province of Sri Lanka," LankaWeb.com, September 28, 2007, http://lankaweb.com/news/items07/090107-1.html.

16. Interview with D. Corea on the NIB versus the LTTE.

17. For more detail, see Debabani Majumdar, "Tamil Charities 'Fail to Monitor Funds,'" BBC, May 30, 2007, http://www.news.bbc.co.uk/2/hi/uk_news/england/london/6669165.stm. Also see Sidharthan Maunaguru and Jonathan Spencer, "'You Can Do Anything with a Temple': Religion, Philanthropy, and Politics in South London and Sri Lanka," *Modern Asian Studies* 52, no. 1 (March 2018): 186–213.

18. Interview with R. Latiff on army special forces and their role in the Eelam war.

19. Interview with S. Jayarathne on the evolution of Military Intelligence.

20. Interview with Merril Gunaratne by Bodhana Perera on Sri Lankan intelligence culture, 2021.

21. Interview with S. Jayarathne on the evolution of Military Intelligence.

22. Interview with C. Wakista, State Intelligence Services, Colombo, 2021.

23. Interview with R. Latiff.

24. Interview with G. Wijesinghe; "The Birth of the JVP: Fear Psychosis," *Daily News*, March 8, 2010.

25. Merril Gunaratne, *Cop in the Crossfire* (Colombo: Merril Gunaratne, 2011).

24

Taiwan: An Intelligence Community in Constant Transformation

Hon-min Yau

Taiwan's intelligence agencies have a reputation for active operations in the Indo-Pacific region. Their alleged covert operations include the failed attempt to assassinate China's premier, Zhou Enlai, in 1955 through the secret installation of explosives on his chartered airplane *Kashmir Princess* in Hong Kong, and the controversial murder of the Taiwanese political dissident Henry Liu in the United States. During the 1995–1996 Taiwan Strait crisis, while China conducted missile drills in areas around Taiwan proper to coerce Taiwan's electoral decisions, Taiwan had the People's Liberation Army (PLA) high-ranking generals acting as covert agents and providing detailed information about the status of the PLA missiles. Given this track record, Taiwan continues to enhance its capabilities in terms of intelligence operations, and numerous expansions have given Taiwan's intelligence services increased roles.

In 2020, the government of Taiwan modified its National Intelligence Service Law (NISL), which is an overarching regulation governing the conduct and the responsibility of intelligence organizations in Taiwan. According to this latest modification, the intelligence community in Taiwan was expanded to eleven agencies covering some members of law enforcement, military operations, and even telecom security experts. The chapter examines this evolution by first exploring the historical transformation of Taiwan's intelligence agencies, then investigates the current culture, and lastly explains intelligence oversight and what challenges lie ahead.

POLITICAL HISTORY

Intelligence is often known as knowledge collected to better respond to one's security threats. To provide leaders with insight into intangible and uncertain threats, a nation or state often creates intelligence services to help respond to threats or emerging security concerns. The way the services are conducted and overseen are guided by its culture of national intelligence.

Cultures of national intelligence do not form in isolation, however, and their development is influenced by their strategic environment. To understand a country's intelligence services, one needs to understand the security circumstances and challenges in the context of its political history. In the case of Taiwan, this refers to understanding the transformation of its political culture (regime type) and how its security threat has been constantly reevaluated by these dynamics. For Taiwan, such an investigation begins with understanding its troublesome relations with China.

The security tension between Taiwan and China was commonly known as a historical relic between the military disputes of the Chinese Communist Party (CCP) and Chinese Nationalists (Kuomintang, KMT) during the 1940s. Immediately after World War II, the Chinese Nationalist leader, Chiang Kai-shek from the KMT, defeated Japan during the Second World War but lost the country to his domestic rival from the CCP, Mao Zedong. As a result of the ensuing civil war in 1949, the defeated Nationalist government retreated to Taiwan and maintained the official name of the "Republic of China" (hereafter Taiwan) on the island. The victor of the civil war, Mao Zedong, established the "People's Republic of China" (hereafter China). Since then, the government of Taiwan has perceived itself as being under a constant security threat from China. The CCP in China is logically the primary target that Taiwan's intelligence agencies need to address, and, not surprisingly, Taiwan's intelligence agencies are the direct descendants of the KMT's security apparatus before 1949 in China.

THE KMT'S INTELLIGENCE AGENCIES BEFORE 1945

The political struggle between the KMT and other political rivals in China in the early 1990s was the main driver for the intelligence services' establishment. In 1928, the KMT created the first intelligence organization within the party, the Investigation Section, through human intelligence (HUMINT) to fight against its political adversaries in the Chinese mainland.[1] By 1931, with the continuous internal armed resistance by domestic dissidents and the looming external military threat in Asia, such as Japan, the KMT government in China had created the Clandestine Investigation Section within the party's armed element to support its military missions. By 1932, both organizations had been merged into the Bureau of Investigation and Statistics within the KMT government; its First Division aimed to counter political threats, and its Second Division was responsible for military threats. Although it is rather ironic, the Bureau of Investigation and Statistics created in China by the KMT is often considered as the first all-inclusive predecessor of the future developments of the intelligence community in Taiwan.

Later, the Marco Polo Bridge incident in 1937 marked a total military confrontation between the KMT government and Japan. At the time, for the KMT leader, Chiang Kai-shek, the Japanese military attacks superseded the threat from the CCP. To consolidate full domestic support to resist the Japanese military invasion, the KMT formed a United Front (a quasi-joint government) with the CCP and established the Central Military Commission to coordinate overall military operations from the Second Sino-Japanese War (1937–1945) until the end of World War II. The Bureau of Investigation and Statistics also remained within the joint government, and it was often called Military Statistics (Juntong) for short. This restructured organization was only responsible for countering the military threat, the original job profile given to its Second Division. The First Division of the Bureau of Investigation and Statistics was believed to hinder the prospect of cooperation with the CCP due to its task of countering political enemies. As a result, the KMT relocated this element to the party's central standing committee. To identify this change, the Bureau of Investigation and Statistics under the KMT's central standing committee is nicknamed Central Statistics (Zhongtong).[2]

After World War II, the postwar political climate in 1945 created immediate momentum in China for an intelligence reform. Not only was there disagreement between the KMT and CCP intensifying, but the reduction of the external threat had given the general public more opportunities for political debate. People eventually started to question the legitimacy of the one-party-state system. The KMT government finally succumbed to public pressure and "nationalized" both the Military Bureau and the Central Bureau. In 1946, the Military Bureau was reformed as the Secrecy Bureau under the Ministry of National Defense (MND), and the Central Bureau was reorganized as the Investigation Bureau under the Ministry of Interior (MOI). By 1949, these two agencies were later moved to Taiwan along with the KMT after its failure in the Chinese civil war from 1945 to 1949.

TAIWAN'S INTELLIGENCE SERVICE FROM
1945 TO THE EARLY 1980S

The Secrecy Bureau and the Investigation Bureau were not the only two intelligence agencies that the people of Taiwan had inherited. Immediately after the Japanese government handed over the administrative control of Taiwan to the Chinese Nationalist government at the end of World War II in 1945, the Taiwan Garrison Command was established on the island for the purpose of maintaining law and order in the region. By 1946, however, the political conflict between the KMT and CCP on the Chinese mainland had deteriorated and escalated to a total armed conflict. Taiwan's relatively prosperous economic system was exploited by the Chinese Nationalist government to fund its wars with the CCP, and this situation, along with growing corruption and mismanagement by the KMT elites, created high unemployment, uncontrolled inflation, and shortages of commodities in Taiwan.

On February 28, 1947, a political uprising occurred in Taiwan after Nationalist government officials killed a bystander while confiscating unlicensed cigarettes in Taipei, the capital city of Taiwan. The event was later called "the 228 Incident" and marked the controversial transformation of the Taiwan Garrison Command into an internal intelligence service, or a type of secret police, which aimed to suppress the separatist agenda of Taiwan independence and democratization of the political system.[3] The major cities on the island were gradually put under curfew by the Taiwan Garrison Command. By 1949, after the retreat of the Chinese National government to Taiwan and its loss of control of the Chinese mainland, the KMT government declared a state of emergency via the creation of the later infamous regulation, the Temporary Provisions for the Period of Mobilization for the Suppression of Communist Rebellion.[4] The whole island was officially under full martial law from May 19, 1949, to July 15, 1987, and political dissidents were stifled so the KMT could maintain political control.

From 1949 onward, the KMT government in Taiwan still suffered from escalating military pressure from CCP-controlled China. In reviewing his failure on the Chinese mainland, Chiang Kai-shek concluded that the success of the future counterattacks would rely on 30 percent military power and 70 percent political power (ideational power). His son, Chiang Ching-kuo, directly pointed out that "the military success of the CCP in 1949 is due to its effective use of its ideational power, and we need to attack the CCP's ideas and safeguard our belief."[5] In 1950, the Political Department in Taiwan's military was created to counter the CCP infiltration into the military, and the organization was later renamed the General Political Warfare Department under the MND in 1951.

Furthermore, the KMT government in Taiwan suffered not only armed attacks by CCP-controlled China but also more complicated regional and international challenges, such as growing international shifts of diplomatic relations from the Republic of China (Taiwan) to the People's Republic of China (China) as well as regional conflicts, such as the Korean War in Asia. In response to these various security challenges, the KMT government further imitated the US National Security Agency and established the National Security Bureau (NSB) in 1955. The newly established NSB is an expansion of the Data Section of the Department of Special Affairs in the Presidential Place, and its six specialized divisions oversee international intelligence collections, intelligence collections in China, intelligence collections in Taiwan (domestic threats), intelligence analysis, signals intelligence (SIGINT), and the development of communication encryption.[6] In addition, from 1950, the KMT government in Taiwan was also a treaty ally of the US military. The United States first provided military consultants to enhance Taiwan's military training and later established the United States Taiwan Defense Command (USTDC) to reinforce Taiwan's national defense. One of the unique units is the 6987th Security Group, which is capable of monitoring radio communications and collecting electronic frequencies (electronic intelligence, ELINT) around East Asia.[7] In 1979, when the United States established formal diplomatic relations with China along with its retreat of military staff from the island, the MND took over this ELINT facility and consolidated it with other domestic SIGINT units. The result was the creation of the Communications Development Office (CDO).

By the early 1980s, the eight major intelligence agencies in Taiwan were as follows. The NSB was the leading organization supervising the overarching affairs of the intelligence operations. The Intelligence Agency, a direct descendant of the Secrecy Bureau under the MND, collected military-related intelligence, mostly through HUMINT against China. The Investigation Bureau was moved from the MOI to the Ministry of Justice (MOJ), and its responsibility was transformed such that it became an organization similar to the US Federal Bureau of Investigation (FBI) to fight against national-level criminal activities. The Taiwan Garrison Command continued to work as an intelligence agency playing the controversial role of the secret police. In addition, there was the Police Agency, under the MOI, working against domestic criminal activities, and the Military Police, under the MND, countering domestic military criminal activities. Finally, the MND also had the CDO for technical intelligence, as well as the General Political Warfare Department for anti-espionage and counterintelligence operations.

RAPID TRANSFORMATIONS DURING THE 1980S AND 1990S

During the martial law period (*Jieyan Shiqi*) from 1949 to 1987, Taiwan's intelligence culture exhibited a significant degree of autonomy and enjoyed excessive privilege under the island-wide martial law. At this time, the national constitution was suspended by the Temporary Provisions for the Period of Mobilization for the Suppression of Communist Rebellion, and national security ranked as the top priority. The fundamental rights, such as freedom of speech, freedom of privacy of correspondence, and freedom of assembly and association, were overridden in the name of national security. The security concerns for the state focused on internal and external threats, and the KMT-controlled government often abused the power of state surveillance to stop the Taiwan independence movement or Communist infiltration in the name of national survival.

The state's suppression of democracy activists on the island was named "White Terror" (*Baise Kongbu*), and the intelligence apparatuses were often used against domestic political dissidents, instead of to resist external threats. In addition, interservice rivalries among different agencies were common, and the intelligence agencies were operated on the principle of "rule by man" instead of "rule by law."[8] As there was no legislative or judicial oversight, securing patronage from the political leadership, such as Chiang Kai-shek or later Chiang Ching-kuo, became the only driven cause for the survival of an intelligence organization.

Three events marked the watershed moments for the modernization of Taiwan's intelligence community. The first event happened in October 1984 when a Taiwanese American, Henry Liu, was shot and killed at his family home in California. Liu was a political critic based in the United States and often published articles criticizing the KMT-controlled government in Taiwan. The US government later discovered from the assassins' testimony that the agents had been directed by Taiwan's Intelligence Agency to stop Liu from publishing an unauthorized biography of the then KMT leader, Chiang Ching-kuo. Although the United States cut off its official diplomatic ties with Taiwan in 1979 due to the establishment of an official diplomatic tie with China, its domestic law, the Taiwan Relations Act, still serves as a US security commitment toward Taiwan. The Henry Liu incident, however, as an extrajudicial killing within the US territory, severely damaged Taiwan–US relations. In 1985, during the aftermath of this foreign relations crisis, the incident forced the government of Taiwan to charge the intelligence officers criminally, replace the leadership within the agency, and rename the agency the Military Intelligence Agency (MIB) while narrowing its activities to the military domain.

The second important event was the political transformation and democratization of Taiwan's political system in the late 1980s. By 1986, the last authoritarian leader of the KMT, Chiang Ching-kuo, had decided to loosen political control of Taiwanese society, and in 1987, the final year of his rule, he ended the thirty-eight-year-long martial law in Taiwan. Freedom of speech, press, and assembly were returned to the public, and the first sizeable opposition party, the Democratic Progress Party (DPP), was allowed to establish and participate in regular national elections. This event promoted the legalization of intelligence operations and marked the first step toward judicial oversight over the intelligence services in Taiwan.

From 1949 to 1987, Taiwan's intelligence agencies were often abused by the state to suppress opposition to the KMT, including Taiwan independence proponents and people who sympathized with Communists. But the democratization movement that started in 1987 gave these various movements the power to orient intelligence agencies and to restrain their operations by regulating new judicial tools. By the early 1990s, the Temporary Provisions for the Period of Mobilization for the Suppression of Communist Rebellion had been revoked, and the National Security Act (NSA) was enacted to prohibit people from conducting espionage for "a foreign country or Mainland China."[9] In 1992, the Taiwan Garrison Command was reorganized as the Coast Guard Administration (CGA) and was made responsible for border security, and its function as the unlawful secret police ceased to exist. The Criminal Code of the Republic of China was also modified to tone down the power of state surveillance.

In 1993, Taiwan legalized the role of the National Security Council as an important advisory committee for the president, and the Organization Act of the National Security Council was also created, specifying regular legislative oversight for the NSB. Later, via the Organization Act of the National Security Bureau, the NSB became the principal agency of all the other intelligence services, and as such, it had to coordinate and direct the intelligence agencies via the National Intelligence Coordination Conference (NICC).

The third event was the financial scandal of the NSB in 2000, which enabled later improvement of legislative oversight. As a result of the political transformation during the 1990s in Taiwan, the funding allocated to the NSB was partially under annual review by the Legislative Yuan (the Taiwanese parliament), but the budget mostly remained secret and was embedded in the fiscal budgets of other government agencies. The protection of its confidential budget and the lack of direct monitoring from the legislative branch gave the NSB excessive autonomy and created space for corruption. In 2000, the Investigation Bureau's anti–money laundering division discovered that a huge number of financial assets had been deposited in a domestic bank by an

NSB financial officer, Liu Kuan-Chun. The scandal made the Taiwan public realize that a large amount of public funds was possessed by the NSB in overseas bank accounts without direct oversight by the legislative process. In 2003, the Organizational Act of the NSB was further modified so as to regulate the overall budgets of the NSB and put them under legislative review, and the NSB chief is required to attend the Foreign and National Defense Committee in the Legislative Yuan since then.

TOWARD THE TWENTY-FIRST CENTURY

Taiwan's intelligence agencies worked in a closed-off sphere prior to the democratization of its political culture, but emerging oversight during the 1990s moved its practices toward greater openness and transparency in regard to the public. In particular, Taiwan's domestic democratization movement enabled pro-Chinese nationalists, pro-Taiwanese nationalists, and pro-Communists to become part of the lawful political discourses within the island as protected by the freedom of expression in Article 12 of the constitution: "The people shall have freedom of speech, teaching, writing and publication." Since then, state prosecutors have not been allowed to stop any unpopular political views as long as no violence or threats are involved. In 1999, the Communication Security and Surveillance Act (CSSA) was also created to regulate state surveillance. Since then, the intelligence agencies have surveyed foreign nationals but must obtain special communication warrants on domestic citizens.

The most noticeable event for overarching intelligence regulation was the creation of the NISL. In the early twenty-first century, Taiwan had multiple intelligence agencies but no integrated intelligence community as the transition of its political climate has been focusing on suppressing the abusive power of state intelligence but has ignored the need to balance the national security needs and protect civil liberty. In addition, the NSB was supposed to be the highest intelligence authority and direct the intelligence mission and oversee the information exchange between agencies, but the legal vacuum inhibited the efficiency of Taiwan's intelligence operations. In 2005, the NISL was created as the overarching regulation to enhance accountability and oversight. This regulation not only requires the political neutrality (Article 6) of the intelligence agencies but also specifies their entitlements (Article 3), defines the roles of their missions (Article 7) and their handling of data (Article 8), creates protections systems for intelligence service agents (Article 9 and 10), reinforces the legislative oversight (Article 4), and establishes an internal accountability mechanism (Article 5). Since then, a Taiwanese intelligence community under the supervision of the NSB (Article 15) has been forged.

INTELLIGENCE COMMUNITY TODAY

By 2020, the NISL had gone through four amendments, in 2010, 2011, 2015, and 2020, and these modifications reflect the globalized transformation of the security threat to Taiwan.

Globalization in the early twenty-first century increased the Cross-Strait's connectedness and economic independence, and Taiwan has become China's number 1 trading partner in terms of the total value of imports. The CCP in China, however, continues to maintain the ambition of bringing Taiwan under its control, and officers from China repeatedly claim that they have never "renounced the use of force" against Taiwan. As real armed conflicts would hinder the economic development of China, intensifying intelligence breaches into the government of Taiwan has become a common strategy for China. In 2010, a senior MIB officer, Lo Chi-Cheng, who was responsible for building an intelligence network in China, was discovered to be a double agent who had been working for China since 2007. In 2011, an army general, Lo Hsien-Che, who was the director of the communications and electronic information department in the Taiwanese army headquarters, was discovered to be passing military secrets to China. Policy makers reacted to such threats by proposing enhancing legal tools, and several amendments of the NISL were later passed by legislators. The 2010 modification of the NISL means to increased salary and welfare treatments for the intelligence officers, and the 2011 and 2015 versions increased the penalty to harden Taiwan's counterintelligence defense. These three amendments reflect the intensifying intelligence breach posed by China's effort at espionage infiltration.

Furthermore, in the era of digitalization, new threats have emerged from cyberspace. Since 2013, the director of the NSB has repeatedly stated in regular hearings at the Legislative Yuan that Taiwan suffers thousands of cyberattacks from China daily. Unlike the challenges of conducting intelligence operations for increasingly vigilant officials within the Taiwanese government agencies, the advent of Information and Communication Technologies (ICTs) and the heavy reliance on technology in the modern social fabric provide the ubiquitous ability to transcend territorial limitations. In 2015, the NSB, as an intelligence agency, established Division 7 to counter China's intelligence services' cyber intrusion.

In 2017, Taiwan also established a new branch of its military force, the Information, Communications, and Electronic Warfare Command, to safeguard Taiwan's digital territory. However, the Information, Communications, and Electronic Warfare Command as a military branch would encounter legal controversy when venturing through the domestic digital world. Not only is Taiwan's military not authorized to be used against its own citizens according to the National Defense Act, its operations over the domestic digital world also have legal ramifications in terms of violating the CSSA. As such, the 2020 modification of the NISL incorporated these new cyber units as intelligence organizations. Currently, among the eleven agencies specified by the NISL, four are official "intelligence organizations," a Taiwanese legal term, as they conduct intelligence-only operations. The other seven agencies, however, are organizations responsible for multiple missions and are guided by NISL and considered "quasi-intelligence organizations," as they conduct activities related to intelligence operations. Their relations are depicted in figure 24.1.

The four agencies designated as the official "intelligence organizations" are:

- The **National Security Bureau** (Guojia Anquan Ju, NSB) is the principal intelligence agency under the National Security Council. The NSB directs the intelligence community in Taiwan and is

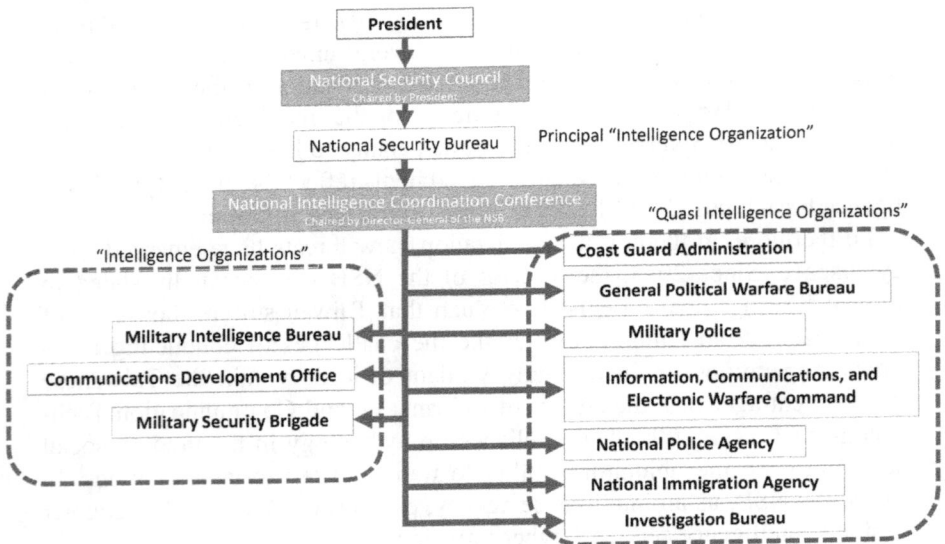

Figure 24.1. The Intelligence Community in Taiwan
Source: Taiwan's National Intelligence Service Law

responsible for strategic-level intelligence and general SIGINT, including cyberespionage.

- The **Military Intelligence Bureau** (Junshi Qingbao Ju, MIB) is a specialized military body under the MND and is responsible for monitoring, collecting, and analyzing the development of external military threats to Taiwan and regional military buildup.
- The **Communications Development Office** (Dianxun Fazhanshi, CDO) is a technical military organization under the MND and is responsible for military SIGINT, image intelligence (IMINT), and ELINT.
- The **Military Security Brigade** (Junshi Anquan Zongdui) is a military element under the MND and is responsible for counterintelligence and espionage in regard to threats coming from both outside and inside Taiwan's military organizations.

In addition, the seven intelligence agencies that contribute to intelligence-related operations are the following:

- The **Coast Guard Administration** (Haixun Shu, CGA) is under the command of the Ocean Affairs Council and conducts law enforcement in the coastal area of Taiwan by pursuing smugglers and illegal immigrants. The CGA could also serve as a resourceful asset to provide general intelligence regarding Taiwan's border area.
- The **General Political Warfare Bureau** (Zhengzhi Zuozhan Ju) is the direct descendant of the General Political Warfare Department under the MND before the democratization movement in Taiwan during the 1990s, and part of its mission is to conduct counterintelligence and serve as the internal security department within Taiwan's military organizations.
- The **Military Police** (Xianbing) is a military body under the MND. It serves as law enforcement within the military and offers security protection details for government leaders and officials. This agency also provides security guards for critical facilities. It is also responsible for counterintelligence missions to stop enemy infiltrations and sabotage in military installations.
- The **Information, Communications, and Electronic Warfare Command** (Zitongdian Jun) is a newly established military branch under the MND that was set up in 2017. This command consolidated the military units of Electronic Warfare and communication and information support from the army, navy, and air force; however, one of the newly established intelligence-relevant capabilities is the command's expansion of its cyber units in information operations.

- The **National Police Agency** (Jingzheng Shu) is the main law enforcement under the MOI, and this agency's mission is to maintain law and order within Taiwan. This agency also serves as a resourceful asset to provide general intelligence within the territorial jurisdiction of Taiwan.
- The **National Immigration Agency** (Yimin Shu), under the MOI, is responsible for border control, immigration management, airport security, and the deportation of illegal immigrants, and this agency serves as a resourceful asset to provide the general status of foreign nationalities in Taiwan.
- The **Investigation Bureau** (Diaocha Ju, MJIB), under the MOJ, deals with corruption, economic crime, organized crime, ICT crime, fraudulence, counterintelligence, and money laundering within the jurisdiction of Taiwan.

Finally, the NSB reports to the president of Taiwan through the advisory organization of the National Security Council. In addition, the director general of the NSB is the chairperson of the NICC and coordinates the actions of the intelligence agencies via this platform.[10] However, depending on the needs of the strategic environment, non-intelligence organizations may be invited to attend the NICC to fulfill a mission-oriented task.

OVERSIGHT

Currently there are three elements in Taiwan's intelligence oversight: judicial oversight, legislative oversight, and departmental oversight.[11] In terms of judicial oversight, the intelligence community is guided by the NISL for specifying the exact roles and responsibilities of the intelligence agencies. The "Organization Act of the National Security Council" and the "Organization Act of the National Security Bureau" specify the overarching hierarchy among the intelligence agencies. The CSSA regulates and constrains the state power of surveillance. "The Classified National Security Information Protection Act" establishes the classification, handling, processing, and transfer of national security information. "The Public Servants' Administrative Neutrality Act" ensures that the intelligence community in Taiwan maintains administrative neutrality without manipulation by any political party. As for legislative oversight, the Legislative Yuan can supervise the intelligence agencies' conduct of secret activities and enforce their accountability by reviewing their budgets, holding public hearings for important events, hosting regular intelligence reviews, and conducting investigations into any incidents. Finally, in terms of departmental oversight, each intelligence agency has its own internal affairs office or inspector's office to maintain professional discipline and organizational integrity.

CHALLENGES

Although Taiwan implemented numerous efforts to enhance its intelligence community, there are challenges that are yet to be answered in this process. The first challenge concerns the deficiency of Taiwan's current intelligence oversight. The success of the intelligence oversight relies on the profession-building and experience-accumulation of members of the oversight boards. However, firstly, Taiwan has no independent intelligence committee in the Legislative Yuan, and the current legislative oversight is handled by the Foreign and National Defense Committee along with other important foreign policy matters. Secondly, the only executive oversight for Taiwan's intelligence agencies is the office of inspectors or internal affairs within each intelligence agency, but these offices often focus on counterintelligence or anti-corruption, instead of scrutinizing the misconduct of surveillance or the malmanagement of intelligence operations. The insufficient experience of oversight members and the lack of centralized executive oversight are potential hindrances for future improvements to Taiwan's intelligence system.

The second challenge is the lack of diversification in the members of the intelligence community. Among all of the intelligence organizations supervised by the NSB as specified by the NISL, six are military bodies under the MND, two are law enforcement under the MOI, another one is the judicial department under the MOJ, and the last one is the CGA under the Ocean Affair Council. No designated intelligence research departments from the Ministry of Economic Affairs, the Ministry of Foreign Affairs, or the Mainland Affair Council (a specialized agency handling relations with China) are part of the intelligence organizations. It is questionable as to how Taiwan's intelligence community could offer policymakers a full picture of the strategic environment when professional intelligence regarding economic activities, diplomacy, and China's development is not covered in any analysis. Currently the NSB is allowed by law to invite representatives arbitrarily to participate in the NICC or communicate with other ministry-level branches via the platform of the National Security Council; however, if the government of Taiwan wanted to improve the interagency synergy and increase data sharing to better "connect the dots," this would be an important area of improvement in the future.

Finally, the last challenge is the need to establish a principal security clearance standard to classify personnel engaged in the handling of sensitive government information. Due to the growing threat of foreign adversaries' infiltrations, government officials handling national security matters are now required to go through polygraph testing regularly, according to Article 28 of the NISL; however, this judicial requirement is only applicable to public servants and does not include politicians or aides and assistants in the Legislative Yuan. In 2020, three legislative aides of KMT and DPP lawmakers were prosecuted for collecting and passing national security information to China between 2012 and 2016. It seems that as Taiwan tightens up its counterintelligence efforts in the executive branch of the government, opponents, like China, have targeted their efforts in regard to the legal loophole in Taiwan's clearance procedure. To safeguard national security secrecy, Taiwan would need to establish a standard vetting process to regulate the appropriate level of information access based on the results of a background review and expectations of nondisclosure obligations.

CONCLUSION

Taiwan's intelligence services and its intelligence culture are dictated by its political culture and how this political culture discerns threats to national security. During the martial law period from 1949 to 1987, the intelligence agencies were used as a state instrument to maintain political control. Both domestic democratic activists and foreign adversaries were perceived as threats to the nation's survival, and the intelligence services were considered by the public as a security threat. After the rapid advancement of Taiwan's democratization movement in the 1990s, however, the accountability and transparency of the intelligence agencies were greatly improved via both judicial tools and legislative monitoring. As diversified discourses and pluralist views were tolerated to a large extent, the power of the intelligence agencies was greatly suppressed, caused by the collected memory of the "White Terror." By the early 2000s, Taiwan formed an official intelligence community by drawing from Western democratic institutions and incorporating various functions of the intelligence providers; however, its recent expansion of the NISL represents the Taiwanese political establishment's acknowledgment of the constant evolution of security threats in the twenty-first century.

Having originated from Military Statistics (Juntong) and Central Statistics (Zhongtong) created by the KMT prior to 1945, today the Taiwanese intelligence community has expanded to eleven agencies. It has technical and nontechnical capabilities to face threats from land, air, sea, and even cyberspace. Although these services are inferior in number when compared with its main adversary, China, they still have charted their way through modern challenges and continue toward a more integrated, cohesive, and capable community operating multiple resources. It is certain that Taiwan's investments in its intelligence community will be a nonstop project as long as the Taiwan Strait remains one of the most likely flashpoints in the world.

NOTES

1. Chen Fu-cheng, *Guojia anquan yu qingzhi jiguan de digui* [A security paradox between national security and intelligence services] (Taipei: Youth Cultural Enterprise, 1998), 4.

2. Chen, *Guojia anquan yu qingzhi jiguan de digui*, 16.

3. Tse-han Lai, Ramon H. Myers, and Wou Wei, *A Tragic Beginning: The Taiwan Uprising of February 28, 1947* (Stanford, CA: Stanford University Press, 1991).

4. The Temporary Provisions for the Period of Mobilization for the Suppression of Communist Rebellion was the emergency legal regulation defined by the KMT's one-party rule of the government from 1948 to 1991 to nullify the fundamental rights protected by the constitution and imposed martial law in Taiwan. The regulation was later revoked in 1991. See *Huazongyiyizi di 2118 hao ling* [Presidential Decree No. 2118], *Zongtongfu gongbao di 5402 hao* [President Office Gazette] 5402 (Taipei, Taiwan: Office of the President, 1991).

5. Chiang Ching-kuo, "*Guojun zhengzhi gongzuo de zhongyaoxing*" [The importance of political education in military], in *Fuxinggang jiangci ji* [The collection of speeches in Fu Hsing Kang], by Chiang Ching-kuo (Taipei, Taiwan: Fu Hsing Kang College, 1951), 1:44.

6. Zhao Ming-yi, *Dangdai guojia anquan fazhi tantao* [The legal aspect of the Contemporary National Security Law] (Taipei: Li-ming Cultural Enterprise, 2005), 80.

7. Guo Nai-ri, *Kan bujian de taihai zhanzheng* [The invisible war across Taiwan Strait] (Taipei: Master Publishing, 2005), 126.

8. Zhang Zhong-yong, *Qingbao yu guojia anquan zhi yanjiu* [A study on intelligence and national security] (Taipei: San-feng, 1993), 13.

9. See Article 2-1 of the National Security Act.

10. Chen Ming-chuan, Xiao Ming-qing, Ceng Wei-wen, and Luo Ping-yi, *Guotu anquan zhuanlun* [A study on homeland security] (Taipei: Wu-nan Cultural Enterprise, 2019), 129.

11. Wang Zheng, *Guojia anquan qingbao jiandu zhi yanjiu* [Study on national security and oversight] (Taoyuan: Central Police University Press, 2015), 348.

Tajikistan: Post-Soviet Intelligence Culture in a Fractured State

Michael Yerushalmi

Tajikistan is the smallest, poorest, and most fractured post-Soviet state in Central Asia.[1] Consequently, intelligence plays an important role in the country's national security to protect Tajikistan's regime and economy. This chapter argues that Tajikistan's experience with intelligence and security is a fusion of multiple influences from pre- and post-Soviet eras, including a strong centralized coercive apparatus along with limited elements of regional autonomy that have marked Tajik intelligence culture. The leadership in Dushanbe has employed hybrid means to ensure stability, though in more recent years the regime has relied to a greater extent on coercive tools and its increasingly adept, more ruthless, security forces. The growing strength of Islamism throughout Central Asia has given form and, at times, increasingly cynical focus to Tajikistan's intelligence apparatus.

This chapter draws from secondary sources, including local news reports and analyses, studies from scholars who had conducted ethnographic research on the security services, and state documents that address security issues. It is organized into five thematic sections. After providing a brief overview of key organizations with intelligence functions, the chapter presents the history that has influenced the current construct of Tajikistan's intelligence services with emphasis on the Soviet period through the 1992 civil war. Next, the chapter examines the current leadership's measures to consolidate power following the war's conclusion and how Dushanbe has exploited the more recent rise of Islamism to further eliminate opposition. It then provides a case study of one region to provide indicators of how the regime in Dushanbe may understand the need for more nuanced intelligence measures. Lastly, it addresses Tajikistan's security ties with foreign partners.

KEY ORGANIZATIONS WITH INTELLIGENCE FUNCTIONS

Tajikistan does not appear to publish an official national security strategy, but the 2011 Law on National Security seemingly provides the parameters for the security forces.[2] Article 9, chapter 2 sets forth numerous organizations as part of Tajikistan's security forces, including internal affairs, military intelligence, emergency and civil defense, tax, customs, and other elements. Tajikistan also passed a law in 2014, amended in 2020, on the protection of state secrets and measures for declassification.[3] Several primary organizations bear the greatest weight for domestic security and neutralizing foreign threats. The State Committee for National Security (Gosudarstveniy Komitet Natsinalnoy Bezopasnotsi, GKNB) is the main service for collecting intelligence from and conducting operations against foreign and domestic adversaries, with branches spread throughout the provinces. The GKNB's structure is similar to its Soviet predecessor, the Committee for State Security (Komitet Gosudarstvennoy Bezopasnosti, KGB), and GKNB chief Saimumin Yatimov, who some critics have likened to Joseph Stalin's ruthless security chief Lavrentiy Beria, has been in the position since 2010. The longest serving of Tajikistan president Emomali Rahmon's cabinet chiefs, Yatimov was a KGB officer who served in the capital Dushanbe and the Gorno-Badakhshan Autonomous Oblast.[4] GKNB includes the Main Border Guard Directorate, which has controlled the border guards since 2005, and even has its own Information and Analytical Department.[5] A holdover from the Soviet period, the Border Guard is also notable because of its corruption and involvement in the lucrative drug trade, and in April 2019, the GKNB arrested its spokesman on charges of disclosing classified material to a "foreign organization."[6] The GKNB's Alpha Squad, also a legacy Soviet unit, conducts counterterrorist and counterinsurgency operations.[7] Researchers portray the GKNB as an omniscient organization that strikes fear into the heart of Tajiks, but there are notable exceptions that will be described later in this chapter.[8] Anna Matveeva has argued GKNB has less influence on policy than its KGB predecessor while advancing its objectives further divorced from adherence to the rule of law.[9]

The Ministry of Internal Affairs (Ministerstvo Vnutrennikh Del, MVD) controls domestic law enforcement and shares responsibilities for counterterrorism. MVD's duties are vast, covering varied tasks such as traffic safety and youth delinquency.[10] MVD's border investigations and the interrogation of opposition figures and local criminals can overlap with GKNB, which has resulted in cooperation and friction between the services.[11] A more recent organization that conducts intelligence is the Drug Control Agency (DCA), established in coordination with the United Nations Office on Drug Control in 1999 to stem the tide of drug importation. In a country where drug trafficking can be lucrative for state entities, scholar Lawrence Markowitz argues that DCA has been a relatively uncorrupted state entity, though questions remain about its staying power.[12] Tajikistan's armed forces also have security departments, though information about them is sparse. The Ministry of Defense's Military Intelligence Directorate provides analysis to the Main Operational Directorate. In May 2019, independent Tajik press reported on legislation authorizing the Military Intelligence Directorate to restrain terrorist sleeper cells within Tajikistan.[13]

Personnel numbers in these organizations are difficult to assess. Estimates, albeit somewhat dated, include 30,000 for the Interior Ministry and 3,800 for its security forces, and 1,200 for the GKNB Border Guards.[14] Coordinating these institutions is the Security Council, a deliberating body.[15] In 2018, the president's Executive Office consolidated control over the council and placed it beyond the purview of parliament.[16] The Security Council mediates between the different security institutions, though Markowitz found it focuses more on topical issues rather than taking a strategic view on their interaction.[17]

Academic scholarship has identified the three tools autocratic regimes use to maintain stability as legitimation, repression, and co-optation.[18] These tools involve patronage to key stakeholders for support or leverage, means of legitimizing a leader's rule, and brute force to counter opposition and maintain power. Tajikistan's intelligence has been part of the country's patronage system. Key elites have used it, along with repression, to marginalize erstwhile allies and defeat domestic opposition. Additionally, as President Emomali Rahmon has entrenched his power, intelligence has also proven crucial in bolstering Rahmon's standing within the population, and thus all three methods of autocratic authority will likely continue to be indispensable to ensuring regime stability into the future.

THE LEGACY OF SOVIET RULE

A proper understanding of Tajikistan's intelligence apparatus must account for the legacy of the Soviet Union's rule. Undoubtedly, Tajikistan's intelligence services draw extensively from their former Soviet masters. At its birth, Tajikistan was a fractured state, lacking a cohesive security apparatus. Together with the KGB Border Troops, Russia's 201st Motor Rifle Division (MRD) was the only noteworthy military formation in the Tajikistan Soviet Socialist Republic on the eve of independence.[19] Moreover, the intelligence structure operating out of Dushanbe was essentially a straight transfer from the Soviets. "Only the nomenclature has changed slightly," Douglas Wayland Foster aptly noted.[20] At the outset, the newly established GKNB struggled following a mass emigration of Slavic intelligence officers.[21]

Soviet changes prior to independence, however, had far-reaching effects on the broader Tajik body politic, which would subsequently leave their mark on the nascent state's security apparatus. The Soviet indigenization effort, begun by Stalin, involved staffing institutions with local power brokers, which in Tajikistan took on clan and regional dimensions.[22] Although ethno-regionalism has exerted significant political consequences in Tajikistan, it was a regionalism not inherent in the Tajik body politic, but one largely inculcated and perpetuated by Soviet overlords as a means of exerting power following the establishment of the Tajikistan Soviet Socialist Republic in 1929.[23] These divisions empowered regional brokers, shored up subnational allegiances, and impeded the development of a strong national identity.[24] The granting of key positions to certain ethno-regional groups at the expense of others exacerbated divisions. During Soviet rule, Khujandis controlled upper levels of the government, while those from Kulob staffed many of the internal affairs and security portfolios, although the historically marginalized Pamiris were given more prominent roles to maintain regional balance following reforms of the 1980s.[25]

These differences laid the ground for the civil war that broke out in 1992. Early on, the real power was wielded by regional warlords tied to the government in Dushanbe, in particular, the brutal Sangak Safarov, head of the Popular Front.[26] By elevating Communist apparatchik Emomali Rahmonov (later changed to Rahmon), who became president in 1994, these warlords thereby entrenched themselves into positions of authority. The five-year civil war between supporters of the nascent government and opposition forces ultimately resulted in the loss of between 35,000 and 157,000 lives, more than 1.5 million internally displaced refugees, and hundreds of thousands more who fled to Afghanistan and other post-Soviet states in the region.[27] Former KGB employees, termed "Yurchiki" after former KGB chairman and later Soviet general secretary Yuri Andropov, staffed key positions in the Popular Front.[28]

At the same time, the war also entrenched the system of divided spoils. State formation took shape as a "bargaining process" between the center and competing power holders in the periphery. After the war, Rahmon used the distribution of rents as patronage to local elites, who used their security forces for resource extraction and power accumulation within their regions.[29] Moreover, warlords aligned with the government were given key positions, notably within the security sectors, fostering a symbiotic patron-client relationship between elites in the capital, headed by the president, and regional strongmen.[30] As a result, Kulob and especially those from Rahmon's native Danghara wielded power in the security services.[31]

POSTWAR CONSOLIDATION

As the only conflict in the postcommunist world resolved through a peace settlement, the peace process and war's end were important early avenues for the Rahmon regime's legitimation. Government outlets routinely described Rahmon as the national peacemaker for ending the civil war, building on his purported lineage to the Samanids and also portraying him as a benevolent father figure.[32] GKNB plays a central role in shaping and even directing the media's representation of Rahmon and Tajikistan to domestic and foreign audiences.[33] Even as Rahmon needed the peripheral elites to sustain his rule and continued to draw Kulobis into the security services, however, he grew more confident in the position and increasingly drew on the third element of stabilization outlined earlier, repression.

In addition to consolidating power by trying to weaken regional elites who had been allies, Rahmon's intelligence services have more aggressively targeted opposition, even those living abroad. After the civil war, the Islamic Renaissance Party of Tajikistan (IRPT), Tajikistan's leading opposition party and one of the key members of United Tajik Opposition, the central force opposing Dushanbe during the civil war, was allowed to operate and field candidates in parliament. In recent years, GKNB has been aggressive in going after its leaders and members, culminating in a regime ban on IRPT's operations in September 2015.[34] The GKNB even sent its officers to befriend and collect on IRPT members abroad.[35] In 2018, one former GKNB official accused GKNB chief Saimumin Yatimov of devising a plan to assassinate IRPT leader Muihiddin Kabiri.[36] More broadly, extraterritorial capture and transfer is practiced as extensively if not more so in Tajikistan than all other Central Asian states.

Scholars have argued that Rahmon's regime has cynically used the threat of the Islamic State as an excuse to target opposition both at home and abroad.[37] Although Dushanbe has tried to capitalize on the growth of Islamist-inspired radicalism to consolidate his power, this does not gainsay the legitimacy of the threat. As of late 2020, Tajik foreign fighters made up a significant per capita contingent in the Islamic State, with more than 2,000 having fought in Syria and Iraq.[38] Tajiks have led Taliban and Islamic State forces, and Tajik-staffed units have conducted attacks both on the border with Afghanistan, within Tajikistan itself, and in Germany.[39] The 2015 defection to the Islamic State of former Colonel Gulmurod Halimov, head of the

Interior Ministry's special forces (supposedly along with fifteen members of the GKNB Alphas), was an especially hard blow. At the same time, the regime has tried to convey a softer image and a more holistic approach to fighting extremism within Tajikistan. A "National Anti-Extremism and Terrorism Strategy for 2016–2020," adopted in November 2016, would supposedly feature Interior Ministry specialists and other security officers, members of the clergy, prosecutors, and local governments working together against extremism.[40] Additionally, the government has announced the pardoning of fighters and dependents who had reportedly not taken part in violence and voluntarily returned to Tajikistan.[41]

It remains unclear to what extent these less coercive measures have actually been carried out in practice, and in any event, the border with Afghanistan will continue to be a persistent thorn for Tajikistan. Personnel who worked for Soviet forces in Afghanistan, the so-called "Afghantsy," may have intimate knowledge of the country and its historical pathologies.[42] Yet a noxious brew of conditions, including insufficient staff, narcotics smuggling, persistent war, and political instability, have made securing the border an almost insurmountable task for Tajikistan. The International Crisis Group called the Tajikistan-Afghanistan border, divided by the Panj River, the "weakest link" in Central Asian security.[43] It is unsurprising that since the resurgence of Islamist violence, Tajik press outlets have more prominently touted the Russian presence and in particular, its 7,000-strong 201st MRD.[44] Foreign countries and intergovernmental organizations such as the Organization for Security and Cooperation in Europe have trained Tajik forces, but little change was seen as of their expected 2020 milestone.[45] The mid-2021 Taliban push toward Kabul caused an influx into Tajikistan of Afghan forces and led to a GKNB reinforcement of the border.[46] For Tajik security forces, the Taliban's swift takeover was surely a cause of foreboding.

Although much of the support from international organizations is aimed at addressing the threats on Tajikistan's borders, these organizations also seek to stem the persistent corruption that plagues the country and its security forces. Transparency International consistently ranks Tajikistan among the most corrupt countries in the world and, in 2020, placed Tajikistan at 149, surpassed regionally only by war-torn Afghanistan and Turkmenistan.[47] Graft is an especially pernicious problem within the security forces. Tajiks say, "If you put epaulettes on a criminal, you'll get a Tajik cop."[48] Corruption affects the intelligence and security sector's culture disproportionately in part because it has historically been so poorly funded by the state.[49] The aforementioned National Strategy cited combatting corruption as an objective in defeating extremism, but these cosmetic measures are unlikely to reverse a phenomenon so deeply rooted in the fabric of Tajik political society.

GORNO-BADAKHSHAN AS A CASE STUDY

Rahmon's autocratic moves demonstrate a concerted effort to gain control over the periphery. Even so, select episodes highlight the different tools the Rahmon regime will continue to employ to sustain its power. Events in Gorno-Badakhshan Autonomous Oblast (GBAO) provide telling indicators of the government's residual dependence on local strongmen in its erstwhile "decentralized authoritarianism."[50] Engagements between Rahmon's forces and local residents also illustrate the limits of a heavy hand and expanded police presence in the periphery. Khorog, the provincial capital, is divided into nine main subdistricts (*Jamoats*), each of which have an informal leader, collectively termed the "Authorities," and even within streets, leaders have their own security force.[51] Due to locals' sense of pride and mistrust of intelligence personnel answering to Dushanbe, residents have sought protection from these local, though unscrupulous, security forces.[52] The dilemma in outlying regions of the GBAO can thus become choosing between the "problematic brother at home and a distant cousin with untrustworthy intentions in Dushanbe."[53]

GBAO comprises 50 percent of the country's landmass, remains functionally independent from the center in Dushanbe, and is run by warlords controlling smuggling routes.[54] A 2018 International Crisis Group report described GBAO as a "microcosm" of Tajikistan.[55] GBAO also is geostrategically important because of its critical location bordering Afghanistan and China. Any suggestion that unrest in GBAO has no meaningful impact on the country's stability due to its remote location therefore seems shortsighted.[56]

The province has witnessed numerous instances of unrest directed against the Rahmon regime. Notably, the 2012 assassination of Major General Abdullo Nazarov, the head of the GKNB directorate in GBAO (who had served as deputy GKNB chief prior to taking his post in 2010), set off a clash with government forces that left twenty-three soldiers and twenty-one civilians dead.[57] Along with other local elites alleged to have been behind his murder, Nazarov was a former commander in the civil war and purportedly involved in GBAO's narcotics industry.[58] Subsequently, riots broke out in Khorog after the May 2014 arrest of a drug dealer, and men with Kalashnikovs and grenades attacked the provincial GKNB office.[59]

After a spate of violent incidents during 2018, Rahmon visited the region and reportedly upbraided local law enforcement for negligence. He later replaced security staff and established a new regional headquarters for security and law enforcement. At the same time, GKNB prepared a television report highlighting its efforts in addressing drug trafficking in the region.[60] Thus, even amid the exercise of more blunt tools of repression, security forces still drew on varied means of legitimation to appeal to the broader populace. Meanwhile, Yodgor Faizov, executive director of the Agha Khan Foundation, which helps administer aid to the GBAO populace and is a large employer of the local population, was appointed GBAO chairman.[61] In mid-2020, the regime faced another test in the region after locals protested the arrest of a purported drug smuggler by the GKNB local branch. Following widespread protests and the forced release of the three men, and through Faizov's intercession, the GKNB backed down with only limited punishments.[62]

FOREIGN INTELLIGENCE AND SECURITY RELATIONSHIPS

The Tajik services rely heavily on human collection and are limited in their conduct of technical surveillance.[63] Yet, in recent years the regime in Dushanbe has grown more adept at using technical means, particularly efforts to monitor and control its population's use of the internet. Although some statistics suggest more expanded internet penetration in 2020, in March 2021 the World Bank country manager in Tajikistan bemoaned limited opportunities for broadband and mobile access, especially in rural areas.[64] Still, Tajik intelligence services have used disinformation online to influence citizens and discredit and isolate adversaries.[65] As part of cementing a broader relationship with China, Tajikistan has also acquired surveillance technology for facial recognition and the expanded collection of biometric data, while Dushanbe is blanketed with CCTV provided by Chinese telecommunications giant Huawei.[66] These tools undoubtedly bolster the regime's control over its citizenry, but as *The Economist* highlighted, such technology may provide the Chinese with backdoor access.[67]

Dushanbe's imports of technology are only one component of its burgeoning ties with China, most prominently demonstrated by China's military base in Tajikistan.[68] In addition to a desire to protect its economic interests in the region, China is concerned about the reports of militants having settled in GBAO and on its own border. Dushanbe's developing relationship with Beijing has included military field exercises and intelligence exchanges.[69]

Tajikistan has other foreign partners. India and Tajikistan have a steady history of amicable ties, and the Indian military maintains an air base in Farkhor, in Tajikistan's southwest.[70] Tajikistan and Iran have long-standing cultural and linguistic ties, yet relations soured after IRPT leader Kabiri attended a 2015 conference in Iran shortly after Rahmon banned the organization.[71] Nevertheless, the countries have since worked to repair relations, and in June 2021, Tajik and Iranian security counterparts signed a memorandum of understanding pledging greater cooperation.[72]

Security and military ties with the United States will continue, not least through US largesse in the interest of bolstering Tajikistan's counterterrorism and counternarcotics capabilities. However, Tajikistan's long-time patron Russia will maintain its preeminent influence within the country, especially in the face of a Taliban-controlled Afghanistan. Indeed, a 2012 agreement extended the presence for Russia's 201st MRD until 2042.[73]

CONCLUSION

As Tajikistan is one of multiple "personalist autocracies" that have prevailed in post-Soviet space, its intelligence culture has been profoundly shaped by its Soviet legacy. Rahmon has used his intelligence services to control patronage networks, crush domestic dissent, and consolidate his position and regime, bolstered by the infusion of foreign support. The efforts that accelerated in 2015 of stifling opposition have continued as Dushanbe's intelligence services work to root out dissent against the president and his family. Even with increasingly brutal means against enemies real or imagined, informal stakeholders will continue to wield influence in peripheral regions such as GBAO. Rahmon likely understands that given the tenuous nature of the state, he needs these strongmen in the periphery as yet one more tool to maintain stability and control.

NOTES

1. The views expressed in this chapter are my own and do not necessarily represent those of the United States government.
2. Marcel de Haas, "Security Policy and Developments in Central Asia: Security Documents Compared with Security Challenges," *Journal of Slavic Military Studies* 29, no. 2 (2016): 205.
3. "Law of the Republic of Tajikistan of July 26, 2014, no. 1095: About the State Secrets (as Amended on 2 January 2020)," CIS Legislation Database, https://cis -legislation.com/document.fwx?rgn=70180.
4. "Tajikistan: Security Services Chief Becomes Old KGB Hand in Overhauled Biography," Eurasianet, November 6, 2020, https://eurasianet.org/tajikistan-security -services-chief-becomes-old-kgb-hand-in-overhauled-biography.
5. "President Shakes Up Senior Border Guard Officials," Asia-Plus, July 10, 2020, https://www.asiaplustj.info/en/news/tajikistan/power/20200710/president-shakes-up -senior-border-guard-officials; Ulan Mukkambaev and Timur Toktonaliev, "The Road of Contention: The Authorities of Kyrgyzstan and Tajikistan Begin Negotiations after a Border Conflict," Central Asian Bureau for Analytical Reporting, March

14, 2019, https://cabar.asia/en/the-road-of-contention-the-authorities-of-kyrgyzstan-and-tajikistan-begin-negotiations-after-a-border-conflict/; "UNODC Programme Office in Tajikistan Organizes a Three-Day Training Course for Tajik Border Troops," UN Office on Drug Control, https://www.unodc.org/centralasia/en/news/unodc-programme-office-in-tajikistan-organizes-a-three-day-training-course-for -tajik-border-troops.html.

   6. "Supreme Court Starts Considering Criminal Proceedings Instituted against Border Service Spokesman," Asia-Plus, July 30, 2019, https://www.asiaplustj.info/en/news/tajikistan/laworder/20190730/supreme-court-starts-considering-criminal -proceedings-instituted-against-border-service-spokesman; "Spokesman for Tajik Border Service Reportedly Arrested on Suspicion of Disclosing State Secret F," Asia-Plus, April 29, 2019, https://www.asiaplustj.info/en/news/tajikistan/security/20190429/spokesman-for-tajik-border-service-reportedly-arrested-on-suspicion-of -disclosing-state-secret-f.

   7. Anna Matveeva, "Tajikistan," in *Intelligence Communities and Cultures in Asia and the Middle East: A Comprehensive Reference*, ed. Bob de Graaff (Boulder, CO: Lynne Rienner, 2020), 408.

   8. Douglas Wayland Foster, "Militarism in Tajikistan: Realities of Post-Soviet Nation Building" (PhD diss., University of Oregon, 2015), 101.

   9. Matveeva, "Tajikistan," 410–11.

   10. "Ministry of Internal Affairs of the Republic of Tajikistan," n.d., https://mvd .tj/index.php/ru/ministerstvo/struktura.

   11. Sophie Roche, "The Fabric of Answer: Constructing a National Facade," *Central Asian Affairs* 5, no. 2 (2018): 97.

   12. Lawrence Markowitz, "The Crystallization of State Security Institutions in Tajikistan and Krygyzstan" (unpublished paper presented at 2017 Annual Convention of Association for the Study of Nationalities, New York), https://ipsr.ku.edu/traffick ing/pdf/ASN2017_Markowitz.pdf (with author's permission).

   13. Matveeva, "Tajikistan," 408; "Tajik Defense Ministry's Military Intelligence Directorate Authorized to Restrain Terrorist Sleeper Cells inside the Country," Asia-Plus, May 29, 2019, https://asiaplustj.info/en/news/tajikistan/power/20190529/tajik-defense-ministrys-military-intelligence-directorate-authorized-to-restrain-terrorist -sleeper-cells-inside-the-country.

   14. Anna Matveeva, *The Perils of Emerging Statehood: Civil War and State Reconstruction in Tajikistan* (London: London School of Economics, Crisis States Research Center, 2009), 48 (citing UN Tajikistan Office for Peacebuilding for figure of 30,000); Matthew Stein, *Compendium of Central Asian Military and Security Activity* (Fort Leavenworth, KS: Foreign Military Studies Office, November 20, 2019), https://community.apan.org/wg/tradoc-g2/fmso/m/fmso-monographs/194880.

   15. "President Convenes Meeting with Senior Security Officials," Asia-Plus, December 20, 2018, https://www.asiaplustj.info/en/news/tajikistan/power/20181220/president-convenes-meeting-with-senior-security-officials.

   16. "Henceforth Security Council Office to Be Subordinate to President's Executive Office," Asia-Plus, June 13, 2018, https://www.asiaplustj.info/en/news/tajikistan/power/20180613/henceforth-security-council-office-to-be-subordinate-to-presidents

-executive-office; Farangis F. Zikriyaeva, "Democratic Control of Armed Forces: A Legal Overview of the Imbalance of Power in Overseeing Armed Forces of Tajikistan," *Revista RyD República y Derecho* 5, no. 5 (2020).

17. Markowitz, "The Crystallization of State Security Institutions in Tajikistan and Krygyzstan."

18. Johannes Gerschewski, "The Three Pillars of Stability: Legitimation, Repression, and Co-Optation in Autocratic Regimes," *Democratization* 20, no. 1 (2013).

19. Tim Epkenhans, *The Origins of the Civil War in Tajikistan: Nationalism, Islamism, and Violent Conflict in Post-Soviet Space* (Lanham, MD: Lexington Books, 2016), 167.

20. Foster, "Militarism in Tajikistan," 100.

21. Matveeva, "Tajikistan," 404.

22. Soleiman Kiasatpour, "Regime Transition in Post-Soviet Central Asia: The Cases of Tajikistan and Kyrgyzstan" (PhD diss., University of California, Riverside, 1998), 87–88.

23. Epkenhans, *The Origins of the Civil War in Tajikistan*, 100.

24. Foster, "Militarism in Tajikistan," 39.

25. Foster, "Militarism in Tajikistan," 50.

26. Carey Goldberg, "The Real Power in Tajikistan," *Los Angeles Times*, January 30, 1993, https://www.latimes.com/archives/la-xpm-1993-01-30-mn-1914-story.html.

27. Bakhtiyor Sobiri, "The Long Echo of Tajikistan's Civil War," Open Democracy, June 23, 2017, https://www.opendemocracy.net/en/odr/long-echo-of-tajikistan -s-civil-war/.

28. Sobiri, "The Long Echo of Tajikistan's Civil War."

29. Lawrence P. Markowitz, *State Erosion: Unlootable Resources and Unruly Elites in Central Asia* (Ithaca, NY: Cornell University Press, 2013), 77, 80.

30. Markowitz, *State Erosion*, 27; Luigi de Martino, *Tajikistan at a Crossroad: The Politics of Decentralization*, Situation Report 4 (Geneva: CIMERA, January 2004).

31. Foster, "Militarism in Tajikistan," 200.

32. "Tajikistan Publishes Book of Wit and Wisdom by President Rahmon," Radio Free Europe / Radio Liberty, July 13, 2017, https://www.rferl.org/a/tajikistan-publishes-book-wit-wisdom-president-rahmon/28613536.html; Rustam Soliev, "Emomali Rahmon: Tajikistan's Architect of Peace," New Europe, June 29, 2015, https://www.neweurope.eu/article/emomali-rahmon-tajikistans-architect-of-peace/.

33. Roche, "The Fabric of Answer."

34. "Three Sons of Late Founding Member of IRPT Reportedly Arrested," Asia-Plus, August 19, 2020, https://www.asiaplustj.info/en/news/tajikistan/laworder/ 20200819/three-sons-of-late-founding-member-of-irpt-reportedly-arrested.

35. "Unsuccessful Refugee or 'GKNB Officer': Who Is Jovidon Ghayurzoda? VIDEO," Radio Ozodi, March 14, 2019, https://www.ozodi.org/a/a-tajik-refugee -claims-worked-with-special-service-to-work-against-opposition/29820822.html.

36. "Tajikistan: Alleged Security Services Agent Reveals Assassination Plot," Eurasianet, August 23, 2018, https://eurasianet.org/tajikistan-alleged-security-services -agent-reveals-assassination-plot.

37. Edward J. Lemon, "Building Resilient Secular Citizens: Tajikistan's Response to the Islamic State," *Caucasus Survey* 4, no. 3 (2016); Kirill Nourzhanov and Amin Saikal, *The Spectre of Afghanistan: Security in Central Asia* (London: Tauris, 2021), 62.

38. Nodirbek Soliev and Raffaello Pantucci, "Central Asia: Kazakhstan, Kyrgyzstan, Tajikistan, Turkmenistan, Uzbekistan," *Counter Terrorist Trends and Analyses* 13, no. 1 (2021): 86; Raffaello Pantucci, "Indians and Central Asians Are the New Face of the Islamic State," *Foreign Policy*, October 8, 2020, https://foreignpolicy .com/2020/10/08/isis-indian-kyrgyzstan-tajikistan-uzbekistan-central-asians-are-the -new-face-of-islamic-state/.

39. Max Taylor, "Analysing the Islamic State Attack in Tajikistan," Intelligence Fusion, November 12, 2019, https://www.intelligencefusion.co.uk/insights/resources/ intelligence-reports/analysing-the-islamic-state-attack-on-tajikistan/; Farangis Najibullah, "Tajik Man Emerges in Afghanistan as Leader of IS Unit of Central Asian Fighters," Radio Free Europe / Radio Liberty, August 12, 2019, https://www.rferl .org/a/tajikistan-islamic-state-central-asia-leader-sayvaly-shafiev/30105372.html.

40. Sherali Rizoyon, "Pros and Cons of the Tajik Strategy against Extremism and Terrorism," Central Asian Bureau for Analytical Reporting, November 15, 2019, https://cabar.asia/en/pros-and-cons-of-the-tajik-strategy-against-extremism- and-terrorism; Negmatullo Mirsaidov, "Clergy, Security Officials Team Up to Fight Extremism in Sughd Province," Caravanserai, August 22, 2017, https://central.asia -news.com/en_GB/articles/cnmi_ca/features/2017/08/22/feature-01.

41. "137 Sughd Residents Suspected of Committing Extremist Crimes Pardoned," Asia-Plus, October 4, 2019, https://www.asiaplustj.info/en/news/tajikistan/ security/20191004/137-sughd-residents-suspected-of-committing-extremist-crimes -pardoned; Farangis Najibullah and Mumin Ahmadi, "Tajikistan Prepares to Repatriate Families of Islamic State Fighters from Camps in Syria," Radio Free Europe / Radio Liberty, December 10, 2020, https://www.rferl.org/a/tajikistan-prepares-to -repatriate-is-families-from-camps-in-syria/30994273.html.

42. Marlene Laruelle, "Assessing Uzbekistan's and Tajikistan's Afghan Policies: The Impact of Domestic Drivers," in *The Central Asia-Afghanistan Relationship: From Soviet Intervention to the Silk Road Initiatives*, ed. Marlene Laruelle (Lanham, MD: Lexington Books, 2017), 119.

43. "Tajikistan Early Warning: Internal Pressures, External Threats," ICG Briefing 78, International Crisis Group, January 11, 2016, https://www.crisisgroup.org/ europe-central-asia/central-asia/tajikistan/tajikistan-early-warning-internal-pressures -external-threats.

44. Alexander Clark, "Tajikistan Is Concerned about Terrorism and Afghanistan— That's Good News for Russia," Medium, March 11, 2021, https://medium.com/the -hillhouse-newsletter/tajikistan-is-concerned-about-terrorism-and-afghanistan-thats -good-news-for-russia-13fd01e9f3f0.

45. Muslimbek Buriev, "Police Reform in Tajikistan: What Should Be the Priority?," Central Asian Bureau for Analytical Reporting, October 21, 2019, https:// cabar.asia/en/police-reform-in-tajikistan-what-should-be-the-priority/; "OSCE: Intelligence-Led Policing Model Presented in Tajikistan," Organization for Security

and Co-operation in Europe, November 27, 2019, https://www.osce.org/secretariat/440321; Muslimbek Buriev, "How Is Tajikistan Entering 2020? Results and Trends," Central Asian Bureau for Analytical Reporting, February 19, 2020, https://cabar.asia/en/how-is-tajikistan-entering-2020-results-and-trends/.

46. "Tajikistan Calls Up Reservists to Bolster Border as Afghan Troops Flee Taliban," Reuters, July 5, 2021, https://www.reuters.com/world/asia-pacific/hundreds-afghan-security-personnel-flee-into-tajikistan-taliban-advances-2021-07-05/.

47. "Tajikistan," Corruptions Perceptions Index 2020, Transparency International, https://www.transparency.org/en/cpi/2020/index/tjk.

48. Kirill Nourzhanov, "Saviours of the Nation or Robber Barons? Warlord Politics in Tajikistan," *Central Asian Survey* 24, no. 2 (June 2005): 119.

49. Markowitz, "The Crystallization of State Security Institutions in Tajikistan and Krygyzstan."

50. Johan Engvall, "The State under Siege: The Drug Trade and Organised Crime in Tajikistan," *Europe-Asia Studies* 58, no. 6 (September 2006): 833.

51. "Rivals for Authority in Tajikistan's Gorno-Badakhshan," ICG Briefing 87, International Crisis Group, March 14, 2018, https://www.crisisgroup.org/europe-central-asia/central-asia/tajikistan/b87-rivals-authority-tajikistans-gorno-badakhshan; de Martino, *Tajikistan at a Crossroad*.

52. Suzanne Levi-Sanchez, "All Institutionalization Is Local: Border (In)security and the Case of Tajik/Afghan Badakhshan" (PhD diss., Rutgers University, 2013), 152, 157.

53. Foster, *Militarism in Tajikistan*, 222.

54. "The Regional Implications of Instability in Tajikistan; Interview with Edward Lemon," National Bureau of Asian Research, June 24, 2019, https://www.nbr.org/publication/the-regional-implications-of-instability-in-tajikistan/.

55. "Rivals for Authority in Tajikistan's Gorno-Badakhshan."

56. Matveeva, "Tajikistan," 402.

57. "Former Tajik Ambassador to Belgium Appointed Deputy Chairman of GKNB," Asia-Plus, May 13, 2010, https://www.asiaplustj.info/en/news/tajikistan/power/20100513/former-tajik-ambassador-belgium-appointed-deputy-chairman-gknb.

58. Markowitz, *State Erosion*, 97.

59. "Tajikistan Early Warning: Internal Pressures, External Threats," ICG Briefing 78, International Crisis Group, January 11, 2016, https://www.crisisgroup.org/europe-central-asia/central-asia/tajikistan/tajikistan-early-warning-internal-pressures-external-threats.

60. Khursand Khurramov, "Special Operations in Khorog for Eight Years: What Has Changed during This Time?" Radio Ozodi, July 22, 2020, https://rus.ozodi.org/a/30740652.html; "SCNS Prepares TV Report on the Situation in GBAO," Asia-Plus, October 11, 2018, https://www.asiaplustj.info/en/news/tajikistan/security/20181011/scns-prepares-tv-report-on-the-situation-in-gbao.

61. "Yodgor Faizov: The Greatest Wealth of GBAO Is Its People," Central Asian Bureau for Analytical Reporting, December 9, 2019, https://cabar.asia/en/yodgor-faizov-the-greatest-wealth-of-gbao-is-its-people/. Faizov was replaced as GBAO chairman in November 2021.

62. "Ministry of Internal Affairs of Tajikistan: The Conflict in Rushan Is Resolved, the Perpetrators Are Punished," Radio Ozodi, June 30, 2020, https://rus.ozodi.org/a/30698903.html; "Five Young Men from GBAO's Rushan District Fined for Obstructing the Work of Police," Asia-Plus, July 1, 2020, https://www.asiaplustj.info/en/news/tajikistan/laworder/20200701/five-young-men-from-gbaos-rushan-district-fined-for-obstructing-the-work-of-police.

63. Matveeva, "Tajikistan," 409.

64. Simon Kemp, "Digital 2021: Tajikistan," DataReportal, February 12, 2021, https://datareportal.com/reports/digital-2021-tajikistan; Jan-Peter Olters, "In Tajikistan, a Digital Future as an Alternative to Unemployment or Migration," World Bank, March 1, 2021, https://www.worldbank.org/en/news/opinion/2021/03/01/in-tajikistan-a-digital-future-as-an-alternative-to-unemployment-or-migration.

65. "Tajikistan's Internet Goes Down Just as Speech by Exiled Opposition Leader Delivered Online," Radio Free Europe / Radio Liberty, September 17, 2020, https://www.rferl.org/a/tajikistan-s-internet-goes-down-just-as-speech-by-exiled-opposition-leader-delivered-online/30844151.html; "Tajikistan: Any Online Action Will Be Used against You," Central Asian Bureau for Analytical Reporting, May 5, 2020, https://cabar.asia/en/tajikistan-any-online-action-will-be-used-against-you-2/.

66. Sergey Sukhankin, "The Security Component of the BRI in Central Asia, Part Two: China's (Para)Military Efforts to Promote Security in Tajikistan and Kyrgyzstan," *China Brief* 20, no. 14 (August 12, 2020), https://jamestown.org/program/the-security-component-of-the-bri-in-central-asia-part-two-chinas-paramilitary-efforts-to-promote-security-in-tajikistan-and-kyrgyzstan/; "The Regional Implications of Instability in Tajikistan: Interview with Edward Lemon," National Bureau of Asian Research, June 24, 2019, https://www.nbr.org/publication/the-regional-implications-of-instability-in-tajikistan/.

67. "America's Approach to Command and Control Goes Peer to Peer: Warfare's Worldwide Web," *The Economist*, January 9, 2021, https://www.economist.com/science-and-technology/2021/01/09/americas-approach-to-command-and-control-goes-peer-to-peer.

68. Suzanne Levi-Sanchez, "China's Gambit in Tajikistan: Partner or Overlord?" *War on the Rocks*, September 23, 2020, https://warontherocks.com/2020/09/chinas-gambit-in-tajikistan-partner-or-overlord/.

69. Laura Zhou, "China Conducts Anti-terror Drill with Tajikistan, as Afghan Spillover Worries Grip Central Asia," *South China Morning Post*, August 18, 2021, https://www.scmp.com/news/china/diplomacy/article/3145532/china-conducts-anti-terror-drill-tajikistan-afghan-spillover; Jacob Levitan, "China Conducts Another Military Exercise in Tajikistan—Should the World Care?" Caspian Policy Center, August 29, 2019, https://www.caspianpolicy.org/research/articles/china-conducts-another-military-exercise-in-tajikistan-should-the-world-care/; "Tajikistan Agrees to More Intelligence Exchanges with China," Reuters, August 31, 2017, https://www.reuters.com/article/us-china-tajikistan-security/tajikistan-agrees-to-more-intelligence-exchanges-with-china-idUSKCN1BC3N5.

70. "Indian Military Base in Tajikistan- Farkhor Air Base Ll India Updated," YouTube, June 28, 2020, https://www.youtube.com/watch?v=KAfFkggzQN4; Ryan

Shaffer, "Unraveling India's Foreign Intelligence: The Origins and Evolution of the Research and Analysis Wing," *International Journal of Intelligence and Counter-Intelligence* 28, no. 2 (2015): 252–89; Muzaffar Olimov, "Tajikistan-India Bilateral Relations: Problems and Perspectives," *Himalayan and Central Asian Studies* 20, no. 2–3 (April–September 2016): 15–27.

71. Ahmad Majidyar, "Tajikistan Closes Iranian Organizations in New Diplomatic Escalation," Middle East Institute, June 30, 2017, https://www.mei.edu/publications/tajikistan-closes-iranian-organizations-new-diplomatic-escalation.

72. "Iran, Tajikistan Sign Security Agreement," Fars News Agency, June 3, 2021, https://www.farsnews.ir/en/news/14000313000319/.

73. "Russia Gets 30-year Extension for Base in Tajikistan," British Broadcasting Corporation, October 5, 2012, https://www.bbc.com/news/world-asia-19849247.

26

Thailand: From Cold War Intelligence to Cyber Surveillance

Michael Landon-Murray and Dao Henry

In what would be the first of roughly a dozen coups, the Siamese monarchy was ousted in 1932, and shortly thereafter the centuries-old Kingdom of Siam was renamed Thailand and governed by a constitutional monarchy. The monarchy has nonetheless remained central in Thai society and politics, developing a mutually beneficial relationship with the military, which itself has governed Thailand for much of its modern history. Thai regimes have monitored and enforced *lèse-majesté*, a "national security" law in Thailand that outlaws any disrespectful, sarcastic, or compromising statement or action regarding the monarchy. In fact, "the military's self-defined top national security mission is to protect the monarchy. It is this mission that has seen the parallel state develop and thrive."[1]

This chapter is organized into four thematic sections. The first part offers an overview of the country and its intelligence services, highlighting the utilization of bilateral relations to improve intelligence capabilities and the use of intelligence for the leaders to maintain political power. The second section analyzes key internal and external influences and events with attention to how particular intelligence practices have shaped security and society in Thailand. The third section explores social media and cyber surveillance, which highlights a technological evolution as well as continuity in using citizens to take actions against one another. Lastly, a conclusion summarizes key aspects of Thailand's intelligence culture and discusses the need for further research.

BACKGROUND

Before addressing key historical and contemporary dimensions of Thai intelligence practice and culture, it is also important to briefly examine underlying political, governmental and bureaucratic dynamics in Thailand. Freedom House has categorized Thailand as "partly free"—earning a 6 out of 40 possible points on political rights—having returned to quasi-democratic governance in 2019 after another five years of military rule.[2] The current prime minister is the former military general who led the 2014 coup. He was "elected" by the Thai National Assembly, whose upper house (the Senate) consists solely of members appointed by the military. It is not surprising, then, that he received 249 of a possible 250 Senate votes, resulting in a majority of total parliamentary votes.[3] It is no wonder that scholars see a muddled picture of principal-agent dynamics between elected politicians and bureaucrats.[4] Atop the Thai bureaucracy sit forty-one cabinet-level positions, thirty-seven of which are filled by men.[5] None of the four women serve in positions with intelligence or security responsibilities.

Thailand's core intelligence activities have been distributed mainly between and within Thailand's interior (i.e., the National Intelligence Agency), police (i.e., the Border Patrol Police and Special Branch Bureau), and military bureaucracies (i.e., the Counter Terrorist Operations Center), often in the absence of civilian, democratic control. These interior, police, and military bureaucracies have operated as the most powerful and influential in Thailand's government and have frequently been in competition with one another.[6] Scholars have described Thailand as a "bureaucratic polity" and even a "military polity" with civil-military relations a perennial challenge.[7] Achieving high-level positions in the bureaucracy is markedly political, and "the system is such that the top bureaucrats exercise firm control over their organizations in crucial matters of budgeting, finance, personnel and policy."[8]

The practices, cultures, and effects of intelligence in Thailand, like in many non-Western nations, have been understudied by intelligence scholars, in part due to common data and access limits.[9] The chapter addresses this issue by examining how the tools and organizations of Thai intelligence and security—ranging from surveillance and collection to covert action and assassination—have been developed and deployed at key junctures in the nation's history. It does not make definitive conclusions on the overall effectiveness of Thai's intelligence services but focuses on the leadership, policy, and the internal and external security objectives for Thai intelligence and security agencies.

Thailand's intelligence apparatus is one of the oldest and largest in Southeast Asia and has been seen as organizationally disjointed and often ineffectual.[10] In part because Thailand has operated so long as a military dictatorship, the intelligence and security services have frequently been used to serve the monarchy and military, which often means suppressing opposition and dissident views. This has included repeated assassinations and campaigns against political opponents, as well as violent or intrusive use of intelligence and security agencies in the context of civil society and universities. Corrupt politicians and members of the military have themselves been involved in drug and arms trafficking.[11]

Domestic political and power dynamics have been influential in the use and control of intelligence tools in Thailand. Foreign relations and regional security dynamics have also been important determinants of the nature and use of its intelligence services. Soon after World War II, Thailand and the United States formed a key political relationship, premised mainly on anticommunism, that would bring millions of dollars of economic and military assistance to Thailand and provide the United States with a platform for its military and covert operations in the region. In the context of this arrangement, the US Central Intelligence Agency (CIA) exerted a formative influence on Thailand's intelligence organizations and practices. Thailand's approach to counterinsurgency was also heavily influenced by its Cold War partnership with the United States.[12] Additionally in waging the global War on Terror, the CIA would in fact return to likely one of the same Cold War locations to establish the first so-called "black site."[13] The enhanced interrogation techniques—torture—used by the CIA at these sites again informed subsequent Thai practices.[14]

WINDOWS INTO THAI INTELLIGENCE AND SECURITY PRACTICE

This section analyzes key internal and external influences on Thai intelligence and security services, and how the use of these services has influenced security and society in Thailand. The subjects are examined through the prism of three key areas: Thailand's Cold War relationship with the United States; Thai efforts to counter the southern insurgency and terrorism; and the suppression of Thai citizens, political dissidents, civil society, and opposition leaders. In doing so, this section highlights the development, application, and effects of Thai intelligence through the prism of some of Thailand's most defining political and security dynamics, historical events, and foreign relations. Some of the most important—and extreme—uses of intelligence tools by Thai authorities will be described in their broader political and policy contexts.

Cold War, Communism, and Thai-US Relations

Though Thailand had declared war on the United States during World War II (which the United States chose not to accept), it quickly formed a close political, military, and economic relationship with the United States as the Cold War emerged amid fears of spreading communism.[15] This arrangement provided the United States with an important regional platform for military and covert operations that helped shore up Thailand against internal and external Communist threats and sent to Thailand tremendous amounts of US military and economic assistance.

These early relations also consisted of the CIA aiding Thailand in the establishment of its first centralized intelligence service, as well as paramilitary and police reconnaissance units.[16] This paramilitary police entity would later be integrated into the Border Patrol Police (BPP),[17] which in 1976 led an armed mob—including the BPP-supported "Village Scouts"—in the heinous killing of student demonstrators (partly in response to allegations of *lèse-majesté*).[18] That event would drive thousands of students to flee into the jungle to join the Communist Party of Thailand (CPT), swelling their insurgent ranks.[19] Earlier assassinations of leaders of the Peasant Federation of Thailand, a movement representing the interests of rural farmers, have been viewed as a prelude to the 1976 urban massacre.[20] More generally, the Thai National Police grew "into a formidable security apparatus, eventually rivalling the army itself."[21] In its history, the police frequently operated with impunity.[22] The United States also provided support to the Thai government in the form of anticommunist, pro-royalist propaganda. Scholar Jim Glassman explained, "Through campaigns such as these, the monarch and military came to be joined at the hip, working in co-ordinated fashion to promote the kind of political regime US counterinsurgents and Thai elites saw as conducive to their agendas."[23] Propaganda from the US Information Service portrayed Communists as "monsters," often being repeated by the Thai press.[24]

Largely due to the tremendous resources flowing into Thailand from the United States and coinciding objectives, Thailand was a willing and compliant US partner in most matters.[25] All of this aid and support made the United States by far Thailand's most important Cold War patron and partner; however, the United States' support of Thailand during the Cold War did more than help establish key intelligence and police services and solidify Thai regimes in the short term. Scholar Kevin Hewison has written that US policies in Thailand contributed to an "emasculation of democratic politics by supporting, bolstering, arming and ideologically cheering 'stable' military and authoritarian regimes."[26] American officials recognized the deleterious effect US support was having on Thai democracy and political development, but Cold War worries about the domino theory outweighed such concerns.

Government assassinations of political rivals—including ex-ministers—were features of this early Cold War period, with the US government aware of this.[27]

Thailand's efforts to contain and manage the CPT also provide insights into Thai intelligence practice and culture during the Cold War. With the CPT declaring armed struggle in 1965, it proved a remarkably difficult intelligence target, being small, disciplined, and evasive, at times creating embarrassment for Thai intelligence services.[28] This was especially so for the civilian Police Special Branch and Directorate of Central Intelligence (currently known as the National Intelligence Agency), which were responsible for the difficult task of discerning the structure, intentions, and capabilities of the CPT. Further, some of the early and unsuccessful efforts to suppress and detain CPT members actually allowed them to network and expand their ideological and organizational influence.[29]

There were successful intelligence and law enforcement operations conducted against the CPT, including the 1972 arrest of virtually all CPT members living in Bangkok.[30] While this operation had little tangible impact on the CPT's capacity, it did prove to be an important source of intelligence. Ultimately, it was CPT defectors who provided Thai authorities with many of the insights needed to effectively understand and address insurgents' conditions and concerns.[31] When Thailand abandoned counterinsurgency strategies borrowed from the United States, it successfully addressed the insurgency with intelligence advisers providing Prime Minister Prem Tinsulanonda some of the most important policy and program ideas.[32] Rather than being military centric, these ideas included amnesty, repatriation, and economic opportunities, as well as simple study abroad programs. Such approaches, which were undoubtedly aided by other circumstances, including the evaporation of Chinese support for the CPT, were counter to the policy preferences of a majority of the Thai intelligence community who had endorsed more conventional counterinsurgency tactics. Additionally, Thai military generals had often called Major General Chavalit Yongchaiyudh—the head of Thai intelligence and a key architect of Thailand's amnesty program—a "Communist." Two decades later, Chavalit for a short time was elevated to address the growing Muslim insurgency in the south.[33]

Contemporary Counterinsurgency and Counterterrorism

Thailand has also encountered counterinsurgency and separatism movements in the post–Cold War era, and it again looked to the US example not only for counterinsurgency practices but also counterterrorism practices, including enhanced interrogation techniques. While the Thai population is mainly Buddhist in terms of religion, its southernmost regions are home to large

numbers of Malay Muslims, especially in the provinces of Yala, Pattani, and
Narathiwat.[34] Generally, Muslims and Buddhists have peacefully coexisted
in Thailand, though that tolerance has likely diminished in recent years.[35]
However, a Malay Muslim separatist movement does extend back decades,
waxing and waning in intensity and violence. The level of violence rose dramatically in 2004, and despite warning indicators, this was to the surprise of
the Thai government.[36] To be sure, the degree of violence was unprecedented.[37] However, the government's 2002 decision to disband the South Border
Provinces Administration Center—established as a component of the Ministry of Interior—is seen as a decision that significantly weakened intelligence
sharing and analysis in southern Thailand.[38]

Southern insurgents had first officially endorsed violent strategies and tactics in the 1960s (though violence predated the 1960s and happened as early
as 1903), around the same time the CPT had declared armed resistance.[39] The
insurgency seemed to be near demise in the late 1990s, but that changed in
the early 2000s.[40] Aurel Croissant's research suggests that, beyond longer
standing issues such as political, religious, cultural, and economic alienation,
three more contemporary developments created the conditions for the spike
in political violence: "(1) Islamization of the Muslim minorities' identity in
Thailand; (2) shifts in government policies after 2001; and (3) the low quality
of the government's conflict management."[41]

Since 2004, government officers, including police and judges, as well as
citizens have been frequent targets of insurgent bombings and shootings.[42]
Insurgent attacks have included numerous beheadings.[43] In addition to this
domestic insurgency and terrorism, Thailand has also been a base of operations for international terrorist organizations, such as al-Qaeda.[44] Civil society groups that have shown support for self-determination and autonomy
in Thailand have often been monitored by Thai intelligence officers.[45] And
more generally, the Border Patrol Police is charged with surveillance of
Thailand's ethnic minorities.[46] Separatist groups have often operated with
extreme secrecy, though the peace negotiations discussed later in the section
did reduce that secrecy somewhat.[47]

When an unanticipated increase in violence occurred during 2004, the
civilian government responded by saturating the region with soldiers and
paramilitary forces affiliated with the Ministry of Interior and military.[48]
Some of the government's responses seemed only to make matters worse, and
Islamic leaders have been disappeared and killed by Thai security agencies.[49]
As Croissant wrote in 2007:

> [C]ultural insensitivity and an increasing number of human rights violations
> committed by the police and the military have provoked both fear and anger
> and strengthened the cause of the insurgents . . . as many as 200 local Malay-

Muslims had been carried away by local police and military or disappeared after the security forces had looked for them. Several other measures taken by the security forces, such as intrusions into the unregistered religion schools, the arrests of teachers, and the army's frequent search and arrest hunts have eroded the local people's will to cooperate with the security forces as well.[50]

Between 2004 and 2012, the government's counterinsurgency policy followed a conventional strategy informed by practices Thailand had borrowed from US Cold War approaches.[51] After briefly experimenting with a more balanced, liberal approach in 2013, the 2014 coup led to the military government again pursuing a more illiberal strategy to address the insurgency.[52] Following the 2014 coup, the peace process was suspended temporarily, and when the military government did reengage, little was achieved.[53] The peace process of the early 2010s was followed by a general reduction of violence in the south, though this is likely more a result of political decisions by insurgents—with the objective of gaining more support internationally—than Thai counterinsurgency policy.[54] Nonetheless, prospects for a peaceful, political settlement in the near term seem remote.[55]

One factor identified by Croissant that has likely contributed to rising Islamist radicalism and insurgency violence in the south has been the Thai government's support for US counterterrorism and military initiatives, including sending troops to the war in Iraq.[56] Thailand is also reported to have hosted the first CIA "black site" in the early 2000s (something the Thai government has denied), where enhanced interrogation techniques were employed by the United States in efforts to extract counterterrorism intelligence.[57] This was during the rule of Thailand's democratically elected prime minister, Thaksin Shinawatra, and was overseen by Gina Haspel, a career CIA operations officer who years later became Donald Trump's CIA director.

While the exact location of that site is unknown, "each of the locations speculated as the CIA black site was associated with USA-Thailand Cold War operations . . . in Laos, Cambodia and Vietnam."[58] Human Rights Watch has found that the torture techniques used by the CIA, including waterboarding, have informed subsequent Thai intelligence practices.[59] Thailand used waterboarding and mock executions to interrogate suspected southern insurgents (and other political dissidents).[60] Just as the Thai government developed intelligence, counterinsurgency, and police practices influenced by the United States during the Cold War, Thailand later emulated some of the most severe practices utilized by the United States in the global War on Terror. The policy and military deference shown to the United States decades earlier also reverberates in the contemporary security landscape.

SOCIAL MEDIA INTELLIGENCE AND CYBER SURVEILLANCE

The Thai government has also made extensive intelligence use of increased online and social media activity, which is especially high in Thailand. The examples discussed previously demonstrate some of the defining uses of Thai security and intelligence services, including brutal treatment of political separatists and opponents. The most extreme security and intelligence tools—i.e., assassinations and torture—have been deployed against insurgents, opposition leaders, and political dissidents.[61] The Thai government has also used intelligence and law enforcement powers to monitor, suppress, and ultimately prosecute the opinions and statements of citizens, protestors, and political opponents. Such efforts have included modern adaptations to enforce long-standing and antiquated laws, including *lèse-majesté*, which in recent years has been applied in especially broad fashion (i.e., cases related to insulting a royal dog and fictitious kings).[62] Even under democratic governance, "the lèse-majesté law was the prime weapon the Bangkok elite and its allies used to clip the leaders of the majority opposition."[63] While perhaps not as shocking or violent as the other instruments of suppression used by the Thai government, contemporary surveillance practices have a deeply chilling effect on free speech, democratic opposition, and privacy.

Before the advent of social media, information to support *lèse-majesté* cases was mainly captured via police recordings or through print media.[64] More recent *lèse-majesté* cases have been driven chiefly by social media intelligence, a relatively recent addition to more established intelligence disciplines (i.e., human intelligence), and a component of open source intelligence.[65] To be sure, the number of *lèse-majesté* cases has dropped in recent years.[66] Nonetheless, the Thai government retains a potent and inexpensive tool for monitoring and surveilling citizens, civil society and academics, political opposition, and anyone else who is perceived to be disrespectful to the monarchy or its pets.

Since 2007, a slate of cybersecurity and computer laws has emerged to limit public and online speech, which included issues pertaining to the military government and public safety and order, broadly defined. For example, Thailand has used powers under the Computer Crimes Act—also known as the "fake news" law—to suppress and prosecute individuals for sharing "false" or "distorted" information in ways that are purportedly damaging to national security. In 2018, prior to the return of quasi-democracy, the deputy chief of Thailand's Cyber-Crime Task Force explained, "To express an opinion honestly is not illegal. However, to share an opinion with a hidden political agenda which could damage the country or national security, is illegal."[67] This has been used as a weapon against those critical of the regime, and many have been arrested for statements made on social media outlets.[68] Social media companies have also been compelled to remove content.[69]

Private citizens and nongovernmental entities have also used social media as a means to reveal the location of dissidents in real time to coordinate attacks and actions against them.[70] In some cases, the Ministry of Interior has even contracted with private citizens (including the so-called Cyber Scouts, schoolchildren tasked to inform on others) to surveil illicit social media activity and content.[71] This represents a technologically updated version of already established practices of supporting private actors in the suppression of activities seen as subversive to the Thai state (i.e., the abovementioned Village Scouts, as well as the state-sponsored Red Gaurs).[72]

Concerns about these various uses of social media are pronounced in Thailand as the use of platforms like Facebook is among the highest in the world. More than half of the Thai population uses Facebook, and citizens spend a tremendous amount of time on social media.[73] It is also worth noting the deeply concerning use of social media intelligence and big data by other governments in the region—namely, China and Singapore—and the increasing technological capacity for mass surveillance.[74]

CONCLUSION

This chapter has provided windows into the development, influences, practices, and societal implications of Thai intelligence and security services. These facets have been explored through the prism of key episodes and dimensions of Thai history, leadership, and policy. The result is a picture of Thailand's intelligence culture as intrusive, suppressive, and often violent. Many of Thailand's early intelligence entities and practices were influenced by the United States—namely, the CIA—which also exported enhanced interrogation practices to Thailand decades later.

To be sure, the picture painted here is not a complete one, and continuing research is needed. Yet in the context of frequent military governments and perennial deference to a monarchy, it is not terribly surprising that Thailand has consistently deployed some of the most extreme intelligence and security tools available. Understanding the focus and limits—or lack thereof—of these tools arguably provides the most important insights into Thai intelligence culture. While often facing difficult targets, Thai intelligence has certainly failed to anticipate key events, not least of which were the 2004 uptick in southern insurgent violence. Intelligence practices in Thailand have also been consequentially adapted to combat long-standing "national security" threats, including the use of social media intelligence to identify and prosecute—or otherwise punish—those who exhibited even the smallest hint of disrespect toward the monarchy or military leadership.

History suggests it is probably a matter of time until the next attempted—and likely successful—coup. But perhaps Thailand will instead find a way to wrest control from the ever-present influence of the military, and democracy will finally get on more solid footing. This would likely improve research conditions for scholars seeking to advance understanding of Thailand's intelligence practice and culture, contributing to the needed and further diversification of the intelligence studies literature. Conversely, academics may look at the potential for military resurgence in Thailand, the recent disappearances, jailings, and murders of political dissidents and security studies scholars—in Thailand and around the world—and "attitude adjustments" courtesy of the military and think twice about such an endeavor.[75] This would represent continuity, as younger Thai scholars have often tended to avoid broaching controversial research questions.[76]

NOTES

1. Paul Chambers and Napisa Waitoolkiat, "The Resilience of Monarchised Military in Thailand," *Journal of Contemporary Asia* 46, no. 3 (2016): 425–44.

2. "Freedom in the World 2020: Thailand," Freedom House, n.d., accessed May 23, 2022, https://freedomhouse.org/country/thailand/freedom-world/2020#PR.

3. "Freedom in the World 2020: Thailand."

4. Jacob I. Ricks, "Agents, Principals, or Something in Between? Bureaucrats and Policy Control in Thailand," *Journal of East Asian Studies* 18, no. 3 (2018): 321–44.

5. "About the Government: Cabinet," Royal Thai Government, 2021, https://www.thaigov.go.th/aboutus/current/cabinet.

6. Bidhya Bowornwathana, "The Politics of Becoming a Top Bureaucrat in the Thai Bureaucracy," *Asia Pacific Journal of Public Administration* 32, no. 2 (2010): 125–36; Paul Chambers, "Securing an Alternative Army: The Evolution of the Royal Thai Police," in *Routledge Handbook of Contemporary Thailand*, ed. Pavin Chachavalpongpun (New York: Routledge, 2020); Aurel Croissant, "Muslim Insurgency, Political Violence, and Democracy in Thailand," *Terrorism and Political Violence* 19, no. 1 (2007): 1–18.

7. Kevin Hewison, "Black Site: The Cold War and the Shaping of Thailand's Politics," *Journal of Contemporary Asia* 50, no. 4 (2020): 551–70; Ricks, "Agents."

8. Bowornwathana, "The Politics of Becoming a Top Bureaucrat," 126; Suehiro Akira, "Technocracy and Thaksinocracy in Thailand: Reforms of the Public Sector and the Budget System under the Thaksin Government," *Southeast Asian Studies* 3, no. 2 (2014); Ricks, "Agents Principals, or Something in Between?"

9. Zakia Shiraz and Richard J. Aldrich, "Secrecy, Spies and the Global South: Intelligence Studies beyond the 'Five Eyes' Alliance," *International Affairs* 95, no. 6 (2019): 1313–29.

10. Croissant, "Muslim Insurgency"; Arne Kislenko, "Thailand," in *Encyclopedia of Intelligence and Counterintelligence*, ed. Rodney P. Carlisle (New York: Routledge, 2004).

11. Croissant, "Muslim Insurgency."

12. Rungrawee Chalermsripinyorat, "Dialogue without Negotiation: Illiberal Peace-building in Southern Thailand," *Conflict, Security & Development* 20, no. 1 (2020): 71–95.

13. Hewison, "Black Site."

14. Shashank Bengali and Chris Megerian, "The CIA Closed Its Original 'Black Site' Years Ago: But Its Legacy of Torture Lives on in Thailand," *Los Angeles Times*, April 22, 2018, https://www.latimes.com/world/asia/la-fg-thailand-cia-haspel-2018 -htmlstory.html.

15. Arne Kislenko, "Thailand's Foreign Policy," in *Routledge Handbook of Contemporary Thailand*, ed. Pavin Chachavalpongpun (New York: Routledge, 2020).

16. Chambers, "Securing an Alternative Army"; Kislenko, "Thailand."

17. Chambers, "Securing an Alternative Army."

18. Bob Bergin, "Defeating an Insurgency—the Thai Effort against the Communist Party of Thailand, 1965–ca. 1982," *Studies in Intelligence* 60, no. 2 (2016): 25–35.

19. Bergin, "Defeating an Insurgency."

20. Jim Glassman, "Lineages of the Authoritarian State in Thailand: Military Dictatorship, Lazy Capitalism and the Cold War Past as Post–Cold War Prologue," *Journal of Contemporary Asia* 50, no. 4 (2020): 575.

21. Chambers, "Securing an Alternative Army," Kindle, 3889.

22. Tyrell Haberkorn, *In Plain Sight: Impunity and Human Rights in Thailand* (Madison: University of Wisconsin Press, 2018).

23. Glassman, "Lineages," 575.

24. Glenn Ettinger, "Thailand's Defeat of Its Communist Party," *International Journal of Intelligence and CounterIntelligence* 20, no. 4 (2007): 661–77.

25. Arne Kislenko, "A Not So Silent Partner: Thailand's Role in Covert Operations, Counter-insurgency, and the Wars in Indochina," *Journal of Conflict Studies* 24, no. 1 (2004).

26. Hewison, "Black Site," 555.

27. Hewison, "Black Site," 555.

28. Chalermsripinyorat, "Dialogue without Negotiation"; Bergin, "Defeating an Insurgency."

29. Ettinger, "Thailand's Defeat."

30. Ettinger, "Thailand's Defeat."

31. Bergin, "Defeating an Insurgency."

32. Bergin, "Defeating an Insurgency."

33. Croissant, "Muslim Insurgency."

34. Anders Engvall and Magnus Andersson, "The Southern Conflict," in *Routledge Handbook of Contemporary Thailand*, ed. Pavin Chachavalpongpun (New York: Routledge, 2020).

35. Engvall and Andersson, "The Southern Conflict."

36. Chalermsripinyorat, "Dialogue without Negotiation"; Croissant, "Muslim Insurgency."

37. Engvall and Andersson, "The Southern Conflict."

38. Croissant, "Muslim Insurgency."

39. Chalermsripinyorat, "Dialogue without Negotiation"; Croissant, "Muslim Insurgency"; Engvall and Andersson, "The Southern Conflict."

40. Croissant, "Muslim Insurgency."

41. Croissant, "Muslim Insurgency," 8.

42. Croissant, "Muslim Insurgency"; Chalermsripinyort, "Dialogue without Negotiation"; Kislenko, "Thailand."

43. "No One Is Safe: Insurgent Attacks on Civilians in Thailand's Southern Border Provinces," Human Rights Watch, August 28, 2017, https://www.hrw.org/report/2007/08/27/no-one-safe/insurgent-attacks-civilians-thailands-southern-border-provinces.

44. Kislenko, "Thailand."

45. Chalermsripinyorat, "Dialogue without Negotiation."

46. Kislenko, "Thailand."

47. Chalermsripinyorat, "Dialogue without Negotiation"; Engvall and Andersson, "The Southern Conflict."

48. Chalermsripinyorat, "Dialogue without Negotiation."

49. Engvall and Andersson, "The Southern Conflict."

50. Croissant, "Muslim Insurgency," 11.

51. Chalermsripinyorat, "Dialogue without Negotiation"; Engvall and Andersson, "The Southern Conflict."

52. Chalermsripinyorat, "Dialogue without Negotiation."

53. Chalermsripinyorat, "Dialogue without Negotiation."

54. Chalermsripinyorat, "Dialogue without Negotiation."

55. Engvall and Andersson, "The Southern Conflict."

56. Croissant, "Muslim Insurgency."

57. Bengali and Megerian, "The CIA Closed Its Original 'Black Site'"; Hewison, "Black Site."

58. Hewison, "Black Site," 552.

59. Bengali and Megerian, "The CIA Closed Its Original 'Black Site.'"

60. Bengali and Megerian, "The CIA Closed Its Original 'Black Site.'"

61. Hannah Beech, "The Dissidents Are Disappearing, and Families Are Fighting for Answers," *New York Times*, June 26, 2020, https://www.nytimes.com/2020/06/26/world/asia/thailand-dissidents-disappeared-military.html; Chalermsripinyorat, "Dialogue without Negotiation"; Hewison, "Black Site."

62. Nash Jenkins, "A Thai Man Faces Nearly 40 Years in Jail for Insulting the King's Dog," *Time*, December 15, 2015, https://time.com/4148911/thailand-bhumibol-tongdaeng-lese-majeste/; David Streckfuss, "Lèse-majesté within

Thailand's Regime of Intimidation," in *Routledge Handbook of Contemporary Thailand*, ed. Pavin Chachavalpongpun (New York: Routledge, 2020).

63. Streckfuss, "Lèse-majesté," Kindle, 5130.

64. Streckfuss, "Lèse-majesté," Kindle, 5130.

65. David Omand, Jamie Bartlett, and Carl Miller, "Introduction: Social Media Intelligence (SOCMINT)," *Intelligence and National Security* 27, no. 6 (2012): 801–23.

66. Streckfuss, "Lèse-majesté."

67. "Are These People Really a Threat to Thai National Security?," BBC News, November 17, 2018, https://www.youtube.com/watch?v=EmGdY4gePrs.

68. "Thailand: Cyber Crime Act Tightens Internet Control: Sweeping Powers to Censor, Stifle Free Speech, Silence Critics," Human Rights Watch, December 21, 2016, https://www.hrw.org/news/2016/12/21/thailand-cyber-crime-act-tightens-internet-control.

69. "Thailand: Cyber Crime Act Tightens Internet Control."

70. Wolfram Schaffar, "The Social Media," in *Routledge Handbook of Contemporary Thailand*, ed. Pavin Chachavalpongpun (New York: Routledge, 2020).

71. Schaffar, "The Social Media."

72. Bergin, "Defeating an Insurgency"; Schaffar, "The Social Media."

73. "Are These People Really a Threat to Thai National Security?"; Schaffar, "The Social Media."

74. Schaffar, "The Social Media."

75. Beech, "The Dissidents Are Disappearing"; Shiraz and Aldrich, "Secrecy, Spies and the Global South"; Streckfuss, "Lèse-majesté."

76. Streckfuss, "Lèse-majesté."

27

Timor-Leste: An Intelligence Culture Developing and Overcoming Politicization

Agnes E. Venema

A relatively new country, Timor-Leste gained independence in 2002 and is situated in the Indonesian archipelago north of Western Australia.[1] The island of Timor consists of an Indonesian western part, including the Timor-Leste enclave of Oecussi, and the independent country of Timor-Leste (previously named East Timor). Unlike Indonesia, which was under Dutch colonial rule, Timor-Leste was a Portuguese colony for centuries until the Carnation Revolution of 1974. What followed was a very brief independence, annexation by Indonesia in 1975 and an often brutal occupation, a popular but violent referendum in August 1999, a large United Nations (UN) deployment and transitional administration (UNTAET) supported by an Australian-led multinational peacekeeping force (INTERFET) from 2000 until restoration of independence on May 20, 2002, and finally a breakdown in law and order necessitating a request for another deployment of the Australian-led International Stabilization Force from 2006 until 2012 and another large UN presence (UNMIT).[2] The overlapping histories of Indonesia and Timor-Leste and the expansive UN and Australian interventions have shaped public Timorese views of the security sector in general and intelligence gathering in particular.

Due to this history of invasion, occupation, and instability, Timor-Leste's intelligence culture had to overcome politicization, a lack of trust, and weariness of outside influence. During the twenty years the country has existed and even before, much of its security sector has been trained by foreign countries, and the capacity building for the country's national intelligence agency is reliant upon receiving training abroad.

This chapter argues, first, that for Timor-Leste's intelligence agency to be truly effective it needs to overcome the image of politicization that has plagued the security sector. Second, Timor-Leste must prioritize counterintelligence to effectively combat regional threats and decrease vulnerability operations by foreign adversaries and nonstate actors. Finally, this chapter demonstrates that, for a small island nation like Timor-Leste, diversification of its intelligence agency's partners is essential in avoiding overreliance on and the undue influence of specific partners.

The chapter is organized in four parts. The first section offers an overview of Timor-Leste's history with attention to recent political events. Then it turns to examining specific intelligence and security institutions. Building from this, it looks at how politics and security culture has influenced intelligence. Next, it explores intelligence and security partnerships, highlighting dependency on foreign actors. Finally, the chapter concludes by analyzing the role of politicization in intelligence culture and recent trends.

BACKGROUND

To fully appreciate the profound impact that the Indonesian occupation has had on Timorese views of security and intelligence gathering, it is important to briefly explore Indonesia's history. Formally known as the Dutch East Indies, present-day Indonesia had been under Dutch rule from the early 1800s until it ended abruptly when Japan invaded Indonesia in 1942. The Japanese occupiers imposed their centuries-old system of community-based policing, which relied on neighborhood associations gathering intelligence and passing this information on to the authorities, effectively creating a highly efficient "neighborhood watch" capable of detecting most pockets of resistance.[3] During and after its independence struggle that ended in 1949, Indonesia adapted this Japanese system to quell cession attempts and uprisings, including the creation of local, village-level links between the military and residents.[4] House visits and regular contact with village elders coupled with group pressure and denunciations were highly effective ways of collecting local intelligence.[5]

The 1974 Carnation Revolution in Portugal resulted in a hasty decolonization process in several former colonies. For Timor-Leste, this resulted in instability and then invasion and annexation by Indonesia in 1975.[6] The Indonesian government introduced a system similar to that of the Japanese in Indonesia: officers were stationed in villages to put local communities under surveillance and detect resistance, local Timorese administrative structures were incorporated into Indonesian information networks, and local Timorese of high standing "were recruited and ordered to forward intelligence about their community members."[7] By the 1980s, Indonesia's military apparatus represented an omnipresent, "smothering intelligence and paramilitary presence made up largely of East Timorese," which bred a culture of suspicion.[8]

In 1999, Indonesia's new president offered the Timorese the choice between autonomy within Indonesia or independence in a referendum that saw enormous voter turnout (98.6 percent) and overwhelming support for independence.[9] The UN mission tasked with organizing the referendum could not prevent Operation Clean Sweep; a deadly scorched-earth campaign by pro-autonomy forces that displaced three-quarters of the population and destroyed the majority of the country's infrastructure.[10] Subsequently, a series of international interventions with peacekeeping and state-building mandates were deployed.

In 2001, Timor-Leste elected a Constituent Assembly, followed by the adoption of a constitution and presidential elections in 2002. With overwhelming support, former resistance leader Xanana Gusmão was elected as Timor-Leste's first president on May 20, 2002, marking Timor-Leste's Independence Day.[11] Independence, however, meant that the new government, supported by international missions, had to build intelligence and security structures and engage in a process of disarmament, demobilization, and reintegration (DDR) of former resistance fighters. The way in which this process was implemented contributed to the 2006 crisis that saw another deployment of an Australian-led stabilization force named Operation Astute.

INTELLIGENCE AND SECURITY INSTITUTIONS

Present-day Timor-Leste has three services that perform security tasks: the military Falintil-Timor-Leste Defense Forces (Falintil-Forças de Defesa de Timor-Leste, F-FDTL),[12] the National Police of Timor-Leste (Polícia Nacional de Timor-Leste, PNTL), and the National Intelligence Service (Serviço Nacional de Inteligência, SNI).[13] Both the military and the national police have their own intelligence services, the Military Intelligence System (Sistema de Informações Militares, SIM) and the Police Intelligence Service (Serviço de Informações da Polícia, SIP), respectively. In 2009 the SNI replaced the postindependence National Service for State Security (Serviço Nacional de Segurança do Estado), which was accused of being used as a tool for partisan politics.[14]

Law 3/2009 created the SNI, which has competence over the entire territorial space of Timor-Leste.[15] It falls under the direct responsibility of the prime minister. The SNI is the only governmental agency charged with producing intelligence to safeguard national independence, national interests, and external security, as well as ensure internal security in preventing sabotage, terrorism, espionage, organized crime, and acts that by their nature may alter or destroy the constitutionally established rule of law.[16] The SNI has an internal and an external intelligence department,[17] yet it does not have any powers to arrest or prosecute.[18] The SNI is led by a director general who is appointed in consultation with the president.[19] Neutrality of the director general is safeguarded by the fact that they may not be affiliated with any political party, nor with any political activities.[20] SNI staff are also prohibited from holding political party positions and participating in political party activities.[21] This is an important step in depoliticizing the intelligence culture in Timor-Leste.

HOW SECURITY CULTURE SHAPED INTELLIGENCE

While the security sector in Timor-Leste is relatively young, three issues profoundly impacted the culture within its institutions and the wider population. The security sector of Timor-Leste had to tackle a lack of delineation in tasks and politicization that is rooted in historic events. Because of this politicization, Timorese citizens have low levels of trust in the state's security institutions. Finally, as a young nation developing its governance and executive institutions, Timor-Leste has been vulnerable to exploitation.

The flawed DDR process in Timor-Leste ignited an outbreak of violence in 2006 that saw the return of an international armed intervention to restore the peace. The direct spark that lit the flame of the 2006 crisis was the dismissal of 591 members (about 40 percent) of the armed forces, the "petitioners," which also drew a response and resulted in the subsequent disintegration of the PNTL, but the roots of this dispute go further back.[22] Upon independence old west-east rivalries in Timor-Leste (the "Loromonu-Lorosae" divide) resurfaced, especially as popular belief held that the Loromonu contributed less to the 1975–1999 resistance than the Lorosae.[23] When the new defense force, which would later become the F-FDTL, was being established in 2001, commanders of the Falintil guerilla force were put in charge of DDR decisions and recruitment, resulting in a force predominantly made up of Lorosae ex-combatants.[24] This process was viewed as biased toward supporters of former Falintil member President Gusmão, fueling the existing antagonism.[25] Complaints of discrimination soon began to surface.[26]

In the same year, the PNTL was officially formed, but here too recruitment led to controversy as the United Nations Transitional Administration in East Timor (UNTAET), mandated to provide an interim civil administration until Timor-Leste's independence, decided to recruit officers who had served with the Indonesian National Police, leading to concerns about putting those responsible for atrocities during the occupation in charge of policing.[27] The perception that PNTL was better equipped and funded than the F-FDTL was cause for further resentment while the politicization of the F-FDLT partially elicited the decision to militarize the PNTL to counterbalance the other.[28] To illustrate this animosity, prior to the 2006 crisis, nearly three-quarters of all F-FDTL disciplinary cases involved confrontations with PNTL members.[29] Furthermore, many ex-combatants were dissatisfied about not being able to secure employment within the F-FDTL or the PNTL and were easily exploited by those with personal agendas.[30] For example, many Martial Arts Groups–affiliated gangs that exist in Timor-Leste today recruited them. Thus, the pre-independence division in the Timorese society was institutionalized in the security sector in the first years after independence.[31]

The 2006 crisis started in early January when F-FDTL members submitted a petition alleging discrimination and poor living conditions to their chief, Brigadier General Taur Matan Ruak, and to their commander in chief, President Gusmão. In February, the petitioners decided to leave their barracks, resulting in the chief dismissing 591 F-FDTL members, the "petitioners," who represent nearly half of the F-FDTL. Violence escalated over the months that followed, which also exposed the internal rift within the PNTL, disintegrating the force in the process and leaving the country on the brink of civil war. By June 26, Prime Minister Mari Alkatiri, caving to political pressure, resigned, and the first 3,200 stabilization troops arrived in Dili. At least 37 people lost their lives in the uprising, while 155,000 were internally displaced due to the violence. On August 25, 2006, the United Nations Integrated Mission in Timor-Leste (UNMIT) was established.[32]

The petitioners' crisis and the disintegration of the PNTL marked the need for security sector reform in Timor-Leste. UNMIT's mandate included a dedicated security sector reform unit, and the United Nations Police (UNPOL) had a direct capacity-building role. One of the efforts toward professionalizing the PNTL was to have its officers work under the mentorship of UNPOL until a policing district was deemed ready for handover, which effectively put PNTL back in charge while receiving backup from UNPOL.[33] The professionalization efforts, however, barely touched upon the intrinsic problems within the PNTL, including its politicization.[34] Furthermore, the delineation of responsibilities between the PNTL and the (peacetime) F-FDTL was not well established.[35] The antagonistic relationship between the two institutions was compounded by the UNTAET decision that border control would fall within the remit of the PNTL, leaving the F-FDTL with a severely diminished role to play in the day-to-day external security of Timor-Leste and a lack of purpose for the garrisoned, often-bored soldiers.[36]

Further compounding the image of a politicized security sector, Timor-Leste's first intelligence agency, the National Service for State Security, was disbanded after complaints of it being used as a partisan tool by the prime minster.[37] Its successor, the SNI, had to overcome the politicized reputation that stuck to all security sector institutions. After a 2008 assassination attempt on President Ramos-Horta and now Prime Minister Gusmão, Operation Halibur saw the establishment of a joint F-FDTL-PNTL command to catch the perpetrators and simultaneously build trust between the F-FDTL and the PNTL.[38] This arrangement helped defuse some of the F-FDTL-PNTL tension and the possibility for future joint commands in cases of national crisis was solidified in the Law on National Security in 2010.[39]

The history of security institutions spying on Timorese citizens and the politicization of the F-FDTL and the PNTL resulted in low levels of civilian trust in the sector. By staffing the PNTL with former *Indonesian* police, the UN's attempt to quickly form a police force led the PNTL to suffer from the Indonesian police's poor example and the stigma of having helped the occupying force.[40] Former resistance fighters who were now part of the police also lacked trust in their PNTL colleagues.[41] This resulted in a "conflicting informal network and party affiliation," which led "to a permanent instability within the Timorese police."[42] Gang affiliation of PNTL officers also contributed to the instability. These internal issues all compounded the 2006 crisis.[43]

The history of informants placed in villages meant that intelligence gathering was extremely difficult, including for foreign peacekeeping units, due to the deep-seated mistrust in security authorities.[44] While the UN, in its various iterations, attempted to instill the idea of community policing into the PNTL through a miscellany of approaches, the Timorese political leadership favored a heavily armed police force.[45] This militarization was both "the dominant culture of policing in Timor-Leste which has been heavily influenced by the Indonesian military during the time of occupation" and an attempt to counterbalance the F-FDTL.[46] The PNTL Organic Law (09/2009) aimed at reforming the PNTL did not change this vision. It did include a small department for community policing, though it was heavily understaffed and lacking in specialized knowledge, most likely reflecting the level of commitment of the Timorese leadership to this endeavor at the time.[47]

When years of training by international community donors did not yield many tangible results nor improve the community's trust in the PNTL, New Zealand deployed two complementing training programs that actively involved community councils and local leaders to better inform citizens about police responsibilities.[48] By encouraging policing contingents to closely interact with traditional dispute resolution mechanisms at the local level, the PNTL established Community Policing Councils and created specialist roles for officers tasked with community liaison duties.[49] In this way, police officers stationed in villages were viewed less through the lens of the Japanese surveillance spectrum but more as an extension of traditional and trusted institutions. Surveyed communities that had this system implemented reported "an increased satisfaction regarding community police relations."[50] The commitment to community policing stuck, and this initiative has since taken root throughout the country.

As for vulnerability, one of the key incidents demonstrating outside meddling was a spying scandal that involved the Australian government.[51] As a small nation with relatively few natural resources and a need to develop, Timor-Leste had to negotiate trade and territorial deals after independence in order to safeguard both fishery and offshore natural resources such as oil and gas reserves. The delineation of the coastal exclusive economic zone (EEZ) of Timor-Leste was subject to bitter negotiations with Australia, finally concluding in the ratification of the Timor Sea Treaty (TST) in early 2003.[52] While the TST created "a revenue-sharing arrangement," it did not establish maritime boundaries between Timor-Leste and Australia.[53] For this, further negotiations were necessary that began in 2004.[54] The negotiations caused an outcry during publication in 2013 because Australia had used the Australian Secret Intelligence Service (ASIS) to gain the upper hand.[55] Australia allegedly made the assessment that its "national security, foreign relations or *economic well-being*" [emphasis added] were threatened by an independent Timor-Leste laying claim to parts of the Timor Sea.[56]

It has been suggested that the case came to light after a witness complained to the Australian intelligence oversight body, the Inspector-General of Intelligence and Security.[57] "Witness K" was concerned that "intelligence assets were being diverted from the War on Terror to the Dili operation."[58] This occurred in the context of Australia stepping up its activities in the region particularly to combat Jemaah Islamiyah, an extremist group with links to al-Qaeda, on the heels of the 9/11 attacks in the United States, the 2002 Bali bombing, and the 2004 bombing of Australia's embassy in Jakarta.[59] At the time of writing (February 2021), Witness K is being prosecuted on charges of "conspiring to reveal classified information" in closed court.[60]

Australia allegedly used the renovation of Timorese government offices under an Australian aid program as cover for ASIS officers to install listening devices, including in the offices used by the intelligence agency.[61] There are indications that Australia's intelligence agencies also recruited informants.[62]

In January 2006, the Treaty on Certain Maritime Arrangements in the Timor Sea (CMATS) was signed, echoing the Timor Gap Treaty maritime boundaries, which were unfavorable for Timor-Leste in comparison to equidistance principle favored in international arbitration of maritime boundaries.[63] When the Timor-Leste political leadership became aware of the spying, it waited for an opportune moment to leverage this information to quietly bring Australia back to the negotiation table without losing face under the guise of a termination clause in the treaty.[64] When Australia denied wrongdoing, Timor-Leste started confidential proceedings at the Permanent Court of Arbitration in order to have the treaty declared void on the basis that Australia had acted in bad faith.[65] On May 3, 2013, the Australian government made the controversy public and further discredited itself in the public eye by searching the offices and residences of both Witness K and their lawyer.[66]

Timor-Leste used a number of international legal and arbitration instruments to bring Australia back to the negotiation table, eventually securing a more favorable sea boundary delineation.[67] While the page was officially turned, the relationship between Australia and Timor-Leste suffered.[68] Moreover, the fact that Australia has brought charges to Witness K for blowing the whistle does not solidify confidence in Australia's assurances that it has not and will not resort to using its intelligence agency for economic gain.[69]

INTELLIGENCE AND SECURITY PARTNERSHIPS

As a small and new nation, Timor-Leste is dependent on partnerships with aligned countries to achieve its strategic goals. Given the fact that the SNI is only about a decade old, intelligence in particular, but also military and policing assistance in general, are priorities for Timor-Leste. This section explores some of the partnerships already in place and those that Timor-Leste would like to develop to join in intelligence sharing with neighboring countries.

Membership of the Association of Southeast Asian Nations (ASEAN) is a key strategic goal for increased defense cooperation with states in the Southeast Asian region. Timor-Leste submitted a formal membership application in 2011.[70] One of the particular benefits of ASEAN membership is the opportunity to partake in the association's Our Eyes initiative intelligence-sharing structure.[71] Our Eyes was initiated by Indonesia as a strategic counterterrorism information exchange among six of the ASEAN countries in early 2018.[72] An ASEAN-wide concept paper, adopted in October 2018, cited the increasingly transnational character of threats facing the region as the reason for establishing the initiative and allowing all members to participate.[73]

The main objective of the Our Eyes initiative is to "enhance strategic information-sharing" and to "share expertise and resources (including technology and experiences)."[74] Particularly for smaller countries, intelligence sharing can have benefits in that it shares the workload and cost among the partners and can diminish the need for national expertise where such knowledge or resources can be accessed through collaboration.[75]

Furthermore, ASEAN membership would allow Timor-Leste to participate in military exercises including those that are focused on maritime border security.[76] ASEAN membership is also likely to open more bilateral opportunities for joint exercises and training as well as enable formal and informal meetings at the level of defense ministers.[77]

ASEAN is not the only multilateral structure with an intelligence branch that Timor-Leste is interested in, however. Timor-Leste hosted the XVI Plenary Meeting of Directors-General and Meeting of Experts of the CPLP Information and Intelligence Services Forum in 2014.[78] The Community of Portuguese-Speaking Countries (Comunidade dos Países de Língua Portuguesa, CPLP) comprises nine members. Timor-Leste has been taking advantage of the opportunities that the CPLP provides to train its intelligence officers abroad, including attendance at intelligence seminars in Brazil.[79]

While multilateral organizations such as ASEAN and CPLP can provide the benefits of scale, bilateral cooperation has also been beneficial to Timor-Leste in terms of receiving training abroad. The governmental budget for 2019 shows that funds were approved to send SNI officers for specialized training to Australia for operations and leadership training and to Indonesia for counterterrorism and organized crime training.[80] Due to Timor-Leste's geography, security ties with Indonesia and Australia are prioritized, as the latter is Timor-Leste's largest security partner.[81] Moreover, China, Japan, and India are also important bilateral partners.[82]

The Philippines is another regional player with whom Timor-Leste has built increasingly close defense ties, including a formal cooperation agreement signed in 2008.[83] Military assistance that Timor-Leste receives from the Philippines focuses predominantly on capacity building for the F-FDTL.[84] In 2013, a specific mechanism for bilateral cooperation at the foreign affairs level was also created, which includes "military consultations and intelligence sharing."[85]

Interestingly and despite the 1975–1999 occupation, Indonesia is an important partner for Timor-Leste. Officers from Timor-Leste train, for example, at the Indonesian Staff and Command College.[86] As early as 2012, a memorandum was signed on security cooperation, military support, and training.[87] This does not mean that the relationship is without challenges, however. Both the maritime boundaries as well as a small portion of the land border around the Timor-Leste's enclave of Oecussi remains disputed even though joint patrols are conducted in the area.[88]

Finally, Malaysia is another key partner in the region. Malaysia's involvement in Timor-Leste goes back to the first UN mission for which it made troops available, as it did for subsequent missions, ranking as the top contributing country of police forces to UNMIT.[89] F-FDTL officers have been able to attend numerous courses as part of the Defense Cooperation Program while Malaysia has also engaged in capacity building of the PNTL.[90]

CONCLUSION

Politicization has been the root cause of distrust and violence over the past decades in Timor-Leste. Though the country has made steps toward the professionalization of the security institutions, this remains a significant issue in the country's intelligence culture and must remain high on the agenda. While politicization is an internal issue, it detracts from Timor-Leste's ability to counter threats. That is not to say that the Australian spying scandal would not have occurred if Timor-Leste was less politicized—after all, the intelligence sector in the country is still in its infancy. The scandal, however, demonstrates that Timor-Leste faces a variety of external threats that must be addressed by a security sector, including an intelligence service focused on detecting and neutralizing operations by foreign adversaries and countering regional threats, not on political turf wars. Politicization affects readiness, and that is not a luxury Timor-Leste can afford. Indeed, then prime minister and minister of defense and security Xanana Gusmão, reflecting on his time in the resistance, insinuated that division and an emphasis on internal security had made Timor-Leste vulnerable to the Indonesian invasion, something that should be avoided in the future.[91] Additionally, if Timor-Leste wants ASEAN membership, it must demonstrate to the current ASEAN partners that it can be relied upon to tackle regional threats.

Finally, Timor-Leste needs to build lasting partnerships that are mutually beneficial and professionalize its security sector, including its intelligence agency. While some scholars feel that truth and justice were sacrificed for a good relationship with Indonesia, the relationship has been beneficial in terms of gaining access to much-needed training of Timorese officers and avoiding border confrontations.[92] As Timor-Leste is a relatively small player diplomatically, however, it may be difficult to obtain a much-coveted "seat at the table," for example, by gaining ASEAN membership. The risk is that Timor-Leste will fall prey to countries who are buying influence, access to resources, or geostrategic positions under the guise of development support, as China is known to be doing. Former president Ramos-Horta does not believe his country is succumbing to greater Chinese influence, for example, but warned Australia, Japan, and the United States that Timor-Leste might look for other partners elsewhere if they did not provide the necessary support.[93]

Timor-Leste has a long way to go to break the grip of partisan politics on its intelligence culture. While off to a good start, it remains to be seen if the SNI can maintain independence from politics as prescribed in its founding documents. The fact that there was a perceived need to explicitly legislate for nonpartisan leadership signals a step forward.

NOTES

1. The views presented here are solely my own. Heartfelt thanks to John Symons for offering his insights and comments on an earlier draft on this chapter and to a former member of the UNMIT mission and another commentator who wish to remain anonymous for their insights and comments.

2. "Global Operations, Timor-Leste," Australian Government, Department of Defence, accessed March 27, 2021, https://www.defence.gov.au/Operations/Past Operations/timorleste/commitment.asp.

3. Deniz Kocak, "On the Spatial-Temporal Diffusion of Community-Based Policing from Japan to Peninsula Southeast Asia: The Case of Timor-Leste," *Journal of Intervention and Statebuilding* 13, no. 1 (January 2019): 28–29.

4. Kocak, "On the Spatial-Temporal Diffusion of Community-Based Policing," 29–30.

5. Kocak, "On the Spatial-Temporal Diffusion of Community-Based Policing," 29–30.

6. Kocak, "On the Spatial-Temporal Diffusion of Community-Based Policing," 30.

7. Kocak, "On the Spatial-Temporal Diffusion of Community-Based Policing," 30.

8. *Chega! Report of the CAVR* (Dili: Commission for Reception, Truth, and Reconciliation Timor-Leste, 2005), 13.

9. Darya Pushkina and Philip Maier, "United Nations Peacekeeping in Timor-Leste," *Civil Wars* 14, no. 3 (September 2012): 329.

10. Pushkina and Maier, "United Nations Peacekeeping in Timor-Leste," 329.

11. Pushkina and Maier, "United Nations Peacekeeping in Timor-Leste," 330.

12. Falintil refers to the Armed Forces for the National Liberation of East Timor (Forças Armadas de Libertação Nacional de Timor-Leste), the main guerilla movement resisting Indonesian occupation.

13. Aurel Croissant and Philip Lorenz, *Comparative Politics of Southeast Asia: An Introduction to Governments and Political Regimes* (Cham: Springer International, 2018), 355–56.

14. Scott Gilmore, "The Time I Started a Spy Agency," *Maclean's*, February 9, 2015, https://www.macleans.ca/politics/worldpolitics/the-time-i-started-a-spy-agency/.

15. Article 6, Decreto Lei 3/2009, Serviço Nacional de Inteligência, 2008, https://www.sni.gov.tl/decreto-lei-3-2009-servico-nacional-de-inteligencia/.

16. Article 3, Decreto Lei 3/2009.

17. Article 13, Decreto Lei 3/2009.

18. Article 4, Decreto Lei 3/2009.

19. Article 9, Decreto Lei 3/2009.

20. Article 11, Decreto Lei 3/2009.

21. Article 17, Decreto Lei 3/2009 I; Article 19, Decreto Lei 3/2009.

22. Sven Gunnar Simonsen, "The Role of East Timor's Security Institutions in National Integration—and Disintegration," *Pacific Review* 22, no. 5 (November 3, 2009): 576.

23. Simonsen, "The Role of East Timor's Security Institutions," 578.

24. Simonsen, "The Role of East Timor's Security Institutions," 579.

25. Alberto Dal Poz, "'Buying Peace' in Timor-Leste: Another UN-Success Story?," *Peace Human Rights Governance* 2, no. 07/2018 (2018): 195.

26. Simonsen, "The Role of East Timor's Security Institutions," 578.

27. Simonsen, "The Role of East Timor's Security Institutions," 579.

28. Simonsen, "The Role of East Timor's Security Institutions," 580; Dal Poz, "'Buying Peace' in Timor-Leste," 195.

29. Simonsen, "The Role of East Timor's Security Institutions," 585.

30. Simonsen, "The Role of East Timor's Security Institutions," 580.

31. Dal Poz, "'Buying Peace' in Timor-Leste," 195–96.

32. Simonsen, "The Role of East Timor's Security Institutions," 580–81.

33. Kocak, "On the Spatial-Temporal Diffusion of Community-Based Policing," 32.

34. Simonsen, "The Role of East Timor's Security Institutions," 587.

35. Simonsen, "The Role of East Timor's Security Institutions," 588.

36. Simonsen, "The Role of East Timor's Security Institutions," 588.

37. Gilmore, "The Time I Started a Spy Agency."

38. Resolução Do Governo 3/2008 (2008).

39. Lei 2/2010, Segurança Nacional, 2010, https://www.sni.gov.tl/lei-2-2010 -seguranca-nacional/.

40. Andrew Goldsmith, "'It Wasn't Like Normal Policing': Voices of Australian Police Peacekeepers in Operation Serene, Timor-Leste 2006," *Policing and Society* 19, no. 2 (June 2009): 128; Natalie Sambhi, "Finding Partners: Timor-Leste's Evolving Security Ties with Southeast Asia," *Maritime Dispute Resolution and the Future of the Asian Order* (Pell Center for International Relations and Public Policy, Salve Regina University, May 2019), 3.

41. Kocak, "On the Spatial-Temporal Diffusion of Community-Based Policing," 31.

42. Kocak, "On the Spatial-Temporal Diffusion of Community-Based Policing," 31.

43. Kocak, "On the Spatial-Temporal Diffusion of Community-Based Policing," 32.

44. Goldsmith, "'It Wasn't Like Normal Policing,'" 128.

45. Kocak, "On the Spatial-Temporal Diffusion of Community-Based Policing," 32.

46. Kocak, "On the Spatial-Temporal Diffusion of Community-Based Policing," 33; Dal Poz, "'Buying Peace' in Timor-Leste," 195.

47. Kocak, "On the Spatial-Temporal Diffusion of Community-Based Policing," 33.

48. Kocak, "On the Spatial-Temporal Diffusion of Community-Based Policing," 33–34.

49. Kocak, "On the Spatial-Temporal Diffusion of Community-Based Policing," 34.

50. Kocak, "On the Spatial-Temporal Diffusion of Community-Based Policing," 35.

51. This case was described at length in Bernard Collaery, *Oil under Troubled Water* (Melbourne: Melbourne University Press, 2020).

52. David Mercer, "Dividing Up the Spoils: Australia, East Timor and the Timor Sea," *Space and Polity* 8, no. 3 (December 2004): 290.

53. Kim McGrath, "Drawing the Line: Witness K and the Ethics of Spying," *Australian Foreign Affairs*, no. 9 (July 2020): 62.

54. McGrath, "Drawing the Line," 63.

55. McGrath, "Drawing the Line," 70–71.

56. McGrath, "Drawing the Line," 63.

57. "The Role of the IGIS," Inspector-General of Intelligence and Security, 2021, https://www.igis.gov.au/about/the-role-of-the-igis.

58. McGrath, "Drawing the Line," 63.

59. McGrath, "Drawing the Line," 63–65.

60. McGrath, "Drawing the Line," 54–55.

61. McGrath, "Drawing the Line," 65; Kate Lamb, "Timor-Leste v Australia: What Each Country Stands to Lose," *The Guardian*, January 23, 2014, https://www.theguardian.com/world/2014/jan/23/timor-leste-v-australia-analysis.

62. McGrath, "Drawing the Line," 66.

63. For a discussion on the legal interpretation of the equidistance principle in the Australia / Timor-Leste case, see Stephen Grenville, "East Timor Maritime Boundary: The 'Equidistance' Principle," *The Interpreter*, February 24, 2016, https://www.lowyinstitute.org/the-interpreter/east-timor-maritime-boundary-equidistance-principle; McGrath, "Drawing the Line," 67.

64. McGrath, "Drawing the Line," 67–69.

65. McGrath, "Drawing the Line," 70.

66. McGrath, "Drawing the Line," 70.

67. McGrath, "Drawing the Line," 71–73.

68. Sambhi, "Finding Partners," 4.

69. McGrath, "Drawing the Line," 73–74.

70. Sambhi, "Finding Partners," 3.

71. Sambhi, "Finding Partners," 6.

72. "2018 'Our Eyes' Initiative Concept Paper," ASEAN, October 19, 2018, https://cil.nus.edu.sg/databasecil/2018-our-eyes-initiative-concept-paper/.

73. "2018 'Our Eyes' Initiative Concept Paper."

74. "2018 'Our Eyes' Initiative Concept Paper."

75. Agnes E. Venema, "The Sum of All Friends: Improving Cross-Border Intelligence Sharing in Europe: The Case of the Benelux," *International Journal of Intelligence, Security, and Public Affairs* 22, no. 1 (January 2, 2020): 9–10.

76. Sambhi, "Finding Partners," 6.

77. Sambhi, "Finding Partners," 6.

78. "Reunião do Fórum da CPLP em Díli," Serviço Nacional de Inteligência, 2021, https://www.sni.gov.tl/reuniao-do-forum-da-cplp-em-dili/.

79. "Orçamento Geral do Estado 2019—Livro 2," República Democrática de Timor-Leste, Ministério das Finanças, 2019, 130, https://www.mof.gov.tl/wp-content/uploads/2019/04/Final_BB2_Port.pdf.

80. "Orçamento Geral do Estado 2019—Livro 2," 130–31.

81. "Timor-Leste Country Brief," Australian Government, Department of Foreign Affairs and Trade, 2021, https://www.dfat.gov.au/geo/timor-leste/timor-leste-country-brief?fbclid=IwAR3nASsgDEp-u7BzsaXpIyqAXN9sozvKEsMMpcx8S4Q2MEiPHELAIvzHZMs.

82. Sambhi, "Finding Partners," 2.

83. Sambhi, "Finding Partners," 5.

84. Sambhi, "Finding Partners," 6.

85. Sambhi, "Finding Partners," 5.

86. Sambhi, "Finding Partners," 4.

87. Rebecca Strating, "East Timor's Emerging National Security Agenda: Establishing 'Real' Independence," *Asian Security* 9, no. 3 (September 2013): 187.

88. Sambhi, "Finding Partners," 5.

89. Sambhi, "Finding Partners," 5.

90. Sambhi, "Finding Partners," 5.

91. Strating, "East Timor's Emerging National Security Agenda," 186–87.

92. Strating, "East Timor's Emerging National Security Agenda," 194.

93. Sambhi, "Finding Partners," 4.

28

Turkmenistan: Analysis of an Enigmatic Intelligence Culture

Réjeanne Lacroix

Turkmenistan is a unitary one-party presidential republic located in Central Asia. It shares land borders with Afghanistan, Iran, Kazakhstan, and Uzbekistan, as well as coastal territory on the Caspian Sea. Turkmenia—as the state is also known—is often acknowledged to have the fourth-largest supply of natural gas reserves in the world.[1] Consequently, much discussion centers on the Turkmen energy industry and its partnerships. Strategically located, Turkmenistan has been at the center of trade routes and cultural interactions for centuries that have later transitioned into geopolitical significance in the contemporary period. A vibrant history marked by dynamic tribal, interethnic, and colonial influences certainly has shaped the development of the modern conception of Turkmenistan and fashioned its intelligence culture.

This chapter has four parts. The first section introduces Turkmenistan's history and lays out the chapter's argument that the country's national intelligence culture is an eclectic combination of history, strongman politics, and international relations. In the second part, it focuses on intelligence history with attention to the mixture of Soviet structures and local culture. The third section focuses on issues specific to Turkmenistan, which include its unique combination of Soviet past, political system, and internationally recognized neutral status. Finally, the chapter highlights the absence of intelligence oversight, limited intelligence reform and international connections.

BACKGROUND

The territory that came to be known as Turkmenistan experienced early history typical of nomadic groups that populated the Central Asian steppes.

Centuries of cross-cultural interactions, such as Arab invaders who brought Islam, the expansion of nomadic agrarian Turkic Oghuz tribes that resulted in the creation of steppe empires, and intertribal conflicts have all left their mark on the subsequent development of Turkmen identity and culture. In regard to the development of the modern Turkmen state, however, the era of Russian imperialism in Central Asia commenced by tsarist forces in the nineteenth century, and the later formation of the Union of Soviet Socialist Republics (USSR) in 1922, is most profound.

In 1881, the Battle of Geok Tepe resulted in a tsarist victory over Teke Turkomens that concluded Russian expansion into Central Asia. Scholars have acknowledged that the consequential involvement of the Russian Empire led to long-lasting changes not only for the region that would later become modern Turkmenistan but also for the local population.[2] Further, historians have argued that Russian officials managing the affairs in the far-flung exotic colonies of Central Asia ensured only conservative Islamic education and traditional social arrangements remained entrenched as a way to prevent the infiltration of outside ideologies that could have led to rebellion.[3] This remains relevant for the study of modern Turkmenistan and its governance.

Modern Turkmenistan, as it is recognized in contemporary scholarship, is undeniably formed in the period during the Russian Revolution (1917–1923) and the subsequent creation of the Soviet Union. A transition of governance from an amalgamation of Turkestan Kray, the Emirate of Bukhara, and the Khanate of Khiva to the Turkestan Autonomous Soviet Socialist Republic (ASSR) (April 30, 1918–October 27, 1924) marked the first geographical arrangement in the journey of the modern nation. The October 1924 dissolution of the Turkestan ASSR resulted in the creation of the Kara-Kyrgyz Autonomous Oblast (now Kyrgyzstan and a section of Uzbekistan), Tajik ASSR (replaced by the Tajik Soviet Socialist Republic in 1929), Uzbek SSR, and the Turkmen SSR—the Soviet Socialist Republic relevant to this analysis.

Power in the Soviet Union was concentrated in Moscow, but its regional republics maintained functional organs to ensure that the massive union of diverse ethnicities united under a centralized government. This had a lasting effect on governance and the formation of intelligence agencies in Central Asia. In fact, Russian influence "was further reinforced during the seventy years of the Soviet Union, which although denounced today by the authorities of independent Turkmenistan, enabled the country to form a modern nation."[4] The Soviet Union underwent birth pangs in the creation of intelligence agencies and secret police forces that resulted in a succession of relevant agencies, but the Committee for State Security (Komitet Gosudarstvennoy Bezopasnosti, KGB) remains the last, most prominent example. Consequently, the national intelligence culture in modern Turkmenistan should be examined in the context of the KGB's local offices that helped provide Turkmenistan with the means for modern intelligence collection and operations.

When the Soviet Union collapsed in 1991, Turkmenistan gained independence as a sovereign state for the first time in its history. First, the secretary of the Turkmen Communist Party, Saparmurat Niyazov, assumed the role as the first president of the new country. Niyazov—often referred to as *Türkmenbaşy* or Head of the Turkmen—installed a unique highly centralized government system that revolved around his personal interests that eventually led to the 1999 decision by the influential legislative branch known as the Mejilis (Assembly of Turkmenistan) to declare him president for life. Under Niyazov, Turkmenistan adopted a foreign policy concept of "permanent neutrality"; however, the Sovietization of the government apparatus and intelligence agencies was entrenched, and intelligence collection and analysis continued operations in this earlier character. The Turkmen KGB became the Committee for National Security (KNB) and, later in 2002, was revamped as the Ministry of National Security.

Niyazov passed away in 2006. Gurbanguly Berdymukhamedov—also known as *Arkadag* or Protector—became the second leader of independent Turkmenistan. The government system installed by his predecessor remains, though some general reforms have been implemented. In regard to intelligence culture, Berdymukhamedov has mostly kept the functions of the Ministry of National Security unchanged but altered its personnel and leadership. Therefore, it is safe to conclude that intelligence culture in Turkmenistan continues to operate in line with its Soviet roots.

This chapter argues that the nation of Turkmenistan has been shaped by the role of Soviet bureaucracy in its national security apparatus development, but it remains an eccentric case study in the decades since its independence. Intelligence culture has certainly been shaped by the KGB's influence and history, but the unitary one-party presidential system also contributes to how intelligence functions, is reformed, and is managed in the Central Asian country. These are relevant points for consideration as Turkmenistan has entered into a new era where the regional security environment is focused on issues such as transnational crime, Islamist extremism, and the competing interests of major regional powers.

HISTORY OF INTELLIGENCE IN TURKMENISTAN

It is general knowledge that during the Soviet Union KGB headquarters were located in Moscow—approximately 3,590 kilometers (about 2,230 miles) from the Turkmen capital of Ashgabat—and the creation of regional offices in the relevant republics was necessary to penetrate areas of the vast Soviet Union. The KGB was a highly centralized agency that practiced a top-down leadership style, which was also implemented in the local offices of constituent republics.

Not only was the agency charged with intelligence collection, analysis, and counterintelligence to ensure national security and the diffusion of Communist ideology abroad, it acted as the secret police. The KGB's introduction to the operational affairs of the Turkmen SSR ushered in the official commencement of intelligence activities in contemporary Turkmenistan. As a result of the installation of regional offices that operated in the same manner across the union, large numbers of KGB-trained intelligence officers remain active in the former Soviet republics, Turkmenistan included.[5] This resulted not only in the lingering effects of a Soviet ethos across numerous intelligence agencies but also a standard of high training and competency. Furthermore, Turkmen intelligence continues to emulate the structure, recruitment strategies, and training that was apprehended during the Soviet period.[6] This was especially evident when the law "On the Organs of State Security of the USSR" seamlessly transitioned as the 1993 legislation "On Organs of the National Security of Turkmenistan"—a document very similar to that of the fallen empire.[7] Therefore, the Soviet experience in the modern development of Turkmenistan is intrinsic to the intelligence culture that has fomented in the Central Asian state.

After the Soviet Union's dissolution, Niyazov supervised the creation of the National Security Committee (KNB) in September 1991. Its responsibilities were nearly identical to that of its KGB forbearers insofar that it was charged with the gathering of foreign intelligence, counterintelligence activities, and the investigation of serious crimes.[8] Due to the professionalism required of the past regime, Turkmen intelligence in the form of the KNB was still regarded as efficient and capable of their tasks. Nonetheless, a new sphere of responsibility materialized in the dawn of the newly independent Turkmen state, and it focused on the preservation of Niyazov as well as his interests. The first Turkmen president bestowed greater powers to the KNB, such as the ability to surveil private citizens and to strongly interfere with opposition forces, and it became an even more formidable force in the supervision of Turkmen society. Simply put, the office of the presidency had to be protected at all costs, including the infringement of personal freedoms of citizens.

Niyazov slightly reformed the Turkmen security sector in 2002. On March 16, the Turkmen president for life stated his intention to improve intelligence and security services in the country since the KNB had grown so powerful that it could not be held accountable to anyone.[9] This commenced a significant purge in which "more than 60 KNB employees, including 36 members of senior staff, were dismissed, demoted or handed down prison sentences for a multitude of crimes, including abuse of power, bribe-taking, drug-trafficking, torture and premediated murder."[10] The charges and convictions demonstrate the ethos of the Turkmen security apparatus and the autonomy with which it operated. Niyazov further expressed that ministries and responsibilities would be broken up insofar as matters of national security would be managed by the security services while issues related to law enforcement (theft, fraud, and drug trafficking) would become responsibilities of the Ministry of Internal Affairs.[11]

It was during the same year that the KNB was reestablished as the Ministry of National Security (MNB). Scholars have summarized Turkmen constitutional legislation in outlining the vast responsibilities and powers of the MNB, such as intelligence and counterintelligence activities; operational searches and investigations; the preservation of state secrets; combatting organized crime, corruption, and drug trafficking; prevention and suppression of civic unrest as well as interethnic conflicts; and border and customs regimes.[12] Undoubtedly, this is a broad mandate that touches every aspect of governance in Turkmenistan. Thus, Turkmen intelligence services are a principal element in the political culture and engagements within the country.

Within this comprehensive directive, the MNB has some key areas of concern based on Turkmenistan's system of governance and regional affairs. For instance, the intelligence agency places a high value on any information about the president, as it is a president-centric arrangement. Complex and strained relationships with neighbors—Azerbaijan and Uzbekistan—compel Turkmen intelligence to look outside their borders and focus on any important developments in those states. This is consequently tied into problematic wider regional affairs that could technically on paper threaten the national security of Turkmenistan, such as military activities (Chinese, Iranian, and Russian maneuvers), hot wars (hostilities in Afghanistan traversing the Turkmen southeast border), the perceived growth of Islamist extremism in Central Asia (development of cells such as Islamic State—Khorasan Province), and transnational organized crime. Typical of other intelligence agencies, the MNB of Turkmenistan must keep eyes within its borders and a keen interest in affairs abroad.

The Berdymukhamedov era has continued with the MNB serving as the top intelligence agency in Turkmenistan. Regional offices can be found cross-country in the western province of Balkan, the southern province (and location of the capital) of Ahal, the northern province of Dashhowuz, and the eastern province of Lebap. While presidential preservation and protection remains the principal priority, in 2018, Berdymukhamedov advised employees of the MNB to emphasize and devote resources to the threats of

international terrorism, extremism, and drug smuggling. Further, he elabo-
rated the need for better interagency cooperation between the intelligence
agency and law enforcement.[13] The ministry continued to grow and mature
in other ways. As a means to create highly skilled and better trained intelligence professionals, the Turkmen government opened the MNB Institute in
August 2012.

While the security apparatus continues to operate as usual, Berdymukhamedov recently made staffing changes that signaled some slight reforms may
be afoot. In early 2020, the president removed the minister of national security, Yaylym Berdiyev, from the State Security Council over accusations of
underperformance in areas that were not specified.[14] A powerful figure across
Central Asia, the long-time security chief was subsequently fired from his
role as minister on February 13. It is unknown what exactly spurred these
decisions, but they were noteworthy as power in Turkmenistan is centralized
on the president and his loyalists.

This overview of Turkmen intelligence history demonstrates that it extends
its Soviet roots into the present as little overall reforms have been attempted.
President-centric systems require a security sector that concurrently focuses
on their preferred matters alongside national security threats; however, Turkmenistan presents a unique case. Its contemporary format is neither completely Soviet nor an ethnic Turkmen creation; rather, it is an amalgamation
of both relevant factors.

ISSUES SPECIFIC TO TURKMENISTAN

Turkmen national intelligence culture is an unique case study as the factors
that contribute to its foundations and functions are currently only found in
that particular state. Turkmenistan is the only country with a Soviet past, an
enigmatic president-for-life governmental system, and a status of permanent
neutrality as acknowledged by international law. Other post-Soviet Central
Asian republics may hold one or two of these variables, but in this case, they
have aggregated and shaped how intelligence is conducted in a specifically
Turkmen way. Simply put, "Turkmenistan's presidential system and status of
permanent neutrality make its security sector unique, even in the context of
Central Asia."[15] It is important to understand each variable.

First, the Sovietization of Turkmenistan laid the underpinnings of intelligence abilities and the wider security sector. Turkmen authorities and scholars hold negative views of this period; however, it was during this almost
seventy-year period that the Central Asian state quickly modernized under the
guidance of Moscow. During this period of forced modernization, Turkmen

political culture and authorities were exposed to bureaucratic systems and a security sector—points not considered in the past. Therefore, such an arrangement meant a Soviet ethos was embedded in the intelligence system. There has been no serious attempt to shun the old system, its structure, or codes of conduct, which means they will remain important elements in Turkmen intelligence culture at least in the near future.

Turkmen conservative cultural norms and adulation of the country's rich history are typical touchstones when discussions center on political messaging. The post-Soviet period is indeed one where Turkmen presidents and their loyal authorities have cultivated the narrative of Turkmen history into one that features a designated hero as a national defender and a steadfast devotion to independence. Titles such as Head of the Turkmen or Protector exemplify this concept. In turn, this has fomented a form of nationalism that is an important political vehicle, especially when a unifying national ideology is lacking. It is vital as the role of intrastate regions and tribal interests need to be considered for continued state development. For instance, it has been remarked that the project of national solidarity has the twofold responsibilities of "the unity of the tribes and gradual socio-cultural de-Russification."[16] With regard to the security sector, scholars note that intertribal relations add complexity to the understanding of Turkmen national security.[17] The question is, at what point will the process of de-Russification—or de-Sovietization—reach the entrenched bureaucracy and the intelligence agencies?

Second, the unitary one-party presidential republican system that has been in place since Turkmen independence plays a significant role in the development of a unique intelligence culture. The president-centric system shapes contemporary intelligence culture insofar as the leadership closely manages the activities of the security agencies, and often, in turn, intelligence is gathered against those who express dissent against the current political framework. It is a highly centralized system where statist principles are strongly upheld, and the president is the ultimate decisive force. Simply put, the intelligence service and law enforcement agencies answer to the president. Whether during Niyazov's or Berdymukhamedov's rule, the president has been involved in the country's inner workings. Thus, Turkmen intelligence directs much of its attention to the preservation of leadership and political stability.

Third, the internationally recognized status of permanent neutrality is yet another factor that differentiates the intelligence culture of Turkmenistan from other sovereign states. On December 12, 1995, the General Assembly of the United Nations adopted Resolution 50/80 on the conviction that the move was a positive step toward Central Asian regional security and signaled that Turkmenistan sought friendly relations across the globe.[18] This means a "permanently neutral State is forbidden from entering into alliances or treaties of guarantee that may involve it in war not involving defense of its own territory."[19] This move aligns with the statist priorities when placed in the context of political affairs and how intelligence is used in Turkmenistan.

For instance, as membership in regional security blocs is prohibited through permanent neutrality status, Turkmen intelligence agencies would not typically accrue or share intelligence data with other member states engaged in active military operations. This could prevent the dissemination of important regional knowledge in regard to specific security threats from active movements of nonstate actors to military involvement countering narcotics trafficking. It seems more appropriate for Turkmen intelligence agencies and the security sector to foster goodwill with regional powers and neighboring states to ensure access to relevant information when needed.

The combination of an imperial past, a strongman political framework, and a neutral status demonstrate that Turkmen is veritably an exceptional case study. Intelligence culture may have had its roots in the creation of a local KGB office, but since the fall of the Soviet Union, Turkmenistan has nuanced its perception of national security to include traditional security threats alongside protection of the current political arrangements. Ashgabat concentrates on matters of Islamist terrorism, extremism, and transnational crime, but intelligence responsibilities have shifted to include the interests of the president as well. Consequently, the professionally trained intelligence forces place a high regard on affairs occurring within the state, rather than those outside Turkmen borders, unless they come into conflict with the agenda of the president.

OVERSIGHT, REFORM, AND INTERNATIONAL CONNECTIONS

Intelligence community and security sector oversight is a straightforward matter in Turkmenistan. In the most elementary terms, all agencies must answer to the president, and he supervises their activities. Nonetheless, presidential powers are assisted by the role of the State Security Council—an elite body that connects high-ranking military officers, the leadership of the security services, and the prosecutorial body of the country. In simplest terms, it is understood that the "security system of Turkmenistan is formally managed through the State Security Council, which in accordance with Article 71 of the Constitution of Turkmenistan is led by the President, who also appoints and dismisses its members."[20] Constitutionally speaking, the president also holds the role of supreme commander of the armed forces and consequently has a keen interest in who holds such esteemed positions on the defense-oriented Security Council.

Turkmenistan has numerous security and defense ministries that fall under the guidance of the Security Council. For instance, the following cooperate in the overall objective of Turkmen state security: Ministry of Defense; Ministry of Internal Affairs and Law Enforcement Agencies; Ministry of National Security; Security Service of the President; State Border Guards Service; State Migration Service; and State Customs Service.[21] The diversity of agencies listed highlight a broad approach to national security and emphasize the statist principles at the center of Turkmen intelligence culture.

More broadly, reform is a relatively undiscussed topic in regard to the Turkmen intelligence services and their operations. Reform has typically manifested by way of purges of high-ranking staff for diverse reasons ranging from unsatisfactory job performance to alleged criminality. Former president Niyazov completed the most noteworthy reforms of the sector nearly two decades ago through expulsion of numerous intelligence professionals, and his successor, Berdymukhamedov, stirred discussion of a similar move after he dismissed senior leadership figures. On the other hand, Central Asian scholars posit that external forces have stifled intelligence reform in autocratic-style governments across the region. Scholars have argued that the global war on terror that commenced in 2001 delayed any possibility of such decisive actions because the threat of Islamist terrorism provided even more incentive to securitize rather than shift intelligence responsibilities.[22]

It is challenging to pinpoint any consequential intelligence-sharing relationships and cooperation for Turkmenistan. Economic agreements—primarily energy deals and transit contracts—are most demonstrative of the state of Turkmen foreign affairs, although the country is located in a geopolitically strategic region. The status of permanent neutrality undoubtedly shapes this predicament, but it is important to observe regional relationships. As a former Soviet republic, the Russian Federation "notes the importance of strategic partnership with Turkmenistan" and underlined "tackling challenges and threats to international security" as central to the bilateral relationship.[23] The two states ratified the "Agreement between the Russian Federation and Turkmenistan on Cooperation in the Area of Security" in 2020, and this document covers numerous opportunities for intelligence sharing, primarily combatting international terrorism, transnational organized crime, and narcotics trafficking.[24] Russia and Turkmenistan may not enjoy an especially close relationship, but it is evident that they work together. Ashgabat and Moscow have mutual interests that intersect at Central Asian regional security as well as advantageous energy sector opportunities.

Relations with liberal democratic states and organizations are apparent, too. For example, Turkmenistan joined the North Atlantic Treaty Organization's

(NATO) Partnership for Peace (PfP) program in 1994. Once again, the status of permanent neutrality obstructs any advanced defensive cooperation, but the intergovernmental military alliance offers educational opportunities in relevant security matters, such as practical techniques to combat terrorism, illegal trafficking issues, border security, and defense budget planning.[25] While these topics may not be directly related to intelligence practices, each of these areas requires skillful agencies to ensure national security.

Relations with the United States follow a similar pattern as engagements with NATO. The United States views Turkmenistan as strategically important as it occupies a "critical geopolitical juncture" linking Central Asia with the South Asian subcontinent.[26] Further, abundant economic prospects in the energy industry, as well as the close proximity to regional powers (and dynamic international actors) China, Iran, and Russia, undoubtedly induce American interests to seek a foothold in Turkmenistan. There are limited opportunities for intelligence cooperation so bilateral relations default to engagement over economic development and advancing regional stability. Permanent neutrality as well as pressure to amend the autocratic presidential system from liberal democratic voices mean that the United States will likely retain a minor security sector role in Turkmenistan for the foreseeable future.

CONCLUSION

Turkmenistan is a secretive society, making public information about its intelligence agencies difficult to obtain. Nonetheless, currently available sources enable the compilation of an overview about how Turkmen intelligence organs operate and the culture that leadership and security professionals have steadily fostered since independence from the Soviet Union.

Turkmen national intelligence culture can be summarized into two developmental periods. First, contemporary Turkmen intelligence continues the traditions and codes of conduct imparted by the KGB. The Soviet Union guided Turkmenistan through modernization during the twentieth century; thus certain elements of its bureaucratic organization remain in place. As a result, the contemporary Ministry of National Security retains elements of its predecessor by way of its organizational structure and operational activities. A lack of meaningful reforms since independence means that Turkmenistan will continue to conduct its intelligence activities in the model of its KGB past for the foreseeable future.

Second, the autocratic and extremely centrist approach to Turkmen governance plays a vital role in the Central Asian republic's intelligence culture. The president's ultimate power and his complete oversight result in a system where his personal security is a national security priority. Regional security threats such as Islamist terrorism, ethnic extremism, and transnational crime compel Turkmen intelligence agencies to focus on traditional security threats, but the complete protection of political security remains central to their activities. Indeed, Turkmenistan intelligence culture is an exceptional area of investigation even in the context of other Central Asian republics.

NOTES

1. İbrahim Arınç and Süleyman Elik, "Turkmenistan and Azerbaijan in European Gas Supply Security," *Insight Turkey* 12, no. 3 (2010): 169.

2. Sébastien Peyrouse, *Turkmenistan: Strategies of Power, Dilemmas of Development* (Armonk, NY: Sharpe, 2012), 24.

3. Alexandre Bennigsen and Chantal Lemercier-Quelquejay, *Islam in the Soviet Union* (London: Central Asian Research Centre, 1967), 15.

4. Peyrouse, *Turkmenistan*, 24.

5. Stéphane Lefebvre and Roger N. McDermott, "Russia and the Intelligence Services of Central Asia," *International Journal of Intelligence and CounterIntelligence* 21, no. 2 (2008): 254.

6. Lefebvre and McDermott, "Russia and the Intelligence Services," 254.

7. Grazvydas Jasutis, Richard Steyne, and Elizaveta Chmykh, *Mapping Study on the Security Sector of Turkmenistan* (Geneva: Geneva Centre for Security Sector Governance, 2020), 16, https://www.dcaf.ch/sites/default/files/publications/documents/security%20sector%20Turkmenistan%2006.07.2020.pdf.

8. Lefebvre and McDermott, "Russia and the Intelligence Services," 280.

9. Annette Bohr, "Independent Turkmenistan: From Post-communism to Sultanism," in *Oil, Security and Transition in Central Asia*, ed. Sally Cummings (London: Routledge, 2002), 12.

10. Bohr, "Independent Turkmenistan," 12.

11. Jasutis, Steyne, and Chmykh, *Mapping Study*, 16.

12. Jasutis, Steyne, and Chmykh, *Mapping Study*, 16.

13. Jasutis, Steyne, and Chmykh, *Mapping Study*, 16.

14. "Turkmenistan's Leader Fires His Longtime Security Chief," AP News, February 13, 2020, https://apnews.com/article/a957eb672ca4704bad740b5e2bbbb6dd.

15. Darko Stancic, foreword to *Mapping Study on the Security Sector of Turkmenistan* (Geneva: Geneva Centre for Security Sector Governance, 2020), https://www.dcaf.ch/sites/default/files/publications/documents/security%20sector%20Turkmenistan%2006.07.2020.pdf.

16. Ahmet T. Kuru, "Between the State and Cultural Zones: Nation Building in Turkmenistan," *Central Asian Survey* 21, no. 1 (2002): 72.

17. Jasutis, Steyne, and Chmykh, Mapping Study, 1.

18. United Nations, General Assembly, *Permanent Neutrality of Turkmenistan: Resolution/Adopted by the General Assembly* A/RES/50/80A, December 12, 1995. https://digitallibrary.un.org/record/284240?ln=en.

19. James Upcher, *Neutrality in Contemporary International Law* (Oxford: Oxford University Press, 2020), 4.

20. Jasutis, Steyne and Chmykh, *Mapping Study*, 1.

21. Jasutis, Steyne and Chmykh, *Mapping Study*, 1.

22. Lefebvre and McDermott, "Russia and the Intelligence Services," 252.

23. "Putin Notes Importance of Strategic Partnership with Turkmenistan," TASS. ru, September 27, 2020, https://tass.com/politics/1205567.

24. President of Russia, "Law Ratifying Russia-Turkmenistan Agreement on Security Cooperation," Kremlin.ru, November 9, 2020, http://en.kremlin.ru/catalog/keywords/82/events/64364/.

25. North Atlantic Treaty Organization, "Relations with Turkmenistan," *NATO-Topic: Relations with Turkmenistan*, September 28, 2018, https://www.nato.int/cps/en/natohq/topics_50317.htm.

26. "U.S. Relations with Turkmenistan," US Department of State, July 27, 2020, https://www.state.gov/u-s-relations-with-turkmenistan/.

29

Uzbekistan: Political Economy of the Intelligence Services

Evrim Gormus

Uzbekistan's intelligence service, the National Security Service (Sluhzba Natsionalnoy Bezopasnosti, SNB), was established on September 26, 1991. The SNB had been largely shaped by the inherited legacy of the Uzbek Republic's Committee for State Security (Komitet Gosudarstvennoy Bezopasnosti, KGB) department, and organizationally structured into three separate departments—namely, foreign intelligence (referred to as the 2nd), counterintelligence, and signals intelligence (referred to as the 6th).[1] The SNB also has its own paramilitary units and controls the Main Border Troops Directorate, but it also operates external intelligence and security activities to remove any threats outside of its borders.[2] The SNB has replicated its domestic surveillance and intelligence-gathering tactics in foreign spaces, and it has been involved in physical attacks and assassination attempts on the regime's opponents in exile. In the absence of effective institutions of governance and the rule of law, the SNB became the most powerful security institution in the country by controlling the other security organs under the rule of President Islam Karimov.

Many scholars and observers believe that the Karimov regime heavily relied on massive networks of the national security service to withstand internal and external threats, especially in the wake of the Andijan massacre in 2005. The reform process launched by President Shavkat Mirziyoyev following the death of Karimov, however, worked to curtail the SNB's power and resources. In March 2018, the SNB was renamed the State Security Service (Sluzhba Gosudarstvennoy Bezopasnosti, SGB), and its special forces were passed under the control of the Interior Ministry. This chapter analyzes the country's intelligence culture by exploring the Uzbek intelligence service's power and excesses in the context of the distorted political and economic transition process in Uzbekistan. The first part of the chapter examines the rentier relationship between the Karimov regime and the SNB and argues that the local elites and the central government agencies aligned with the SNB to extract resources and to maintain social control. In return for providing the regime with coercive instruments to eliminate internal and external threats, the SNB has been incorporated into rent-seeking activities that itself became rentier in the post-Soviet Uzbekistan. The second part of the chapter analyzes the SNB's reorganization and assesses the extent of the success and challenges in reforming intelligence service under President Mirziyoyev's rule in Uzbekistan.

THE NATIONAL SECURITY SERVICE UNDER THE KARIMOV REGIME: A PROTECTION RACKET

In the process of the Soviet Union's dissolution, the Republic of Uzbekistan declared its independence on August 31, 1991, and embarked on a number of political and economic reforms during the tumultuous decade of the 1990s. The first presidential election was held in December 1991, and Islam A. Karimov who was formerly president of the Uzbek Soviet Socialist Republic (SSR), obtained 86 percent of the popular vote. After being elected president, Karimov launched a crackdown on all opposition and independent civil society and established a personalistic regime in which he could appoint all ministers, judges, and administrators.[3] Karimov justified the executive branch's excessive power to achieve political stability and economic development in the process of transition from communism in Uzbekistan. Karimov further stated that the "western notion of democracy couldn't be applicable to the situation prevailing in the Republic as it is likely to promote political instability and developmental process will be at stake."[4]

As opposed to the shock therapy approach to economic reform applied in the various postcommunist states, Karimov presented his economic reform strategy as "a unique Uzbek road" in which state-led gradual transition from command economy to a market economy had been sought to preserve stability and to avoid social unrest in the country.[5] Karimov's economic reforms also entailed achieving self-sufficiency in food and energy production to protect domestic prices from fluctuations in world prices. In the course of economic reforms, consumer prices were liberalized, and small-scale enterprises and retail were privatized; however, the central government maintained a significant amount of control over strategic sectors, such as agriculture, fossil fuels, energy, foreign trade, and banking.[6] By the end of the 1990s, major price controls remained on cotton, interest rates, and foreign exchange. In

2013, Uzbekistan was recorded as the worst of 189 countries in terms of ease of cross-border transactions.[7]

By keeping the state's pivotal position in the production processes, rent-seeking opportunities continued to be promised to "the central apparatus, the associated bureaucracies, and the regional agriculture-based elites."[8] The local elites' access to state rents, which had increased after the nullification of the anticorruption measures in 1989, drastically expanded during the economic reform processes in the early 1990s. As scholar Lawrence Markowitz explained, "densely concentrated resources, access to patrons, and open rent-seeking opportunities promote the co-optation of local elites to the regime, encouraging them to use local law enforcement and security bodies as tools of extraction to exploit lucrative rent-seeking avenues."[9] The SNB's power, along with other security organs, expanded to control the economic activities through the legal changes in 1997. State officials, businessmen, and clan leaders used their links with the SNB to launch raids aimed at extorting firms, expropriating enterprises, and crushing competitors.[10] Furthermore, as in other Central Asian countries, Uzbekistan's authoritarian leadership saw the SNB as the assurance of the regime to provide internal and external security. In exchange for supplying the regime with the coercive instruments to remove internal and external threats, the SNB itself engaged in rent-seeking activities through coercive methods, such as threats, torture, arbitrary arrests, detention, and rigged trials, which enabled it to become a powerful economic actor.[11] It is not without reason that Colonel General Rustam Inoyatov, who was appointed as the head of the SNB in 1995, came to be seen as one of the most corrupt people, if not the most feared man in Uzbekistan.

The SNB's repressive control has been explicitly spatialized in a traditional community-based organization, called the *mahalla*. The *mahalla*, coming from an Arabic word, was integrated into an official public administration system in the postindependence period in Uzbekistan.[12] As the lowest unit of state administration, the *mahalla* had been entitled to run the social welfare system and maintain social control through changes in public administration law, known as the Mahalla Law, in 1993. The law was revised after the bombing attacks in Tashkent during 1999, and it made the failure to comply with any decisions of the *mahallas* a state crime. Article 12 of the Mahalla Law charged the *mahalla* committees to "take measures to stop the activity of non-registered religious organizations, to ensure observance of the rights of citizens for religious liberty, non-admission of forced spreading of religious views, to consider other issues related to the observance of legislation on freedom of conscience and religious organizations."[13] The Cabinet of Minister decree further introduced the *mahalla*-based civilian police force, called the *posbon*, to increase the role of the *mahalla* in surveillance and law enforcement in 1999.[14] The *mahalla* then successfully functioned as an effective instrument of monitoring local communities in which the Uzbek people experienced their first encounter of the surveillance state orchestrated by the SNB. In 2003, Human Rights Watch reported abuses committed by the *mahalla* authorities, such as surveillance and information gathering on *mahalla* residents sent to the SNB, discretionary decisions for social assistance that excluded certain groups, and political positions as well as extrajudicial punishments.[15]

The dependence of the central government on the regional elites and security apparatus to ensure revenue increased predatory behaviors of these actors and hindered economic development. The economy, which was based on the agricultural and natural resource sectors, was unable to create job opportunities for unemployed youth, and real wages for workers continued to decline. While the average wage decreased from US$54 per month in 1996 to US$39 in 2001–2002, the savings rate went down by 20 percent.[16] Due to residency restrictions that prevented the mobility of the unemployed people, many Uzbeks sought employment opportunities abroad. It was estimated that migrant remittances constituted 10 percent of the Uzbek gross domestic product (GDP). From 2002, the regime introduced new tariffs and government licenses for *bazaaris* (small merchants) to control foreign currency demand and cross-border trade. These measures worsened the living standard for most of the population at an unprecedent level, which eventually culminated into massive protests in Ferghana Province during November 2004, in Jizzax Province during March 2005, and the most prominent one, in Andijan during May 2005, sparked by an arbitrary prosecution against twenty-three middle-class businessmen.[17]

Markowitz aptly argues that "as resource extraction became more coercive and the instruments of coercion became more corrupt, Uzbekistan's solution for averting state security fragmentation has increasingly fostered discontent. Rising popular dissent not only targets governors but also offices of local law enforcement and security bodies."[18] It was not surprising that armed protestors attacked the SNB headquarters and the prison to express their discontent in Andijan. Having been alarmed by the color revolutions in the region, the Karimov regime tasked the four separate units of special forces of the SNB, Ministry of Interior's internal troop, and the Seventeenth Air-Assault Brigade and a battalion of specialized operations from the Eastern military district to suppress the uprising. Estimates suggest that around 12,500 soldiers were deployed in the region.[19] The Andijan uprising was brutally crushed by these forces without discriminating civilians from armed insurgents and resulted in massive civilian deaths. Karimov rejected an independent inquiry demanded by the European Union, United Nations, and United States. Karimov's uncompromising stance on the international investigation significantly worsened Uzbekistan's relationship with the West and made the regime even more dependent on the SNB to combat internal and external threats in the Andijan massacre's aftermath.

The SNB inherited the institutional legacy of the Uzbek Republic's KGB as the majority of its staff were trained by KGB, which had significant implications on the intelligence culture. From the onset of its creation, the SNB kept close connections with the Russian intelligence agencies. Yet the SNB sought to develop its own independent threat assessments and nurtured close intelligence relationships with other countries. The SNB started collaborating with the intelligence services of the Commonwealth of Independent States (CIS) countries as early as April 1992.[20] Sharing intelligence among the CIS member-states was further formalized through the establishment of a Counter-Terrorism Center in Moscow in June 2000. Uzbekistan also joined the Shanghai Cooperation Organisation (SCO) in 2001 and signed the SCO Convention of Combating, Terrorism, Separatism and Extremism for further regional security cooperation and intelligence gathering.[21] Following the opening of the US air base in the southern town of Khanabad in Uzbekistan in 2001, the intelligence relationship between the United States and Uzbekistan also intensified. The US Central Intelligence Agency and the National Security Agency were allowed to install a surveillance system intended to intercept communications between the Taliban and al-Qaeda.[22] In response, critics accused the United States of collaborating with a brutal regime where torture is frequently used as a "routine investigation technique."[23] Despite reports that the SNB extensively used torture as a method of gathering intelligence for itself and its allies with impunity, the United States continued to transfer terror suspects to Uzbekistan for detention and interrogation.[24] Craig Murray, the British ambassador to Uzbekistan between 2002 and 2004, was one of the vocal critics of the methods employed by Uzbek intelligence and who publicly discussed the problem. He explained:

> The torture record of the Uzbek security services could hardly be more widely known. Plainly there are, at the very least, reasonable grounds for believing the material is obtained under torture. Nonetheless, I repeat that this material is useless—we are selling our souls for dross. It is in fact positively harmful. It is designed to give the message the Uzbeks want the West to hear. It exaggerates the role, size, organization and activity of the IMU [Islamic Movement of Uzbekistan] and its links with Al Qaida. The aim is to convince the West that the Uzbeks are a vital cog against a common foe, that they should keep the assistance, especially military assistance, coming, and that they should mute the international criticism on human rights and economic reform.[25]

The relationship between the United States and Uzbekistan continued to intensify in which the Declaration on Strategic Partnership was signed between the two countries during Karimov's visit to Washington, DC, in March 2002. Uzbekistan joined the North Atlantic Treaty Organization's Partnership for Peace, and the Uzbek Ministry of Defense received US security assistance, including a total of US$516,638 worth of equipment for border protection in 2004.[26] In the aftermath of the Andijan uprisings, however, Uzbekistan's relations with the United States deteriorated as a result of Karimov's refusal to collaborate with the international community to inspect the Andijan events in 2005. Karimov wanted the public to believe the Andijan events were a Western-sponsored color revolution and asked the United States to dismantle its base in Khanabad within 180 days. The SCO convened its annual meeting in Astana in July 2005 and further issued a declaration concerning the removal of the US military forces from the Central Asian region.[27]

Following the Andijan massacre, the SNB had undergone significant organizational changes aiming at expanding its power and influence over the society in Uzbekistan. The Interior Ministry troops were dissolved, and its antiterrorism and extremism units were placed under the authority of the SNB and the Ministry of Defense.[28] Such a shift in the security forces denoted the victory of Inoyatov, the head of the SNB, over Zokir Almatov, the minister of interior, in their fight for power and resources. The SNB's privileged position among security organizations remained unchanged until Shavkat Mirziyoyev, the former prime minister in the Karimov government, came to power after Karimov's death in September 2016.

THE REORGANIZATION OF THE SNB
UNDER THE NEW LEADERSHIP

In the December 2016 elections, Mirziyoyev was elected president with 88.6 percent of the popular vote. Mirziyoyev accelerated his reform agenda that he already started as interim president in September 2016. As an interim president, Mirziyoyev heralded the start of a new era in state-society relations in Uzbekistan by signing a presidential decree called "the measures on further reforming the judicial system and strengthening the guarantees of reliable protection of the rights and freedoms of citizens."[29] As a newly elected president, Mirziyoyev introduced the "Five Point Development Strategy Plan of Policy Priorities for the Next Five Years" and identified five reform areas in governance, administration, rule of law, economy, and foreign policy.[30]

Economic liberalization was one of the most important goals in the strategy document. To achieve this aim, price and exchange rates were liberalized, restrictions on foreign trade were removed, and custom tariffs on imported goods were reduced. Foreign investment was also encouraged and even provided incentives, such as the provision of special tax preferences and the relaxation of visas. Foreign direct investment reached US$4.2 billion, which was the highest level of all time in 2019. Uzbekistan further received financial and technical assistance from international financial institutions and jumped up eight places in one year to be sixty-ninth in the World Bank's 2020 Ease of Doing Business Index.[31] A new anticorruption law passed in January 2017 increased economic efficiency and ensured accountability of state officials both at the central and regional level. In the first half of 2017, more than 1,566 corruption cases were investigated, including Karimov's daughter Gulnara Karimov, who was sentenced to ten years in jail for fraud and money laundering.[32]

Mirziyoyev took a number of measures to strengthen further the central government's power and restrict the arbitrary rule of regional leaders. He reshuffled and dismissed many regional and district *hokims*, based on corruption allegations. In August 2017, legislation was changed to allow the direct elections of regional leaders, as well as setting a date for Tashkent city elections to be held on December 24, 2017.[33] Mirziyoyev, however, was convinced that "the anarchy in local governments created by the SNB which *de facto* ran a region by slandering, threating, and imprisoning hokims." In one of his speeches to the parliament in late 2017, Mirziyoyev stated that "a hokim is the representative of a president and any actions against hokims without a due process, including their imprisonment, will trigger equal punishment."[34] Curtailing the SNB's power and resources became an urgent necessity for the success of his reform program. He explained the reasons for restructuring of SNB:

The bodies of the National Security Service have been acting until the present day on the basis of a regulation approved by the government 26 years ago. This regulation has not been changed for a quarter of a century. Every ordinary issue has been regarded as a threat to national security, which led to the expansion of the agency's powers. Giving this, and also taking into account all the threats arising in an era of globalization, it is time to reform the National Security Service. In this regard, I propose to draft and adopt laws "On Law Enforcement Bodies" and "On the National Security Service." I believe that the adoption of these laws will create a legal basis for further strengthening the constitutional rights and freedoms of citizens and guarantees to them of a prosperous life.[35]

To restructure the SNB, Mirziyoyev ordered that the SNB's special forces of around 20,000 men be put under the control of the Interior Ministry in May 2017. Then, Inoyatov, the long-serving head of the SNB, was ousted on January 31, 2018, and replaced by Prosecutor General Ichtiyor Abdullaev. Shortly after, the SNB was renamed as the State Security Service (Sluzhba Gosudarstvennoy Bezopasnosti, SGB), and its headquarters were moved from the center of the capital to outside the city through a presidential decree in March 2018. Mirziyoyev justified the renaming of the intelligence service from SNB to the SGB on the grounds that the term national security was too broad, and "any local issue could be seen as a national security threat." He further stated that "this reorganization will draw the attention of the agency to the real state-level threats."[36] The parliament passed a new law that specified the legal status, powers, and responsibilities of the SNB in March 2018.[37] Mirziyoyev also publicly revealed the SNB's legal and moral violations, and that myriad numbers of its staff as well as the custom and tax agencies were prosecuted. The use of torture that the SNB often practiced to collect evidence for court proceedings was prohibited. The notorious Jaslyk prison, known as the SNB's "house of torture," was closed. Mirziyoyev also ordered the SNB to remove the blacklist status of 18,000 Uzbek citizens and withdraw the SNB officers from the Uzbek embassies.[38] Mirziyoyev also made an international investigation dealing with human rights issues possible, allowing the United Nations High Commissioner for Human Rights and Human Rights Watch to resume their activities in Uzbekistan.[39]

CONCLUSION

The extent to which Mirziyoyev's reforms successfully achieve political liberalization remains to be seen. What has been observed is Mirziyoyev is in the process of establishing a dependent network of relations through institutional reshuffling and the appointments of new loyalists, including family members, to consolidate his power. After having degraded the SNB's power, Mirziyoyev empowered the National Guard and the State Security Service of the President (GSBP) to play the pivotal role in the intelligence and security domain in Uzbekistan.[40] In August 2017, the National Guard was removed from the military and given an independent status through a presidential decree. The National Guard is now responsible for ensuring the country's territorial integrity and defense as well as controlling the import and export of weapons. Through the changes in the criminal procedure legislation in July 2019, the National Guard has also been entitled to conduct pretrial investigations and detain people.[41] In a similar vein, in 2019 the GSBP, which is responsible for providing the security for the president and his family, was given authority for overseeing criminal investigations. At the time of this writing, there are many incidents indicating that journalists, academics, civil society representatives, and opposition politicians are still being persecuted and surveilled, and independent nongovernmental organizations continue to be denied registration.[42] After a long period of repression, it is clear that Uzbekistan is not undergoing a democratization process; rather, it is moving toward an authoritarian upgrading that entails partial implementation of political and economic reforms to pacify the people's demand for democratization. As scholar Edward Lemon argues, "[A]s citizens are given greater freedoms while expecting the government to deliver on its promised reforms, the potential for opposition to the government will grow."[43] The extent to which the regime will respond to the growing opposition through the repressive apparatus of the state will determine the course of democratization in Uzbekistan.

NOTES

1. The 2nd and the 6th departments were transferred to the SNB from military intelligence in 1996. Roger N. McDermott, "Central Asian Security Post-2014: Perspectives in Kazakhstan and Uzbekistan," DIIS Report 2013:12, Danish Institute for International Studies, 2013, https://ciaotest.cc.columbia.edu/wps/diis/0028709/f_0028709_23303.pdf.

2. McDermott, "Central Asian Security Post-2014."

3. Martin C. Spechler, *The Political Economy of Reform in Central Asia: Uzbekistan under Authoritarianism* (New York: Routledge, 2008), 4:29.

4. Nalin Kumar Mohapatra, "Dynamics of Democratization and Political Process in Uzbekistan," *Himalayan and Central Asian Studies* 9, no. 1–2 (2005): 47.

5. Spechler, *The Political Economy of Reform in Central Asia*, 33.

6. Andrea Schmitz, "Uzbekistan's Transformation: Strategies and Perspectives," SWP Research Paper 12 (Berlin: German Institute for International and Security Affairs, 2020), 9, https://www.swp-berlin.org/publications/products/research_papers/2020RP12_Uzbekistan.pdf.

7. World Bank, cited in David Lewis, "'Illiberal Spaces': Uzbekistan's Extraterritorial Security Practices and the Spatial Politics of Contemporary Authoritarianism," *Nationalities Papers* 43, no. 1 (2015): 144.

8. Schmitz, "Uzbekistan's Transformation," 9.

9. Lawrence P. Markowitz, *State Erosion: Unlootable Resources and Unruly Elites in Central Asia* (Ithaca, NY: Cornell University Press, 2013), 6.

10. There are numerous credible accounts by the human rights organizations about how the SNB administered such actions with the participation of "government agencies, including the tax authorities, fire inspection and regulatory agencies, police,

prosecutors, and courts." For example, "Submission on 'Corruption and Human Rights in Uzbekistan,'" 30th Session of the UPR Working Group, Uzbek-German Forum for Human Rights, 2018, https://ccprcentre.org/files/media/Joint_submission _Corruption_and_Human_Rights_in_Uzbekistan_FINAL1.pdf.

11. Kristian Lasslett, Fatima Kanji, and Daire McGill, "A Dance with the Cobra: Confronting Grand Corruption in Uzbekistan," International State Crime Initiative, 2017, 33, http://statecrime.org/data/2017/08/Full-Report-with-Executive-Summary .pdf.

12. Uzbekistan has around 12,000 *mahalla*, and each contains approximately 400 households. John Micklewright and Sheila Marnie, "Targeting Social Assistance in a Transition Economy: The Mahallas in Uzbekistan," *Social Policy & Administration* 39, no. 4 (2005): 431.

13. "Uzbekistan: From House to House: Abuses by *Mahalla* Committees," Human Rights Watch, September 22, 2003, 9, https://www.hrw.org/report/2003/09/22/ house-house/abuses-mahalla-comittees.

14. "Uzbekistan: Role of 'Mahalla' in Uzbek Society; Whether Mahalla Are Involved in Extortion; State Protection," Immigration and Refugee Board of Canada, April 7, 2004, https://www.refworld.org/docid/41501c6f23.html.

15. "Uzbekistan: From House to House," 12.

16. Spechler, *The Political Economy of Reform in Central Asia*, 46.

17. Fiona Hill and Kevin Jones, "Fear of Democracy or Revolution: The Reaction to Andijon," *Washington Quarterly* 29, no. 3 (2006): 113–14.

18. Markowitz, *State Erosion*, 69.

19. Rustam Burnashev and Irina Chernykh, "Changes in Uzbekistan's Military Policy after the Andijan Events," *China and Eurasia Forum Quarterly* 5, no. 1 (2007): 68.

20. CIS countries in 1992: Armenia, Belarus, Georgia, Kazakhstan, Kyrgyzstan, Moldova, Russia, Tajikistan, Turkmenistan, Ukraine, and Uzbekistan.

21. Stéphane Lefebvre and Roger N. McDermott, "Russia and the Intelligence Services of Central Asia," *International Journal of Intelligence and CounterIntelligence* 21, no. 2 (2008): 261.

22. Steve Coll, *Ghost Wars: The Secret History of the CIA, Afghanistan, and Bin Laden, from the Soviet Invasion to September 10, 2001* (New York: Penguin, 2005), 952.

23. Nick Walsh, "Uzbekistan Kicks US Out of Military Base," *The Guardian*, August 1, 2005, https://www.theguardian.com/world/2005/aug/01/usa.nick patonwalsh.

24. Don van Natta Jr., "Growing Evidence US Sending Prisoners to Torture Capital: Despite Bad Record on Human Rights, Uzbekistan Is Ally," *New York Times*, May 1, 2005.

25. Craig Murray, *Dirty Diplomacy: The Rough-and-Tumble Adventures of a Scotch-Drinking, Skirt-Chasing, Dictator-Busting and Thoroughly Unrepentant Ambassador Stuck on the Frontline of the War against Terror* (New York: Simon & Schuster, 2007), 885.

26. Jessica N. Trisko, "Coping with the Islamist Threat: Analysing Repression in Kazakhstan, Kyrgyzstan and Uzbekistan," *Central Asian Survey* 24, no. 4 (2005): 382.

27. Charles J. Sullivan, "Uzbekistan and the United States: Interests and Avenues for Cooperation," *Asian Affairs* 50, no. 1 (2019): 102.

28. Burnashev and Chernykh, "Changes in Uzbekistan's Military Policy after the Andijan Events," 71.

29. "Substantial Reforms in Judicial and Legal System Are Forthcoming," Regional Dialogue, October 22, 2016, https://www.regionaldialogue.org/single -post/2016/10/22/Substantial-reforms-in-judicial-and-legal-system-are-forthcoming; "Судебно-правовую _систему _ждет _серьезное _реформирование" [The judicial system is undergoing serious reform], Gazeta.uz, October 21, 2016, https://www .gazeta.uz/ru/2016/10/21/courts/.

30. "Uzbekistan's Development Strategy for 2017–2021 Has Been Adopted Following Public Consultation," *Tashkent Times*, February 8, 2017, http://tashkent times.uz/national/541-uzbekistan-s-development-strategy-for-2017-2021-has-been -adopted-following.

31. Kate Mallinson, "The Investment Climate in Uzbekistan," Foreign Policy Centre, July 14, 2020, https://fpc.org.uk/the-investment-climate-in-uzbekistan/.

32. Edward Lemon, "Mirziyoyev's Uzbekistan: Democratization or Authoritarian Upgrading?," Central Asia Papers (Philadelphia: Foreign Policy Research Institute, 2019), 5.

33. Anthony C. Bowyer, "Political Reform in Mirziyoyev's Uzbekistan: Elections, Political Parties and Civil Society," Central Asia-Caucasus Institute, Silk Road Studies Program, March 2018, 6, https://www.silkroadstudies.org/resources/pdf/Silk RoadPapers/1803-Bowyer-Uzbekistan.pdf.

34. Umida Hashimova, "Hokim Hubbub: Making Sense of Local Government Shuffles in Uzbekistan," *The Diplomat*, August 6, 2018, https://thediplomat.com/2018/08/ hokim-hubbub-making-sense-of-local-government-shuffles-in-uzbekistan/.

35. Mjusa Sever, "Judicial and Governance Reform in Uzbekistan," Central Asia-Caucasus Institute, Silk Road Studies Program, March 2018, 14–15, https://silkroad studies.org/resources/pdf/SilkRoadPapers/2018-03-Sever-Uzbekistan.pdf.

36. Timur Toktonaliev and Turonbek Kozokov, "Uzbek President Reins in Security Service," Institute for War and Peace Reporting, April 4, 2018, https://www.ref world.org/docid/5b8660b8a.html.

37. Schmitz, "Uzbekistan's Transformation," 16.

38. Jonathan Z. Ludwig, "Uzbekistan's Second Chance," SAGE International Australia, May 29, 2018, 3, https://ethz.ch/content/dam/ethz/special-interest/gess/ cis/center-for-securities-studies/resources/docs/SIA_Uzbekistan's%20Second%20 Chance.pdf.

39. Bowyer, "Political Reform in Mirziyoyev's Uzbekistan," 9.

40. Schmitz, "Uzbekistan's Transformation," 17.

41. Bruce Pannier, "Uzbekistan's New Security Powerhouse: The National Guard," Radio Free Europe / Radio Liberty, August 31, 2019, https://www.rferl.org/ a/the-nationalguard-uzbekistan-s-new-security-powerhouse/30139322.html.

42. Dilmira Matyakubowa, "There Won't Be Political Reform in Uzbekistan: Here's Why," *The Diplomat*, December 22, 2020, https://thediplomat.com/2020/12/there-wont-be-political-reform-in-uzbekistan-heres-why/.

43. Lemon, "Mirziyoyev's Uzbekistan," 14.

Vietnam: Intelligence-Led Policing Culture at the Borderland

Hai Thanh Luong

This chapter examines intelligence culture in Vietnam by exploring intelligence-led policing (ILP) in antinarcotics efforts. It situates ILP in the context of the wider intelligence culture to understand how it developed strategies and capabilities to stem illegal drug imports from Laos with attention to overt and covert efforts. The chapter has four sections. The first part provides a background about Vietnam's intelligence history with attention to postcolonial structures and the role of the Communist Party. The second section examines narcotics smuggling and its challenges to intelligence in the country. The next part analyzes ILP efforts against drug trafficking by looking at methodologies and practices. The fourth section explores oversight with attention to authorities and efforts to safeguard privacy. Finally, the conclusion highlights continuing transparency issues and how effectiveness of ILP against drug trafficking is unknown due to the lack of data for analysis.

BACKGROUND

In 1945, the August Revolution's success in Hanoi led to officially establishing the Democratic Republic of Vietnam. Although Vietnam became an independent country on September 2, 1945, after two long wars (France in 1946–1954 and the United States in 1965–1975), the early state faced several challenges in integrating the country after 1975.[1] In the intelligence domain, the first effort to build state intelligence structures originated in early Vietnam's independence.[2] Along with the August Revolution in 1945, both Public Security (started on August 19) and the Defense Forces (started on December

22) in Vietnam were established to protect their new government and the party through these new special task forces.

Excluding military intelligence, the Vietnam People's Public Security Force (Công an Nhân dân Việt Nam, PPSF) was not initially a united organization.[3] Rather, it was three agencies with different names in three separate regions, including the Security Service Bureau in the North (Sở Liêm phóng Bắc Bộ), Scout Bureau in Central (Sở Trinh sát Trung Bộ), and National Self-Defense Force in the South (Quốc gia tự vệ cuộc Nam Bộ).[4] Nevertheless, the three agencies had the same functions and missions, such as fighting counterrevolutionary and hostile organizations, maintaining social order and security, and protecting the Communist Party. On February 21, 1946, President Ho Chi Minh signed Decree No.23/S.L. to unify the three forces into the Vietnam People's Police Department.[5] Employing a model similar to the former Soviet Union's intelligence services, this department was supervised and controlled by the Ministry of Internal Affairs.[6] There were three levels for its organizational structure: Vietnam Police, Regional Police, and Provincial Police, focusing on protecting national security and maintaining social order.[7]

After 1954, Vietnam was temporarily divided into north and south with two strategic missions and different approaches. The PPSF fulfilled its given tasks in various fields and fought enemies on the southern battlefield and protected the socialist rear in the north.[8] In the north, the security and police forces used various methods and forms to implement their tasks to prevent, detect, and crack down on foreign spy organizations.[9] Under the requirements of the Communist Party of Vietnam (CPV), the intelligence services worked with PPSF's units to investigate and arrest thousands of enemy scouts and suppressed emerging reactionary organizations.[10] Whereas in the north, police forces were instrumental in responding to psychological war and sabotaged the enemy's forces; protected the internal security, national defense, the armed forces, and the socialist property; and engaged in crime solving.[11] The south's intelligence services also contributed to the victory of the 1968 Tet Offensive, the 1972 Strategic Offensive, and the Great Victory in spring 1975.[12]

On April 30, 1975, the country was unified, which led to the merging of all of PPSF's regions. Although the PPSF no longer had to fight foreign enemies on the battlefield, it suffered hardships and faced new challenges. Under the direct, centralized, and united CPV leadership and in close coordination with the Vietnam People's Defense Force, the PPSF participated in building and consolidating the revolutionary government in the newly liberated areas. The PPSF's successes had significant political and social meaning with the particular case named Plan CM12.[13] This counterintelligence operation involved the PPSF's intelligence department and dismantled the antirevolutionary network named the National United Front for the Liberation of Vietnam led by Le Quoc Tuy and Mai Van Hanh, which was sponsored by hostile international forces.[14]

Since 1986, Vietnam has been carrying out the Renovation Period (*Doi Moi*). When the Soviet Union and Eastern Europe socialist models collapsed in the early 1990s, it led to questions about the PPSF intelligence services' ability to deal with new challenges.[15] Born in the revolution and developed since 1975, the PPSF continuously grew to protect the country's national security.[16] Although the police investigated and solved crimes, most of their ideologies and plans were according to CPV provisions and directions.[17] This helps shape the PPSF's unique culture. In Vietnam, the PPSF is considered the sword and shield of CPV to protect the Communist regime by policing crime control and safeguarding national security.

TRANSNATIONAL NARCOTICS TRAFFICKING AND ITS CHALLENGES IN INTELLIGENCE SERVICES

More than 12,400 kilometers (about 7,700 miles) in total length connect the mountains and hills to create distinct geological characteristics between Vietnam and three neighboring countries, Cambodia, China, and Laos. With an altitude at the northern locations of approximately 600 meters (about 2,000 feet) above sea level, it is suitable for opium poppy growing, including Dienbien and Sonla that share borders with Phongsaly, Luangprabang, and Houaphan of Laos.[18] Vietnam-Laos is bordered by ten provinces, including sixteen national border gates and thousands of trails spreading out over 2,340 kilometers (about 1,500 miles) of porous borderlands. These natural geographical variations and geological features led to its positive contributions to economic development, social management, and international integration.[19] Located in the proximity of the Golden Triangle, including Laos, Myanmar, and Thailand, one of the world's primary poppy sources and amphetamine-type stimulants (ATS) has led to long-term threats for Vietnam's national security and social order.[20]

The types of drugs transported in the area vary, including mostly heroin, but also ATS in the form of stones and slate. Criminal methods for smuggling are sophisticated.[21] Drug criminals on the border are mainly ethnic minorities, border guards, brokers, and transporters hired for and use border facilities to transit the narcotics.[22] From 2010 to June 2020, the Counter-Narcotics Police Force (CNPF) investigated 208,059 cases, arrested 310,124 subjects related to drug crimes, and seized about 24 tons of heroin, 5.8 million tablets and 152 tons of synthetic drugs, 1,195 guns, 13,251 bullets of all kinds, and other related items.[23]

Vietnam is a destination and transit point for illicit drugs, which has been challenging for Vietnam's police forces to combat transnational narcotics trafficking (TransNT) across the border. The country is one of five current countries in the world that has continued under Communist Party rule.[24] Vietnam's current constitution confirms CPV's ultimate role in the political and socioeconomic system. To protect the government and the party, the PPSF is the sword and the shield. It protects national security, ensures social order and safety, fights crime, and enforces national security, social order, and safety laws.[25]

The PPSF is composed of two leading branches under the Ministry of Public Security (MPS)—the Vietnam People's Security Force (An Ninh nhân dân, VPSF) and the Vietnam People's Police Force (Cảnh sát nhân dân, VPPF)—and has the two largest training systems.[26] The People's Security Academy trains public security agents in intelligence collection and analysis to prevent, investigate, and defeat potential enemies to protect national security. The People's Police Academy trains ILP for law enforcement, including police agents, to combat drug trafficking.[27] The VPPF's role and functions, specifically the CNPF, which was established in 1997, applies ILP for combating TransNT across the borderland between Vietnam and Laos.

Under the current legislation, the CNPF is considered one of the essential bodies for investigating police agencies' methods related to drug trafficking involving TransNT. According to the 2018 PPSF's Law, those forces cover twenty-one specific duties and powers, including carrying out intelligence activities and its related operations to combat and prevent crimes and violations through seven specific measures.[28] One of the CNPF's tasks is to investigate all drug cases, which includes the TransNT across Vietnam's borderland with Laos. The CNPF can use deterrent measures (i.e., arrest, custody, temporary detention, ban from travel outside one's residence, guarantee, the deposit of money or valuable property as bail), initiate criminal proceedings, interrogate the accused, take witness statements, conduct identification, and search or seize property.[29]

Vietnam's law for antinarcotics ILP has stipulated the powers of the agencies responsible for the CNPF. Among the six main powers' groups, the police are permitted to conduct reconnaissance measures to detect drug-related crimes, including confidential informants and undercover operators' networks, technical equipment recording (audio and video), uninterrupted reconnaissance techniques, and mixed-method operations.[30] These special ILP measures assist the CNPF's efforts to collect information; documents; financial situations of individuals, families, agencies, and/or organizations; and seize bank accounts of those whom police believe are involved, either directly or indirectly, in TransNT activities. Besides that, ILP tactics also allow CNPF to request post offices open parcels for inspection when there are grounds to believe they contain narcotic substances, presubstances, addictive medicines, and centripetal neurotropic medicines.[31] ILP and related methods play a crucial central effort in exploring and investigating the drug trafficking organizations from two sides.

INTELLIGENCE-LED POLICING TO COMBAT DRUG TRAFFICKING

In Vietnam, most intelligence activities of MPS (and also the General Directorate II, GD II, military intelligence; Ministry of Defense, MOD) are recognized as the professional intelligence collection techniques regulated in internal documents.[32] Likewise, special measures in ILP are secretive requirements of CNPF and its relevant counterparts.[33] The nature of the CNPF's criminal intelligence to combat TransNT is utilizing reconnaissance strategies, both covert and overt forms, for collecting and analyzing information and situations relating to drug trafficking groups.[34] For example, police can use technical equipment and intelligence from a network of informants to deploy their surveillance process to pursue TransNT.[35] Therefore, criminal intelligence analysis in Vietnam's ILP should be understood as a concept that frames how CNPF can approach the investigation of TransNT and its related entities by using intelligence and information that have been collected.

Utilizing ILP is crucial for antinarcotics police agents' ability to combat TransNT in three major perspectives. First, ILP permits CNPF officers to establish a proactive response to crime, enabling them to determine and understand drug trafficking operating in their areas, Vietnam and Laos territories.[36] It enables police to identify and understand criminal groups operating. Once criminal groups are identified and their habits are known, CNPF officers can assess current crime trends to forecast and hamper the development of perceived future criminal activities.[37] Second, ILP provides the knowledge on which to base decisions and select appropriate targets for investigation. While the use of ILP is suitable to support investigations, surveillance operations, and the prosecution of cases, it also provides CNPF with the ability to manage resources, budget effectively, and meet its responsibility for fighting TransNT.[38] Third, information technology in ILP is key to intelligence sharing between two CNPF sides when they jointly investigate a TransNT case.[39] Indeed, CNPF needs forward-looking, proactive, and comprehensive strategies to counteract the threat of those illegal drug groups and share intelligence effectively.[40]

National legislation dictates the ways intelligence can be used for law enforcement purposes, including antinarcotics.[41] The intelligence collection process in a specific investigation is usually a prelude to any evidence-gathering activity.[42] Legislation, either evidence law or criminal procedure code (CPC), also dictates whether intelligence material gathered during an investigation is protected from disclosure in criminal proceedings.[43] In Vietnam, Chapter XVI in the 2015 CPC officially regulate ILP techniques and related procedures for investigation and proceeding methods in drug-related offenses.[44] It is conducted based on scientific and technical achievements in ICTs, including collecting information and documents related to drug trafficking cases. On the one hand, based on the 2015 CPC regulations, CNPF agents can apply special methods of the ILP techniques, including physical surveillance (audio and video) and electronic surveillance (trap and trace or wiretap).[45] These measures allow the recording of high-resolution images, high-quality audio, and other information and documents while ensuring confidentiality from the applicable audience and those who are irrelevant.[46] On the other hand, based on the 2018 PPSF Law, as part of the essential operations in professional reconnaissance methods, police also can apply their undercover operators and confidential informants' networks to support the process of data collection. To combat TransNT effectively, CNPF applies both overt and covert forms of ILP under the law.

OVERSIGHT OF INTELLIGENCE-LED POLICING

Based on legislative regulations, there are two primary forms to supervise the ILP of CNPF during TransNT cases. First, confidential informants and undercover operators of CNPF are supervised by internal authorities. It is regulated in the 2018 PPSF Law with its specific instructions; however, documents relating to the process of applying ILP's measures are classified and shared in internal channels among CNPF's agencies. In Vietnam, before the 2015 CPC took effect, all the ILP findings were transferred from reconnaissance activities (covert ways) to criminal procedure measures (overt ways). Any breached regulations and leaked material, either deliberately or involuntary disclosed, could be dealt with as a crime. Accordingly, those who deliberately disclose classified information or appropriate, trade, or destroy classified documents could be charged with a maximum of fifteen years' imprisonment, with a seven-year jail term for involuntary disclosure activities. As a secretive organization, the CNPF rarely makes any public arguments or specific reports in ILP oversight. This is a barrier to objectively review and assess the intelligence management system.

Second, for the overt form, all three methods in the special investigation activities (i.e., secret recording by sound or by sound and visual means;

secret phone tapping; and private collection of electronic data) is supervised by the relevant procuracy agencies. As a unique representative of Vietnam's government-state, the procuracy exercises the power of prosecution and supervise judicial activities, including all special investigation methods of CNPF in drug-related offenses. Procurators strictly manage the principles, grounds, conditions, order, procedures, the time limit for application for unique methods of investigation and proceedings, and oversight for the use of information and documents collected by the CNPF. Under the supervision of prosecutors, the types of information and documents when collecting via ILP's measures have to be processed in two directions. First, documents and information related to the case can be used as evidence in the investigation, prosecution, and adjudication of criminal cases. Second, all documents and information excluding the case must be promptly destroyed. This helps to avoid abuses by ensuring privacy.[47]

After prosecuting the drug-related case, to avoid abuse or negatively affect individuals' personal lives, Vietnam stipulates the role of procuracy oversight for the CNPF's intelligence methods. The time limit for applying and utilizing special methods cannot exceed two months from the Procurator General's date of approval; however, almost all TransNT cases are complex with extended investigations among two countries and need more time for collecting intelligence. Therefore, police can request an extension for using ILP tactics at least ten days before expiring.

Special ILP investigations often relate to the individual's right to confidentiality and privacy data. To avoid rampant use and ensure efficiency in applying special investigation methods and proceedings, some cases will withdraw ILP efforts. If so, the head of the procuracy can request ending ILP in the following cases: (1) there is a written request from the CNPF leaders, (2) there are violations in the process of special methods of investigation and proceedings, and (3) there is no need to continue to apply special measures of investigation and proceedings. To promote the supervisory role, the code stipulates that the approved procurator general must be notified immediately about the intelligence activities' results.

CONCLUSION

Like other countries that combat transnational crimes, particularly with cross-border drug trafficking, Vietnam needs to apply professional and productive intelligence measures as much as possible. Nonetheless, ILP with specific methods in both overt and covert forms is an essential part of CNPF's intelligence culture. It facilitates security by actively collecting evidence and identifying suspected offenders in investigating each TransNT. Yet, overt intelligence measures under the 2015 CPC may breach privacy information and personal data, and Vietnam is also a member of several international treaties to protect human rights. Indeed, information and documents gathered from ILP measures are related to individuals' privacy, and the CNPF and its relevant procuracy authorities must analyze, evaluate, and select what and which are valuable resources to prove criminal acts as legal evidence. Therefore, in the intelligence culture in Vietnam transparent approaches and objective assessments of the CNPF and relevant authorities are still in question even after the 2015 CPC took effect on January 1, 2018.

Unlike the intelligence of military and public security activities to protect national security and counter foreign spies, the ILP is mainly deployed for collecting and analyzing information for crime prevention. While the former is often requested and supervised under secretive regulations with the highest confidence level for VPSF (MPS) and GD II (MOD) to look for potential threats from external spies, the latter ILP is part of the flexible strategies of police to anticipate and investigate TransNT complex cases. Although both separate functions and responsibilities in applications, the new changes in the recent laws affect CNPF activities. Accordingly, ILP methods to apply to a TransNT case, including foreigners across the borderland, have to be approved and overseen by relevant procuracies before conducting investigations. In some cases, in collaboration with border guards (MOD, but not belonging to GD II) and customs (Ministry of Finance), CNPF could deploy ILP measures by establishing a joint investigation team (JIT) to monitor and arrest traffickers at the border areas. Notably, those JITs permit both covert and overt forms to utilize ILP in their investigations to share information among those agencies. If applying ILP as covert measures, those resources have to ensure confidential factors and only use it as physical evidence unless transferring from reconnaissance ways to conduct criminal procedure measures under the 2015 CPC. On the other hand, if conducting ILP as overt measures, those resources are considered as legal documents.

Currently, ILP is monitored by the VPPF (MPS) based on the 2018 PPSF Law and the 2015 CPC, which differ from national security intelligence. In Vietnam, each agency could use intelligence measures without illegally breaching personal privacy. If this information is valuable to support the process of investigation, prosecution, and conviction of a TransNT case, CNPF can call for other agencies to share the intelligence's outcomes as specific references of ILP tactics; however, the ILP of police and national security intelligence does not overlap and has different authorities. As for overt forms based on the 2015 CPC regulations, there needs more research and analysis about how those measures contributed to fighting TransNT and understand why Vietnam changed from covert intelligence (under internal police rules) to overt intelligence (under public regulation).

NOTES

1. Carl Thayer, "One Party Rule and the Challenge of Political Civil Society in Vietnam" (paper presented at the Seminar of the Like-Minded Donor Countries, Royal Norwegian Embassy, Hanoi, Vietnam, 2008); Carl Thayer, "Political Legitimacy in Vietnam: Challenge and Response," *Politics & Policy* 38, no. 3 (2010): 423–44; Tuong Vu, "Vietnamese Political Studies and Debates on Vietnamese Nationalism," *Journal of Vietnamese Studies* 2, no. 2 (2007): 175–239.

2. Carl Thayer, "Vietnam's Security Outlook," in *Security Outlook of the Asia Pacific Countries and Its Implications for the Defense Sector* (Tokyo, Japan: National Institute for Defense Studies, 2012), 69–89; Tuong Vu, "Persistence amid Decay: The Communist Party of Vietnam," in *Politics in Contemporary Vietnam: Party, State, and Authority Relations* (New York: Springer, 2014), 21–41.

3. Within this chapter's scope, all military forces' intelligence activities (General Directorate II, Ministry of Defense) will be excluded. As Larry Berman reviewed the role of an intelligence agent in the US-Vietnam War and explained, "Intense consciousness of the communist ideal, extreme loyalty to the Party, utmost devotion to the people, great courage in the fight and diligent creativeness . . . deserving confidence, love, and respect from all people" (cited in Larry Berman, "Author," Perfect Spy, accessed May 25, 2022, http://larrybermanperfectspy.com/faq2.html#q4). For more information about Vietnam's military forces' intelligence services, see Larry Berman, *Perfect Spy: The Incredible Double Life of Pham Xuan An, Time Magazine Reporter, and Vietnamese Communist Agent* (New York: HarperCollins, 2007).

4. "History of Establishing and Developing of People's Public Security Forces," Ministry of Public Security of Vietnam, December 10, 2019, http://en.bocongan .gov.vn/news/top-stories/history-of-peoples-public-security-forces-of-vietnam-4446 .html.

5. February 21, 1946, was recorded as the official date for the establishment of the intelligence service in the PPSF.

6. Bob de Graaff and James M. Nyce, introduction to *Handbook of European Intelligence Cultures*, ed. Bob de Graaff and James M. Nyce (New York: Rowman & Littlefield, 2016), xxiv–xlvi; Prokop Tomek, "Czechoslovakia: The Czech Path between Totalitarianism and Democracy," in *Handbook of European Intelligence Cultures*, ed. Bob de Graaff and James M. Nyce (New York: Rowman & Littlefield, 2016), 81–94; Iztok Prezelj, "Slovenia: The Intelligence System, Its Development, and Some Key Challenges," in *Handbook of European Intelligence Cultures*, ed. Bob de Graaff and James M. Nyce (New York: Rowman & Littlefield, 2016), 347–58.

7. Bui V. Nam, "Intelligence Service Has to Rely on the People: Lessons of 75 Years of Establishing, Fighting and Developing of the Intelligence Unit in the People's Public Security," People's Public Security, December 11, 2019, http://cand

.com.vn/Cong-an/19-8-tr10-Tinh-bao-phai-dua-vao-dan-Bai-hoc-tu-truyen-thong-75-nam-chien-dau-xay-dung-truong-thanh-cua-Tinh-bao-CAND-607653/.

8. "History of Establishing and Developing of People's Public Security Forces."

9. MPS, *People's Public Security Forces: Fighting for the Country, Serving for the People* (Hanoi, Vietnam: People's Public Security, 2017).

10. Nam, "Intelligence Service Has to Rely on the People."

11. Trinh Q. Do and Nguyen T. H. Anh, "Vietnam People's Police Force: Smart and Brave, Doing for Country, for People without Personal Motivations," People's Police Academy, December 10, 2019, http://csnd.vn/Home/Truyen-thong-ve-vang-luc-luong-Canh-sat/6231/Canh-sat-nhan-dan-Viet-Nam-Muu-tri-dung-cam-vi-nuoc-vi-dan-quen-than-phuc-vu.

12. MPS, *People's Public Security Forces.*

13. Tuan Anh, "Officers Participating in Counter-intelligence Plan CM12 Gather in Ca Mau," Ministry of Public Security of Vietnam, September 5, 2019, http://en.bocongan.gov.vn/tintuc/Pages/news-events.aspx?ItemID=5926.

14. Nguyen P. Ta and Nguyen K. Duc, *Counterintelligence Plan CM-12: A Professional Memoir* (Hanoi, Vietnam: People's Public Security, 2003); Nguyen K. Duc, *CM-12: Behind the Plan of Counterintelligence* (Hanoi, Vietnam: People's Public Security, 2020).

15. Thayer, "Vietnam's Security Outlook"; Vu, "Persistence amid Decay."

16. Thayer, "One Party Rule and the Challenge of Political Civil Society in Vietnam"; Thayer, "Political Legitimacy in Vietnam"; Vu, "Vietnamese Political Studies and Debates on Vietnamese Nationalism."

17. Thayer, "One Party Rule and the Challenge of Political Civil Society in Vietnam"; Thayer, "Political Legitimacy in Vietnam"; Vu, "Vietnamese Political Studies and Debates on Vietnamese Nationalism."

18. Luong T. Hai, "Drug Trafficking Trends and Its Responses: A Case Study of Vietnam," in *Cybercrime, Organized Crime, and Societal Responses: International Approaches* (Cham, Switzerland: Springer, 2017), 201–19.

19. Luong T. Hai, "Drug Production, Consumption, and Trafficking in the Greater Mekong Sub-Region," *Asian Survey* 59, no. 4 (2019): 717–37.

20. Luong T. Hai, "Drug Trafficking in the Mainland Southeast Asian Region: The Example of Vietnam's Shared Borderland with Laos," *International Annals of Criminology* 58, no. 1 (2020): 130–51.

21. Luong T. Hai, *Transnational Drug Trafficking across the Vietnam-Laos Border* (Cham, Switzerland: Palgrave Macmillan, 2019).

22. Luong T. Hai, "Transnational Crime and Its Trends in South-East Asia: A Detailed Narrative in Vietnam," *International Journal for Crime, Justice and Social Democracy* 9, no. 2 (2020): 88–101.

23. Thai Son, "Bilateral Cooperation between Vietnam and Laos to Combat Drug Trafficking," *Tieng Chuong*, January 1, 2021, http://tiengchuong.vn/Nghien-cuu-Chuyen-de/Hop-tac-chat-che-trong-phong-chong-ma-tuy-o-bien-gioi-Viet-Nam-Lao/39082.vgp.

24. There are five remaining Communist countries globally—namely, China, Cuba, North Korea, Lao PDR, and Vietnam.

25. Martin Grossheim, "The Sword and Shield of the Party: How the Vietnamese People's Public Security Forces Portray Themselves," *Intelligence and National Security* 33, no. 3 (2018): 439–58.

26. MPS, *People's Public Security Forces.*

27. Tran D. Quang and Nguyen X. Yem, *Vietnamese Public Security Science,* vol. 6, *Theory of Vietnamese Intelligence* (Hanoi, Vietnam: People's Public Security, 2017); Tran D. Quang and Nguyen X. Yem, *Vietnamese Reconnaissance Science,* vol. 3, *Reconnaissance Activities in Anti-crime* (Hanoi, Vietnam: People's Public Security, 2017).

28. Seven measures of PPSF include (1) mass mobilization, (2) legal, (3) diplomatic, (4) economic, (5) scientific-technical, (6) professional operation, and (7) armed measures to protect national security, maintain social order and safety, and combat, prevent, and control crimes and violations of laws on national security, social order, and protection.

29. Hai, "Drug Trafficking Trends and Its Responses."

30. Tran D. Quang and Nguyen X. Yem, *Vietnamese Reconnaissance Science,* vol. 3, *Reconnaissance Activities in Anti-crime* (Hanoi, Vietnam: People's Public Security, 2017); Tran D. Quang and Nguyen X. Yem, *Vietnamese Reconnaissance Science,* vol. 2, *Method and Tactics of Reconnaissance Operations* (Hanoi, Vietnam: People's Public Security, 2017).

31. Luong T. Hai, "Drug and Drug Trafficking in the Greater Mekong Sub-regional: A Case Study of Vietnam and Its Shared Borders" (paper presented at the 10th Annual Conference of the International Society for the Study of Drug Policy, Sydney, Australia, 2016); Luong T. Hai, "Transnational Narcotics Trafficking and Law Enforcement: A Perspective of Vietnam" (PhD diss., RMIT University, Melbourne, 2017).

32. Carl Thayer, "The Apparatus of Authoritarian Rule in Vietnam," in *Politics in Contemporary Vietnam: Party, State, and Authority Relations* (New York: Springer, 2014), 135–61; Quang and Yem, *Vietnamese Reconnaissance Science,* vol. 3, *Reconnaissance Activities in Anti-crime*; Quang and Yem, *Vietnamese Reconnaissance Science,* vol. 2, *Method and Tactics of Reconnaissance Operations.*

33. Thayer, "The Apparatus of Authoritarian Rule in Vietnam."

34. Ibid.

35. Helen McKernan and Dean McWhirter, "Policing Communities in Vietnam: Intercultural Lessons for Community Policing with Vietnamese Australians" (paper presented at the Future of Sociology, Canberra, Australia, 2009).

36. Hai, "Drug and Drug Trafficking in the Greater Mekong Sub-regional"; Hai, "Transnational Narcotics Trafficking and Law Enforcement."

37. Nguyen V. Vien, "Main Achievements in International Cooperation to Counter Narcotics between Vietnam and ASEAN," People's Public Security, November 24, 2020, http://cand.com.vn/Hoat-dong-LL-CAND/Ket-qua-noi-bat-trong-hop-tac-dau-tranh-phong-chong-toi-pham-ma-tuy-giua-Viet-Nam-voi-cac-nuoc-ASEAN-620950/.

38. Hai, "Drug Trafficking in the Mainland Southeast Asian Region."

39. Jurgen Kapplinghaus, "Joint Investigation Teams: Basic Ideas, Relevant Legal Instruments and First Experiences in Europe," in *Visiting Experts' Papers* (Japan: UNAFEI, 2007).

40. Nam, "Intelligence Service Has to Rely on the People."

41. Marilyn Peterson, "Intelligence-Led Policing: The New Intelligence Architecture," US Department of Justice, Office of Justice Programs, December 10, 2017, https://www.ojp.gov/pdffiles1/bja/210681.pdf.

42. United Nations Office on Drugs and Crime, *Criminal Intelligence: Manual for Front-Line Law Enforcement* (Vienna, Austria: United Nations, 2010).

43. United Nations Office on Drugs and Crime, *Policing: Police Information and Intelligence System* (Vienna, Austria: United Nations, 2007).

44. Investigation methods and proceedings concerned national security, drug-related crimes, corruption crimes, terrorism crimes, and money laundering crimes. For more detail on the process, see Mai Nga, "Special Criminal Investigation's Measures and Its Related Managements to Apply in the Drug-Related Cases," Supreme People's Procuracy, July 28, 2019, https://vksndtc.gov.vn/tin-tuc/cac-bien-phap-dieu-tra-to-tung-dac-biet-va-kiem-sa-t8131.html.

45. Nga, "Special Criminal Investigation's Measures."

46. Duong V. Hung, "Special Investigation's Measures in Criminal Procedure," People's Court Press, May 10, 2019, https://tapchitoaan.vn/bai-viet/phap-luat/bien-phap-dieu-tra-to-tung-dac-biet.

47. Quang Linh, "Workshop on Personal Data Protection on Cyberspace," Ministry of Public Security of Vietnam, October 20, 2020, http://en.bocongan.gov.vn/news-events/workshop-on-personal-data-protection-on-cyberspace-t7542.html.

Index

Border Security Force, in India, 84
Border Troops, in Mongolia, 203, 205
Born, Hans, 185
Bo Xilai, 74
BPI. *See* Badan Pusat Intelijen
BPP. *See* Border Patrol Police
BRANI. *See* Badan Rahasia Negara
  Indonesia
Brazil, North Korea and, 245, 249
BRD. *See* Brunei Research Department
BRI. *See* Belt and Road Initiative
Britain. *See* United Kingdom
British East India Company (BEIC),
  Bhutan and, 33
Brooks, T. B. Henderson, 86
Bruneau, Thomas, 177–78
Brunei, 43–49; background on, 44–46;
  intelligence culture of, 46–48;
  Malaysia and, 284; oversight and
  foreign relations in, 48–49
Brunei Investment Agency, 44
Brunei Research Department (BRD),
  47–48, 49
BSPP. *See* Bahagian Staf Perisikan
  Pertahanan
BTF. *See* Bhutan Tiger Force
Bureau of Intelligence, Research and
  Documentation, in Cambodia, 58
Bureau of Internal Affairs (BIA), in
  North Korea, 242
Bureau of Investigation (BI), in the
  Philippines, 270–71
Bureau of Investigation and Statistics,
  of KMT, 325
Bureau of Special Investigations, in
  Myanmar, 216, 219
Burma Independence Army (BIA), in
  Myanmar, 215
Bush, George W., 7

Cabinet, in North Korea, 244
Cabinet Intelligence Research Office
  (CIRO), in Japan, 119, 126
Cambodia, 55–65, *64*; history and
  intelligence services of, 56–60;

intelligence culture issues in, 60–62;
  oversight, reform, and control in, 62;
  Singapore and, 281; Vietnam and,
  57, 58, 60, 61, 62, 65, 409
Cambodian National Rescue Party, 63
Cambodian People's Party (Kanakpak
  Pracheachon Kampuchea, CPP), 55,
  59, 61
Canada: Brunei and, 49; Singapore and,
  280
Cao de Benós, Alejandro, 245
Capiral, Christopher John, 271
Capstone Doctrine 2020, in Maldives,
  190, 196n12
Carnation Revolution, in Portugal, 369,
  370
CBI. *See* Central Bureau of
  Investigation
CC/ID. *See* Central Committee
  Investigation Department
CCP. *See* Chinese Communist Party
CCTV. *See* video surveillance
CDO. *See* Communications
  Development Office
Central Asia Regional Information and
  Coordination Centre, in Kazakhstan,
  134
Central Bureau, of KMT, 325
Central Bureau of Investigation (CBI),
  in India, 87, 90
Central Committee Investigation
  Department (CC/ID), in China, 76
Central Intelligence Agency, US (CIA,
  US): in Afghanistan, 4–5, 6, 7; in
  Cambodia, 57; in China, 73–74, 75;
  in Laos, 162; in Malaysia, 176; in
  Myanmar, 217, 219; in Pakistan,
  257; in South Korea, 300; in Sri
  Lanka, 314, 316; in Thailand, 356,
  361; Uzbekistan and, 399
Central Intelligence Agency (Badan
  Pusat Intelijen, BPI), in Indonesia,
  105
Central Intelligence Bureau (CIB), in
  Nepal, 229, 230–31

DDGNI. *See* Deputy Director General Naval Intelligence

DDGs. *See* deputy directors general

DDR. *See* disarmament, demobilization, and reintegration

DDSI. *See* Directorate of Defence Services intelligence

Declaration of Strategic Partnership, of US and Uzbekistan, 400

Deep Penetration Units (DPUs), in Sri Lanka, 316–17

Defence Image Processing and Analysis Centre, in India, 88

Defence Intelligence Agency (DIA), in India, 84, 88

Defence White Paper of 2021, in Brunei, 46, 48

Defense Agency (Bōeichō), in Japan, 119

Defense Forces, in Vietnam, 407

Defense Intelligence Headquarters (DIH), in Japan, 122

Defense Intelligence Staff Division (Bahagian Staf Perisikan Pertahanan, BSPP), 178; in Malaysia, 172, 176

Defense Ministry: of Afghanistan, 7; in Cambodia, 61

Defense of Political Security Directorates, in Cambodia, 59

Defense Security Command (DSC), of South Korea, 293, 295, 297

Democratic Choice of Kazakhstan (DVK), 137

Democratic People's Republic of Korea (DPRK). *See* North Korea

Democratic Progress Party (DPP), in Taiwan, 329, 336

Den Fa, 72

Deng Xiaoping, 73, 76, 77

Department of Military Intelligence (DMI), in Nepal, 227, 229, 231, 234

Department of Revenue Intelligence (DRI), in India, 84

Department of Special Affairs, in KMT, 327

Deputy Director General External, in Pakistan, 260

Deputy Director General Naval Intelligence (DDGNI), in Pakistan, 261

deputy directors general (DDGs), in Pakistan, 260, 262

Desai, Morarji, 87

Designated State Secrets Law, in Japan, 124

Detective Branch (DB), in Bangladesh, 20

Deuve, Jean, 161

DFI. *See* Directorate of Foreign Intelligence

DGAI. *See* Director General Air Intelligence

DGFI. *See* Directorate General of Forces Intelligence

DGIB. *See* Director General Intelligence Bureau

DGIS. *See* Director General Intelligence and Security

DGMI. *See* Director General Military Intelligence

DGNI. *See* Director General Naval Intelligence

DGSE. *See* Direction Générale de la Sécurité Extérieure

Dhaka Metropolitan Police (DMP), in Bangladesh, 18, 25

Dhar, Maloy Krishna, 84, 91

DI. *See* Division of Investigation

DIA. *See* Defence Intelligence Agency

Diamond, Larry, 56

Dianxun Fazhanshi (Communication Development Office, CDO), in Taiwan, 327, 333

Diaocha Ju (Investigation Bureau), in Taiwan, 334

Digital Security Act of 2018, in Bangladesh, 25

DIH. *See* Defense Intelligence Headquarters

Economic Espionage Act, of US, 73
Edmunds, Timothy, 175, 177
Edussuriya, Bandu, 311
Eelam Revolution Organization of
 Students (EROS), in Sri Lanka, 315
EEZ. *See* exclusive economic zone
Egmont Group, Bangladesh and, 26
e-government, in Kazakhstan, 133
EISS. *See* External Intelligence and
 Security Service
Election Commission, in Bhutan, 37
electric intelligence (ELINT): in
 Singapore, 285; in Taiwan, 327, 333
Emergency Regulations, in Singapore,
 283
Employment Tribunal, in Maldives, 193
encryption: in India, 84; in KMT, 327
EROS. *See* Eelam Revolution
 Organization of Students
Ershad, H. M., 24
ETLO. *See* East Turkestan Liberation
 Organization
European Union (EU): Bangladesh
 and, 26; Mongolia and, 204–5;
 Uzbekistan and, 398
Evidence Act, in Maldives, 193
exclusive economic zone (EEZ), in
 Timor-Leste, 375
External Documentation and Counter-
 Espionage Service (Service de
 Documentation Extérieure et de
 Contre-Espionnage, SDECE): in
 Cambodia, 57; in Laos, 161
external intelligence agency, in India, 83
External Intelligence and Security
 Service (EISS), of South Korea, 293,
 298–99
Extraordinary Commission to Combat
 Counter-Revolution (Cheka), in
 Kyrgyzstan, 144

facial recognition: in Kazakhstan, 137;
 in Tajikistan, 346
Faizov, Yodgor, 346

Falintil-Forçasde Defesa de Timor-
 Leste, F-FDTL (Falintil-Timor-Leste
 Defense Forces), 371–74
FATF. *See* Financial Action Task Force
Federal'naya sluzhba bezopasnosti
 Rossiyskoy Federatsii (Federal
 Security Service, FSB), in
 Kazakhstan, 135
Federal Security (Sûreté Federale), in
 Laos, 161
Federal Security Service (Federal'naya
 sluzhba bezopasnosti Rossiyskoy
 Federatsii, FSB), in Kazakhstan, 135
Federal Security Service (FSB), in
 Kyrgyzstan, 149–50
F-FDTL. *See* Falintil-Forçasde Defesa
 de Timor-Leste
FID. *See* Financial Intelligence
 Department
Financial Action Task Force (FATF), in
 Bhutan, 37
Financial Intelligence Department
 (FID), in Bhutan, 36
Financial Intelligence Unit (FIU): in
 Bangladesh, 20, 25, 26, 28n24, 49;
 in Bhutan, 36–37; in Brunei, 49;
 in India, 84; in Malaysia, 172; in
 Maldives, 188, 189, 190, 192, 193
Financial Service Act of 2018, in
 Bhutan, 36
FireEye, 250
FIU. *See* Financial Intelligence Unit
"Five Point Development Strategy Plan
 of Policy Priorities for the Next Five
 Years," in Uzbekistan, 400
Forces de Gendarmerie Laotiennes
 (Laotian Gendarmerie Forces), 160
Forces Goal 2030, in Bangladesh, 24
Foreign and National Defense
 Committee, in Taiwan, 335
Foreign Intelligence Service (SVR), in
 Kyrgyzstan, 149–50
Foreign Ministry (Gaimushō), in Japan,
 119

Gusmão, Xanana, 371, 372, 374

Hadi Bin Haji Hussin, Abdul, 178
Haixun Shu (Coast Guard
    Administration, CGA), in Taiwan,
    329, 333, 335
Halimov, Gulmurod, 343–44
Hamid, Shahid, 257
Hannan, Mufti Abdul, 19
Harkat ul Jihad al Islami Bangladesh
    (HUJI-B), 19, 21
Hasanuddin, Tubagus, 107
Hasina, Sheikh, 22, 25–26
Haspel, Gina, 361
Hazaraas, 5
Hedman, Eva-Lotta, 270
Henderson Brooks-Bhagat Report, 86,
    98n40
Herath, Cyril, 313
Hezb-e Islami (Party of Islam), 6
Hezbollah, in Nepal, 230–31
Hobbes, Thomas, 310–11
Ho Chi Minh, 408
Hok Chendavy, 63
Hok Lundy, 62
Home Affairs Ministry, in Myanmar, 221
Hong Kong, China and, 71, 72
HRW. *See* Human Rights Watch
HUJI-B. *See* Harkat ul Jihad al Islami
    Bangladesh
human intelligence (HUMINT): in
    Bangladesh, 16, 17, 18; in India, 93,
    100n71; in Indonesia, 112; in Japan,
    121, 125; in KMT, 325; in North
    Korea, 245, 248–49; in Pakistan,
    260; in South Korea, 294; in Sri
    Lanka, 311; in Taiwan, 327
Human Rights Commission, in
    Malaysia, 178
Human Rights Watch (HRW): on CIA,
    361; on Indonesia, 111–12; on
    Uzbekistan, 398, 402
human trafficking: in Malaysia, 177; in
    Mongolia, 207; in Nepal, 228; in the
    Philippines, 270

Hun Manith, 63
Hun Sen, 58–63, 65
Hyon Yongchol, 247

IB. *See* Intelligence Bureau;
    Investigation Bureau
Ibrahim, Anwar, 176
IEDs. *See* improvised explosive devices
IFS. *See* Indian Foreign Service
Ignacio, Jeffrey, 271
IGP. *See* inspector general of police
ILEA. *See* International Law
    Enforcement Academy
ILP. *See* intelligence-led policing
image intelligence (IMINT): in Japan,
    121; in Taiwan, 333
IMET. *See* International Military
    Education and Training program
IMINT. *See* image intelligence
improvised explosive devices (IEDs), in
    Bangladesh, 21
IMTRAT. *See* Indian Military Training
    team
IMU. *See* Islamic Movement of
    Uzbekistan
India: Bangladesh and, 17, 25–26, 94;
    Bhutan and, 33, 37; Brunei and,
    49; history of, 86–88; intelligence
    performance in, 88–89; key
    intelligence services and structure
    in, 83–86, 85; Myanmar and, 213,
    214, 223; Nepal and, 229, 234;
    operational issues in, 90–94; Pakistan
    and, 85, 86–87, 94, 255, 256–57,
    263; South Korea and, 300; Sri
    Lanka and, 314, 318–19; successes
    in, 94–95; Tajikistan and, 346;
    Timor-Leste and, 377
India-China war, 86
Indian Foreign Service (IFS), 89
Indian Military Training team
    (IMTRAT), in Bhutan, 34
Indian Peace Keeping Force (IPKF), Sri
    Lanka and, 319

and, 1, 2, 3, 5, 6; China and, 72; in Kyrgyzstan, 144; Kyrgyzstan and, 143, 145–46, 149, 153; Laos and, 163, 164; Mongolia and, 200–201, 207, 210n7, 211n16; North Korea and, 243; Tajikistan and, 341–43; Turkmenistan and, 383–88; Vietnam and, 409. *See also* Komitet Gosudarstvennoy Bezopasnosti
United Arab Emirates, India and, 95
United Front, in KMT, 325
United Front Department (UFD), in North Korea, 244–45
United Kingdom (UK): Afghanistan and, 1, 6, 11n1; Bangladesh and, 17; Bhutan and, 33; Brunei and, 43, 44, 46, 49; Gamma Group in, 111, 112; India and, 84, 95; Indonesia and, 103, 105; Japan and, 119; Malaysia and, 173–74; Myanmar and, 214–15; North Korea and, 245; Singapore and, 280, 283, 285; Sri Lanka and, 312–13, 316; Suu Kyi and, 220. *See also* Secret Intelligence Service; Security Service
United Liberation Front of Assam (ULFA), 26, 37
United Malay National Organization (UMNO), 174–75, 179
United Nations (UN): in Bangladesh, 15; Brunei in, 48; Mongolia and, 204, 206; North Korea and, 250; Timor-Leste and, 369; Turkmenistan and, 389; Uzbekistan and, 398
United Nations Command (UNC), in South Korea, 300
United Nations Integrated Mission in Timor-Leste (UNMIT), 371, 373
United Nations Office on Drugs and Crime (UNDOC): in Kazakhstan, 134; in Kyrgyzstan, 151; in Tajikistan, 340–41
United Nations Police (UNPOL), in Timor-Leste, 373

United Nations Transitional Administration in East Timor (UNTAET), 371, 372
United Nations Transitional Authority in Cambodia (UNTAC), 59
United Revolutionary Front of Bhutan (URFB), 38
United States (US): Afghanistan and, 1; Bangladesh and, 17; Brunei and, 48, 49; Cambodia and, 60, 65; China and, 77, 328; India and, 95; Indonesia and, 104, 110, 111, 113; Japan and, 119, 120, 124; Kazakhstan and, 129, 136; Kyrgyzstan and, 152–53; Laos and, 162–63; Mongolia and, 206; Nepal and, 235–36; North Korea and, 248, 249–50; Singapore and, 280; South Korea and, 296; Sri Lanka and, 314, 319; Taiwan and, 328; Taiwan Relations Act of, 328; Tajikistan and, 346–47; Thailand and, 358–59; Turkmenistan and, 392; Uzbekistan and, 398, 399–400; Vietnam and, 407. *See also* Central Intelligence Agency, US
United States Taiwan Defense Command (USTDC), 327
United Tajik Opposition, 343
United Wa State Army (UWSA), in Myanmar, 217
UNMIT. *See* United Nations Integrated Mission in Timor-Leste
UN Office on Drugs and Crime, Bangladesh and, 26
UNPOL. *See* United Nations Police
UNTAC. *See* United Nations Transitional Authority in Cambodia
UNTAET. *See* United Nations Transitional Administration in East Timor
URFB. *See* United Revolutionary Front of Bhutan
US. *See* United States

About the Contributors

ASM Ali Ashraf is professor of international relations at the University of Dhaka, Bangladesh. He holds a PhD in international security policy from the University of Pittsburgh, United States. His teaching and research interests are broadly in the fields of security and intelligence studies, public policy, and international migration. He was a Fulbright fellow and a European Union Center of Excellent dissertation fellow at the University of Pittsburgh. He often lectures at the Defence Services Command and Staff College, Foreign Service Academy, and National Defence College in Bangladesh. He is a member of the International Institute for Strategic Studies (IISS), London.

Matthew Brazil is a fellow at the Jamestown Foundation and a former US Army military intelligence officer, diplomat, and corporate security investigator. He lived in China for eight years, first as a commercial officer at the US embassy, Beijing, where he both promoted and controlled American high technology exports, and then as the security manager for an American semiconductor factory. With Peter Mattis, he is the coauthor of *Chinese Communist Espionage: An Intelligence Primer* (2019). His next book will be a narrative describing the world reaction to China's developing espionage offensive.

Mark Briskey is associate professor at Murdoch University, Australia. He was previously employed by the Australian government where he served in Australia and on several overseas postings. Briskey was decorated for his work by the Australian and Indonesian governments for his role in counterterrorism as well as for work in Pakistan, Afghanistan, Bangladesh, and Sri Lanka.

Paul Chambers serves as lecturer and special adviser in international affairs at the Center of ASEAN Community Studies, Faculty of Social Sciences, Naresuan University, Thailand. He is also a senior fellow at the Cambodian Institute for Cooperation and Peace in Phnom Penh, Cambodia. In addition, he is the executive editor of the journal *Asian Affairs: An American Review*. His areas of research are civil-military relations, democratization, and international relations in Southeast Asia. He has written six books and numerous journal articles, book chapters, and reviews relating to these issues.

Elizabeth Van Wie Davis is professor of international politics and security at the Colorado School of Mines and holds a PhD from the University of Virginia. Davis also serves as a fellow at the Payne Institute for Earth Resources, the Center for Asian Studies at University of Colorado Boulder, and at the Center for Chinese Studies, University of Hawaii Manoa. Her third book is on Central Asia after September 11, 2001, while her other books and dozens of articles specifically focus on the nexus between security and religion in the context of terrorism. Davis's fifth book is *Shadow Warfare: Cyberwar Policy in the United States, Russia, and China* (Rowman & Littlefield, 2021).

Julian Dierkes is associate professor in the Institute of Asian Research at the University of British Columbia in Vancouver, Canada. Originally focused on sociological research on the Japanese education system, Dierkes has paid close attention to Mongolia's economic, political, and social developments for the past ten years. He edited *Change in Democratic Mongolia* (2012) and frequently writes about Mongolia in the media and online. Dierkes also coordinates the Program on Inner Asia and maintains the *Mongolia Focus* blog.

Scott Edwards is a postdoctoral research associate for the Transnational Organized Crime at Sea project, led by SafeSeas, based at the University of Bristol, United Kingdom. Edwards completed his PhD at the University of Birmingham, where he analyzed the role of trust in Southeast Asian international relations. His research interests include maritime security, interstate cooperative mechanisms for countering maritime security issues and organized crime, and interagency coordination and management. He has a particular emphasis on the Malaysian and Indonesian security sectors. He has consulted for Transparency International, Geneva Centre for Security Sector Governance, and the International Committee of the Red Cross.

Joseph Fitsanakis is professor of intelligence and security studies at Coastal Carolina University, where he teaches courses on intelligence analysis, intelligence dissemination, intelligence operations, human intelligence collection, and intelligence in the Cold War, among other subjects. He has written extensively on intelligence policy and practice, intelligence collection, information security, communications interception, cyber espionage, and transnational criminal networks. His writings have been translated into several languages and referenced by media outlets such as the *Washington Post*, NPR, BBC, ABC, and *Newsweek*. Before joining Coastal Carolina University, Fitsanakis built the Security and Intelligence Studies program at King University, where he also directed the King Institute for Security and Intelligence Studies. He is also deputy director of the European Intelligence Academy and senior editor at intelNews.org.

Evrim Gormus is assistant professor at the Political Science and International Relations Department of MEF University in Istanbul, Turkey. Gormus holds a PhD from the Interdisciplinary PhD Program in Near and Middle Eastern studies, University of Washington, Seattle; an MSc in Russian and Eastern European studies, University of Oxford; and a BA in political science and international relations, Istanbul Bilgi University. Her research interests are political economy of the Middle East and North Africa, comparative Middle East politics, state-society relations, social and economic inclusion, and female labor force participation. She has published in *Journal of Refugee Studies*, *Journal of International Relations and Development*, *Mediterranean Politics*, *Journal of North African Studies*, and *Forum for Development Studies*.

Rohan Gunaratna is an honorary professor at the Department of Strategic Studies, General Sir John Kotelawala Defence University, Sri Lanka.

Dao Henry is an analyst with a local government in the western United States. Previously, Henry was a criminal investigator for the US federal government before relocating to the United States. She is now also pursuing a postgraduate degree in data science and security.

Praveen Kumar is associate professor and head at the Department of Political Studies, Central University of South Bihar, Gaya, India. He has a PhD in political science from Jawaharlal Nehru University, New Delhi. Formerly Kumar was associate professor in the Department of Geopolitics and International Relations at Manipal University, Karnataka, which he had joined in 2014 after twelve years of research experience in the areas of national security and counterterrorism with institutions of repute including the New Delhi–based (Manohar Parrikar) Institute for Defence Study and Analyses and Institute for Conflict Management (South Asia Terrorism Portal). Kumar has written about applying Kautalyan principles to understand regional geopolitics in national and international journals.

Réjeanne Lacroix holds a master of arts degree in international security studies from the University of Leicester, United Kingdom. Lacroix's area of focus is the post-Soviet space, primarily de facto states and unresolved conflicts, as well as the Balkans. She has contributed thoughtful and balanced analysis on such matters to various sources. Lacroix has been affiliated with nonprofit organizations that have tackled issues such as counterterrorism, counterextremism, and foreign policy in the roles of research fellow, adviser, and editor in chief.

Michael Landon-Murray is assistant professor at the University of Colorado, Colorado Springs, where he teaches intelligence studies, intelligence analysis, and public policy. His research focuses on intelligence education, analysis, and oversight with an emphasis on emerging technology. He is coeditor of *Researching National Security Intelligence: Multidisciplinary Approaches* (2019) and certification chair for the International Association for Intelligence Education.

Hans Lipp studied economic and tourism geography at the universities of Bayreuth and Trier and received his doctorate from the University of Tuebingen, Germany. After working in tourism IT, he is affiliated with the University of Tuebingen and is active as a specialist for the region of Southeast Asia / Laos / northeast Thailand in the areas of economic, tourism, and infrastructure development, especially in human security issues.

Charlie Lizza holds a master's degree in intelligence and security studies from King's College London. His research interests include organizational learning within intelligence and security agencies, as well as the practice and theory of intelligence.

Hai Thanh Luong is research fellow in cyber criminology at the School of Social Science, the University of Queensland, Australia. He has a bachelor's of law in criminal investigation and has more than fifteen years of research and lecturing experience at the People's Police Academy of Vietnam. Luong completed a master's degree at the University of Wollongong and a PhD at RMIT University. His areas of interest are the death penalty in Vietnam, transnational organized crime in Asia, intelligence-led policing, harm reduction, and police training. In 2021, Luong earned the Asian Young Criminologist award from the Asia Society of Criminology. His latest book, *Transnational Drug Trafficking across the Vietnam and Laos Border*, was published in 2019, and he has published in *Asian Survey, International Journal of Drug*

Policy, International Journal of Cyber Criminology, Journal of Justice and Crime, and *Trends in Organized Crime,* among others.

Prem Mahadevan is a researcher in intelligence, terrorism, and organized crime. He is the author of two academic books on intelligence agencies in India and Pakistan, respectively, and has taught at universities in Switzerland, the Czech Republic, and Austria.

Nasir Mehmood is assistant professor at the Department of Strategic Studies, National Defence University, Islamabad, Pakistan. He was an international visiting fellow at James Martin Center for Nonproliferation Studies in Monterey, California, United States. He completed his PhD at the Department of Politics and International Relations, University of Reading, United Kingdom. His research focuses on arms control, military doctrine, military strategy, and intelligence studies.

Jargalsaikhan Mendee is a PhD student in political science at the University of British Columbia, Canada. Holder of a BA in social sciences from the Mongolian Defense University, he received an MA in international security and civil-military relations from the Naval Postgraduate School and in Asia Pacific policy studies from the Institute of Asian Research, University of British Columbia. Prior to joining the PhD program, Colonel Mendee served as a defense attaché to the United States and senior research fellow at the Mongolian Institute for Strategic Studies.

Sameer Patil is senior fellow at the Observer Research Foundation, India, where he researches India's defense and national security policies. He has previously worked at the National Security Council Secretariat and Gateway House. At the National Security Council Secretariat, he handled counter-terrorism and regional security desks. Sameer has written extensively on various aspects of national security, including counter-terrorism, cyber security, Kashmir issue, border security, and defense industrialization. He is also a dissertation advisor at the Indian Naval War College.

Amador IV Peleo is an independent researcher based in the Philippines. He has an MA from the Graduate School of International Relations of the International University of Japan and a PhD from the School of Political, Social and International Studies of the University of East Anglia, United Kingdom. He was a research fellow at the Center for Southeast Asian Studies and an assistant professor at the Graduate Institute of Marine Affairs of the National Sun Yat-Sen University in Kaohsiung, Taiwan.

Bodhana Perera is an independent researcher interested in the study of intelligence and strategic security.

Abdulla Phairoosch holds a PhD in law enforcement intelligence from Macquarie University, Australia. He is a graduate of the FBI National Academy and National Police Academy of India. Phairoosch served in the Maldives Police Force from October 1998 to January 2021. During this period, he held command of a range of functions including investigation, major events and operations, intelligence, counterterrorism, crime prevention, administration, resource management, and future planning. He led the effort in restructuring and professionalizing police intelligence in 2012 as the head of intelligence command. He developed force policies on surveillance, lawful interception, and auditing of special funds, and he contributed to many national policies on security. He collaborated closely with many intelligence and security agencies on the issue of global terrorism and violent extremism.

Richard J. Samuels is Ford International Professor of Political Science and director of the Center for International Studies at the Massachusetts Institute of Technology.

Ryan Shaffer is a historian with expertise on political violence and security. Shaffer has a PhD in history and has written for international magazines, including *Reader's Digest* and *Homeland Security Today*, and his academic research has appeared in journals, such as *Intelligence and National Security* and the *Journal of Intelligence History*. His books include *African Intelligence Services: Early Postcolonial and Contemporary Challenges* (2021) and *The Handbook of African Intelligence Cultures* (2022).

Alexander Nicholas Shaw is a historian of intelligence and diplomacy specializing in Singapore and Southeast Asia. He gained his PhD from the University of Leeds in 2019 where his thesis, funded by the Arts and Humanities Research Council and the White Rose College of the Arts and Humanities, explored the world of British intelligence in Singapore from 1946 to 1959. Shaw has previously published articles in *Intelligence and National Security*, *Small Wars and Insurgencies*, and the *Journal of Intelligence History*.

Owen Sirrs is associate professor at the University of Montana's Defense Critical Language and Culture Program. Sirrs previously served as an intelligence analyst at the Defense Intelligence Agency and authored a book on Pakistan's Inter-Services Intelligence Directorate.

Adiya Tuvshintugs has served as director of the Mongolian National Intelligence Academy of the General Intelligence Agency of Mongolia since 2009. Professor Tuvshintugs received an MA in technical sciences from the Military Telecommunication Institute, Ulyanovsk, USSR, and a PhD from the Military Communication Academy, Saint Petersburg, Russia. Previously, he taught at the Mongolian National Defense University. Colonel Tuvshintugs was an adviser for the Foreign Cooperation Department of the Ministry of Defense (2008–2009), deputy director of the Institute for Strategic Studies (2003–2008), and deputy director of the Institute for Defense Studies (1997–2001).

Bishnu Raj Upreti has a master's degree in sociology from Tribhuvan University of Nepal, and a master's degree in management of agricultural knowledge systems and a PhD in conflict management from the Wageningen University, Netherlands. He completed a post-doctoral fellowship from the University of London (King's College) / Centre for Environmental Studies, University of Surrey, United Kingdom. Since the early 1980s, Upreti has engaged in professional activities at local and international levels in Europe, Latin America, Asia, and Africa. He has published more than sixty books and hundreds of articles about conflict, peace, and unconventional security including water, food, health, and environmental security. Upreti supervises PhD students in different universities and currently leads a think tank. He is frequently quoted nationally and internationally about Nepal's armed conflict and peace process.

Agnes E. Venema is a doctoral candidate in the field of intelligence and national security and the recipient of a Marie Skłodowska-Curie scholarship awarded by the European Commission on the "*E*volving *S*ecurity *S*cience through *N*etworked *T*echnologies, *I*nformation Policy *a*nd *L*aw" (ESSENTIAL) project. Her research focuses on the use of emerging technologies in the identification of people in crowded spaces, and she has published on the role of emerging technologies in security, as well as on intelligence- and security-sharing structures. Venema is conducting her doctoral studies at the "Mihai Viteazul" National Intelligence Academy in Bucharest, Romania, and the Department of Information Policy and Governance, University of Malta. Prior to her doctoral studies, Venema worked in the field of international security policy, including with the Security Sector Support Unit of the United Nations Integrated Mission in Timor-Leste (UNMIT) in 2010.

Arun Vishwanathan is associate professor at the Centre for Security Studies, School of National Security Studies, Central University of Gujarat, Gandhinagar. Previously he was assistant professor in the Department of Defence and Strategic Studies, Savitribai Phule Pune University, and at the International Strategic and Security Studies Program, National Institute of Advanced Studies (NIAS), Bangalore. Vishwanathan also served as assistant director in the National Security Council Secretariat, Prime Minister's Office, and he was an associate fellow at the Indian Pugwash Society, IDSA Campus, New Delhi.

Hon-min Yau is associate professor and the director of the Graduate Institute of International Security (GIIS), College of International and National Defense Affairs (INDAC), National Defense University (NDU), Taiwan. He teaches courses at War College and Air Command & Staff College, NDU, Taiwan. He received his Ph.D. from the Department of International Politics, Aberystwyth University, Wales, UK. He also holds a Master of Science in management and information system from Cranfield University, UK. He has been affiliated with Taiwan's military for more than 25 years and has participated in both domestic and overseas positions. Hence, his research interests focus on investigating the intermingled relations among national security policy, international relations, and technologies."

Michael Yerushalmi is an analyst with the US Department of Defense. He is a graduate of Georgetown University and previously worked as a fellow with a nongovernmental organization and assistant editor with an academic journal. He conducts research on Asian and Middle East intelligence and political affairs.